CHOOSINGWAR

CHOOSINGWAR

The Lost Chance for
Peace and the Escalation
of War in Vietnam

FREDRIK LOGEVALL

University of California Press
Berkeley   Los Angeles   London

University of California Press
Berkeley and Los Angeles, California

University of California Press, Ltd.
London, England

© 1999 by
The Regents of the University of California

Library of Congress Cataloging-in-Publication Data
Logevall, Fredrik, 1963–
    Choosing war: the lost chance for peace and the escalation of war
in Vietnam / Fredrik Logevall.
        p.   cm.
    Includes bibliographical references and index.
    ISBN 0-520-21511-7 (alk. paper)
    1. Vietnamese Conflict, 1961–1975—United States.   2. United
States—Foreign relations—Vietnam.   3. Vietnam—Foreign relations—
United States.   4. United States—Foreign relations—1963–1969.
5. United States—Politics and government—1963–1969.   I. Title.
DS558.L6   1999
959.704'3373—dc21   99–18674
                                                                        CIP

Printed in the United States of America

9 8 7 6 5 4 3 2 1

For my parents

Contents

Acknowledgments

In completing this study, I have incurred numerous institutional and individual debts I would like to acknowledge here. As anyone who works on the Vietnam War knows, the documentary records are voluminous, and in a very basic way, archivists at a number of institutions in several countries have made my work possible. In particular, I wish to thank Regina Greenwell and Linda Hanson Seelke of the Lyndon Baines Johnson Library for their expert assistance and unfailing good cheer. John Armstrong of the National Archives of Canada also went beyond the call of duty in helping me to get access to documents.

Several organizations have supported my research and writing. From the Lyndon Baines Johnson Foundation I received a grant-in-aid to defray travel and research expenses. The MacArthur Foundation provided crucial assistance in the form of a travel grant and a generous dissertation fellowship. A postdoctoral year at Yale University in 1993 and 1994 was essential in allowing me time to conduct in-depth research. The Academic Senate of the University of California at Santa Barbara provided a timely research grant, as did the same institution's Interdisciplinary Humanities Center (IHC). The IHC's associate director, Leonard Wallock, has been a constant source of support and encouragement.

Numerous scholars have facilitated my work. Edwin Moïse, Robert Schulzinger, and Larry Berman, all accomplished scholars of the war, read the manuscript and provided a large number of helpful suggestions. Though my interpretation of events differs from each of theirs in important respects, all three have made this a better book. Kenneth Pomeranz is not a specialist in the study of Vietnam or American foreign relations, but his detailed and penetrating comments were extremely helpful—as helpful as any I received. The dean of American historians of the Vietnam War, George Herring of the University of Kentucky, commented on several draft chapters and provided encouragement at many points along the way: it was always a special thrill to get a letter postmarked Lexington. John Lewis Gaddis provided characteristically cogent and incisive comments on an early draft and affirmed my belief in the importance of putting American policymaking in its wider domestic and international contexts.

The Chinese position on the war was made clearer to me through discussions with two experts on China's foreign policy in the Cold War, Chen Jian and Qiang Zhai, both of whom also generously shared research materials with me. H. R. McMaster and I racked up sizable phone bills discussing and debating various aspects of the war—more than once I put down the phone after a "brief" call and realized an hour had gone by. My friend and fellow historian Anne Blair provided penetrating comments on several draft chapters, along with periodic email messages of encouragement that always seemed to arrive just when I needed them most. Others who helped in various ways and to varying degrees include Timothy Naftali, Steven Schwartzberg, Zachary Karabell, Robert David Johnson, John Mueller, Ronald Steel, Arthur Combs, William Gibbons, Kurk Dorsey, Phillip Hughes, Fermina Murray, David Humphrey, Laurence Juarez, Judith Steedman, Patrik Andersson, and Daniel Philpott. At the University of California Press I wish to thank Director James Clark for his enthusiasm for the project as well as managing editor Monica McCormick and production editor Scott Norton for their patience and skill in guiding me through the shoals of publishing a first book.

Two colleagues at UC Santa Barbara deserve special mention: Laura Kalman and Kenneth Mouré. Both kindly agreed to read a large chunk of the manuscript, and the time and thoughtful effort they put into their lengthy commentaries far exceeded any reasonable expectations I might have had in anticipating critical feedback. Three other colleagues, John E. Talbott, Lawrence Badash, and Tsuyoshi Hasegawa, provided important assistance at various points. The faculty and graduate students who make up the UCSB Cold War History Group provided a forum in which I could test my ideas on a couple of occasions. I would also like to thank Kathryn Statler and Kimber Quinney of UCSB for their expert research assistance. John Coleman, a combat veteran of the Vietnam War as well as a historian-in-training, helped in innumerable ways in the final stages of the project, from tracking down obscure citations to tidying up the bibliography. A heartfelt thanks, John, from "The Big Lacuna."

This study began as a dissertation at Yale University, and I am indebted to committee members Paul Kennedy, Diane Kunz, and Gaddis Smith for their counsel and support. As the director of the committee and my main adviser in graduate school, Gaddis Smith shaped this study in countless ways, many of them indirect but all of them important. At an earlier stage of my academic training, my interest in the history of American foreign relations was deepened and broadened by Glenn Anthony May, model scholar and teacher.

Finally, I want to acknowledge the devoted support of my family. My parents, Bengt and Louise Logevall, never flagged in their enthusiasm for the project, never failed to offer just the right words of encouragement. This book is dedicated to them. Most of all, I want to thank my wife, Danielle, and our beautiful children, Emma and Joseph. Danielle is my best friend and my most unsparing critic; she, more than any other person, made it possible to complete this work through her faith in me and her keen editorial eye. Emma and Joe, who arrived in this world in the project's middle stages, reminded their dad time and again of the importance of putting scholarly obsessions into proper perspective.

Preface

The Vietnam War. A quarter of a century has passed since it ended for the United States, but it is with us still. It is the modern American tragedy, the costliest, most divisive conflict since the Civil War. It took the lives of close to sixty thousand Americans and perhaps three million Vietnamese. That the American decision for war was the wrong decision is today taken as axiomatic by a large majority of both lay observers and scholars, myself included, who see the U.S. intervention as, at best, a failure and a mistake, at worst a crime. "We were wrong, terribly wrong," former Secretary of Defense Robert McNamara, one of the architects of the escalation, intoned in his 1995 memoirs.[1] So why did the war happen? Might it have been averted? If so, how? These are the questions that led me to research the war and to write this book. Its focus is on what I call "The Long 1964," the roughly eighteen months from late August 1963 to late February 1965. This period, I argue, is the most important in the entire thirty-year American involvement in Vietnam, the period in which the Second Indochina War began in earnest. At the start of it, in the summer of 1963, Vietnam for the first time became a top-priority, day-to-day foreign-policy issue for the United States. At its end, in the late winter of 1965, American officials under Lyndon Johnson had made the decision to "Americanize" the war, to essentially take over from their South Vietnamese allies the fighting against the North Vietnam–sponsored insurgents known as the Vietcong.*

To argue for the distinctiveness and primacy of The Long 1964 is not to deny the import of the earlier history of American involvement in Vietnam, which has been the subject of detailed and essential scholarship.[2] But comprehensiveness in some dimensions requires concision in others. To best

---

*This is the derogatory name for the National Liberation Front coined by South Vietnamese leader Ngo Dinh Diem and commonly used by American and international officials and reporters. Because it is the term familiar to many readers, its use is retained here.

understand the Americanization of the war, I realized I would have to place U.S. decision making in its wider context—wider both in the international political and domestic American political senses—which necessitated narrowing my periodization to what I determined to be the most vital period. That period began in mid 1963 and ended in early 1965.[3]

The international context of American policy making has received scant attention from students of the war. Scholars tend to discuss the conflict in a vacuum, concentrating almost exclusively on events as perceived in Washington and, to a lesser extent, Hanoi and Saigon.[4] The result is a skewed picture of the environment in which key decisions were reached. Unless we extend our frame of reference beyond America's borders and beyond the boundaries of South and North Vietnam, we cannot fully understand the sources and consequences of American officials' decisions, the options they faced, and the choices they did or did not have.[5] I have sought throughout this book to bring U.S. officials' foreign counterparts—both hostile and friendly—into the picture, to consider how these leaders approached the Vietnam issue and how their policies influenced, or did not influence, Washington's thinking.

The importance of viewing the war through this wider lens becomes starkly clear when we consider that U.S. officials typically explained their decision to escalate the war in international terms. Both at the time and later, these officials claimed that the demands of American "credibility" necessitated standing firm in Vietnam, even if that meant committing U.S. ground troops to fight and die there.[6] U.S. prestige was on the line in Southeast Asia, they said, as a result of ten years of steadily expanding involvement in the struggle and constant public assertions of South Vietnam's importance to American security. An early withdrawal from the war would cause allies elsewhere in Asia and around the world to lose faith in the dependability of America's commitments and would embolden adversaries in Moscow and Beijing to pursue aggressive designs all over the globe.

Was this true? Was American credibility really at stake in Vietnam in the months leading up to the outbreak of major war? Determining the veracity of this claim is impossible within the purely national framework most authors have utilized. Only by examining how the war played in other capitals—in London and Paris, in Ottawa and Tokyo, in Moscow and Beijing—can we make meaningful assertions about how the world looked upon what Washington sought to achieve in Vietnam. And only by looking at how accurately American officials understood these foreign views, and how much importance they attached to them, can we determine how much explanatory power to attach to the notion of credibility and the need to preserve it by fighting in Vietnam.

A more international emphasis is also essential if we are to get a meaningful answer to the second core question: could the escalation of the Vietnam conflict into a large-scale war have been prevented? "Was there a point when the looming collision might have been averted?" a prominent diplomatic historian has recently asked, without offering an answer.[7] This is a crucial question, as it always is when the issue is war and peace. (The editor of a recent volume on the various explanations for American intervention opened by noting the centrality of this question in the existing literature.)[8] All the more amazing, then, that the diplomacy prior to major war should have received so little detailed scholarly attention. To really answer the question of whether the 1965 escalation of the war could have been prevented, we must look closely at the efforts to prevent it. In this book, I attend to the attempts at finding a diplomatic solution in the year and a half before Americanization. Hence the second reason why our story begins in August 1963: the same month that saw America's Vietnam problem become acute also witnessed what Jean Lacouture has accurately called the "diplomatic kick-off" in Vietnam, as French President Charles de Gaulle publicly called for an end to foreign intervention there.[9] The efforts of de Gaulle and others to bring about a political solution to the conflict in the months that followed, perhaps through the reconvening of the 1954 Geneva Conference, and the reactions to those efforts by the principal belligerents are a central part of our story.

Is this therefore a full-fledged "international history" of the Vietnam War in 1963 to 1965? Not if that means giving more or less equal treatment to all of the main actors. Though based on research in the national archives of several countries, this book centers on the United States. Notwithstanding my belief in the essential importance of placing American decision making in its international context, my primary concern is understanding and explaining how and why leaders in Washington chose to commit the United States to war in Southeast Asia. An international history of the war in this period that made Washington just one of several major players would run the danger of distorting history, by giving greater influence to some of them than they in fact deserve. Any satisfactory history of the conflict in The Long 1964 has to be American-centered to some degree. As U.S. officials themselves knew, and as observers in other locales—London, Paris, Tokyo, Moscow—understood, the resolution or expansion of the conflict depended to an inordinate degree on decisions in Washington.

The international observers also understood something else. They understood that for both American presidents in this period, and especially for Lyndon Johnson, the Vietnam conflict's importance derived in large measure from its potential to threaten their own political standing—and their party's standing—at home. Comprehending the decision to Americanize the war in Vietnam requires comprehending the domestic political context out of which that decision emerged, a context shaped to a great degree by the November 1964 presidential election. Here, too, as with the international context, I perceived early on the importance of utilizing a wider lens than have previous authors, of going considerably beyond the top-level deliberations in the Oval Office and in the State and Defense Departments and considering how the Vietnam conflict was perceived in the halls of Congress, in the media, and in public opinion.[10] The concept of "credibility," I discovered, mattered at least as much in domestic terms as in international terms—only now it was the Democratic Party's credibility, and the personal credibility of leading officials, rather than the credibility of the United States. Nor did the passing of the election cause these domestic political considerations to lose power in American policy making; they remained paramount in the all-important three months thereafter, when the decision to escalate the war was made.

Three interconnected themes run through the narrative. The first is the theme of contingency, by which I mean that the period prior to the spring of 1965 was to a considerable extent a fluid one, with several options open. The second theme is the rigidity that characterized American decision making on the war, especially with respect to diplomacy, throughout the eighteen months under study. The third theme is the failure of the large and distinguished group of opponents of escalation to fully commit themselves to preventing it. The first theme suggests that the American war in Vietnam was an unnecessary war; the second and third themes help explain why it nevertheless occurred.

Elaboration on these themes is warranted. In arguing for contingency, I am saying that there was nothing preordained or inevitable about the slide into major war in Vietnam in 1965. The roots of the American intervention were deep, to be sure, but the ultimate decision to Americanize the conflict was highly dependent on individual decisions. The importance of human agency, of contingency, was paramount. Viable alternatives existed for American policy makers, not merely at the beginning of the period under study but also at the end—alternatives advocated at the time by important voices at home and abroad.

The argument that these were viable alternatives runs counter to the predominant view in the existing literature. A quarter century ago, Leslie H. Gelb and Richard K. Betts observed: "To argue that American leaders *could* have withdrawn or had the opportunity to begin disengagement from Vietnam at various stages is not sufficient. Of course, they could choose, but that does not mean they possessed *real* choice."[11] Gelb and Betts were correct: the nub of the matter is indeed whether a real choice existed, and for how long. To pose the question differently, although alternatives might have existed (they always do in history), were these practical alternatives in the actual situation in late 1963 to early 1965, or merely alternatives in theory? For Gelb and Betts, and for the majority of authors who followed them and who have examined the issue at length, the practical alternatives to a stand-firm U.S. posture had disappeared by the latter part of 1964, if not before (for many, the American-backed coup against Diem on 1 November 1963 is the point of no return).[12]

These authors are far from monolithic in their analyses of the war, but they agree that by 1964, a reorientation in U.S. policy leading to disengagement, though certainly preferable in hindsight, is very difficult to imagine. Too much of a commitment to South Vietnam's survival had by then been made, too much credibility was at stake, for *any* American president to realistically have altered course. Even if he had sought to do so, bureaucratic inertia (or, some would say, momentum) would have prevented him from being successful. And besides, virtually no one was asking him to change course: a core component of the "inevitability thesis" is that American public opinion embraced a "Cold War Consensus" in this period and thus wholeheartedly supported a staunch commitment to defend South Vietnam, indeed saw that defense as vital to U.S. security. The Americanization decision thus overwhelmingly represented conventional thinking.[13] Among its international allies as well, so the theory goes, Washington had broad (if not always enthusiastic) backing. Add to all this the Hanoi government's unshakable determination to persevere in the conflict, and it becomes clear that there existed no realistic way of averting war. If one extends this line of analysis far enough, one could logically conclude, as a distinguished scholar recently has, that the Americanization of the Vietnam War is not of major historical interest. If the thing was overdetermined, after all, why study it?[14]

Why indeed. But what if it was not overdetermined? The argument is seemingly compelling, but it ultimately fails to satisfy.[15] Too many of its components crumble when subjected to close scrutiny. At no point during The Long 1964 were American leaders hemmed in on Vietnam. They always had considerable freedom about which way to go in the war. They always possessed real choice. Neither domestic nor international considerations compelled them to escalate the war. At home, they confronted not an all-powerful Cold War Consensus, fully committed to thwarting communist designs in Southeast Asia, but a pronounced fluidity in nonofficial thinking about the conflict, with little support for a larger war.[16] The strong consensus habitually referred to in the literature does not appear until after the Americanization decisions had been made and U.S. ground troops were on the scene. (Vietnam 1965 provides a textbook example of the rally-around-the-flag effect.) In the months prior, opposition to escalation was widespread on Capitol Hill, and numerous newspapers across the United States, including the *New York Times,* the *Washington Post,* and the *Wall Street Journal,* editorialized against any deepening of American involvement. Many prominent columnists did the same. The prevailing myth of a Congress and mainstream press that in late 1964 to early 1965 overwhelmingly favored a firm commitment to the defense of South Vietnam deserves to be discarded.[17]

In the international community, the United States was largely isolated on the Vietnam issue by the end of 1964. The key allies opposed escalation and refused strong U.S. pressure to take part in it, because of deep doubts about both Vietnam's importance to western security and the possibilities of any kind of meaningful "victory." The Chinese and Soviet governments, meanwhile, were supporters of North Vietnam but anxious to avoid a direct military confrontation with the United States. Both were careful in this period not to pledge full-scale support to Hanoi in the event of large-scale American intervention. The Soviets, committed to continuing the moves toward détente with Washington begun in 1963, hoped for a political solution to the conflict, perhaps by way of a reconvened Geneva conference. More important, neither Moscow nor Beijing, nor most American allies, nor indeed many U.S. officials, believed Washington's global credibility would be crippled if it failed to stand firm in South Vietnam, particularly given the poor performance of the Saigon regime.

More than anything, it was this utterly dismal political situation in South Vietnam, and the apparent unwillingness of southern leaders to work to rectify it, that gave American leaders maneuverability on the war. Lethargy, corruption, and in-fighting characterized the political leadership in Saigon, and the Army of the Republic of Vietnam (ARVN) was plagued by high rates of desertion among soldiers and a general reluctance among officers to engage the enemy. In the larger population, war-weariness, induced by twenty years of fighting, was endemic. And underneath it all existed a latent, but potentially powerful, anti-Americanism. Able and dedicated anti-communists committed to the war effort certainly existed in the South, but not in large enough numbers. For scores of independent observers, the implications were clear: there would be no hope for American intervention on any scale unless the South Vietnamese leaders and people themselves first became fully committed to the struggle, something there was no reason to think would happen.

Did senior American officials grasp this reality? The unqualified answer is that they did. A startling aspect of the war in these months is the pronounced pessimism at the center of American strategy on Vietnam.[18] U.S. officials certainly hoped that the new military measures they implemented in 1965 would compel North Vietnam to cease its support of the insurgency in the South and thereafter allow ARVN to turn the tables on the enemy—but they were far from confident that this would actually happen. The hubris so often ascribed to these officials is seldom seen, at least with respect to military prospects. The bulk of intelligence reports told them that Hanoi was in it for the long haul, and allied observers suggested likewise. In low voices among themselves, officials conceded that even if the Ho Chi Minh government could somehow be induced to end its support of the Vietcong, the insurgency would, in the best of circumstances, take several years to stamp out. Most were aware, even as they made the escalation decisions, that an increased U.S. presence in South Vietnam would likely stir widespread resentment among southerners.

Add these elements together—severe doubts both at home and abroad about Vietnam's importance to American and western security; a South Vietnamese ally incapable and apparently unwilling to live up to its end of the bargain; and pessimism among senior American policymakers about the prospects in the conflict—and you have an Americanization decision that could hardly be called overdetermined. This is not to suggest it was *under*determined—given the trajectory of American involvement in Vietnam since 1950, escalation was bound to be one of the options before policymakers in the grim setting of 1964. It is to suggest, however, that American leaders were less constrained by that long involvement than usually is suggested, a reality that, in turn, makes their choice of war less easy to explain.

Which brings us to the book's second major theme, the consistent rigidity in official American thinking about Vietnam. The fluidity that marked assessments about the war outside the halls of power was not present inside. Top officials did not dispute the view that the picture in the South looked grim, or even the argument that long-term success might be impossible regardless of what they did. Nor did they disagree with independent observers who said time and again that the United States faced a stark choice in Vietnam: to dramatically escalate American involvement, thereby changing the very character of the war, or to negotiate some kind of fig leaf for withdrawal. Indeed, among themselves senior policymakers often described their choice in precisely these terms. What they never did, however, was expend equal effort on each of these possibilities. One of the salient characteristics of the massive documentary record for these eighteen months is the gross disparity between the amount of American contingency planning for military escalation and that for a possible diplomatic solution to the conflict; huge stacks of reports on the former, barely a single folder on the latter.

This does not mean that U.S. leaders ignored the subject of negotiations—one can fail to plan for an eventuality and still spend much time thinking about it. Senior officials may have refused to seriously explore avenues for disengagement from the war, but they worried plenty that pressure for such disengagement through diplomatic settlement would become too great to resist. Fear of early negotiations is everywhere in the internal record. American policymakers knew that domestic and international support for the commitment to Saigon, although in general quite broad, was also shallow and could evaporate quickly. Hence they expended a phenomenal amount of energy trying to convince influential critics—that is, those with the capacity to sway large numbers of others—to come around to the administration's point of view, or at least keep their objections quiet. Here, perhaps, is the best proof of all for the absence of any domestic or allied consensus on what to do in the event of collapse in Vietnam: American leaders themselves did not believe such a consensus existed.

Even the demonstrated lack of South Vietnamese commitment to the war effort could not move senior American officials to think about alternatives to a military solution. The coup against Ngo Dinh Diem in November 1963 happened in part because Kennedy administration officials feared that Diem might opt for an end to the war through an agreement with the enemy. Reports that the successor government led by Duong Van Minh might have similar intentions caused Washington to become disenchanted with it as well. And when the popular clamor among South Vietnamese for an early end to the war increased in the latter part of 1964, Lyndon Johnson and his top Vietnam aides became acutely concerned and worked to prevent the ascension to the top of the Saigon regime of anyone who might contemplate a deal with the National Liberation Front (NLF) or Hanoi. The possibility that such a deal might nevertheless be struck caused Washington to speed up its plans for escalation. Nor did Washington follow up when Hanoi, at various points in 1963–1965, indicated a desire to enter talks. Said a State Department intelligence report at the end of the period under study: "Has Hanoi shown any [serious] interest in negotiations? Yes, repeatedly." The same thing could never have been said of the United States.[19]

This American aversion to early negotiations on Vietnam, and even to planning for such a development, suggests the importance to our story (in a negative sense) of the State Department and of the nation's chief diplomat, Secretary of State Dean Rusk. During the mid 1960s, observers took for granted that Rusk occupied a key role in the Vietnam policy-making apparatus—along with Johnson, Secretary of Defense Robert McNamara, and National Security Adviser McGeorge Bundy, he was deemed by Washington scribes to be one of the "Awesome Foursome." Most historians would say that he was very much the junior member of that foursome in terms of influence, at least through the end of 1964—both Bundy and McNamara held greater sway over decision making in these months.[20] But that was at least partly because Rusk allowed them to take control; he preferred to remain in the background, in large part because he believed his department's work would not begin until the war had been turned around (that is, until victory was ensured). In this way, and much more than the recent scholarship has allowed, Rusk's role in the buildup to war was essential, though more for what he did not do than for what he did.[21] As the head of the Department of State, Rusk had a responsibility to explore possible political solutions and speculate imaginatively about ways to get the United States out of what all agreed was a difficult situation, with a minimum of bloodshed and with its honor and prestige largely intact. But Rusk, doggedly committed to a stand-firm policy in the war, engaged in no such speculation and failed to investigate the viability of various attempts to negotiate a settlement in the period prior to escalation. If the mark of the true statesman is the ability not merely to take advantage of existing diplomatic opportunities but to create new ones, Dean Rusk failed the test.

The great tragedy is that Rusk's successive superiors also failed it. To understand the rigidity of American policy on Vietnam during The Long 1964, and the resultant Americanization of the war in 1965, we must understand the aversion to negotiations of John F. Kennedy and the inflexible foreign-policy mind of Lyndon Baines Johnson. Kennedy was never the arch Cold Warrior some have labeled him, and he possessed a better grasp of the dynamics of Southeast Asian politics than his successor. More than Johnson he worried about the lack of allied support for major intervention in Indochina; more than Johnson he sought to keep Vietnam from overshadowing other foreign policy priorities. At various points, notably in the fall of 1961, Kennedy withstood strong pressure from senior subordinates for a large-scale escalation of U.S. involvement in Indochina. But Kennedy nevertheless allowed the American presence in South Vietnam to increase dramatically on his watch, and he rejected numerous appeals that he pursue a political settlement to the conflict. At the time of his death, in November 1963, JFK still sought to temporize on Vietnam, to postpone the truly difficult choices—go in much deeper, or get out—for another day.

For a time Johnson too could temporize, but only for a time. Eventually he had to choose, and for that reason it is he who must loom largest in this story. Many authors, implicitly or explicitly endorsing the argument that

Americanization was overdetermined, have (not surprisingly) viewed the LBJ of 1964–1965 with genuine empathy, as a leader taking the only path open to him in the domestic and foreign political contexts of the time.[22] The evidence, however, shows that Johnson was not pulled into war by deep, structural forces beyond his control; nor was he pulled into it by overzealous advisers from the Kennedy era. He inherited a difficult situation in Vietnam, in large part because of the policy decisions of his predecessor, but he made that situation far worse with his actions, not merely before the November 1964 election but, more important, in the three months thereafter. This period represented the last good chance to withdraw the United States from Vietnam. In those ninety days, Johnson deceived the nation and the Congress about the state of the war and about his plans for it. He, more than his top advisers, feared a premature move to negotiations; he, more than they, ensured that all options to an escalated U.S. involvement were squeezed out of the picture.

It should come as no surprise that the "heroes" of this story are the large number of voices who understood already in 1964 the essential futility of what the United States was trying to do in South Vietnam and who believed that Vietnam was in any case not crucial to American or western security. By the end of that year, the group included most allied governments as well as key members of the Senate Democratic leadership, numerous second-tier officials in the State Department, the National Security Council, the Central Intelligence Agency, and dozens of editorial writers and columnists across the United States.

These were flawed heroes, however, as heroes usually are. The third and final general theme in this book is that so many of the proponents of a political solution failed to challenge the administration in Washington directly with their views on the conflict and what should be done to settle it. Indeed, those domestic and foreign voices who would have had the greatest potential impact on top officials were the most reticent to speak out. Thus, whereas the Paris government of Charles de Gaulle forcefully disputed the U.S. position at every turn, the more important American ally in London consistently refrained from doing so, despite the fact that officials there largely shared the French leader's views. Whereas Senate mavericks like Wayne Morse and Ernest Gruening boldly criticized every aspect of the intervention, their more influential colleagues, such as Majority Leader Mike Mansfield and Foreign Relations Committee Chairman J. William Fulbright, always took care to keep their concerns private and even occasionally to do the administration's bidding. United Nations Secretary General U Thant, convinced already in 1963 that any major American intervention would

fail, and by the late summer of 1964 that Hanoi leaders were willing to enter talks with the United States, acceded to American requests into 1965 that
he not push publicly for negotiations. Undersecretary of State George W.
Ball, though genuinely opposed to an expanded war, willingly became the
designated in-house "dove" on Vietnam and always put careerist ambition
and loyalty to Johnson before principle; outside high-level meetings, few administration aides in 1964 and early 1965 were more hawkish than he. Even
the columnist Walter Lippmann, the earliest and most prescient of all prominent American critics, for a long time valued his insider status too much to
break completely with Johnson over the war; when he finally did so in the
spring of 1965, Americanization was a reality.[23]

The critics failed in another sense as well. Nearly all of them, including
de Gaulle, were much better at pointing out the flaws in current American
policy and the likely futility of escalation than at identifying alternative
solutions and the means to achieve them. Though it would be unfair to insist that the proponents of a political settlement should have stated precisely what such a settlement would have looked like and how it would
have been reached (the advocates of escalation were certainly no better at
explaining where their preferred course was likely to lead), it is nevertheless true that they tended to be vague about what they meant by terms
such as *neutralization* and *negotiation*. They proclaimed that a "political
solution" was the answer but said relatively little about the difficulties involved in reaching such a solution. Realists such as Lippmann offered the
"national interest" as the key criterion for effective policy making without
sufficiently acknowledging that the phrase is open to varying interpretations and is therefore an imperfect guide to the dilemmas of policy.

Ironically, the same shortcoming is evident in previous studies that, like
this one, see options to an Americanized war in the first half of 1965. To
argue for contingency, for realistic alternatives to an American war in Vietnam, brings with it an added responsibility, one with which proponents of
inevitability need not concern themselves. That responsibility is to subject
these alternatives to analytic scrutiny, to give attention to what would
have been required to implement them and what would likely have resulted if they had been. It will not do to merely state that a face-saving
American disengagement could have been arranged in, say, late 1964, after
LBJ had been safely returned to the White House. Precisely *how* could it
have been arranged? What would likely have happened if it had been? In
his memoirs, Robert McNamara suggests that there were several "missed
opportunities" for an American withdrawal in 1963 to 1965. He further
notes, accurately, that he and his colleagues failed to explore those opportunities. Unfortunately, he then commits the same error again, saying next

to nothing in his book about what choosing an alternative path would have meant. Others who have argued for "missed opportunities" have likewise failed to say much about how reasonable these were and what might have been the result had they been adopted.[24] It is a counterfactual question, resistant to conclusive answer, but it is no less important for that.[25] It shall get significant attention in this book.

Consider again the three core questions listed at the outset: Why did the United States opt for large-scale war in Vietnam? Could the war have been averted? If so, how? To a degree I did not initially realize, my ultimate answer to the second question, a resounding yes, complicated my task with respect to the other two. It forced me to think about and frame an answer to the third question, and it required that I think more deeply about the first one. The "structural forces" explanation for Americanization, which had initially struck me as intellectually sophisticated, proved intellectually insufficient, even lazy, particularly after I examined the wider context— domestic and foreign—of American decision making. The reality was more human, more messy, more interesting.

It was also more disturbing. Writing this book stirred strong emotions in me, for reasons that should become clear but to a degree that I had not anticipated. I knew of the passionate nature of the debate over the war, but I thought my background and approach would allow me to remain above the fray. Born in the same year that John F. Kennedy and Ngo Dinh Diem met their deaths, in a place—Stockholm, Sweden—about as far removed from the scene of the fighting as one could be, I had no memories of the Vietnam War or the controversy surrounding it (even the considerable internal Swedish debate over the struggle in the late 1960s and early 1970s went completely by my young mind). When as a graduate student in the United States I began my inquiry, I thus had no irreducible existential stake in the subject, unlike so many of an earlier generation. I also knew the dangers of presentism, of judging the past by the mores of the present, and I knew of the capacity of hindsight to falsify our picture of the past. I was determined to fulfill the historian's obligation to explore what people did— and what they thought they were doing—in the context of their own time.

But herein lay the key. My findings were so troubling precisely because they were not dependent on hindsight. Too many folks *at the time*, in too many important locales, foresaw the essential futility of what Washington sought to achieve. Too many were convinced, *at the time*, that it was unnecessary even to try. This realization, along with the finding that U.S. officials were themselves pessimistic about the prospects and, in many cases, dubious of Vietnam's importance, raised questions in my mind not merely about the wisdom of America's Vietnam policy during The Long 1964 but also about the motivations behind that policy; I questioned not merely the practicality of the chosen course, but also the morality of it. There was no avoiding these larger implications, and I will address them in the concluding chapter. First, however, a more immediate task awaits: to examine the history of these crucial months and the developments that would make Vietnam an American war.

Abbreviations Used in the Text

The following abbreviations are used throughout the text:

AFC	Armed Forces Council
AFP	Agence France Presse
ARVN	Army of the Republic of Vietnam
BRIAM	British Advisory Mission to South Vietnam
CFR	Council of Foreign Relations
CIA	Central Intelligence Agency
Desoto	U.S. destroyer patrols into the Gulf of Tonkin along the coast of North Vietnam
DRV	Democratic Republic of Vietnam
EEC	European Economic Community
ExCom	Executive Committee (of the NSC)
FRC	Senate Foreign Relations Committee
GVN	Government of Vietnam
ICC	International Commission on Supervision and Control
INR	Bureau of Intelligence and Research, U.S. State Department
JCS	Joint Chiefs of Staff
JFK	John F. Kennedy
LBJ	Lyndon B. Johnson
MACV	U.S. Military Assistance Command in South Vietnam
MLF	Multilateral Force
MRC	Military Revolutionary Council
NATO	North Atlantic Treaty Organization
NLF	National Front for the Liberation of South Vietnam
NSAM	National Security Action Memorandum
NSC	National Security Council
Oplan	Operations plan

PAVN	People's Army of Vietnam
RFK	Robert F. Kennedy
RVN	Republic of Vietnam
SEA	Southeast Asia
SEAD	South-East Asia Department at the British Foreign Office
SEATO	Southeast Asia Treaty Organization
SNIE	Special National Intelligence Estimate
SVN	South Vietnam
UN	United Nations
USG	U.S. government
USIS	U.S. Information Service
VC	Vietcong
VOA	Voice of America

1 The Kickoff

We begin not in Washington or Saigon or Hanoi but in Paris: Paris with its long and tangled attachment to the affairs of Vietnam, Paris where French leaders had ruled Indochina for three-quarters of a century and where generations of privileged Vietnamese had gone to be educated. The imperial relationship was no more; the Vietnamese had learned more than they were supposed to, and a long and bloody war of independence had ended in a French defeat at the hands of the Vietminh in 1954.[1] Yet the French social and cultural influence in Vietnam remained significant, which ensured that any official pronouncement out of Paris relating to the former colony was bound to attract notice. There would be such an announcement on this day, 29 August 1963. France's president, General Charles de Gaulle, believed that a major crisis threatened in Vietnam, one that again involved a western power, this time the United States.

The general was far from alone in this view. The international community's attention was riveted on Vietnam in a way it had not been since the time of the 1954 Geneva Conference that ended the Franco-Vietminh War. Yet there was always a sense that this day might come, because the signing of the peace accords had not ended the struggle for Vietnam. The conferees at Geneva had divided Vietnam at the seventeenth parallel, with the communist Vietminh assuming power in the North and noncommunist forces retaining control in the South, and with the understanding that there would be elections for reunification in 1956. The elections did not take place, and the division remained. The United States, determined after 1954 to create and sustain a noncommunist bastion in the South, threw its backing behind the government of Ngo Dinh Diem, supported his decision to bypass the elections, and steadily expanded its involvement in South Vietnamese affairs. Without American aid, the Catholic-dominated Government of Vietnam (GVN) would have foundered because it faced not only a hostile North

1

under Ho Chi Minh but, beginning in the late 1950s, a Hanoi-supported insurgency in South Vietnam.[2]

By the start of 1963, the American presence in the South had grown to more than sixteen thousand military personnel, some of whom took part in combat operations, and U.S. expenditures totaled more than one million dollars per day. And yet political stability remained elusive. The insurgency continued to grow in intensity, fueled by the government's repression and by its growing dependence on American largesse. Then, in May 1963, when government troops opened fire on observers of a Buddhist holiday, a full-blown crisis erupted. An escalating spiral of Buddhist demonstrations and regime countermeasures caused South Vietnam to move, by late August, to the verge of chaos. Reports proliferated in the world press and among the Saigon diplomatic corps about growing American dissatisfaction with the Diem government and especially the increased power within it of Diem's brother, Ngo Dinh Nhu, the mastermind behind the crackdown against the Buddhists. There were rumors of an impending coup d'état against the government by dissident generals of the Army of the Republic of Vietnam (ARVN).

De Gaulle's statement, made in a cabinet meeting on 29 August and then (in a highly uncommon procedure) cited verbatim to the press by Minister of Information Alain Peyrefitte, contained no specific policy proposals. But there was no mistaking its central message. "The serious events taking place in Vietnam are being followed in Paris with attention and emotion," de Gaulle declared. The long history of French-Vietnamese relations and the close ties that France retained in "the country as a whole" led the French people to "understand particularly well, and share sincerely, the hardships of the Vietnamese people." This understanding, he continued, also allowed Frenchmen to perceive the positive role that Vietnam could play in Asia, "for its own progress and for the benefit of international understanding, once it is able to carry on its activity independent of outside influences, in internal peace and unity, and in concord with its neighbors." Today more than ever, France wanted such a result for "all of Vietnam," de Gaulle said, and he offered his country's help to realize it: "Naturally, it is up to [the Vietnamese people] and to them alone to choose the means to bring this about. But every national effort which might be undertaken in Vietnam toward this end would find France ready, to the extent she is able, to set up a cordial cooperation with this country."[3]

The implications were clear. Without mentioning the United States by name, the general had left no doubt that he opposed the American commitment to preserve an independent, noncommunist South Vietnam. Vietnam was one country, he had suggested, and it should be reunited. The country moreover ought to be "independent of outside influences," by which he presumably meant both the American commitment in the South and the Chinese and Soviet influence in the North. Finally, the Vietnamese could count on French support should they opt for reunification and independence. Though contemporaneous observers understood full well the importance of these assertions—the story made the front page of several major newspapers around the world the following day, and in Saigon rumors spread like wildfire that de Gaulle was laying the groundwork for a proposal to reunify Vietnam through a Laos-type neutralization—they loom even larger in hindsight, because of what we now know about policy deliberations in Washington at exactly the same time.

When the day began in Washington on 29 August, Charles de Gaulle's statement was still a few hours away from being issued. Already, however, it was shaping up to be a day of reckoning. Overnight a cable had arrived from the U.S. ambassador in Saigon, Henry Cabot Lodge, which minced no words: "We are launched," Lodge wrote, "on a course from which there is no respectable turning back: the overthrow of the Diem government." John F. Kennedy had this cable before him early in the day. No doubt he had already seen that day's *Washington Post*, which included large headlines on the previous day's civil rights march in the city and two smaller ones from Saigon: "Nhu Called Real Viet-Nam Ruler," and "Vietnamese Regime Headed for Showdown with U.S." He had certainly seen an article that appeared on the front page of the *New York Times* the previous day, for he now called senior State Department official Roger Hilsman about it. The article, titled "Long Crisis Seen on Vietnam Rule," and written by reporter Tad Szulc, reported that high officials in Washington believed that removing Ngo Dinh Nhu alone or both Nhu and his brother Diem was the only way to solve America's Vietnam problems. "He seems to be getting pretty close to things," Kennedy said of Szulc in asking who might be the source for the story. Pretty close indeed. A few hours later, an "eyes only" cable from Washington to Saigon gave the presidential approval for a coup d'état. Late in the day, Kennedy followed this cable to Lodge with one of his own, which affirmed U.S. support for a coup but also emphasized that he, Kennedy, reserved the right to reverse course. "When we go, we must go to win, but it will be better to change our minds than fail," the president wrote.[4]

Thus the logic of beginning our story at the end of August 1963: it represented a key juncture in the war. Both the documentary record and later testimonials make this clear. In retrospect, certainly, it can be said that the latter part of August brought two critical and interconnected changes with respect to the war, critical in particular given our aim of establishing why major war erupted in Vietnam in 1965 and whether that war could have been prevented. First, after mid August Vietnam for the first time became a high-priority, day-to-day issue for America's foreign policymakers, and it would remain such for the next ten years.[5] In the last week of the month the Kennedy administration reaffirmed its commitment to defeating the insurgency in South Vietnam and demonstrated this commitment in the starkest of ways: by seeking to oust the sitting government in Saigon in favor of a new regime, one that Washington hoped would be more able and more willing to prosecute the war.

Second, the month witnessed, in de Gaulle's pronouncement, the first major attempt at diminishing the tensions and preventing the resumption of large-scale war—what Jean Lacouture later called the "kick-off" of the diplomatic game in Vietnam.[6] The French president had summoned the Vietnamese to be independent at the very moment Americans were moving to replace Diem with a leader more able (in their view) to pursue the war effort. He had chosen to speak of peace when the overriding concern in Washington was how to best prosecute the war. In the eighteen months that followed, more and more observers would come to share the essentials of de Gaulle's vision of the conflict, until, by the spring of 1965, most world leaders embraced them, together with important voices in the United States. In the months and years that followed, many opponents of the war would make a point of invoking his name in laying out their arguments against a military solution.[7]

Of course, it was one thing to endorse the French president's analysis in 1966 or 1967, when full-scale war raged in Vietnam and the end seemed nowhere in sight, and quite another to do so in mid 1963. How reasonable was de Gaulle's call for a political settlement in the context of that summer? It is a large question in history, for if the general saw things correctly it means that the Second Indochina War might have been ended before it really began, before the destruction of large portions of Indochina and the deaths of millions. To answer the question requires examining the perspectives in North and South Vietnam in the middle of 1963, as well as the thinking among the major actors in the larger international community—by common agreement, these were France, Great Britain, the Soviet Union, China, and the United States.[8] It is to that task we now turn. We shall find that the thinking in several of the key capitals was fluid that summer—partly because of important changes in the international system—with considerable support for the French president's analysis, including his belief in the need for a political solution. We shall also find, however, little inclination among these governments to work for a negotiated settlement, and determined opposition to negotiations from the most important player of all: the United States. It is no contradiction to say that the summer of 1963 constituted one of the great missed opportunities to prevent the tragedy that was the Vietnam War, and one that never came close to being realized.

The proximate cause of both de Gaulle's pronouncement and Kennedy's coup decision was the grave crisis in U.S.–South Vietnamese relations. The Buddhist affair had brought those relations to their lowest point ever, but the warning signs had been there long before. From the moment of Ngo Dinh Diem's appointment as prime minister in 1954, American officials had been concerned about his shortcomings as a leader—his political myopia, his tendency toward paranoia, his unwillingness to delegate authority beyond his immediate family. Nevertheless they had stuck with him, partly because they thought his staunch anticommunism and fervent nationalism might make up for those weaknesses, and partly because no adequate replacement appeared anywhere in sight. "Sink or Swim with Ngo Dinh Diem" became the defining slogan. As late as April 1963, in meetings with British officials, Kennedy administration representatives stuck to this line.[9]

Already then, however, in the weeks *before* the Buddhist crisis broke, U.S.-GVN relations were poor. The Americans were distressed by the wastefulness and inefficiency with which the Vietnamese handled the material aid they received, by the regime's unwillingness to implement political reforms, and by the growing power of Ngo Dinh Nhu. For the past year, Nhu had told British and French officials that there were too many Americans in South Vietnam, and he had become more insistent on the issue in the spring of 1963. On 1 April Nhu told Australian officials in Saigon that the American "way of life" was completely inapplicable to an underdeveloped but ancient society like Vietnam and that it would be good if half the U.S. personnel currently in the country went home. He repeated the claim several times that month. Diem adhered to a more circumspect position, but it was well known to diplomats in Saigon that the president, too, chafed under the weight of the American presence.[10]

Then came the eighth of May and the crackdown on the Buddhists. American officials were perplexed and irritated at this government action in a country in which 80 percent of the population practiced some form of Buddhism. Ambassador Frederick Nolting was instructed to remonstrate with Diem and urge him to reduce Buddhist irritation and calm the crisis. But following some halfhearted government attempts at conciliation, the tension continued to escalate. There were more protest demonstrations, and more Nhu-orchestrated police suppression. American contingency plans for the possible emergence of a new government, already in existence but for a long time dormant, were revived. As the weeks passed and the crisis deepened, and as Diem proved resistant to following U.S. advice (American pressure in fact seemed only to make him and his brother more stubborn, with Nhu now openly sneering at Washington), a consensus developed among several senior State Department officials that the regime should be ousted.[11] The members of this group, which included Undersecretary of State George W. Ball and Assistant Secretaries Roger Hilsman Jr. and W. Averell Harriman, won a crucial ally in their cause in Henry Cabot Lodge, the prominent Republican named by Kennedy to replace Nolting as ambassador. Firmly convinced that Nhu and, if necessary, Diem had to go, these men managed by the last week of August to get the rest of the administration to go along.[12]

How did the Diem government respond to all this? Did the severe downturn in U.S.-Saigon relations in the summer of 1963 make the Ngo brothers receptive to a separate peace with North Vietnam (formally the Democratic Republic of Vietnam, or DRV)? The question has long intrigued students of the war. That some contacts between Nhu and individuals from the DRV took place in this period seems clear.[13] On 10 August, in talks with British diplomats Lord Selkirk and Donald Murray, Nhu spoke of having regular meetings with members of the "Dien Bien Phu" generation in North Vietnam. He told Selkirk that there was a considerable body of patriotic individuals in Hanoi who were nationalists first and communists second, men who were in their midforties and who had fought against the French and who naturally had been in the ranks of Ho Chi Minh's forces because he had provided the power and organization to bring about the liberation. They were persons who rightly sought a Vietnamese solution to the Vietnamese problem, and, Nhu added, "I have had some of them sitting in this room." Selkirk and the British embassy found Nhu's claims credible, including his assertion that the visitors were actual representatives of the Hanoi government rather than private citizens. Other believers included French ambassador Roger Lalouette and Mieczyslaw Maneli, the new Polish delegate to the International Commission for Supervision and Control (ICC),* both of whom had indeed encouraged Nhu to seek a dialogue with

---

*The ICC was created by the Geneva Accords of 1954. Its three members—one each from communist Poland, anticommunist Canada, and neutralist India—were ostensibly in place to prevent outside powers from violating the Accords by providing arms to either the North or the South. The commission proved largely powerless, and few inspections took place. But the delegates did have the privilege of being able to travel easily between Hanoi and Saigon and were thus believed to be informed about the thinking on both sides of the war.

Hanoi. "Saigon is buzzing with rumors about secret contacts between Diem-Nhu and Ho Chi Minh," Maneli reported to Warsaw and the Soviet embassy in a top-secret cable. "On the basis of information I have received strictly privately in the North, it is possible to conclude that some kind of Ngo-Ho talks have begun, through direct emissaries in the North."[14]

The historian would like to know more, of course, including where in the Hanoi bureaucracy these officials toiled. More important, it remains to be determined what Ngo Dinh Nhu hoped to achieve with his gambit. American officials professed to believe, then and later in the fall, that his motive was merely to secure increased leverage with Washington, in effect to blackmail the Kennedy administration into retreating from its efforts to reform the Ngo family.[15] No doubt this was part of it. It also seems likely, however, that by late July or early August Nhu had concluded that U.S. hostility toward him had risen to the point that an accommodation with his Vietnamese opponents might be his only chance for political survival. His wife, Madame Nhu, who in early 1964 was to affirm that talks had been going on, cited this latter motivation as most important. She even revealed that she and Nhu were prepared to send their two oldest children to school in Hanoi as a "fraternal gesture." Brigadier Robert G. K. Thompson of the British Advisory Mission to South Vietnam (BRIAM) told officials at the U.S. embassy that Nhu's only trump card was an American withdrawal from Vietnam, a point also made by F. A. Warner, head of the South-East Asia Department (SEAD) at the British Foreign Office. "In the long run," Warner told colleagues in London, "the only thing that can save Nhu and Diem would be an accommodation with North Vietnam, for this would produce a completely new state of affairs in which they could try and pull people together again in the South."[16]

There is much to commend in this argument. The idea that Nhu and his brother could long have survived in power following any kind of deal with Hanoi seems altogether doubtful, but it is not so crazy to think Nhu would give it a try if he knew—as he surely did by the last half of August—that Washington was determined to remove him from all political power, through a coup if necessary.[17] The prospect of, say, twelve or eighteen months in power following an accord would look quite appealing if the alternative might be an ouster within weeks. Whether Diem would have gone along with such a scheme is, of course, anything but certain. Given Diem's unshakable anticommunism throughout his nine years in power, it indeed may be doubted. Opposition from Diem may have mattered less now than it would have a few months earlier, however, given Nhu's growing power in the Saigon government. By the middle of August, the diplomatic community in Saigon appears to have been in broad agreement that the man now in effective control of the government of Vietnam was Ngo Dinh Nhu.

Nhu's claims regarding the existence of North-South contacts take on added credibility when one considers that it was in North Vietnam's interest to explore the thinking of the de facto leader of the southern regime. The available evidence suggests strongly that Hanoi leaders in this period were broadly sympathetic to a negotiated settlement of the conflict. Well before this point, in fact, northern officials had expressed hopes for a settlement. In March 1962, for example, while the negotiations for a neutral Laos were still ongoing, North Vietnamese foreign minister Ung Van Khiem had formally asked the cochairs of the 1954 Geneva Conference, Britain and the USSR, to "proceed to consultations with the interested countries to seek effective means of preserving the Geneva settlement of 1954 and safeguarding peace." The following month another senior Hanoi official had suggested publicly that a new Geneva conference be called to discuss South Vietnam, on the theory that the "Laotian model" could be applied there as well. The same appeal was made in midyear by the National Front for the Liberation of South Vietnam (NLF), the political arm of the Vietcong. And at the end of 1962, Ho Chi Minh advocated peaceful reunification of North and South Vietnam through negotiation.[18]

Leaders in the North appear to have reasoned that, although Washington was more committed to the Vietnam conflict than to the one in Laos, the administration was reluctant to intervene directly in the struggle against the Vietcong. According to William J. Duiker, an authority on Hanoi's strategy in the war, the North Vietnamese in 1962 believed that the Kennedy administration might be willing to accept a diplomatic solution, even if it were really a disguised defeat. Such a solution would allow Hanoi to meet one of its core aims—to avoid a direct military confrontation with the United States—and satisfy demands from both Beijing and Moscow that the Indochina conflict not be allowed to get out of hand. In July, senior Politburo member Le Duan accordingly instructed the leadership of the southern resistance to avoid a major escalation of the war by keeping the fighting confined to the mountain and rural areas of South Vietnam (direct attacks on the cities could result in the Americans intervening directly in the war) and to work for a negotiated settlement and a U.S. withdrawal.[19]

In March 1963 Premier Pham Van Dong elaborated on Hanoi's vision for negotiations. In a meeting with the Polish diplomat Maneli, Pham Van

Dong said a Geneva conference on South Vietnam should be convened, with the aim of establishing a neutral South Vietnam led by a coalition government. This government would include the NLF as well as other groups. There would be no need to adopt neutralization also for North Vietnam, since there were at present no foreign troops or foreign bases on North Vietnamese soil. (On the issue of DRV infiltration of men and supplies into the South, the premier was silent.) Pham Van Dong emphasized, however, that he understood that the United States could not be expected to lose face and must be allowed to "withdraw with honor satisfied"; as a result, reunification of the two zones of Vietnam would take place only gradually, and the coalition government would be a democratic one (in the "western" sense of the word, he said). J. Kenneth Blackwell, who headed the small staff at the British consulate in Hanoi, gave a very similar sense of North Vietnamese intentions. Hanoi leaders, he told London in April, "are now clearly working towards a negotiated settlement through an international conference and are apparently prepared to accept . . . the indefinite neutralisation and independence of South Vietnam."[20]

Blackwell had some reason to speak with such confidence about Hanoi's intentions: at various times in the early months of 1963 he spoke with Foreign Minister Ung Van Khiem, with the Soviet ambassador in Hanoi, and with members of the French delegation there. All suggested to him that North Vietnam, though in no way slackening in its commitment to ultimate victory (which meant reunification under its control), sought to give the Americans a face-saving way out of the war and was prepared to delay reunification—an important concession, in Blackwell's view, given the emotional appeal of making Vietnam one nation again—in order to achieve this result.[21]

The question is why. In Blackwell's view, two main motives moved the DRV leadership in this direction. First, though they remained fundamentally confident about long-term trends in the war effort, they had concluded to their dismay that the large-scale increase in the American advisory presence during 1962 had made an important difference on the ground, improving to some extent the military position of the GVN. The result, northern strategists surmised, could be a lengthy stalemate in the South, with the Vietcong controlling much of the countryside and the Diem regime maintaining its grip on the cities. (Recall Le Duan's directive to the Vietcong to refrain from launching major attacks on urban areas.) For this reason alone, exploring the possibilities of negotiated solution made sense—if such a deal would get rid of the Americans, all other problems were soluble.[22] In addition, Blackwell believed that the deepening Sino-Soviet split had affected Hanoi's thinking. He saw the North as walking a "tightrope" between the two Communist powers, and that, notwithstanding the pro-Chinese rhetoric coming out of Hanoi at various times in 1963, its leaders were anxious to avoid unduly alienating Moscow.[23] Like his colleagues at the Foreign Office, and indeed virtually all international observers, Blackwell thought the Vietnamese basically anti-Chinese, and his contacts with northern leaders convinced him they were acutely concerned about the prospect of becoming a vassal of Beijing, and about the possibility of a major war between China and the United States fought on North Vietnamese soil and using Vietnamese men.

The growing rift between Washington and the GVN in the spring and summer may also have inclined Hanoi to probe for an early settlement. North Vietnamese leaders could reasonably expect any successor government in Saigon to be too dependent on the United States to agree to a compromise settlement, and conclude that the time to act was now, especially given the rising tenor of Ngo Dinh Nhu's anti-American outbursts. (One can imagine their satisfaction at hearing Nhu declare the American way of life inapplicable to Vietnam and asking for half of the American contingent to leave.) In addition, the North, with much less arable land than the South, was that year experiencing the worst drought it had known since the end of the war against France, in 1954. All available hands, including schoolchildren and office workers, were pressed into service to dig canals and to irrigate the fields. Nevertheless, more than two hundred thousand hectares of rice paddy were ravaged, and in many areas river levels dropped too low for the water to reach the rice fields. Hanoi was forced to ask China and the Soviet Union for food aid, which only left it even more at the mercy of their growing rivalry. According to procommunist Australian journalist Wilfred Burchett, Ho Chi Minh told him all this was an added incentive for making a deal with Saigon. Similarly, Hoang Tung, the Communist Party head of propaganda, confirmed to journalist Stanley Karnow in Hanoi in 1981 that it was partly because of the drought that the North Vietnamese had tried to "probe the depth of differences" between the Ngo brothers and the United States.[24]

The skeptical reader may wonder why, if this analysis is correct and the Hanoi leadership favored a diplomatic settlement to the conflict in this period, it did not work harder to try to get one. There was no full-fledged campaign by DRV officials for a Geneva conference in 1962–1963, after all, no strong efforts through diplomatic channels to get talks going. Probably the answer is that the foregoing is not the whole picture. Even as Hanoi saw the benefits of negotiations, it also saw dangers. Its leaders knew from

1954 that victories gained on the battlefield could be taken away at the conference table, and they were reluctant to put forth proposals that might bind them to a specific course of action or to dealing with a specific group. They therefore may have preferred clandestine bilateral talks with Saigon to reactivating the Geneva conference machinery, as the latter could be cumbersome and less responsive to their desires. A bilateral deal would also avoid the DRV having to face charges from the world community that it was violating the Geneva Accords by having troops in neighboring Laos. Moreover, the North Vietnamese were not yet desperate. As concerned as many senior officials were about various developments—about the deepening Sino-Soviet split; about perhaps falling under Chinese control in the event of an expanded war; about the prospect of future droughts like the current one; and about the likelihood of a coup in Saigon that would bring in a regime wholly dependent on the United States—they also had reason to feel pretty good about the overall course of the war in the South. True, the influx of Americans had improved the Saigon regime's military position and made the prospect of an early GVN collapse less likely. But the Vietcong continued to apply pressure on the government, continued to score military victories, continued to win recruits. The Diem regime, meanwhile, continued to lose support among the people, to the point that—as both Hanoi officials and foreign diplomats in Saigon knew—very few southerners were willing to fight and die for its survival. Hanoi leaders could also take comfort in the fact that the fighting had not yet put much strain on North Vietnamese resources—the insurgency in the South was to a large extent self-sustaining. All this helps explain the apparent lack of urgency with which the DRV approached the issue of diplomacy. After all, why strive for an accommodation with Ngo Dinh Nhu when he and his brother were in the process of antagonizing so many important segments of the southern population?

Finally, and paradoxically, it may be that the Sino-Soviet split, while on the one hand making the North Vietnamese more attracted to a political solution in the South, also may have inhibited them from actually pursuing one. Notwithstanding their determination to avoid antagonizing either side in the ideological dispute and to make decisions in terms of what best served the DRV's interests, they saw no reason to alienate the powerful neighbor next door unless absolutely necessary. More often than not, North Vietnamese public statements in 1963 echoed the Chinese position in the Sino-Soviet dispute—that is, as good Marxist-Leninists they claimed that the USSR under Nikita Khrushchev had deviated from pure doctrine in supporting "revisionism" in Yugoslavia and in espousing "peaceful co-existence" and "world peace." Though European diplomats were correct in not reading too much into this rhetoric, it does suggest that North Vietnamese officials were skittish about sounding too accommodating with the West, too eager for a peaceful resolution to the conflict in South Vietnam.

Nevertheless, the original point stands: the period from early 1962 to mid 1963 witnessed a more forthcoming North Vietnamese position on the subject of diplomacy than had been seen previously. If Hanoi officials were sufficiently suspicious of diplomatic bargaining generally, and sufficiently pleased with the state of the insurgency, to prefer a wait-and-see approach over an active *search* for negotiations, there can be little doubt that they were more open than hitherto to the idea of shifting the struggle to the political plane. More than that, key elements in the northern leadership in mid 1963 sincerely hoped for a political solution to the conflict and were prepared to compromise—by agreeing to a delay in unification—in order to get it. The potential benefits of such a move were too obvious for them to rule out.[25] Thus in August, Ho Chi Minh suggested publicly that a cease-fire be worked out in the South. Robert Thompson captured the DRV's basic motivation well: to ensure an American withdrawal, he told officials at the American embassy, Hanoi would pay almost any price. Poland's Maneli and France's Laloulette believed likewise, as did Ramchundur Goburdhun, the Indian delegate to the ICC who spoke to Hanoi leaders on a regular basis.[26]

The constellation of forces within Vietnam thus suggested the possibility in the middle of 1963 for fashioning some kind of political solution to the Indochina conflict, whether by way of a bilateral North-South deal or a multipower conference. What about the position of forces outside the country? Here, too, informed observers saw genuine possibilities for a negotiated solution. This was a sound interpretation, though it also contained a certain degree of wishful thinking, at least if these observers expected such a solution to be actually implemented. It was sound because several of the world powers that would have attended a reconvened Geneva conference were broadly supportive of attempting a negotiated settlement to the conflict. It was wishful thinking because each of these governments preferred to adhere to the same wait-and-see attitude adopted by the North Vietnamese, and because the United States was resolutely opposed to an early political settlement.

Among the major world powers, France felt most strongly that no reasonable alternative existed to some kind of peaceful resolution, whether by a bilateral accord between Saigon and Hanoi or via an international meeting. De Gaulle's pronouncement of 29 August came as no surprise to close observers of his foreign policy. For years he had been convinced that the

United States–Ngo Dinh Diem alliance was destined to fail.[27] This conviction grew in part out of his low opinion of Diem; he had always seen the Saigon leader as the wrong man for the job, neither popular among his people nor capable of uniting the various political factions in South Vietnam. More important, de Gaulle determined in the late 1950s that the United States would not succeed in Indochina where France had failed, even with superior military power, because the struggle in Vietnam was fundamentally a political and not a military problem—a struggle for the minds and hearts of the people of South Vietnam—and one that demanded an internal solution. Therefore, the Americans and not the North Vietnamese were the outsiders in the conflict. De Gaulle was convinced that in an age of decolonization, nationalism would prevail even over a superpowerful United States, and thus some form of neutralization was the best that could be hoped for. Neutralization would not be tantamount to the surrender of Southeast Asia to communism, as Americans believed; even should all of Vietnam become communist, neighboring countries would not necessarily follow suit. Above all, neutralization would bring peace to the region without substantially endangering the West's position in the world balance of power. On each of these points de Gaulle had the support of the French representatives in Saigon and Hanoi as well as Foreign Minister Maurice Couve de Murville and other top officials at the Quai d'Orsay.[28]

Neutralization is a protean term, and de Gaulle did not specify precisely what he meant by it. Fundamentally, he used the term to describe a situation in which the Vietnamese themselves would settle their conflict without external interference. In terms of how that settlement would be reached, de Gaulle had in mind an end to the war against the Vietcong insurgents by the Saigon government and a move to more normal contacts with Hanoi, the creation of a coalition government in Saigon including the Vietcong, the reduction of and eventual ending of the American military presence in the South, and the eventual negotiating of a North-South confederation and perhaps unification. The process might begin with a Geneva-type conference of major powers, or a bilateral deal between Saigon and Hanoi.[29]

De Gaulle saw little to fear in the prospect of a reunified Vietnam under communist control, which he conceded was the most likely ultimate outcome in the event of an American withdrawal. For de Gaulle, ideologies were passing phenomena in the life of nations, which he saw as the only realities. He reasoned that traditional Vietnamese animosity toward China would make Chinese control of Indochina highly unlikely and that a unified Vietnam suspicious of the West and led by Ho would likely turn to the USSR as the most trusted and geographically remote friend. The Soviets, with no territorial ambitions in the region, would welcome an ally there.

As a result, Chinese ambitions would be checked, and peace would come to Southeast Asia.

De Gaulle grew more confident as 1963 progressed that, for the first time in many years, there might be an opportunity to fashion a political settlement. A key issue for him appears to have been the deepening of the Sino-Soviet split that occurred in the spring and summer. For de Gaulle, the split had important implications for the Vietnam conflict. The USSR, anxious to keep Chinese influence from spreading in the region, would welcome a negotiated settlement. More important, North Vietnam would be more amenable to it than previously. De Gaulle knew from the French delegation in Hanoi that the North Vietnamese felt squeezed between Moscow and Beijing and that key elements in the DRV leadership, though still wholly committed to achieving eventual reunification of the country under communist control, were beginning to look for relief in the fighting in the South as a means of reducing the pressure from Beijing and lowering the chances of North Vietnam becoming a Chinese satellite. "It is not improbable," a late-summer assessment by the British embassy in Paris said, "that some time during August General de Gaulle decided that for the first time since 1954 it was possible to believe that the North might be willing to lower the temperature in the struggle with the South in order to avoid a further escalation of the guerrilla war which would force them further into the arms of the Chinese."[30]

The Saigon leadership would have far less to gain from any talks, but de Gaulle believed that it, too, might be amenable to some kind of deal, given the increased pressure from Washington and the rumors of coup plotting by ARVN generals. He received encouragement on this point from the French ambassador in Saigon, Roger Laloulette. Like de Gaulle, Laloulette had long been dubious about the prospects for the U.S.-GVN alliance, and he thought that Ho Chi Minh might be prepared to accept a cease-fire in the conflict rather than run the risk of being forced by China into a gradual escalation of hostilities. In addition, Laloulette believed that war-weariness among the South Vietnamese people had become so deep and pervasive that an early end to the war was essential, and he dismissed the notion that any successor regime the Americans might bring in could hope to bring the war to a successful conclusion. Beginning in early 1963 Laloulette warned the Ngos against allowing too many Americans into the country and advised them to open a dialogue with Hanoi. Then in early August he returned to Paris for consultations, and a decision was made that he would promote the concept of neutralization with Diem and Nhu. He did so on at least one occasion in late August. Laloulette told the brothers it would be in their interests to distance themselves from the United States by requesting that

some American advisers leave South Vietnam. Following that action, Laloulette suggested, a negotiated settlement with the NLF and perhaps Hanoi
could be reached. Diem and Nhu sounded receptive, Laloulette reported.[31]

What about the United States? Did the general believe that the Kennedy administration would seriously consider abandoning America's long-
standing pursuit of a military solution in Vietnam in favor of a political one,
especially in view of the weak negotiating position held by the South Vietnamese and United States? It is difficult to say. Probably he doubted it. But
de Gaulle could point to the Laos crisis of 1961 as a situation that bore important similarities to the current one in Vietnam, and in which Kennedy
had opted for negotiations rather than war, in part because of the advice
he received from France and Britain. If JFK had shown such wisdom once,
why not again? In addition, de Gaulle may well have surmised that the
evident oppressiveness of the Saigon regime, together with its blatant disregard of American advice, made disengagement for Kennedy a much less
costly proposition, in domestic political terms, than at any time previously.
Finally, it is also possible, perhaps likely, that de Gaulle did not much concern himself with the American position. After all, French interests would
be advanced regardless of how Washington responded. If the administration
agreed to negotiate for a withdrawal, France would get worldwide credit for
helping to facilitate that result and would be in a position to increase its
own influence in Southeast Asia; if it declined, the Paris government would
still win kudos from nonaligned nations everywhere, particularly in the
Third World, and de Gaulle would have furthered one of his chief aims
since taking power in 1958: to distance his country from the American co-
lossus and stake out a more independent French position within the western alliance.[32]

Herein lies the main reason for the general lack of urgency in the French
government's pronouncements on the war, not only in 1963 but later as
well. Serene in the conviction that his analysis of the Vietnam situation
was correct, and that French interests would be served regardless of how
Washington responded to his appeals, de Gaulle was content to be vague in
his comments and to see how events played themselves out in Saigon before becoming more centrally involved. He was no agitator for negotiations.
In mid 1964 an American official would say after a meeting at the Elysée
Palace that on Vietnam the general was "merely waiting for things to come
his way."[33] The phrase aptly describes his policy a year earlier. His statement of 29 August was an unmistakable critique of American policy in
Vietnam, but it did not, it will be recalled, explicitly demand negotiations.

The French approach to the war matters especially because of the unique
relationship that existed between France and its former colony, which would

have increased the potential impact of a determined effort out of Paris to promote negotiations. It was not uncommon for foreign diplomats in both Saigon and Hanoi to remark on the powerful hold of the French language and culture on the country, and on how the passage of time appeared to have blunted the feelings of bitterness toward France engendered by the Franco-Vietminh War. ("Already a [North] Vietnamese Minister can talk of having fought the French with 'tenacity' but fighting the Americans with 'hatred,'" one British observer noted in May 1963.) The Vietnamese, according to this view, no longer feared France as a colonial power and were, after several generations of French education, more prepared to listen to the French than to any other western people. Kenneth Blackwell marveled at the genuine sympathy that existed between the French delegation in Hanoi and the leading Vietnamese officials, including Ho Chi Minh and his chief ministers. French correspondents were among the few foreign journalists allowed in Hanoi.[34]

The French connection was particularly close in the South. Some 17,500 French citizens lived there in mid 1963, about 6,000 of them born in France. Eleven thousand Vietnamese children, including those of the ruling Ngo family, attended French-run primary schools and *lycées*, and when they fell ill they often were treated by French doctors in hospitals built by the French. Several members of Diem's cabinet were married to French women. France's economic presence in South Vietnam remained considerable, with French citizens in 1963 owning most of the public utilities, hotels, breweries, cigarette factories, and rubber plantations. About 85 percent of the GVN's foreign earnings came from rubber, and three French companies produced about 95 percent of the annual rubber crop. France was South Vietnam's best customer, buying 43.6 percent of its exports in 1962. Then there were the less tangible ties, unmistakable to any perceptive visitor. Bouillabaisse and bifteck–pommes frites were common features in Saigon restaurants, along with Algerian vin ordinaire. For young urbanites French was still the language to learn, not English, and Paris was the city a student dreamed about, not New York or San Francisco. The French capital, as a result, had a large South Vietnamese émigré population in 1963, much of which was clamoring for an end to the war through negotiations.[35]

If the French were circumspect in their public pronouncements on the conflict and what ought to be done to settle it, the Soviet Union and Great Britain were doubly so. As cochairs of the 1954 Geneva Conference, these two powers would be expected to occupy an important role in any international effort to end the war. In mid 1963, both saw a good deal of merit in the French analysis (though both were suspicious of de Gaulle's motives in speaking up), but they were more reluctant than the Paris government to state their position publicly. Indeed, what is fascinating about the Soviet and British outlooks on Vietnam is the degree to which both shared a general desire to maintain as low a profile as possible, not only in the summer of 1963 but also in the eighteen months that followed. As such, they would be highly important players in the diplomatic game leading up to the 1965 outbreak of large-scale war, but in the negative sense—like the dog that did not bark, they would be important for what they did not do rather than for what they did.

The Soviet Union's outlook on Southeast Asia was no mystery to western observers. Moscow had traditionally favored negotiated settlements in this part of the world, if only because such settlements reduced the chance of a major great-power confrontation resulting from a head-on collision between the United States and China; from the Kremlin's perspective such a conflagration would be a disastrous development. Now, in the middle months of 1963, with the worsening Sino-Soviet relations and the welcome moves toward détente with Washington, the Khrushchev government was even more desirous of lessening the tensions in the region— any escalation of the fighting, whether in Laos or Vietnam, would in the Kremlin's estimation only benefit the Chinese. A settlement would also provide another token of East-West agreement in an area of lesser Soviet interest. Accordingly, in early 1963 the Kremlin tacitly encouraged a political settlement leading to neutralization, and it probably encouraged Mieczyslaw Maneli's efforts to facilitate North South contacts in the summer.[36]

At the same time, Khrushchev had to worry about appearing too intent on seeking accommodation with the western powers, because such a posture would solidify Beijing's claim to being the true champion of national liberation movements around the world. The pressure increased after the signing of the partial Test Ban Treaty in midsummer, as both Beijing and Hanoi denounced the "modern revisionists" in Moscow for dealing with the imperialists at the expense of the Vietnamese people. This was the dilemma that would bedevil Soviet officials for years to come: how to keep the Vietnam conflict from escalating to a major war while affirming Soviet support for Hanoi's struggle for national liberation. It proved an insoluble dilemma, and it suggested to Kremlin leaders that the best posture on Vietnam was a low-profile posture.[37]

The London government of Harold Macmillan felt very much the same, though for different reasons. British thinking on the war was not yet as uniformly pessimistic as it would be a year later—whereas a Kenneth Blackwell in Hanoi even now thought the American-sponsored effort in the South was destined to fail, others, including BRIAM's Robert Thompson, in the spring of 1963 thought the war effort was going reasonably well. (By mid 1964, Thompson would be converted to the Blackwell point of view.) Still, British officials were in general agreement among themselves on several key propositions. One was that any American decision to step up U.S. involvement in South Vietnam would be unwise; if the war was to be won, the South Vietnamese themselves would have to win it. Harry F. Hohler, the British ambassador in Saigon, spoke for many when he said in April 1963 that there were already too many Americans on the scene and that Washington's policy was based on the dubious premise that "if a large gift does not produce results, a larger one must."[38] British officials were also in full accord that there should be no significant increase in the United Kingdom's commitment to the war effort, regardless of how much pressure Washington might apply in that direction. This conviction grew in part out of the belief that more westerners in Vietnam were not the answer and indeed would worsen things by making southerners too dependent on outside aid. In addition, Vietnam was not perceived by the Macmillan government to be a vital theater in the Cold War, either for Britain alone or for the West as a whole. One finds nary a reference in the large British internal record to the idea that preserving a noncommunist South Vietnam ought to be a strategic priority for the West. Ever since the Korean War, in fact, British leaders had consistently seen Asian communism as less of a threat to world peace than did their American counterparts. They did not see communism as monolithic and were dubious about notions of falling dominoes. As a result, from the time of the Geneva Conference of 1954 important differences separated London's and Washington's thinking on the nature of the struggle in Indochina. Harold Macmillan gave some sense of his thinking a few days after de Gaulle's August pronouncement: "I agree with the Foreign Office," Macmillan scribbled at the bottom of one internal memo. "With so many other troubles in the world we had better keep out of the Vietnam one."[39]

Macmillan's choice of words was important, for by "keep out" he meant not merely that his government should steer clear of a deeper involvement in the cause of the GVN but also that it should avoid deeper diplomatic engagement to try to end the conflict. Great Britain should stay out, period. This aversion to working for a negotiated settlement did not arise out of a belief that such a pursuit would necessarily fail. Indeed, most London officials appear to have seen early negotiations as imperative if the GVN did not soon show a capacity to beat back the Vietcong challenge—and on its own, without increased American participation. "If the conclusion is reached that the Viet Cong are not being beaten," one analyst at the Foreign Office wrote in late summer, "the only alternative is negotiation." The West's bargaining position would be poor, this and other British analysts agreed, but the likely end result, a reunified, Titoist Vietnam, would be acceptable. ("The prize of a Tito-istic Vietnam would be a great let-out for the West," as one put it.) Moreover, given Hanoi's desire to be rid of the Americans, it ought to be possible at a conference to negotiate a concession that would help the Americans save face—the most likely such concession being a delay in reunifying the two halves of the country. Like de Gaulle, Harold Macmillan appears to have seen the Laos example as something that could be duplicated for Vietnam, even after tensions among the factions in Laos intensified in April 1963. In talks with Canadian prime minister Lester Pearson in London in early May, Macmillan agreed with Pearson's concerns about the growing American involvement in South Vietnam and said that President Kennedy had been very sensible in Laos in choosing a political solution over a military one.[40]

Why, then, the Macmillan government's total lack of interest in using its cochair role to facilitate negotiations on Vietnam? In large part it resulted from a long-standing agreement with Washington that Britain would refrain from pushing for negotiations until the war was clearly on the path to being won. "The policy which we have agreed with the Americans is to avoid international discussion on Vietnam until the military situation has been restored," F. A. Warner wrote in mid 1962, succinctly summarizing the British position. Nine months later, he spoke to the issue again: "We must be careful not to say anything about future possibilities of negotiation, because this would only upset the Americans and make them think we want to sell out South Vietnam to the Communists." Warner was not unduly bothered by implications of this Anglo-American agreement—in early 1963, he was one of those Britons skeptical of the potential for a diplomatic solution to the conflict—but his choice of words was telling. Even talk of *future* negotiations, he had indicated, was out of bounds. Edward H. Peck, a Foreign Office specialist on Southeast Asia, acknowledged in an internal memo in April 1963 that there were indications of the possibility of negotiation between North and South under international auspices. But he, too, warned against any British initiative in that direction. "If the Americans start talking of a negotiated settlement, we may need to reconsider," Peck noted, but in the meantime the best policy was to wait and see.[41]

This unwillingness of London officials to challenge the Americans over Vietnam, even privately in diplomatic channels, would remain largely intact in the months and years to come, with highly important implications. Understanding the phenomenon requires understanding the quandary in which successive British governments found themselves in the 1960s: how to preserve Britain's great-power role in the context of the nation's shrinking economic—and hence military—power. It was not merely that the economy was in frequent trouble in these years, but that Washington had to be asked to come to the rescue. As London grew ever more dependent on American financial largesse, and its military contribution to the western alliance diminished, British leaders were little inclined to try to influence U.S. foreign policy. The Anglo-American "special relationship," they knew, had become a client relationship. On top of all that, the Macmillan government sought American backing in handling Britain's own emerging Southeast Asian problem, the defense of the newly created Malaysia Federation against aggressive designs by Sukarno's Indonesia. A quid pro quo— U.S. support on Malaysia for British support on Vietnam—seemed the order of the day.[42]

Internal dissenters against this hands-off policy were few, but they did exist. Kenneth Blackwell in Hanoi, confident that the DRV sought a compromise settlement, thought it foolish to say that there would be no negotiations until the military situation improved; no such improvement was likely, and therefore the time to pursue an international agreement was now, when the two sides were at least somewhat evenly matched. "We have avoided all reference to negotiations or neutrality as dirty words, chiefly, I imagine, so as to give Diem and the Americans the chance to show whether they could achieve a military solution, and not sabotage their efforts in the meantime," Blackwell wrote London. Now that such an outcome seemed utterly remote, however, Britain "should feel justified in recommending measures which seem more likely to produce results, and which would take the heat out of this potential point of conflict between the East and West blocs." The measure Blackwell had in mind was a Laos-type agreement, which would bring peace to Vietnam and give the actual 1962 Laos agreement a proper chance to work. The recommendation found few takers among Blackwell's colleagues, whether in Vietnam or in London. Some rejected his gloomy analysis in favor of Robert Thompson's argument that the war effort was in fact starting to go better, which meant that it was still premature to seek negotiations; others thought the absence of a centrist, Souvanna Phouma–type figure in South Vietnam made the Laos model more problematic than Blackwell allowed. Almost all were loath to do anything that might annoy Washington.[43]

This *tour d'horizon* of the Vietnam policies of several of the major world powers provides part of the answer to why, despite the considerable discussion about an international effort to find a political solution to the war, nothing in that vein materialized. Leaders in Hanoi, Moscow, and Paris were supportive of negotiations but not prepared to work for them, whereas their counterparts in London, many of whom also showed considerable faith in what diplomacy might bring, were not about to initiate anything that might provoke the ire of the Kennedy administration. The Foreign Office's South-East Asia Department, in a report on the British response to international pressure for a conference on Vietnam from the start of 1960 through August 1963, captured the mood well: "We agreed with the apparent calculation of the Communists [from early 1962 onward] that their cause would almost certainly be forwarded by a conference," the report said, "and in consultation with the Americans decided that the demand for a conference should if necessary be strongly resisted, at least until circumstances—particularly the military situation in Vietnam—altered substantially; but we feared that the demand might in the end prove irresistible. We were thus relieved when in the end the demand was not pressed, or indeed ever specifically formulated, by the Communist side."[44]

It will not do to stop the analysis here, of course. In order to fully understand the failure of diplomacy in Vietnam in 1963, it is necessary to expand the focus to include the remaining two great powers most dominant in the region, China and the United States. The Beijing government's posture on the war in 1962–1963 is not easily defined. The SEAD study included China among the countries hopeful for a reconvened Geneva conference—when the report spoke of "the Communists" being supportive of, and well served by, a conference, it referred to the governments in Hanoi, Moscow, and Beijing. This determination was correct, at least for 1962. Several times that year, Beijing made clear its desire for an international meeting. On 24 February, shortly after the creation of the Military Assistance Command, Vietnam (MACV), created to coordinate the growing American presence in the conflict and for Beijing a potent symbol of Washington's commitment to the struggle, the Chinese government called on the "Geneva co-Chairmen and countries concerned" to "hold prompt consultations and take appropriate measures" to eliminate the serious danger of war in the area. The following month, Beijing reportedly encouraged Cambodia's Prince Norodom Sihanouk in his plea for an international conference on South Vietnam. In July and again in August, Chinese foreign minister Chen Yi said publicly that his government supported neutralization for Vietnam, and he added that a conference was sooner or later inevitable.[45]

Over the following months, the Chinese position appears to have hardened, which suggests that Chen Yi and his colleagues perhaps decided that later might be better than sooner. Beginning in late 1962, they became less forthcoming on the subject of a conference and more belligerent in their rhetoric, and over a number of months they made several security commitments to the DRV. In March and again in May 1963, high-level Chinese delegations visited Hanoi and pledged to officials there that if the war expanded to North Vietnam, they could count on China as the strategic rear. In late August Chinese leader Mao Zedong received a delegation representing the NLF and issued a statement proclaiming support for its cause.[46] No doubt the worsening relations with Moscow were mostly to blame for this alteration in China's posture, encouraging Beijing to seize the chance to proclaim its leadership of Third World revolutions. Also, the Diem government's growing problems in the South in 1963 may have encouraged the Chinese to adopt a more aggressive stance—they could smell a Vietcong victory and wanted to claim part of the credit. Does this mean that Beijing authorities had renounced the idea of a great-power meeting on the war? Not necessarily. Since 1954 these leaders had counseled Hanoi to avoid a dramatic escalation of the war, and they were no less anxious than the North Vietnamese and the Soviets to avoid a direct military confrontation with the United States. They were careful, both now and in 1964, to avoid making specific pledges of support to the DRV in the event of an expanded war. They also avoided specifically ruling out a negotiated settlement, and it may be, as the Southeast Asian specialists in the British Foreign Office surmised, that Beijing in the summer of 1963 still saw a conference as forwarding its cause.

Certainly, China's position on negotiations in Vietnam was more equivocal than that of the United States. In 1963, the Kennedy administration opposed any move to bring about an early diplomatic settlement, as it had since it came into office and as its predecessor had done before that. From January 1961 to November 1963, the administration adhered firmly to the position that the insurgency in the South had to be defeated and that no diplomacy should be undertaken until that result was ensured. Negotiations should be entered into only when there was nothing to negotiate. Note here that American officials were not merely skeptical of what negotiations might bring; they were downright fearful of the likely results. Far from merely hoping a meeting would not be convened, they actively sought to prevent it. This acute American concern about the prospect of early negotiations, which would become much stronger after August 1963, is in itself indirect but powerful additional evidence of such negotiations' viability. Washington officials fretted about negotiations on Vietnam in The Long 1964 precisely because they recognized that diplomacy represented a workable—if from their position also odious—means to bring the conflict to an end.

It was not that John F. Kennedy was eager to take on the communists in Vietnam. Quite the contrary. Some critics, reading too much into a few passages of his inaugural address and into the decade-long record of the international affairs team that he brought to Washington, have depicted him as an exceptionally aggressive foreign-policy president, a kind of Cold Warrior par excellence.[47] This picture is flawed for his foreign policy as a whole, and it is flawed for Vietnam. Kennedy, it is now clear, sought to make important departures in the superpower relationship in order to lessen the tension with Moscow, to the point that by 1963 détente was the most important element in his foreign policy, and he proved increasingly reluctant to engage American fighting forces in war, whether in Cuba or in Southeast Asia. Even in the administration's early months, he did not practice the simple and reflexive anticommunism so often attributed to him.[48] In general, Kennedy was much less prone than many of this senior aides to seek military solutions to foreign-policy problems. Notwithstanding his aversion to negotiations in Vietnam, he had greater faith in the possibilities for diplomacy in foreign affairs than, for example, his chief diplomatic representative, Secretary of State Dean Rusk.

Right from the start in 1961, Kennedy clashed with top military and diplomatic advisers over the proper course in Southeast Asia. That year, the main trouble spot was not Vietnam but neighboring Laos. The Laotian analogy would hover near the surface in all discussions regarding Vietnam negotiations in the coming years, and thus it warrants examination here. Under Dwight Eisenhower, the United States had rejected a neutral government for Laos in favor of a pro-American regime under Phoumi Nosavan. By the end of 1960, the Phoumi government faced imminent defeat at the hands of the communist-backed Pathet Lao. At a meeting the day before Kennedy's January inauguration, Eisenhower stressed the strategic importance of Laos, calling it the key to all of Southeast Asia and apparently warning Kennedy that if it fell, the United States would have to "write off the whole area." He expressly ruled out neutralization. "It would be fatal," Eisenhower told Kennedy, "for us to permit Communists to insert themselves into the Laotian government."[49] But though senior advisers at various times in the months that followed recommended military intervention, Kennedy never authorized it. He quickly came to doubt the intrinsic importance of Laos to U.S. security. He worried about its difficult geography, about the likely lack of public support for a long-term commitment, and about the lack of an "exit strategy" for any such commitment. Instead he opted for a diplomatic solution, despite warnings that he would pay a domestic political price for it.[50]

Kennedy was influenced in this decision by the misgivings expressed by America's leading allies. They believed that the West's stake in Laos was small, the chances of success minimal. During talks at Rambouillet on 28 January, Charles de Gaulle and Harold Macmillan agreed that the Phoumi government was a disaster and that the new American president, if he were wise, would pursue a political solution. In the ensuing weeks, both leaders worked to convince Kennedy to move in that direction, with considerable success. In discussions with senior British officials in Washington on 28 February, Kennedy said that he had made a fundamental change in U.S. policy toward Laos, abandoning the Eisenhower administration's insistence on getting a Laos that was 100 percent prowestern in its "neutrality" in favor of one that recognized a key place for the Pathet Lao. He said that he would be amenable to a conference if the Russians would do their part in bringing about a prior cease-fire. Four weeks later, at a hastily convened meeting with Macmillan in Key West, Florida, the president reiterated these points and professed agreement with Macmillan's contention that there could be no long-term military success for the West in Laos. At the same time, Kennedy continued, it would be unwise to let Laos be completely overrun by the communists. If the Soviets failed to agree to a cease-fire, he asked, would Britain commit troops to a limited Southeast Asia Treaty Organization (SEATO) military intervention? Macmillan dodged a firm answer and said that he would like to ask Kennedy the "really important" question: "Was the thing worth doing at all?" Even if a military intervention brought momentary stabilization, would that make any real difference, insofar as those Laotians supported by the United States did not seem disposed to do any fighting at all, whereas the other side did? Kennedy agreed that this was the key question and, although avoiding a direct response, implied that the answer was no. A great-power conference, he suggested, was the best option available. Macmillan, upon his return to London, wrote de Gaulle: "I think that the President really accepts the necessity for a political solution if we can get one. I hope therefore that we may succeed on the lines which you and I discussed [at Rambouillet]."[51]

In May, after Moscow at last agreed to a cease-fire and negotiations, Kennedy met with de Gaulle in Paris. The Frenchman told him Laos did not offer a good terrain for western troops, nor indeed for western politics. The French experience in the region made clear that military action could never achieve lasting results, and therefore the best solution to the Laos problem was neutralization. When Kennedy responded that if the negotiations faltered at least the threat of American military intervention might be necessary, de Gaulle shook his head. "For you," he said, "intervention in this region will be an entanglement without end." Nationalism would always prove stronger than "any foreign authority," and "you are going to see this." The French president's words apparently made an impression on Kennedy. When General Maxwell D. Taylor and Walt W. Rostow of the National Security Council (NSC) staff urged him to intervene with U.S. forces if the communists renewed their Laotian offensive, Kennedy reportedly balked, replying that de Gaulle had "spoken with feeling of the difficulty of fighting in this part of the world."[52]

Kennedy thus spurned the advice of several of his senior advisers and Eisenhower, and sidestepped Laos. In late May, a Geneva conference on Laos convened for the purpose of negotiating a settlement among the communists, neutralists, and American-supported military that were contending for power in the country. Kennedy assigned the veteran negotiator Averell Harriman as the U.S. representative. The thirteen months of negotiations that followed brought forth a consensus that the only compromise with any chance of success was one wherein the procommunist Pathet Lao and the neutralist faction were given positions reasonably commensurate with their actual power. The final agreement, signed in July 1962, created a "neutral and independent" Laos led by a coalition government under neutralist prime minister Souvanna Phouma but in which the Pathet Lao shared power. To what degree the settlement can really be called a "success" is a question we shall return to; here it will suffice to say, first, that de Gaulle, Macmillan, and Khrushchev believed, both then and later, that it was about the best that could be achieved under the circumstances; and second, that Kennedy thought so as well.[53]

In the interval between the start of the Laos conference in 1961 and the final agreement in 1962, Kennedy made policy decisions with respect to Southeast Asia that revealed much about his attitude both to military intervention and to diplomacy. The decision to opt for neutralization in Laos unsettled the South Vietnamese government, which was already suffering under the onslaught of the Vietcong. Partly to reassure Saigon of America's steadfast commitment to the cause, and partly to mollify domestic critics who might think him too accommodating to communists, Kennedy in May 1961 signed off on National Security Action Memorandum (NSAM) 52, which described the U.S. objective as preventing communist domination of South Vietnam. At the same time, however, he faulted what he saw as the undue military emphasis of an interagency task-force report on Vietnam and deleted those passages that discussed the insertion of U.S. ground forces.

In succeeding months, combined problems in the Laos negotiations and in South Vietnam led to several proposals for a larger American military and political commitment in both countries.[54] Kennedy rejected them. He had no desire to send American troops to the Asian mainland. Even as a senator in the 1950s, when he advocated strong support for the Diem regime and warned of dire consequences should South Vietnam fall, he stated publicly that the disastrous French experience in Indochina showed that Americans should never fight there. Likewise, the Korean War experience taught Kennedy that public opinion in the United States would quickly sour on a similar commitment in that part of the world. Perhaps most important, already in the 1950s he insisted that no American-backed government in Southeast Asia could survive without broad-based popular support. Once he reached the White House, he frequently invoked General Douglas MacArthur's admonition against the U.S. fighting another land war in Asia. Now, in the fall of 1961, he expressed grave doubt to a group of reporters that the United States should interfere in "civil disturbances" caused by guerrillas, adding that "it was hard to prove that this wasn't largely the situation in Vietnam." This was Kennedy's dilemma: he did not want to expand the American military commitment, but he feared a continued military and political deterioration in South Vietnam.[55]

In October 1961, with the deterioration occurring more rapidly than ever, both the Joint Chiefs of Staff and the National Security Council leaned toward the introduction of sizable American combat forces into Vietnam. Kennedy sent a team headed by his personal military adviser, General Maxwell D. Taylor, to Vietnam to get a firsthand look at the war and consider U.S. options. Significantly, however, when Taylor wrote draft instructions for himself to "evaluate what could be accomplished by the introduction of [SEATO] or United States forces into South Vietnam, determining the role, composition, and probable disposition of such forces," Kennedy rewrote them, eliminating any specific reference to SEATO or U.S. forces. Kennedy also added that "the initial responsibility for the effective maintenance of the independence of South Vietnam rests with the people and government of that country." When the Taylor team returned with a report calling for an initial force of eight thousand Americans, Kennedy rejected it again.[56]

He may have been influenced by rumblings of discontent among some whose opinions he respected. Senator Mike Mansfield, a long-time supporter of Ngo Dinh Diem and a former professor of Asian history, wrote Kennedy a memorandum advising caution on the question of ground troops. If American forces were dispatched, Mansfield wrote, they would enter Vietnam without much allied support and would, by their mere presence, heighten the possibility of a major intervention by the communist powers. The result would be an open-ended commitment for the United States, one in which the United States would be at a serious logistical disadvantage and that would weaken American positions elsewhere around the globe.

Mansfield, still unwilling to counsel a withdrawal from Vietnam, favored increasing military and economic aid to the GVN but leaving the burden of the actual fighting to the South Vietnamese. In the same vein, Assistant Secretary of State for Economic Affairs George W. Ball told Kennedy that American prestige was sure to suffer if the United States became too deeply committed, and he warned that the Vietnamese topography was "totally unsuitable for the commitment of American forces." Of the Taylor plan, Ball said prophetically, "If we go down that road, we might have, within five years, 300,000 men in the rice paddies of the jungles of Vietnam and never be able to find them."[57] Jawaharlal Nehru, prime minister of India, also warned Kennedy against sending American ground forces. On a visit to Washington at the start of November (precisely the time when administration officials were considering the Taylor report), Nehru told Kennedy that the dispatch of U.S. troops would only turn most South Vietnamese against Diem—he would never again be able to command their respect, Nehru said—and would provide Hanoi with an excuse to move troops to the South.[58]

Though rejecting the commitment of American ground troops, Kennedy agreed in November to an important increase in the U.S. advisory effort and to an active American air combat role, as promulgated in NSAM 111 on 22 November. It bears emphasizing, however, that this was a smaller expansion than most of JFK's top advisers wanted—several told him that the war would be lost without a large infusion of U.S. troops. Kennedy said he instinctively opposed the use of American forces, and he pointedly cut the section in the memorandum that committed the administration to preventing South Vietnam's fall. It would be wrong, he told senior aides in a meeting on 15 November, to take a direct role in a conflict that, unlike Korea, did not represent a clear case of aggression. The obscurity of the issues in Vietnam contrasted sharply with the clarity of the positions in Berlin, which meant that American intervention might bring strong opposition from major allies (almost certainly he had France and Britain in mind) and raise hackles on Capitol Hill. A good case could be made, Kennedy declared, against intervening in a place ten thousand miles away, where millions of dollars had already been spent supporting a native army of two hundred thousand soldiers against sixteen thousand guerrillas without any success. Several advisers, including Secretary of State Dean Rusk, Secretary of Defense Robert McNamara, and General Lyman Lemnitzer, the chairman of the Joint Chiefs of Staff, voiced opposition to these assertions, but Kennedy held his ground.[59]

At the same time, and complicating any effort to get a clear picture of his thinking in this period, Kennedy showed no interest in pursuing in

Vietnam the kind of conference-table settlement that was then in the process of being agreed to with respect to Laos. He expressly ruled out such a
solution, despite urgings in that direction from several quarters. Chief Laos
negotiator Averell Harriman, with whom Kennedy had formed a rather
unique bond—they were about the only two in the upper levels in the administration who had any faith that something would come of the Laos
talks—pressed for a vigorous attempt to pursue a similar agreement for
Vietnam. Harriman met with Nehru at the Geneva airport on the morning of 4 November, shortly before the Indian flew to the United States.
Hawkish advisers were pushing Kennedy in the wrong direction, Harriman
lamented, and he urged Nehru to use his "fresh, authoritative voice" to
convince the president to give negotiations a chance, with respect to both
Laos and South Vietnam. Extending the Geneva talks to include Vietnam
would, in fact, make any deal on Laos much more workable, Harriman
said. The Russians would be helpful, and the Chinese, too, would come
around.[60]

In a memo to Kennedy a few days later, Harriman elaborated on his vision: he wrote that a diplomatic settlement for Vietnam based on the 1954
peace accords was America's best option, if only because the Diem regime
was "repressive, dictatorial, and unpopular." The United States should not
"stake its prestige" on such an entity. Moreover, the Soviet Union was
interested in stabilizing the Southeast Asian situation, which made the
prospects for negotiations infinitely better. Harriman suggested that the
United States agree to reduce its military presence in South Vietnam as
peace was restored in the area. For their part, the North Vietnamese and
the NLF would agree to a cease-fire, accept a strong United Nations Control Commission, and achieve eventual reunification, possibly through elections. In addition to this memo, Harriman may also have made his pitch to
Kennedy in person. He told the British representative at Geneva, Malcolm
MacDonald, that he had suggested to JFK that the two Geneva cochairs,
Britain and the USSR, should begin by consulting with one another on
the best approach to take on Vietnam and then expand the discussions to
include the United States, China, South Vietnam, and North Vietnam. The
French and the Indians could also be included, if necessary, and later the
remaining Geneva delegations. Harriman envisioned a formal agreement
that both Hanoi and Saigon would accept and that would include elections
for reunification at some point down the road. Kennedy, Harriman told
MacDonald, was considering the proposal.[61]

Kennedy heard essentially the same message from his ambassador to
India, the economist John Kenneth Galbraith, and from the number-two
ranking official in the State Department, Undersecretary Chester Bowles.

Galbraith's concerns echoed Nehru's, and he traveled to Washington for the Indian leader's meeting with JFK. On the evening of 8 November, during after-dinner conversation at the White House with Kennedy, McGeorge Bundy, presidential aide Arthur M. Schlesinger Jr., and the British ambassador, David Ormsby-Gore, Galbraith spoke out forcefully against American military intervention in Vietnam and in favor of broadening the discussions at Geneva to include South Vietnam. Ngo Dinh Diem was a broken reed, Galbraith said, and Vietnam was not worth a major investment. Schlesinger expressed support for the idea of negotiations, but Bundy and Kennedy were unmoved. When Ormsby-Gore said that talk of a diplomatic settlement was, in his view, still premature, Kennedy and Bundy voiced agreement.[62]

Bowles fared no better. A figure of rapidly declining influence in the administration—he had never earned the trust of the president or his brother, Attorney General Robert F. Kennedy, and had been unable to establish a close working relationship with Dean Rusk—Bowles had long harbored doubts about the ability of the United States to achieve foreign-policy successes in the Third World by military means.[63] He urged Kennedy in late November to remember France's experience in Indochina. Bowles warned that a similar troop commitment by the United States would almost certainly result in another long and bloody war that pitted white outsiders against "anticolonial" guerrillas. Any expansion of the American commitment to the GVN could lead the United States "full blast up a dead end street" and "constitute a long step toward a full-blown war of unpredictable dimensions," which meant that the best solution would be neutralization of the whole Indochina region by way of a negotiated settlement.[64]

The advocates of disengagement were prescient. They understood the almost certain futility of attempting a military solution in South Vietnam, understood the central relevance for the United States of the French analogy, and understood the chronic weaknesses of the Saigon government. They understood, in other words, that American power, however great in relative terms, was ultimately limited, and that in such a situation, the best option for the administration was to draw up stakes and take its stand elsewhere. But there was also a major flaw in these critics' articulations, a flaw that we shall encounter repeatedly in the pages that follow. So incisive and cogent in analyzing the current state of affairs and the outlook for the future (their ability to consider matters in the long term set them apart from most of their contemporaries), they tended to become tongue-tied on the subject of how exactly a "political solution" would be reached and with what terms. One reads the many long memoranda Chester Bowles penned on the subject in 1961–1962, for example, without ever getting a clear sense of what exactly he envisioned on this score. Galbraith, for all his acute insight and keen wit, likewise gives little clue on the matter. Harriman acquitted himself better—he spelled out how the negotiations would start and what might follow—but he too raised as many questions as he answered, about how long the process might take, about who would ultimately rule Vietnam, and about the implications for America's standing on the world stage and the Democratic Party's standing at home. Certainly for Bowles and Galbraith, but even to some degree for Harriman, neutralization was less an actual plan than a lofty concept, a noble idea that lacked a mechanism for implementation.

This argument should not be taken too far. It would be unfair to demand of the advocates of a negotiated settlement that they spell out exactly how such a deal would be reached, much less that they guarantee a priori that the terms of the agreement would be advantageous to the United States—an inherently impossible task. It was not their responsibility but that of their superiors to order teams of researchers to consider in detail the ins and outs of the negotiating option. Certainly Galbraith and Bowles and their like-minded colleagues (including some, like Mike Mansfield and George Ball, who were broadly sympathetic but in late 1961 said nothing explicit about negotiations) hurt their cause by their fuzziness on the particulars, but they no doubt expected, and rightly so, that the specifics could be provided in due course.

Moreover, even if they had laid out a specific point-by-point plan for a political solution, it is doubtful that the Kennedy inner circle would have been any more interested. Senior policymakers in Washington in late 1961, facing a severe crisis and possible government collapse in South Vietnam, were asking not whether but how to commit increased U.S. resources. Robert McNamara, McGeorge Bundy, and Dean Rusk differed among themselves on the speed and scale of deepened American involvement, but all three favored standing firm in Vietnam and argued against initiating negotiated withdrawal.[65] Kennedy agreed. He plainly shared a number of the conerns expressed by the likes of Mansfield, Nehru, Ball, Harriman, and Galbraith—it is not hard to imagine him nodding solemnly as they articulated their positions. It is clear from the record that he was more skeptical than most of his key advisers on the advisability of a major American role in the conflict. He not only rejected the proposal to send U.S. combat forces but also questioned the political, strategic, and even moral purpose for their being there.

But he was not prepared to alter course. Still mindful of the humiliation caused by the failed attempt to oust Castro in the Bay of Pigs operation back in April, and nervous about conservative criticism of the handling of the Berlin crisis, Kennedy worried about how altering course might belie administration promises to wage the Cold War vigorously. After leaving office, Eisenhower had vowed to keep a close eye on Kennedy's foreign policy, and throughout 1961, Republicans and right-wing Democrats had charged the administration with weakness and vacillation. Kennedy appears to have feared that a decision to negotiate on Vietnam would harm his credibility and provoke a domestic political attack similar to that which Harry Truman had endured after the "fall of China" a dozen years earlier.

This domestic dimension of credibility no doubt mattered most to Kennedy, but he was not unmindful of Vietnam's potential impact on America's international position. Notwithstanding his claims that one could make a good case against major intervention ten thousand miles away and that the defense of Berlin was not synonymous with the defense of Saigon, he still felt it important to consider the credibility of America's commitments, felt it necessary to convince adversaries and allies alike of American firmness, determination, and dependability. The moves the United States made, Kennedy told Rusk and McNamara in mid November, would be scrutinized on both sides of the Iron Curtain, and if it chose to negotiate in Vietnam, it might "in fact be judged weaker than in Laos" and cause "a major crisis of nerve" throughout Southeast Asia. Similarly, a Rusk-McNamara report warned the same month that "the loss of South Viet-Nam would . . . undermine the credibility of American commitments elsewhere."[66] This "doctrine of credibility" had by the fall of 1961 supplanted the domino theory in American thinking on Vietnam, or at least altered the way that theory was conceived. Kennedy administration officials were less concerned than their predecessors had been that each nation that fell to communism would endanger its immediate neighbor; they were less attached, in other words, to the notion of what one might call a "territorial domino theory." Instead, Kennedy and (probably more so) his advisers feared the impact of one nation's fall on other nations the world over; by merely watching the spectacle, these other nations would lose confidence in the power of the United States. It amounted to a kind of "psychological domino theory," to use Jonathan Schell's apt phrase.[67]

In retrospect, there is much to question in these assertions about Vietnam's importance to America's larger strategic interests. In the context of late 1961, however, they made sense in a way they would not in, say, 1971, when the Nixon team still persisted in articulating them, or even in 1964–1965, when the Johnson administration did. Nineteen-sixty-one was a tense time in the Cold War, a year in which superpower tensions can be said to have reached their apogee, as symbolized by the construction of the Berlin Wall in August. The Sino-Soviet split was not yet the wide chasm it would become—some in the administration still believed that it did not exist—and any relaxation in Soviet-American relations seemed to most observers hard to imagine, at least in the short term.[68] In American public opinion, the Cold War Consensus that had undergirded American foreign policy since the mid 1940s remained intact in 1961, as could be readily seen on the editorial pages of elite newspapers. The *New York Times,* which a couple of years later would ask large questions about the nation's Vietnam commitment and whether it was worth maintaining, still took for granted that the United States must do its utmost to prevent further "Red" penetration of Southeast Asia. The *Washington Post,* whose questioning of a full-fledged commitment to the GVN would commence in late 1964 (and then abruptly cease when U.S. ground troops began arriving in 1965), believed likewise.

Nor was there yet the international allied criticism of the Vietnam commitment that there would be two or three years later. Great Britain, for example, Washington's most important ally in the post-1945 period, feared the prospect of a dramatically expanded American involvement, but London officials were not yet asking the kinds of fundamental questions—Is Vietnam worth it? Can the Vietcong ever be defeated? Will the GVN ever shape up?—that they would pose repeatedly to each other in 1964 and 1965. Most took for granted that the commitment to Saigon would be, and should be, maintained.

In this way, Kennedy's decisions on Vietnam in the closing weeks of 1961 can be considered, if not courageous or farsighted, at least reasonable. He rejected the alternatives of negotiating a peace settlement or deploying combat forces and chose instead a down-the-middle approach of increasing aid and advisers. He understood that these steps by themselves were not enough to save South Vietnam, but he chose them because they bought him time: they left him free to expand or contract the U.S. military commitment. This made sense given the domestic and international political contexts of the time, and given the fact that the Diem government had not yet been clearly revealed as the hopeless cause it in fact was. (Few informed contemporary observers would have seconded Lyndon Johnson's mid-1961 description of Diem, during a visit to Saigon, as "the Churchill of Asia," but the appellation did not seem as ludicrous then as it would a couple of years later.)[69] It is a prudent leader, so the saying goes, who keeps his options open, and that is what Kennedy believed he did with NSAM 111. He did what Lyndon Johnson at the start of 1965 would not have the luxury of doing: he chose to postpone the tough decisions.

What Kennedy perhaps did not understand, and what made November 1961 so historically important, was that even a relatively modest increase in the U.S. commitment to South Vietnam would make any future contraction of that commitment more difficult. Not impossible—those authors who suggest that the NSAM 111 decisions marked the point of no return do not convince[70]—but significantly more difficult. Like Hanoi, Washington had never been a faithful adherent of the 1954 Geneva Accords, but now, as a result of Kennedy's November decisions, the American flouting of the agreements was plain for all informed observers to see. Three thousand American military personnel would now move about the South Vietnamese countryside, and some of them would be authorized to take part in combat. (British officials, aware that both sides had been quietly violating the accords for years, expressed great concern about the new measures precisely because they removed any chance of deniability.) Henceforth the prospect of violating the accords would not give U.S. officials much pause. The creation of a formal military command in MACV also carried symbolic importance, suggesting as it did that Washington would now assume more responsibility for the war effort—Hanoi evidently made just this deduction, as evidenced by its expressed interest in a negotiated settlement immediately following MACV's formation. America's stake in the war had deepened.

Having lingered for a considerable time on these November 1961 decisions and their meaning, we can move more swiftly through the period that followed. Beginning in early 1962 and continuing until the Buddhist crisis in 1963, Vietnam ceased to be a front-burner issue for the Kennedy administration. Top officials were preoccupied with more pressing matters, including the Soviet military buildup on Cuba, and they devoted little attention to Vietnam. The war appeared to most of them to be going much better. An early GVN collapse no longer threatened. And, indeed, the infusion of American aid and advisers in late 1961 and early 1962 yielded immediate (if temporary) results in the war against the Vietcong. The deployment of American helicopters dramatically increased the mobility of Diem's troops, allowing them to leapfrog and surround Vietcong military detachments. The result was a number of successful large-scale operations against enemy strongholds in the first half of 1962. Not surprisingly, the administration saw this as proof that its policy was working—in one of several public expressions of confidence made by officials in early 1962, Attorney General Robert F. Kennedy told a Saigon audience that "we are going to win." Privately, too, senior officials expressed confidence. Robert McNamara, at a meeting among top officials in Honolulu in July, reported "tremendous progress" in bringing the insurgency to an end.[71] On Kennedy's orders, McNamara that same month made operational a plan for the phased withdrawal of American forces from Vietnam. The plan called for the withdrawals to begin at the end of 1963 and continue for several years—provided the war was going well.[72]

The optimism was unfounded. Militarily, the ARVN may have seized the initiative, but it meant little because Vietcong bases remained almost impossible to locate amid the dense forests and swampy paddylands of South Vietnam. Guerrillas would often merely wait for government troops to withdraw from conquered territory and then reoccupy it. More important, the 1962 American-Diem military offensive did nothing to stem the political revolution against the Saigon regime that was taking place in the countryside. The much-vaunted strategic hamlets program, based roughly on a proposal by Robert Thompson of BRIAM and designed to insulate and protect the peasantry from the NLF militarily in a way similar to what had been done in Malaya and the Philippines, served primarily to alienate peasants from the Diem regime—scores of villages were uprooted, and their inhabitants were forced to relocate.[73] Funds that were supposed to provide for the villagers all too often went into the pockets of Diem's officials. More and more peasants refused to pay land taxes, and many chose to back the NLF, with its aggressive land-reform platform and anti-Diem line.

The question is when and to what degree these realities were known to Kennedy and his chief Vietnam lieutenants. Historian George C. Herring, in his landmark history of American involvement in the war, titles a section on 1962 "Optimism and Uncertainty," and those words do capture the predominant perceptions in official Washington circles during much of that year.[74] The problems in the war effort were to a large extent masked, in part because of Vietnam's low importance in 1962 and in part because of the steady drumbeat of optimistic pronouncements from embassy staffers and the military command in Saigon. To some degree, at least, this picture of progress appears to have been deliberately fabricated by American military and diplomatic sources in Vietnam who faced tremendous pressure from McNamara's Pentagon to report such improvements. (As early as March 1962, British officials in Saigon were alarmed to hear Ambassador Frederick Nolting tell them that he was under pressure to show results.)[75] Whatever the truth of this charge, there can be no disputing that Nolting and MACV head General Paul D. Harkins too readily accepted these reports at face value, though it should be said that the conflict in that year did not lend itself to easy analysis. It was logical to believe that something must have changed for the better since the fall of 1961—whereas then the Diem regime had appeared on the verge of collapse, no one now saw that as an immediate danger. Others besides Nolting and Harkins—including independent observers such as BRIAM's Robert Thompson—argued that the policy was working, that, notwithstanding Diem's weaknesses, there now existed a fairly good chance that the war could be won.

But it would take time. No one disputed that. In the meantime, senior American analysts agreed, no negotiations should be undertaken. Averell Harriman, more hopeful about the prospects in the war than previously (and perhaps sensing that the issue had been decided in JFK's mind), now categorically opposed the solution he had urged back in November: to extend the Laos discussions to include Vietnam, with an eye toward gaining a neutralist settlement. Back then, Harriman had joined John Kenneth Galbraith in urging a diplomatic offensive, but no more. When Galbraith told Kennedy in April 1962 that the Diem government was corrupt and contemptible and not worthy of American support, and that therefore the administration should seek a negotiated withdrawal and instead make its stand in Thailand, Harriman registered strong opposition.[76] He urged JFK to avoid a dramatic deepening of the American commitment to the war but also steer clear of an early settlement. Harriman argued that major decisions of that kind should be postponed until the new measures had been given a chance to work. Robert McNamara also attacked Galbraith's proposal, as did the Joint Chiefs of Staff. The Chiefs warned Kennedy that any departure from the Vietnam commitment would be a major blow to America's strategic interests all over the globe. Nor did Galbraith find meaningful support for his ideas within his own State Department—only the increasingly marginalized Chester Bowles shared his perspective. Roger Hilsman, one of Dean Rusk's top deputies on Vietnam, attacked Galbraith's interpretation of the war and urged that the war be prosecuted. Rusk himself felt the same. When top British officials, including Macmillan, asked Rusk during talks in London in May if the emerging settlement on Laos suggested the possibility of something similar being arranged for Vietnam, Rusk responded with an emphatic no. Peace would come to Southeast Asia when the communists left it in peace, he said.[77]

It was a curious thing about Rusk: as secretary of state he was the nation's chief diplomat, and yet he had little faith in the power of diplomacy to settle international disputes, at least where communists were involved. In 1947, the distinguished journalist Walter Lippmann, distraught at the military emphasis of the emerging containment policy, addressed this line of thinking in memorable fashion. "The history of diplomacy is the history of relations among rival powers, which did not enjoy political intimacy, and did not respond to appeals to common purposes," Lippmann declared. "Nevertheless, there have been settlements. Some of them did not last very long. Some of them did. For a diplomat to think that rival and unfriendly powers cannot be brought to a settlement is to forget what diplomacy is all about. There would be little for diplomats to do if the world consisted of partners, enjoying political intimacy, and responding to common appeals."[78]

No settlement possible; little for diplomats to do: Lippmann anticipated perfectly the essence of Rusk's approach to diplomacy on Southeast Asia (and perhaps other areas—Kennedy was continually frustrated in 1961 by Rusk's unwillingness to come up with diplomatic options for the German problem). Rusk had from the start been deeply skeptical of Kennedy's decision to seek a compromise political settlement on Laos, and though he ultimately pledged his support to the Geneva effort, he never expected the talks to succeed. He decided early that the State Department should occupy a secondary position to McNamara's Pentagon in setting policy on Vietnam, at least until the GVN's survival had been ensured; only after that point would the State Department's work really begin. Only then could the United States be in a position to dictate the terms (and that is really what he had in mind) to the leaders in Hanoi.[79]

Rusk's decision to have his department take a lower profile on the war had hugely important implications as U.S. involvement deepened, and it provides a large part of the explanation for one of the central features of American Vietnam policy in 1961–1965: the striking absence in the massive internal record of even rudimentary contingency planning for negotiations to end the conflict. It was not that Dean Rusk was eager for war. Far from it. He sincerely hoped that American assistance could be kept limited, and he understood better than many the weaknesses of the Diem regime. But Rusk also felt certain that the United States had to maintain its commitment to the GVN, for reasons both moral and geostrategic, and he felt this more deeply than any of his fellow senior decision makers. More than they, Rusk could be counted on to say essentially the same things in private that he said in public—a sure mark of the true believer. And although the depth of his hostility to exploring diplomatic alternatives would be revealed only later, as pressure in that direction increased—in 1964 he would greet the diplomatic proposals of U Thant and French foreign minister Henri Couve de Murville, for example, with scarcely concealed contempt—a close observer could see the basic outlines of his vision even in 1962. Already he was utilizing the stock phrase that would become his mantra in the coming years, that peace would come to Vietnam when the DRV ceased its unprovoked aggression against the South. "There can be peace overnight in Vietnam if those responsible for the aggression wish peace," he told a press conference at the beginning of March 1962.[80]

Kennedy could and did make virtually identical comments publicly (with important ramifications), but he was much slower than Rusk to make them privately. That was the great difference between them. Whereas Rusk made quite clear, both on the record and off, that he saw little effective difference between the defense of Berlin and the defense of Saigon, Kennedy explicitly denied that they were the same. Much more than his senior Vietnam advisers, Kennedy appears to have been impressed with the force of the arguments in Galbraith's April memo, with his description of large and perhaps insurmountable problems ahead. After reading the memo, JFK told Harriman and Michael Forrestal of the NSC staff that the United States should "be prepared to seize upon any favorable moment to reduce our commitment, recognizing that the moment might yet be some time away."[81] He also asked several of his senior Vietnam advisers to read and comment on the memo. Although Kennedy in mid 1962 appears to have bought into the reports of a dramatically improved battlefield situation, he clearly retained many of the fundamental concerns he had articulated the previous autumn—about the absence of allied and public support for a larger war, about the danger of repeating France's mistakes in the region, and about the shortcomings of the GVN.

And yet. Whatever his continuing doubts, JFK still sought victory in Vietnam—with "victory" defined as "not losing," as ensuring the survival of a noncommunist bastion in the southern part of Vietnam. Had he lived past November 1963, the fundamental differences in his and Rusk's respective outlooks might have manifested themselves in a meaningful way; he did not, and they did not. Both men favored the middle path between major American intervention and outright withdrawal, and both of them opposed early negotiations. (Disengagement "might yet be some time away," as JFK said to Harriman and Forrestal.) Kennedy's sympathy for Galbraith's ideas did not prevent him from allowing the ambassador's plan to be shelved at a high-level meeting on 1 May. His concerns about too large a U.S. commitment to the war did not keep him from telling Rusk privately and American journalists publicly that month that the United States would not end its assistance to South Vietnam.[82]

Even as Kennedy's doubts about the long-term prospects in Vietnam deepened in the last half of 1962 and the first half of 1963, as the illusions of significant progress in the war gradually were stripped away, he continued to adhere to the middle course and to avoid exploring negotiations.

True, in July 1962 he accepted a Burmese proposal to have Averell Harriman meet with his North Vietnamese counterparts at Geneva to discuss not only the Laos talks but also the situation in South Vietnam, which would seem to suggest that he might be willing to make a genuine attempt to reach an accommodation on the war. But there is no indication that JFK saw the meeting as significant. Harriman took an utterly intransigent line with DRV foreign minister Ung Van Khiem, demanding from Hanoi what would have amounted to a complete capitulation and abruptly ending the meeting when Khiem challenged his interpretation of events.[83]

It is also true that Kennedy reacted with alarm to the gloomy report produced by Mike Mansfield after a mission to Vietnam near the end of the year. ("It is their country, their future which is most at stake, not ours," Mansfield wrote in recommending against a deeper commitment and in favor of a "vigorous diplomacy.") The president reportedly told aides in December that he agreed with the senator, and in January he assured Mansfield that there would be a complete U.S. withdrawal, though not until after the 1964 election. But Kennedy said other things to other people. At a press conference on 6 March, he declared: "I don't see how we are going to be able, unless we are going to pull out of Southeast Asia and turn it over to the Communists, how we are going to be able to reduce very much our economic programs and military programs in South Viet-Nam, in Cambodia, in Thailand."[84]

Ultimately, unambiguous public statements such as these are probably the best evidence that John F. Kennedy in 1963 contemplated no major alteration in American Vietnam policy in the near term. A statesman thinking about disengagement would have made sure to speak more elliptically and would have instructed his underlings to do likewise. Instead, administration officials continued through the summer to make categorical statements. Kennedy himself did so, as in July when he vowed to journalists, "We are not going to withdraw from [this] effort. In my opinion, for us to withdraw would mean a collapse not only of South Vietnam, but of Southeast Asia. So we are going to stay there."[85] The private record is murkier, though it too ultimately shows no flagging in the administration's determination.[86] Kennedy was unhappy with the war but also committed to it, for reasons that lay not in Vietnam or in the international community primarily, but at home. His oft-quoted assertion to newspaperman Charles Bartlett in late April 1963 (that is, shortly after Ngo Dinh Nhu stepped up his anti-American campaign), which may be apocryphal but rings true, captures this point well: "We don't have a prayer of staying in Vietnam," Bartlett quotes JFK as telling him. "Those people hate us. They are going to throw our asses out of there at almost any point. But I can't give up a piece of territory like that to the Communists and then get the people to reelect me."[87]

Was this true? Did Kennedy really possess no freedom to maneuver on policy toward Vietnam in 1963? This question would not be particularly important had Kennedy felt differently about the war—had he felt confident about the long-term prospects; had he not feared a repeat of the French debacle, and the stalemate in Korea; had he felt a strong sense of personal commitment to the GVN; or had he cared less about the importance of maintaining strong allied support for the war effort. Freedom to maneuver is immaterial when one is doing what one wants to do, or at least feels that it is the right course for its own sake. Precisely because JFK revealed a distinct lack of optimism ("We don't have a prayer") and a clear skepticism about Vietnam's importance, and precisely because he worried about the French and Korean analogies as well as the absence of strong allied support, the question matters a great deal.

Was Kennedy as hemmed in as he claimed to Bartlett (and to Mansfield and others)? Almost certainly not, at least not after the spring of 1963. If he had been looking for a face-saving and domestically defensible way out of Vietnam, the Diem regime presented it to him during the spring and summer of that year with Nhu's anti-American pronouncements and with the attacks on the Buddhists. The American news media, led by the likes of David Halberstam of the New York Times and Neil Sheehan of United Press International, gave extensive coverage to the viciousness of the regime's campaign, presenting to the American people irrefutable evidence of heavy religious persecution. Many who had been apathetic about the conflict and about the Diem regime's harsh rule were outraged, and though few were prepared to advocate a U.S. withdrawal from South Vietnam, the idea no longer seemed wholly far-fetched. As journalist Bernard Fall remarked shortly thereafter, the Buddhist uprisings were an unmistakable symptom of the unraveling of the South Vietnamese social fabric, and they gave Kennedy an avenue for disengagement that risked considerably less domestic political damage than ever before. The "perfect pretext" for a U.S. withdrawal, two respected authors have called the cycle of uprisings and crackdowns.[88] Kennedy could have claimed that Diem and Nhu had flagrantly violated the stipulations for aid laid down by Eisenhower in 1954— continued aid, Eisenhower had said, depended on the implementation of meaningful reform. He could have publicized far and wide Nhu's anti-American pronouncements and his contacts with Hanoi. ("Mr. Nhu says we do not understand his country and apparently wants us to leave, and I see no option but to abide by his wishes," JFK could have announced.)

No doubt Kennedy would have paid a political price for opting for dis-engagement, whether through a unilateral withdrawal combined with a conspicuous boosting of the U.S. commitment to Thailand, or through a face-saving Geneva-type agreement. But it bears noting that his decision to cut losses and negotiate on Laos caused far less ruckus on the homefront than many of his aides had feared and anticipated. The silence was deafen-ing on Capitol Hill in the wake of that decision. Likewise, some advisers worried about a conservative backlash to his conciliatory speech at Ameri-can University in June 1963 ("Let us reexamine our attitude toward the Cold War," he declared), yet very little backlash occurred. Kennedy, it is worth remembering, was in a strong political position in mid 1963 as far as foreign policy was concerned, with some legitimate achievements un-der his belt. Less than a year earlier he had showed strength and gained prestige in forcing Khrushchev to withdraw Soviet missiles from Cuba; regardless of whether JFK's tough stance was wise or necessary, few could question his steadfastness after that point. In mid 1963 he signed the Test Ban Treaty with Moscow, which he could cite as his commitment to peace. Well aware by then of the depth of the Sino-Soviet split, and of the Soviet concerns about the expansion of Chinese influence in Asia, he could have backed up his stated commitment to peace and improved Soviet-American relations by taking the Vietnam problem to an international conference (a move Moscow would have welcomed).[89]

What would have resulted from such a conference cannot be stated with certainty, but a few observations are in order. Hanoi's vision of a settle-ment involved a coalition government in the South patterned on the Laos model, together with the withdrawal of the United States. The Soviets, the French, and most British officials also envisioned an agreement along these lines. Most of these observers understood that the Laotian model was an im-perfect fit—that unlike Laos, South Vietnam did not have a readily identifi-able centrist candidate for any coalition government who occupied the mid-dle between two extremes (there was no Vietnamese Souvanna Phouma); that the Laos settlement had not in fact ended the conflict in that country, because tensions remained and fighting continued; and that for both the DRV and the United States the stakes were much greater in South Viet-nam in mid 1963 than they had been in Laos in 1961. But these observ-ers nevertheless believed that, as with Laos, a settlement was possible on Vietnam that would allow the United States to disengage gracefully. There can be little doubt that they were correct. In both 1954 and 1962, the west-ern powers had emerged from Geneva with deals more favorable than their positions on the battlefield should have allowed them to expect; it is rea-sonable to assume that they could have done so again, particularly given the Soviet Union's interest in gaining a settlement and given North Vietnam's strong desire to avert a major American military intervention. In great-power conferences, the greatest powers invariably get at least some of what they want.[90]

The 1962 settlement on Laos was indeed considerably more advantageous to the West than is often assumed; it got the Soviets more or less out of the conflict and committed to working for a settlement, and it got Souvanna Phouma to switch to a much more prowestern orientation. If the agreement did not end the fighting in Laos, it certainly reduced it considerably, and it removed Laos as a major issue in superpower relations. Few informed observers doubted that the long-term result of a Vietnam settlement would be a reunified country under Hanoi's control, but most outside the United States thought that this result would be at least some years away and even then not a major concern for the West, because a Hanoi-ruled Vietnam would be a Titoist Vietnam standing clear of Chinese domination.[91] Particularly for those doubtful of the GVN's chances and dubious about the ultimate importance of the outcome in South Vietnam (a group that probably included John F. Kennedy himself), an American withdrawal by way of a fig-leaf negotiated settlement made a good deal of tactical and strategic sense.

All that said, it is not easy to imagine Kennedy taking this step and cutting his losses, for the simple reason that the down-the-middle path he had followed for so long on Vietnam still remained open to him. He was no profile in courage on Vietnam, and if indeed his thoughts were already on the November 1964 election, it made all the sense in the world for him to keep the war as much as possible on the back burner in 1963, which meant no dramatic departures of any kind. When next we consider the freedom-of-maneuver question in detail (in chapter 9, covering the final weeks of 1964), we will find a very different objective situation, both on the ground in Vietnam and in the domestic American and international arenas. At the start of 1965 continuing on the middle path would be impossible, which meant that the disengagement option demanded (or should have demanded) much closer attention.

In August 1963 the situation was very different. Expert opinion in August 1963, both in the United States and abroad, was far less pessimistic about the trends than it would be a year and a half later. Anti-Americanism in South Vietnam was far less pervasive, notwithstanding Ngo Dinh Nhu's periodic outbursts. The Saigon political upheavals of 1964, with governments coming and going seemingly by the week, had yet to occur. International allied opposition to America's deepening involvement in the war had yet to become widespread—before de Gaulle's August pronouncement, there was hardly any at all. In the United States, meanwhile, virtually no one in Congress and in the mainstream media that summer doubted that the defense of South Vietnam should remain a high American priority—the famed Saigon correspondents who reported the repression of the Buddhists and battlefield developments questioned how the war was being fought, not whether it should be.[92] Consensus reigned in the East Coast "Establishment." Finally, unlike Lyndon Johnson in December 1964, John Kennedy in 1963 still had the election in front of him. The safe course, in his view, was to stay the course, even if this required engineering a (preferably bloodless) coup in Saigon. It could be considered an example of breathtaking callousness and self-serving cynicism, this willingness to prolong a military commitment—and thereby endanger the lives of many Vietnamese and Americans—primarily to serve one's own political ends. So indeed it was. But it defines, to a considerable extent, Kennedy's thinking as the summer drew to a close.

We have come full circle. In late August 1963, as the United States moved to oust the South Vietnamese leader it had backed for the past nine years, Charles de Gaulle chose to speak out in favor of a political solution leading to a Vietnam free of outside intervention. American officials, always opposed to an early settlement and possessing an agreement with London to work to prevent one, had seen no reason to feel particularly fearful of the prospect. The pressure in that direction had never been significant. Until now. The Kennedy administration, faced with determined opponents in both Hanoi and Saigon, now would face one also in Paris.

2 Breaks and Continuities

There would be no coup d'état in South Vietnam in the late summer of 1963. The generals backed off. John F. Kennedy had signed off on the coup on August 29, but he had reserved the option of pulling back, telling Henry Cabot Lodge in Saigon that it would be better "to change our minds than fail." The generals perceived the vacillation in American policy that Kennedy's words indicated—the administration had been sending mixed messages for several days—and they shared his basic concern: that the balance of forces in South Vietnam might still be in favor of the government.[1] They even suspected one another's loyalties. Neither the generals nor the American president had scruples about their plan to overthrow a sitting Saigon leader who had occupied his office for close to nine years and who had been praised by successive American administrations as a crucial ally in the East; their worry was merely that the effort might not succeed. Little wonder, therefore, that in September and October, as U.S.-GVN relations continued to plummet, as Diem became ever more dependent on Nhu, and as Nhu continued to flirt with a possible deal with Hanoi, the plans for a coup would revive. This time there would be no retreat. On 1 November 1963, Ngo Dinh Diem was ousted from power. On the following day, he and his brother were killed.

Three weeks later, Kennedy himself lay dead. His image glittered with triumph after the Cuban Missile Crisis, and with hope after the Test Ban Treaty. Over the previous months, much of the tension in the Soviet-American confrontation had drained away, as Kennedy and Khrushchev took steps to reverse the direction of the previous two years and to lay the foundation for a future of peaceful coexistence rather than inevitable conflict. Certainly in hindsight but probably also in the context of the time, the foreign-policy issue that loomed largest for the administration in those fateful months of late 1963 was Vietnam—or, at least, none could be said to have loomed larger. William P. Bundy, then a McNamara deputy at the Pentagon, has described the changed atmosphere well. "Whereas the successive Vietnam decisions in 1961 had been handled in the shadow of apparently graver crises elsewhere, this was no longer the case in the summer or fall of 1963," Bundy wrote a few years later. "Particularly after mid-August, the senior levels of the US Government from the President down were more preoccupied with Vietnam than at any previous time."[2]

To a considerable extent, it is the developments of these eleven or twelve weeks leading up to Dallas that are responsible for making Vietnam the most controversial aspect of John F. Kennedy's image and record. September and October witnessed a worsening crisis in South Vietnam, as well as the first significant stirrings of discontent in American elite opinion and growing concerns in the international community. November saw a U.S.-sponsored coup and the violent deaths of two presidents. The very suddenness of Kennedy's death has added fuel to the controversy. His admirers, seeking to insulate JFK from the subsequent debacle in Southeast Asia, have asked us to judge him by his intentions rather than his accomplishments because, they have argued, his good intentions would have reached fruition had he not been cut down so suddenly in November 1963. For Vietnam, this would have meant a de-escalation of the American involvement in the war, not a massive expansion as occurred under Lyndon Johnson.

Many Kennedy defenders go further, arguing not merely that Kennedy would have avoided Americanizing the war in 1965 but that he had already decided to get out of the war prior to leaving on that fateful trip to Texas.[3] At first glance this "incipient-withdrawal thesis" would not seem unreasonable, given the ambiguities that characterized Kennedy's Vietnam policy from the start and that we examined in the last chapter. But there are problems. Evidence for the thesis is slim, to say the least, and to be plausible, the thesis must somehow overcome the two central themes of American policy making in the fall of 1963, to be examined in this chapter: first, a pronounced fear of a premature negotiated settlement; and second, a strong determination to remove Ngo Dinh Nhu from effective policy-making power, if necessary by removing President Diem himself.[4] The two themes are closely connected: the administration's fear that Nhu and Diem might opt for a deal with the enemy, perhaps with French help, made the administration all the more determined to oust them.[5]

The fear of negotiations was evident from the moment that de Gaulle's call for a reunified, independent Vietnam became known in Washington. Senior American officials immediately began discussing the implications and planning a response. In a top-secret memorandum on 30 August, As-

sistant Secretary of State for Far Eastern Affairs Roger Hilsman, a key figure on Vietnam policy in these months, warned Dean Rusk that Diem and
Nhu, in an effort to ensure their political survival and thwart a possible
coup, might appeal to de Gaulle for support in pursuing neutralization for
South Vietnam. "In response," Hilsman advised, the United States "should
point out publicly that Vietnam cannot be effectively neutralized unless
the Communists are removed from control of North Vietnam." Should the
brothers make a "political move" directed to Hanoi, Hilsman suggested that
Henry Cabot Lodge "give Diem a clear warning of the dangers of such a
course and point out its continued pursuit will lead to a cessation of U.S.
aid."[6] Hilsman conceded that such efforts might not be sufficient to thwart
an agreement between Saigon and the communists, and he argued that the
United States should "encourage the dissident generals to move promptly
with a coup" if the Saigon regime showed signs of negotiating with the
North. In the event that Hanoi intervened militarily to save Diem, he wrote,
the United States should launch military strikes against North Vietnam.[7]

From Saigon, Lodge also expressed his concern. On 30 August, he made
note of French ambassador Laloulette's efforts to promote negotiations and
warned that de Gaulle's views could cause trouble for America's mission in
Vietnam. In a follow-up cable the next day, he stated that he was "reliably
advised" that Nhu was in fact considering a rapprochement with North
Vietnam. Lodge suggested that the United States might have to enlist special help to bring forth a change in de Gaulle's policy. "I have good reason
to believe," he said, "that the Holy See would be willing to intervene with
de Gaulle."[8]

Later the same day, Secretary of State Dean Rusk met with French ambassador Hervé Alphand at the State Department. Rusk told him that it
was the other side, not the United States, that was seeking to impose a military solution. The United States would be happy if South Vietnam could
be nonaligned, but the fact was that Hanoi-supported communist guerrillas were attempting to subjugate the country. This the United States had
to resist. Alphand said that he understood the American position, but he
maintained that a neutral solution for Vietnam was better than any alternative. More than that, such a solution was possible, given the limited influence of the USSR in the area and the anti-Chinese mindset of Ho Chi
Minh. The Laos neutralist settlement was not perfect, Alphand conceded,
but at least it had ended the great-power confrontation there. Rusk was
unpersuaded, but he plainly revealed his concern about de Gaulle's statement and its potential impact. He asked for, and received, Alphand's promise to announce that it represented long-term French thinking, not something that could be put into effect in the near future.[9]

The administration also expressed its worry to the British. As so often during The Long 1964, London officials possessed keen insight into American thinking and choices. British analysts believed that three courses were open to Washington: to make peace with Nhu, to replace the whole regime by way of a coup, or to clear out of Vietnam altogether. The analysts were divided among themselves on which of the first two options was more likely but saw little chance that Kennedy would consider negotiations. Washington's negative response to de Gaulle's intervention, as expressed to British officials in Washington at the start of September, was ample proof of that. "The State Department are thoroughly alarmed [by the general's intervention] and have asked us to pass on to them everything about French views and activities which we can," the Foreign Office cabled the embassy in Saigon early in the month.[10]

But perhaps the clearest sign of the extent of U.S. concern over de Gaulle's comments was the attention that the administration gave the matter in preparing Kennedy for a CBS interview with Walter Cronkite on 2 September. Policymakers sought to use the interview to put pressure on the Diem regime, but they also wanted to publicly refute the overtures from Paris. In a memorandum to Kennedy on "suggested comments" for the interview, National Security Adviser McGeorge Bundy dealt at considerable length with the general's statement and the ways in which the administration could gently but clearly distance itself from it. He cautioned, however, against a detailed reply by Kennedy, on the grounds that "only our own personal irritation" is an argument against the "well-established conclusion that we do best when we ignore nosey Charlie."[11]

Cronkite asked two questions on Vietnam, both of them prearranged. In response to the first, on the current situation on Saigon, the president voiced displeasure with the Saigon government's prosecution of the war and followed with a thinly veiled threat. "I don't think that unless a greater effort is made by the government to win popular support that the war can be won out there," he said. "With changes in policy and perhaps in personnel, I think [the government] can win. If it doesn't make those changes, I would think that the chances of winning would not be very good." When Cronkite followed with a question on the de Gaulle pronouncement, Kennedy pointedly noted that although the United States was glad to get counsel from its allies, it should take the form of "assistance, real assistance. . . . It doesn't do us any good to say: 'Well, why don't we all just go home and leave the world to those who are our enemies.'" It would be a mistake, Kennedy said, for the United States to withdraw from Vietnam.[12]

It is not difficult to see why the Kennedy team viewed de Gaulle's statement with such concern. He had introduced a dangerous new element—the prospect of North-South peace—at a time when U.S. officials were work-ing feverishly to strengthen the war effort. Prior to this, they had not been particularly worried about the prospect of a push for early negotiations, but de Gaulle had changed all that. Senior policymakers knew that the French leader, though he could not pretend to compete with the substantial economic and military aid programs they could offer, still carried real if in-calculable influence in Vietnam because he appealed to older ties that still linked the Vietnamese and the French. They knew of French ambassador Roger Laloulette's efforts at promoting talks, and they knew of the consid-erable international interest in a diplomatic solution. And, no less impor-tant, they knew of the Ngo brothers' determination to preserve a measure of independence from Washington, and of Nhu's growing anti-American agitation. De Gaulle's message was therefore a boost to the regime, at least in the short term. Add to this the concerns about the American people's commitment to the Vietnam cause, and the administration's trepidation is rather easy to explain. They realized that the fuzziness of de Gaulle's lan-guage, far from weakening his message, might strengthen it to a significant degree, because it could allow both sides to read into it what they wanted.

We see here the establishment of a pattern that would persist through the Americanization of the war in 1965 and beyond. American planners would spend much time discussing the French leader's actions and ideas, but only in terms of how best to counter them. The substance of his ar-gument was not closely examined, then or later, partly because that argu-ment was anathema to American officials and partly because they were convinced he had ulterior motives in opposing U.S. efforts in Vietnam. Many of them saw his 29 August intervention as having little to do with Vietnam and a great deal to with his longtime aim of gaining greater in-dependence for France within the western alliance. In this formulation his pronouncement was merely one more in a long line of specific policy deci-sions that flowed from that larger objective—others included his continu-ation of the nuclear weapons development program initiated by his prede-cessors in the Fourth Republic; his push for greater French influence over decision making within the NATO alliance; and his rebuffing of Anglo-American attempts to admit Britain into the European Common Market.[13] U.S. policymakers also reasoned that de Gaulle was embarrassed by the French defeat in the region and did not want the United States to succeed where France had failed. And they were convinced that what they saw as de Gaulle's own negative view of the United States—dating back to his troubled relationship with Franklin Roosevelt in World War II—contrib-uted to the French position. Many were certain that de Gaulle would auto-matically oppose *any* American initiative that did not immediately benefit

France, and often speculated that Franco-American friction would end once de Gaulle left office.[14]

Unfortunately for these officials, in September there were more signs that leaders in both North and South Vietnam were interested in pursuing the kind of accommodation envisioned by de Gaulle. Hanoi that month made no public comment on de Gaulle's statement but privately expressed sympathy. On 11 September Premier Pham Van Dong told Jacques De Buzon, the head of the French *délégate-général* in Hanoi, that his government would like to see a neutral South as an interim step toward reunification. The premier professed puzzlement at the meaning of de Gaulle's statement, but he added that France could be helpful in bringing about a peaceful resolution of the crisis, particularly given its continued cultural and social influence in the country. Respected Vietnam watcher Bernard Fall declared in late September that, on the basis of his discussions with Ho Chi Minh and other DRV leaders, he was convinced that Hanoi would agree to a delay in reunification. Its leaders, Fall maintained, sought to avoid a war with the United States since it would make them "dependent on Red Chinese aid and cost North Viet-Nam its delicately sustained independence." The marked slow-down in insurgent military activity in the late summer and early autumn likewise may have signified a desire on Hanoi's part to keep the wobbling Diem regime in power, on the theory that the Ngos, increasingly at odds with the Americans, might opt to take their chances on a North-South deal.[15]

In Saigon, meanwhile, Nhu continued in September to insist to virtually all comers that he was not against negotiations and cooperation with the North; to most of them he also said that contacts had begun and would continue.[16] By all accounts the contacts, if they existed at all in September or October, were of a very preliminary nature, and the question remains: did Nhu really want a deal in this period, or was he merely trying to blackmail the Americans? It is difficult to be sure. His leaking of the existence of the contacts to the rabidly anticommunist American journalist Joseph Alsop, who wrote a column on it in midmonth, suggests that he was trying to scare Washington, and it is probably true that, as Mieczyslaw Maneli would later put it, "he was playing on many instruments at the same time." And yet he almost certainly perceived genuine advantages in professing interest in talks, particularly because they offered a means by which to potentially reduce South Vietnam's dependence on the United States.[17]

More important for present purposes than the question of whether Nhu was serious about wanting a deal with Hanoi is the fact that the United

States thought he was. Throughout September, as the Kennedy administration considered ways to strengthen the war effort, there was growing consensus in Washington that Nhu was becoming increasingly anti-American and that a rapprochement between North and South was possible. At the start of the month, the CIA learned from an unidentified source that Nhu's dealings with Hanoi were an "open secret" in Saigon diplomatic circles. On 13 September Director John McCone said that he was increasingly concerned about the possibility of Nhu making a deal with Hanoi.[18] On 19 September McCone received an agency memorandum authored by staffer Chester Cooper, which said that a DRV-GVN agreement was possible and advised that "Ngo family actions in this realm merit continuing close attention." The memo noted that the usually secretive Nhu was now openly acknowledging contacts with Hanoi and dropping "transparent hints that the GVN would not necessarily refuse to consider overtures from Hanoi." Such a move would not be made out of any affection for the Hanoi regime—the Vietminh had reportedly tortured and killed their oldest brother. "Nevertheless," Cooper claimed, "it would be quite in character for Nhu—and Diem—to seek some measure of maneuverability vis-à-vis the U.S. to avoid being boxed in between two unacceptable alternatives: abject surrender to U.S. demands or loss of all political power." He thought that it was in this context that the likelihood of Ngo-family dealings with North Vietnam should be assessed. "We believe that if Nhu and Diem feel themselves soon to be faced with such extreme alternatives, they might well cast about for some sort of agreement with Hanoi," the memo continued. "If the Ngos were moved to seek a rapprochement with the DRV on terms less than reunification—e.g. a cease fire—they might seriously entertain the almost certain minimum DRV demand for the removal of U.S. forces."

North Vietnam, too, had an incentive to make a deal, Cooper continued. Though Hanoi remained confident of ultimate victory and therefore felt no pressure to agree to a settlement on any but its own terms, it "might be willing to consider something less than reunification, particularly if it thought that its aims could be achieved more quickly and cheaply than by continuing a campaign for armed insurgency. Hanoi's conditions for such a more modest rapprochement might be considerably less stringent." In another report, this one from its station in Saigon, the CIA reported that many Americans and Vietnamese were concerned over "additional evidence [that] Nhu [was] negotiating for a settlement with the North." The agency warned that its assessment was based on the assumption that the Ngos, though operating under tremendous pressures, "remain essentially rational." But if, as some observers believed, they no longer were rational, then the "likelihood of Nhu's endeavoring to seek an accommodation with Hanoi must be assessed considerably higher; and to a somewhat lesser extent the same would have to be said of Diem."[19]

Similar fears were expressed by officials in the State Department. They may have been influenced by Robert G. K. Thompson's assertion to personnel at the U.S. embassy that Nhu's only "trump card" was an American withdrawal and that Hanoi would pay almost any price to achieve such a result. Ambassador Lodge no doubt had Thompson in mind when he cabled Washington on 13 September: "Hope some study will be given to what our response should be if Nhu, in the course of negotiating with North Vietnam, should ask the U.S. to leave South Vietnam or to make a major reduction in forces. This is obviously the only trump card he has got and it is obviously of the highest importance. It is also obvious to me that we must not leave. But the question of finding a proper basis for remaining is at first blush not simple."[20]

Roger Hilsman, in a top-secret memorandum to Rusk on 16 September, speculated that Nhu had "already decided on an adventure," one with a minimum and a maximum goal. The minimum goal would be to reduce sharply the American presence in politically significant positions; the maximum goal would be "a deal with North Vietnam for a truce in the war, a complete removal of the U.S. presence, and a 'neutralist' or 'Titoist' but still separate South Vietnam." Similarly, Thomas L. Hughes, the director of the department's Bureau of Intelligence and Research, told Rusk of "proliferating reports of varying credibility" alleging that Nhu was negotiating with Hanoi, "with or without French connivance." De Gaulle's 29 August statement, Hughes maintained, provided a basis for Ngo Dinh Nhu to threaten, directly or indirectly, that clandestine contacts between Saigon and Hanoi might arrange a settlement contrary to U.S. interests. "Conceivably," Hughes continued, "the mixture of truth and rumor, contrived and accidental, could bring about diplomatic pressures for an international conference on Vietnam. Soviet Russia might back such a move; Communist China would reluctantly go along if it thought this could force a withdrawal of the United States from South Vietnam."

Hughes emphasized the "overweening self-confidence" and growing anti-Americanism of Nhu, which together could lead Nhu to conclude that a deal with the North Vietnamese was desirable. Diem was unlikely to support such a view, but Hughes argued that he too desired to reduce American pressure on his regime and therefore might agree to at least exploratory talks with Hanoi. For its part, Hanoi would likely welcome bilateral talks with Saigon, given their primary goal of reducing the American presence in Vietnam.[21]

Hughes's words spoke right to the heart of the issue, as Kennedy and his advisers well knew. A compromise settlement between North and South would have forced an American withdrawal from Vietnam, a prospect most policymakers found too frightening to contemplate, much less to pursue. In late 1963, senior U.S. officials remained in nearly unanimous agreement that the American presence must be preserved. As the chroniclers of the *Pentagon Papers* put it, they believed that an independent noncommunist South Vietnam was too important an interest to abandon.[22]

Just how important was made clear at an extraordinary State Department meeting on 31 August. Word had come that the generals in Saigon had decided against a coup, and McNamara and Rusk now argued for getting back to business as usual and getting on with the war. Nhu's intentions and growing influence over Diem remained a problem, they agreed, but there was no choice but to reopen lines of communication with the government. A lone contrarian voice spoke up. Paul Kattenburg, a veteran State Department official who was chair of the Interdepartmental Working Group and who was considered a leading department expert on Vietnam, said his recent trip to Saigon had convinced him that Diem was hopeless and had made the people of South Vietnam unwilling allies of the Vietcong. The conclusion that both he and Lodge had reached, he told the group, was that the situation would continue to unravel and that the United States would be booted out of the country within six months to a year. Because Diem would not change and would not get rid of Nhu, there was only one wise thing to do: withdraw in a dignified way. It was a key moment: the unthinkable proposition—to get out of Vietnam—had been made at a high-level meeting by a man widely respected for his deep knowledge of Vietnamese society.[23]

The moment did not last long. Rusk, McNamara, and Vice President Lyndon Johnson immediately blasted Kattenburg's claims. Rusk called his assertions "largely speculative" and said that it would be much better to proceed from the assumption that "we will not pull out . . . until the war is won." After all, there was "good proof" that the war effort was going well. McNamara seconded Rusk's views, affirming that "we have been winning the war." And Johnson, a seldom-heard voice on Vietnam issues in these months, said that it would be a "disaster to pull out. We should stop playing cops and robbers and go about winning the war."[24]

It was a textbook example of how to silence a midlevel official, even one respected for his expertise on the issue in question. Kattenburg was rarely heard from again in policy deliberations that autumn. By early 1964 he was gone from Vietnam decision making altogether.[25]

John Kennedy also ruled out a withdrawal. His rejection of de Gaulle's plan in the Cronkite interview on 2 September was followed a week later by an even more categorical rejection of disengagement on NBC's *Huntley-Brinkley Report*. Speaking with more certainty than he likely privately felt, Kennedy said he fully accepted the validity of the domino theory as it applied to Southeast Asia ("I believe it. I believe it"). When David Brinkley asked whether a reduction of U.S. aid to South Vietnam was likely, Kennedy responded at length. "I don't think we think that would be helpful at this time," he said. "We must be patient, we must persist. What I am concerned about is that Americans will get impatient and say because they don't like events in Southeast Asia or they don't like the government in Vietnam, that we should withdraw. . . . I think we should stay." During a press conference on 12 September, Kennedy announced that he was "for those things and those policies which help win the war there. That is why some 25,000 Americans have traveled 10,000 miles to participate in the struggle. What helps to win the war, we support; what interferes with the war effort, we oppose. . . . We are not there to see a war lost."[26]

Consider the impression such stark language must have left on anyone who heard it. Would a president privately scheming for disengagement from the war make such a categorical comment? Hardly. Kennedy was too smart to miss the degree to which such statements can reduce a leader's maneuverability. An official at the British Foreign Office, commenting on the press conference in an internal memo, understood the implications: "The criterion 'what helps the war we are for, what hinders we are against' is O.K. as a formula for the present, but it will lead to nasty come-backs when, as is likely, things go badly in the field over the next two months. The critics can then justly say 'The war is now going worse—what are you going to do about it?' "[27]

Privately, too, Kennedy remained committed to staying in Vietnam. On 3 September, at a White House meeting attended by all of his top Vietnam aides, he dismissed de Gaulle's plan and said that Alphand likely lacked the courage to respond to his criticism of the French proposal in the Cronkite interview. The same day, he helped in the wording of a cable to Ambassador Lodge that restated the importance of victory in the war. In a follow-up cable of his own, Dean Rusk described Kennedy's Cronkite interview as setting the "general objective of U.S. policy, i.e., to secure a victory in [the] war against [the] Viet Cong. It is in that context that [the president] expressed our sense of need for change in GVN policies and perhaps in personnel so as to regain touch with people." And Averell Harriman, who had more access to Kennedy's thinking than most in the administration, assured Lodge that "from the President on down everybody is determined to support you and the country team in winning the war against the Viet Cong. . . . There are no quitters here."[28]

But if there was general agreement among U.S. policymakers that a negotiated American withdrawal should be excluded from consideration, there was no such unity of opinion on what should be done to stabilize the situation in South Vietnam. Indeed, in mid September, bureaucratic opinion was significantly divided about the preferred course in the war. The State Department, led by Rusk, Hilsman, and Lodge, argued that lasting stability would be impossible as long as Nhu remained, that he was likely to remain because actual power rested with him rather than Diem, and that Nhu's dealings with Hanoi would only intensify over time. They concluded that the administration should adopt a policy of "pressures and persuasion" (including cuts in economic aid) against Diem to compel him to remove Nhu and to adopt the policy changes needed to defeat the Vietcong. If Diem resisted the pressures, the United States should work for his ouster. Supporters of this strategy conceded that it contained risks and might bring about the very North-South accord it sought to prevent. "Our problem," Hilsman told Rusk and McNamara, "is to implement this policy of persuasion coupled with pressure in such a way as to avoid triggering either civil violence or a radical move by the government of South Vietnam to make a deal with the DRV and remove the U.S. presence."[29]

The "pressures" group was opposed by one centered in the Defense Department and advocating "reconciliation." Its members included the Joint Chiefs of Staff, CIA director John McCone, and General Harkins. They were certain that the failure of the August coup made it clear that no viable alternative to Diem existed. He was unlikely to remove Nhu, upon whom he depended more and more, and even severe cuts in aid would only harm the war effort, antagonize the South Vietnamese populace, and further destabilize the country. In addition, it might lead the Ngos to seek a deal with Hanoi. Diem may not be ideal, they acknowledged, but he represented the best chance for victory.[30]

This was the internal schism that confronted Kennedy. He had to choose between two contrasting views, both of which sought the same goal, victory in Vietnam, but which differed dramatically on how to get there and how far away it was. The president too wanted victory, but he also wanted consensus among his advisers on a course of action. He refused to proceed without it. In late September, he dispatched a team headed by Robert McNamara and General Maxwell Taylor, his most trusted military adviser, to make an on-the-spot assessment.[31]

The trip proved an eye-opener for McNamara. He had been among those favoring a pro-Diem policy in the weeks prior, but the mission changed him. Discussions in Saigon, notably one with Vice President Nguyen Ngoc Tho and one with a British observer code-named "Professor Smith" (in reality, Patrick Honey of the University of London), convinced him that reports of great military progress had been exaggerated, that the statistics had been wrong, that Diem was totally dependent on Nhu, and that Nhu probably was in contact with the North Vietnamese. McNamara concluded that Hilsman and Lodge were correct: the prospects for success would be much greater without the Ngos in power. At the same time, he found no solid evidence that a coup would be successful, or that a successor regime would be better. Maxwell Taylor, too, was ambivalent. He did not doubt the weakness of the Diem regime, or the growing influence of the unpredictable Nhu. But his findings in the field led him to agree substantially with the contention by Harkins and other military officials that the war was being won and that the Vietcong could be reduced to banditry within two years—by the end of 1965.[32]

This ambivalence found its way into the bulky, ten-thousand-word report the two men submitted on their return to Washington on 2 October. Simultaneously optimistic about the state of the military campaign and deeply concerned about the political situation, the report clearly aimed to satisfy both the "pressure" advocates and the supporters of "reconciliation." Lauding the "great progress" in the military campaign, the report proposed that one thousand U.S. advisers be withdrawn by the end of the year and speculated that the "bulk" of the American force could be pulled out by 1965. McNamara and Taylor found no good evidence of the possibility of a successful coup d'état, and they recommended that "at this time, no initiative should be taken to encourage actively a change in government." At the same time, however, they counseled "to let the present impression stand that the U.S. would not be averse to a change in government" and called for the United States "urgently to identify and build contacts with an alternative leadership if and when it appears." Though concluding that the probability of an early coup was not high, McNamara and Taylor conceded that American support could make an important difference to the chances for a coup. No doubt their coolness toward a change in government grew out of their conclusion that a replacement regime stood only a fifty-fifty chance of being an improvement over Diem. The best course for the United States, the report concluded, was one of "selective pressures," including modest cuts in economic aid, applied against the regime. Such pressure would probably fail to induce Diem to remove Nhu, but the South Vietnamese president might "at least be deterred from resuming large-scale oppressions."[33]

The McNamara-Taylor report was a remarkable document, both for its importance in subsequent American policy decisions and for what William P. Bundy, an assistant secretary of defense, who was a member of the delegation, later called its "internal inconsistency." Though the military section of the report was optimistic, predicting victory *once the political situation righted itself,* the political section maintained, in Bundy's words, that "such a righting was unlikely, and that on the contrary there was a serious prospect that an unreformed Diem would bring on chaos or an unpredictable change of regime."[34] Nor was the report accurate in its rendering of the military situation. It grossly underestimated the problems in the strategic hamlets program and incorrectly attributed the relative quiet in the countryside to the success of the counterinsurgency program. Equally significant, it overestimated the potential impact that aid cuts would have on Diem, underestimated the possibility of a coup, and failed to anticipate that such a coup, sanctioned by the United States, would tie Washington ever more closely to South Vietnam.

Nevertheless, McNamara and his team had accomplished the major task set for them by Kennedy: to produce a consensus paper and bring back from Saigon a plan he could call a policy. Upon landing back in Washington on 2 October, McNamara went straight to the White House, where Kennedy approved the recommendations and ordered the gradual implementation of a "selective pressures" policy. "As of tonight, we have policy," he told those present. It was a policy designed to bring forth changes in Saigon, without in any way impairing the war effort. The following week, the president signed National Security Action Memorandum 263, the document that officially made the McNamara-Taylor report national policy.[35]

While American policymakers moved to reaffirm their commitment to the war against the Vietcong, others were increasingly coming to question that commitment. Here we come to another important new development in the late summer of 1963: the much greater attention paid to the war by both domestic and international audiences than at any time before, and the growing misgivings among many of these observers. A State Department survey of U.S. public opinion in mid September found "widespread concern about U.S. Vietnam policy and considerable confusion" among Americans.[36] Key elements of the American press, though opposed to a unilateral American withdrawal, began in September to emphasize the need for diplomacy. *Newsweek* and *The New Republic* welcomed de Gaulle's initiative and questioned the administration's determination to preserve an independent South Vietnam, as did the dean of American columnists, Walter Lippmann. "If there is no settlement such as General de Gaulle proposes, then a protracted and indecisive war of attrition is all that is left," Lippmann declared in his syndicated column (which appeared in nearly two hundred newspapers) on 3 September. Two days later he wrote: "The price of a military victory in the Vietnamese war is higher than American vital interests can justify." The columnist maintained that the very fact that the administration had kept the U.S. commitment limited showed that it saw South Vietnam as "an important secondary interest but . . . not a primary vital interest of the United States."[37]

In its 14 September issue, *The New Republic* called reunification the only way to bring "order and prosperity" to Vietnam and criticized the Kennedy team for having no program for reunification. What, the magazine asked, justified the American commitment to South Vietnam? Certainly not the immediate danger to the rest of Indochina; because the communists had already moved through Laos into both South Vietnam and Cambodia, "it is hard to see how a new [Hanoi-supported] government in Saigon could make matters worse. The real importance of South Vietnam, so far as we can discover, is psychological. If Diem falls, the world may be somewhat more convinced that Communism is the wave of the future." The editors conceded that there was some sense in this argument, but, they asked, just how much sense? "Would other Asian leaders really feel as incompetent, and hence as insecure, as they think Diem is? Might they not expect to do somewhat better? Certainly none of them faces such intractable problems. Also, would they see Hanoi's victory as a victory for Communism, or only for national unity? If for Communism, would the stock of Moscow, Peking, or Hanoi rise?"[38]

These were penetrating questions, exactly the questions that would be asked time and again later in the decade, as more and more observers came to share the assumptions that underlay them. Then came this remarkable passage:

> The US hope ought to be the creation of a stable, non-aligned Vietnam, looking to Moscow, Paris, and Washington as well as Peking. There is no reason to suppose that this is impossible once Hanoi's *casus belli* with the West is gone. So long as America props up Diem, Ho will share the militance of Peking. But once Ho's country is united under his rule, he could become another Tito. Indeed, it might be worth discussing the subject directly with the Soviets, for they have every reason to want an independent government in Hanoi. If they are prepared to join the Americans in giving India hardware to fight China, they would surely be willing to join in keeping Vietnam independent. "But," it will be answered, "we cannot in good conscience betray our promises of the past ten years and sell the people of South Vietnam

into slavery in the North." To this there are two answers. The first is that it seems increasingly unlikely that we can prevent this from happening, even if we try. The second is that the difference between the regimes in Hanoi and Saigon is not sufficiently great to justify continuing the present war.

The magazine, in short, saw little to fear in a communist Vietnam, particularly given the historic Vietnamese hostility to China. It urged Washington to think of Ho Chi Minh as the leader who would be "most likely to serve America's primary purpose in Southeast Asia: stopping Chinese expansion. It seems increasingly possible that Ho is America's best bet."

Few publications were willing to second the idea that Ho Chi Minh was America's answer in Vietnam, and the editorial's larger assertions about the U.S. commitment and whether it ought to be continued were not widely shared in the print media in the late summer of 1963—such comments would not become commonplace until about a year later, in the autumn of 1964. A clear majority of editorial writers across the country, to the extent that they expressed an opinion on the matter, favored standing firm in the war. But the editorial is highly noteworthy nevertheless, both for its extraordinary prescience and for the sizable hole it by itself punches in the long-standing myth that Vietnam was "The Liberals' War." *The New Republic* in the 1960s (unlike in the 1980s and 1990s) was a beacon of American liberalism. As will become clear in the pages that follow, liberals in America were divided on the war from an early stage, and many were among the first to challenge the need for a continued commitment to the GVN.

Expressions of alarm came also from more unexpected places. *U.S. News & World Report* had traditionally been a strong supporter of the American commitment to South Vietnam, and it would continue to be in the months to come. But in September it too expressed nervousness about the direction of events in Vietnam and posed tough questions for the administration. "Can a war against the Communists be won when the Diem government is preoccupied with a political struggle for survival against a non-Communist opposition that is increasing, rather than decreasing, in strength?" the magazine asked. "If the war cannot be won under these circumstances, would it be better to cut losses and get out, or hang on and hope for a change for the better? It's a choice that may have to be faced sooner than many think."[39]

Not long after these magazine issues appeared, the *New York Times*, far and away the most influential press organ in the country, began to encourage a greater American effort in the direction of negotiations. In October

1963, the paper's editorials urged the administration not to exclude the idea of an independent, neutral Vietnam from its current policy appraisal, and it wondered if Nikita Khrushchev might be induced to "take an interest in keeping Vietnam out of Peking's grasp." Smaller regional papers also began expressing concerns. The *Salt Lake City Tribune* declared that the United States should not remain in South Vietnam "to fight a war that cannot be won. . . . Withdrawal would be a defeat for the U.S. but it would not be nearly as disastrous as continuing a hopeless struggle to help those who will not help themselves." The *Milwaukee Journal* said that withdrawal might be the only option: "The U.S. is being made to look silly as it pours in money and extreme effort to bolster a regime that does little but insult us and terrorize its own people." The *New York Journal-American* took a similar line. The State Department kept careful tab on these press attitudes. Its secret American Opinion Survey for the week ending 2 October referred to "the withdrawal talk being heard in some quarters." A week later, it noted that although most of the press remained supportive of the American commitment, there was a growing emphasis on the need for diplomacy.[40]

The weeks of late summer and early autumn also witnessed the first stirrings of significant congressional questioning of the commitment to South Vietnam. Here, too, as with the press, the concerns were not nearly as widespread or deeply felt as they would be a year later; but here, too, they are of historical importance. An important shift, largely evident only in hindsight, was occurring: administration representatives for the first time had to endure tough questioning not merely about the conduct of the war, but also about its viability and importance. After an appearance before the Senate Foreign Relations Committee's Far East subcommittee, Roger Hilsman reported "far-reaching doubts regarding not only [the] Diem-Nhu leadership but also [the] advisability of continued U.S. participation in the Viet-Nam War."[41] Research by Robert David Johnson makes clear that several centrist and left-of-center Senate Democrats in this period cast considerable doubt on the long-term prospects in the war effort—Albert Gore of Tennessee, Wayne Morse of Oregon, and George McGovern of North Dakota, for example, advocated using the Buddhist crisis as an excuse to get the United States out of what they saw as a hopeless mess. Arkansas's J. William Fulbright, chairman of the Foreign Relations Committee, worried about the prospect of an open-ended commitment, as did Majority Leader Mike Mansfield of Montana, whose doubts had increased since his trip to South Vietnam a year earlier. An important rationale for including the one-thousand-man withdrawal plan in the McNamara-Taylor report, it is clear, was growing cognizance on the part of Kennedy and his aides that they would have to make a strong case to Congress for continuing U.S. involvement—a partial withdrawal, so the theory went, would suggest to lawmakers that the current course was the correct one and that the administration did not plan for Americans to take over the main burden of the fighting.[42]

To be sure, most congressional skeptics were still focused more on salvaging a bad situation than on initiating immediate disengagement from South Vietnam. Most still desperately wanted to support the administration's position. This was true of Frank Church of Idaho, one of the leading congressional figures of the period. Bitterly critical of Diem's repressive policies ("There has been nothing like him since the Borgias," Church declared in executive session on 5 September), he moved in early September to introduce a resolution to end U.S. aid to South Vietnam if the regime's harsh methods continued. The administration, which had contemplated just such a resolution as a means of putting pressure on Diem, encouraged Church to proceed but asked him to work in concert with the White House. The senator agreed. In late 1963, he still believed in the Vietnam commitment, albeit with greater misgivings than before. The resolution, drafted by the State Department and introduced on 12 September, called for condemnation by the Senate of Diem's repressive handling of the Buddhist issue and an end to American aid unless he changed his policies. This was a tough warning, but one that meant little. The Kennedy team wanted Diem to feel the heat but also wanted to avoid actually cutting U.S. aid significantly—such action would hurt the war effort and could well push Diem and Nhu into the arms of the communists. The administration made sure that Church's resolution never reached a vote. In a scene that would be repeated several times in The Long 1964, a prominent Senate Democrat had allowed himself to be used, to be co-opted by an administration intent on pursuing the war.[43]

Some of the same co-opting was occurring in the international arena, though here, too, one finds increased talk in this period of finding a negotiated solution to the conflict. *U.S. News & World Report* noted in mid September that de Gaulle's point of view was supported by many of the western diplomats stationed in Saigon. One of these diplomats told the magazine: "A Geneva-type settlement could easily result in all the peninsula going Communist. But at least the Americans then would be getting out of a dirty and expensive war, and one which you probably now cannot win under any circumstances." On 30 September, the State Department's William H. Sullivan reported that the French chargé d'affaires in Saigon and the Indian and Canadian representatives to the ICC had informed him that the United States should not discount the possibility of a Nhu-Ho deal if present trends continued for three to four months. The next day, Roger Hilsman warned that increased calls for a political solution to the conflict might be forthcoming from an increasingly restless United Nations General Assembly. Secretary General U Thant of Burma was known to favor an early move to negotiations.[44]

Among western allies the restlessness, though real, was kept largely hidden—note that the "western diplomat" above did not wish to be identified. Few governments were prepared to risk Washington's ire over the issue of Vietnam. Such was certainly the case with Great Britain. London officials were suspicious of de Gaulle's motives in issuing his pronouncement, but they were in general sympathetic to his gloomy outlook on the GVN's prospects. It is a safe bet that exceedingly few of them would have objected to anything in the aforementioned editorial in *The New Republic*—that is, they were dubious about the validity of the domino theory and pessimistic about the GVN's prospects, and they thought that a Titoist Vietnam was not a bad deal for the West. Almost to a person, they also believed that a coup would be disastrous, that it would result in chaos in Saigon and in the provinces and thereby benefit the Vietcong. Gordon Etherington-Smith, Her Majesty's ambassador in Saigon, a man more sympathetic to American aims in Vietnam than many of his compatriots, told the Foreign Office in mid September that the French proposal merited consideration. Hanoi would welcome an agreement, the ambassador declared, and it ought to be possible to get an agreement that would allow the Americans to save face. If the war effort continued to go badly, negotiations should be pursued. London officials agreed, but they were no more willing now than earlier in the year to press this point on Washington. The long-standing Anglo-American agreement to work to prevent early negotiations remained sacrosanct in late 1963. A move by London to abandon it could threaten U.S. support for British policy in Malaysia and complicate other bilateral issues as well.[45]

Across the channel in France, officials were less reticent about speaking out, though they continued to prefer generalities to specifics. In September, de Gaulle reiterated his desire for a peaceful settlement during a speech in Lyon, and Prime Minister Georges Pompidou, in an interview with the French weekly *Paris-Match*, criticized U.S. policy and called for a political settlement via a Geneva-type conference. At the beginning of October, Foreign Minister Maurice Couve de Murville declared that "the only valid objective in Viet Nam is reunification and independence, and if there is a movement in this direction it will have the support of France." France was not insisting on such a development right away, he added, but saw no other long-term solution. Couve emphasized that the problems in Indochina were linked, that the continuing uncertainty in Laos was caused in significant part by the struggle in Vietnam.[46]

Just what to do about the de Gaulle problem continued to vex American policymakers. His 29 August statement continued to reverberate weeks after the fact and further convinced them of the harmful impact that his views could have in South Vietnam and on world opinion.[47] The news had not been all bad. Roger Laloulette, the French ambassador in Saigon, had been recalled to Paris for consultations in mid September following a spate of press reports detailing his support for a North-South agreement and alleging that he was leaning on other western diplomats to back Nhu against the Americans. Without him on the scene—he would in fact never return to Saigon—France's capacity for direct influence on the GVN had been diminished.[48] Still, this was small consolation to American planners. Already suspicious of the Diem regime's intentions, and aware of the French president's potential influence in Saigon and Hanoi, the Kennedy administration determined that "selective pressures" of a different, more subtle, kind should be placed on Paris.[49]

As a first step, Kennedy instructed Rusk to have the American ambassador in Paris, Charles E. Bohlen, meet with de Gaulle. In a top-secret cable to Bohlen outlining the purpose for the meeting, the State Department told the ambassador to tell de Gaulle that it was imperative that Washington understand French "purpose and policy" in this area. Kennedy certainly had not forgotten de Gaulle's warnings of June 1961, the cable continued, "but he does not understand just how General de Gaulle envisages the development of a unified and neutralized Vietnam without the development of a strong non-communist society in the southern part of the country." In a clear reference to the 29 August statement, the cable also instructed Bohlen to ask the general to confine his misgivings to closed-door meetings with American officials: "Private discussions [are] less likely to lead to misunderstanding than public declarations with respect to an area where an ally is carrying the major responsibility." At the meeting that followed, Bohlen did as instructed, but de Gaulle refused to budge. He reiterated that France had learned that political questions could not be solved by force, even when that force was superior; and he refused to give assurances as to what he might say or do in the future.[50]

Kennedy made clear American unhappiness with the French policy in a 7 October meeting with French foreign minister Maurice Couve de Murville. Kennedy said bluntly that de Gaulle's August statement had been unhelpful, particularly with regard to its timing. The United States had been trying to stabilize South Vietnam, and de Gaulle's intervention made the task more difficult. When Couve pointed out that the situation in South Vietnam had been going steadily downhill for some time and continued to do so, Kennedy replied that he thought it was being made to appear much worse than it actually was.[51]

Couve's assessment was closer to the mark. Despite (or because of) the implementation of the "selective pressures" policy, the situation in the South continued to unravel in late September and early October. Intelligence analysts at the CIA and the State Department presented a bleak picture. "We are substantially worse off today in our relations with, and influence on, the Diem/Nhu regime than we have been since Diem came to power," a CIA report prepared for Director McCone declared. "Meanwhile, with each day that passes, there is an increasing danger that the GVN's deteriorating relations with the South Vietnamese people will begin to produce a general sag of enthusiasm for continuing the war against the Viet Cong, both among the populace and the armed forces. Should this occur, the likelihood of achieving ultimate U.S. objectives in South Vietnam will have virtually disappeared." The report warned that the situation was now so fluid that "sudden, unanticipated, and radical changes may occur which could render *any* U.S. policy for the area somewhat academic." Such changes, it said, could take any of several forms: riot, assassination, capitulation, dramatically stepped-up Vietcong activity, a GVN rapprochement with Hanoi, and revived plotting by disaffected ARVN generals for a coup.[52]

The last of these possibilities was in fact already under way when the report was written. Already in mid September the dissident generals had renewed their scheming. Once aware of these plans, the Kennedy administration did not discourage them. Lodge was authorized to inform the plotters that although the United States did not "wish to stimulate a coup," it would not "thwart a change of government or deny economic and military assistance to a new regime if it appeared capable of increasing [the] effectiveness of the military effort, ensuring popular support to win [the] war and improving working relations with the U.S."[53]

Diem and Nhu did not back down. Rather than yield to the "selective pressures" policy and initiate reforms, they escalated the anti-American rhetoric and accused CIA operatives and other Americans in Saigon of organizing a coup to overthrow them. By mid October the situation had taken on the appearance of war, this time not between the South and the communists, but between the United States and the Diem government. A remarkable CIA "situation appraisal," read by Kennedy, put the matter starkly. "Recent developments," it warned, "convey the unmistakable impression that the Diem/Nhu combine are prepared to dig in for a protracted war of attrition with the United States, resisting pressures for reform." The report spoke of "several sources in Saigon" who confirmed that "the government is indeed cutting back on functionary salary payments. The policy may merely reflect an anticipatory GVN response to a possible US-initiated cutback in aid. A lesser possibility, but one which cannot be overlooked, is that Ngo Dinh Nhu is conditioning officials to an eventual full break with the United States, brought about at the initiative of the Diem regime."[54]

This last possibility continued to alarm American officials in October and added urgency to the need for a coup. William Sullivan, in a memorandum to Roger Hilsman, said that indications were that Nhu would "eject" the United States "by a deal with North Vietnam when he feels he has adequate means to continue in power without its assistance." Sullivan argued that the United States thus had only one choice: to make "common cause" with the dissident generals and "overthrow the current regime." From Saigon, Ambassador Lodge warned that "we should consider a request [from the GVN] to withdraw as a growing possibility" and that the United States therefore had no choice but to back a coup. Lodge cited a Nhu interview with the Italian weekly *Espresso*, in which Nhu said, in effect, that he could and would like to get along without the Americans. "If the Americans were to interrupt their help," Nhu said, "it may not be a bad thing after all." Officials at the British embassy in October received new reports that Nhu had regular contacts with North Vietnamese representatives, reports they probably passed on to Lodge.[55]

At the White House, too, the Diem-Nhu team's intransigence added to the sense that a coup was urgently needed. But what if the coup failed? Just as they had done in the last week of August, Kennedy and his lieutenants in October spent much time debating the implications of a takeover attempt that did not succeed. They were convinced that a failed coup would be disastrous for America's image abroad and would almost certainly bring about the very thing that a coup was intended to prevent: an ejection of the United States from South Vietnam by the Diem regime. This fear of failure and its implications were the dominant theme in the hundreds of pages of cable traffic sent by Washington to the embassy in Saigon in the last half of October. It was a fear bluntly articulated by Robert Kennedy at a top-level meeting on 29 October. "If the coup fails," he warned those around him, "Diem throws us out."[56]

At the same time, no one in the Kennedy inner circle was prepared to alter course. As always, their concern was pragmatic, not ethical—not whether the United States had any business getting involved in the overthrow of a foreign government, but whether that overthrow would work.

The administration pressed forward with the "selective pressures" policy, and it continued to promise the coup plotters that a new government could count on full U.S. support. At home, officials emphasized that the one-thousand-man withdrawal plan was conditional on success in the war and that it marked no change in American policy. They publicly repeated the president's line that "what helps win the war we support, what interferes with the war effort we oppose."[57] Finally, Kennedy made one decision that plainly revealed that, whatever his reservations about a coup, he was determined to get rid of the Ngos: he left in the hands of Lodge—whose anti-Diem views had been unambiguously clear since he set foot in Saigon in August—the final decision on whether to try to call off or delay the coup. Lodge did neither. By the end of the day on 1 November, a new regime had taken power in Saigon. Its first order of business was to make absolutely certain that the old one could never return.[58]

The era of Diem was over. His regime had from the start depended for its existence on the support of the United States; when that support evaporated, so did any hope of the regime's staying in power. The regime's repressive actions helped ensure its demise. Particularly in the final weeks the government seemed bent on alienating all educated Vietnamese. Schoolchildren, students, and professional people were arrested en masse, universities were closed, absurd morality laws were enforced, and the quality of South Vietnamese life took on some of the worst aspects of the totalitarianism that the Diem regime was ostensibly fighting. But if this political and religious repression and reluctance to implement reforms contributed significantly to the American dissatisfaction, an important additional factor was the possibility that Diem and Nhu might be abandoning the war effort altogether in favor of a negotiated settlement. Not for the last time, Washington would engineer the removal of a Saigon leader it perceived to be insufficiently committed to the war effort, a reality that makes a mockery of official claims, both then and in the years to follow, that the United States sought only to preserve freedom in South Vietnam, sought only to allow southerners to enjoy the blessings of self-determination.[59]

It is one of the supreme ironies of American Vietnam policy in the Kennedy years that the same fear of negotiations resurfaced almost immediately after the new government, headed by General Duong Van Minh, took over. U.S. officials assumed that because it comprised military men, the junta, which also included Generals Nguyen Ngoc Tho, Tran Van Don, Ton That Dinh, Mai Huu Xuan, and Le Van Kim, would be implacably anti-communist and opposed to any form of compromise with the National Liberation Front (NLF) and Hanoi. They also assumed that the new government would provide a more aggressive military challenge to the Vietcong and accept a greater American direction of the fighting. A State Department cable summed up the American view on 4 November, expressing with satisfaction the administration's "feeling that [the] change in regime ends any thought in Saigon of accommodation with North Vietnam on [the] basis of neutralization[,] which idea the previous regime may have toyed with."[60]

Very soon, it became clear that these American assumptions were mistaken. From the start, the junta wanted, as George McT. Kahin has put it, "to move as rapidly as possible towards transferring the struggle for power in the South from the military to the political level."[61] It was not that they sought to abandon the conflict against the Vietcong, or even that they no longer saw any use for military action; rather, they saw it as imperative to expand the political base of the Saigon government and offer new initiatives for solving outstanding problems through nonmilitary means. Doing so would not be easy, they conceded, but they felt certain that they could negotiate with the NLF from a position of strength by building a rapport with those groups alienated by the Ngos—students, urban professionals, members of the Cao Dai and Hoa Hao sects, and, most important, the Buddhists. Junta leaders believed strongly that these groups had been attracted to the NLF not out of a commitment to communism but because the NLF was seen as a symbol of opposition to the Diem regime. The new government pledged to be prowestern but not a vassal of the United States.[62]

It would take some weeks before the Kennedy inner circle perceived the strength of the new regime's commitment to shifting the arena of struggle to politics, but the Central Intelligence Agency saw warning signs. On 6 November, just five days after the coup, the CIA warned of the "pro-French nature of the new government" and the trouble this could cause for American efforts in Vietnam. Most of the members of the new regime, the agency noted, began their careers under French colonial administration, were thought by observers to be steeped in the French tradition of government, and though not necessarily pro-French, were "probably innately open to French example and influence." According to a "respected business source," the new government was "70 percent pro-French."[63] Ten days later, the CIA noted that Mai Huu Xuan was being viewed with alarm in many quarters for his past reputation of strong pro-French sympathies. And on 26 November, in a memorandum titled "South Vietnamese Government Contacts with the Vietcong and the Liberation Front," the agency again spoke of pro-French sympathies among junta leaders and reported that the change in government in Saigon had not ended the contacts with the NLF and Hanoi.[64] The State Department, though still optimistic about the junta's determination to pursue victory in the war, also worried about

French influence in Saigon. In the week after the coup, Ambassador Bohlen had once again met with de Gaulle to try to induce him to change his policy on the war; as before, Bohlen did not succeed. A department cable noted the following week that France and the United States were moving along "divergent paths" with respect to Vietnam.[65]

That was putting it mildly. The Paris government was certain that Washington was behind the Diem overthrow and that the new regime in Saigon was, as Foreign Minister Maurice Couve de Murville put it in a cabinet meeting, no real government at all. When de Gaulle and Bohlen met at the Elysée a few days after the coup the French leader spoke in harsh tones. "You will be blamed for the deaths of Diem and Nhu," he told the American. "You may do and say what you like; no one will believe you. It is you who will be held responsible." Afterward de Gaulle told his cabinet that the new government in Saigon would be closer to the United States and would step up military operations (like the Americans, he wrongly assumed that a government run by generals would focus its energies on the battlefield) and that, as a result, the South Vietnamese people would turn against it. "The population just wants peace," de Gaulle declared. Nevertheless, the Americans would become more engaged, and the results would be disastrous. The only real solution, de Gaulle said, was for all foreigners to leave Vietnam—as had been prescribed at Geneva in 1954—so that the country could regain its liberty, unity, and neutrality.[66]

Unfortunately for the Kennedy administration, de Gaulle's line on Vietnam was gaining adherents in the United States in the wake of the coup. In the Senate, Mike Mansfield was increasingly inclined to agree with Paris that a neutralist settlement was the only real solution to the conflict. Walter Lippmann believed likewise, more strongly than ever. In December, both would press for such a solution.

Of more immediate concern to the White House, the *New York Times* began in November to promote neutralization. The paper in fact was schizophrenic in its judgments in the first part of this month, which suggests that it was undergoing a far-reaching and perhaps painful transition. On 3 November, the headline for an article by Max Frankel blared, "Vietnam Holds Strategic Importance for West," and a lead editorial declared that "the loss of South Vietnam to the Communists would raise doubts around the globe about the value of U.S. commitments to defend nations against Communist pressure. Fortunately, the new Vietnamese rulers are dedicated anti-Communists who reject any idea of neutralism." On 10 November, however, another lead editorial said that "such concepts as a negotiated settlement and 'neutralization' are not to be ruled out." There was an important role, "too long ignored," for international diplomacy, the paper now said, and the administration ought to move swiftly to the conference table. The 180-degree turn might be partly explained by the line taken by a *Times* heavyweight, James Reston, in a column on 6 November. Reston castigated the administration for not even exploring the prospects for negotiations with the DRV. "Everybody here [in Washington] is just settling down behind Duong Van (Big) Minh in Saigon and insisting that only a military settlement is feasible," Reston charged. Why not make a serious effort, in concert with allies and with the USSR, to see if an agreement could be reached?[67]

With hindsight it can be said, with only slight exaggeration, that the week of 3–10 November was the week when the *New York Times* changed its editorial stance on Vietnam. Not unequivocally, not wholeheartedly—already in October it had urged that negotiations be considered, and the schizophrenia would occasionally return, especially in mid 1965, when the paper's by-then-ingrained pessimism competed with its desire to. rally around the arriving U.S. ground forces—but more than enough to convince top administration officials that the *Times* was now an adversary. By early 1964, these officials would take for granted that the paper opposed a larger war and supported de Gaulle's position that only a negotiated U.S. withdrawal made sense. Later claims that the *Times* was slow in opposing the war in Vietnam, and therefore should be considered an accomplice to the Americanization of 1964–1965, are mistaken.[68]

The one-two punch of the Reston column and the 10 November editorial shook the administration. First Lippmann, now Reston and the *New York Times*, had questioned its policy. Policymakers were acutely aware of the *Times*'s leading place in the country's press hierarchy, of its unmatched ability to shape press attitudes all across the country and overseas as well. On 7 November NSC staffer Michael Forrestal told his superior McGeorge Bundy that he thought an administration response to the Reston column necessary, ideally by the president himself, to the effect that the United States was in South Vietnam to resist aggression from the North and that once that aggression ceased the United States would withdraw. Bundy agreed, and the following day Dean Rusk told the press that "there can be peace in Southeast Asia if others would leave South Viet-Nam and Laos alone, and let the people of those countries work out their own future." Neutralization was not the answer, Rusk said. When the *Times* editorial followed two days after that, Joseph Mendenhall of the Far East desk told Roger Hilsman that he thought a meeting should be set up with the newspaper to try to "set them straight" on the situation in Vietnam and on U.S. policy there. Rusk's comments had helped, Mendenhall noted, but he added that continued criticism "by highly reputable journalists" could create uncertainty in Saigon. Hilsman agreed. He talked it over with Rusk, who then instructed Forrestal to seek a meeting as soon as possible.[69]

On 13 November, Forrestal met with the paper's Robert Kleiman. He found little sympathy for the administration's views. Kleiman suggested strongly that the United States should move as rapidly as possible to reconvene the Geneva Conference and to negotiate settlement of the differences between the two Vietnams. Now was the time to pursue such a settlement, he argued, because the regime in the South would never again be as politically strong as it would be in the coming few months. Therefore, the United States should seize this opportunity for negotiations before the situation deteriorated and led to a ten-year, Malayan-type effort.

Forrestal replied that negotiations were not the answer. Not now. South Vietnam was still not strong enough to approach the bargaining table "with any hope of coming away whole." Moreover, an American move to reconvene the Geneva Conference would be viewed by "responsible Vietnamese" as a complete sell-out by the United States. Forrestal then voiced what had become the standard administration reply to suggestions of negotiation. He told Kleiman that the president had made very clear that "the United States was prepared to withdraw its presence from South Vietnam as soon as Hanoi ceased its interference in the South or as soon as the South was able to handle the problem on its own." The meeting apparently did not draw the two sides together: in a summary memorandum to Bundy, Forrestal correctly predicted that Kleiman and the *Times* would continue to peddle the Geneva Conference idea and that "we should be preparing ourselves to counter it."[70]

The administration was not content to leave it there. Senior officials feared the impact that the *Times*'s advocacy might have in South Vietnam and elsewhere, and they instructed Lodge to inform the new Saigon government that the paper's "Nov. 10 editorial and the Reston column [a] few days earlier do not represent U.S. policy." The cable reiterated the promise that the United States would withdraw as soon as North Vietnam would "cease and desist in subversive aggression" against the South, and it said that international negotiations were not necessary to achieve peace. "We cannot," the message concluded, "envisage any points that would be negotiable."[71]

Those words serve as a succinct summary of the Kennedy administration's approach to negotiations throughout its three years in office. Only days later, Kennedy was shot to death in Dallas. A number of individuals inside and outside the administration—among them Charles de Gaulle, Jawaharlal Nehru, Mike Mansfield, Walter Lippmann, George Ball, Chester

Bowles, and John Kenneth Galbraith—had since 1961 warned Kennedy against deepening America's involvement in Vietnam and had urged him to seek negotiated withdrawal. Instead, the president chose to steadily increase the U.S. commitment. By the time of his death, more than sixteen thousand American military advisers were in Vietnam.

What, then, of the incipient-withdrawal thesis? It ultimately fails to persuade. The pieces of evidence usually cited by its proponents are JFK's deep ambivalence about the U.S. commitment; his continual refusal to commit American ground troops, despite the urgings of top advisers; his skepticism about a coup against Diem; his belief, stated most notably in his 2 September 1963 interview with Walter Cronkite, that in the end this was a war that the South Vietnamese themselves would have to win; and, most important, his administration's October 1963 declaration that a thousand U.S. military advisers would be withdrawn at the end of 1963. Some also cite private comments made by Kennedy to the effect that he was determined to get out of Vietnam, come what may.

The first of these pieces of supposed evidence is incontrovertibly correct. Kennedy was ambivalent, more so than many of his top aides. He also was more resistant than most to making an unequivocal American pledge to preserve an independent, noncommunist South Vietnam, and he repeatedly made clear his opposition to using American ground troops in the war. He wanted out of the war and probably said so privately to like-minded people. But this says little about his actual intentions in the autumn of 1963. The assertion regarding Kennedy's thinking with respect to the coup is not so much wrong as it is misleading. If Kennedy was uncertain about a coup against Diem after the beginning of September, it was only because of a fear that it might fail. His comments to Cronkite must be set against the rest of that interview and his other comments in the September–October period, both public and private. His remarks set for delivery on 22 November at the Dallas Trade Mart, a destination he never reached, included the words: "We in this country in this generation are the watchmen on the walls of freedom. . . . Our assistance to . . . nations can be painful, risky and costly, as is true in Southeast Asia today. But we dare not weary of the task."[72]

As for the one-thousand-man withdrawal plan, it must be understood as being primarily a device to put pressure on Diem, as appearing at a time of general military optimism (or at least nonpessimism) in the war, as being wholly conditional upon battlefield success, and as designed to neutralize growing domestic American concerns and counter the appearance that Washington was taking over the war effort. A year earlier, in September 1962, Robert Thompson of the British Advisory Mission, an early proponent of a partial reduction in the American presence, left no doubt as to the rationale for such a withdrawal after meeting with Maxwell Taylor. "I also raised again [with Taylor] the possibility of a *token* American reduction, perhaps just as a result of house cleaning, some time next year at a suitable opportunity," Thompson wrote his superiors in London. The move would defuse communist charges that the war was becoming an American affair and would "keep the Communists in the dock with a finger clearly pointed at them." Thompson emphasized that the reduction "should be entirely a unilateral move, well thought out and timed, so that it achieved the maximum effect *without taking any of the pressure off here*. We had to think of both winning political advantages as well as military ones." In a meeting with Kennedy at the White House on 4 April 1963, Thompson repeated the suggestion, using similar language.[73]

Nothing in the voluminous internal record for 1962 and 1963 suggests that any of the top American officials, including Kennedy, ever differed from Thompson in their rationale for a "token" withdrawal—the move would have political benefits, at home and abroad, and would be implemented in such a way as to have no deleterious impact on the war effort. Some authors nevertheless have pointed to the one-thousand-man withdrawal as showing that Vietnam policy changed dramatically after Kennedy's murder. Specifically, they assert that NSAM 263, the final policy directive of the Kennedy administration on Vietnam, differed in critical respects from NSAM 273, the first such directive of the administration of Lyndon Johnson.[74] Though desirous of a partial early withdrawal for domestic political reasons, Kennedy was skeptical that it could be sustained, which obviously makes this argument highly problematic. When judged together, the McNamara-Taylor report, NSAM 263, and the accompanying documents all demonstrate clearly that the one-thousand-man withdrawal signaled no lessening of the American commitment to South Vietnam.

A high-level cable to Lodge on 5 October is especially instructive here. Read and approved by Kennedy, it noted that the NSAM sought to indicate to the Diem government the American displeasure at its policies and activities and to make South Vietnamese leaders uncertain about Washington's future intentions. "At the same time," the cable continued, the "actions are designed to have at most a slight impact on the military and counterinsurgency effort against the Vietcong, at least in the short term," and the president intended, at his next press conference "to repeat his basic statement that what furthers the war effort we support, and what interferes with the war effort we oppose." Kennedy did indeed make that point in a meeting with the press on 31 October. Tellingly, he also expressed caution on the issue of removing some U.S. advisers. "*If we are able to do that,*" he said in reference to an end-of-the-year one-thousand-man withdrawal, "that would be our schedule. I think the first unit or first contingent would be 250 men who are not involved in what might be called frontline operations. *It would be our hope* to lessen the number of Americans there by 1000, as the training intensifies and is carried on in Saigon."[75]

In sum, NSAM 263 hardly represented the far-reaching policy initiative that the incipient-withdrawal proponents suggest. It was but one part of a larger "selective pressures" policy designed to push the Diem regime into greater effectiveness in both governing and prosecuting the war against the Vietcong. No further withdrawals were envisioned; more advisers could be sent in the future, if the situation demanded. The "fundamental objective of victory," as Kennedy told Lodge, remained paramount. As for NSAM 273, issued on 26 November 1963, four days after JFK's death, it did not institute any kind of reversal of the one-thousand-man reduction. The withdrawal, it read, would "remain as stated" in NSAM 263, and the thousand men in fact were removed at the end of the year. There were actually two drafts of NSAM 273, one penned on 20 November—two days before Kennedy's death and intended for his signature—after a meeting among senior U.S. officials in Honolulu, and the other the final version approved by Johnson six days later. The two were essentially identical, except for a paragraph pertaining to military action against North Vietnam (which had been going on covertly and under U.S. direction, it should be noted, since 1962). Even here, the differences were insignificant. More important, neither draft signaled a significant departure from NSAM 263, or from the various other high-level documents in October and November.[76]

To further complicate the picture, several other top aides have dismissed the idea that Kennedy had decided to get out. Secretary of State Dean Rusk argued forcefully in the late 1980s that Kennedy had made no decision to disengage from the war after the 1964 election. "I talked with John Kennedy on hundreds of occasions about Southeast Asia," Rusk noted in his memoirs, "and not once did he suggest or even hint at withdrawal." In what appears to be a direct reference to the incipient-withdrawal school, Rusk pointed out that "Kennedy liked to bat the breeze and toss ideas around, and it is entirely possible that he left the impression with some that he planned on getting out of Vietnam after 1965." But that did not mean Kennedy had made any such decision. "Had he done so," Rusk asserted, "I think I would have known about it." Midlevel officials Walt W. Rostow and William P. Bundy voiced similar sentiments after Oliver Stone's *JFK* appeared. To be sure, these men might have had ulterior motives of their own—as active participants in the escalation decisions under Johnson, they might wish to emphasize the continuities between the two administrations, and indeed between all the post-1945 administrations. But consider also the comments of Robert F. Kennedy, who would appear to have had no such agenda, and who presumably knew his brother better than anyone. In a 1964 oral history interview, the younger Kennedy confirmed that the administration had not seriously considered a withdrawal. When asked what the president would have done if the South Vietnamese had been on the brink of defeat, Robert replied: "We'd face that when we came to it."[77]

Dean Rusk is surely correct in arguing that Kennedy's Vietnam policy must be judged on what "he said and did while president, not on what he may have said at tea table conversations or walks around the Rose Garden." Judged in that light, the evidence points not in the direction of an American withdrawal at the time of Kennedy's death but to a continued commitment to the war. Consider again the two central themes of this chapter. First there is Kennedy's quiet but firm endorsement and encouragement of a showdown between Diem and dissident generals. From late August onward, Kennedy's actions indicate that he had resigned himself to the necessity of removing Diem. Though his administration appears to have given astonishingly little sustained thought to whether the successor regime would be better able (or more willing) to defeat the Vietcong, or to the increased responsibility that Americans would henceforth have for developments in Vietnam, he surely knew that a coup with American fingerprints all over it would make any U.S. withdrawal more difficult, at least in the short term.[78]

No less important, but largely ignored in the existing literature, is the second theme: the Kennedy administration's complete rejection of exploring the possibilities for a political solution to the conflict. There was virtually no American diplomacy with respect to Vietnam in 1961 to 1963, and administration aversion to any compromise settlement grew stronger as the Vietnam issue heated up in the last half of 1963. What is most striking here is not the Kennedy team's rejection of de Gaulle's vaguely worded neutralization proposal; rather, it is that they refused to even consider resolving the conflict at the conference table and indeed worked to thwart any and all efforts in that direction. The vagueness of de Gaulle's plan might have been imaginatively utilized by an administration genuinely interested in negotiations; it would certainly have been utilized by a president determined to withdraw from South Vietnam. Most telling of all, when Ngo Dinh Nhu began exploring a settlement on his own, the administration, far from being encouraged or relieved, was deeply worried. The outrage in American public opinion at the GVN's policies in the fall of 1963 represented the golden opportunity—even more so than earlier in the summer—for the Kennedy team to throw up its hands and say that it had no option but to withdraw all U.S. assistance. Instead, Nhu's actions only made Washington more determined to overthrow him and his brother. His attempt at blackmail, if indeed that is what it was, failed catastrophically, but not for the reason it might have failed—with the administration calling his bluff.

That is all very well, it could be argued in response, but surely the administration deserves at least some sympathy, for the simple reason that no one of consequence was at the time asking it to consider disengagement. But in fact they were. Influential commentators at home and abroad began in the autumn of 1963 to suggest that America's commitment to South Vietnam ought to be fundamentally reevaluated, that a major war on behalf of the GVN might be neither necessary to western security nor winnable in any meaningful sense of the term. These voices were not as numerous as they would be a year later, but they were audible enough to cause the administration to take notice and to fret about the implications. The CIA's Vietnam Working Group got it exactly right when it said, in a lengthy report dated 30 September 1963, that all options, including immediate disengagement from the war or disengagement via a conference-table settlement, should be closely examined.[79]

In all likelihood, John F. Kennedy on the day of his death had not decided what to do with his Vietnam problem. Like many politicians, he liked to put off difficult decisions for as long as possible, and he no doubt hoped that the crisis in Indochina would somehow resolve itself, if not before the 1964 election, then after. His decisions on Vietnam since 1961 had led to a significantly expanded American presence in the war, but they had usually been compromise decisions, between the extremes of an Americanized war and an American withdrawal, both of which he seemed to fear in equal measure. He always sought to preserve his flexibility. "We'd cross that bridge when we came to it," was his brother Robert's description of the administration's thinking about the prospect of a complete deterioration in South Vietnam. It is an expression that effectively summarizes Kennedy's entire approach to the war.

This suggests that the most interesting question with respect to John F. Kennedy and Vietnam is not what his immediate plans were in November 1963, when he could still temporize, but what he would have done later, when the difficult choices could no longer be postponed. (We examine this question in chapter 12.) An impressive array of authors have said otherwise, have argued that American involvement in Vietnam was essentially sealed with the coup against Diem; after that, they maintain, American disengagement from the conflict is virtually impossible to imagine, regardless of who occupied the Oval Office.[80] They do not persuade. When John F. Kennedy arrived in Dallas that fateful day in November, the most important Vietnam decisions still lay in the future.

But not that far in the future. The day before the assassination, Kennedy's top Vietnam advisers wrapped up a series of meetings in Honolulu, at which they determined that the situation in the South had deteriorated— Vietcong attacks had risen sharply since the coup, and large chunks of territory had fallen out of the government's control. The United States could anticipate a long, difficult period in Vietnam, they agreed, but it was vital to persevere.[81] They were preparing to bring that message to John Kennedy. They would bring it instead to Lyndon Johnson.

3 "I Will Not Lose in Vietnam"

It was an unfortunate irony for Lyndon Johnson that the Vietnam problem loomed large from the very beginning of his presidency. Since the start of his political career in the 1930s, the issues that engaged him most were domestic ones—rural electrification, social security, unemployment, and education. Though not ignorant of world affairs[1]—he had spent more than two decades involved in defense and foreign-policy questions as a member of the House Naval Affairs and the House and Senate Armed Services Committees—Johnson found the realm of diplomacy and statecraft complicated and frustrating. When as vice president he visited Bangkok, he exploded in anger when a U.S. embassy official counseled him against shaking hands with the Thais, who traditionally recoil from physical contact with strangers. Dammit, Johnson exploded, he shook hands with people everywhere, and they loved it.[2] Nor could he comprehend the way in which diplomacy seemed to be above politics, immune to the haggling he had perfected with American politicians, businesspeople, and labor leaders. Little wonder that he entered the White House with his eyes on matters at home—his main goal, he told aides only hours after being sworn in, was to enable all Americans to share in America's bounty. His first State of the Union address, delivered in January 1964, was the first since Franklin Roosevelt's to stress, by placement and by language, domestic affairs.

Yet Johnson knew from the start that the war in Southeast Asia would demand a great deal of his attention. Since visiting the country on Kennedy's behalf in May 1961, he had followed the course of the war and the evolution of American policy and had sat in on many White House meetings. In the late autumn of 1963, he understood well the scope of America's commitment in Vietnam and the potential trouble the war could pose for him. When U.S. Ambassador Henry Cabot Lodge reported on the situation in Saigon on 24 November, Johnson said he felt like a catfish that had just "grabbed a big juicy worm with a right sharp hook in the middle of it." In a memorandum a few days later to Maxwell Taylor, the chairman of the Joint Chiefs of Staff (JCS), the new president noted that the more he looked at it, "the more it is clear to me that South Vietnam is our most critical military area right now."[3]

Johnson was determined to stand up to the challenge. Though he had opposed the coup against Diem, he was determined to carry out his predecessor's policies, particularly in the foreign arena. More important, he came to the White House with a deep and unquestioning commitment to the posture of staunch anticommunism, as well as to presidential supremacy in foreign affairs. The same was true of his predecessors in the office, but with Johnson the commitments were more deeply ingrained, more unalterable. Throughout his career he had always rallied behind the flag, making it his first rule to support the president whenever a foreign-policy crisis arose. "It is an American, not a political foreign policy that we have in the United States," he declared in 1948. "This is a question of patriotism, not politics." Six years later, when the Eisenhower team engineered a counterrevolutionary coup in Guatemala, Johnson said, "We've got to be for America first." On those occasions in the 1950s when he faulted presidents on foreign policy, it was usually for being insufficiently aggressive in waging the Cold War. He criticized Harry Truman for not destroying the Chinese in the Korean War, and he blasted Dwight Eisenhower for tolerating a supposed "missile gap" with the Soviet Union.[4]

On Vietnam Johnson strongly backed first Eisenhower's and then Kennedy's attempt to create an anticommunist bastion in the southern half of the country. In 1961 he returned from Saigon militant about the need to persevere in the conflict and warning darkly that failure to act decisively could force the United States to retreat to San Francisco and "leave the vast Pacific . . . a Red Sea."[5] There is no reason to think that Johnson had modified that view by the time he assumed the presidency. Like many of his generation he was marked by the failure of the allies to stop Hitler at Munich, and he often declared that he would not reward "aggression" in Vietnam with "appeasement." He also invoked the mythology of the Alamo, where, as he said, Texas boys had "fought for freedom." Moreover, history taught Johnson that right-wing adversaries would finish him politically should South Vietnam fall to communism—just hours after taking office, he vowed that he would not be the president who saw Vietnam go the way of China. As he later said to biographer Doris Kearns, in a dubious interpretation of the past: "I knew that Harry Truman and Dean Acheson had lost their effectiveness from the day that the communists took over in

China. I believed that the loss of China had played a large role in the rise of Joe McCarthy. And I knew that all these problems, taken together, were chickenshit compared to what might happen if we lost Vietnam."[6]

Johnson opted to keep Kennedy's top foreign-policy advisers, and all of them recommended staying the course in Vietnam. It was Johnson more than his lieutenants, however, who set the tone for Vietnam policy in the early days after the assassination. At his first meeting on Vietnam, on 24 November, he voiced concerns about the direction of American policy, and about growing congressional sentiment in favor of withdrawal, but then quickly affirmed that America's long-standing objectives could not be abandoned. The most important task, he said, was to win the war. Too much effort had been placed on "so-called social reforms," not enough on battling the enemy. Johnson instructed Henry Cabot Lodge, who was present at the meeting, to return to Saigon and tell Duong Van Minh and the other generals who made up the ruling Military Revolutionary Council (MRC) two things: that the bickering among them must stop, and that the United States would make good on its promise to provide them with economic and military assistance. "Lyndon Johnson intends to stand by our word," he told Lodge to say, and he added, "I will not lose in Vietnam." In a National Security Action Memorandum (NSAM 273) released two days later, Johnson reiterated that the United States would assist the South Vietnamese to "win their contest against the externally directed and supported Communist conspiracy."[7]

"Win the war." That was the essential message Johnson conveyed to his foreign-policy advisers in those early days after Dallas. He left little room for uncertainty about America's task in the struggle. According to one of the participants at the 24 November meeting, Johnson urged people to devote "every effort" to the conflict. "Don't go to bed at night until you have asked yourself, 'Have I done everything I could to further the American effort to assist South Vietnam?'" A few days later, when Johnson met with David Nes, who had been chosen as Henry Cabot Lodge's new deputy chief of mission in Saigon, he said failure was not an option against the Vietcong. "Lyndon Johnson is not going down as the president who lost Vietnam," Johnson said as Nes prepared to leave. "Don't you forget that."[8]

Determination was thus the watchword of the new administration from its first days. There was no fundamental reassessment of the rationale behind the U.S. commitment to preserving a separate, noncommunist, South Vietnam; no examination of whether such an objective was vital to U.S. security, or whether it was even attainable; no serious investigation of possible alternative solutions to the conflict. Assistant Secretary of State Roger

Hilsman assured a visiting South Vietnamese official on 27 November that Johnson not only supported Kennedy's policies toward Vietnam, but helped in making them. As a result, the Saigon government could count on strong U.S. support in the war. Hilsman added that though the thousand-man withdrawal set for the end of the year would go ahead as planned, South Vietnamese leaders could rest assured that the United States would keep in Vietnam whatever forces were needed for victory. Ambassador Lodge, in a meeting with Minh three days later, also emphasized Johnson's commitment to the struggle against the Vietcong. And Dean Rusk, in a top-secret cable to Lodge on 6 December, stressed Johnson's "deep concern that our effort in Viet-Nam be stepped up to the highest pitch and that each day we ask ourselves what more we can do to further the struggle."[9]

There was continuity here, but also change. It is no contradiction to say that Lyndon Johnson sought to maintain his predecessor's policies in Vietnam and that there occurred a subtle but crucial shift when he took office, in the form of a greater presidential insistence on preventing defeat in Vietnam. It may be, as some have suggested, that Johnson had an excellent opportunity to withdraw from Vietnam immediately upon entering the White House, but it is virtually impossible to imagine him actually taking such a step. Perhaps *any* successor would have been inhibited from dramatically altering the slain leader's policy in those difficult weeks of transition; it was certainly out of the question for Johnson. Every fiber of his being compelled him to proceed. His reading of history told him to continue in the war, as did his calculations of what would serve him best in the 1964 presidential campaign—avoid radical departures in foreign affairs, play to the strength of domestic policy. Already suspicious to the point of paranoia about Robert F. Kennedy's ambitions and designs, he believed he would be opposed by RFK and his associates—Robert McNamara, Walt W. Rostow, McGeorge Bundy—if he did not pursue Kennedy's policies in Southeast Asia.[10]

For that matter, Johnson's temperament was the type to avoid the kind of reexamination of policy assumptions that would have been needed to initiate disengagement. His mind was excellent, fast and resourceful, but he had no interest in, or patience with, intellectual give and take. He sought only solutions to problems and tried whenever possible to avoid listening to the underlying rationales. As longtime assistant George Reedy would later put it, LBJ "could think but not reflect; devise ingenuous schemes for achieving goals but not ponder the validity of the goals; outguess his fellow human beings in playing the game of one-upmanship without realizing that the game might not be worth playing." In foreign-policy matters, especially, Johnson lacked a detached critical perspective, which left him vulnerable to clichés and stereotypes about world affairs. Neither diplomatic history nor current international politics interested him (as more than a few visiting diplomats were quick to notice), and he was deeply insecure about his abilities as a statesman. Though he had gained valuable experience on his eleven goodwill trips abroad as vice president, many of these had been frustrating affairs for him as well as for his hosts (he often came across as a boor) and had aggravated his sense of being an interloper in the world arena. "Foreigners," Johnson quipped early in the administration, only half-jokingly, "are not like the folks I am used to."[11]

This insecurity, well documented in the reflections of those who knew him well, helps explain two closely related tendencies in Johnson's approach to Vietnam that were evident early and would prove highly important to policy making as time went on. One was his aversion to meeting with foreign diplomats or consulting with allied governments. McGeorge Bundy learned right away that one of his tasks would involve seeing to it that few foreign dignitaries made it into the Oval Office.[12] In the years that followed Johnson would seldom welcome, much less seek out, the opinions and advice of allied government leaders on what should happen in Southeast Asia. As more and more of them came to oppose his Vietnam policy he looked for ways to avoid even speaking to them. Second, Johnson's lack of confidence in foreign policy helped fuel his well-documented dislike of dissension on Vietnam policy, even among his closest advisers. All politicians like consensus, but LBJ craved it more than most. Reedy again: "He abhorred dissent to a point where he sought to quell it long before the protagonists had taken themselves out." Early in the administration top aides began the practice of meeting among themselves before entering the Oval Office, in order to work out what they were going to say. Johnson, these advisers knew, would want various policy options articulated but, given both his temperament and his unambiguous exhortations in those first days, would not want deep and wide-ranging discussion of those options.[13]

Johnson's craving for internal consensus led him to try to limit Vietnam policy formulation to a small group of advisers, smaller than the one utilized by John F. Kennedy.[14] From the start, the three key figures in that group were Secretary of Defense Robert McNamara, Secretary of State Dean Rusk, and National Security Adviser McGeorge Bundy. All three had helped shape the policy under Kennedy and thus had a stake in making sure the policy succeeded; all three would be key players, along with Johnson, in the decisions that over the next fifteen months would make Vietnam an American war. Others would contribute to the fateful decisions, of course, and help in implementing the policies—notably the chief deputies of the three advisers, as well as the successive ambassadors in Saigon—but this group was supreme.

Despite his determination to continue the Kennedy policies, Johnson encountered a steadily disintegrating situation in South Vietnam. On the battlefield, the picture was grim. The new president had barely settled into the Oval Office before the CIA, the JCS, and the embassy in Saigon began issuing reports of virtually unchecked momentum by the Vietcong in almost all parts of South Vietnam. According to Defense Department figures presented at a high-level interdepartmental meeting in the first week of December, Vietcong incidents had skyrocketed since the Diem coup, going as high as 1,000 in one week, as compared to the 1962 average of 363 per week, and the first-half-of-1963 average of 266 per week. The picture was especially bleak in several key provinces around Saigon. "The only progress made in Long An Province during the month of November 1963," Lodge reported, "has been by the Communist Viet Cong."[15]

Troubling as these trends were to U.S. officials in Washington and Saigon, even more disconcerting was the Minh government's ambivalence with regard to the war effort—an ambivalence that had first materialized in early November but accelerated in December. The military situation could be turned around, Americans were convinced, but only if the Saigon regime was committed to doing so. Some American officials clung to the belief that the will was there, that present problems were the inevitable but short-term result of the transition to a new government. But a growing number of officials ascribed the lack of progress to the MRC's reluctance to initiate offensive military actions. Among the latter were General Harkins and the rest of the American military in Vietnam. Harkins had opposed the overthrow of the Ngos, and he made no secret of his dislike of Minh. He inundated administration officials in Washington with detailed information on the junta's nonaggressiveness; with time, many of those who had most opposed Diem and most welcomed the change in government would be converted to this view.[16]

It was not just Harkins's claims that convinced them. The Minh government took a number of specific actions contrary to American wishes and designed to shift the struggle to the political plane. To begin with, it announced its intention to implement a rural-welfare program designed to eventually supersede the strategic hamlets program instituted under Diem. Minh officials felt certain that the hamlets only exacerbated dissatisfaction in the countryside; they were convinced that the new program, which would permit peasants to remain in their scattered homes under the administration of local leaders, was more likely to win peasant allegiance than the American-backed strategic hamlets program, with its barbed-wire-enclosed compounds and aggressive military activity. In addition, the government refused to go along with a new Pentagon plan to improve the military situation by bombing the North. At a meeting with American officials, Minh argued that such bombing would be a mistake for the most fundamental reasons: it would hurt innocent people, it would alienate popular opinion in the South, and it would likely have no real effect on Vietcong troops fighting in the South.[17]

If Minh government officials disagreed with Americans on key issues of policy, they also disagreed among themselves. They could not reach an accord on the best way to approach those groups most discriminated against by Diem—the Buddhists above all, but also the students and urban professionals. More important, although there was general agreement on the need to emphasize the political dimension of the struggle, there was little unity of thought on how fast or how far to proceed in that direction. Whether key government leaders such as Minh were prepared to consider a neutralist settlement to the conflict in this period is unclear. Publicly they denied it, and Minh told British Ambassador Gordon Etherington-Smith at the start of December that neutralism was not a practicable solution for South Vietnam, given that communists controlled North Vietnam. Nevertheless, in the latter part of November and early December, reports proliferated in Saigon intellectual circles and in the South Vietnamese press that leading members of the junta were sympathetic to such a solution. In mid November French officials in Saigon reported to Paris that many junta members were distraught at the delay in French recognition of the new government, particularly because they sought to move the GVN closer to France and away from the United States. The report noted that there appeared to be a division of opinion within the junta, with some members sympathetic to a neutralist settlement and others, including Minh, committed to pursuing the war against the Vietcong.[18]

As it had when Diem and Nhu appeared to consider the idea, the prospect of an early political settlement struck fear into American officials. The notion of a negotiated settlement between the Saigon regime and the NLF or Hanoi was anathema to them, and they were determined to prevent it. At the same time, American intelligence continued to find signs of MRC support for accommodation. In late November, the CIA reported that contacts between the Saigon regime and the NLF were taking place. The State Department's Bureau of Intelligence and Research, citing "reliable sources," made the same claim. And in fact, the NLF had issued a number of conciliatory statements in the weeks after the Minh government assumed power, all of which called for negotiations to reach a cease-fire, free general elections, and the subsequent formation of a coalition government "composed of representatives of all parties, tendencies, and strata of the South Vietnamese people." Reunification, the NLF declared, would be neither immediate nor automatic but something to be realized "step by step on a voluntary basis." This would be the official NLF line throughout the junta's time in office.[19]

Not all American officials believed that the top government leaders were prepared to agree to an immediate political settlement—Lodge, for one, thought Minh would likely veto any move in that direction. However, even Lodge readily conceded that the junta, given its desire to focus its energies on the political plane, might opt for political settlement eventually, perhaps within a matter of weeks. Perhaps neutralists would gain the upper hand in the decision making, or perhaps Minh and other leaders would move in that direction on their own. Equally worrisome, continued instability in Saigon might bring forth a new regime dedicated to ending the war. U.S. officials understood perfectly well that in this kind of fluid situation, in which anything was possible, pressure for negotiations from outside Vietnam could have enormous influence.

And indeed, as 1963 drew to a close, such pressure was gaining momentum. In the United States, public and press opinion remained mostly supportive of the war, but murmurings of skepticism continued to be heard on Capitol Hill, as Johnson himself indicated on 24 November. The White House was particularly concerned about the growing concerns expressed by three key Democratic members of the Senate, Johnson's mentor Richard Russell, Majority Leader Mike Mansfield of Montana, and J. William Fulbright of Arkansas, chairman of the Senate Foreign Relations Committee. All three had grown increasingly dismayed with the direction of U.S. policy in recent months, and all three had the capacity to strongly influence thinking on Capitol Hill. In a telephone conversation with LBJ on 2 December Fulbright recommended that the administration opt for a negotiated settlement via a reconvened Geneva Conference. On 7 December Russell told Johnson, "We should get out [of Vietnam], but I don't know any way to get out." On another occasion in December Russell reportedly advised LBJ to "spend whatever it takes to bring to power a government that would ask us to go home."[20] Mansfield, meanwhile, chose this time to launch a personal campaign to convince the president to pursue a political solution. It was a campaign he would not relinquish until Johnson opted to Americanize the war in the spring and summer of 1965.

In a 7 December memorandum to Johnson, Mansfield suggested that two core administration assumptions—that the war could be won in South

Vietnam alone, and that it could be won at a "limited expenditure of American lives and resources somewhere commensurate with our national interests in south Viet Nam"—might be mistaken. The war, he argued, might extend beyond South Vietnam, and "what national interests in Asia would steel the American people for the massive costs of an ever-deepening involvement of that kind?" Mansfield described the situation as increasingly similar to the Korean War of a decade earlier, and he reminded Johnson that Eisenhower did not pursue that war to victory but went to Korea "to make peace, in reality, a truce." As then, Mansfield suggested, "there may be a truce that could be won now in Viet Nam alone and eventually a peace which might be won throughout Southeast Asia at a price commensurate with American interests. That peace should mean, in the end, a Southeast Asia less dependent on our aid-resources and support, less under our control, not cut off from China but, still, not overwhelmed by China."[21]

The way to achieve such a peace, Mansfield argued, was, first and foremost, to encourage the new Saigon government to shift its primary emphasis from the military to the political side (he was apparently unaware that the new regime was planning to do just that). Such "political and social acts of popular benefit" were imperative, "even if it means curtailing the present elusive and so far unsuccessful chase of the Viet Cong all over the land." Second, the United States should take part in an "astute diplomatic offensive," along with France, Britain, India, and perhaps Russia and others, with the aim of making "a bonafide effort to bring about an end to the North-South Vietnamese conflict. . . . *France is the key country*."[22]

American officials agreed that France was the key country, and it worried them. Concerns about pro-French sympathies in the Minh junta, first expressed in the immediate aftermath of the Diem coup, had not disappeared but had intensified in late November, despite the fact that de Gaulle proved slow in recognizing the new government. Lodge did not hide his concern. He worried that neutralist sentiment was growing in Saigon, and he implored Washington to intensify its efforts to persuade the French president to keep quiet before the entire South was converted to neutralism. CIA director John McCone was similarly troubled and told Johnson that it might be time for the United States to get tough with the French. But Johnson was reluctant. He later noted that from the start he "made it a rule for myself and the U.S. government simply to ignore President de Gaulle's attitudes on our policies." Johnson had little of Kennedy's interest in Europe, knew little of its history, and concerned himself mainly with keeping the western alliance on an even keel. He often said that the French president reminded him of his baseball-playing days: "I was feared as a power-hitter," he would explain, and rival pitchers (de Gaulle) would "try to dust me off, but I would just lean back and let the ball go into the catcher's mitt." This patience came as a surprise to presidential advisers, who had often seen Johnson take almost irrational offense at even minor criticism. A number of these individuals would later comment on the exceptional way in which Johnson seemed to view de Gaulle, even as the frequency of the French leader's criticisms increased. No one was more surprised than Undersecretary of State George Ball: "He incessantly restrained me from making critical comments, even though he would never have taken the general's constant needling from any other foreign leader."[23]

Charles Bohlen, the American ambassador in Paris, played a significant role in convincing Johnson to avoid a public confrontation with de Gaulle. In a memorandum sent soon after LBJ took office, Bohlen made note of the general's almost complete control over French foreign policy and recommended "great care in the avoidance of any derogatory statements in regard to de Gaulle which he will be able to use for his own purposes." Bohlen was convinced that de Gaulle, whom he described as "highly egocentric with touches indeed of megalomania," actually wanted strained relations with the United States. The general, Bohlen argued, viewed the nation as the only real international unit. He therefore disliked any form of integration or other association that watered down the sovereignty of the country; consequently, it was natural that he would stress the independence of France on all matters. It followed that the United States would be playing into de Gaulle's hands if it confronted him, whether on Vietnam or on any of the other issues that plagued Franco-American relations in the 1960s. The ambassador would later claim that it was he who convinced the president to "avoid fighting de Gaulle."[24]

If American policymakers agreed among themselves on the need to avoid a dramatic showdown with de Gaulle, they also agreed that he could not be ignored. The Johnson administration was no less determined than the Kennedy team had been to use diplomatic channels to bring forth a change in Paris's Vietnam policy. In mid December, Ambassador Bohlen met with French foreign minister Maurice Couve de Murville, and Rusk met with de Gaulle while in Paris for the annual North Atlantic Treaty Organization (NATO) meeting, to once again explain American policy and urge a French disavowal of neutralization. They got nowhere. Couve and de Gaulle insisted that U.S. policy was destined to fail and that only negotiations presented a viable solution to the conflict. To the administration's chagrin, that message continued to find support. The esteemed columnist Walter Lippmann, who was to become a leading proponent of negotiations, extolled the general's plan in a column in the *Washington Post* syndicate. Mansfield, backed by Russell, again urged Johnson to solicit French help in securing a settlement even if the possibility of getting it offered "only a faint glimmer of hope." And the *New York Times*, read not only by leaders in Washington but also by those in Saigon and Hanoi, invoked de Gaulle in editorializing that "a negotiated settlement and 'neutralization' of Vietnam are not to be ruled out."[25]

The administration did rule them out, and nothing demonstrated that more starkly than its reaction to events in another place where de Gaulle's influence was deemed to be great: Cambodia. U.S.-Cambodian relations had grown increasingly strained in 1963, largely as a result of the neutralist policy followed by Cambodian leader Prince Norodom Sihanouk. Sihanouk had since the mid 1950s accepted American military aid, but he was from the start distrustful of Washington's intentions in Southeast Asia and highly skeptical that the U.S.-backed government in neighboring South Vietnam could ever achieve a victory over the insurgents. Sihanouk's policy of taking American aid and yet distancing himself from Washington's policies made a good deal of sense; it allowed him to equip his armed forces, balance Cambodia's budget, and simultaneously neutralize the appeal of anti-American left-wing Khmers. Nor did the policy hurt him with Cambodian public opinion in general, which tended to fully share his mistrust of the United States. The policy did, however, lead to increasingly strained relations with the United States in the late 1950s and early 1960s. Concerned about the prince's drift toward what U.S. officials called "pro-communist neutrality," Washington sought noncommunist forces to act as a counterweight to him. Sihanouk, for his part, blamed the United States for the conflict in Vietnam, which by the early 1960s was encroaching on his own borders, and he increasingly resented American interference in Cambodian affairs.

By the late autumn of 1963, Sihanouk was ready to break from Washington. Two developments in particular propelled him. The first was de Gaulle's effort, begun in August, to de-Americanize Southeast Asia. Sihanouk had long been an admirer of the French president, and he welcomed the idea of neutralization for South Vietnam, particularly because such a plan might eventually spread to include Cambodia. Second, the prince was deeply affected by the overthrow and killing of the Ngo brothers. He had never been close to Diem and Nhu, but their assassinations confirmed his belief that the United States could not be trusted. On 19 November, Sihanouk renounced American military and economic aid and requested a curtailment of diplomatic relations. He knew that France and China would approve of these actions, and he hoped that Paris and Beijing would step in and provide a good chunk of the aid he had been getting from Washington. Then, on 30 November, Sihanouk went one step further, invoking de Gaulle's name in calling for a conference to neutralize Cambodia under international guarantees. Sihanouk said that he would welcome the creation of a federation of neutralized Indochinese states.[26]

These actions came as a shock to American policymakers. Vietnam had long since superseded Cambodia in terms of importance to them, and they had failed to perceive the depth of Sihanouk's hostility to the growing U.S. presence in the region. There was also a good dose of ethnocentrism in American assumptions about the prince; as David Chandler has noted, U.S. officials "ignored the possibility that Sihanouk's neutralist policies might be less dangerous for Cambodia than a full-blown alliance with the United States."[27] But if developments in Cambodia were of decidedly secondary importance to Americans, Washington was nevertheless profoundly concerned by Sihanouk's actions, precisely because of their likely impact on the situation in Vietnam. Sihanouk's timing could not have been worse—he had chosen to act at the very time these advisers were trying to convince Johnson of the need for a more aggressive American policy in Vietnam and at the very time political instability in Saigon was rising.

For this reason, Sihanouk's request for a conference on Cambodia was especially disconcerting. The initial public American response to the announcement in Phnom Penh was one of support for the idea of a conference, but policymakers were privately anything but enthusiastic, fearing that such a gathering would inevitably increase support for a similar one for Vietnam. Henry Cabot Lodge, concerned that his superiors might agree to Sihanouk's request, pressed this theme of inevitability in several cables. On 3 December, after conceding that he was "unable to predict [the] new GVN's reaction to [the] specific Cambodian neutrality proposal," Lodge warned that if the United States agreed to sit down at a table with communist powers to discuss threats to Cambodian neutrality and territorial integrity from its neighbors, "we shall undermine the confidence of the new Vietnamese leadership in the firmness of our purpose here and play into the hands of the advocates of neutralism in South Vietnam."[28]

Lodge must have thought about the issue further that night, for the next day he dispatched another message to Washington. "The more I think about the proposed conference on Cambodia," he said, "the more disastrous I think it would be. . . . It is inconceivable to me that a conference like this could do other than foment and encourage the neutralism which is always present in varying degrees here in South Vietnam. . . . Obviously, any encouragement of neutralism must impair the war effort." Lest there be any doubt of his position, the ambassador stressed that "this emphatically is not the time even to discuss the question of unifying North and South Vietnam." It would be "most imprudent" to consider unification until the South was in a position of superior strength at the conference table, and "obviously this state of affairs is not now even in sight." Sounding a familiar refrain, the ambassador warned of the certainty of France's participation at any conference and of the French desire to "hamper all of our major policy objectives" in Vietnam. He wondered "why we should hand them this juicy favor by putting them into the game."[29]

Lodge's sense of alarm was fully shared in Washington. A State Department cable instructed him to "categorically, and in [a] manner most likely to convince them, say to the generals that the U.S. government in no way favors neutral solution for South Vietnam." The cable noted that "powerful voices" such as Lippmann and the *New York Times* had been pressing for such a solution, but emphasized that the U.S. government, "from the top down," was committed to a "win-the-war policy." In a "for your information only" conclusion, the department reported "little disposition" in Washington for attending a conference on Cambodia and expressed confidence that one would not be held. The task would be to convince Britain and France, who were inclined to agree to Sihanouk's proposal, "of the dangers inherent in a conference."[30]

An internal report prepared for Secretary of State Rusk took a similar line. "With respect to South Vietnam," the report read, "an even broader question arises—the possibility that a conference neutralizing Cambodia under international guarantees would add pressure for a similar arrangement for Vietnam." Even if Sihanouk were to refrain from using the occasion to press for neutralizing South Vietnam, this did not lessen the possibility that it would be used by others as a precedent for such proposals. The report did not mention who the "others" might be, but administration officials were particularly concerned about the proconference noises coming out of London and Moscow—the British and Soviets had been cochairs of the 1954 Geneva conference, and their endorsement would greatly improve the odds of a conference coming off. Washington officials moved quickly to dissuade them from doing so. The Soviets were unreceptive. On 16 December, six days after U.S. ambassador Foy Kohler, on State Department instructions, had inquired if the Kremlin could be "induced" to cooperate in avoiding a Cambodia conference that could cause "serious problems" for the United States and South Vietnam, Soviet officials told Washington that the USSR had decided to accept Sihanouk's proposal and was awaiting word from London. On that very day, as it turned out, Rusk met with British officials in Paris to discuss Cambodia and convey American concerns.[31]

His words had the desired effect. Britain chose not to press for a conference, despite the prevailing opinion among senior officials in London that such a meeting should be convened. Not for the first time, and not for the last, Britain gave top priority to its desire for good relations with Washington. In the first days of December, London officials made several internal arguments in favor of a conference: that it would soothe Sihanouk's ego and keep him from drifting closer to Beijing; that it could stabilize Cambodia's relations with its neighbors; and that, if nothing else, it would "give us a breathing space of many months while the conference is deliberating." These officials did not deny that the talks at such a conference could well end up including the Vietnam conflict, and some saw this as yet another reason to view the prospect favorably. "If there is any likelihood at all (as I think there is) that we might want to consider an international conference for Vietnam during 1964," James E. Cable of the Foreign Office wrote, "then this is a further argument for persisting in our present policy of keeping the door open for a conference on Cambodia. One of the main American objections to this policy—that it would encourage people to regard a conference as a solution for Vietnam as well—could turn into one of the strongest supporting arguments if it became clear that military victory in Vietnam was impossible."[32] There was a world of difference, of course, between "keeping the door open" for a conference and actually working to get one; the British government, to Washington's relief, chose the former position.

Lodge was not satisfied. His doubts about the Minh regime's commitment to the war had not abated, and he implored Washington to issue a definitive rejection of Sihanouk's proposal. He warned that, without such a rejection, "there is going to remain in Viet-Nam a large residue of doubt about our ultimate intentions. And this doubt will inevitably have a bad effect on the determination of the new Vietnamese leadership to pursue the war effort vigorously." Lodge used a specific example to buttress his point. He reported that the government's minister of security, General Ton That Dinh, "is so concerned over Sihanouk's conference proposal that he is considering how to accommodate himself to a neutral solution for Vietnam." The State Department responded immediately. It instructed the ambassador to "make a special effort to reassure Dinh and others who may also be concerned. Nothing is further from USG [the U.S. government's] mind than [a] 'neutral solution for Vietnam.' We intend to win."[33]

So determined was Johnson to hammer home that message to the Saigon leadership that he opted to send Defense Secretary McNamara to do so in person. The United States was not doing all it should in the war, the president lectured McNamara in ordering him to go to South Vietnam directly from the NATO meeting in Paris. McNamara's task would be to give Johnson a fresh view of the state of the war and lay the groundwork for an expanded campaign against North Vietnam. Even more important, however, was the need to counter the growing clamor for a conference-table settlement for Vietnam and the need to convince the Minh regime that such a solution must be resisted. In a memo to McGeorge Bundy, the NSC's Michael Forrestal succinctly summarized the rationale for the trip, reporting that he had just cleared a cable to Lodge "telling him that we are against neutralism and want to win the war, and that is why McNamara is coming out."[34]

This deep fear among American officials of indigenous South Vietnam neutralism is a predominant theme in the internal record in these weeks, as it would be right up through the Americanization of the war in 1965. But what did the concept of "neutralism" mean in the South Vietnamese context at that particular time? Here it is necessary to distinguish between, on the one hand, neutralism as a conscious political line that would seek to steer a middle path between both East and West, and, on the other, a less political and less coherent attitude springing from weariness of war and lengthy suffering at the hands of both sides. By all accounts it was the latter of these variations that mushroomed in the South near the end of 1963 and caused such trepidation in Washington. The concern was well founded. "Intense and increasingly hopeless war-weariness certainly prevails among the great bulk of the peasantry, who ache to be free of the increasing demands made on them by both the Government and the Viet Cong," the British ambassador cabled London a few days before McNamara arrived. "The peasants do not want Communism, but if the Government cannot protect them they will support the Communists. There is no middle way." French officials likewise found evidence of an epidemic of war-weariness and speculated that the euphoria in many quarters immediately after the Diem coup resulted from expectations that the war would soon end. These assessments jibed with what American officials in Saigon were learning.[35]

McNamara arrived in Saigon on the afternoon of 18 December and was immediately rushed into meetings on the situation in the field. What he heard confirmed the administration's worst fears. The enemy controlled ever greater sections of the countryside. Strategic hamlets were overrun or in ruins. (The McNamara team asked to visit one district where eighteen hamlets were said to be functioning and the general area pacified; the visit was discouraged on the grounds that safety could not be ensured. When the team pressed to visit at least one hamlet, it emerged that not one of the eighteen in fact existed.) In the northern Mekong Delta, the Vietcong roamed with impunity by night. Even during the day, they had effective control over many densely populated rural areas, notably in Long An and Dinh Tuong provinces. In the four northern provinces and in Quang Ngai and Binh Dinh, as well, the insurgents were gaining. In Saigon, meanwhile, the government was ineffectual and badly divided. The news proved for McNamara what he had been fearing for several weeks: that the optimistic appraisals provided to him by Harkins earlier in the fall had been wrong, and that the Kennedy team's one-thousand-man withdrawal plan had been based on false reports. John McCone, who accompanied McNamara on the trip, began his report of the visit with the stark observation, "There is no organized government in South Vietnam at this time." McCone bemoaned the absence of leadership in Saigon and concluded with the comment that the war effort probably could not succeed "under present programs and with moderate extensions to existing programs."[36]

The grim findings did not affect McNamara's determination to pursue the war effort. Before departing South Vietnam he told Saigon government leaders of the need to step up military activity, in part through increased covert activity against the North. Neutralism was not the answer, he assured them, because any negotiation for neutralism was actually negotiation for servitude. Privately, however, McNamara clearly feared the prospect of some kind of early settlement among the warring parties—on his return to Washington, he informed Johnson that the situation was "very disturbing. Current trends, unless reversed in the next 2–3 months, will lead to neutralization at best and more likely a Communist-controlled state."[37]

Thus, less than a month after taking office, the Johnson administration faced a problem of mammoth proportions in Vietnam. On the military side, the immediate outlook was grim. On the political side, it was not much better—*ambivalence* and *drift* remained words that aptly described the Minh government's approach to governance. Equally disturbing—and a direct result of the political and military situations—was that a political settlement to the conflict was finding increasing favor in the international community, in the United States, and in South Vietnam. De Gaulle's position on the war continued to gain adherents in December, and Norodom Sihanouk's conference proposal was received with sympathy by several key governments worldwide. In the United States, the voices expressing sympathy for a negotiated settlement were in the minority, but they were influential—notably Walter Lippmann and the *New York Times* in the press community, and Mike Mansfield and William Fulbright on Capitol Hill. In South Vietnam, neutralism had gained significant appeal among many in the war-weary general population, among elements of the Buddhist leadership, and evidently among some in the Minh government. The NLF also professed to support the concept on several occasions in November and December.[38]

Among America's Vietnam policymakers, however, there were no such sentiments. Robert McNamara's position was made clear in the last part of his mission report. He wrote: "We should watch the situation very carefully, running scared, hoping for the best, but preparing for more forceful moves if the situation does not show early signs of improvement." John McCone, while noting that there were more reasons to be pessimistic than optimistic, advised standing firm in the war. And Dean Rusk, in a memo he delivered personally to the president at the LBJ Ranch on 27 December, counseled steadfastness and suggested the need for a presidential letter to Duong Van Minh. The letter, Rusk advised, should stress "the urgency of action to reverse the adverse trend in the war as well as reaffirming the United States policy of complete support for the Vietnamese government." He noted that "public uneasiness and confusion in both the United States and Vietnam" necessitated an authoritative statement of American war aims and policy on neutralization.[39]

Johnson needed no convincing. He fully shared his aides' determination to find a winning formula in Saigon. "If we can have victory in Vietnam there will be praise enough for all of us," he said in a year-end letter to Lodge. "So I rely on you to do all in your power to achieve it, and to be alert and demanding in telling all of us in Washington how and what more we can do to help." In his New Year's Eve letter to Minh, Johnson said that the U.S. government "shares the view of your government that 'neutralization' of South Vietnam is unacceptable," because it "would only be another name for a Communist take-over." More portentously, given that the letter was also released to the press, LBJ gave Minh a "pledge" that the United States "will continue to furnish you and your people with the fullest measure of support in this bitter fight."[40]

If Johnson needed any further assurance on the dangers of compromise, the blistering attacks on neutralization delivered to him in early January 1964 by his three principal foreign-policy advisers, McNamara, Rusk, and Bundy, no doubt sufficed. The pretext for their onslaught was a second memorandum from Mansfield to the president that favored such a solution. After reiterating many of the points of his earlier effort, the majority leader suggested that there should be less talk of American responsibility in Vietnam and more talk of the Vietnamese themselves and that there should be a great deal of thought given to the possibilities of a negotiated solution. "We are close," he warned Johnson, "to the point of no return in Vietnam."[41]

The ferocity with which the trio of top officials countered Mansfield's claims is stark evidence of their concerns about his influence on Capitol Hill and about the growth in pronegotiation sentiment in general, both at home and abroad. Bundy warned Johnson on 6 January that moving in the direction of withdrawal by way of neutralization would mean:

a) A rapid collapse of anti-communist forces in South Vietnam, and a unification of the whole country on Communist terms.
b) Neutrality in Thailand, and increased influence for Hanoi and Peking.
c) Collapse of the anti-Communist position in Laos.
d) Heavy pressure on Malaya and Malaysia [sic].
e) A shift toward neutrality in Japan and the Philippines.
f) Blows to U.S. prestige in South Korea and Taiwan which would require compensating increases in American commitment there— or else further retreat.

Bundy did not neglect the potential domestic implications. He warned ominously that if the United States followed Mansfield's advice and moved toward neutralization, that move would be seen as a "betrayal" by "all anti-communist Vietnamese," and "there are enough of them to lose us an election." In a second, shorter, memo three days later, Bundy, referring to himself as an "ex-historian," noted that Harry Truman had suffered politically from the fall of China because most Americans came to believe that he could and should have done more than he did to prevent it. "That is exactly what would happen now if we seem to be the first to quit in Saigon. . . . *When* we are stronger, *then* we can face negotiation."[42]

The same concerns dominated the McNamara and Rusk memoranda. In the longer of the two, the secretary of defense echoed many of Bundy's claims and bluntly told the president that any deal to neutralize South Vietnam would inevitably mean "a new government in Saigon that would in short order become Communist-dominated." That result, in turn, would create a "serious problem" not only for the rest of Southeast Asia but also for the United States and its position in Asia and the world. Therefore, McNamara concluded apocalyptically, "the stakes in preserving an anti-communist South Vietnam are so high that, in our judgment, we must go on bending every effort to win." For his part, Rusk called the neutralization proposal "a phony" and argued that negotiations should not be undertaken until the South was in a much stronger position militarily.[43]

Johnson received similar warnings from two others whose opinions he respected. The State Department's Walt Rostow, in a memorandum addressed to Rusk but intended also for the president, cautioned that three forces were converging and could cause the "greatest setback to U.S. interest on the world scene in many years." The first force was the rise in the South "of a popular mood" that "a neutralized South Vietnam was the only

way out," the second was a "spread of neutralist thought in Thailand as
well as Cambodia," and the third was de Gaulle's campaign "to encourage
neutralist feeling in Southeast Asia." Rostow encouraged Johnson to initiate "a direct political-military showdown with Hanoi" and to renounce
any attempt at imposing communist-inspired neutralism. Theodore Sorensen, one of Kennedy's top aides, advised Johnson to reject Mansfield's analysis. He warned that neutralization would lead to a communist takeover of
Vietnam, a weakening of American prestige and security in Asia, and domestic political trouble for Democrats.[44]

Three decades later Robert McNamara would express regret at the "limited and shallow" nature of these arguments against neutralization or withdrawal at the start of 1964 and would acknowledge that they demonstrated
graphically the unalterable American opposition to any kind of early negotiated settlement in Vietnam.[45] But the analyses also revealed something
else: the continuing American fear that the momentum for such a settlement might become too great to stop. The neutralization proposals put forth
by Charles de Gaulle and Norodom Sihanouk were vague, but Americans
knew that this vagueness was precisely why the concept might appeal to
many in South Vietnam and elsewhere. And indeed, as 1964 began, reports
flowing into Washington pointed to increased neutralist sentiment in various parts of South Vietnamese society.[46] Where Minh and other top leaders stood on the issue remained uncertain to U.S. officials, but the junta's
continuing emphasis on the political struggle was cause for alarm, as was
the MRC's ambivalence about an increased American presence in the South.
In meetings with Lodge in early January, Minh made clear that he was
troubled by the U.S. commitment envisaged in Washington. On 10 January,
Lodge reported that Minh and Le Van Kim had told him of the "extreme
undesirability" of American advisers going into villages and districts, because they would be perceived as "more imperialistic than the French" and
would add weight to charges that the Saigon government was an American
"lackey." Minh also objected to the scope of a joint U.S.-MRC "brain trust"
proposed by officials in Washington. He was, according to Lodge, loath to
follow up on the proposal and refused to view it as a businesslike proposal.[47]

Despite Minh's ambivalence (or because of it) the Johnson administration pushed ahead with the "more forceful moves" that McNamara had
hinted at in his 21 December report. On 2 January, an interdepartmental
committee that was formed to study the proposed Oplan 34-A issued its report to Johnson. The report recommended the implementation of the plan,
which, by "progressively escalating pressure . . . to inflict increasing punishment upon North Vietnam," might convince Hanoi "to desist from its

aggressive policies." The plan was to be directed by the military and was to consist of three phases over the next calendar year, each phase progressively more punitive. Top administration officials doubted that the measures would cause Hanoi to cease its support for the Vietcong, but they counseled Johnson to approve the plan nonetheless. He obliged, signing off on the scheme on 16 January.[48]

That Lyndon Johnson was as committed to achieving victory in Vietnam as his predecessor was not lost on leaders in North Vietnam. They had greeted the events of November 1963—first the overthrow of Diem, then the death of Kennedy—with mixed feelings. The coup against Diem was certainly a victory for the revolution, validating Hanoi's long-standing assertion that his government was corrupt and unresponsive to the people. And yet North Vietnamese leaders knew that for that very reason his ouster could also pose a problem, because if Diem was widely believed to be responsible for what was wrong in South Vietnam, it followed that his successors would be welcomed as heroes. Nor could northern leaders predict the reaction of the United States to the changes in Saigon. Initial hopes that Washington would accept the inevitability of defeat and withdraw from the South soon disappeared, as the Kennedy administration moved quickly to announce its support for the Minh government and the war effort. When Johnson advanced to the presidency three weeks later, he wasted no time affirming his intention to stand firm in Vietnam.

These developments necessitated a change in strategy, North Vietnamese officials decided. In December 1963, at the Vietnamese Workers' Party (Lao Dong) Central Committee meeting in Hanoi, leaders expressed satisfaction with the current state of developments in the South, in particular with the low morale of the Saigon regime's armed forces. At the same time, they anticipated that Johnson would probably continue and, if necessary, expand the Kennedy commitment. Because the Vietcong would be hard pressed to overcome such a challenge alone, it was necessary to increase the matériel and personnel assistance to the NLF and to press the NLF to increase its political agitation and military operations against the Saigon government. Hanoi leaders made these decisions not because they saw a military confrontation involving large-scale units as inevitable but because they hoped a forceful response would prevent such a confrontation from occurring. Their fundamental objective remained unchanged: to prevent an Americanization of the conflict. For that reason, they continued to look favorably upon a negotiated settlement that would allow an American withdrawal from South Vietnam. Resolution 9 of the meeting spoke of the possibility that the revolution might have to go through a lengthy period of "complex forms and methods" of struggle before victory was attained, which William Duiker has called "an obvious allusion to the possibility of a negotiated settlement." Final victory would be reached via an incremental "step-by-step" process, a "transition period" of uncertain length.[49]

American intelligence was not unaware of these North Vietnamese attitudes with respect to a diplomatic settlement. A mid-January report prepared for Dean Rusk by the State Department's Bureau of Intelligence and Research argued that although Hanoi was unlikely to actively seek a conference-table solution to the war under present conditions, it was not opposed to one. The report noted that Premier Pham Van Dong had in November expressed gratitude for de Gaulle's pronouncement as a reaffirmation of French support for the Geneva agreements, and that Hanoi had greeted Sihanouk's conference proposal sympathetically. Given their bitter memories of the 1954 negotiations and their concerns about appearing too eager for diplomacy, northern leaders would be unlikely to press for a settlement unless it became "clear that the United States was seeking a graceful exit from its commitments to the GVN." Alternatively, the report continued, "should pressure for neutralization develop among non-communist powers, in a situation where Hanoi feels the Vietcong has been stalemated, the North Vietnamese might see such a settlement as a relatively cheap method of removing the United States from the scene."[50]

Rusk was no doubt comforted by the prediction that Hanoi was unlikely to press for negotiations in the immediate future, particularly given that he and other U.S. officials had their hands full in mid and late January dealing with others who were pushing for such a solution. De Gaulle remained the main problem. His name continued to be invoked whenever the subject of negotiations came up in the United States and South Vietnam, and he showed no signs of acceding to American requests to adopt a lower profile on the war. In fact, as 1964 began he moved closer to an action designed in part to increase his presence in the Vietnam picture: recognition of Communist China. It was not a sudden development. During the previous year, Beijing and Paris had moved closer together; since mid 1963, in particular, contacts between them had accelerated, culminating in an October 1963 visit to China by former French premier Edgar Faure. De Gaulle's motives were complex. On a most basic level, he believed that it was unrealistic to ignore the existence of a rising power in Asia. Chiang Kai-Shek's band of aging generals was unlikely ever to set foot on the mainland again, he knew, and in opting for recognition he was simply following the path Britain had cut more than a decade before. De Gaulle also felt strongly that the Chinese had adopted communism not out of ideological conviction but as a way of disciplining and organizing their vast country and that the clear conflict between Beijing and Moscow guaranteed the independence of Chinese foreign policy. In addition, there can be no doubt that de Gaulle was motivated by the situation in Southeast Asia. He believed that China had to be part of any lasting settlement to the war, and he hoped that closer ties with Beijing, when combined with French historical ties to both Vietnam and the United States, might allow Paris to play a mediating role in settling the conflict, in the process boosting French influence in Southeast Asia.[51]

American intelligence had known of the increased Sino-French contacts for some months but had misjudged both the contacts' seriousness and the American administration's ability to dissuade the French from going as far as recognition—as late as mid December 1963, after Rusk's meeting with de Gaulle in Paris, Washington believed that French recognition of Beijing was unlikely until late 1964 at the earliest.[52] In the days and weeks that followed, however, speculation increased that France was getting ready to move, perhaps before the end of January.

The possibility made American policymakers shudder. Already alarmed by the level of Gaullist involvement in the Vietnam conflict, they knew that the China initiative would likely raise it still further. Equally important, French recognition of China would deliver a direct blow to their much-trumpeted rationale for standing tough in Vietnam: checking expansionist Chinese ambitions in Southeast Asia. U.S. officials were not unaware of the mistrust that existed between Hanoi and Beijing; they understood that, helpful though it might be, Chinese material assistance and verbal support to the North were not yet instrumental. They also thought that Beijing would try to avoid a major confrontation with the West over Indochina. Nevertheless, many officials insisted that China had aggressive designs on its southern neighbors and that it would try to exploit any far-ranging and rapid change in the region's status quo. As it had with Kennedy, the notion of credibility played a key role here. Many in the Johnson administration declared that standing up to China was a test of American resolve, one that could decisively influence the attitudes of both friends and foes in Asia and across the world.[53] French recognition of China would demonstrate to the world that de Gaulle disagreed. Recognition would signify a rejection not only of the contention that Beijing had expansionist aims in Southeast Asia, but also of the idea that Vietnam was vital to western security. As had been the case with the French leader's August 1963 proposal, American officials were particularly incensed by de Gaulle's timing. Rumors of endemic war-weariness and neutralist sentiment in Saigon had been gaining momentum for weeks in early January 1964, and U.S. decision makers did not doubt that a Paris-Beijing rapprochement would strengthen the momentum for an early negotiated settlement and inevitably fuel speculation that the West's opposition to Chinese support of Hanoi was diminishing.

Lyndon Johnson and his top aides knew the task before them: to persuade de Gaulle to abandon his plan, or at least delay implementing it until the situation in Vietnam had stabilized. On 3 January, Rusk instructed Bohlen to seek an appointment with the general as soon as possible to convey American concerns and elicit a promise from him to discuss the issue with Washington before proceeding with recognition. De Gaulle, it turned out, was away from the capital, so Bohlen met with Foreign Minister Maurice Couve de Murville. He did not get the response he wanted. Couve told him that no military victory was possible for the West in Indochina and that France therefore supported the neutralization of the whole region, including Thailand. The foreign minister did not object to the American desire to keep Vietnam divided, but he said that any long-term division could come only by way of negotiation, not by military force. French recognition of China, he insisted, would enhance the prospect of successful neutralization.[54]

Couve's intransigence was highly discouraging to Bohlen and policymakers in Washington, and they were uncertain how to proceed. Some favored a letter from Johnson to de Gaulle, on the grounds that only direct presidential intervention could induce the general to reconsider. Rusk appeared to endorse this view, as did Undersecretary of State for Political Affairs W. Averell Harriman, who told Rusk that de Gaulle had "to be faced up with the fact that if he recognizes Red China this year he will do so in direct opposition to the wishes of the President of the United States." But others, including Bohlen and National Security Adviser McGeorge Bundy, were not certain that a presidential communication would do any good; experience had shown, they believed, that the French president did not respond to that kind of pressure, and an unsuccessful effort would reflect badly on Johnson. "You yourself will want to be in a position to shrug this off if it happens," Bundy counseled the president. Instead, the State Department should continue to press for a delay until 1965 and should "generate as many expressions of concern to Paris from other countries as possible."[55]

The Bundy argument won the day. Johnson evidently shared Bundy's concern that all efforts to persuade de Gaulle might fail and that, therefore, he should avoid any personal involvement. It soon proved to be an accurate assessment—by the middle of January, despite continued State Department pressure to prevent it, all signs pointed to a French announcement of recognition before the end of the month.[56] U.S. officials quickly shifted to a second objective: to convince allies and the Minh government that de Gaulle's China initiative would not alter American commitments in Vietnam. Key U.S. embassies were instructed to emphasize that the administration intended to stand firm and that French thinking on the situation was mistaken. The administration's position was represented by Undersecretary of State George Ball in a White House conversation with Canadian external affairs minister Paul Martin on January 22. Ball said that French recognition of China would "upset a few apple carts" and would lead to increased speculation in South Vietnam that neutralization was in the offing, but would not diminish U.S. determination to help the Vietnamese achieve a victory over communism. A neutralist solution was no solution at all, Ball maintained, and would serve only to facilitate a takeover by China. When Martin asked about Washington's view of the proposed Cambodia conference, Ball's response was blunt: the administration did not want one but had to be careful not to appear directly opposed to Sihanouk's proposal.[57]

Top American officials took the same hard line in nondiplomatic venues. On 22 January, Rusk told an audience at Barnard College that the United States was in Vietnam to fulfill its obligation in the struggle against communism and that "no new conference or agreement [on Vietnam] is needed. All that is needed is for the North Vietnamese to abandon their aggression." Five days later, McNamara, appearing before the House Armed Services Committee, told members that the situation in South Vietnam "continues grave" but that "the survival of an independent Government in South Vietnam is so important to the security of all Southeast Asia and to the free world that I can conceive of no alternative other than to take all necessary measures within our capability to prevent a communist victory." He emphasized that the year-end, one-thousand-man withdrawal decided upon in October 1963 had never been intended as a first step in an irrevocable withdrawal from Vietnam—withdrawal had always been, and would continue to be, contingent upon the battlefield situation.[58]

The administration understood perfectly well that none of these affirmations of American determination would mean anything unless the South Vietnamese were persuaded that neutralization was disastrous and that the U.S. support for the war remained firm. Already uncertain about the Minh government's commitment to a military solution, the Johnson team worried about the impact that de Gaulle's China initiative might have on its thinking. By mid January, Saigon was awash in rumors involving de Gaulle, Beijing, and Indochina. On 18 January, an Agence France Presse (AFP) article that was widely circulated in Saigon said that France planned to use its impending recognition of China to bring about a negotiated settlement in Indochina. The article equated American actions in the war with those of the Vietcong and North Vietnam and called a cease-fire an essential first step on the road to peace. Lodge was outraged. He moved quickly "to repudiate French plans to recognize Peiping and the whole line of thought contained in the AFP article." On 21 January, he met with the top Saigon leaders, including Minh, Prime Minister Nguyen Ngo Tho, Foreign Minister Pham Dang Lam, and General Le Van Kim. The ambassador assured them that Lyndon Johnson was committed to their struggle and had no interest in any solution proposed by Paris. Indeed, so determined was the president, Lodge pointed out, that he had approved "a plan for expanded operations against North Vietnam [Oplan 34-A]."[59]

Lodge was evidently uncertain about the junta members' reaction to his comments, because he gave contradictory reports of the meeting. In the first, submitted the same day, he conceded that the South Vietnamese had criticized the rationale behind Oplan 34-A (most significantly, they rejected the notion that bombing would demoralize the North) but said that he "had the sense" that Tho and Kim were disturbed by the AFP article and by de Gaulle's plans, and he remarked that Minh was "greatly reassured and relieved that we did not take the French maneuvers too seriously." However, in recalling the meeting some ten days later (after the junta had been ousted from power), the ambassador wondered about the eagerness with which Minh and the others had wanted to discuss de Gaulle and neutralization. General Kim, in particular, had been "obviously eager to discuss it," and Lodge now wondered if it might have been because Kim supported such a solution. Similar concerns shaped Lodge's continuing opposition to a conference on Cambodia. On 21 and 23 January, he urged his superiors to resolutely oppose "Sihanouk and his 'neutrality conference,'" on the grounds that any sympathy for the idea would sap "the will to win" in Saigon.[60]

The unceasing American concern about an absence of will among the South Vietnamese and their leaders pointed to the fundamental problem the United States continued to face in Vietnam: finding a government committed to producing political stability in Saigon and to waging war against the Vietcong. Doubts about the Minh regime's determination on both counts (and about the Diem regime before it) had existed since it came to power; now, some ten weeks later, a growing number of Americans in South Vietnam, particularly in the military, were convinced that the commitment was not there and that new leadership had to be found. In mid January 1964, many of these officials believed that they had found such leadership in the figure of General Nguyen Khanh, widely regarded as the most hawkish and pro-American military officer in the South. Ambitious and unscrupulous,

Khanh had supported the coup against Diem but had turned against the new government when Minh failed to appoint him to a key post in the MRC. Khanh saw a chance to advance his cause by spreading word around Saigon that Paris was behind a conspiracy to bring to power a procommunist South Vietnamese government that would carry out de Gaulle's call for neutralization. On 28 January, a day after the French Foreign Office announced that France would establish diplomatic relations with China, Khanh informed American officials that the key Vietnamese in this plot were Don and Kim, both of whom had served in French colonial administrations, and Mai Huu Xuan. Khanh charged that, along with Minh, they were "pro-French and pro-neutralist" and that they firmly supported de Gaulle's plans. As proof, he noted that Don had recently held a dinner for two Gaullist deputies from the French National Assembly and had invited Minh and Kim.[61]

The CIA's Saigon station gave considerable credence to these claims. It noted that Foreign Minister Lam had recently returned from Paris, where he was reportedly "empowered, presumably by the French, to spend [a] substantial sum (two billion piastres) to achieve neutralization of SVN [South Vietnam]"; that an American observer had witnessed numerous military vehicles bringing weapons and ammunition to Xuan's headquarters; and that a top South Vietnamese military man, Major General Le Van Nghiem, had charged that Kim and Don, as well as their associates Nguyen Van Vy and Duong Van Duc, were pro-French and privately in favor of neutralization. Just how much validity to grant these reports was difficult to determine, the agency continued. Personal disgruntlement and ambition on the part of Khanh and Nghiem might be important, but the phenomenon appeared larger than these two men, as evidenced by the "noticeable rise in uneasiness, rumor-mongering, and political maneuvering" in recent days. The neutralization issue and de Gaulle's China initiative, along with the continuing political confusion in Saigon, had fueled the restiveness, and the CIA pledged to watch the situation closely. The report concluded by returning to Khanh and his allegations against Minh, Don, and Kim: "It is possible that he feels this alleged [neutralist] tendency on their part is becoming so pronounced that he and his like-minded military associates must act to prevent a neutral solution."[62]

Khanh repeated his claims in a meeting with Lodge on 29 January. Though the ambassador had little if any prior awareness about the plans for a coup (four days earlier, he had suggested that Johnson send a letter of encouragement to Minh), he was sympathetic and urged Washington to warn France that neutralization for Vietnam was not a good idea and would not be allowed to happen. Indeed, even before meeting Khanh, Lodge had suggested that Washington tell de Gaulle that the United States had secret information indicating that people "purporting to be under the strong influence of the French government" were working "directly against U.S. vital interests in Viet-Nam" and that de Gaulle should "call off his dogs."[63]

Lodge's superiors rejected the suggestion, telling him that Franco-American relations had declined to a level where any "approach to [de Gaulle] would be fruitless." But Lodge was undaunted—after meeting Khanh, he again recommended telling the French president that the United States had reports of "French neutralist plot, French money, and French agents" and that he should cease his activities. The ambassador said that Khanh thought a move toward neutralism by the Minh regime was very likely within the next day or two and that, given the war-weariness among the Vietnamese, including among junior ARVN officers, the move might very well succeed unless "vigorously crushed." Lodge was impressed by what he heard. In his cable, he noted that Khanh was considered the "most capable general in Vietnam," with a reputation for political shrewdness. "I continue to believe that Generals Don and Kim are patriotic Vietnamese," Lodge concluded, "but General Khanh's reputation for perspicacity gives me pause."[64]

But perhaps the surest sign that the American ambassador to South Vietnam was sympathetic to a coup was his decision not to tell the Minh government of his conversation with Khanh. It proved a fateful decision, because less than twelve hours later, in a hastily executed action, Khanh and a group of officers toppled the three-month-old government. Khanh and other sources in Saigon told American officials the same day that the coup was intended to save South Vietnam from a neutral settlement like the ones suggested by de Gaulle and Sihanouk. The settlement, Khanh said, was to have coincided with France's recognition of China and would have been announced by Minh on 31 January or in the first few days of February.[65]

In Washington, administration officials followed the unfolding events in Saigon with rapt attention. When news of the coup reached the White House in the late afternoon on 29 January, Washington time, the immediate reaction was one of satisfaction that a new leader had taken over, along with concern that the United States would be implicated. The Minh junta's alleged sympathy for neutralization figured prominently in the administration's analysis. In relaying the news to Johnson via telephone, Acting Secretary of State George Ball said that Khanh had moved to thwart Xuan and Kim, "who have been flirting with the French on the neutralist line," and to convince Prime Minister Tho to "take a much stronger anti-neutralist line." If the coup succeeded, Ball told the president, "it is probably a good thing." Ball had scarcely hung up with Johnson when his phone rang. It was Robert McNamara.

MCNAMARA: What's going on in Saigon?

    BALL: I don't know. The best that we can read is that this fellow Khanh is in control of the situation. He is more our boy than the other side.

MCNAMARA: He's the ablest of the generals in my opinion.

    BALL: It looks as though it may be a bloodless one. [And?] that he'll get rid of these boys that were allegedly flirting with the French. Now whether he has achieved this or not I don't know.

The two men agreed on the need for the administration to "play stupid" on the developments—Washington, they felt, should "not know of this until the story actually breaks out of Vietnam." Ball instructed aide Ted Clifton to get the word out: the United States knew nothing about the coup and had played no part in it. He then cabled Lodge with the same directive.[66]

That American officials should at once welcome the coup and want to distance themselves from it is not difficult to understand. They perceived the potential public-relations problem of a second coup in South Vietnam so soon after the first, with inevitable questions about U.S. involvement and about extending recognition to a regime that had just forcibly taken power from a U.S.-supported government. At the same time, the problems that had characterized the Diem regime had not appreciably lessened under Minh; many, indeed, had grown more severe. General Khanh was committed to the war, and he appeared willing to allow a greater American presence in the war effort and in South Vietnam than Duong Van Minh and his cohorts had been. He also appeared resolutely opposed to neutralization. Though there is little evidence that the Minh regime was "flirting with the French" in a serious way in late January, U.S. policymakers were prepared to believe that it was or that it might in the near future.[67] Americans conceded that Khanh was certainly power-hungry and unscrupulous, but that fact did not lessen the potential validity of his charges.

Henry Cabot Lodge, who was as close to events in Saigon as any American, emphasized the neutralist dimension in his post-coup cables. In the first, on 30 January, he reiterated Khanh's rationale sympathetically and emphasized that the transfer of power had been bloodless and quietly done. The following day he reminded Washington that Don and Kim "had never at any time forsworn the possibility of a neutral solution at what might seem to them to be the proper time." Though they had been working to strengthen the position of the government in the struggle against the Vietcong, no one had ever considered what might happen after that. "Perhaps they did favor the French neutrality solution at that time." Furthermore, Lodge added, Ambassador Giovanni D'Orlandi of Italy, "one of the shrewdest men here," had on numerous occasions said that the Minh government "was actively in support of General de Gaulle's ideas and would become overtly neutralist at the proper time." The regime's ouster was therefore welcome. Lodge remained furious at Paris for meddling in the conflict, but in the wake of the coup he felt confident that, at last, de Gaulle had been thwarted. "The spurious idea of a neutralized Vietnam will now die," he assured Rusk.[68]

Rusk and others in Lyndon Johnson's inner circle were not so sure. On 31 January, just one day after the coup, there were renewed calls for a neutralist settlement to the conflict from two sources that these officials deemed important: the *New York Times* and the French government. In the *Times*, Washington bureau chief James "Scotty" Reston urged the United States to seek a negotiated settlement to the conflict and claimed that the administration was "actually on record as favoring the neutralization of the whole country, North Vietnam as well as South." Johnson's aides assured him that the United States was on record arguing no such thing, but they were alarmed. "I don't know where Scotty gets this, but he should be knocked down," NSC staffer Michael Forrestal advised the president.[69]

In Paris, Charles de Gaulle drew a direct link between his government's recognition of China and the war in Vietnam during a much-publicized news conference. "There is no political reality in Asia," he said, "which does not interest or touch China. Neither war nor peace is imaginable on that continent without China's becoming implicated. Thus it is absolutely inconceivable that without her participation there can be any accord on the eventual neutrality of Southeast Asia." De Gaulle insisted that, with Beijing on board, the prospects for such a successful neutralization were excellent, provided that the agreement was guaranteed on the international level, that it outlawed "armed agitations" by the states involved, and that it excluded "the various forms of external intervention." Such a neutrality, the general concluded, "seems, at the present time, to be the only situation compatible with the peaceful existence and progress of the peoples concerned."[70]

There was fuzziness here, deliberate fuzziness. De Gaulle spoke of the "eventual neutrality of Southeast Asia" as the desired goal but gave little sense of how it would be reached. Would the process begin with an agreement neutralizing just South Vietnam, or would it apply to the North as well? He did not say. Privately de Gaulle believed, and had believed for some time, that the concept should initially be confined to the South alone. The Hanoi leadership would refuse to agree to any kind of formal neutralization, he felt certain, and would get support in this position from Beijing and Moscow. This reality did not concern him particularly—the DRV, he believed, would be effectively neutral regardless, in view of the historic Sino-Vietnamese friction and the deepening Sino-Soviet split. Ultimately, Hanoi might gain control of all of Vietnam, but it would take time and would in any event not be a big blow to the West. In the long run, de Gaulle was certain, Vietnam would be more Vietnamese than communist.

De Gaulle conceded that this line of thinking would not find favor in Washington, but, he asked, what choice did the Americans really have? The reports from Vietnam and from Vietnamese émigré groups in Paris showed that the peace movement in the South was growing stronger each day and that no U.S.-backed government could ever win broad popular support. Americanizing the war thus offered no hope for success. "If the Americans are not too stupid they will put an end to this absurd Vietnam War," Gaulle told information minister Alain Peyrefitte after a cabinet meeting on 22 January. "The only way to get out is through an agreement for neutrality." France could play a role by facilitating discussion between Beijing and Washington, de Gaulle noted, but should the Johnson administration reject this option and instead choose escalation, the results would be disastrous for all involved.[71]

Why, given the strength of his convictions on these core propositions, did de Gaulle not call explicitly for the neutralization of South Vietnam? Because vagueness suited his purposes, just as it had suited him in his statement in August 1963. Well aware that France's continuing cultural and social presence in Vietnam gave his pronouncements outsized attention, he could afford to be ambiguous—his comments would reverberate throughout Vietnam whatever their level of specificity. Thus he saw no reason to give either side specifics on which to attack him and torpedo the prospects for talks. A certain blurring of categories was essential to get negotiations started. In addition, de Gaulle felt no particular sense of urgency about the situation. Not altogether displeased to see the United States floundering in its efforts to achieve what he had long said it could never accomplish, he was content to wait and see how things developed, meanwhile giving tacit support to neutralist forces in the South and issuing periodic calls for a political settlement.

American analysts paid close attention to the French president's press conference and struggled to come up with an effective response. When Johnson in a press conference on 1 February appeared to give a qualified endorsement to the notion of a neutralized Vietnam, aides became alarmed, despite the fact that Johnson also said that de Gaulle was hurting U.S. efforts in the region. The remarks could be twisted any number of ways by the press both at home and abroad, these aides thought, and could make the

United States appear to support a neutral solution. Secretary of State Rusk immediately instructed subordinates to prepare a clarifying statement indicating that the administration had been and remained strongly opposed to the French position and was determined to press ahead with the war. He then instructed Lodge to make the same clarification in Saigon. "It would be incorrect," Rusk emphasized, "to read any change in policy into the President's remarks." Johnson himself took an unambiguous tone in a hand-written letter to Khanh the same day. "I am glad we see eye to eye on the necessity of stepping up the pace of military operations against the Vietcong," Johnson wrote. "We shall continue to be available to help you carry the war to the enemy and to increase the confidence of the Vietnamese people in their government." And Lodge, in early meetings with Khanh, assured him that U.S. policy was unchanged and warned that he would "rise or fall, as far as American opinion was concerned, on the results he obtained in the effort against the Vietcong."[72]

A clear pattern can at this point be discerned. If American fear of what Jean Lacouture has termed a neutralist "plot between Paris, Hanoi, and Nhu" predated the coup that ousted the Ngos, and may have helped precipitate it, much the same fear predated the coup that overthrew the Minh junta. It was fueled to a large degree by suspicions on the part of American civilian and military leaders and disaffected South Vietnamese leaders that the Minh regime might, with French support, be moving toward a compromise with the enemy.[73] Kennedy, Johnson, and their advisers were convinced that a military solution was needed in Vietnam, and when the Diem and Minh regimes expressed doubts about such a solution, or at least appeared incapable of pursuing one effectively, the United States aided in their overthrow.

It was this single-minded American determination to pursue a military solution in Vietnam that was most troubling to the proponents of a negotiated settlement. For these critics, the central weakness in the U.S. position was not so much that Washington had strong doubts about the prospects for diplomacy, or even that it insisted on continuing to equip and train the South Vietnamese army to fight the Vietcong; it was, rather, that the Johnson administration, like its predecessor, was averse to even considering possible diplomatic alternatives. The administration's claim that mere talk of negotiations would destroy the fighting will of the South Vietnamese did not impress the critics; any government that would crumble under such conditions, they argued, was not worth fighting for in the first place. "General de Gaulle's argument is unanswerable unless we are able to persuade ourselves that the civil war can be won," Walter Lippmann asserted in his syndicated column on 4 February. "The official American view is that we have to say unreservedly that the war will be won and refuse to think about what we shall do if it cannot be won." In other words, Lippmann argued, the United States had one policy; if that policy failed, all was lost. "We have staked everything on one card," he wrote, and "this is a reckless and unstatesmanlike gamble. A competent statesman, like any competent military strategist, never locks himself into a commitment where there is no other position on which he can fall back. In Southeast Asia we have bolted the doors and do not have that indispensable part of any strategy, a fall-back position."

De Gaulle was in fact "rendering us a signal service" by unbolting those doors, Lippmann continued. The general was suggesting a way to save Southeast Asia from Chinese domination, by way of political moves that could be initiated and diplomatic bargaining that could be undertaken. He argued that now was the time for an imaginative diplomatic approach, because de Gaulle was surely correct in claiming that the United States was heading for a "disaster which will leave us an intolerable choice between a humiliating withdrawal and engaging in a much larger war, at least as large as the Korean War." Best of all, such an approach had a good chance of success, given Vietnamese war-weariness and historical Chinese-Vietnamese friction. What was needed, Lippmann concluded, was for Americans to demonstrate the cardinal virtues of the successful diplomat, namely patience and a willingness to compromise: "In all this we should not confuse ourselves with the notion that General de Gaulle has offered a 'plan' for the neutralization of Southeast Asia which we must accept or reject. We must not be in too much of a hurry. General de Gaulle has not proposed a plan. He has proposed a line of policy and a mode of thinking which we cannot afford to dismiss lightly."[74]

Dismiss it lightly is, of course, precisely what America's Vietnam policymakers had done. In the wake of the coup, they worried about the implications of de Gaulle's China initiative, and it dismayed them that he had found support for his views among influential voices on Capitol Hill and in the press. The prospect of a Cambodian neutralization conference, which might unavoidably be expanded to cover the entire region, also continued to concern them. But Lyndon Johnson and his advisers were determined to press on with the war, in expanded form if necessary. And in the early days of February 1964, they felt relatively good about their prospects. A new man was on the scene in Saigon, one who professed support for an expanded war and pledged to follow American advice to a greater degree than his predecessors. As had been the case with Duong Van Minh, U.S. officials knew little about Khanh, but they hoped that he could bring stability to Saigon and leadership to the war effort, which would reduce the international and domestic pressure for a reevaluation of policy and thereby allow Johnson to focus his energies on his ambitious legislative agenda. They hoped, in other words, that with Nguyen Khanh they could finally get the Vietnam problem under control.

The day after the coup, Johnson summed up administration thinking for Walker Stone, editor in chief of the Scripps-Howard Newspapers. "This Khanh is the toughest one they got and the ablest one they got," Johnson declared. "And he said, 'Screw this neutrality, we ain't going to do business with the Communists, and get the goddammned hell out of here. I'm pro-American and I'm taking over.' Now it'll take him a little time to get his marbles in a row, just like it's taking me a little time. But it's de Gaulle's loss and the neutralists' loss, not the Americans' loss, and we're going to try to launch some counterattacks ourselves. . . . We're going to touch them up a little bit in the days to come."[75]

4 "A Deeply Dangerous Game"

McGeorge Bundy, when asked years later to assess Vietnam developments in the year 1964, said it was a "year off." "It was so under Johnson, and it would have been under [a surviving Kennedy] as well. Neither man wanted to go to the election as the one who either made war or lost Vietnam. If you could put it off you did."[1] Bundy's remark carries immense historical importance, not because he was wholly correct but precisely because he was both right and wrong. Lyndon Johnson, it is clear, in 1964 sought above all else to keep Vietnam from complicating his election-year strategy, which aimed at winning him the White House and thereby allowing him to emerge from the shadow of his slain predecessor. This consuming desire of Johnson's, this obsession with keeping Vietnam from making major trouble for him in November, is not plainly revealed in the massive documentary record of policy making in the eleven months after Dallas—such motivations are hardly the type to be put down on paper—but it was there and it was overriding. Presidential aides did not doubt its central importance, even if they were prepared to admit it only later; international observers, both allied and hostile, understood it as well.[2] White House telephone transcripts, though never stating the point baldly, likewise leave little doubt that the president judged all options on the war in terms of what they meant for November.

But though the strategy worked—Johnson and his advisers succeeded in keeping the war from becoming a major issue in domestic politics in the months leading up to polling day—only by the most tortured logic can 1964 be called an "off year" in Vietnam. As we shall see in the pages and chapters that follow, the administration proved skilled in giving the appearance of keeping the war on the back burner for much of that year, but behind closed doors Vietnam was in fact on the front burner and rapidly reaching full boil. As late as December 1964 the administration could convince most Americans that it envisioned no dramatic escalation in the American involvement in the war (even many informed observers were ready to believe this), whereas secretly a general consensus had been reached already by the spring that major escalatory moves would in all likelihood have to be undertaken by late in the year or early in 1965.

For the historian, there are additional reasons why 1964 must rate as crucial. It was the year in which pessimism about the prospects in Vietnam became endemic among senior American officials, including Lyndon Johnson, but also when the administration stepped up its efforts to prevent early negotiations. It was the year in which key voices in American society, including the Senate Democratic leadership and editorial writers and columnists at various newspapers across the United States, came fully to question the necessity and wisdom of a full-fledged American defense of South Vietnam. In the international community, meanwhile, 1964 witnessed the depletion of allied support for American policy in the war, to the point that by January 1965 international backing had all but ceased to exist. The year also featured significant efforts by French president Charles de Gaulle, United Nations secretary general U Thant, and others to facilitate negotiations. As it turned out, these would be the last best efforts at peace—by the end of February 1965 the best chance for a negotiated settlement had passed.

Most important, 1964 proved a pivotal year in the internal politico-military situation within South Vietnam itself. The military history of that year is a story of almost unrelieved decline in the GVN's fortunes and the ARVN's will to fight, a story of growing war-weariness and attachment to "neutralism" (meaning, in this context, a swift end to the war on whatever terms) among the peasantry and many in the urban areas of the South. Many in the international diplomatic corps in Saigon, thoroughly alarmed at the overthrow of the Minh junta so soon after the ouster of Ngo Dinh Diem—two such upheavals in the span of three months might just prove too much for the South's fragile political structure to bear, these observers believed—began in February to speak of the very real possibility of a third coup engineered by neutralist forces committed to an immediate end to the war. Already in the first weeks of the year, one finds evidence of what will become starkly apparent by year's end: that decision makers in Washington were more committed to the war effort than the mass of the South Vietnamese they were ostensibly working to help. Even Nguyen Khanh, the new leader of the GVN, would in time fall out of favor with American officials for failing in their eyes to be vigorous enough in prosecuting the war. Like the Diem regime and Minh junta before him, Khanh would learn that his ability to win broad-based domestic support would be directly linked to his ability to preserve a degree of independence from the Americans.

It would take time for Khanh to come to this realization. Initially, he pinned his hopes on the opposite strategy, of cementing the GVN's ties to the United States. Khanh understood that American relations with the Minh regime had deteriorated primarily because the junta refused to accede to U.S. leadership in the war effort, and he moved quickly to make good on his midcoup promise to cooperate fully with the United States. He revamped the MRC according to American wishes and agreed to a U.S. demand that he retain Minh in a figurehead capacity to foster the appearance of governmental continuity. More significant, Khanh readily agreed to two key policy changes—one civilian and one military—consistently vetoed by the Minh regime. First, he agreed to the placement of more American advisers in subunits of the GVN. On 3 February, the day before he formally took office, Khanh approved U.S. ambassador Henry Cabot Lodge's suggestion that U.S. advisers be placed in key districts throughout South Vietnam, and he even asked for the ambassador's advice in choosing members of his cabinet. Second, the new leader reversed Minh's policy of strictly limiting the number of U.S. military advisers in the bottom levels of the armed forces. At the same time, he authorized the initiation of American-directed covert operations against the North, as outlined in Oplan 34-A and as approved by Lyndon Johnson in mid January. The scheme involved intelligence overflights, the dropping of propaganda leaflets, and commando raids by South Vietnamese forces. These raids, the centerpiece of the plan, were designed to "result in substantial destruction, economic loss, and harassment" and commenced on 1 February.[3]

Johnson administration officials had every reason to be encouraged. In the figure of Nguyen Khanh they finally had a leader committed to doing America's bidding in Vietnam, one who would not only listen to their advice but willingly follow it. Two things stand out about this American satisfaction with the Khanh takeover. The first is how much it contrasted with the views of other western governments. To British, Australian, and French officials, for example, the coup was a disastrous development, not only because of the tumult it generated throughout the governmental structure in South Vietnam, but because of what they saw as Khanh's grave shortcomings as a leader. Those things that Americans had seen as negatives in Duong Van Minh—his determination to keep the United States at arm's length and to shift the struggle from the military to the political plane to some degree—these foreign observers tended to see as positives, while the attributes in Khanh that appealed to the Johnson administration they saw as weaknesses. "In General Khanh, the Americans appear to have found the kind of man whom they think they can understand and appreciate and who, so they believe, understands and appreciates them," British ambassador to Saigon Gordon Etherington-Smith cabled London, in speaking of Khanh's "bounce and fluency" and "no-nonsense" approach. "To us here," he said, "it seems increasingly probable that the very qualities which make Khanh attractive to American soldiers and politicians render him unpleasing to a very great many Vietnamese." The ambassador was convinced that the Johnson administration, even if it did not instigate the January coup, could and should have prevented it. He wrote the Foreign Office on 12 February: "[The U.S.] failure to support Minh against Khanh has made many people draw bitter conclusions regarding American loyalty. United States prestige as a whole has suffered and, if the situation were to deteriorate further, the Americans might well find that the influence they can now exert on the Vietnamese is less than it was." The same point of view emerged at quadripartite talks in Washington early in the month, where officials from Australia, New Zealand, and Great Britain made clear their uneasiness about the new developments and their skepticism regarding Khanh.[4]

The second striking aspect of this American optimism in the immediate postcoup period is how fleeting it proved to be. By mid February, less than three weeks after the new government had taken over, it was starkly clear that the coup had not slowed enemy advances in the field or stemmed the growth of neutralist sentiment in South Vietnam. In Washington, NSC staffer Michael Forrestal warned Defense Secretary Robert McNamara that time was short, that the coming few months were critical for America's efforts to prevent defeat in Vietnam. McNamara needed little convincing. A Special National Intelligence Estimate (SNIE) prepared for him by the Defense Intelligence Agency had concluded that "the situation in South Vietnam is very serious, and prospects uncertain. Even with U.S. assistance approximately as it now is, we believe, unless there is a marked improvement in the effectiveness of the South Vietnamese government and armed forces, that the South Vietnamese have at best an even chance of withstanding the insurgency threat during the next few weeks or months." Secretary of State Dean Rusk received a similar evaluation from Richard Helms, the CIA's deputy director for plans. The strategic hamlet program was in shambles, Helms pointed out, with the result that in several key provinces, the amount of Vietcong-controlled area now approached 80 percent. So minimal was the government's presence in many provincial areas that the Vietcong was the first to inform the populace of the coup on 30 January.[5]

Helms relied for his information on data gathered by the CIA's Saigon station, which, in a series of remarkable reports of its own, described a situation that had reached a crisis point. The South Vietnamese population was apathetic, the station warned, with ever greater numbers leaning to the NLF. Even with the increased U.S. aid and the closer cooperation between American and GVN officials, the prospects were not encouraging. "In critical areas near Saigon," a 20 February report stated, "U.S. officials note a general lack of urgency and direction, and no real progress." The problems extended to the northernmost provinces of the South, "long considered one of the country's least troublesome areas," where Vietcong gains had accelerated alarmingly. Lyman D. Kirkpatrick, a top CIA official in Saigon, reported that he was "shocked by the number of our people and of the military, even those whose job is always to say that we are winning, who feel that the tide is against us."[6]

But the clearest affirmation of concern came from the deputy chief of mission in Saigon, David Nes. Nes had been in Vietnam less than two months, during which time he had grown more and more pessimistic about the long-term viability of any policy that involved aiding a corrupt and chronically incompetent South Vietnamese government to defeat the Vietcong. Nes was convinced that Vietnam was embroiled in a civil war and that the United States was backing a side that was unlikely to ever win a lasting victory. Khanh's lack of political experience, Nes told Briton Robert G. K. Thompson over dinner a few days after the coup, together with the inevitable chaos caused by a second coup so soon after the first, made the outlook especially grim.[7] These realities led Nes to an uncomfortable conclusion: Charles de Gaulle's position on the war might be the only viable one, at least absent a major American escalation. On 17 February, Nes penned a lengthy memorandum to his superior, Henry Cabot Lodge. The memo opened and closed with de Gaulle.

"Although I have only been directly associated with this area for some two months," Nes began, "my reading of developments over the past year and recent experiences here lead me to fear that General de Gaulle may be right in his belief that we are faced with the choice between accepting the possible collapse of our counter-insurgency efforts here or the escalation of the conflict toward a direct military confrontation of the DRV and China by the U.S." Present policy would in all likelihood never succeed, so long as the Vietcong was backed "politically and psychologically and to a lesser extent militarily by Hanoi and Peking." The outlook was particularly poor in the countryside, Nes continued. The peasants, who formed the mass of the South Vietnamese population and who had received neither political leadership nor orderly and just administration from the GVN, were "exhausted and sick of twenty years of civil conflict. . . . They have enjoyed little if any social or economic betterment." The Vietcong therefore had a huge natural advantage because it represented a grass roots movement, one that was determined and disciplined and was certainly ruthless but also "easily identifiable with the desires of the peasantry."

Here Nes reached the heart of his message, and he minced few words: "I do not see in the present military regime or any conceivable successor much hope in providing the real political and social leadership or the just and effective country-wide administration so essential to the success of our counter-insurgency program." As a result, the United States would be "naive in the extreme" to believe that any number or quality of U.S. advisers could successfully alter, in a reasonable period of time, the attitudes and patterns of thinking of senior Vietnamese military and political officialdom. Much as the French claimed, the United States had accomplished little in its advisory capacity, and another coup could cause swift and total disintegration. "Should this in fact happen," Nes concluded, "we will be faced either with turning the [Southeast Asian] ball game over to de Gaulle in the hope that his policy can salvage something from the wreckage or of rapidly escalating our efforts toward a final military showdown with China. [I recommend] that we seize every opportunity to warn Washington that escalation may be the only alternative to inevitable neutralization."[8]

It was an extraordinary memorandum. The second-ranking American diplomat in South Vietnam had described a war effort that was floundering and might within weeks collapse completely. The Vietcong were winning not only the military struggle but also the struggle for the allegiance of the war-weary peasantry. The Khanh government, meanwhile, was no improvement over its predecessors; it was out of touch with its constituents and appeared incapable of providing even the rudiments of leadership. Nes maintained that the French government's position on the war thus contained considerable wisdom, which the United States could ignore only at its own peril. The best proof of that wisdom was the continuing appeal in South Vietnam of de Gaulle's neutralization proposal.

Nes may have been influenced on this point by a report the embassy received the same day from Georges Perruche, the French chargé d'affaires in Saigon. Perruche requested the meeting to inform American officials that because of South Vietnamese war-weariness, a neutralist coup could come at any time, and that such a coup would have widespread public support. Indeed, the support would extend all the way to Paris. Perruche insisted that the West should not be fooled into thinking it could win either a political or military victory in Vietnam, but instead should employ the American military presence as a bargaining chip to obtain an internationally guaranteed diplomatic settlement. The end result might be a communist Vietnam, Perruche conceded, but even so, "Vietnam would remain the most Western-oriented part of Southeast Asia."[9]

The Nes memorandum did not take long to reach top administration officials in Washington—as part of his effort to "seize every opportunity to warn Washington," the diplomat had sent a copy to Roger Hilsman, the outgoing assistant secretary of state for Far Eastern affairs, who then passed it along to his designated successor, William Bundy. By the middle of February, top aides around Lyndon Johnson were under no illusion about what they confronted in Vietnam. Pessimistic analyses from the CIA, the Pentagon, and the number-two man at the embassy in Saigon had presented them with a grim picture of what portended in the war. What is more, the evidence is powerful that they accepted this baleful interpretation, and that they were inclined to agree with David Nes's assertion that "escalation may be the only alternative to inevitable neutralization." In February we find both the beginning of serious preliminary contingency planning for an escalation of the war into North Vietnam and, no less important, a near-obsessive concern on the part of senior American officials about de Gaulle and neutralization and about how the concept might win support among war-weary southern Vietnamese and the larger world community. It is the presence of both of these features in U.S. policy making that makes the late winter and spring of 1964, which are the focus of this chapter and the next, so important in the making of large-scale war in Vietnam.

That this aversion to even considering any alternative to standing firm in Vietnam guided the thinking of all the principal elements in American decision making, including the chief executive himself, is beyond doubt. Time and again in the wake of the Khanh coup Lyndon Johnson articulated his resoluteness on this point to both hawks and doves (as the supporters and opponents of the war were coming to be known). Judging by his assertion to one newspaper executive in early February, he understood even now the truth of David Nes's assertion that the administration likely faced a fundamental choice in the war. "It really boils down to one or two decisions—getting in or getting out," Johnson told John S. Knight of the *Miami Herald*. But Johnson hoped to postpone having to make that choice for as long as possible, ideally until after the November election. He therefore told many people of his preference for a third path between escalation and withdrawal. This policy involved continued assistance to the Saigon government and continued affirmations of America's staunch commitment to

South Vietnam, in the hope—and hope was the word, not certainty, not expectation—that southerners would stand and fight.[10] Johnson liked to think of this as a middle-of-the-road policy, and in a general sense it was, but it was a policy that operated much closer to the "escalation" side of the street than the "withdrawal" side. Expanding the war always constituted a legitimate option for Lyndon Johnson and his chief Vietnam lieutenants in the winter and spring of 1964; disengagement never did.

Thus at the quadripartite meetings in Washington on 11–12 February, and at the Anglo-American talks the following day, administration officials made amply clear their determination to remain steadfast in the war effort and gave hints that, if the deterioration in the South continued, they would likely move to wider military measures. At a luncheon at the British embassy on 13 February, Dean Rusk informed British officials that, although no decision had yet been made regarding initiating military measures against North Vietnam, the present mood of the administration was to take such action if defeat threatened. On 18 February, Johnson assured Lodge in Saigon that the United States would contribute additional economic and military assistance to South Vietnam if Lodge deemed such aid necessary. Two days later, at a White House meeting of the NSC, the president ordered his aides to accelerate "contingency planning for pressures against North Vietnam." And on 21 February at the University of California, Los Angeles, in his first major pronouncement on Vietnam since taking office, Johnson vowed to uphold America's commitment to the conflict and warned that "those engaged in external direction and supply would do well to be reminded and to remember that this type of aggression is a deeply dangerous game."[11]

Johnson's tough talk fell on welcome ears at the American ambassador's residence in Saigon. Henry Cabot Lodge believed strongly in a program of expanded action against the North. In several key respects, his analysis of the war differed from that of his deputy, David Nes. In contrast to Nes's fundamental pessimism, the ambassador saw matters moving in the right direction, or at least said so to Washington; on 19 February, he told Johnson that "persistent and patient execution of current civil and military plans will bring victory—provided external pressures would be about as they were when I got here last summer." Whereas Nes saw the Vietcong as essentially an indigenous force, relying only marginally on outside support, Lodge emphasized the central role played by the government in Hanoi. And whereas Nes showed scarcely concealed contempt for the Khanh government and its commitment to reform, Lodge continued in late February to praise the new leader. "I continue to be favorably impressed by him," the ambassador told Rusk. "He is invariably good humored, intelligent, unruffled, and quickly comprehending. He is really very much more able than the Minh, Don, and Kim group and, of course, he is so far above Diem and Nhu that there is no comparison."[12]

Even as he professed optimism about the prospects for Khanh and for the war effort, however, Lodge continued to worry about the activities of those agitating for neutralization. He realized now that the prediction he had made hours after Khanh took power had proven false—"the spurious notion of a neutralized Vietnam" had not, in fact, died. Indeed, the idea had continued to gain support among a South Vietnamese population weary of war and of government unresponsiveness. Lodge feared that the conference proposals of Charles de Gaulle and Norodom Sihanouk could boost such sentiments even further, as could the proneutralization positions taken by influential American voices such as Walter Lippmann and the *New York Times*. As he had done in the Minh period, the ambassador urged Washington to work hard to prevent an early settlement. The point is worth emphasizing: what concerned Henry Cabot Lodge in the late winter of 1964 was not so much those forces that might get the United States into a war but those that might keep it out of one.

The French president was the key. Lodge must have found Nes's reference to Gaullist wisdom on Vietnam particularly irritating, because even after the Minh junta's overthrow he continued to fume about French obstructionism—in a series of cables in February he hammered away at the possible implications of de Gaulle's policy for South Vietnam. The French were meddling in matters that did not concern them, Lodge charged on 10 February, and may even have provided the "direction and inspiration" for a number of "recent [presumably verbal] barbaric attacks against Americans." Even worse, he warned a few days later, de Gaulle's declaration on neutralism "is having a demoralizing effect on the will to win of both senior and junior officers, and of the politically conscious population generally. . . . It starts a line of thinking which runs: 'It was Laos last year; this year it will be Cambodia; and next year it will be us.' Obviously such thinking does not make for bravery and for hard fighting." The ambassador urged Johnson to tell de Gaulle that "all men of good will" must desire an end to "the Viet Cong war," that the word *negotiation* made no sense when one side was much weaker than the other, and that, therefore, South Vietnam could never agree to an international conference. Adopting a now-standard American theme, Lodge complained that de Gaulle's words were coming at the worst possible time: they sapped the will to win in the South at precisely the moment that determination was required. (Just why the will should sap so easily Lodge evidently did not ask.) The French president had to be told, ideally by Johnson himself, to declare publicly that his comments about neutralism "were not meant to apply to the present time."[13]

It was a remarkable claim, this suggestion that de Gaulle was all but single-handedly destroying the will to win in South Vietnam, and it resonated with Lodge's superiors in Washington. Indeed, the frequency with which Johnson and his top aides mentioned de Gaulle's name in this period suggests just how much they worried about him and his influence. What they were not prepared to do, however, any more than the Kennedy administration had been, was to seriously consider de Gaulle's proposals. This distinguished them from other western governments, many of which were far from convinced of the ultimate viability of any neutralization scheme, whether for the South alone or both halves of the country, but believed that the French proposals merited serious examination. Australia is especially noteworthy in this regard, given that Canberra ranked second only to Washington in its desire to forestall communist expansion in Southeast Asia. (A year later, Australia would be the only country to wholeheartedly support the major U.S. escalation.) "De Gaulle's proposals merit serious study," a report by the country's Department of External Affairs said in mid February, "because they are not put forward irresponsibly or capriciously. De Gaulle believes that it is impossible to go on ignoring the fact of China's great power status, that it is possible to exploit the Sino/Soviet split [to gain a settlement], and that, as there is no prospect of Western military victory over the Viet Cong, America's allies must find some way of enabling her to disengage militarily in South Vietnam before the situation worsens." The Australians were not prepared to say that the prospects for victory were zero, and they considered it important to try to buck up the Saigon government and military. But the Canberra government showed a willingness to entertain the French proposals wholly missing in the Americans.[14]

On 22 February, after discussing the French problem with Dean Rusk while vacationing in Palm Springs, Johnson sent Lodge a reply in which he assured the ambassador that, as they had done repeatedly for months, Rusk and Bohlen would work to impress upon the French "the futility and danger of empty talk of neutralization of South Viet Nam." The president emphasized that Americans had to "expend every effort and mobilize every resource to get Vietnam strong enough to be independent and feared by any aggressor," and he instructed Lodge to inform him of "any evidence of local French activity" that undercut those efforts.[15]

The presence of Rusk in Palm Springs may have had more than a little to do with the tenor of Johnson's cable, because the secretary of state had been having his own apprehensions about the French policy and the apparent growth of neutralist sentiment in Vietnam. He voiced these concerns in the quadripartite and Anglo-American discussions early in the month, and later in a circular telegram to the key American embassies in Ottawa, London, Paris, Bonn, and Tokyo. In the telegram he advised the ambassadors of the possible impact on Vietnam of de Gaulle's efforts and of Sihanouk's continuing demand for Cambodian neutralization. Rusk warned that "with his neutrality thrust de Gaulle has greatly complicated our already difficult problem in Vietnam," and he pledged that the administration would do nothing to aggravate the problem "by our actions vis-à-vis Sihanouk's demand . . . which fits into de Gaulle's scheme and in [the] French view is a desired preliminary step to [the] neutralization of all Indochina."[16]

Rusk's complete lack of interest in exploring the possibilities for a political solution in Vietnam, already evident in the Kennedy administration, in 1964 became if anything even more pronounced. He had not shaken off his conviction that the State Department's task would only begin after Robert McNamara and the Pentagon had turned the war around—only then could the State Department negotiate an acceptable peace. Vietnam thus was essentially a military problem for Rusk, and he was content to stay in the background during policy discussions, to play a dormant role, and to let McNamara assume the leadership. Where others might balk at such a subordinate position, Rusk welcomed it. Though he got on well with Lyndon Johnson, better than he had with John Kennedy, and was not averse to articulating his views (though preferably one-on-one with the president), he was never comfortable in the role of forceful policy advocate. When journalists in the spring of 1964 began referring to Vietnam as "McNamara's War," Rusk did not mind at all.

No doubt Rusk's view of the negotiations issue was colored by his intense personal dislike for Charles de Gaulle, a dislike he maintained throughout his term as secretary of state. Rusk described the French leader as "living in an anachronistic dream world of the France of Joan of Arc and Louis XIV." De Gaulle's grandiloquence and his policies concerning NATO, the proposed Multilateral Force, and the German rearmament question greatly irritated Rusk, but he seemed especially put off by de Gaulle's meddling in Vietnam. Rusk saw no connection between the French failure to win in Southeast Asia and the efficacy and correctness of the American effort. He thought France a moribund and fading power that had been trying vainly to defend a colonial possession; the United States, in contrast, had no territorial or economic ambitions in the area and was merely doing its part in the global fight for freedom. Rusk refused to take seriously de Gaulle's warning that the struggle in Vietnam would be a never-ending one for the United States. Rusk concluded that France did not want the United States to succeed where France had failed.[17]

Rusk's attitudes and disposition had important implications for American Vietnam policy in 1964. Early in the year, with the political situation in Saigon deteriorating, the Vietcong gaining in strength, and neutralization talk heavy in the air, the State Department could logically have been expected to look hard, harder than any other organ of government, for political alternatives, to issue warning after warning to the White House that there might be no light at the end of this very long, very dark tunnel, and to step back and pose fundamental questions about the reasons for America's commitment to the conflict and about whether any long-term victory was possible. It did not do so. David Nes's pessimistic analysis, one that contained precisely such questions, was read by his superiors in Washington but generated no significant discussion; the memorandum, in Nes's words, "disappeared without a trace." Fundamental questions were not on Dean Rusk's mind in the early months of 1964. Staying the course was; upholding America's commitment was. He saw no reason to explore what kind of deal might be worked out with Hanoi in this period, or what precisely neutralization might mean in the Indochina context.[18]

The secretary of state thus saw Lodge's view as a confirmation of his own, and he supported the ambassador's call for renewed pressure on Paris. The president agreed. But what kind of pressure? A presidential letter, as suggested by Lodge, would have the most impact, but it could also prove embarrassing if leaked to the press or if ignored by de Gaulle. The best bet, Johnson and Rusk agreed, was to have Bohlen make the case to the French president. To underscore the seriousness of the matter, the administration sent an "eyes only" message over Johnson's name to the ambassador on 25 February, which said that the "difficult and dangerous situation in South Vietnam is being made still more difficult and dangerous by impressions and rumors of French policy." De Gaulle's utterances, precisely because they were imprecise in their prescription for neutralism, had caused "great uncertainties" in South Vietnam and would continue to do so, because of the continuing French social, economic, and cultural presence in the South. The president instructed Bohlen to assess how best to persuade de Gaulle that "unless he takes action to correct the current impression in Saigon, the influence of France will work toward the disintegration of the only forces which can prevent a Communist take-over there." In a separate cable, Rusk instructed Bohlen to "give this problem your most imaginative attention."[19]

Charles Bohlen was not keen on the idea of another meeting with de Gaulle. He knew the French president, knew him better than anyone in the administration, and knew that he was unlikely to be swayed on the question of Indochina. Since 1961, Bohlen had heard de Gaulle assert that U.S. policy in the region was destined to fail and that some form of neutralization was the proper solution, first for Vietnam and eventually for the whole of Indochina. The end result might be a unified Vietnam under communist control, but it would be neither Moscow- nor Beijing-directed and thus would pose no significant threat to the West. In view of these oft-stated French claims, Bohlen found Lodge's demand for a public clarification of French policy somewhat puzzling; true, de Gaulle had stated his prescription in rather vague, typically Gaullist terms, but about his fundamental views there could be no doubt. It was even possible that a request for a public declaration from him, as urged by Lodge and endorsed in Washington, could backfire, because it might offer him a chance to restate his position and his differences with American policy.

Bohlen therefore suggested that he call instead on Foreign Minister Maurice Couve de Murville, to convey American concerns and to gently inquire if a public statement indicating French opposition to neutralization was possible; failing that, perhaps Couve would pledge to "refrain from *any* statements in regard to Vietnam during this critical period." Should Couve prove uncooperative, Bohlen suggested that he return to Washington to discuss the issue more fully and to consider what pressures might be applied to the Elysée. Johnson and Rusk agreed, and on 4 March, the U.S. ambassador and the French foreign minister met for an extended conversation on their countries' deepening rift over Vietnam. Couve professed sympathy for the American dilemma but called a political solution the only viable one. He ruled out the idea of any public French declaration. A dejected Bohlen made plans to return to Washington.[20]

The continuing American anxiety about pressures for a political solution is not difficult to understand, especially given the simultaneous reports of increased neutralist sentiment in South Vietnam itself. The CIA reported on 28 February that war-weariness was endemic in the countryside, with growing numbers favoring neutralism, not because of any intrinsic attachment to the concept but because they perceived it as an end to the conflict. The agency also cited reputable Vietnamese sources that noted increased sympathy for neutralism among students in Saigon, most of whom lacked confidence in the Khanh government, and reports of coup plotting against Khanh by dissident, pro-French military officials. According to the *New York Times*, U.S. military officers in the field were finding increased sentiment throughout South Vietnam for an end to the fighting via neutralization. "Neutralism seems to many in South Vietnam to represent a device to end the bloodshed and strife that has marred their lives for more than twenty years," the paper's Saigon correspondent Peter Grose reported.[21]

This was welcome news indeed to the NLF and to Hanoi, whose leaders continued to see neutralization as a way to further their aims in South Vietnam while preventing an Americanization of the Saigon war effort. Earlier in February, voicing support for de Gaulle's efforts, the Front had put forth a "Minimum Two-Point Program" that called for (1) the United States to withdraw, and (2) "all parties and forces in South Vietnam" to negotiate together for a "policy of peace and neutrality." Late in the month, a clandestine Vietcong radio station said that only neutralism could bring peace and that "attention must be paid to the views recently expressed by de Gaulle." Perhaps in order to encourage Paris, the Front released four French citizens they had held prisoner.[22]

The Hanoi government, meanwhile, issued a statement that, while careful to limit the issue to South Vietnam, praised the French president's proposal and welcomed "initiatives contributing to a solution for South Vietnam which conforms to the aspirations of the overwhelming majority of the South Vietnamese people." One government radio broadcast declared that "opposition to neutrality means opposition to all the people's aspirations," while another praised the "neutralization plans worked out by the National Liberation Front." North Vietnamese officials were in regular contact with the Paris government in this period, promoting the line that both they and the NLF were "national communists" and that they were eager to maintain their independence from Beijing. On 11 February Ho Chi Minh and Pham Van Dong met with officials of the French délégate-général in Hanoi and expressed their desire to have close relations with France. According to the French record of the meeting, the two DRV leaders indicated support for de Gaulle's position on the war and said they were prepared to let South Vietnam choose its own political system pending reunification. If the Americans chose to fight, however, Hanoi was ready. Pham Van Dong concluded by urging France to continue its efforts for peace and said: "We don't want Americans in the South, but we are in no hurry, and we know how to wait. When the time comes, we will talk around a table. The reunification of the country presupposes a single government, but we will respect the interests of the South, sincerely, without any pressure."[23]

How much importance to attach to these Hanoi-Paris contacts is a matter of debate, but their mere existence added to Washington's concerns. When Nguyen Khanh issued a public threat to break relations with France over de Gaulle's sponsorship of neutralization, U.S. officials moved quickly to kill the idea, not because they disagreed with his assessment of the French leader's plans but because they believed a break would do nothing but embolden Paris and the South Vietnamese neutralists to push still harder for such a solution. The roughly seventeen thousand French citizens still living in Vietnam would be infuriated by the move, and the chances for a French-supported neutralist coup would be that much greater.[24]

As the winter of 1964 gave way to spring, America's Vietnam policymakers thus faced a problem of monumental proportions: how to turn around a war effort that was fast disintegrating, at a time when two vital preconditions for such a turnaround—a Saigon government possessing widespread popular support, and a South Vietnamese populace dedicated to the war—were missing, and a leading European statesman was working in opposition to U.S. policy. What to do? The top men around Lyndon Johnson were of one mind that swift action might be necessary to keep the war effort from collapsing completely, but they also knew that their leader would accept no drastic escalation—at a meeting with the Joint Chiefs of Staff on 4 March, Johnson repeated that Vietnam must not be lost before the November election, but must not become a full-scale war either. The situation had to be salvaged, but quietly. Accordingly, the administration opted for continued preparations for selective and carefully controlled bombing of the DRV; made plans to send Defense Secretary Robert McNamara on another mission to South Vietnam; and recalled Bohlen to Washington for top-level meetings on how to most effectively confront General de Gaulle. In public forums senior officials, including Johnson and Rusk, tried to paint the best possible picture of the state of the war and rejected neutralization as a viable option. At a news conference on 7 March, the president pledged greater U.S. aid to Saigon if the war effort required it.[25]

The growing attraction among top policymakers for bombing the North was a graphic demonstration of their desperation about the state of the war. To be sure, it was not a sudden development—during his December 1963 trip McNamara had talked at length with the military about a range of operations against the North, and Oplan 34-A had represented an expansion of the war beyond the seventeenth parallel. The Joint Chiefs of Staff were on record as favoring such action, as were a few junior civilian analysts such as Walt W. Rostow of the policy planning staff at the State Department. But the most senior officials had consistently resisted calls to bring U.S. air power to bear on the North. Until now. Now that option seemed viable, and worthy of serious consideration.

There was a kind of logic to the shift. If the antiguerrilla measures in the South were failing and Khanh's government was faltering, despite America's best efforts, it stands to reason that U.S. officials would shift their attention to an area where they might have more influence: North Vietnam. The same Americans who had always believed that the war could only be won or lost in the South now began to argue that the Hanoi government's role in the insurgency was crucial and that bombing, or the threat of bombing, could affect its willingness to support the NLF. Thus began in March 1964 a pattern that would persist right up until the initiation of major bombing of the North in early 1965: Hanoi would grow as a villain in direct proportion to U.S.-GVN failures in the South.

In a greater sense, however, the shift in strategy was not logical at all. The Johnson team made these determinations even though its own intelligence community was arguing that bombing the North would not have the desired impact because the problems were political and in the South, not military and in the North. Even if you somehow sealed South Vietnam off, therefore, the war would continue at roughly the same rate. This had been the CIA's line for the better part of a year. Nor would bombing appreciably affect North Vietnamese policy. In early March the Policy Planning Council produced a lengthy—and prescient—study that concluded that bombing would not work because Hanoi's determination was such that it would not be affected by even extensive physical destruction. If anything, bombing might strengthen the regime's control, while doing nothing to improve South Vietnamese morale. The main effect of the policy would be to increase America's stake in Vietnam and make any future extrication more difficult. Sigma I-64, a war game conducted by the Joint Chiefs of Staff on 6–9 April, achieved similar results. Air power against the North, almost all the participants concluded, would not cause Hanoi to give up the fight or do much to help matters in the South.[26]

This was essentially the same argument that Charles de Gaulle had been making. Significantly, it also corresponded closely with the analysis in London. It is striking to observe how differently from the Johnson administration the British interpreted the recent developments and future prospects in the war. Already in mid 1963 London had indicated its opposition to any expansion of the war into North Vietnam and voiced its belief that a face-saving American withdrawal under cover of an agreement was a viable option; on both these points British authorities grew more convinced in the early months of 1964. The communiqué issued after the Anglo-American talks in Washington in mid February affirmed both nations' commitment to thwarting aggression in South Vietnam and Malaysia (the confrontation between the newly formed Malaysian federation and Indonesia had in the preceding months pinned down large numbers of British forces in and around Singapore), and Lyndon Johnson got Prime Minister Alec Douglas-Home to agree that neutralization was no solution at present in Vietnam.

Behind the scenes, however, major differences were emerging over how best to approach the developments in Indochina. In the talks the British continued to disagree with the administration's determination to prevent a reconvened Geneva conference on Cambodia, which Prince Sihanouk had been urging since late 1963 and which London had agreed to forestall. Moreover, Douglas-Home, while declaring staunch British support for South Vietnam in its defense against the Vietcong, expressly ruled out any significant increase in British military assistance to the cause.[27]

In the weeks that followed, as reports flowed into London that the administration contemplated hitting North Vietnam, British analysts grew alarmed. Like the French, they had grown more convinced that such action would fail to yield the desired result. A study by the government's Joint Intelligence Committee (JIC) in late February concluded that even a complete severance of all links between North Vietnam and the Vietcong in the South (which the report called virtually impossible to bring about) would not significantly reduce the difficulty of defeating the insurgents, given their basic self-sufficiency. Moreover, an attack on the North would strengthen Hanoi-Beijing relations, would bring increased Chinese and Soviet assistance to the DRV, and would generate widespread condemnation in the international community. From the consulate in Hanoi, J. Kenneth Blackwell reported that dropping bombs on North Vietnam would do little to stop the transport of personnel and matériel from North to South and would not induce the Hanoi leaders to "throw in the sponge"; on the contrary, it would make them more determined to resist and less willing to reach a compromise agreement. A major war might well ensue. It was in any case moot to talk of North Vietnam's reaction to any attack, Blackwell added, since the Vietcong could and would carry on very effectively even without northern assistance. Therefore, "the appalling risks which an American attack on North Vietnam would run would have been incurred to little purpose. I sincerely hope the American Government will think many times before committing themselves to such a disastrous policy."[28]

Blackwell's superiors agreed. On 29 February Foreign Secretary R. A. B. Butler informed Dean Rusk that British support for U.S. policy in South Vietnam, as affirmed in the Washington communiqué, was based on the assumption that this policy would remain defensive in character and not involve any kind of expansion of the fighting—the same defensive posture, Butler said, that Britain adhered to in Malaysia. Should the administration opt for escalation, Butler emphasized, his government would have to reevaluate its position. Part of the concern in London stemmed from fears of increased domestic criticism against the government for its public backing of U.S. policy—rumors of possible impending action against the DRV received widespread play in the British press—but there can be no doubt that Butler and his colleagues endorsed the basic findings of the JIC study. That is, they believed that the southern insurgency was largely self-sustaining; that the Khanh government lacked the requisite ability and popular support to meet the challenge; that the North Vietnamese would not buckle in the face of military pressure; and that escalation across the seventeenth parallel therefore made little sense.[29]

Butler's intervention no doubt had the desired effect. Lyndon Johnson had been annoyed by Douglas-Home's refusal during the Washington talks to increase British aid to the GVN,[30] but London's clear opposition to bombing the North probably reinforced his determination to avoid any immediate expansion of the fighting if at all possible. Butler's letter added to long-standing administration concerns about the impact of an expanded war on opinion in the world community and in the United States. Bombing North Vietnam would cause considerable international outcry, some officials feared, with both foes and friends around the world seeing it as disproportionate to what the North was doing in the South. The result was sure to be increased sympathy for a political settlement along the lines proposed by de Gaulle. "What is worse," Roger Hilsman warned in a widely circulated memorandum penned shortly before he left the administration, "I think that premature action will so alarm our friends and allies and a significant segment of domestic opinion that the pressure for neutralization will become formidable." Here Hilsman undoubtedly had in mind not merely the major Western European allies but also the skepticism among some leading Democrats on Capitol Hill and elements in the media such as Walter Lippmann and the *New York Times*.[31]

Even before McNamara departed for Vietnam on 9 March, therefore, the decision had tacitly been made to hold off on attacking the North by air. But the trip was nevertheless deemed important, ranking with McNamara's visits the previous September and December. Unlike those two missions, however, which were to a large extent aimed at fact-finding, this one was not principally about gathering information, despite administration claims to the contrary. Washington officials knew very well what was happening in the war—no expedition was necessary to determine that war-weariness was endemic among the populace, that Khanh lacked popular support, and that the Vietcong continued to score gains. Rather, the chief purpose was public relations, as McNamara aimed primarily to convey to the main actors in Vietnam the administration's determination to persevere in the war. These actors included the beleaguered Nguyen Khanh and any politicians in Saigon who might be contemplating a neutralist coup. They included the leaders of the NLF and the Hanoi government. And, not least, they included the most prominent American in Saigon, Ambassador Henry Cabot Lodge.

Lodge had been among those favoring taking the war to North Vietnam, in order to send a message to Hanoi, bolster the sagging spirits in the South, and prevent any move toward a neutralist settlement. Lodge was also a leading candidate for the Republican presidential nomination, which for Lyndon Johnson made it essential that he be handled carefully. (For Johnson the most important figure in Vietnam in the early part of 1964 was not Nguyen Khanh or Ho Chi Minh; it was Henry Cabot Lodge.) Many senior officials in the administration, including LBJ, had long since grown disenchanted with Lodge's performance as ambassador, his mercurial, lone-wolf nature, his lack of management skills, his generally poor relations with underlings. But there could be no serious thought of removing him because away from Saigon he posed such a political threat to the president. In Johnson's nightmare Lodge would run for the GOP nomination as the war effort disintegrated completely, whereupon Lodge would proclaim that Vietnam could have been saved if only the administration had followed his recommendations. Little wonder that Johnson made clear that every effort must be made to mollify the ambassador, to seek his advice, to assure him that the administration was no less determined than he to see the struggle through. A principal task for McNamara on the trip would be to get Lodge to go on record as agreeing with the mission's recommendations.[32]

That the visit was not about gathering facts was clear from the start. Immediately upon arriving in South Vietnam McNamara pledged full American support for Khanh and vowed that the United States would provide South Vietnam with as much aid as necessary for as long as necessary. This method of stating conclusions before asking questions struck some observers as odd. "It is strange, on a 'fact-finding' mission, to announce decisions on arrival," remarked Gordon Etherington-Smith in a cable to London. The Briton also found it disconcerting that McNamara visited fewer provinces than on previous visits, that his stays in each were so short as to limit business to the most perfunctory briefing, and that, given the high-powered McNamara entourage, which included Khanh as well as senior American military officials, the junior officers who gave the briefings could hardly have felt free to speak their minds. Nor did the defense secretary make any effort to seek out the views of the allied diplomatic community in Saigon. Etherington-Smith expected at any moment to be summoned to meet McNamara. He waited in vain.[33]

What did McNamara actually think about the war at this point? As leader of the mission and as Johnson's most trusted Vietnam adviser, his views at the time of arrival in Saigon obviously mattered a great deal, especially in view of the predetermined "findings" of the expedition. The McNamara of 1964 has come down in history as a kind of super-technocrat, a man with an almost religious faith in the ability of number-crunching to generate success in the war, and the hubristic belief of the "Best and the Brightest" in the ultimate invincibility of American power. Most authors date his first real pessimism about the enterprise to late 1965, well after the onset of large-scale war.[34] But McNamara appears to have been beset by deep doubts even now, in early March 1964, as he boarded the plane for South Vietnam—deep doubts not merely about the outlook for the existing policy of providing aid and advisers to the GVN, but about the merits of going North. His famed hawkishness on the war in this period likely resulted not from optimism about the outlook or conviction that America's national security was at stake but from his almost slavish loyalty to his president. Lyndon Johnson had made clear he would not countenance defeat in Vietnam, and McNamara aimed to ensure it would not happen.

A close examination of the internal record gives evidence of McNamara's pessimism. In a telephone conversation with the president on the morning of 25 February he conveyed clear concern about the war and irritated Johnson by saying that he did not know what could be said publicly about the situation that could be construed as hopeful. The following week he again advised LBJ that the less said publicly about the situation, the better. "The signs I see coming through the cables are disturbing signs—poor morale in Vietnamese forces, poor morale in the armed forces, disunity, a tremendous amount of coup planning against Khanh," McNamara said. Maybe the hoped-for results would come, "but it's a very uncertain period." The secretary was even more downbeat during a dinner conversation with British ambassador Lord Harlech on the evening of 5 March, immediately before his departure for Saigon. "[McNamara] was more despondent about the situation [in Vietnam] than I have ever seen him," the ambassador reported to London. "He clearly thought that the departure of Diem but not of Nhu had on balance done harm to the Western cause." According to Harlech, McNamara said he frankly wondered whether the Khanh regime would be able in the coming months to restore morale and achieve significant popular support. If it could not, war-weariness among southerners, already rampant, would become more widespread and the outlook would be utterly bleak. "McNamara was not in a belligerent mood,"

Harlech concluded, "and although he had spoken to me previously about examining the possibilities of hurting the North Vietnamese, I gained the strong impression that unless he came back feeling that there was a reasonable chance of pulling the situation round in South Vietnam there would be no value in risking a further extension of American military commitments in the area such as would result from trying to carry the conflict over the border into the North."[35]

McNamara made a great show of being bullish on the war effort as he barnstormed the South Vietnamese countryside with Khanh and spoke to carefully choreographed crowds, but it is doubtful that the visit changed his outlook in any significant way. The mission report he presented to Johnson at a White House meeting on 16 March contained a now-familiar mixture of gloom and determination. (It speaks volumes about the mission's aims that a draft of the report was completed well before the team even arrived in Saigon.) The situation had grown much worse, McNamara noted, especially in the past ninety days, with unchecked Vietcong successes in the countryside and no signs of improved performance by the government of Nguyen Khanh. Though the United States should not at present initiate bombing of North Vietnam, it should continue to plan for such action, both through "quick reaction strikes" and in more sustained actions, as part of an intensification of pressure against Hanoi. Such escalation would be warranted, McNamara argued, because saving South Vietnam was the key to saving Southeast Asia, and because the conflict was a "test case" of American determination to thwart wars of liberation. To demonstrate that determination, the United States should make clear that it was prepared to stay in Vietnam "as long as it takes to bring the insurgency under control." In addition, it should fully support Khanh and oppose more coups, increase military aid to the Saigon government, and reject calls for neutralization.[36]

At a meeting of the NSC the following day, Johnson asked McNamara if the proposals could reverse the trend in South Vietnam. Yes, the defense secretary replied, the tide could be turned in four to six months, provided the administration moved energetically to implement the proposals. After Maxwell Taylor affirmed JCS support for the report, the president summarized the alternatives to the proposed program: putting in more American forces, withdrawal, or neutralizing the area. None would work, he said. "The course we are following is the only realistic alternative. It will have the maximum effectiveness with the minimum loss." He added that adopting the plan would not foreclose going to an alternative in the future if the situation did not improve. Johnson asked if anyone objected to the proposals. No one did. That day the McNamara report was implemented verbatim as NSAM 288.[37]

The importance of NSAM 288 in laying the foundation for major escalation that followed a year later can scarcely be exaggerated, as the chroniclers of the *Pentagon Papers* well understood. The document, they wrote, "outlined a program that called for considerable enlargement of the U.S. effort. It involved an assumption by the United States of a greater part of the task, and an increased involvement by the United States in the internal affairs of South Vietnam, and for these reasons it carried with it an enlarged commitment of U.S. prestige to the success of our effort in that area." Henceforth the United States would be committed not merely to advising the Saigon government but to maintaining it. Max Frankel of the *New York Times*, though not knowledgeable about the NSAM or its particulars, understood that an important moment had come. "The decision to hold the line," he wrote in the paper on 21 March, "lies at the end of a long reasoning process by which the administration has rejected all thought of a graceful withdrawal."[38]

It came through loud and clear in the report and in the discussion surrounding it, this continuing American opposition to a negotiated disengagement. Also unmistakable was the continuing fear that the momentum for such a solution might be unstoppable. McNamara told Johnson that the United States must steer clear of a negotiated settlement involving neutralization and a withdrawal of the American military presence, because this "would simply mean a Communist takeover in South Vietnam." He conceded, however, that a French-inspired neutralist plot to overthrow Khanh was possible, because de Gaulle's policy and the anti-Americanism in Saigon provided "constant fuel to neutralist sentiment and the coup possibility." A CIA report the same week was still more alarming, speaking of "various reports" out of Saigon that even Khanh himself, the man to whom McNamara had pledged full and complete U.S. support and who in January had appealed to Washington because of his anti-neutralist stance, might consider neutralization. According to these reports, Khanh had long-standing close ties with the French and was "capable of changing sides." Though the CIA found the reports unconvincing, their mere existence certainly added to American apprehension.[39]

But the question remained: how precisely was the pressure for an early end to the war to be contained? The proposals in NSAM 288 needed four to six months to work, and it was imperative to delay any negotiations for at least that long. After high-level meetings with Bohlen in mid March, the administration opted for more of the same: efforts in Saigon to prevent a neutralist coup and more pressure on the Paris government. So anxious were U.S. officials to make an impression on de Gaulle that they not only decided to have Bohlen meet with the French president when the latter returned from the Caribbean, but also considered having Lodge fly to Paris "to explain the realities of the situation to de Gaulle." Only Lodge's strong and repeated objections, on the grounds that his visiting Paris would send the wrong message to Khanh, killed the idea, but Johnson refused to rule it out for the future. A presidential cable reminded Lodge on 20 March that there was much work to be done in Saigon. "Your mission," Johnson wrote, "is precisely for the purpose of knocking down the idea of neutralization wherever it rears its ugly head and that on this point I think that nothing is more important than to stop neutralist talk wherever we can and by whatever means we can."[40]

Lodge did as ordered. In the weeks that followed, he worked hard to thwart any coup plotting by disaffected South Vietnamese officials, held meetings with potentially neutralist Buddhist leaders, and sought repeated assurances from Khanh that he did not favor an accommodation with the communists. But the ambassador did not stop there. It pleased him that the Johnson message included the phrase "wherever we can," and he took it as evidence of Washington's determination to continue to work on de Gaulle. To spur the administration on, he continued to warn of Gaullist machinations. "France and the U.S. are headed for a collision as regards Vietnam," he warned in one cable. "The French can do a tremendous amount of damage here," he noted in another, "and they are doing it every day in many subtle but effective ways. . . . [T]he tremendous American outlay of effort and blood make it impossible to condone what they are doing." Lodge also enlisted the help of Averell Harriman. The veteran diplomat, no longer the proponent of early negotiations he had been early in the Kennedy years, urged Rusk to tell de Gaulle that his actions were looked on with great displeasure in Washington. "I am not suggesting threats because I do not know anything we can do against him, but he should know that he faces American displeasure including that of the President. He has been allowed so far to get away with his actions without the slightest personal embarrassment. I think we are only encouraging future difficulties if we allow this to continue."[41]

Rusk agreed, but the question was what exactly could be done. At lunch on 24 March Rusk, McNamara, McGeorge Bundy, and the president discussed this issue in the context of the impending Bohlen–de Gaulle meeting. The four men agreed on a set of instructions from the president, which were dispatched to Bohlen later that day. "You should point out," the cable said, that "we have come to this determination [to stand firm] after having thoroughly examined and rejected arguments for disengagement or for political negotiation starting from current circumstances." It was for this reason that the United States had implemented NSAM 288. The cable instructed Bohlen to seek a public statement from the general, prior to the up-coming SEATO meeting in Manila, "that the idea of 'neutralization' does not apply to the attitudes or policies of the Government of Vietnam or its friends in the face of the current communist aggression." De Gaulle did not need to drop this idea "for eternity," Johnson continued. "What we want is a statement that he does not think it applies now." The cable left it to the ambassador to decide how best to frame these arguments but emphasized that he had to make clear that Washington expected the Paris government, "as an ally, to adopt an attitude of cooperation rather than obstruction-ism in this critical area of United States interest." The following day, as if to underline the importance of getting exactly the right message across to de Gaulle, Rusk sent Bohlen a cable of his own.[42]

All the American preparations came to naught. When Bohlen called on de Gaulle on 2 April, he carefully outlined American concerns as instructed and requested that the French president make a public statement in sup-port of the joint U.S.–South Vietnamese efforts. De Gaulle refused, agree-ing only to say that he saw neutralization as the best hope—slim though it was—to prevent a Hanoi takeover. Did this mean neutralization of both Vietnams? Bohlen asked. Not as a first step, the general responded; initially only the South should be neutralized. There was no real government in Saigon, he declared, and thus no substantial support for the Khanh regime among the people. The war was essentially the same one the French had been waging since the end of World War II, and the Vietnamese people were weary of two decades of fighting. The sooner Americans agreed to neutralization for Vietnam—perhaps through the mechanism of a Geneva-type conference including the Chinese—the better off they would be.[43]

The full extent of the administration's failure to influence French think-ing was demonstrated in the Philippines a couple of weeks later, during the annual meeting of the SEATO alliance.[44] On 12 April, before the meeting began, Secretary of State Rusk and French Foreign Minister Maurice Couve de Murville discussed the issue at length, with only minimum staff pres-ent. "Extremely frank" is how one of the staffers described the conver-sation. The United States was in a hopeless situation in Vietnam, Couve began, because it had mistaken a political conflict for a military one. The political situation in South Vietnam was "rotten," with an army but no government, and with a populace that did not want to fight. In essence, therefore, the United States had no policy. In fact, Couve went on, the sit-uation was exactly the same as the one the French experienced in Vietnam in 1954 and in Algeria in 1962. In the latter case, France had complete physical control of the country, "but in spite of that we lost the battle. You can't win without the people." But, Rusk asked, were there large numbers of Vietnamese and Algerians fighting with the French in those instances? Yes, Couve replied: two hundred thousand Vietnamese and large numbers of Algerians.

But what was the French alternative, Rusk demanded to know. The key was China, Couve said. China was an imperialist, expansionist country, rightly feared by the peoples of Southeast Asia, but China's main interests lay in internal development and in reducing threats to its geographic approaches. More than anything, the Beijing leadership feared an American presence close to its southern borders, and it would, Couve predicted, renounce any claims to Southeast Asia in exchange for a secure southern flank. The Chinese, in other words, would agree to the kind of neutralization proposed by France. "It was a *tour de force* of simple logic, if the premise of Chinese policy was correct," Assistant Secretary of State William Bundy, who was one of those present, later wrote. But it failed to move Rusk (or Bundy) at the time. The secretary, as he was wont to do when the subject of a political settlement came up, pointed to the Laos agreements as evidence that neutralization would not work. Couve responded that it was the Vietnam conflict that had complicated the Laos situation. Besides, he added, Laos was no longer a Cold War crisis in the way that Vietnam was. On the most basic level, therefore, Laotian neutralization had been a success.[45]

The French foreign minister could scarcely have been more forthright in articulating his country's position on the war. He had dismissed the entire rationale behind American policy as mistaken and argued that, as a result, the U.S. effort could never succeed. As France had failed when it pursued a military solution in Indochina, so would the United States.[46] Any hopes Rusk may have had that Couve would downplay the disagreement in the SEATO sessions that followed were soon dashed. When a communiqué was drafted affirming the vital importance of preserving the independence of South Vietnam, France, alone among the participants, chose to abstain (Pakistan, also opposed to U.S. policy, opted to stay away from the meeting altogether).[47] The action greatly irritated Rusk—according to a British official in attendance, Rusk was openly contemptuous of Couve during the sessions—but he tried to put the best face on the situation. The prospect of French cooperation might be lost for the foreseeable future, he told Johnson in cable, but the other allies were on board. "There is no disposition among others, " he said, "to let France set the tone."[48]

That claim was not false, but it was not entirely true either. Even though the SEATO members and others in the western alliance were unwilling to let Paris "set the tone" on the Vietnam question, a growing number of them were coming to share the basic thrust of de Gaulle's position. The

British had joined in isolating the French at Manila, but as Rusk well knew, the London government shared both Paris's low opinion of the GVN and its wholesale opposition to any expansion of the war into North Vietnam. Among Canadian and West German officials, as well, there were growing doubts about Vietnam's importance to western security and deep doubts that a stable Saigon government could ever be created. What is more, a study by the State Department's Intelligence and Research desk indicated that a number of Asian countries, among them India, Pakistan, Burma, and Cambodia, would welcome neutralization, either for South Vietnam alone or for a unified Vietnam.[49]

This unwillingness of America's friends to see the importance of preserving an independent, noncommunist South Vietnam rankled Rusk more than perhaps any other issue during his entire tenure as secretary of state. (Angered by London's policy, he once told a British journalist: "When the Russians invade Sussex, don't expect us to come and help you.")[50] In April 1964 he could be thankful that few of these governments were prepared to follow France's lead and publicly come out against American policy, but he knew just how thin the veneer of support was. Moreover, Rusk understood that, in the event of an escalated war, it would be essential to have the backing of the major western governments, and that the best way to ensure this would be to make them actual partners in the war effort. Greater allied involvement would also please lawmakers on Capitol Hill and send a powerful message to the Hanoi leadership. And so, in April the State Department quietly launched a "more flags" campaign designed to get greater allied contributions to the war effort. Officials knew from the start that it was going to be a hard sell indeed.

5 Rumblings of Discontent

Lyndon Johnson shared his top diplomat's frustration with the tepid response from friends abroad. But Johnson could take comfort in the fact that at home his policies, both domestic and foreign, continued to receive broad public support. Indeed, in retrospect it could be said that the spring months of 1964 were among the best of his entire presidency. His legislative agenda was on track, his public approval ratings were high, and he received high marks for his handling of the difficult months following the assassination. It had taken some time, but he and his wife, Lady Bird, had begun to feel at home in the White House. In foreign affairs, Johnson's emphasis on continuity with the policies of his predecessor had worked well. Though he and his advisers were laying plans for an escalated American commitment to Vietnam, they worked hard to prevent any major public debate on the matter. To a large extent, they succeeded—less because of their skill at deception, it should be noted, than because of public apathy. Warnings of impending defeat and rumors of wider military action were not hard to come by in the nation's press in the spring of 1964, but for most Americans, Vietnam remained a place and an issue of which they knew little and cared less. Most people, envisioning a U.S. commitment that stayed more or less the same, supported the effort to preserve a noncommunist South Vietnam.

Even now, however, a close observer could see ominous rumblings of discontent among influential voices in American society on the subject of Southeast Asia. For these observers, who *were* paying close attention to developments, it was by now starkly clear that neither the coups against Diem and the Minh junta nor the steadily increasing American commitment to South Vietnam had turned the military situation around; on the contrary, these actions had been accompanied by a progressive deterioration of the Saigon government's position in the war. Some clung to the hope that the current course could be successful, even as they conceded that the prospects

for that did not look good. The *Christian Science Monitor* said that a precipitate American withdrawal would be disastrous and that only the Vietnamese themselves could win the war. "A safe way must be found," the
paper declared, "to lessen rather than increase United States military involvement in a war that can never be won by military action alone." The
Los Angeles Times also preached staying the current course in an editorial
notable for its lack of confidence and conviction: "Present U.S. forces, with
the new Khanh government apparently trying to pull its own weight, may
be able to do the job of halting the Red putsch. It is worth a try." And veteran columnist Emmet John Hughes acknowledged the seriousness of the
situation but counseled patience. He assured readers that "no one close to
the President can imagine his risking such military action as could turn
Vietnam into another Korea."[1]

Others, however, saw the time for patience ending fast, saw the outlook as so grim that the United States would soon be faced with a critical
choice: whether to drastically escalate the American presence in the war,
thereby changing its very nature, or to move in the other direction, toward
some form of negotiated withdrawal.[2] Already in early March *New York
Times* reporter David Halberstam wrote of this stark and looming choice,
and in the succeeding weeks many others followed suit.[3] Some of these observers favored escalation. The syndicated columnist Joseph Alsop, for example, consistently pressed for a greater application of American military
power in Indochina, as on occasion did columnists David Lawrence and
C. L. Sulzberger. Once and future Republican presidential candidate Richard Nixon, who since February had warned against any move toward neutralization, returned from a visit to Saigon in early April and derided Johnson's policy as "soft" and overly defensive-minded; he strongly hinted that
he favored taking the war to the North. Arizona senator Barry Goldwater,
a leading candidate for the Republican presidential nomination, tended toward a more cryptic approach in these weeks, but he too spoke of the likely
need for wider military action, as did Democratic senator Thomas Dodd of
Connecticut. *Time* and *U.S. News & World Report* adhered to a similarly
tough approach, with the latter declaring that Vietnam was being lost and
that the war should be "carried to North Vietnam—the base of key manpower, supplies, and training."[4]

These pro-escalation voices were formidable elements in elite American
opinion, and the administration paid them due attention. Yet what is most
striking is how few individuals and publications in the spring of 1964 were
willing to go on record favoring escalation in Vietnam. Nixon's calls for
expanded action were echoed by virtually none of his fellow Republican
leaders, some of whom, indeed, wanted to pull out of Vietnam. (The *Los*

Angeles Times and the *Christian Science Monitor* in April spoke of internal GOP divisions on Vietnam and its importance to U.S. security.) Alsop likewise was almost alone among prominent journalists in his stridency.[5]

In comparison, those who took the other side on the escalate/de-escalate question, in favor of a reduced American commitment to South Vietnam, were more numerous and more vocal—and more of a concern to the Johnson administration. They were, to be sure, not a large group in absolute terms—the vast majority of Vietnam watchers in the press and on Capitol Hill still avoided casting the Vietnam options in dramatic either/or terms—but merely that they outnumbered the advocates of escalation is significant. These critics foresaw trouble ahead for any policy that relied on military means to salvage the situation, and they rejected the assertion the conflict was the result of outside aggression against South Vietnam. Many were fast coming to the conclusion that the war simply could not be won at any price acceptable to the United States, which meant that the only viable policy was one emphasizing diplomacy and disengagement. The end result would likely be a communist Vietnam under Hanoi rule, but this result would not necessarily affect other parts of Asia. Moreover, it ought to be possible to delay reunification long enough to shore up other, more vital, parts of the region. This kind of "defeatist" thinking was anathema to the president and his advisers (the Nixon-Alsop analysis was not; as we have seen, the administration was secretly planning precisely the kind of expansion of the war advocated by Nixon), but they were concerned about the problems it could generate for their efforts to raise support for an expanded war.

On Capitol Hill, discontent was growing among many in Johnson's own party. Democratic senators Wayne Morse of Oregon and Ernest Gruening of Alaska spoke out almost daily against a wider war and in favor of negotiations. The two charged that the conflict was a civil war between "two tyrannies," and that the United States was unjustifiably participating in an unnecessary war, which it could never hope to win. "We have no more right to be in South Vietnam," Morse argued, "than Russia has in East Germany." Any expansion of the war to North Vietnam would make the United States an aggressor under the UN charter. The senator said that the conflict was "not worth the life of a single American boy," and he blasted the administration for adopting an antidiplomacy position during the recent SEATO meeting in Manila. That almost all of the SEATO allies refused to commit themselves in a meaningful way to the war was dramatic proof of the hopelessness of the American cause, Morse charged, and he called on the administration to fully explore de Gaulle's proposals and to commit itself to negotiations leading to a Laos-type neutralization. Gruening spoke in similar terms and said in a 10 March Senate speech that the time had come for a "little hard rethinking." The war was not winnable in any meaningful sense, he declared, which meant that the nation should opt for withdrawal "with the knowledge that the game was not worth the candle." A continuation of the U.S. commitment could only hurt America's image abroad, Gruening charged.[6]

Morse and Gruening were not among the august body's more influential members. Still, administration officials paid close attention to the two lawmakers' campaign and how it played in the Senate.[7] James C. Thomson Jr., an Asian specialist who was William Bundy's deputy at the State Department's Far East desk, noted in an internal memo that although the two senators "appeared to have made no admitted converts in this period, they have encountered little rebuttal from their colleagues." In fact, Thomson added, much of the questioning they had received from colleagues had been friendly, which added credence to reports that "a growing number of Senators are privately sympathetic with the Morse-Gruening position."[8]

This was true. Growing numbers of senators were privately sympathetic to the thrust of what Morse and Gruening were saying—that Vietnam was not worth the loss of American lives, that the outlook in the war effort was exceedingly bleak, that avenues of disengagement should be actively explored. By late spring this group included Democrats Frank Church of Idaho, Allen Ellender of Louisiana, William Fulbright of Arkansas, Albert Gore of Tennessee, Mike Mansfield of Montana, John McClellan of Arkansas, George McGovern of North Dakota, Gaylord Nelson of Wisconsin, Richard Russell of Georgia, and (according to Thomson) Russell Long of Louisiana and Stuart Symington of Missouri, as well as Republicans Len Jordan of Idaho, John Sherman Cooper of Kentucky, and George Aiken of Vermont. Church, for example, wrote to one constituent that any expansion of the war would be a mistake since, unlike the conflict in Korea, the conflict in Vietnam was not a war of external aggression but primarily "a civil war fought between the South Vietnamese." To another he expressed the fear that the more the United States, as a "White Western nation," committed to the war, the more it would benefit communist propaganda. Nelson declared that unless the South Vietnamese showed more of a commitment to the fight there was "no reason to continue pouring money down a rat hole" and that the United States needed to "face up to the question right now of whether it would be wise to disengage and extricate ourselves." McGovern, also privately, said that Charles de Gaulle's call for negotiations leading to neutralization should be actively investigated.[9]

Publicly, these and other Democrats kept largely silent, much to the administration's relief. Church told Armed Services Committee chairman

Richard Russell that he wanted the United States to get out of Vietnam but did not want to make a speech about it. Russell understood completely. One of Lyndon Johnson's closest confidants, he shared Church's sentiments and agreed with much of what Morse and Gruening were saying—after Gruening's 10 March speech Russell called the Alaskan to praise his comments and even sent him a congratulatory note. But Russell was not prepared to offer that praise on the Senate floor. Like many of his Democratic colleagues he was anxious to avoid a party rift on Vietnam, particularly with Johnson still fairly new to the presidency and about to enter a tough election campaign—and particularly given the president's frequent private assertions to them that he saw no option but to maintain the American commitment. Russell also felt genuinely confused about exactly how U.S. disengagement could be brought about, which no doubt further inclined him to stay mum.[10]

In a telephone conversation in late May Russell told the president that he thought the outlook in the war was near hopeless ("It's the damn worst mess I ever saw"), that Vietnam did not matter ("It isn't important a damn bit"), and that a lot of people agreed with Wayne Morse's position. The South Vietnamese could not be depended on to fight, Russell told LBJ, and the American people were in no mood to send U.S. troops. But the Georgian did not insist on the need to withdraw. "If it got down to . . . just pulling out, I'd get out," Russell said. "But then I don't know. There's undoubtedly some middle ground somewhere. If I was going to get out, I'd get the same crowd that got rid of old Diem to get rid of these people and get some fellow in there that said he wished to hell we would get out. That would give us a good excuse for getting out." Russell concluded, "I wish I could help ya. God knows, I do. It's a terrific quandary that we're in over there. We're just in the quicksands up to our very necks."[11]

Russell made up one third of the Senate Democratic leadership on foreign policy. The other two in the group, Senate majority leader Mike Mansfield and Foreign Relations Committee chairman William Fulbright, also opposed a wider war and favored greater efforts in the direction of a negotiated settlement. Mansfield's attraction to neutralization and opposition to escalation had if anything increased since the start of the year, and his position was well enough known that the press could write of it in general terms. White House officials understood what kind of impact the widely respected leader of the Senate (who also happened to be a former professor of Asian history) could have if he challenged administration policy in the Morse-Gruening fashion. They worked hard in the spring months to keep him contained, to convince him that a party split on the matter would only play into the hands of the GOP at home and the communists in Southeast

Asia. To a large extent the strategy worked; Mansfield made few critical comments in public, even as the war effort deteriorated rapidly in April and May.[12]

As for Fulbright, he had for at least a year been dubious about America's prospects in Vietnam, and he had given much thought to the prospects for some kind of negotiated extrication. In December 1963 administration officials had worried that he might come out in opposition to the war. In the months that followed, however, the Arkansan stayed on board in support of U.S. policy, much to the administration's relief. Convinced that any kind of Americanization of the war would be grave mistake, Fulbright accepted White House promises that it sought no escalation of the fighting. Uncertain about the prospects for any kind of neutralization formula, and intensely loyal to his friend and fellow southerner Lyndon Johnson, he avoided raising the large questions. When a journalist asked him why he kept his reservations quiet, Fulbright responded: "I don't think Senators spouting off help the situation." On the rare occasions when Fulbright spoke out publicly on the war in this period, he tended indeed to express support for U.S. policy. In a much-publicized 25 March speech entitled "Old Myths and New Realities," Fulbright called for greater U.S. flexibility in dealing with the communist world, but in Vietnam he saw no option but to maintain the current policy of aid and advisers to the Saigon government. Negotiations were at present not a feasible option, he declared, and he noted that "it should be clear to all concerned that the United States will continue to meet its obligations and fulfill its commitments with respect to Vietnam."[13]

This unwillingness of top Democratic lawmakers to join Morse and Gruening in publicly opposing the war was vital in allowing the administration to keep Vietnam from becoming a major national issue, not only in the spring of 1964 but throughout the year and into 1965. But it in no way diminishes the accuracy and importance of James Thomson's point that support for the war effort was thin and getting thinner on Capitol Hill, with much private support for the views of Wayne Morse and Ernest Gruening. What is more, administration officials were well aware of this, which was why they were so pleased with Fulbright's comments on Vietnam in the "Old Myths" speech—such forthright and supportive language was seldom heard from prominent legislators in the spring of 1964. Had Lyndon Johnson opted for disengagement via a great-power conference, or at least chosen to give that option serious consideration, or followed the Russell plan of finding a South Vietnamese leader who would ask the United States to leave, he would have encountered little opposition from the leading figures in his own party; of that there can be little doubt.

Other prominent voices in American society were also coming in this period to echo the Morse-Gruening line. In the academic community the respected political scientist Hans J. Morgenthau and the veteran Vietnam-watcher Bernard Fall, among others, became more vocal in opposing a military solution to what they perceived to be a civil conflict. In a 15 March *Washington Post* op-ed piece that some administration aides deemed important enough to circulate among themselves, Morgenthau attacked the idea that Vietnam was a war of external aggression against South Vietnam and that therefore neutralization equaled surrender. "The war," Morgenthau argued, "is first of all a South Vietnamese civil war, aided and abetted by North Vietnam but neither created nor sustained by it. Anybody who has traveled in Vietnam must recognize that anything more than token support extended by North Vietnam to, say, the guerrillas in the Mekong Delta, over a distance of 1,000 miles and carried by human bodies, is a physical impossibility."[14] Fall was more ambivalent about the nature of the war, but he too advocated a greater American effort in the direction of diplomacy. "There must be negotiation and settlement sooner or later," he wrote the same week in *The Reporter*, "unless the Johnson administration wishes to leave the Vietnamese war in what has been called the shadow-land between unattainable victory and unacceptable surrender."[15]

Equally worrisome to policymakers were the growing concerns expressed by important elements in the American press. In March *The New Republic* laid out the choices facing the administration and concluded that only one, negotiations leading an internationally guaranteed neutralization agreement, made sense. In May the magazine said the White House "runs the risk of being successfully accused of wasting American lives in a war that will last another 10 years or more." *Newsweek* subtly questioned whether the administration was doing enough to promote a diplomatic solution and spoke of "growing and disturbing similarities" between the French and American experiences in Indochina. Columnist Joseph Kraft likewise wondered why the administration seemed to be ignoring diplomatic avenues.[16] Then there was the *New York Times*, which had continued, despite administration pressure, to press in its editorials for a political solution to the conflict. U.S. officials were worried, as they had been the previous autumn—the amount of time they spent fretting about the *Times*'s pronouncements on the war throughout 1964 is graphic evidence of the respect they accorded the paper and its ability to shape elite opinion.[17]

In mid April National Security Adviser McGeorge Bundy, as he had the previous November, dispatched Michael Forrestal to the paper to explain the administration's policy and how opposition to that policy could be harmful. In a contentious discussion with the paper's Robert Kleiman, Forrestal bluntly asked if the *Times* was contemplating a change in its editorial policy. Kleiman answered no and even said he was in the process of writing an editorial attacking the concept of total victory in Vietnam. The administration had not set any real goals for its efforts in Vietnam, he complained, with the result that Hanoi had no choice but to continue to escalate its efforts every time Washington did. What was needed, therefore, was an affirmation by the administration that it was interested in eventual neutrality and willing to return to the 1954 Geneva Conference. Kleiman conceded that de Gaulle was a "kibitzer at the bridge game" but argued that the French leader had stimulated discussion on the core questions of U.S. policy and should be listened to. A frustrated Forrestal charged Kleiman with distorting the American position and warned that irresponsible talk of neutralization was not only unrealistic but dangerous.[18]

If the *Times*'s editorial policy was problematic for the administration, so was the ever mounting criticism from Walter Lippmann. Lippmann had become more outspoken in his criticism of American policy since the previous summer, much to the dismay of Johnson officials. Lippmann's influence on his journalistic peers, viewed in hindsight, had probably waned somewhat by the mid 1960s. But to White House officials at the time he remained a profoundly important voice in the nation's press corps, capable of shaping media opinion on a wide variety of issues. Lippmann's syndicated column appeared in well over a hundred American newspapers, they knew, and was required reading in chancelleries all over the globe. To Lyndon Johnson, certainly, no one was as important.[19] Little wonder, therefore, that Lippmann's frequent pronouncements on the Vietnam issue during the first half of 1964 (he devoted more columns to it than to any other single issue) resulted in considerable consternation among American policymakers and to concerted efforts to persuade him to change his tune. It began as a courtship in early 1964, with Bundy and other senior aides using lunches, dinners, and private White House briefings to woo the columnist with assurances that they welcomed his advice and shared many of his concerns. It ended in 1966 and 1967 (by which time Johnson and Lippmann had broken completely) with the "Lippmann Project," in which a team of aides combed through everything the columnist had written since the 1930s, looking for errors, inconsistencies, and failed predictions that could be used to publicly rebut his arguments.[20]

Lippmann still believed, in the spring of 1964, that Lyndon Johnson could be persuaded to find a way to extricate the United States from the conflict. But he was worried that Johnson, faced with a rapidly deteriorating situation in South Vietnam, was actively considering expanding the war. He determined that he would have to step up his opposition to such a move.

Now was the time to move energetically in the direction of diplomacy leading to an eventual U.S. withdrawal, he believed, because once American troops were committed, withdrawal would be almost impossible. A Francophile and a longtime admirer of de Gaulle, Lippmann was more and more convinced that the French view of the conflict was correct, a conviction that was strengthened in early May during a series of meetings in Paris with top French officials, including Pompidou and Couve de Murville. (He did not see de Gaulle, who was recovering from prostate surgery.) The columnist returned to Washington determined to voice his support for disengagement in print and perhaps at the White House, even as he sensed that the administration was moving in the opposite direction, toward an enlarged war.[21]

Lippmann's suspicions seemed borne out when he met with McGeorge Bundy at the White House on 19 May. "Well, what's the French plan?" Bundy, in a belligerent mood, said as soon as Lippmann walked in the door. Startled, Lippmann replied that he did not answer questions posed in such a tone, and that Bundy was clearly not in the proper frame of mind to listen in any case. Bundy apologized but kept pressing, insisting that de Gaulle's neutralization was merely a formula for a communist takeover. "Mac, please don't talk in such clichés," Lippmann countered. A Titoist government, he said, was the best the United States could hope to get. Bundy replied that it would be awful if Americans died in Vietnam only to see the communists take power, but Lippmann was undaunted. The next morning he rose early and wrote a column that extolled neutralization as the best means for the United States to extricate itself from an incipient disaster.

"We are missing the main point and we are stultifying our influence," he wrote, "when we dismiss the French policies as not really serious, as expressions of personal pique or personal vanity on the part of General de Gaulle, as inspired by 'anti-Americanism' and a wish to embarrass the U.S." The French leader at least had a framework, however sketchy, whereas the Johnson administration had "no credible policy for winning the war or for ending it." Indeed, the only end envisioned by Washington, Lippmann charged, was "the unconditional surrender of the enemy," a stance that served only to lower the morale in Southeast Asia. "We are supporting and promoting a cruel and nasty war that has no visible end," he wrote. "There is no light at the end of the tunnel. I have heard it said by people in Washington that we must fight on in South Viet-Nam for 10 or 20 years. That may sound stout-hearted in Washington but it is a dismal prospect for the villagers of Vietnam. What we are offering the Vietnamese people is altogether demoralizing."[22]

Three days later Lippmann had a long talk with Fulbright about neutralization, and on the twenty-seventh he was again called to the White House for an afternoon meeting. At 11:30 that morning, Bundy and Johnson discussed the columnist's position on the phone:

LBJ: What does Lippmann think [we] ought to do?

BUNDY: . . . What he really thinks is that you should provide a diplomatic structure within which the thing can go under the control of Hanoi and walk away from it. . . .

LBJ: You mean he thinks that Hanoi ought to take South Vietnam?

BUNDY: Yes, sir—diplomatically.

LBJ: Um-hmm.

BUNDY: Maybe by calling a neutralization and removing American force and letting it slip away the way Laos did—[corrects himself:] *would*, if we didn't do anything, and *will*, if we don't do anything. And we would guarantee the neutrality in some sort of treaty. . . . I'm sorry. I'm not sure I'm the best person to describe Lippmann's views because I don't agree with them.[23]

A little after four o'clock, Lippmann was ushered into the Oval Office. Johnson, McNamara, Bundy, and Undersecretary of State George Ball were waiting for him. Like Bundy the week before, Johnson asked Lippmann how neutralization could keep the communists from taking power. There was no guarantee, the columnist replied, but neither was there a viable alternative. Any military approach would fail, just as it had failed for France. Johnson was unconvinced. He restated what by now had become the standard administration line whenever the French analogy was offered: America's power was far greater than that of France, and its objectives more noble. On the central question of the progress of the war effort, the two men also disagreed. Johnson pushed a stack of top-secret reports across his desk, which, he said, showed that the tide was turning against the communists. Lippmann replied that he had been told by French officials and American journalists that the war was continuing to go badly.[24]

The journalist left the Oval Office further convinced that Johnson was leaning toward a military solution. He hit the idea hard in his column the following day. "In spite of the endless official assurances of how the struggle [is] being won, there has never been a time when a military victory, or anything like a military victory, has been possible," he wrote. "It is not easy for any country to repair its mistakes, especially those in which it has invested lives, money, and moral judgments. But the original mistake [of intervening] in Southeast Asia must be repaired. The way to do this is to go to a conference. . . . [E]ven if the prospects of a conference are not brilliant, the military outlook in South Viet-Nam is dismal beyond words."[25]

"Dismal beyond words" was not a phrase U.S. officials would utter in public in midspring 1964, but it pretty much summed up their private assessment of the war. McNamara had visited Saigon again in May and had come away convinced that the situation had worsened since his last visit.[26] Hardly a week now went by without a major Vietcong attack, and the number of people and amount of territory under Vietcong control had increased steadily.[27] ARVN desertion rates remained high. Frequent leadership changes continued at the province level (in Long An alone, there had been six province chiefs in recent weeks), and the Khanh government remained fragmented by dissension and distrust. Rumors of an impending neutralist coup continued to circulate in Saigon. McNamara also found morale at the U.S. embassy to be at an all-time low, with officials divided on how to turn the situation around. Some, such as Ambassador Lodge, favored extending the war to the North; others thought such action could not be attempted until the South was politically stable. On his return, the secretary of defense briefed top officials at an NSC meeting on 15 May and later discussed his findings further with Bundy, Rusk, and the president. The Vietnam problem, he told them, showed no signs of diminishing. McNamara reiterated the point in a follow-up draft memorandum coauthored with William Bundy and CIA director John McCone on 18 May. In the absence of American action against North Vietnam the battle for Indochina could very well be lost by the latter part of 1964, the three warned Johnson. "In Viet-Nam, the likely sequence would be the replacement of Khanh by a neutralist regime that would ask us to leave."[28]

The same grim message was articulated by other American observers in Washington and Saigon. A 15 May CIA memorandum prepared for Director McCone labeled the situation in Southeast Asia "extremely fragile," with no signs that the various adverse trends (Vietcong successes, GVN dissension, popular war-weariness) were yet "bottoming out." McCone, in discussing this memo on the telephone with Dean Rusk, called the situation on the ground much more critical than indicated by McNamara's trip report. In another mid-May memorandum, put together by staff in Saigon, the Agency said the Khanh government was "confronting great odds" in its efforts to survive and warned that a sudden and complete collapse of morale in South Vietnam was possible. By the end of the year, the memo cautioned, the United States might be "unable to rally effectively the friendly forces necessary" to preserve a noncommunist South Vietnam. The State Department, in its correspondence with the U.S. embassy in Saigon, struck a similar tone. And Lodge, in a series of cables in the middle of May, wondered if defeat could be averted much longer in the absence of dramatic and substantial American action. He warned of the growing religious dissension in South Vietnam, the anti-Khanh machinations of the Buddhists, and the possibility of a Duong Van Minh–directed coup against Khanh, a development that "might create the very [neutralist] developments we wish to discourage."[29]

Lyndon Johnson needed no convincing. To Lippmann he had claimed that the military outlook in Vietnam was brightening, but inside he knew better. "We're not getting it done," Johnson had told McNamara at the end of April. "We're losing. So we need something new." Two weeks later, on 13 May, he told McGeorge Bundy of the need to "get the Joint Chiefs to start stepping that thing up and do some winning and do a little stuff in the North . . . some way or another. . . . We just can't sit idly by and do nothing." One possibility, he told Bundy a week after that, would be to have Americans assume much of the responsibility for running South Vietnam's government.[30]

Johnson did not relish this prospect. He hoped it could be avoided. More than he had let on to Lippmann, he shared the journalist's pessimistic diagnosis of the Vietnam situation, shared his and other skeptics' fears that the United States might be slipping into another major war on the Asian mainland, one that might well be unwinnable. Even on the question of whether Vietnam was worth fighting for LBJ could sound much like these critics. "What the hell is Vietnam worth to me?" he bellowed at Bundy in late May. "What is Laos worth to me? What is it worth to this country? Now, we've got a treaty but, hell, everybody else's got a treaty out there and they're not doing anything about it." Even as he said those things, however, Johnson could not bring himself to give serious thought to disengagement. "I don't think it's worth fighting for and I don't think we can get out," he told Bundy in a line that summarized his state of mind on the war. Time and again in the spring he would say that America had stark options in Vietnam, including withdrawal and escalation, but he would always frame these choices in such a way that standing firm appeared the only reasonable option. Withdrawal was equated with "cutting and running," with being chased out by the communists, with appeasement. Of Mansfield's plan for neutralization, Johnson told Bundy, "it's just as milquetoast as it can be. He['s] got no spine at all." A conference, he assured Russell in late May, "ain't gonna do a damn bit of good."[31]

The advocacy of top presidential aides mattered here. Bundy, McNamara, and Rusk all advised sticking it out in Vietnam, through escalation if necessary. Had the three of them marched into the Oval Office one spring day and declared that disengagement via a conference was the only sensible option, no doubt Johnson would have listened. Perhaps he would have followed their advice. But perhaps not. The role of the three advisers in the

decision making was not quite as important as is often suggested. The vast
internal record does not reveal a president who was intimidated by these
men to any significant degree; indeed, the one who more often than not
did the intimidating was Johnson.[32] Nor does the record reveal a president
who had to be persuaded on the war and how to manage it. Johnson was as
committed to the defense of South Vietnam as anyone in his administration—not as optimistic as some, not as convinced that the outcome was
crucial to America's national security, but just as committed. Talk of disengagement he equated with softness, with being weak. Withdrawal might
start the dominoes falling and would certainly lead to a loss of prestige
abroad. More than that, it would lead to a loss of the Democratic Party's
prestige at home, and his own personal prestige. Averse as he might have
been to expanding America's involvement in the fighting, he always preferred that option to getting out.

The administration's fear of traveling down any road that might lead to
neutralization for Vietnam and withdrawal for the United States was amply demonstrated when the crisis in Laos flared up again in mid May. A
large-scale offensive by the communist Pathet Lao and disruptive activity by the right wing threatened the very survival of the fragile government of neutralist prime minister Souvanna Phouma. France, which had favored great-power action on Laos for some time, immediately issued a formal
proposal that the 1962 Geneva Conference be reconvened. Within days India, Cambodia, and the Soviet Union announced their support. For months
Americans had worried about precisely this scenario—a sudden deterioration in Vientiane and in the countryside, followed by international pressure for a conference. As had been the case during the Cambodian crisis
some months earlier, U.S. officials viewed the events in Laos through the
lens of Vietnam: they were convinced that any conference on Laos would
inevitably grow to encompass its neighbor to the east, and the prospect made
them shudder. The administration moved quickly to thwart the French proposal. It attached a set of preconditions for any conference that it felt confident would never be accepted.[33] It leaned hard on Souvanna, who was
sympathetic to the idea of a return to Geneva, to fall in line on the need
for preconditions ("We cannot of course afford to have Souvanna get off
the train at this point," a State Department cable stated). And it put pressure on the British and the Canadians to veto the Paris plan unless and
until the preconditions were met. The pressure tactics worked. Ottawa
and London, though dismayed by U.S. intransigence, agreed to forestall a
conference. The French proposal was dead.[34]

So serious was the combined deterioration in Laos and South Vietnam
that the administration in the last ten days of May gave serious thought to

initiating immediate military measures against North Vietnam. On 20 May Johnson directed aides to prepare plans for how to proceed in Vietnam, both politically and militarily. Four working groups labored day and night to produce the plans, which together made the case for "selected and carefully graduated military force against North Vietnam." Bundy, Rusk, and McNamara, together with the other principal members (called the Executive Committee, or ExCom) of the NSC, urged Johnson to accept the recommendations.[35] The president did so, and his thinking was summarized in a cable to Lodge. The president was convinced, the message read, of three basic propositions. First, the United States could not let Southeast Asia go to the communists. Second, time was presently not on the American side, which meant that the United States was in danger of losing, "unless we can produce a turn-around on the ground." And third, the administration should be prepared to "ask Congress to join in a national decision authorizing all necessary action, including military force, to make the Communists stop their subversion," unless through other means the current trends could be soon be reversed.[36]

The telegram, which barely mentioned South Vietnam or its people, formed a blueprint of sorts for American policy in the months to come. The president and his aides, it made clear, were convinced of the need for a congressional resolution authorizing wider action.[37] It further showed that, armed with such a resolution, the administration was prepared to use "all necessary action" to achieve victory. In subsequent cables the State and Defense Departments were more specific about what the phrase meant, outlining a policy of carefully graduated military force against North Vietnam (ninety-four targets were selected) and, if necessary, the introduction of American ground forces. Even the "selective use" of nuclear weapons was considered, though only briefly.[38]

Even as they made these determinations in favor of escalation, senior American officials knew there were serious problems with moving to implementation. Dire as the situation in South Vietnam might be, there were compelling reasons, most agreed, to hold off launching the new initiatives as long as possible, until the end of the summer or later. The war would need to be escalated, in other words, but not just yet. Though the ostensible reason for the decision to delay was confidence that the South Vietnamese could, in Henry Cabot Lodge's words, continue to "jog along" for another few months, much more important were continuing American concerns about how an expanded war would play with major constituencies in the United States and in the international community, especially in the absence of some compelling pretext (for example, an all-out communist drive to take over Laos, or evidence of massive North Vietnamese infiltration into

South Vietnam). William Bundy admitted as much during meetings with senior British officials in London on 28–29 May: military action against North Vietnam would in all likelihood be initiated, he told his hosts, but not before important groundwork had been laid in the U.S. Congress.[39] When Bundy and other top U.S. military and civilian officials met in Honolulu in the first week of June they affirmed American determination in the war ("Our point of departure," a State Department guidance cable said, "is and must be that we cannot accept the overrunning of Southeast Asia by Hanoi and Peiping") but agreed that more time was needed to make the case for escalation to Congress, to the American public, and to key allied governments.[40]

It was a telling admission. U.S. officials were conceding that crucial domestic and international constituencies were not yet convinced that Vietnam was worth fighting for. "We must get at the basic doubts of the value of Southeast Asia and the importance of our stake there that are besetting and confusing both key members of the Congress and the public," William Bundy wrote in a memorandum titled "Highlights of the Honolulu Conference."[41] Signs pointing to such doubts were plentiful. On Capitol Hill, where civil rights was the dominant issue of the day, there was no more enthusiasm at the end of May than in March or April for a major U.S. effort on behalf of South Vietnam. Most in Congress "are cautious or noncommittal," Frederick Dutton, the head of the State Department's office of congressional relations, reported in a memo to McGeorge Bundy on 2 June. "Even most of those supporting the Administration's course are often wary about it." Dutton noted that the level of interest in Southeast Asia was "not at all high," which suggested "not merely political caution in an election year but low understanding or care about the problem." Given lawmakers' historic reluctance to challenge executive branch foreign-policy initiatives, Dutton predicted that a resolution would pass overwhelmingly, but he added that legislators would likely "try to keep sufficiently remote to be able to second-guess if things went bad or were prolonged." Among those few who actually had a deep interest in the issue, Dutton might have added, many, including influential Senate Democrats, were actively opposed to any form of escalation.[42]

Nor did public opinion polls offer much support for a wider war. A Gallup poll conducted in late May revealed that only 37 percent of Americans followed events in Vietnam, a figure that, according to the chroniclers of the *Pentagon Papers*, caused great concern among policymakers, particularly since a large portion of those 37 percent "desir[ed] our withdrawal" from the region.[43] Though presidential aides could point to other polls that showed larger percentages deeming it important to keep Southeast Asia from falling to communism, they were under no illusion that the mass of Americans wanted, or would necessarily support, a significantly enlarged U.S. military presence in Vietnam. Assistant Secretary of State for Public Affairs Robert J. Manning, whose job it was to know such things, pointedly reminded Johnson in mid June that little could be done "to make Americans feel happy or confident about the situation" as it then appeared. "The memories of Korea, the bitter French experience in Southeast Asia, the ugliness and brutality of the war in Viet-Nam, mixed with the odor of confusion and frustration that seeps out of Saigon, are poor material on which to build understanding and confidence. Too many available answers are unfavorable answers." To make matters worse, Manning added, important elements of so-called elite opinion favored finding a means to disengage the country from the war; in the event of escalation, they would surely become more vocal, more critical, more troublesome. "We have already lost important elements of the press, for example, the *New York Times* and Walter Lippmann," he told the president. "The situation is looked on with skepticism and/or suspicion by the rest of the news media. We are confronted by the persistent undermining tactics of President de Gaulle."[44]

For Lyndon Johnson, with his eyes on November, these realities only strengthened the case in favor of delaying new initiatives, either until the Saigon government reached the very brink of collapse, or until public opinion had been brought around to the importance of the struggle.[45] In the meantime, the plans for hitting the North could be further refined, and he could gain political advantage by portraying as a saber rattler the hawkish Barry Goldwater, his likely Republican challenger, who had called for the use of more force in Vietnam. This policy of delay should extend to the congressional resolution, Johnson decided. Some in the administration continued even after Honolulu to favor going to Congress right away. But to Johnson, who knew what kind of splash such a measure would make, and who feared the potential for obstructionism among skeptics in his own party, no new initiatives meant no new initiatives. By 15 June the resolution, too, was on the shelf.[46]

Important as these domestic considerations were in the decision to delay expanding the war, international concerns may have mattered even more, if not to Johnson himself then to his foreign-policy advisers. The State Department's "more flags" campaign was off to a disastrous start. When Dean Rusk asked NATO members for at least token matériel and personnel participation in the conflict at an alliance meeting at The Hague in May 1964, he found a decidedly unenthusiastic response. Some members agreed to provide very modest amounts of nonmilitary support to the

South Vietnamese regime, but all refused to send any troops, and they steadfastly maintained that position even as the war intensified in the months that followed. In the wake of the meeting, Rusk ordered embassy staff in key capitals to press the host governments for greater participation in the struggle. The cable to the Bonn embassy, for example, instructed staffers to inform German officials that their country's contribution to the war effort was insufficient; that a German embassy in Saigon needed to be constructed immediately and "with suitable publicity and fanfare"; and that Bonn needed to make a "public commitment of additional aid to GVN."[47]

The administration did not stop there. In May Robert McNamara visited Bonn and tried to impress on his hosts the need for all western allies to share in the effort to combat communism wherever necessary. McNamara said he understood that Bonn could not contribute military assistance to South Vietnam, but he asked for the dispatch of a German medical unit. The Germans were noncommittal. Chancellor Ludwig Erhard said he was supportive of American policy, but officials in the Ministry of Foreign Affairs were skeptical that allied help of any sort would do much good in view of the situation on the ground—only a massive Korea-type American commitment could have any hope of turning the tide, most appear to have believed. A few weeks after the defense secretary's visit, a State Department cable to the U.S. embassy in Bonn would summarize well the tepid nature of German support. German officials, it said, "have on several occasions agreed in principle to increased support for Southeast Asia but have not repeat not fulfilled these increases." The generally pro-American Hamburg daily *Die Welt* defended Bonn's policy, noting that Germany could not be expected to "take upon itself the burdens of a policy [about which] it has never been consulted in the slightest." On 26 May, the Foreign Ministry in Bonn made known that it had resisted heavy U.S. pressure for stepped-up West German aid to the Saigon regime.[48]

In London, policymakers ruled out any significant increase in the British presence in South Vietnam. But they faced a dilemma that would bedevil them for the next year: how to reconcile a firm opposition to increased British involvement in the war and a preference for a negotiated settlement, on the one hand, with a desire to preserve good relations with Washington, on the other. Already in early March James E. Cable, head of the South-East Asia Department in the Foreign Office, had framed the issue in a secret memo. "The moment may be rapidly approaching at which we should urge our views on the U.S. Government, both in order to dissuade them from courses liable to lead to dangerous increases in international tension and also to make clear that we are unwilling to extend our support for their existing policy to embrace hypothetical new policies of this [escalatory] kind," Cable noted. "The timing of the approach is a little difficult to judge. Should we make it before the U.S. Government have reached a decision (at the risk of irritating them by displaying premature and perhaps needless alarm) or should we make it when they have reached their decision (at the risk of being too late to exert any influence)?"[49]

British officials would have reason to ask themselves this question again and again in the months to come. Adding to their uncertainty was Britain's role as cochair of the 1954 Geneva Conference; should tensions continue to rise, London's policy of supporting publicly one side in the struggle would become harder to sustain. For the moment, neither Alec Douglas-Home nor R. A. B. Butler was prepared to initiate a confrontation with Washington (which, of course, was itself an answer to Cable's question). For them a policy of linkage still made sense: British public support for the defense of South Vietnam, American backing for British involvement in Malaysia. They clung to the possibility that they could still have it both ways: they could postpone the showdown with Washington and still retain the chance to have influence. More and more convinced of Lyndon Johnson's obsession with the November election and his desire to avoid any major decision on Vietnam until after that event, London leaders aimed to keep a low British profile until the fall. "We should probably be thinking of a continuing stalemate until the U.S. elections," one Foreign Office member observed, "[anticipating] that thereafter all sides might in fact welcome a negotiated 'Geneva' solution in which the co-Chairmen could play their traditional roles. But it would be unwise to breathe a word of this to the Americans at present." Until the U.S. election, London officials could agree, Britain should voice rhetorical support for current American policy, work behind the scenes to prevent an escalation of the war, and resist pressure from Washington for significantly increased British participation in the war effort.[50]

It was not quite universal, this unwillingness of allied governments to become meaningfully involved in supporting the Saigon government. Australia boosted its financial and personnel commitment significantly in early June and urged Washington in the strongest terms to continue steadfast in the war.[51] But Canberra was exceptional. Other governments declined altogether to provide assistance or made vague pledges of limited future support, almost invariably of a token character and in the end often not kept. Americans understood only too well that these attitudes represented further proof of fundamental allied doubts about the importance of Indochina to the West's security, as well as concerns about the dangers of an escalated war, and that any U.S. expansion of the war was therefore a perilous proposition—as Roger Hilsman had warned back in March, premature action would surely increase international pressure for precisely what Washington did not want: a conference-table solution to the conflict. McNamara, McCone, and William Bundy, in their 18 May draft memo to the president, put the matter bluntly:

> The NATO nations as a whole are only passively in sympathy with our position, and the French drumfire of gloom and doom is having a serious effect principally in Europe but to some extent in other areas. Even the British, although they recognize the direct link to their own struggle in Malaysia, would probably have to buck a very weak public opinion to stick with us, and would exert major pressures from the outset toward a negotiated solution.
>
> The above attitudes simply highlight the great difficulty we would have, once we initiated action, in resisting pressures for premature and unsatisfactory negotiations that would leave us short of our goal of an independent and secure South Viet-Nam. While we can in theory stick to our guns and refuse to negotiate until Hanoi agrees to our essential terms, the damage to our worldwide relationships will be substantial.[52]

And so, for the second time in less than three months the United States decided to delay a policy initiative that all top officials agreed would in all likelihood eventually have to be implemented: taking the war to North Vietnam. Both times the decision to delay was based not on assessments of the military situation on the ground but on concerns that critical constituencies around the world would not support such action, and that some would respond by increasing the pressure for a negotiated settlement. Decision makers in Washington continued to believe, as Hilsman had put it some time before, that "De Gaulle, Lippmann, and Mansfield [had] set the neutralist hares running," and they wanted to do nothing that might make them run faster—at least for the immediate future.[53]

There was nevertheless much to be done in that immediate future. Efforts to forestall any conference on Vietnam until after "D day" (as the day of launching action against the North was now called in internal documents) had to continue. Plans for an expanded war had to be revised. Drafts of a congressional resolution authorizing a wider war had to be fine-tuned, ready to be introduced quickly if the situation warranted. Just as important, a public information campaign had to be launched, aimed at convincing Congress and the American public that the defense of South Vietnam was essential to the country's security (on 22 June this campaign, to be discussed in the next chapter, was officially implemented as NSAM 308).[54] And the State Department had to press on with its own information campaign, aimed at convincing allies to either step up their support for the Saigon government or, in the case of France, reduce its interference with American objectives. In South Vietnam, too, large tasks remained, chief among them improving the performance of the Khanh government and the coordination between GVN/ARVN officials and their American advisers, and convincing the South Vietnamese that U.S. determination was unshakable and that theirs must be too.

It would not be enough, of course, to assure the South Vietnamese of American determination; North Vietnam had to be convinced as well. Lest Hanoi conclude that Washington's reluctance to expand the war signified an absence of U.S. steadfastness, the Johnson administration set for itself one additional task in the spring of 1964: to make an overture of sorts to the North Vietnamese government. The purpose of the effort, to be made through a Canadian diplomat, was to warn Hanoi against supporting the Vietcong's campaign in the South, and to make clear that, if it failed to heed that warning, America was ready and willing to escalate the conflict. The administration may have had no interest in backing down, but it hoped that Hanoi would.

6 Campaigns at Home and Abroad

"The problem of a U.S. information program supporting our involvement in Southeast Asia," Assistant Secretary of State for Public Affairs Robert J. Manning told Lyndon Johnson in mid June 1964, "falls into three major categories: first, the on-the-scene information program for consumption in South and North Viet-Nam, Laos, and other Southeast Asian nations; second, the case to be made in the international arena; and third . . . the case to be made to our own people and Congress." With these words, Manning neatly summarized the massive information effort on Vietnam that the Johnson administration launched in the summer of 1964. *Massive* is the right word, because the program's parameters extended to the four corners of the globe. While Manning and his Public Affairs team worked the home front, allies around the world would be pressed for support, and foes in Moscow, Beijing, and Hanoi would be warned that Washington's commitment to South Vietnam was total. In South Vietnam itself, a new Saigon Mission team would assure the Khanh government of the same thing. The gigantic scope of the program revealed just how isolated the administration perceived itself to be in the late spring of 1964—the president and his top aides feared they could not count on the American people or the vast majority of America's allies to support the war effort. They even worried about the level of commitment among the South Vietnamese.[1]

Manning's phraseology is important for an additional reason: it spoke to the interconnectedness of the domestic and foreign components of the program. American policymakers understood that one could never succeed if the other failed. Domestic audiences would question a war that allied governments refused to commit to; individual allied governments would be heavily influenced by what other countries did; and the communists would inevitably question how committed Washington could really be over the long term if it could not convince its own allies or the American public of the importance of the cause. Also, the already questionable South Vietnamese willingness to persevere in the war effort would inevitably suffer if American public opinion appeared indifferent or, worse, hostile to a heavy American presence in Southeast Asia.

The importance of the information program can thus scarcely be exaggerated. It was the centerpiece of the administration's Vietnam policy that summer. (Remarkably, it has received almost no attention from students of the war.) Its outcome would determine when and how to launch the wider military action that top officials now saw as nearly inevitable to prevent a collapse in South Vietnam (recall that the conferees in Honolulu in early June opted to delay such action in large part because of concern about how these crucial audiences would react). Ideally, any expansion of the war could wait until the November election was safely passed. But perhaps it could not. Events could force America's hand. An immediate expansion of the war might be imperative. Hence the need for a lobbying effort of vast proportions, to lay the groundwork for escalation with both friends and foes. On 22 June, NSAM 308 officially launched Manning's domestic campaign. A few days later, a new mission team, headed by General Maxwell Taylor, took the helm in Saigon. And simultaneously, the State Department stepped up its "more flags" campaign, which was designed to win support in the international arena.

Even before these efforts got under way, Washington made an overture to the other crucial target audience, the leadership in North Vietnam. The idea of sending an emissary to Hanoi was not a sudden development. It had taken shape over several months, as a corollary to the planned expansion of the war to the North. American officials reasoned that, in advance of such an expansion, it would be useful to probe the North Vietnamese leaders' attitudes on developments in the South and to inform them directly of Washington's determination to prevail in the conflict. That the notion of a contact with Hanoi should arise only in conjunction with plans for escalation tells much about what policymakers hoped to accomplish by the visit. The emissary's lone and essential purpose would be to issue a warning to his hosts: end the insurgency in the South or face certain punishment. His task, in other words, was not to promote negotiations but to practice intimidation; not to compromise but to coerce. For the United States to make an overture to Hanoi through an interlocutor would suggest neither a negotiation nor a dialogue, Ambassador Henry Cabot Lodge said at a meeting among U.S. officials in Saigon on 19 April: "It is more nearly an ultimatum." Lodge granted that perhaps there should be a carrot to go along with the stick, but the emphasis had to be on the stick. The purpose of the mission was to frighten Ho Chi Minh and Pham Van Dong, to compel them "to call off the V.C." Under no circumstances should the interlocutor agree to a great-power conference on the war.[2]

Not a negotiation but an ultimatum: what Lodge was describing was a strategy of coercive diplomacy, or *compellance*, in which a state employs threats or limited force to persuade an opponent to cease its aggression. (Compellance should be distinguished from pure coercion, in which crude force is used to bludgeon an opponent into ceasing its aggression.) For great powers, coercive diplomacy has often been a beguiling strategy—these states tend to believe that they can intimidate weaker states to give up their gains and objectives. This was certainly the assumption that American policymakers clung to, right up through the time they Americanized the war in the first half of 1965. Until then, coercive diplomacy would be the only diplomacy they would employ.[3]

In the weeks following the 19 April meeting in Saigon, the State Department laid the groundwork for the contact. The first question was which country's representative should serve as interlocutor. A number of possibilities, among them Poland, Yugoslavia, Britain, and Japan, were considered and rejected, all because they could not be trusted to represent the administration's position effectively. (For example, U.S. officials asked London about the suitability of Her Majesty's representative in Hanoi, J. Kenneth Blackwell, and were told that he would not be appropriate. The reason: Blackwell was too sympathetic to the Hanoi regime.) In Lodge's view, that left only one suitable candidate: Canada. No country was a closer ally of the United States; none had over time been more dependable. Lodge even saw an ideal emissary in J. Blair Seaborn, a veteran diplomat who had recently been appointed the Canadian representative to the ICC, a post that allowed him unrestricted travel in both North and South Vietnam. Lodge assured Rusk that the United States could trust Seaborn.[4]

Rusk agreed. On 30 April, he flew to Ottawa and broached the idea with Canadian prime minister Lester Pearson and minister of external affairs Paul Martin. They were receptive. Pearson assured Rusk that Canada would provide the interlocutor and agreed that Seaborn was the logical choice and that Seaborn should try to establish ready access to and close contact with Ho Chi Minh and Pham Van Dong. The prime minister's readiness to help may have resulted at least in part from Rusk's reassuring tones. Rusk said that the United States saw no reason to fight a war in that part of the world and that it sought no bases and no military position in the region. Nguyen Khanh was a relatively able leader, and the administration felt confident that under his leadership events in South Vietnam would take a turn for the better. As for Washington's goals in the conflict, these were merely that all sides comply with the 1954 and 1962 Geneva agreements. Rusk then went over what Washington felt should be the main objectives for the visit. Seaborn should try to uncover what was on Ho's mind, notably whether he saw himself as overextended and exposed, or whether he felt confident that his Chinese allies would back him to the end. More important, Seaborn should make clear to the Hanoi leaders that the United States was fully determined to "see this thing through," and he should warn them that if "they did not put a stop to their operations they would be in trouble." Should North Vietnam agree to leave its neighbors alone, it could be assured that Washington would consider facilitating trade between the DRV and the West. Pearson agreed to this agenda, but not before he and Martin expressed doubts about Khanh and about the prospect for political stability in Saigon.[5]

In Saigon, Lodge received a copy of the Rusk-Pearson meeting notes. He was dissatisfied. The instructions for Seaborn sounded too timid, he thought. First in a cable to Rusk and then in one to Johnson, the ambassador urged that Seaborn be told to tell Ho that if the United States had to choose between withdrawal and escalation, it would escalate. The Canadian should be perfectly clear, Lodge told the president: "The Americans are determined to win the struggle in South Viet Nam and will do whatever is necessary to win it." Unless the North Vietnamese ceased their "murderous intrusion into South Vietnam," they could expect an expansion of the war north of the seventeenth parallel; if they did cease it, they could expect a withdrawal of *some* Americans from the South (only those, Lodge advised, whom the administration had decided to remove anyway), as well as food and economic aid for themselves. Lodge had one final recommendation: in the event of a significant Vietcong attack prior to Seaborn's arrival in Hanoi, the U.S. should launch a concentrated bombing attack on a target in the North, in planes flown by South Vietnamese pilots.[6]

Rusk and Johnson evidently welcomed the Saigon ambassador's tough language, because much of his phraseology was included in the internal plans for the mission drawn up in the ensuing weeks. It is a measure of the importance the administration attached to securing Canadian agreement on the purpose of the mission that it arranged for a meeting between Johnson and Pearson in New York City on 28 May to discuss Seaborn's message. In a suite at the Hilton Hotel, Johnson told Pearson that the United States was interested not in starting wars but in keeping peace. At the same time, he emphasized that North Vietnam's aggression had to be confronted. Hence the need for a confidential and responsible interlocutor to carry a carrot-and-stick message to North Vietnam, to the effect that although Lyndon Johnson was a man of peace he would not stand by and let the South be overrun. Johnson said that, given the seriousness of the situation in both

Vietnam and Laos, it was imperative that Seaborn go soon. Pearson was wary. In the four weeks since his meeting with Rusk, he had apparently grown concerned about the nature of the "stick," and he cautioned the president about the inherent risks of an American policy of expansion, especially if that policy could include nuclear weapons. (This caution was probably a reference to a recent comment by GOP presidential hopeful Barry Goldwater that the nuclear option should be considered.)[7] Any drastic escalation of the war, Pearson warned Johnson, would cause great problems in Canada and internationally. Johnson reiterated that he was a man of peace and vowed that if, against his own hopes and desires, action against the North became necessary, it would be kept strictly limited.[8]

Pearson's suspiciousness with respect to American plans for the war was not unexpected. In the days before the meeting, State Department officials had determined that Ottawa would have strong reservations about any policy departure that carried the war to North Vietnam. "In light of present Canadian attitudes," Rusk informed Lodge in a top-secret cable on 22 May, "we tend to see real difficulty in approaching the Canadians at this time with any message as specific as you suggest, i.e. that Hanoi be told by the Canadians 'that they will be punished.'" Indeed, Rusk noted, the more specific Washington was with regard to its plans, the more difficult the dialogue with Ottawa would be. This time Lodge was persuaded. In a return cable he agreed that Seaborn should not tell North Vietnamese leaders of American plans for bombing their territory. Lodge still advocated a bombing run just prior to Seaborn's arrival in Hanoi, but he added, "There is no question whatsoever of consulting the Canadian."[9]

It was a revealing exchange. Canadian reservations about a wider war had led America's top diplomat to conclude that Washington would have to be circumspect in its discussions with Ottawa. The instructions for Seaborn had to be long on broad generalities, short on specifics. And so they were. Johnson mentioned the possibility of limited escalation in his conversation with Pearson, but only in response to a query by the prime minister; in the rest of his comments, Johnson emphasized his desire for peace. At precisely the same time that Johnson and Pearson were meeting, lower officials from the two countries convened in Ottawa to hammer out the details of Seaborn's instructions. (Seaborn himself was among those present.) Here, too, the American team, led by the State Department's William H. Sullivan, head of the interagency Vietnam Coordinating Committee and Rusk's "Special Assistant" on Vietnam, described U.S. determination only in general terms.

Still, for the Sullivan team the carrot remained much less important than the stick. Working from a talking paper prepared by the State Department and approved by the White House, Sullivan remarked that Seaborn should "hint" at the economic and other benefits enjoyed by communist countries such as Yugoslavia that "had not sought to expand into other areas," and that Seaborn could "state that the U.S. does not seek military bases in the area and is not seeking to overthrow the Communist regime in Hanoi." At the same time, Seaborn should stress that Lyndon Johnson's patience was growing thin, that the United States was in the war to stay, and that it would sooner escalate than withdraw. It was Hanoi that was responsible for the fighting in the South and therefore Hanoi's responsibility to end the fighting. Sullivan underlined the importance of Hanoi understanding that Washington's Vietnam commitment had relevance far beyond Indochina, indeed to every corner of the globe. For the United States, therefore, the stakes were extremely high. In addition to delivering this message, Sullivan asked Seaborn to do one other thing while in Hanoi: to keep his eyes and ears open and to assess the North's morale and war capability. How extensive was the frustration and war-weariness among the North Vietnamese? Were there cliques or factions in the party or government? How did the Sino-Soviet split influence Hanoi's thinking? Was there evidence of differences between the political cadres and the military group?[10]

The Canadians, led by External Affairs Minister Martin, raised no major objections to the "instructions" as outlined by the Sullivan team. But the prospect of an American escalation of the fighting concerned Martin. Canadians would not look kindly on the prospect of an enlarged war, he told Sullivan, and he insisted that Seaborn not have to "agree with or associate his Government with the substance of some of the messages" he would be transmitting, as long as he transmitted them faithfully. Martin further said that he agreed with Walter Lippmann's most recent column, in which Lippmann stated that even an imperfect political settlement via a conference was preferable to pursuing a costly and unwinnable war. How could the administration avoid a conference, Martin asked, particularly when the only alternative seemed to be direct military intervention? Sullivan's response was telling. These were "extreme alternatives," he said, and the administration hoped to find a middle way. But he acknowledged that intervention seemed a more likely course than a conference at the present time. Martin was unmoved. He repeated Canadian objections to direct intervention and repeated his view that a conference, perhaps including the whole of Indochina, was the best bet.[11]

More than any desire to come to the aid of an ally, it was these concerns about a larger war that motivated the Canadian government to agree to act as a go-between, as Seaborn himself said later. "All of us had doubts right along the line that a large increase of American force" could produce an eventual settlement between North and South. At the same time, "all of us were so concerned and preoccupied with the possibilities of a great escalation of the military situation in that area and what it might lead to." In such circumstances, Seaborn maintained, his assignment was "something which no Canadian government could refuse."[12]

In Washington, meanwhile, several officials were worrying about what they considered an absence of meaningful carrots in the American negotiating position on Vietnam. At a State Department meeting on 30 May, W. Averell Harriman argued that too little work had been done on what might be offered to Hanoi in exchange for ceasing aggression in South Vietnam. The same day, Marshall Green, who was William Bundy's deputy at the Far East desk and who had attended the meeting, penned a memo to Bundy in which he seconded Harriman's claim. "We have the problem," Green wrote, "of the carrot as well as the stick in inducing the desired response from Hanoi in connection with [escalatory] actions we have under contemplation." After noting that no one at the meeting had any ideas of what the carrot should be, Green suggested one possibility, a kind of Marshall Plan for Southeast Asia should Hanoi cease its "current direction and support of aggression." Two other officials present at the meeting that day, George Ball and Harlan Cleveland, likewise lamented the absence of an olive branch to go along with the sword. Cleveland, who as assistant secretary of state for international organization affairs knew firsthand the growing skepticism in the world community about American prospects in the war, noted in the meeting that Washington would have a hard time convincing the rest of the world that it could succeed in Vietnam. After the meeting adjourned, he and Ball talked on the phone. "We really have no peace proposals here," Ball said. Cleveland agreed. The carrot, he said, was the missing link in all the discussions he had taken part in.[13]

It was certainly the missing link in the Ottawa meetings. At several points, Canadian officials asked Sullivan what inducements Washington could offer the North Vietnamese in exchange for ceasing their support of the insurgency. Sullivan replied that the administration would accept the independent existence of the two Vietnams and hold out the hope for ultimate unity. In addition, Hanoi leaders might be looking to obtain American foodstuffs, and thus Washington could dangle the prospect of increased trade. Seeing the Canadian expressions of disbelief, Sullivan quickly conceded that Hanoi might see neither of these offers as genuine U.S. concessions.[14]

This general fuzziness in the American position, with respect both to the stick and to the carrot, had a profound influence on the message that

Blair Seaborn carried with him as he flew to North Vietnam in mid June, the result of which was to make that message neither tempting nor intimidating to the Hanoi leadership. Though Canadian officials had no knowledge of the detailed contingency plans then being drawn up in Washington for bombing the North, they knew in general terms about the bombing possibility—it had, after all, been touched upon in the Pearson-Johnson meeting. But Seaborn was not instructed to warn specifically of this possibility. He was to say only that American patience was growing "extremely thin." Likewise, he was only to "hint" in general terms about the economic benefits that might come the North's way if it called off the war in the South. The result of this ambiguity would be that Hanoi would have nothing firm to consider, which is another indication that Washington had no real intention of seeking negotiations at this time. Certainly the ambiguity would have a deleterious effect on Washington's attempt at coercive diplomacy, because that strategy has in practice been far less effective when the demand on the opponent lacks clarity or specificity.[15]

On 18 June, in an antique-filled ballroom at the former French governor's palace in Hanoi, Seaborn met with North Vietnamese prime minister Pham Van Dong. Seaborn wasted little time getting to the issue at hand. The Canadian government was convinced that Lyndon Johnson was a man of peace, he began, a man who would take great pains to avoid a major military confrontation among world powers. But he was also a man of his word, and he remained fully committed to keeping Southeast Asia from falling under the control of communism. He could not go back on his country's promises to South Vietnam. Moreover, Johnson's patience was not limitless. If he had to choose between withdrawal and escalation, he would choose escalation. Seaborn stressed that Washington considered the Vietnam conflict as part of the larger East-West confrontation; as a result, the U.S. stake in the region was of worldwide proportions.[16]

Pham Van Dong did not dispute that the stakes for the United States were high, but he reminded Seaborn that they were high also for the NLF and its supporters—hence their determination to continue the struggle regardless of cost. "It's impossible," the premier said, "for you Westerners to understand the force of the people's will to resist, and to continue. The struggle of our people exceeds the imagination. It has astonished us too." The premier rejected the implication that Hanoi directed and controlled Vietcong activity in the South, and he assured Seaborn that his government would not "force or provoke the U.S." by escalating its "limited" role in the conflict. As to the possibility of great destruction for North Vietnam, Pham Van Dong was not concerned. He assured Seaborn that his people could withstand whatever the Americans threw their way. Whereas the southern "mercenaries" and U.S. soldiers did not have their hearts in the fighting, the NLF was steadily increasing its popular support.

Despite his confidence that the Washington-Saigon forces would eventually be defeated, Pham Van Dong did not close the door on a diplomatic settlement. He said that all the parties in the conflict had to learn to coexist and find a solution to the problem that had wracked Southeast Asia for twenty-five years. But it had to be a just solution. It had to involve an American withdrawal from Indochina, as well as a neutralist settlement arranged by the people of the South. The NLF must naturally have a say in that settlement, he emphasized, because "no other group represents the broad wishes of the people." Finally, there must be a reunification of the country.

Perhaps because he sensed that these conditions for a "just solution" would receive a negative reaction in Washington, Pham Van Dong emphasized that Hanoi was in no hurry. Reunification need not take place immediately, he told Seaborn, this being a matter for negotiation, "without military pressures," between North and South. When Seaborn noted the Johnson administration's concern about the NLF's ultimate intentions, Pham Van Dong acknowledged that the NLF did not represent all South Vietnamese, but he maintained that there was no reason to fear that it would take over any government established after the settlement. On the important issue of whether his government would support the kind of international negotiations for Vietnam envisioned by Charles de Gaulle, Pham Van Dong said nothing (and Seaborn failed to probe him on the issue), but it is telling that he voiced firm support for a new Geneva conference on Laos—surely he knew that de Gaulle and others felt confident that such a meeting would almost certainly be expanded to include all of Indochina. The premier concluded the ninety-minute meeting with an invitation for further talks. "Next time you will meet Ho Chi Minh," he promised Seaborn. "The President is on leave at present, but has sent his greetings."[17]

By emphasizing his government's patience and its determination not to provoke the United States, Pham Van Dong appears to have been trying, as Wallace J. Thies has put it, to "sketch out a solution allowing the U.S. a face-saving exit from the war." Bringing about such an exit remained a key goal among Hanoi strategists: they were well aware of the immense military capabilities of the United States and wanted to do nothing that might encourage Washington to drastically escalate its role in the war. Thus, although Pham Van Dong showed little concern about, or even interest in, Seaborn's carrot-and-stick message and professed confidence that combined

American and South Vietnamese efforts would ultimately fail (he even quoted Walter Lippmann's 21 May column, which said "there is no light at the end of the tunnel"), he issued no threats, and he stressed the likelihood of a delay in Vietnamese reunification. The neutralization of South Vietnam, he told Seaborn, would not necessarily be merely a first step toward unification; it could persist indefinitely.[18]

Blair Seaborn filed two lengthy reports on the meeting. In these reports, he intimated that Hanoi seemed open to a settlement and said that Pham Van Dong gave "the impression of quiet sincerity, of realization of the seriousness of what we are discussing and of lack of truculence or belligerency." At the same time, Seaborn cautioned, the premier exhibited little fear at the prospect of the United States taking the war to the North. Indeed, the general mood in the northern capital seemed to Seaborn one of unyielding commitment to the war. There was no evidence of war-weariness, "and indeed all Vietnamese emphasized quiet determination to go on struggling as long as necessary to achieve objectives which they said they were bound to achieve in the long run." The city itself was "much less run down" than Seaborn had expected, and its people did not appear discontented. As for his own views, the Canadian left little doubt that he thought an enlarged war was neither warranted nor manageable, and he closed the second report by reiterating the Hanoi leadership's belief in the certainty of ultimate victory: "[I] think DRVN leaders are completely convinced that military action at any level is not, repeat not, going to bring success for the US and government forces in South Vietnam. They are almost as completely convinced that the Khanh government is losing ground on the local political front and are confident that in the fullness of time success is assured for the Liberation Front supported by the DRVN."[19]

Senior strategists in Washington were not prepared to consider the complexity of Seaborn's message, with its description of a DRV both determined and restrained, both supremely confident of eventual victory and committed to not provoking the United States. What Seaborn and other Canadian officials saw as both a positive and a negative picture, they saw as almost wholly negative—William Sullivan told Ottawa's ambassador in Washington that Seaborn's assessment provided a "sobering" picture, one in line with the "least optimistic" among the various possibilities.[20] What mattered to U.S. policymakers was that their attempt at coercive diplomacy had failed, not that Pham Van Dong seemed to leave the door open for further dialogue. The Johnson administration in mid 1964 was not interested in dialogue, not interested in seeking a face-saving exit from the war, and not interested in going to Geneva. Senior officials knew that to negotiate now would be to negotiate from weakness; not only that, the mere mention of talks might cause the collapse of the fragile Saigon government. Beyond that, they remained committed to riding out the four and a half months remaining until the November election without any dramatic new policy departure. The administration therefore chose not to issue a formal response to Pham Van Dong's message. Concerned about appearing too eager to negotiate, the Johnson team opted to have Seaborn postpone a return trip to Hanoi from mid July until mid August, on the grounds that the delay would allow more time to reinforce U.S. steadfastness.[21]

One way Washington hoped to demonstrate that steadfastness was through a change in its Saigon team. On 20 June, William Westmoreland succeeded Paul Harkins as head of the Military Assistance Command in South Vietnam (MACV). Three days later, Johnson announced the resignation of Henry Cabot Lodge as ambassador to South Vietnam and the appointment of General Maxwell Taylor as his replacement. It was a revealing selection. For several weeks, top aides around Johnson had suggested that a new ambassador might be just what the war effort needed. Lodge, these men believed, was tired, had run out of ideas, had stopped communicating with the American military in Vietnam, and had at least one eye on the Republican presidential nomination. Thus even before Lodge announced his intention to leave Vietnam, McGeorge Bundy sent Johnson a list of potential replacements, including Robert McNamara, Robert Kennedy, and himself. (The interest of these men in taking on the assignment is graphic proof of how important Vietnam had become in official Washington by mid 1964.)[22] Johnson bypassed them all in favor of Taylor, the man he trusted more than any other, with the possible exception of McNamara. Taylor was ideal for the post, the president believed. As chairman of the Joint Chiefs of Staff, as the most prestigious American in the armed services, he was as likely as anyone to meet Johnson's election-year goal for Vietnam: to organize an effective prosecution of the war and to do so quietly—Taylor could "move things in Vietnam without really touching them, affect events while doing nothing," as David Halberstam has put it. Taylor went to Saigon with unhampered authority: an agreement between the Pentagon and the State Department gave him the full civil and military authority of a proconsul. Thus although Westmoreland succeeded Harkins as supreme commander, he was in fact Taylor's subordinate.[23]

Taylor's appointment was important for an additional reason: he had a stake in this war. He had trumpeted Vietnam as a "test case" early in the Kennedy administration, a test of America's ability to fight and win limited wars in remote regions of the world. He had influenced Kennedy's decision to make a stand in Vietnam, had traveled to the country with Rostow

in the autumn of 1961, and had counseled an expanded American commitment. Since then Taylor had accompanied Robert McNamara to Saigon on
four separate occasions; each time, he had advocated a firm U.S. posture in
the war. Taylor was also, it is true, a charter member of the "Never Again
Club," a group of military officers who took from the Korean War the lesson that the United States should never again fight a land war in Asia, at
least not without nuclear weapons. But that conviction only made Taylor
more determined to make the existing policy work, to find some way to
whip the Khanh government and ARVN into shape. Had he been less inti-
mately tied to the war effort, had his reputation not been on the line that
summer, he might have cited his Never Again Club credentials and initiated a searching review of the American presence in Vietnam, whereupon
he might have found that all the objective signs pointed to continued futility in the war effort. As the nation's most respected military man, his
would certainly have been a powerful voice for disengagement, either right
away or after the November election. But Taylor was not interested in
searching reviews. As the months passed and the war effort deteriorated, he
would even abandon, reluctantly, his opposition to the commitment of major American ground forces. By July 1965, he had renounced his membership in the Never Again Club.

When he departed for Vietnam in the early summer of 1964, Maxwell
Taylor was confident that drastic departures from current policy would not
be needed; he felt he could work within the "wait and see" strictures laid
down in Honolulu and later endorsed by the president.[24] All things considered, the situation could have been much worse, Taylor believed. True,
chronic factionalism and religious strife continued to wreak havoc on political stability and undermine the effectiveness of the regime. But Khanh
appeared to have a reasonably firm grasp on power in the capital and seemed
anxious to cooperate with the new U.S. ambassador (both questionable assumptions, Taylor would soon learn). True, Vietcong activity had increased
in recent weeks, and the number of desertions from the ARVN had also
risen. But there were no signs that a major campaign was imminent and
no indication that main force troops from the People's Army of Vietnam
(PAVN) had begun to appear in the South. Pham Van Dong's comments to
Blair Seaborn seemed to indicate that Hanoi would do nothing that might
provoke American escalation. So there was time, the new ambassador believed, time for him to use his broad powers over all U.S. operations in
Vietnam to organize an effective war effort.

Many inclined to take a longer-range view than Taylor were much less
optimistic. To them, the key indicators pointed not in the direction of gradual progress but continual decline. Willard Matthias, an analyst with the

CIA's Board of National Estimates, argued in a June 1964 internal memo (a draft of which he had completed earlier in the year) that the United States faced exceedingly poor prospects in Vietnam and should therefore consider seeking "some kind of negotiated settlement" to the conflict. "The guerrilla war in South Vietnam is in its fifth year and no end appears in sight," Matthias wrote. The Vietcong, under the direction of the Hanoi government but dependent largely on their own resources, were pressing their attack more vigorously than ever, and with greater success, while the "counter-guerrilla effort" by the GVN was continuing to flounder. Matthias expressed "serious doubt that victory can be won" and argued that, at best, a "prolonged stalemate" might be achieved (and this only if the United States continued to provide massive assistance to the Saigon regime). A cover note by Sherman Kent, chairman of the board, indicated that the memo, which also dealt with other global issues, had received "general board approval."[25]

Similarly, David G. Nes, Lodge's deputy at the embassy in Saigon, who, like his boss, was departing from Vietnam, remained as pessimistic as he had been early in the year; he had seen no progress in the war in his six-month stint in the country. In late May, Nes had complained to Lodge about the optimistic assessments of the war effort put out by the State Department in Washington. This optimism was not warranted, Nes had argued. "The over-all political situation is extremely fragile. We *hope* we can keep it stabilized but there is no assurance that this will be possible." The Saigon government and army were declining in strength, whereas the Vietcong strength and capability continued to grow, he had warned Lodge. Now, a month later, on the eve of his departure, Nes gave a similar assessment to the man who was to be his functional successor in Saigon, U. Alexis Johnson. None of the crucial prerequisites for a successful counterinsurgency effort were present, Nes told him, including the most important one of all: a "reasonably cohesive national anti-Communist base" with a "universally popular leader." Nor was there much that Americans could do to change this abysmal state of affairs. Indeed, Nes warned, U.S. officials had to recognize that "more dollars, more Americans, and more publicity can be counterproductive in supporting the GVN's efforts to cope with the insurgency." No doubt aware of the contingency plans being laid down, he warned against an expanded American role in the war.[26]

The Matthias and Nes claims that the prerequisites for a successful prosecution of the war had not yet been met were echoed publicly by a ranking U.S. military adviser. Speaking on the condition that he not be named, the adviser, identified as being either a major or colonel, told an Associated Press reporter in Saigon in mid June that the communist threat to South Vietnam was much more severe now than it had been when he first came to the country three years earlier. The Vietcong controlled huge areas of the countryside, he noted, and were "much better armed and professionally more competent" than they had been in 1961. More than 90 percent of their weapons came from the U.S. military aid program for Vietnam. Though there had been a marginal improvement in the quality of ARVN since the coup against Ngo Dinh Diem the previous November, the rate of improvement was not enough to win the war.[27]

These were strong words, and they received wide circulation—the *New York Times* ran the story under a large headline on the front page, and a number of other major newspapers carried it as well. The comments came at a particularly poor time for the Johnson administration, which was in the process of launching the public information campaign aimed at solidifying support for the commitment to Vietnam, in anticipation of an expanded American role in the war. As the designated head of this effort, Robert J. Manning already had his hands full dealing with continued skepticism in the press, in the academic community, and on Capitol Hill. He had been forced to react, for example, to a 12 June *Times* lead editorial warning against U.S. pursuit of a military solution. "There is no ideal solution," the paper asserted, "but it has seemed to this newspaper that the most practicable one is, in the broadest possible terms, a guaranteed neutralization of all the states that formerly made up Indochina." The United States, the People's Republic of China, and the Soviet Union would all agree to withdraw from the region and would at the same time guarantee the independence of the respective states, perhaps with a United Nations presence to enforce it. No doubt there were risks in such a scenario, the *Times* admitted, but the risks "will be great no matter what is done, and will be still greater if the outcome is left to the hazards of military escalation." Manning, aware that *New York Times* editorials circulated in Saigon, immediately fired off a cable to the embassy there, assuring staffers that Washington was working to ensure that "counter-arguments" to the editorial were aired, and soon.[28]

The *Times* and other papers also gave front-page coverage to an eighty-six-word petition signed by more than five thousand scholars at American universities and colleges; the petition urged the administration to work for the neutralization of both North and South Vietnam. University of Chicago political scientist Hans J. Morgenthau, spokesperson for the group, told a press conference that it was "not impossible" to visualize "a kind of Titoist Vietnam"—a country, led by Ho Chi Minh, in which neither China nor the United States retained dominant power. Escalating the American presence was assuredly not the answer, Morgenthau said. Manning's office responded immediately. The government would "welcome, of course, an end to terror and suffering in Vietnam and the loss of Vietnamese lives," a spokesman told reporters. But it was not clear precisely what the educators meant by neutralization and, further, how it was to be achieved given the continued communist violation of the 1954 Geneva Accords. (Morgenthau's more accurate position was that both sides had violated them.) Disingenuously, the spokesperson insisted that no thought was being given to expanding the war to North Vietnam.[29]

Disgruntled academics, even when speaking en masse and when represented by Hans Morgenthau, were not a central concern for the Johnson administration in the summer of 1964. They were intellectuals; they were supposed to complain. Much more important was the mood among the general public and among legislators on Capitol Hill. Accordingly, Manning's campaign called for administration representatives to fan out across the country to sell the importance of the conflict and demonstrate American resolve. At Williams College on 14 June, Dean Rusk told an audience that the United States would not abandon its commitment to South Vietnam and Laos. He issued a warning to Hanoi and Beijing: "Leave your neighbors alone." At a news conference five days later, Rusk repeated the warning and called the defense of South Vietnam as important as the defense of West Berlin. In an address the following week in Minneapolis, Lyndon Johnson vowed that the United States would not hesitate to "risk war" to preserve the peace in Southeast Asia. And in two speeches in late June, Robert McNamara called it imperative that the United States live up to its responsibilities in Vietnam. In addition, Johnson ordered the State Department to arrange meetings with powerful lawmakers in order to answer their questions and secure support for a congressional resolution. In June and July Johnson, Rusk, and Undersecretary of State George Ball met individually with several prominent legislators.[30]

Rusk and other administration representatives also appeared before the Senate Foreign Relations Committee in two executive session briefings in the last half of June. Manning's team attached great importance to these briefings, and for good reason: they would reveal much about congressional attitudes on the war. At the session on 15 June, Dean Rusk and his special assistant for Vietnamese affairs, William Sullivan, testified for the administration. Both vigorously defended U.S. policy and assured committee members that progress was being made in the war effort. Idaho Democrat Frank Church was skeptical. The war would be won or lost by the South Vietnamese, Church said, and there was little that American military intervention could do to fundamentally affect the outcome. Moreover, such an intervention could involve the United States in a war with North Vietnam, or China, or both. J. William Fulbright, chair of the committee, appeared to be sympathetic to Church's views but did not offer his own opinion. On 30 June, Henry Cabot Lodge took his turn before the committee. Reflecting on his recently completed term as ambassador in Saigon, Lodge professed to see light at the end of the tunnel but at the same time counseled patience—it would take time, he told the senators, to develop the necessary political strength in South Vietnam. This time only the irascible Wayne Morse spoke up in opposition and repeated his long-standing demand for a negotiated settlement.[31]

But Frank Church remained troubled. For several months his skepticism about the American effort had been growing, but he had stayed quiet until now. He could stay silent no longer. In a major Senate speech, he said experience had made one thing clear: no unilateral intervention by any white nation could achieve long-term success in the developing areas of the world. "The empires which Western power could not hold, that power cannot now pacify," Church declared, and yet the United States appeared to believe that it could. The senator did not counsel an immediate withdrawal from Vietnam, but he advocated a greater role for the United Nations in bringing peace to Indochina. He attacked the notion that an escalated war was the answer. "What troubles me is that if this war—which is essentially a political war, that can be won only by the people of South Vietnam—is being waged on terms so advantageous, with the enemy restricted to 25,000 hard core Vietcong, how on earth will the situation be improved by extending the war to the north?" Would it really help, he continued, to take on the army of North Vietnam? "Do we think the bombing of North Vietnam will break the spirit of the Government, and cause it to discontinue to aid and abet the insurrection in the south? Why should we? The bombing of North Korea never broke the spirit there. And we bombed every house, bridge, and road until there was nothing left but rubble. Expanding the war is not getting out, Mr. President. It is getting further in."

In sum, Church concluded, a heavy American presence in Southeast Asia would solve nothing. A U.S. war would result in the "wast[ing] of our troops in the interminable jungle," would lack international support, and would run counter to the history of two decades of decolonization. Did the United States really believe that Asians would be thankful for such an intervention and for the American occupation that would inevitably follow? "Why, the tides of history will wash over us in time. For Asia does belong to the Asians now, and will forevermore."[32]

Senator Hubert H. Humphrey, soon to be nominated as Lyndon Johnson's running mate for the upcoming campaign, voiced general support for Church's comments. He said that the United Nations could indeed play a role in settling the conflict and that an American escalation of the war would be a mistake. "What is needed in Vietnam," Humphrey added, "is a cause for which to fight, some sort of inspiration for the people of South Vietnam to live and fight for." (The marvelous irony of this statement appears to have escaped him.) In a memo to Johnson outlining his views on the war, Humphrey said that the South Vietnamese should get American guidance but little else. Only they themselves could win their war, and to be able to do so they needed a stable political base. Without such a base, Humphrey warned, "no additional military involvement can be successful. . . . Direct U.S. military action against North Vietnam, U.S. assumption of command roles, or the participation in combat of U.S. troop units is unnecessary and undesirable."[33]

Church and Humphrey were prescient. They correctly identified many of the core problems that would bedevil American policymakers throughout the war. Church's extraordinary Senate speech contained arguments and language, indeed exact phrases, that congressional critics would voice countless times in later years. In mid 1964, however, the speech did not cause a groundswell of opposition to the direction of American policy, despite the fact that a sizable and growing number of senators shared the essence of Church's views (see chapter 5). Even though Church's speech did not generate strong criticism from colleagues (a telling fact in itself), it generated little outward support among them, either, for several reasons. For one thing, the dominant issue on Capitol Hill at this time was not Vietnam but civil rights; domestic issues in general, including an upcoming election, were at the forefront of legislators' minds. War in Southeast Asia was a cloud on the horizon—an increasingly ominous cloud, to be sure, but still some distance away. In addition, except for Morse and Gruening, these Democrats were acutely uncomfortable about challenging a Democratic president's foreign policy, even when they disagreed with it.

That 1964 was a presidential election year obviously mattered a great deal in this regard. The notion of handing the Republicans a juicy election issue by openly criticizing Johnson seemed impossible to these senators, especially if doing so might help elect hawkish Senator Barry Goldwater, the favorite to get the Republican presidential nomination at the party's July convention. Goldwater's rhetorical stridency on foreign policy in general, and his calls for a greater application of American force in Vietnam in particular, made many of these Democrats shudder. Nor was it just Goldwater. In late June, a thirteen-member group of House Republicans, led by Representative Gerald Ford, called for a stronger U.S. stand in Vietnam, labeled the Kennedy-Johnson policies in Southeast Asia a failure, and threatened to make the war an issue in the upcoming campaign. The group charged that the administration was following a "Why Win?" policy in Vietnam, suggested that the time had come for a congressional resolution on the war, and called for an absolute commitment "to insure a victory for freedom." A centerpiece in that commitment should be American command of all military operations in the struggle. Efforts by fellow Republican Lodge to get the group to alter its stance, to convince its members that politics should stop at the water's edge, were to no avail.[34]

The great irony, of course, was that the Johnson administration was secretly planning to do more or less exactly what the Ford group was demanding, as Lodge himself knew. Indeed, though major initiatives had to be delayed until the election or until South Vietnam appeared about to collapse, several smaller policy departures had already been made, all of them designed to demonstrate U.S. determination to the key constituencies at home, in Vietnam (North and South), and in the world community, and to lay the foundation for a future increase in the American role in the war. Among these were the reinforcing of military stockpiles in Thailand and the Philippines, the deployment of five thousand U.S. troops in Thailand, the forward deployment of a carrier task force and land-based tactical aircraft within striking distance of Vietnam, and the assignment of an unprecedentedly high-level team under Maxwell Taylor to the embassy in Saigon.[35]

In addition to these highly publicized actions, the United States also undertook a number of covert and more provocative ones. Desoto patrols (U.S. destroyer patrols venturing deep into the Gulf of Tonkin along the coast of North Vietnam) were stepped up, both in order to gather intelligence and to show American determination. Likewise, officials increased the number of Oplan 34-A raids by South Vietnamese guerrilla units into North Vietnam. American-led South Vietnamese forces increased the pace of cross-border operations against Vietcong infiltration routes in Laos, accompanied by American air strikes. And the United States launched operation Yankee Team, which consisted of low-level photo reconnaissance missions over Laos; these missions were conducted by U.S. aircraft, with fighter escorts to allow suppressive or retaliatory actions against enemy ground fire.[36]

The Laos actions were intended as much to boost morale in South Vietnam as they were to materially disrupt the Vietcong infiltration routes. That the morale still needed boosting so long after the overthrow of the Diem government ("the real problem" in Vietnam), and so long after the advent of Nguyen Khanh ("the best man for the job"), showed just how little progress had been made in bringing cohesion and purpose to the southern populace. In the last half of June, foreign diplomatic observers in Saigon saw daily evidence of Khanh's plummeting prestige and of what one British official called "a marked deterioration in public morale." The situation, the official said, had gone "from bad to worse. None of the essential requirements—the creation of a strong and unified central government and the implementation of a progressive pacification plan—show any signs of being met. On the contrary, nothing is to be seen but drift, back-biting, corruption—and worse."[37]

The contrast with Blair Seaborn's picture of Hanoi could hardly have been starker. Whereas Seaborn saw no evidence of war-weariness or apathy in the North, no one could dispute that both were endemic in the South. Whereas he encountered the calm and resolute determination of Pham Van Dong, others marveled at the utter lack of such steadfastness among southern leaders. At precisely the time Seaborn dispatched his reports of the Hanoi meeting, Gordon Etherington-Smith, the British ambassador in Saigon, dispatched to London some hot news of his own: Khanh government representatives were secretly meeting with elements of the Vietcong. At a dinner on 22 June, Minister of State Dr. Le Van Hoach told Etherington-Smith that he had initiated the meetings with the tacit consent of Khanh and that he hoped they would eventually lead to a negotiated settlement. The war could not go on too much longer, Hoach said. Etherington-Smith thought the news highly significant: "While the existence of widespread feeling of war-weariness has been known to us for some time, this is the first positive evidence of a disposition on the part of the present government to negotiate with the Vietcong. It confirms a previous report that Khanh was contemplating an eventual deal with the insurgents." Even if Khanh did not intend an imminent move to negotiations, Hoach's revelations showed the present government position "to be even more brittle than we had thought."[38]

True to form, American officials, who were informed of the Hoach contacts by the British, never saw this dreary state of socio-politico-military affairs as a reason to ask fundamental questions about the U.S. commitment to the Saigon government, or as an opportunity that could be exploited to allow for a disengagement from what most agreed was a mess. To them it was merely another problem to be addressed. Hence the need for Robert Manning's domestic information campaign, to keep Cassandras like Lippmann, Church, Mansfield, and the *New York Times* (who *were* asking the fundamental questions) from gaining more support. Hence the need to continue to work against a large-scale, Geneva-type conference on Laos (such a conference would inevitably grow to encompass Vietnam, which was anathema) and instead to plug the Polish Plan, which was strictly limited to Laos, involved only a few countries, and could be strung out indefinitely while the situation in South Vietnam righted itself or, more accurately, was righted.[39]

And hence the need to kick into high gear the effort to get greater international support for South Vietnam and for the U.S. commitment there. Since its launching in April, the State Department's "more flags" campaign had accomplished next to nothing, and officials continued to put most of the blame on the French government. It was Charles de Gaulle, they argued, who was largely responsible for the tepid response from other western governments. The belief was erroneous, of course—the British and Canadians, for example, were coming to their interpretations on their own, thank you—but it was strong. Washington officials also were convinced that de Gaulle was largely responsible for the neutralization rumors enveloping Saigon and other cities in South Vietnam. The question was, what could be done? The French president had brushed off all previous American attempts, dating back to August 1963, to get him to change his tune or at least stop singing it.

The only answer was to try, try again. It was a remarkable phenomenon, this American persistence in attempting, time and again, to convince the French president, to cajole him, to get him to see things from Washington's perspective. Almost every time policymakers approached the Paris government in the mid 1960s, whether over Vietnam or one of the other issues that embroiled Franco-American relations—NATO, the French nuclear weapons program, and British entry into the European Economic Community (EEC), among others—they came away disappointed, sometimes with only a little of what they wanted, often with nothing. But they did not give up. Convinced of the damage that de Gaulle was doing on the Vietnam question, and how much additional trouble he could stir up if he chose to, the Johnson team in June made what would be its most determined overture yet to the Paris government; never again would it make such a concentrated effort. The timing for this push made eminent sense: the administration was in the midst of planning an enlarged American presence in the struggle, and it was imperative to find out how de Gaulle might react.[40] In addition, prior to any escalation it was important to show the leading domestic skeptics that a real effort had been made to at least hear the French out. "We don't want [Lippmann and Mansfield] to have the easy score that we didn't even try to talk to the French," Bundy said to LBJ on 1 June. The individual selected to carry out the assignment: Undersecretary of State George Ball.[41]

At first glance, it seemed a bizarre choice. Though Ball had uttered nary a word of reservation about U.S. Vietnam policy in the previous six months, he had in recent days begun to dredge up some of the arguments he made under Kennedy. Still fundamentally pessimistic about American prospects in any military confrontation in the region, Ball worried about plans to expand the U.S. commitment to the Saigon regime. The plans were going forward too precipitously, he believed, with too little attention paid to costs and alternatives, and too little to the lukewarm attitudes of America's allies. As undersecretary, Ball interacted with high-level foreign officials on an almost daily basis, and his conversations with them convinced him that the western world would not, either from self-interested or altruistic reasoning, support an Americanized war. Such a war would also exact a heavy price at home. It might be true, Ball conceded, that military failure or a compromise settlement would harm the administration domestically, but that would be nothing compared to the domestic political hazards of waging a land war in Asia.

Ball expressed his misgivings in a letter he wrote to Rusk in the wake of Johnson's 27 May meeting with Lippmann, which Ball had attended. Policy making on Vietnam had been marred, he began, parroting Lippmann, by an unwillingness to ask the hard questions about the nature of the conflict and its importance to American interests—by "an inarticulate wish to sweep difficult issues under the bed." Planning had proceeded not on the basis of addressing these core questions but on the assumption that, because the war might be lost under the present policy, the administration should move to increase its commitment, "even though (a) no one could be sure that the new plan of action would have the desired effect and (b) the risks of a major catastrophe might be vastly enlarged." Ball acknowledged that the questions might appear "negative and defeatist," but he proceeded to raise them anyway. Why was action against the North being contemplated? Was it because it had a realistic chance of working, or because the present course was not working and no one had thought of anything else to do? What did the United States hope to achieve by bombing above the seventeenth parallel? Was it realistic to expect such action to appreciably reduce Vietcong activity in the South? And what would such action say about American intentions? Would it signify an open-ended commitment by the United States to defend South Vietnam with U.S. troops, a key consideration "in light of the deep aversion of many Americans to the commitment of U.S. ground forces to the Asian mainland"? And what would be the effect on the South of an enlarged American presence? Might it not raise the "old colonial bogey" or, alternatively, persuade the mass of South Vietnamese that the United States would do the fighting and they need do nothing?[42]

Here was a foretaste of the George Ball who would become the most prominent in-house critic of escalation in the coming year: skeptical, searching, incisive, and prescient. Though Ball carefully avoided directly endorsing Lippmann's analysis of the conflict, he indicated the same deep-seated suspicions and asked the same fundamental questions as the columnist and, for that matter, Charles de Gaulle. Why Johnson nevertheless chose Ball to meet the French president is not entirely clear, though it was a familiar Johnson stratagem to send dissenters to argue on his behalf. Ball's loyalty was unswerving, and Johnson felt certain that he could count on Ball to defend government policy, whatever it might be. Johnson told him: "George, you're like the school teacher looking for a job with a small school district in Texas. When asked by the school board whether he believed that the earth was flat or round, he replied: 'Oh, I can teach it either way.' That's you. You can argue like hell with me against a position, but I know outside this room you're going to support me. You can teach it either flat or round."[43]

Armed with instructions from Johnson to emphasize the administration's peaceful intent but also its determination to meet its commitments to South Vietnam, Ball flew to Paris for a meeting on 5 June with the French leader.[44] In the splendor of the Elysée Palace, Ball outlined the U.S. position, telling de Gaulle that the administration's only objective was the preservation of a viable government in South Vietnam. The United States had only two choices, he said. It could do everything possible to strengthen the Saigon government politically and militarily, or, failing that, it could throw the weight of American military power onto the scale. Naturally the United States desired a diplomatic solution, but the situation in the South was so fragile that even the mention of negotiations might lead to its collapse and an immediate Vietcong victory. Consequently, the United States would not agree to negotiate until the situation on the battlefield had improved sufficiently to force the enemy to make the requisite concessions. In short, said Ball, "we would have to teach the North Vietnamese a lesson" before any talks could begin. He noted the need to prove American determination to the Chinese, likening them to the Bolsheviks of 1917: primitive and aggressive toward their neighbors.[45]

De Gaulle disagreed. In addition to the two policy options described by Ball, de Gaulle maintained that there existed a third: the United States could avoid further involvement and agree to the convening of an international conference similar in kind to the one held in Geneva in 1954. The United States could not win with force in Vietnam, even with its superior striking power, because the problem was not military but political. To the Khanh regime and to the people of South Vietnam, America was a very big, very foreign power, and the more force the United States committed, the more the population would turn against it. Washington was therefore pursuing the same illusions in Vietnam that had doomed France to such an unwinnable situation, believing that it could succeed by force. De Gaulle said that he sympathized with Johnson's dilemma but that the American president needed to know something about Vietnam: it was a hopeless place to fight. Vietnam is "rotten country," he said, a phrase Ball would never forget. France would never again become involved there, nor would it ever support any American escalation.[46]

The French president also doubted that China resembled the Soviet Union in 1917—intransigent, warlike, and expansive. If anything, he argued, China was weak and backward, lacking the military, industrial, and intellectual resources that the USSR had even in 1917. China would therefore not become aggressive until after it had consolidated its power, something that would require decades. Consequently, Beijing would in all likelihood accept neutralization for Vietnam, if only because it would secure its southern border. De Gaulle concluded by again urging the United States to agree to a Geneva-type conference. France had learned in Vietnam and Algeria that only negotiations could bring lasting results, and de Gaulle felt confident that all parties would agree to such a conference. The longer Americans stayed in the war, he intoned, the more humiliating their withdrawal would be.[47]

Ball left the meeting convinced that de Gaulle was "merely waiting for things to come his way," certain that the United States would soon begin "to consider seriously his suggestion of a conference." The undersecretary's own difficulty, of course, was that he agreed substantially with the French president's view. As he had indicated in his 31 May memo to Rusk, Ball felt certain that any American attempt to impose a military solution on the conflict was destined to fail, and he shared de Gaulle's conviction that an increased U.S. military commitment to the South would only increase Vietnamese anti-Americanism. And although he doubted somewhat de Gaulle's claim that the insurgents would willingly lose their momentum by accepting a cease-fire, he thought the risk worth taking. Thus, although Ball's cable to Washington said that the meeting had not brought the American and French positions closer together, his own views differed very little from those of the French leader. "Since de Gaulle's views supported what I had been arguing to my colleagues," he later wrote, "I hoped they would reinforce my position."[48]

Whatever he may have hoped, Ball gave no hint of it in reports to his superiors. In the cables he sent to Johnson and Rusk on 5 and 6 June, he adhered to standard diplomatic practice and said nothing about his own position on the war. If anything, he distanced himself from the French position, and in subsequent weeks he seemed intent on hiding his actual support for de Gaulle's suggestions. No doubt Ball's impatience with France's

European policies colored his thinking; as a strong advocate of European federation, he was irked at the French attempts to pursue an independent foreign policy, and he resented de Gaulle's efforts to damage American prestige. Most of all, Ball was unshakably loyal to his president; he could indeed "teach it either flat or round" and always did so, not only in Paris in June 1964 but on countless other occasions. Lyndon Johnson prized this attribute in people, and Ball knew it. He acted accordingly. He would remain ever the loyal servant in the fateful months that followed, even as the war he so abhorred came to consume the administration.

The failure of the Ball mission to move Paris and Washington closer together on the Vietnam issue distressed Johnson and his top aides, even if they had not been exactly hopeful going in. Little did they know that the Franco-American conflict on the war would soon become even more sharply delineated. De Gaulle, sensing an American escalation in the offing, as well as an opportunity to insert France more deeply into the Southeast Asia picture, in late June launched his most determined push yet for a reconvened Geneva conference. Three weeks after Ball returned home, de Gaulle, at a Paris dinner given in honor of the visiting Prince Norodom Sihanouk of Cambodia, assailed the "cruel divisions" of Southeast Asia, which he said were exacerbated by "unending foreign intervention." To Americans these comments were a double blow: the general had once again dismissed the legitimacy of the U.S. presence in the area, and had done so in front of Sihanouk, long a thorn in Washington's side. Even worse, Sihanouk endorsed de Gaulle's comments.

Dean Rusk was particularly outraged. It was vintage de Gaulle, he thought, arrogant grandstanding, delighting in causing grief to France's principal ally. In the days that followed Rusk held two contentious meetings with the French ambassador in Washington, Hervé Alphand, but these too failed to yield any change in the French position.[49] The schism that had developed between the two countries over the war was too wide. Washington and Paris shared one fundamental goal: preventing China from taking over Southeast Asia. On everything else, they differed. De Gaulle and Alphand insisted that Beijing's ambitions in Southeast Asia were limited, and that Washington therefore had options. For the student of American policymaking in Vietnam, this split is noteworthy not merely because it was so wide, or because Washington was unable or unwilling to really grapple with the particulars of the French position; equally important is the mere fact that Washington continued to attach so much importance to this French "obstructionism." To summarize how a hypothetical U.S. official might have put it, "There is no question of us adopting the French view of the conflict, but others might. We must work to prevent it." De Gaulle's name invariably came up when Americans fretted about premature negotiations, about the lack of allied support in general, and about the skepticism of important voices in the United States. And indeed, those skeptics (Lippmann, Morgenthau, the *New York Times*, and several Senate Democrats) invoked the general's name at almost every turn. In Southeast Asia, Norodom Sihanouk in Cambodia and Souvanna Phouma in Laos publicly welcomed his efforts. In Vietnam itself, the lingering French influence in all sectors of society, especially in the South, ensured that de Gaulle's every pronouncement received wide attention. Even Hanoi and the NLF uttered sympathetic noises about his position.

No wonder, then, that concerns about the far reach of French influence permeated the campaign to get increased allied involvement in the Vietnam struggle. In July, State Department officials urged other governments to not only provide greater material and rhetorical support for the war effort, but also publicly distance themselves from the French position. Johnson tried to reinforce the seriousness of the campaign with a long, impassioned circular cable of his own, distributed to eleven key embassies.[50] "I am gravely disappointed," the president wrote, "by the inadequacy of the actions by our friends and allies in response to our request that they share the burden of Free World responsibility in Vietnam." Johnson professed to be puzzled by this allied attitude and ordered his envoys to work even harder to change it: "I am charging you personally with the responsibility of seeing to it that the Government to which you are accredited understands how seriously we view the challenge to freedom in Viet Nam and how heavily the burden of responsibility for defending that freedom falls on those Governments who possess freedom in their own right," he wrote. "They must, if necessary, be reminded that their share of this burden is increased proportionately where they owe their own freedom to assistance they have received from others."

As for how much these governments should contribute, the president ordered the envoys to work out an "adequate program." "Our interest," he said, "is that this contribution should be as large and visible as possible in terms of *men on the scene*, in each case." Given that more than sixteen thousand American military personnel were on the scene, the allies, especially the larger ones, should be thinking in terms of hundreds of men each, not mere dozens. Johnson hammered home the importance of the effort: "I know of no other task imposed upon you in your current assignment which . . . precedes this one in its urgency and its significance. I therefore ask you personally to undertake this task in working with the highest levels of the Government to which you are accredited." To underscore the gravity of the situation, the president concluded with a none-too-subtle warning: "I will review reports of the progress being made responsive to this cable at regular intervals . . . [and] hope to see evidence of your success in the very near future."[51]

The recipients of this presidential directive could not have been happy when it came over the wire. Embassy staff in the various capitals knew that Johnson would not get to see evidence of their success "in the very near future" or, very likely, ever. Australia had agreed in June to send six air force transport planes and thirty additional army instructors (for a total of sixty). Infinitesimal though this military aid was compared to that of the United States, it was nevertheless larger than that of any other western nation. Not one of the eleven countries targeted in the Johnson cable was prepared to contribute personnel. Despite strong American pressure, West Germany had already ruled out even a small military presence in South Vietnam (as noted in chapter 5), as had other European allies including Britain, the Netherlands, Denmark, and Italy.[52]

Sympathetic to Washington's problem in Vietnam, not opposed per se to what the United States sought to accomplish, these governments nevertheless doubted that it could be done, for the same reasons that de Gaulle had. ("Most people," one British official wrote Prime Minister Douglas-Home, "feel that if the South-Vietnamese cannot cope [even] with American help, it is because they are war-weary, apathetic, and fed-up.") Like the French leader, these governments also downplayed Vietnam's importance to western security. They remained unwilling to openly challenge Washington over the war, and on occasion made tepid public professions of support, but they ruled out even a token military contribution to the war. Their pledges to provide a few million dollars in economic aid to Saigon meant little to a Johnson administration already spending more than one and a half million dollars a day in Vietnam.[53]

More embarrassing still to the administration, Asian allies were also lukewarm in their support for the war effort. Several of the countries that Johnson railed against in his cable were in Asia. The two most important, from Washington's perspective, were Pakistan and Japan. Karachi's position mattered primarily because Pakistan was a member of SEATO. As such, its opposition to American policy, like that of Paris, created an immense headache for U.S. officials trying to use America's SEATO "obligations" to justify and rally support for the war effort. A State Department memo in late July put it well: Pakistan's "increasing support for French neutralization proposals enhance the likelihood of a Karachi-Paris breach in the

SEATO front vis-à-vis South Vietnam." The government of President Mohammad Ayub Khan had not arrived at this policy suddenly—since February 1964, the State Department had warned of Pakistani support for de
Gaulle's proposals. The Ayub government had applauded the French president's recognition of China in January, and Foreign Minister Zulfikar Ali
Bhutto had made numerous visits to Paris in the first months of 1964. In
July, Bhutto announced that the question of Southeast Asia "should be settled on the conference table, not on the battlefield." That same month, Ayub
himself declared that Pakistan was in effect neutral as far as Vietnam was
concerned. Because it was his country's policy to avoid war unless attacked,
he said, "I don't see why we should get involved." Ayub did not mention
an additional rationale for his policy: a desire to foster good relations with
China. The Karachi government, obsessed with the danger to Pakistani security posed by India, believed that close ties with Beijing could bring more
protection than SEATO or other defense arrangements alone.[54]

Japan in mid 1964 had a more ambiguous position on the war. The
government of Ikeda Hayato prized close relations with Washington and
worked hard to maintain them. But it also sought a measure of independence from American tutelage, and the result was Japanese-American friction over several issues: over the status of Okinawa, which the United States
occupied but which Tokyo wanted returned to Japanese control; over the
presence of U.S.-controlled nuclear weapons on Japan's territory; and over
Japan's desire to increase trade with Beijing, despite Washington's objections.
By and large, however, relations between the two countries were harmoni-
ous in the summer of 1964. The close ties, coupled with Japan's proximity to Vietnam, led Johnson administration officials to assume that Tokyo
would make a sizable contribution to the "more flags" campaign. It did not
happen. The Ikeda government agreed in August to send a small medical team to Saigon and to provide the Khanh regime with one and a half
million dollars in aid, in the form of medicines, prefabricated buildings,
twenty-five ambulances, and twenty thousand radios. Although U.S. officials certainly welcomed this aid, it was not what they had in mind—it was
not the "large and visible" contribution Johnson had wanted, with "men
on the scene."[55]

Tokyo had strong doubts about the enterprise that the United States had
undertaken in Vietnam. Few Japanese had a taste for communism or wanted
a North Vietnamese victory in the conflict, but many on all parts of the political spectrum were haunted by memories of Japan's own misadventure
in China a quarter century earlier; they predicted that, much as Japanese
forces had bogged down then, Americans would bog down now if they
chose to fight. The imbalance of forces in Vietnam, with a shockingly weak

GVN aligned against a strong, determined adversary in the NLF and Hanoi, impressed the Japanese and pointed to the futility of what Washington sought to achieve. Much as France had failed earlier, the United States would fail now. And the Japanese feared that an escalated war, which looked increasingly likely, could eventually grow to include China. Officials in Tokyo thus ruled out both a vigorous rhetorical defense of the American effort and a significant material contribution to the war effort. When U.S. ambassador Edwin O. Reischauer pressed Tokyo officials for a more substantial involvement, they steadfastly refused. Before long, Reischauer later recalled, Vietnam would "cast a dark shadow over all Japanese-American relations."[56]

The same mixture of skepticism and fear permeated Southeast Asia itself. It is surely one of the startling realities of the war: if anyone should have been wholehearted in supporting the American mission in Vietnam, it should have been the noncommunist countries of this region. If European disaffection could be chalked up to remoteness, such was not the case with them. They were on the war's doorstep. They were the dominoes that Washington insisted would fall if the free-world bastion in South Vietnam collapsed. But the governments there saw the struggle differently. Washington's strenuous and continuous attempts to characterize the struggle against communism in Southeast Asia as a defense of all its allies in the region did not impress them. Whether the dominoes fell depended on the balance of forces in the individual country in question, they were convinced, not on what happened in Vietnam. In addition, these governments were concerned about antagonizing China, the big kid on the block. And, no less important, they were deeply pessimistic that the American and South Vietnamese forces could prevail in the conflict. Why commit to a losing cause, they asked, especially if doing so could raise the hackles of Beijing? For that matter, why antagonize Hanoi, the almost-certain victor in the war?

A few of these governments, notably Sihanouk's in Cambodia and Sukarno's in Indonesia, had by mid 1964 publicly declared their opposition to Washington's aims. Most, following the model of the Europeans, were content to stay silent or even offer public support for the war effort, all the while making private predictions of defeat and refusing to become meaningfully involved.[57] Even those few Asian nations that did eventually make significant contributions to the war effort (and thus were constantly brought forth by Washington as proof of an "international" war effort) exacted a heavy price for doing so—South Korea, the Philippines, and Thailand each demanded and received high remuneration for their personnel commitments.[58]

All the evidence, then, pointed to a "more flags" campaign that was floundering. When Lyndon Johnson in mid July asked aides to update him on the state of the campaign, they could only mumble that no real progress had been made. The Australians had come through with a personnel contribution, but no one else had. Many American policymakers, never expecting the campaign to be easy, were nevertheless taken aback by the difficulties they encountered. It did not seem to them that they were asking much of the allies—notwithstanding Johnson's talk of a "large and visible" presence, Washington would have been satisfied if the other governments had merely matched Canberra's modest commitment.

Herein lies an important truth about the "more flags" operation: the flags were needed in South Vietnam not for material, military reasons but for symbolic, psychological ones. Even a small allied presence, U.S. officials reasoned, would demonstrate to nervous South Vietnamese, to an ambivalent American public, and to the enemy the commitment of the anticommunist world to the struggle. And yet, ally after ally said no. Perhaps, American strategists hoped, the pressure tactics called for by Johnson in his cable just needed more time to work—only a couple of weeks had passed, after all, since the message went out. But they knew there was little reason to be optimistic.[59]

Fundamental though they were, these problems in the drive to get global support for U.S. policy were slow to manifest themselves, much to the administration's relief. The reluctance of most allied governments to openly confront Washington with their doubts and fears, and the willingness of several to offer rhetorical support for the American position and make vague pledges of economic assistance to Saigon, allowed Washington in 1964 to maintain the facade of noncommunist unity on the war. The administration could publicly claim, disingenuously but with little fear of protest, that the free world backed its policy. Still, U.S. policymakers were correct to attach great importance to the "more flags" campaign and to worry about the consequences of its failure. Robert Manning's parallel domestic campaign could never hope to fully succeed if Washington failed to get allied governments on board. Skeptics in Congress, the press, and the general population could rightly ask how the administration could wax rhapsodic about defending the western world in Vietnam and yet find almost total unwillingness among fellow western nations to join the team. Likewise, they might ask, why did the U.S. government seem more keen on fighting the war than those in Southeast Asia itself, those in the near vicinity of Vietnam, who presumably had the most at stake? That few Americans were asking these questions yet was scant comfort to officials; they knew that could change, especially if more countries joined France's lead and made a public break with the administration.

What is especially startling about what one might call the "few flags problem" is not that it complicated the effort to win support for the war among Americans, important as that was; rather, what really stands out is that it threatened to do the same thing in South Vietnam itself. Indeed, boosting the morale of the South Vietnamese had been a key rationale behind the effort to get allies to commit personnel to the conflict. The argument went roughly as follows: the allies will make a commitment; the Saigon regime will see that the free world is behind it; and the government, army, and people of the South will become more committed to the struggle. That Americans should need to worry about the commitment of the people they were fighting for pointed, as noted, to the fatal flaw at the center of the war effort. War-weariness and apathy among the South Vietnamese were a constant source of concern to U.S. officials in both Washington and Saigon in June and July, more so even than they had been earlier in the year. As always, concern about neutralist sentiment followed closely behind.

Fear of neutralism: it is everywhere in the administration cables, memoranda, and meeting notes that summer—sometimes spoken, sometimes implicit, always there. The fear existed on two levels: the fear that voices outside Vietnam preaching neutralization might reach a crescendo and force a return to Geneva, and the fear that the Vietnamese themselves might find neutralism preferable to a continuation of the war. The CIA warned in July that the mass of southerners were tired of twenty years of war, were anxious to end it, and might well view neutralization with sympathy. Canadian and British diplomats told their respective governments the same thing. When Nguyen Khanh in July began pressing for an expansion of the war to North Vietnam, U.S. officials speculated that he might be doing so because of "pressure from the neutralist-minded." The State Department instructed Ambassador Taylor to watch "as closely as possible for neutralist thinking in Vietnamese circles" and for signs of possible contacts between Hanoi and Saigon officials or former members of the Minh junta.[60]

Taylor shared these concerns. Barely into his term as ambassador, anxious to get the war effort moving, he was distressed by Khanh's evident inability to bring effective leadership to the struggle against the Vietcong (Taylor had been among those who had cheered Khanh's assumption of power six months earlier). Khanh faced significant opposition from within the military, Taylor reported, and "on the civilian side he has been unable to achieve any real unity of purpose and action among his official family."

He seemed obsessed with political intrigue and backbiting. Khanh's talk of a "march to the North" particularly angered Taylor, because it represented an act of open defiance on the part of a Saigon government that owed its existence to the United States. Khanh, in other words, had embarrassed the United States and wreaked havoc on Lyndon Johnson's plans to avoid if possible any drastic foreign-policy departures in Vietnam before November, at least those departures not of his own choosing.

Khanh could be forgiven for feeling confused. Had not expanding the war to North Vietnam been an American idea in the first place? Was he not now merely repeating what U.S. officials had long said might be necessary? Why this hostile reaction? There was, indeed, eminent logic in Khanh's proposal, as independent observers could plainly see. "The irony," said a Canadian official, "is that, having launched the idea of retaliation against North Vietnam, United States officials are now embarrassed and disquieted at the success their propaganda has had on the South Vietnamese authorities themselves." Khanh knew that Americans were laying plans for an expanded war. He knew that the Johnson administration had staked its support on his leadership and that this gave him substantial leverage. He knew that Barry Goldwater had recently won the nomination to head the Republican ticket, a sign, perhaps, that there was support in the United States for a more aggressive war policy, including attacks outside South Vietnam's frontiers. And he knew, as did Americans, that the Sino-Soviet split was deepening and that this reduced the risk of Chinese or Soviet intervention in the event of a march to the North. Desperate for a way to revive his fortunes, Khanh no doubt believed that his open advocacy of expanded action might draw the Americans in, or might give them an excuse to escalate, if that was what they wanted.[61]

It was not an auspicious start for the Taylor-Khanh relationship, and it augured worse to come. For the moment, however, Taylor saw no alternative to a Khanh-led government. He warned of war-weariness among other leaders in Saigon and cautioned that there were generals and senior officials who were "of a neutralist bent." Khanh's government might be shaky, Taylor told Rusk, but it was better than any conceivable alternative. The "march to the North" problem thus had to be handled carefully. "If [Khanh and his colleagues] are unsuccessful in getting the U.S. more directly involved," the ambassador warned, "it is difficult to judge at this stage how strong pressures would become within the GVN to seek a negotiated solution. However, there are signs that this possibility cannot be excluded." Accordingly, Taylor proposed, and the State Department endorsed, the initiation of joint U.S.-GVN contingency planning for numerous forms of extended action against the North. Such planning would defuse the clamor for going north and would buy more time to stabilize the situation in South Vietnam and to neutralize the neutralist elements. Most important, it would allow American officials to reestablish decision-making control in the war effort.[62]

While Americans fretted about neutralism in South Vietnam, they also had to observe another international figure step forward to endorse the concept and to call for a reconvened Geneva conference. This time it was United Nations Secretary General U Thant. A former foreign minister of Burma with widely respected neutralist credentials, Thant had for some months been growing increasingly alarmed about the escalation of the fighting. In late 1963, he had hoped that the overthrow of the Diem regime would facilitate the emergence of a more representative government in the South. In a talk with Adlai E. Stevenson, the American ambassador to the UN, Thant had urged the formation of a broad-based government that would include exiles in Paris and elsewhere and begin to enact much needed reforms. He continued to make that pitch privately in the spring of 1964.[63]

Thant grew more worried as spring turned to summer and as Johnson, Rusk, and others in the administration talked tough and vowed American steadfastness in the war. He believed that the more the United States intervened, the more it would be resented by Asians, which meant that failure was inevitable. (If Burma in 1947 had received U.S. aid or advisers, Thant liked to say, the country would have been lost to the communists.) By midsummer, he determined that he would have to speak out publicly. On 8 July, Thant told a news conference that the 1954 Geneva Conference should be reconvened to negotiate peace in Southeast Asia. For ten years, Thant told the reporters, he had been convinced "that military methods will not bring about peace in South Vietnam." The "only sensible solution," therefore, "even at this late hour," was negotiations. Thant rejected a UN role in these negotiations, in view of the fact that "more than one" of the parties concerned (North Vietnam, South Vietnam, and China) were not members of the organization, but he offered UN assistance in monitoring any agreement. "Of course, if there is an agreement by the parties primarily concerned," he said, "the UN can be involved at that stage to see that any agreement is observed." The secretary general also offered to lend his personal efforts to the negotiations; he felt that as secretary general, and as a native of neutral Burma, he could talk to persons and parties who would not talk to one another. His strength, he said, lay in his impartiality. Thant concluded on a personal note: "Whenever I read of the death of an American or the death of a Vietnamese my heart bleeds. To me it makes no difference whether the man killed is an American or a Vietnamese."[64]

The State Department immediately rejected the proposal with the brief comment that what was needed was not a new conference but communist compliance with previous accords. If the intention was to downplay the significance of Thant's comments, it failed—his news conference received wide play in the press, with lead articles on the front page of the *New York Times, Le Monde,* and the London *Times* the following day. The *New York Times* extolled his pronouncement in a lead editorial that blasted the State Department's "frigid response." So what if past agreements had been violated? the paper asked. That fact did not negate "the kernel of the Secretary General's statement, the need for negotiations." A key figure on Capitol Hill also took favorable notice. Senator J. William Fulbright, increasingly concerned about the war and about the direction of U.S. policy but still unwilling to challenge his own president openly, told Johnson at a White House dinner in late July that he welcomed the idea of a negotiating track with Hanoi via Thant.[65]

The entry of U Thant into the fray was thus another blow to American efforts to build support for its policy and to discourage talk of a return to Geneva. Dean Rusk was especially put off. He had little respect for Thant and thought him a weak secretary general, a man much too inclined to accommodate communists. It annoyed him that Thant was injecting himself into the conflict. "Who does he think he is?" Rusk would ask. "Does he think he's a country?" But as the United Nations' top diplomat, Thant could not merely be ignored. Rusk therefore sent Adlai Stevenson to try to talk sense into him. Stevenson had been having his own fears and doubts about the war. He believed that all alternatives looked unpalatable.[66]

Stevenson and Thant met on 11 July. Thant began by assuring Stevenson that he had not meant to suggest that a return to Geneva had to happen immediately. He was sympathetic to the American position, he added, even though he did not agree with it. But then Thant turned somber and warned of dire consequences if Washington continued to pursue a military solution. "I am fearful that the more the U.S. becomes involved, the weaker its cause will become, he said. "Hanoi is broadcasting stories about desertions to the Vietcong. The more experience the Vietnamese have with the war and the terrorism, the more fed-up and fearful they will become, with consequent desertions." Thant noted that the situation had not improved "from the viewpoint of democratic institutions," and he speculated that it would deteriorate and not improve the bargaining position of the United States. "The communists insist it was the U.S. which violated the 1954 accords by giving massive support to South Vietnam in violation of the neutrality provisions. It is a chicken and egg sequence, as usual."

In phrasing the issue this way, Thant struck a blow at the heart of the administration's policy vis-à-vis diplomacy. Since at least 1961, Americans had maintained that negotiations could not be undertaken until the Saigon government's bargaining position improved. This was not an unreasonable position to hold, but there was one problem: that bargaining position could not improve unless the United States maintained an active, perhaps central, role in the struggle. U.S. officials understood this reality and accepted it; they were prepared to expand the American presence as much as necessary. U Thant, in contrast, told Adlai Stevenson that such action would inevitably doom the South Vietnamese cause. An Americanized war, he believed, would have precisely the opposite effect of what was intended.

Thant told Stevenson that Ho Chi Minh was no puppet of the Chinese ("he is more Russian than Chinese"), but that geography kept the North Vietnamese leader from making his position clear. Ho's views should be sought in confidence, Thant suggested, and he said that he would consult with Ne Win, the premier in his native Burma, who "is in contact with all of the parties," about who might be a suitable channel. Later, the United States could consult with Paris, London, and Moscow about the best way to get to the conference table.[67]

Consult Paris? About the best way to get to Geneva? Nothing was further from the minds of Lyndon Johnson and his Vietnam advisers. De Gaulle was a large part of the problem, they reasoned, and certainly not the solution. They wondered if the French president's large frame was not standing directly behind the diminutive Thant, pushing him, urging him to speak out publicly against American aims. They may have been right. The secretary general got on well with de Gaulle, had visited Paris on several occasions, and was a big believer in the concept of neutralism in world affairs. He certainly shared the French pessimism about the prospects for the Washington-Saigon war effort. On 21 July, Thant returned to Paris for a meeting with de Gaulle on a broad range of subjects, among them Vietnam. The two agreed that neutralization was the best bet and that a conference ought to be convened. After the meeting, Thant told the press that the problem in South Vietnam could not be settled by military means but only by "political and diplomatic means, negotiations and discussions." The hope for a settlement, he said, rested in the reconvening of the 1954 Geneva Conference.[68]

Perhaps not coincidentally, de Gaulle issued the same plea two days later at an extraordinary news conference watched closely by American officials. The troubles in Indochina had their root, he began, in the failure of both sides to respect the Geneva agreements of 1954. Pressure by the new communist regime in North Vietnam against South Vietnam brought in the

United States, which at that time gave aid to anyone who opposed communism. Herein lay the explanation for America's intervention: "I believe that one can add, without hurting our American friends, that their conviction that they were fulfilling a sort of vocation, and also their aversion to all colonial activity which was not theirs, and finally the very natural desire in such a powerful people to take up new positions, all this determined them to take over Indochina from France."

The trouble was, de Gaulle continued, that Washington's subsequent heavy commitment to the regime of Ngo Dinh Diem, and to two successor regimes, had not checked the Vietcong advance or the decline in support among southerners for "an authority and a cause" that appeared to them to be that of a foreign state. A continued application of American policy would thus inevitably fail. There could be no military solution in South Vietnam for the United States, regardless of how much force it applied. Thus, "since war cannot bring a solution, one must make peace," and the best way to do so would be a return to Geneva. This time the agreements would have to be respected; that is, this time no foreign power would intervene in the "unfortunate countries" of Indochina.

De Gaulle had said much of this before. What was new was the explicit suggestion that the conference agenda should cover the whole region—previously he had tended to speak of a meeting only on Laos (though he no doubt believed, as did Americans, that a Laos conference would inevitably address South Vietnam as well). In addition, this time de Gaulle provided specifics to go along with his usual vague generalities. Two things, he said, were needed for a new Geneva conference to be successful: first, the meeting would have to include "in principle the same participants" as in 1954; and second, "everyone should go on the condition he wants peace . . . without preconditions and without claims." Once in Geneva, the United States, China, the Soviet Union, and France should agree to get out and stay out of Indochina, as a means of ending the fighting in South Vietnam and Laos, and should agree to the neutralization of the region. On top of that, de Gaulle proposed, there should be a massive technical and economic aid program for the whole of Indochina, provided by the "states that have the means, in such a way that development should replace destruction."[69]

Nervous American officials went over de Gaulle's comments line by line and debated how to respond.[70] As always, they viewed the French president's position primarily as a public relations problem to be dealt with, not as a proposal to be genuinely explored. Lyndon Johnson expressed the administration's position with stark finality the following day; addressing de Gaulle's pronouncement, the president told reporters, "We do not believe in conferences called to ratify terror, so our policy is unchanged." The next day the Saigon government, with Ambassador Taylor's urging, issued a statement of its own: "The Republic of Vietnam unequivocally rejects the proposition directed toward the convening of a new Geneva conference, and is wholly committed to pursuing its struggle against the aggressors, in spite of colonialist [in other words, French] and communist efforts." On 28 July, in an apparent effort to underscore the administration's rejection of negotiations (and to encourage Khanh), Johnson announced that the size of the U.S. military mission in South Vietnam would be increased by close to a third, from sixteen thousand to almost twenty-two thousand military advisers.[71]

What should we conclude about this flurry of activity in mid 1964 geared to finding a political solution to the conflict? It is an intriguing question, and it is made more so by the communist world's hints during this period of support for a conference-table settlement. Analysts at the State Department's Bureau of Intelligence and Research (INR) speculated that encouragement from communist governments had motivated de Gaulle to speak in such detail at his 23 July press conference. There were signs, these analysts reported, that the relevant Asian communist regimes were more willing than previously to "consider the idea of the peninsula's neutralization at a Geneva-type conference."[72]

The Hanoi government, for example, followed up Pham Van Dong's conciliatory encounter with Blair Seaborn by voicing support in July for a conference-table settlement. In Paris in midmonth, Mai Van Bo, the head of the North Vietnamese trade delegation in Paris, told a news conference that his government favored another meeting of the Geneva powers, though preferably with eleven rather than the original fourteen members (he excluded without elaboration the three members of the ICC, India, Poland, and Canada). The NLF, too, spoke out in favor of reconvening the Geneva Conference. On 20 July, Le Monde printed an undated interview with NLF leader Nguyen Huu Tho in which he expressed willingness to have other countries present in negotiations between Vietnamese for the neutralization of South Vietnam. Tho said that, after the settlement, these countries could help guarantee its continued neutrality. Five days later, after de Gaulle's press conference, Tho praised the French leader's comments and said that the NLF was prepared "to begin negotiations with all parties, groups, religious sects, and patriotic persons, without regard to differences of political views or past actions."[73]

Beijing, too, made sympathetic noises. Early in the year, Chinese officials had supported Sihanouk's appeal for a meeting to guarantee Cambodia's neutrality; in late May, they had called for a reconvening of the

1962 Geneva Conference on Laos. In July, Beijing indicated a willingness to extend such a conference to include Vietnam, even as it reaffirmed its commitment to help North Vietnam if it were attacked by the United States. On 10 July, Premier Zhou Enlai and Foreign Minister Chen Yi traveled to Rangoon and reportedly urged support for U Thant's proposed international conference on Vietnam. The Sino-Burmese communiqué that resulted from the meeting called for a conference specifically on Laos but framed this call with an expression of "deep concern over the deteriorating situation in Southeast Asia, particularly in South Vietnam." About a week later, Zhou told visiting members of the Japan Socialist Party that de Gaulle's conference idea constituted a clever way by which the United States could gracefully withdraw from the war. (Revealing himself to be a student of American domestic politics, Zhou noted that such a move would be sure to encounter the opposition of Barry Goldwater.) Zhou told his guests that his government supported the convening of a fourteen-member conference as soon as possible to settle the problems of Laos and Indochina, and he added that the number of nations calling for such a meeting increased daily. Some who had remained silent, such as Britain and Canada, would feel compelled to attend if the meeting were called: "If the problems are placed before [London and Ottawa] of whether to expand the war or hold a conference, they will [have] no choice but to advocate the opening of the conference." Zhou said that in such a situation, only three nations, the United States, South Vietnam, and Thailand, would remain opposed to a conference.[74]

This is not to suggest that Beijing was actively seeking a conference, or that it had in any way mellowed its harsh denunciation of American involvement in Southeast Asia. On the contrary, Chinese officials in June and July condemned U.S. policy in Laos and Vietnam more vigorously than ever and worked to increase their coordination with the North Vietnamese. On 5–8 July, Zhou Enlai visited Hanoi and discussed the recent developments in Laos and South Vietnam with DRV leaders. On 6 July, Chen Yi declared that the Chinese people could not be expected "to look on with folded arms" in the face of aggression against North Vietnam. A *People's Daily* article three days later made the same point. At the end of July, when American and Chinese representatives held one of their periodic meetings in Warsaw, the exchanges were sharp, despite assurances from both sides that they did not intend to provoke hostilities with each other. Still, in assessing the Chinese posture it is important to distinguish between words and actions, between the bark and the bite, between Beijing's confrontational rhetoric and its desire to avoid direct confrontation because of its military weakness vis-à-vis the United States. (Note that the "folded arms" statement did not actually commit China to doing anything.) Almost certainly, Zhou Enlai meant what he said: Beijing supported a return to Geneva. According to INR, recent developments suggested that all three of the adversaries in the region—Beijing, Hanoi, and the NLF—appeared more sympathetic than previously to the convening of an international conference, on the grounds that it was "preferable to accepting the risks of escalation."[75]

What about the Soviet Union? North Vietnamese leaders had long distrusted the Soviets and Nikita Khrushchev for capitulating to the United States in the Cuban Missile Crisis and for signing the Kennedy-initiated Test Ban Treaty. Following the Ninth Plenum of the Lao Dong party in December 1963, which resulted in a pro-Chinese orientation in Hanoi's posture, Moscow's influence plummeted. The first half of 1964 thus marked a low point in the Soviet–North Vietnamese relationship, as the two governments squabbled over Hanoi's closer relations with Beijing and over the best way to advance the socialist struggle. (North Vietnamese leaders maintained that the principal role had to be played by national liberation movements, not by Moscow or other socialist countries.) For Khrushchev and other Soviet officials, an international conference to neutralize the region thus marked an opportunity to reassert their political influence over Indochina. Neutralization also had a more basic attraction: it would prevent an expanded war. Moscow viewed Washington's recent tough talk on the conflict with alarm and, according to both the CIA and the State Department, sought a way of alleviating the crisis. The Soviets, the latter predicted, might not provide explicit approval for a return to Geneva, but they would work to keep the proposal alive. On 25 July, echoing de Gaulle and U Thant, Moscow expressed support for a reconvened Geneva conference.[76]

An enticing proposal that might have had a good chance of resolving the Vietnam conflict before the eruption of major war—that is how one might describe the push in July 1964 for a reconvened Geneva conference. In this way the summer of 1964 was like the summer of 1963, a time of missed opportunity for a political solution to the conflict. But also as in 1963, it was a solution that never really had a chance of being realized, despite the momentum behind it in much of the international community. For the United States government, Geneva was a nightmare destination, to be avoided at any cost, even if elements in South Vietnam expressed a willingness to go. On 25 July, a State Department intelligence report warned that Saigon leaders were beginning to believe they had only two alternatives: either an attack on the North, or negotiations. (On the same day, Maxwell Taylor reported the same thing from the Saigon embassy.) Should these leaders conclude that Washington had precluded going North and that the U.S. commitment to South Vietnam was less than total, "they might well reach the point of seeing negotiations as the only feasible option."[77]

Other observers, too, saw events at the end of July moving to a climax of one kind or another. Several pointed to a *Saigon Daily News* article of 26 July, which said that, without an attack on the North, neutralism would triumph. "Who can blame [the people], then, if they succumb to the temptations of de Gaulle's promises?" the paper asked. On 30 July, the *News* said that the South Vietnamese people were tired of dying in an apparently hopeless cause. Canada's Seaborn saw the danger signs in these and other expressions of desperation. He told Ottawa that Khanh, who seemed himself to be tired of the struggle, might abandon the premiership if he could not get Washington to go along with an attack on the North. The British embassy on 30 July informed London of numerous reports in recent days of peasant demonstrations in favor of peace and U.S. withdrawal, and pointed to Khanh's "growing realisation that he lacks the prestige and experience to unite his government and to lead his tired people through a long war." Khanh's hope: to "escape from the realities of the situation" through an attack on the North. Unless his demands for a march to the North were met, the embassy predicted, Khanh might well opt for a deal with the NLF through his already-established contacts.[78]

All observers could agree that something had to happen. Certainly the senior officials in Washington thought so. They knew that the information campaign they had launched two months earlier had not yet succeeded in demonstrating to the key audiences around the world America's determination to stick it out in Vietnam. They knew that they would have to demonstrate that determination again, forcefully and soon, but without a "fundamental change in policy," without unduly disrupting the president's keep-Vietnam-quiet election strategy for November. In a few days they would get their chance, as a result of murky developments in the waters of the Gulf of Tonkin.

7 Provocations

In the early days of August 1964 the Johnson administration launched the first American air strikes ever against North Vietnam. Shortly thereafter it rammed through Congress the Gulf of Tonkin Resolution, giving it carte blanche to "take all necessary steps" to defend South Vietnam. Major signposts on the road to full-scale war in Vietnam, these developments marked the beginning of a highly important period in the conflict in Indochina, a period that would culminate in early November, when Lyndon Johnson achieved what had been his all-consuming goal since ascending to the White House a year earlier: a massive election victory that made him president in his own right (and thereby removed the chief restraint on expanded American action in Vietnam). These three months are the subject of this chapter and the next.

In the international arena these months witnessed a serious effort by the United Nations secretary general to bring about negotiations on the war, and much strategizing about Vietnam in Moscow, Paris, London, Beijing, and other capitals. Canadian diplomat J. Blair Seaborn made a second visit to Hanoi, and North Vietnamese officials traveled to Beijing to talk strategy with Mao Zedong. In South Vietnam, the last vestiges of governmental authority in Saigon all but disappeared, as a series of regimes rose and fell, as religious tensions flared up anew, and as the Vietcong continued to pile up victories in vital areas of South Vietnam. For American officials, the time of decision had arrived. "The Vietnam War as it has been fought in the last three years seems to be drawing to a close," Peter Grose accurately noted in the *New York Times* in early September. "To replace it by a costly new effort with more direct American participation or to cut losses in a negotiated peace—that is the larger policy question." To escalate or get out: that was indeed the central, inescapable question, as it had been for the previous twelve months. The difference now was that it had to be fully confronted, because the war was, as Grose perceived, at a turning point.

The president and his top men never doubted which way they would go: they would escalate. Neither the mounting chaos in South Vietnam nor the refusal of Hanoi to bend to American threats diminished their determination. Never in this period did these men question the American commitment as outlined in NSAM 288 back in March. Their only concern was how to retrieve the situation. U.S. officials understood that the old palliatives—more aid, more advice, and more threats to Hanoi—would no longer suffice. And although they were not yet thinking in terms of a massive escalation of the war, including the introduction of U.S. ground troops and the massive bombing of North Vietnam, they were agreed that new measures were needed, new measures designed to increase the pressure on the North. As Ambassador Maxwell Taylor put it in mid August, to avert certain defeat "something must be added in the coming months."[1]

But not before the election. At the beginning of August, Lyndon Johnson had his eyes on the prize that would be his in three short months, provided he played things safe. Finally he would be elected president, would emerge from John Kennedy's shadow, and would be able to emulate his hero, Franklin D. Roosevelt, by making his Great Society the successor to the New Deal—provided he played things safe. Dramatic new measures, at home or abroad, were to be avoided if at all possible. "D day" in Vietnam, as aides now routinely called the day for initiating the bombing of North Vietnam, would have to await the president's own D day, 3 November. Johnson wanted not merely to win this election, but to win big. At the beginning of August, as he surveyed his chances, he had reason to feel confident. The momentous civil rights bill, which skeptics had said would never survive, had become law a few weeks earlier. Public opinion polls showed that he was popular, even among voters who had supported Richard Nixon in 1960—especially welcome news given the Deep South's defection from Democratic ranks to the independent candidacy of George Wallace, governor of Alabama. The nomination of Arizona senator Barry Goldwater to head the Republican ticket also pleased Johnson. Seasoned politician that he was, Johnson knew better than to take any opponent lightly, but he felt confident that Goldwater's far-right pronouncements would alienate the mass of voters and would allow him, Johnson, to continue to position himself as a moderate, middle-of-the-road leader who could be trusted. On Vietnam in particular, Goldwater's belligerent language would allow Johnson to sell himself as the candidate of firmness and restraint.

Honest and blunt-spoken, a reserve general in the air force, Goldwater was the inspirational leader of the conservative movement in the United

States. Faith in God, love of country, anticommunism, and opposition to modernism in art and religion—these were the basic themes he hit upon in frequent speeches to conservative audiences and in his manifesto, *The Conscience of a Conservative*. Time and again Goldwater asked Americans to consider the fundamental question: were enough of them willing to die to keep communism from spreading over the entire globe? Only if the answer was yes could American liberty be preserved. "We are in clear and imminent danger of being overwhelmed by alien forces," he wrote in his book. "We are confronted by a world revolutionary movement that possesses not only the will to dominate absolutely every square mile of the globe, but increasingly the capacity to do so." In a typical speech to an audience in Los Angeles in March 1964, Goldwater charged that American "backdownsmanship" was the defining characteristic of the Johnson administration's foreign policy. There was only one way, he said, for the United States to deter war and keep the peace: "to make sure the enemy knows he cannot and will not win any war that he might be tempted to start. But our enemy will never know that—our enemy will never respect that so long as the architects of defeat are in power in Washington."[2]

In his acceptance speech after nomination at the party's convention in San Francisco, Goldwater made clear that his campaign would not shy away from fundamental questions about the war. "Yesterday it was Korea, tonight it is Vietnam," he warned the delegates. "Make no bones of this. Don't try to sweep this under the rug. We are at war in Vietnam. And yet the president, who is commander-in-chief of our forces, refuses to say—refuses to say, mind you—whether the objective there is victory, and his Secretary of Defense continues to mislead and misinform the American people, and enough of this has gone by."[3]

Lost in the hubbub surrounding the convention and his nomination, Goldwater's pointed words about Johnson's Vietnam policy received little attention. But, of course, he had it exactly right. The United States was involved in a war in Vietnam, and administration representatives, including the president, were withholding from the public crucial information about the war and about the contingency plans to expand the conflict to North Vietnam. It was a deliberate strategy, adhered to with scrupulous care since the beginning of the year and aimed at keeping Vietnam in the background until polling day. The administration was anxious to preserve the deception until November, even as it laid the groundwork for new military measures. But a policy of delay generated a problem of its own, one that had bedeviled U.S. officials for months and had become acute in July. What if South Vietnamese leader Nguyen Khanh or other Saigon officials, sensing the war-weariness among their people and perhaps seeing accommodation with the enemy as the best of a set of bad alternatives, gave up the fight? What if they opted to end the war through a political solution? The possibility was very real, as the CIA, the intelligence analysts at the State Department, and Maxwell Taylor had indicated in separate analyses in late July.

Note that the concern was not military. American officials were quite confident that the military situation, though poor and getting worse, was not in danger of collapsing entirely, at least for the remainder of 1964. They surmised that the Vietcong, despite its formidable strength, was not yet capable of conquering all of South Vietnam. The problem, rather, was that the Vietcong might not *need* to conquer it; the Saigon government might collapse on its own, or might opt for accommodation with the NLF (a possibility that was not lost on the NLF and Hanoi: why launch a major military offensive, they reasoned, if it might not be necessary?). Though top U.S. policymakers were loath to admit it, they were more committed to this war than were their clients in South Vietnam, and they were anxious to once again demonstrate that commitment, to convince Nguyen Khanh that Lyndon Johnson was determined to stick it out, so that Khanh could be determined too. Such a demonstration might also quiet Republican charges that the administration was not doing enough to win the war. Johnson's July decision to raise the U.S. personnel count from sixteen thousand to twenty-two thousand had been one demonstration of America's resoluteness, but something else would clearly be needed before long.

Which brings us to the Gulf of Tonkin episode, destined to become one of the most controversial episodes in a controversial war.[4] Understanding what happened in the gulf and why requires understanding this urgent administration need to reaffirm its commitment to the struggle and find a way to jump-start the flagging effort in South Vietnam. It also requires understanding that, contrary to the administration's claims, the incident had in fact been provoked, consciously or not, by the United States. And it requires understanding that American officials engaged in deliberate and repeated deception about what went on in the gulf in the days surrounding the affair.

The administration's retelling of events went roughly as follows: on 2 August, the U.S. destroyer *Maddox*, innocently traversing international waters in the Gulf of Tonkin off the central coast of North Vietnam, was attacked without provocation by three North Vietnamese patrol boats. The *Maddox* returned fire, but the United States, anxious to avoid war and willing to treat the incident as an isolated, one-time mistake on the part of the authorities in Hanoi, chose only to issue a warning to the attackers. But when the North Vietnamese launched a second unprovoked attack in the gulf two days later, Washington had no choice but to respond, in the

form of limited and appropriate air strikes against North Vietnamese patrol boat bases and other targets on the northern coastline. A second unprovoked attack so soon after the first was a sure sign of Hanoi's aggressive
intentions, officials said, and it necessitated a congressional resolution authorizing the president to take required action to defend U.S. interests in
Southeast Asia.

This account was wholly correct about the first point: North Vietnamese
vessels did attack the *Maddox* on 2 August, inflicting minor damage. After
that, however, the government's version of events is problematic. The question of whether the *Maddox* had been in international waters at the time
of the attack, as the Americans claimed, or in the North's territorial waters,
as Hanoi claimed, is open to interpretation. The attack occurred about ten
miles off the coast. U.S. officials ostensibly assumed a three-mile territorial
limit, such as had been set by the French in the colonial period. But they
could just as easily have assumed the more common twelve-mile limit, such
as China observed. Hanoi did claim a twelve-mile limit but did not make it
public until September 1964, a month after the attack.[5]

The more serious question concerns the supposed innocence of the *Maddox*'s presence in the gulf, and the related issue of whether the attack on
the destroyer was unprovoked. Here the administration's case is shaky indeed. The *Maddox* was not merely transiting the gulf, as the White House
claimed. It was there to engage in eavesdropping activities as part of the
Desoto spy mission of the National Security Agency (before entering the
gulf, the destroyer had stopped in Taiwan and picked up a van of electronic
gear and seventeen specialists to operate the equipment). In addition, while
the *Maddox* was beginning its zigzag course and scanning the North
Vietnamese littoral, U.S.-directed South Vietnamese units were launching
Oplan 34-A guerrilla raids against offshore islands nearby. Though conceding that they knew of Oplan 34-A operations taking place in the vicinity of
the Desoto patrols, senior American officials denied that the two operations were connected. However, a State Department cable to the Saigon
embassy written right after the attack indicated something else: "We believe the present Oplan 34-A activities are beginning to rattle Hanoi, and
Maddox incident is clearly related to their effort to resist these activities.
We have no intention of yielding to pressure." The two activities were
also linked in the sense that the Desoto patrols gathered intelligence useful
to the Oplan 34-A raids, and the raids brought enemy responses that
could in turn be monitored by the technicians aboard the destroyer. In
any event, North Vietnamese military commanders undoubtedly thought
the two programs were related, and they acted accordingly. What is more,
the administration knew that they thought so.[6]

Then there is the issue of the alleged second attack, on 4 August. Whether it in fact occurred has long been a source of controversy, but the appearance of a major study by historian Edwin Moïse almost certainly has settled the issue: no attack on American ships occurred that day.[7] That evening, the *Maddox*, which had returned to the gulf, and another destroyer, the *C. Turner Joy*, reported that they were under attack. Just a few hours later, however, Captain John Herrick, head of the Desoto mission on the *Maddox*, cabled that because of "freak weather effects" and "overeager sonarmen," a number of the supposed contacts may not have been contacts at all. Herrick advised a thorough evaluation before any further action. As Moïse demonstrates, physical evidence for a second incident is exceedingly slight, whereas the evidence that it did not occur is very strong. It was a stormy, moonless night, and although several men on board the *C. Turner Joy* reported a torpedo wake, others were doubtful. Two U.S. airmen flying overhead for much of the alleged encounter saw nothing. Several U.S. officials, among them Deputy Director of the CIA Ray Cline, who studied the matter in detail, concluded that no second attack had occurred. Even Johnson himself told an aide a few days later: "Hell, those dumb, stupid sailors were just shooting at flying fish."[8]

On the actual day of this "incident," however, Johnson and his advisers were anxious to believe that the two destroyers had come under fire, or at least to say that they believed it. According to National Security Adviser McGeorge Bundy, Johnson decided early in the day—possibly even before the shooting started, when all he had were reports that an attack on the destroyers might be imminent—to use the incident as a means to get a congressional resolution passed. And the machinery for a retaliatory attack was set in motion almost immediately after the first reports came in, which left no time to conduct the evaluation that Herrick had suggested. Indeed, his cable advising delay arrived after the decision to retaliate had been made, though early enough that Johnson could easily have halted the plans, had he wanted to. He did not. Ascertaining the facts, finding out what actually happened or did not happen, was by all accounts a low priority at the White House that day. Johnson did pressure McNamara to find verification of the 4 August incident, but again only after the retaliation decision had been made, which suggests that his primary concern was to guard against future charges that he had acted with undue haste.

With sketchy information, the president convened sixteen congressional leaders in the early evening of 4 August and told them that he had ordered retaliation. Rusk, McNamara, CIA director John McCone, and Joint Chiefs of Staff chairman Gen. Earle Wheeler also spoke. Each emphasized the unprovoked nature of the attack and the need for a quick demonstration of

American resolve. Their words had the desired effect: only Senate Majority Leader Mike Mansfield voiced opposition to retaliation. ("The Communists won't be forced down," he said, and any attempt to do so would cost "a lot of lives.") All the others were in favor. The discussion turned to the subject of a congressional resolution, which Johnson had already broached with some of them earlier in the day. Everyone, including Mansfield, said that they would support a resolution. "I have told you what I want from you," Johnson declared and then proceeded to go around the room asking each legislator to state his view. It was a tough spot for members of Congress to be in, a point not lost on a clearly dubious George Aiken, Republican senator from Vermont. "By the time you send [the resolution] up here there won't be anything for us to [do] but support you," he told Johnson. After the meeting adjourned, the president talked by telephone with Barry Goldwater. He, too, said that he backed the air strikes.[9]

With that, Johnson had the congressional backing he so desperately wanted. At 11:37 P.M. that night, after the first planes had left the USS *Ticonderoga* (but before any had left the USS *Constellation*) to begin the bombing, Johnson spoke to the nation on television: "Aggression by terror against peaceful villages of South Vietnam," he said, "has now been joined by open aggression on the high seas against the United States of America. . . . [The] repeated acts of violence against the armed forces of the United States must be met not only with alert defense but with positive reply." Johnson then reassured the country: "We know, although others appear to forget, the risks of spreading conflict. We seek no wider war."[10]

Maybe not, but the president and his chief advisers did seek what perhaps only a show of military muscle could bring them: a clear demonstration to South Vietnamese leaders of Washington's steadfast commitment to the struggle, and a simultaneous inoculation against Republican charges that they were "soft" on communism. No less important for the long term, the crisis allowed them to introduce the congressional resolution that they had been holding for several months.[11] The Tonkin Gulf affair was tailor-made for them, a golden opportunity to accomplish several objectives with one decision. "It is certainly true," McGeorge Bundy later said, "that the Gulf of Tonkin incident was seized by the president as a time for him to take his resolution on Vietnam to the Congress. And he made that decision and arranged that broadcast [to the nation] before there was really absolutely clear-cut evidence as to what had happened out there. And I think that was a mistake. . . . He made a quick decision on an incompletely verified event."[12]

This all leads inexorably to one very large question: Did U.S. leaders engineer the crisis in the Tonkin Gulf? Did they, in other words, deliberately seek to provoke a North Vietnamese reaction in order to secure a casus belli? The provocative nature of the Oplan 34-A raids and Desoto patrols is beyond dispute, but provocation can be deliberate or incidental, intended or unintended. Was it deliberate in this case? Certainly with respect to the alleged second attack, on 4 August, a good case can be made that it was deliberate. Consider, first, that the *Maddox* was sent back into the Tonkin Gulf just a few hours after the attack on 2 August, along with the *C. Turner Joy.* Captain Herrick was instructed to operate in zigzag fashion in the general vicinity of the first attack for *two days,* spend an additional day off one of the offshore islands, and still one more day coming south past two other islands. Concludes historian John Prados: "A two-destroyer force to sail in close proximity to the North Vietnamese coast for ninety-six hours? Rationalize as you may, it was taunting Hanoi to do so."[13]

Captain Herrick appears to have understood that his ship was being used as bait. Anticipating another North Vietnamese attack and feeling that his ship had been put at unacceptable risk, he requested on 3 August that the patrol be terminated. The request was denied. To further ratchet up the pressure on the North Vietnamese, U.S. officials launched another Oplan 34-A raid on the night of 3 August, the details of which Johnson and McNamara discussed earlier that afternoon. Shortly after 9:00 the next morning, 4 August, McNamara phoned Johnson and told him of a message from Herrick that said that radio monitoring suggested an impending attack on the *Maddox* and *C. Turner Joy.* Though no attack had yet occurred, Johnson told several congressional leaders who were in the Oval Office at the time that if one occurred, he thought the United States would have to retaliate. He received their promise to support a congressional resolution. The tone of that meeting, and the swift decisions that followed it, reveal how anxious Johnson and his lieutenants were to launch a retaliation, with or without verification of an attack.[14]

Looking at the affair as a whole, including the developments of 2 and 4 August and what happened in between, there are additional reasons to suggest that the administration was looking for a pretext to flex American strength in Vietnam and hoped to find it in the gulf in early August. First, recall that top policymakers had long since coalesced around the need for a congressional resolution authorizing an expanded war, and that in mid June they chose to delay introducing it partly because they wanted to wait until civil rights was off the legislative calendar and the GOP convention had ended. By late July, both had occurred. The timing was perfect for another reason: the Democratic Convention was scheduled for mid August, and officials knew that the party's members of Congress would feel especially duty-bound to support a resolution brought up mere days before that celebratory event.

Second, consider the point with which we began this discussion: the growing crisis in South Vietnam, and the concern that the Khanh government might seek an end to the war through an accommodation with the enemy, or might be overthrown by one that did. Khanh's growing agitation in the last half of July for action against the DRV, on the grounds that both he and his people were tired and needed the war to end soon, caused much speculation in the diplomatic community in Saigon that events were moving to a climax. (Recall the Canadian and British claims to this effect on 27 and 30 July.) The Johnson team wanted desperately to show that it was in the war to stay. In this context, it is extremely interesting that Lyndon Johnson reportedly told influential Senator J. William Fulbright at a White House dinner on 26 July—a week before the American destroyer came under attack—that the Saigon regime was floundering and that he would soon go before Congress and ask for a resolution. Fulbright had already been approached about a resolution a few days before that dinner, by Undersecretary of State George Ball. Both Johnson and Ball assured the senator that a resolution could prevent an escalated war by taking the "soft on Communism" issue away from Goldwater. In Saigon, meanwhile, Alexis Johnson said privately that the United States was prepared for wider action, but only in response to new moves initiated by Hanoi. On 27 July Maxwell Taylor, acting on Rusk's instructions, assured Khanh that the United States was laying plans for air attacks and that joint planning between the United States and Khanh's government might begin soon.[15]

Finally, note once again the heavy activity initiated by the United States in the Tonkin Gulf beginning on 31 July. Despite later denials, top officials appear to have known very well that the Oplan 34-A raids and Desoto patrols occurred in close proximity to one another and would be interpreted by Hanoi as being connected—in addition to the State Department's 3 August cable to Taylor, there is the following comment by CIA director McCone at a meeting of the NSC the next day: "The North Vietnamese are reacting defensively to our [Oplan 34-A] attacks on their off-shore islands. They are responding out of pride and on the basis of defense considerations."[16]

International observers, too, emphasized Hanoi's defensive posture. British officials in Vietnam, convinced that North Vietnam wanted to do nothing that might provoke the United States, were dumbfounded when reports of the second attack, on 4 August, came in. It made no sense for Hanoi to strike at the Americans in this way, these officials reasoned, especially at the very symbol of U.S. military might, the Seventh Fleet. The only possible explanation was that an American-inspired war of nerves, culminating in the heavy activity in the gulf in the days leading up to the incidents, had caused the North Vietnamese to lash out. The Americans and not the North Vietnamese, therefore, were the provocateurs. Kenneth Blackwell, head of the British Consulate-General in Hanoi, put it bluntly: "The only plausible explanation of the incident," he cabled London, "seems to be that it was a deliberate attempt by the Americans to provoke the North Vietnamese into hostile reaction so that, by their counter-reaction, the U.S. representative [presumably Canada's J. Blair Seaborn, who was scheduled to return to Hanoi in a few days] could ensure that their message to the North Vietnamese and Chinese got through." A senior French official likewise told a British counterpart that it looked as though Washington had taken advantage of an error in order to take firm action. And Australian officials in Vietnam, although not prepared to state that the United States had deliberately provoked the incident, concurred that the large number of recent raids and intrusions from the South made the 2 August attack on the *Maddox* understandable.[17]

It may be objected here that if Lyndon Johnson had really been so desperate to create a crisis necessitating a show of American military power, then he would have ordered retaliation right away, after the initial attack on 2 August. Fair enough, but it is worth noting that officials, in deliberating the previous spring about the question of air strikes against the North, had spoken of such strikes as taking place only *after* Hanoi had been appropriately warned. Precisely what they meant by this is not clear. They may have been thinking primarily in terms of the kind of warning issued by J. Blair Seaborn on his mission to Hanoi in June (cease support of the insurgency or face certain punishment), but they may also have had in mind a direct warning in response to a specific act of aggression, such as the attack on the *Maddox*. Either way, the warning had now indisputably been issued. Johnson could thus appear the model of restraint, content after the 2 August attack to merely shake his finger at Ho Chi Minh and to warn of dire consequences should another attack occur.

Ultimately, the question of whether the United States deliberately planned its operations in the Gulf of Tonkin as a means of provoking North Vietnam to retaliate remains elusive, especially with respect to the first incident, on 2 August. For the historian, there is insufficient evidence to suggest that the whole affair, from beginning to end, was staged for the purpose of justifying an American retaliation. But there is compelling circumstantial evidence that, at the very least, government officials entered the month of August hoping desperately for a pretext that would allow a show of U.S. strength and determination. If those officials were genuinely surprised by the 2 August attack (as they claimed but as appears contradicted by the evidence), they certainly realized very quickly the opportunity that had presented itself, and they acted accordingly. As General Alexander Haig later put it: "If [Johnson] had not found the Gulf of Tonkin there would have been another excuse. This was tailor-made. It gave him an excuse and it gave him a massive level of support from the legislature."[18]

Massive indeed. The president had been assured in his meeting with congressional leaders on 4 August that the resolution would pass overwhelmingly, and it did. When hearings on the measure began on 6 August, administration officials continued their policy of deception. Rusk and McNamara told the House Foreign Affairs Committee that the *Maddox* had been on a "routine patrol" and that the two North Vietnamese attacks were "deliberate and unprovoked." When, at a joint meeting of the Senate Foreign Relations and Senate Armed Services committees later that day, Oregon senator Wayne Morse, tipped off by a Pentagon staffer, correctly suggested that there was a connection between the *Maddox* and the South Vietnamese Oplan 34-A raids, McNamara shot back: "Our Navy played absolutely no part in, was not associated with, was not aware of, any South Vietnamese actions, if there were any. . . . I say this flatly. This is a fact."[19]

When Congress convened the following day to vote on the Southeast Asia Resolution, as it was formally called, things went better for Johnson than he ever could have dreamed. He had charged Fulbright with the responsibility of securing quick passage by the largest possible vote, knowing that liberal Democrats in the Senate, many of whom had already expressed misgivings about the enterprise in Southeast Asia, respected Fulbright and would listen to him. Fulbright performed beautifully. He knew that many senators were privately critical of the measure—that these senators felt that it gave the president too much power to make war at his own discretion, bypassing a power that constitutionally belonged to Congress. Fulbright urged them to think of the resolution as a moderate measure "calculated to prevent the spread of war." He worked hard on doubters such as Mansfield, George McGovern, and Frank Church, assuring them that the president would consult fully with Congress before embarking on any escalation of the conflict. When Wisconsin senator Gaylord Nelson declared his intention to introduce an amendment calling for efforts to avoid "a direct military involvement" in the region, Fulbright successfully moved to prevent the amendment, on the grounds that it was unnecessary. After all, he told Nelson, "the last thing we want to do is to become involved in a land war in Asia."[20] That was the pattern: almost every time a senator expressed reservations (and a significant number from both parties did so), Fulbright would rise and say that he shared their concern, that he opposed a wider war, and that as far as he knew, the administration did not plan a wider war. In the end, only Morse and Alaska Democrat Ernest Gruening in the Senate raised serious objections to the resolution (Gruening called it a "predated declaration of war"), and the Senate voted eighty-eight to two in favor. In the House it was unanimous.[21]

Morse did not go down without a fight. For three days, on 5, 6, and 7 August, he railed against the resolution and challenged the administration's account of what actually happened in the Gulf of Tonkin. He predicted that Johnson would use the resolution as a functional declaration of war. Read today, Morse's lengthy diatribes are uncanny in their accuracy, more so than he himself could have known at the time. Had they been delivered by someone else, anyone else, they might have influenced more members of the august body to reconsider their position. But Morse was not influential. Considered dour and humorless, too sanctimonious by half, too prone to reveling in trivia, he did not move many colleagues to his position. They endured him rather than listened to him. When he spoke, the Senate chamber was often nearly empty.[22]

Morse predicted that his colleagues would live to regret their votes, and many of them did. Most would in later years explain their vote by pointing to the administration's deception and withholding of crucial information, and that is no doubt part of it—had they been aware that the United States was a provocateur in the gulf, had they been aware of the long-standing administration plans to introduce a resolution, many would likely have voted differently, or at least insisted on a meaningful debate. That scores were unenthusiastic in casting their "aye" votes is clear. But the fact is that legislators, with the notable exception of Morse, did not ask the hard questions, despite opportunities to do so and despite the capacious language of the resolution. It is no doubt true that most never expected the resolution to become the functional declaration of war that it did, but all knew that its language could allow the landing of large American armies in Vietnam. Fulbright admitted as much during the floor debate in the Senate.

That said, it is not difficult to comprehend why these legislators voted the way they did. It was, to begin with, a time in the nation's history when national interests seemed perpetually under threat, and Congress was accustomed to backing presidential initiatives without serious question. More important, Johnson's position was difficult to attack. He had asked Congress to approve an action he had already taken, and members felt compelled to go along. The flag of the country was involved. The administration had skillfully cultivated a crisis atmosphere that seemed to leave little time for debate. And, of course, there was the looming election, perhaps the most important consideration of all. Every House member and a third of the senators had their own election to worry about and did not want to be charged with helping to put the flag in danger. ("Hell, Wayne," a fellow lawmaker told Morse, "you can't get in a fight with the president at a time when the flags are waving and we're about to go to a national convention.")[23] With mere days until the Democratic convention, most in the majority party would have considered it unthinkable to deny Johnson his request, especially since the dangerous Goldwater stood to benefit.[24]

Johnson was delighted with the broad authority the resolution gave him. "Like grandma's nightshirt," he later quipped, "it covered everything." Even more pleasing, the public evidently shared Congress's approval—overnight his ratings in a Louis Harris public opinion poll shot up 30 percent. For the general public, confused about what was happening in South Vietnam, the North Vietnamese attack and massive U.S. retaliation must have seemed satisfyingly clear. Of course, like members of Congress, the people had not been told the whole story. Few understood the implications of the administration's actions.[25] And that was just the way the president and his men preferred it. In their view, they could scarcely have scripted the affair any better, for not only did Johnson now possess unsurpassed authority to wage war in a remote region far from America's shores, but his popularity had skyrocketed. "I didn't just screw Ho Chi Minh, I cut his pecker off," Johnson whispered to a reporter the day after the air strikes.[26]

In time, however, Lyndon Johnson's easy victory would return to haunt him. The administration had accomplished what it sought, to dramatically demonstrate America's commitment to South Vietnam, but in the process it had broken a long-standing barrier to taking the war to the North. A line had been crossed. "The sword, once drawn in anger, will tend to be unsheathed more easily in the future," the New York Times prophetically warned on 6 August. Moreover, when subsequent investigations showed that the administration's case for retaliation in the Tonkin Gulf had been considerably less than airtight, legislators correctly concluded that they had been deceived, and Johnson's "credibility gap" with the press and public was exacerbated.[27] Perhaps most crucial, the tenor of the congressional resolution, with its vow to "take all necessary steps" to defend a "vital" area, dramatically raised the publicly articulated stakes in Vietnam, which ensured that any future move to disengage from the conflict would be that much more difficult. An Australian government report, analyzing developments in the gulf, said that the U.S. commitment had now "deepened appreciably," particularly because of the resolution's "firm language about American national security interests in Southeast Asia." Or as a chronicler of the *Pentagon Papers* put it: "Greater visible commitment was purchased at the price of reduced flexibility."[28]

Greater visible commitment equals reduced flexibility. A simple theorem, it explains much about the momentous Vietnam policy decisions made in Washington in 1964 and 1965. Neither in August 1964 nor in the months that followed, it seems, did Johnson and his close advisers closely reflect on this equation and its applicability. Other contemporaneous observers did. Several Senate Democrats, even as they voted for the resolution, openly worried that one result would be a limiting of American options. The *New York Times* cautioned that "the lines have hardened" in Vietnam and that the reprisal strikes underscored American opposition to an Indochina peace conference. In the international community, such fears were even more pronounced. The administration had hoped for a strong show of support for its actions in the gulf, but allied backing was tepid at best. The British government of Sir Alec Douglas-Home, gloomy about the war but anxious as always to preserve good relations with the United States, pronounced itself satisfied that Washington had acted properly in the affair.[29] In Bonn, Chancellor Ludwig Erhard's government, though apprehensive about the prospect of an enlarged war, expressed its "understanding" of the U.S. retaliatory action. The Australian, Philippine, Italian, and Japanese governments likewise announced their support, though Rome and Tokyo made their backing conditional upon the conflict not spreading. Nonaligned nations were quiet or critical. Several charged that U.S. warships had no business in the Gulf of Tonkin and that their presence thus constituted a provocation. Some echoed France in stating that the crisis was further proof of the need for a greater effort in the direction of a diplomatic settlement. Small anti-American demonstrations were reported in New Delhi, Tokyo, Glasgow, Toronto, Melbourne, Algiers, and Stockholm.[30]

Given Washington's previous difficulties in winning allied support for its Vietnam policy, this lukewarm-to-critical international reaction probably did not come as a major surprise to American policymakers. Still, they moved quickly to counter the trend. For a Johnson address at Syracuse University on 5 August, speechwriters inserted a passage specifically for the Europeans; the passage sought to portray once again the defense of South Vietnam as a defense of the West. Declared Johnson, "So, to our friends in the Atlantic Alliance, let me say this this morning: The challenge that we face in Southeast Asia today is the same challenge that we have faced with courage and that we have met with strength in Greece and Turkey, in Berlin and Korea, and in Lebanon and in China." On 7 August, after the world reaction had become further clarified, Johnson and Rusk decided to send a prominent envoy, in the person of former ambassador to Saigon Henry Cabot Lodge, on a lengthy tour of European capitals to explain the U.S. actions in the gulf and enlist more third-country assistance for South Vietnam. Press reports tended to describe the move primarily as a clever campaign ploy—sending a leading Republican on a high-profile mission made it difficult for the GOP to make an issue of Johnson's conduct of the war. No doubt it served that function, but only as a bonus to the main objective: getting "more flags" involved.[31]

For both supporters and critics of the American actions in the gulf, the key question was what North Vietnam thought of them. Leaders in Hanoi appear to have drawn two principal lessons from the developments. First, the American air strikes were dramatic proof of their vulnerability to U.S. military power. In internal directives Hanoi officials cautioned that "our initial experiences in fighting were inadequate," and they redeployed their defense units and tightened discipline. Second, northern leaders, who knew that there occurred no DRV attacks on U.S. ships on 4 August, viewed the "retaliatory" bombings and the congressional resolution as demonstrations of Johnson's determination to maintain the American presence in Vietnam. No doubt this American resoluteness disappointed them, given their long-standing hope of avoiding a direct U.S. intervention in the war and their belief that Washington would ultimately not wish to tie itself to a wholly ineffectual Saigon regime. But if Ho Chi Minh and his associates were let down, they were not deterred. If Washington was willing to bear the costs of escalation, so were they. At high level meetings in mid August, senior officials decided to expand insurgency activities in the South in the hope of winning a "decisive victory in the next one or two years." They opted to increase aggressive actions against the strategic hamlets, to expand liberated areas, and to increase propaganda and agitational activities in the cities of the South in preparation for a general uprising.[32]

No doubt the North Vietnamese were bolstered by the support they received from their Chinese allies in the aftermath of the U.S. air strikes. Within forty-eight hours of the bombing raids, three dozen MIG aircraft had been flown in from China to be stationed at Phuc Yen airfield near Hanoi. This show of support may in fact have been less than Beijing had promised—according to one North Vietnamese official the Chinese had said that they would also provide the pilots for the MIGs in such a situation, but only the planes were provided—but it was significant nonetheless. The Chinese also issued scathing denunciations of the American actions. "Aggression by the United States against the Democratic Republic of Vietnam means aggression against China," the government declared on

6 August. "The Chinese people will absolutely not sit idly by without lending a helping hand. The debt of blood incurred by the United States to the Vietnamese people must be repaid."[33]

Strong words, though as with all Chinese pronouncements in these months they did not commit Beijing to any specific course of action. In the wake of the gulf incidents Chinese leaders still sought to avoid a direct military confrontation with the United States, as Mao Zedong made clear in a meeting with senior DRV official Le Duan in Beijing on 13 August. Mao said his intelligence information suggested that the 4 August incident was "not an intentional attack by the Americans" but was caused by "the Americans' mistaken judgment, based on wrong information." On whether the United States might expand the war into North Vietnam, Mao was doubtful. "It seems that the Americans do not want to fight a war, you do not want to fight a war, and we do not necessarily want to fight a war"; as a result, "because no one wants to fight a war, there will be no war."[34]

Hanoi leaders may have been slightly less confident than Mao on this score, but they certainly hoped he was right. Hence they continued even after the air strikes to leave the door at least slightly ajar to a negotiated settlement of the conflict. A forthcoming posture on negotiations made eminent sense for them, in view of their dual objectives of achieving victory and preventing an Americanized war. In the late summer of 1964, the timing was right, from Hanoi's perspective. The American air strikes had been a rude awakening and had demonstrated Washington's capacity to inflict immense military damage. At the same time, the situation on the ground in South Vietnam had never been more favorable, with widespread popular war-weariness and a virtually unchecked political disintegration in Saigon. Hanoi's position in any negotiations would thus be commanding, likely much more so than after an increasingly plausible direct U.S. intervention in the conflict. If the result of such negotiations might be a delay in reunification of the country, it seemed a small price to pay.

This complex North Vietnamese reaction to the Gulf of Tonkin affair—at once apprehensive and undeterred, yet still receptive to diplomacy—was on display when Canadian diplomat J. Blair Seaborn returned to Hanoi on 10 August for a second meeting with Pham Van Dong. Seaborn encountered a different atmosphere than during his previous visit in June: air-raid drills were constant, and throughout the city people were digging street trenches and brick bunkers. A crisis atmosphere prevailed. Seaborn, operating on American instructions, said that the U.S. position was that it had responded in a limited and fitting matter to the deliberate and unprovoked attacks on 4 August. He offered Pham Van Dong the same deal as previously: if Hanoi ceased its support of the insurgency in the South, there would be financial and other benefits; if it did not, it would "suffer the consequences." The premier reacted with outrage. There had been "no DRV provocation" for the air strikes, the premier said, and no North Vietnamese attack on the *Maddox* and the *Turner Joy* on 4 August. Rather, the United States had found "it necessary to carry the war to the North in order to find a way out of the impasse in the South." In addition, he added, "Johnson worries also of course about the coming electoral battle in which it is necessary to outbid the Republican candidate."

Pham Van Dong warned that sustained American attacks against North Vietnam would create a dangerous situation, one that would also be the product of "real miscalculation." The result would be war that would cover not only Vietnam but the whole of Southeast Asia, with unforeseeable consequences. If the United States was thinking in terms of a Korea-type war it should think again, he continued; Korea was a peninsula, which simplified the American task there enormously. In Vietnam there was no military solution for the United States, a fact that Walter Lippmann realized when he said that there was "no light at the end of the tunnel." The only answer, therefore, was for all parties to pursue a diplomatic solution. The premier assured Seaborn that North Vietnam wanted the channel kept open and that it was not opposed to a return to Geneva. "General de Gaulle has some good ideas and some of them are appreciated by political leaders elsewhere, even in the United States," he said.

Veteran diplomat that he was, Seaborn had undoubtedly heard this kind of rhetoric before; he had reason to be skeptical. In his report of the meeting he said that Pham Van Dong still appeared broadly confident, still seemed to see things moving North Vietnam's way in the war, which meant that Hanoi likely would have little incentive to compromise its ultimate objective of reunification of the country under its control. Still, Seaborn continued, Pham Van Dong's comments were encouraging. The premier seemed sincere in claiming that, despite the air attacks, his government wanted to preserve the channel to Washington, wanted the negotiations option left alive. (Perhaps, Seaborn wrote a colleague at the end of the month, the DRV wanted it kept alive to give Johnson a face-saving way out of Indochina after the election in November.) Seaborn concluded by advising that the necessary preparations be made so that he or another Canadian could return to Hanoi "in case of urgent need."[35]

He need not have bothered. Upon receiving Seaborn's report, Ottawa passed it on to Washington. The Johnson administration, fundamentally uninterested in any negotiations except those involving the modalities of North Vietnam's capitulation, chose not to respond. Canadian officials were not really surprised. They had been unhappy with Washington's suggested talking

points for Seaborn, seeing them as hastily drafted and as merely repeating the warnings and threats Seaborn had been asked to deliver during his
June visit to Hanoi. Two new talking points were sufficiently problematic
that Ottawa had instructed Seaborn to avoid mentioning them: the first
read that North Vietnam "knows what it must do if the peace is to be restored"; the second that the United States "has ways of and means of measuring [the] DRV's participation in, and direction and control of, the war
on South Vietnam and in Laos and will be carefully watching [the] DRV's
response" to Seaborn's points. Such vague assertions would make Canadians seem like mere "unthinking mouthpieces" and do little but anger
Pham Van Dong, officials believed, and might well cause Hanoi to close
down the Seaborn channel. Add the fact that the talking points arrived late
and only after repeated Canadian requests, and it should come as no surprise that Ottawa would conclude that Washington did not take the mission very seriously, despite its timing mere days after the incidents in the
Gulf.[36]

Nor did Washington respond the following month when Hanoi made a
more concrete offer to negotiate by privately agreeing to U Thant's proposal for secret bilateral U.S.–North Vietnamese talks on neutral territory.
This intriguing proposal grew out of Thant's efforts in July. Shortly after
his press conference and his talks with de Gaulle and Adlai Stevenson that
month, during which he emphasized the need for negotiations, Thant traveled to Moscow to discuss the Vietnam issue with Soviet leaders. Nikita
Khrushchev was sympathetic to his views, shared his apprehension about
a wider war, and encouraged him to proceed with his efforts. On 6 August,
mere hours after the American retaliatory bombings on North Vietnam and
with Congress yet to vote on the resolution, Thant flew to Washington for
previously arranged meetings with top administration officials. Thant was
unhappy about the reprisals, and his hosts were unhappy about his meddling, but the tension was masked by the pomp surrounding the visit. A
Marine Corps band played for Thant as he arrived. There were ceremonial
speeches in the Rose Garden. There was a luncheon at the State Department
and, that night, a state dinner in the White House for 140 persons, among
them several senators and governors. Like any visiting monarch, president,
or prime minister, Thant was put up overnight at Blair House, an honor accorded no previous secretary general.

In his welcoming remarks and later in a toast at the dinner, Johnson extolled the guest of honor's commitment to bringing peace to the world's
trouble spots and promised complete American support in that effort. "The
will for peace in the world is a will that springs from the soul of the human race," Johnson said in his toast. "That will is stronger tonight, stronger

in this decade, I think, than ever before in the human race. Willful men may still design willful schemes for war, but they will meet today the strong and the steadfast will of men everywhere who reject war as an acceptable instrument of national policy."[37]

The secretary general may have squirmed in his seat as he listened to these words, because in closed-door meetings earlier in the day, administration officials had shown no interest in his efforts on Vietnam; instead, they revealed a pronounced willingness to employ the very instrument of policy that the president was now denouncing. That morning, before Thant arrived, National Security Adviser McGeorge Bundy had assured Johnson that, when it came to Vietnam, Thant acted "more like a neutralist Burmese than like a spokesman for the world" and thus could be spoken to in frank terms. "You will want him to carry away a clear impression of the confident determination of the United States," Bundy advised. Johnson agreed. When Thant at a pre-lunch Oval Office meeting suggested bilateral talks between Hanoi and Washington, the president replied, "We are ready to get out tomorrow if [the communists] behave." In the meantime, America had to stand firm. There had been no sign, Bundy piped in, of a North Vietnamese desire for political discussion.

At the State Department luncheon that followed, Thant repeated the suggestion of bilateral talks and added that there need not be an agenda for them, merely a face-to-face exchange of views at, say, the ambassadorial level. Echoing de Gaulle, he said that the United States need not fear a Chinese takeover of Southeast Asia, because Beijing would likely welcome a neutralization of the region as a means of gaining a secure southern flank. Thant reiterated his view that an internationally guaranteed neutrality was the best answer for Southeast Asia and told Dean Rusk that if there were a consensus including Hanoi, but not necessarily Beijing, the UN could take some responsibility for administering agreed arrangements. Rusk threw cold water on the idea. There was no reason to believe such discussions would be fruitful, he told Thant, though he added that the secretary general could by all means continue his explorations, if he so chose.[38]

It was anything but a ringing endorsement of his efforts, but Thant left Washington determined to press ahead. He turned to the Soviets for help. Thant knew that Soviet–North Vietnamese relations had deteriorated steadily since the beginning of the year, but he also knew that Khrushchev shared his fear of an escalated war, and he reasoned that as the world's leading communist power the USSR was the right vehicle to convey a message to Hanoi. Accordingly, Thant asked an official with the Soviet mission at the UN to find out, through Moscow and Hanoi, if Ho Chi Minh would agree to send an envoy to talk with an American at a neutral site. The terms were those he had suggested in Washington: agendaless, open-ended discussions, conducted in secret.

The Soviets were receptive. The Gulf of Tonkin incident had alarmed them, seeming to confirm their fears of an incipient conflagration. At the same time, it had left them with the problem of how to reconcile their twin objectives: to end the war (on terms not disadvantageous to Hanoi) while also reinjecting Soviet influence over Ho's government (in part as a means of reaching the first objective). In the wake of the incident, Moscow thus had to play a delicate game of reducing world tension over the war and at the same time allying itself squarely with North Vietnam. The result was predictable: an initial, very moderate Soviet response to the U.S. air strikes, which was followed a few days later, after complaints from Hanoi, by a much harsher condemnation of Washington's "imperialist aggression." (Even then, the Kremlin was careful to avoid a clear commitment to defend the DRV.) This schizophrenic policy did little to enhance Moscow's prestige in Hanoi, but the North Vietnamese nevertheless agreed to the Soviet appeal that they take part in bilateral talks with Washington.[39] They had their own reasons to be forthcoming on the question of diplomacy, as we have seen, and Khrushchev sweetened the deal by promising increased Soviet military assistance in return. Moscow also at last appointed a new ambassador to Hanoi, Il'ia Shcherbakov, who arrived on 23 September. (The post had been vacant for months, a sure sign of the poor state of relations.)[40]

By mid September, U Thant thus had what he wanted: explicit North Vietnamese agreement to take part in talks with the United States. He passed on the news to Stevenson, who was reportedly "favorably surprised." Stevenson, in turn, informed Rusk that Hanoi had agreed to take part in secret, low-level, exploratory talks. Thant expected a swift administration response, but none came. Several weeks went by. Finally, in early October, Stevenson received word that the Thant initiative would have to wait because Johnson was preoccupied with the election campaign, which of course was merely a polite way of telling U Thant to go away. Whether Rusk and other officials deliberately withheld from Johnson news of Hanoi's positive response, as some have alleged, is not clear; what is clear is that neither the president nor his top Vietnam aides were interested in talking to Hanoi, in any forum, in the late summer of 1964. When the Canadian government on several occasions in late September and early October offered to send Blair Seaborn back to Hanoi on short notice to discuss the war and convey an American message, it received from the administration the same response as Thant: in effect, no thanks. If not an early trip by Seaborn, the Canadians persisted, what about one in November, after the presidential election? The United States likely would have little to say to Hanoi then either, came the reply. "*When* we are stronger, *then* we can face negotiation," is how McGeorge Bundy had put it back in January. It remained the guiding principle six months later.[41]

Had the "we" in Bundy's dictum referred primarily to the United States, there might have been good reason for the administration to feel rather confident in the wake of the Gulf of Tonkin air strikes, and thus less fearful of negotiations. The United States, after all, had shown its strength, and Hanoi had taken notice. But the Vietnam War was never really about America's strength, never really about Lyndon Johnson's ability to deliver, with the wave of a hand or a nod of the head, military punishment on a scale the world had never seen. The war was about South Vietnam's strength. It was about the political strength of the Saigon government, the ability of the regime to win the allegiance of the mass of the southern populace. The NLF understood this reality, as did the Hanoi leadership. Much of the world community understood it, as did skeptics in the United States. The Duong Van Minh junta, deposed in January 1964 after only three months in office, appears to have understood it as well. And indeed, top American policymakers understood it, on some level at least. Even as they drifted closer and closer to taking the war to North Vietnam, these officials conceded that, ultimately, the keys to victory were in the South and were political. They may have been much more confident than the skeptics that American power could help strengthen the Saigon regime, but they fully agreed that such strengthening was essential.

Hence the mixture of satisfaction and trepidation that characterized administration thinking in the aftermath of the Tonkin Gulf affair. On the one hand, Johnson and his aides were jubilant at the incident's domestic American impact—they had been given the congressional resolution that they had long coveted; they had won widespread public approval; and they had effectively removed Vietnam as a campaign issue for Goldwater—and they savored the opportunity to deliver a military blow to North Vietnam. On the other hand, these men swiftly discovered that the U.S. air strikes had done little or nothing to bolster Khanh's government. In that respect, the flexing of American muscle in the gulf had actually been spectacularly unsuccessful in accomplishing its most important purpose: boosting the morale in South Vietnam and thereby solidifying the political foundation of the Saigon government. There occurred no lasting increase in morale, and except to Khanh and a handful of other hawkish military officers, the dropping of bombs on compatriots and relatives in the North was not popular among southerners (according to the CIA's own study, only one in twenty-five South Vietnamese registered unequivocal support for the air strikes).[42]

As a result, Americans in Saigon and Washington continued in August and September to fret, even more incessantly than before, about low morale among South Vietnamese, about growing neutralist sentiments, and about Khanh's weaknesses. On 10 August, in his first official Mission Report from the U.S. embassy, Maxwell Taylor painted a gloomy picture of the war. "The best thing that can be said about the present Khanh government is that it has lasted six months and has about a 50-50 chance of lasting out the year," Taylor wrote. The regime, exhibiting symptoms of defeatism, had failed to win significant support from a public that was itself "confused and apathetic." The bombing of North Vietnam had given Khanh and his associates a brief boost, but they were clamoring for more. "In the coming months," the ambassador warned, "we may expect to face mounting pressure from the GVN to win the war by direct attack on Hanoi which, if resisted, will create frictions and irritations which could lead local politicians to serious consideration of a negotiated settlement or local soldiers to a military adventure without US consent." William Bundy of the State Department's Far East desk echoed these themes in a carefully written (it went through at least three drafts) top-secret memorandum dated 13 August and titled "Next Courses of Action in Southeast Asia." "South Vietnam is not going well," Bundy bluntly reported. The chief problem was low morale among the South Vietnamese, with the result that local forces might opt for negotiations if things continued to go poorly. Even if the situation improved slightly, the administration "would still have a major problem of maintaining morale."[43]

The implications were clear: without continued U.S. pressure on the North, morale in the South would sag further. The worst possible outcome, a GVN accommodation with the enemy, could result. In this context, both Taylor and Bundy placed considerable emphasis on the growing international clamor for a great-power conference on Laos and the need to work against it. Ever since the fighting in Laos resumed the previous May, Washington had successfully fended off efforts to reconvene such a conference, in large part by pressuring Britain and Souvanna Phouma to insist on a prior Pathet Lao withdrawal from the positions taken in the spring. By early August, however, pressure from the key players in the international community—the USSR, China, and France, above all, and also Canada and India—left both London and Souvanna inclined to waive this precondition. Souvanna, who had always been more open to the idea of a conference than Americans would have liked, in August had additional incentive to look with favor on negotiations: a string of recent military successes for government forces west of the Plaine des Jarres yielded significant territorial gains and ensured access between the two capitals (Vientiane and Luang Prabang) for the first time in three years. Souvanna thus felt confident that he could negotiate from strength. He also knew that if he continued to insist on a Pathet Lao withdrawal from the Plaine des Jarres, he would face pressure to reciprocate by giving up the government's recently won gains. Much to Washington's chagrin, Souvanna took the initiative in getting the diplomatic wheel turning. Through the British, he arranged to have the three factions in Laos meet for preliminary talks in Paris in late August.[44]

As always, American officials viewed the developments in Laos through the prism of Vietnam. The recent success of Laotian military efforts pleased them and might under different circumstances have propelled them to strongly endorse a great-power conference on that country, on the grounds that Souvanna now had trump cards to play. But they continued to be animated by fears that negotiations on Laos would inevitably grow to encompass Vietnam, a disastrous prospect. William Bundy articulated this close Laos-Vietnam linkage in administration thinking in a mid-August conversation with a senior official at the British embassy: the United States sought to delay any Laos conference, Bundy said, because of concerns about its impact on South Vietnamese morale. From Saigon, Taylor declared that U.S. participation in any Laos meeting would represent a calamity for America's interests, because it would cause the communists to believe that the American show of power in the Gulf of Tonkin had been a transient phenomenon and that Washington had reverted to being a "paper tiger." It would also lead to a further lessening of "morale and will to fight" among the South Vietnamese and would cause increased support for the "pro-Gaullist" contention that the Saigon government should follow the Laotian lead and seek a negotiated settlement. Moreover, it would cause the already weak Khanh to "slump into the deepest funk."

The ambassador found it interesting that the intensified pressure for a conference came "almost entirely from those who are opposed to U.S. policy objectives in Southeast Asia (except possibly the UK which seems prepared to jump on the bandwagon)." This meant that there was little reason to see anything good coming out of such a meeting, and little reason to think it could be limited to Laos. Taylor urged that less attention be given to finding a "safety valve" to the growing world pressures on Southeast Asia and more to channeling those pressures against North Vietnam: "We should continue to focus attention in all forums on Communist aggressive actions as the root cause of tension in Southeast Asia and reinforce our current stance."[45]

Taylor's exhortations carried great weight in Washington. Less than two months into his tenure as ambassador, he was at the peak of his policy-making influence, still possessing an aura of infallibility in the eyes of many, including Johnson. That aura would in time dissipate, as it inevitably does, but in August 1964 it was still strong. This is not to suggest that Taylor's views on the war and on negotiations were unrepresentative; they were not. But they served as a powerful reinforcing mechanism for senior civilian and military officials. William Bundy, in his "Next Courses" memo, employed more restrained language than the ambassador but clearly followed his cue: the United States should work to prevent a Laos conference, Bundy urged, or, if that proved impossible, delay it as long as possible. Bundy understood that the effort might be in vain. "If, despite our efforts, Souvanna on his own, or in response to third-country pressures, started to move rapidly toward a conference, we would have a very difficult problem," he cautioned. "If the timing of a Laos conference, in relation to the degree of pressures we had then set in motion against the DRV, was such that our attending or accepting the conference would have major morale drawbacks in South Vietnam, we might well have to refuse to attend ourselves and to accept the disadvantages of having no direct participation. In the last analysis, GVN morale would have to be the deciding factor."[46]

How little things had changed. Low South Vietnamese morale had been a central American concern in June and July, before Tonkin Gulf; it remained no less a preoccupation afterward. Though it is possible that hawkish American officials sought to exaggerate the depth of this indigenous defeatism in order to hasten wider military action, all indications are that the situation was precisely as they described it: very bad, and getting worse. To independent observers, this reality foretold gigantic, perhaps insurmountable, problems in any defense of South Vietnam (running through the whole body of *New York Times* reporting of the war in the last half of August is the haunting question: how can a successful war be fought in the vacuum of a society that no longer seems to care about winning?); to the top figures in the Johnson administration, it necessitated merely a redoubled effort.[47] Just how it could be that South Vietnamese motivation depended so thoroughly on what Americans did or did not do went unexamined by these officials, at least at the time—some three decades later Robert McNamara would conclude that the war had been unwinnable, in large part because the South Vietnamese lacked the necessary motivation.[48] In 1964, neither McNamara nor his associates would allow themselves to believe that, or, if they secretly did, to act on that belief.

Instead, they pressed ahead. In doing so, however, they faced a dilemma directly related to the dismal picture in South Vietnam. On the one hand, U.S. officials were in agreement that, in order to boost southern morale and strengthen the steadily weakening Saigon regime, the Tonkin Gulf air strikes had to be followed with additional pressures against the North. On the other hand, that same governmental weakness precluded a drastically enlarged war effort, because the inevitable reverberations of such an enlargement might cause the complete collapse of central authority in Saigon. Too much action might be as deleterious as too little. Then there was the November election to think about. Its importance was seldom stated, but it was always understood: any expansion of the war would have to wait until after election day. (Occasionally, this imperative was articulated, though quietly—during a mid-August White House meeting, McGeorge Bundy whispered to the CIA's Ray Cline, "We know we're not going to do a goddamn thing while this election is on.")[49] The rationale was, as always, twofold: that Johnson should avoid dramatic foreign-policy departures in an election year, and that the American public, though supportive of the Tonkin Gulf air strikes, might not yet be willing to back an expanded war.

Until election day, then, the only solution was the middle road of graduated, carefully controlled military pressure on North Vietnam, what William Bundy referred to as "limited pressures." Slated for August through, tentatively, December, this program called for, among other things, the continuation of Oplan 34-A and Desoto operations against North Vietnam, joint U.S.–South Vietnamese operations into Laos, and more tit-for-tat retaliations—à la Tonkin Gulf—for "any special VC or DRV activity." Ever mindful of the negotiations problem, Bundy emphasized that these actions were "in general limited and controllable," but he conceded that they could bring increased pressure for negotiations. This pressure had to be resisted. "These actions are not in themselves a truly coherent program of strong enough pressure either to bring Hanoi around or to sustain a pressure posture into some kind of discussion. Hence, *we should continue absolutely opposed to any conference*" (emphasis added). But what if "limited pressures" proved insufficient? In that case, Bundy inevitably advised, the administration should move to "more serious pressures" that involved "systematic military action" against North Vietnam. Following Taylor's suggestion, Bundy posited 1 January 1965 as a good contingency date ("D day") for initiating such action.[50]

Here, then, were the "Next Courses of Action in Southeast Asia," as drawn up by the State Department's top official on Southeast Asia with input from several other officials. It was a highly important document, produced in response to Johnson's request for a summary of options on Vietnam, and the main topic of discussion at a top-level, off-the-record meeting at the White House on 14 August. It also circulated among the other elements of the policy-making establishment. The memorandum formed a blueprint of sorts for American policy in the weeks that followed—Robert McNamara later called it "the focus of our attention" until January 1965. Johnson signed off on it. The Joint Chiefs of Staff signed off on it, provided the administration would not hesitate to move to the "more serious pressures" plan if the situation demanded it. And Ambassador Taylor, with his certainty that "something must be added in the coming months," signed off on it, though like the Joint Chiefs he wanted assurances that the United States would go to "Plan B" if necessary.[51]

One of Bundy's recommendations, also urged by Dean Rusk and eventually implemented as policy, called for a brief "holding pause" of some ten days, or until about the twenty-fifth of August, on the grounds that it was vital to avoid actions that would in any way take the onus off the communist side for escalation. Ten days is a short time, and yet so severe was the political turmoil in South Vietnam that Americans in Saigon feared that a pause of that length might cause a complete governmental and military collapse. And indeed, in the last half of August it appeared that South Vietnam's ten-year history might be swiftly careening to an end. Khanh's own actions had something to do with it. The possibility that Hanoi might retaliate for the Gulf of Tonkin air strikes provided him with the excuse to consolidate his power by decreeing a state of emergency that gave him, in the CIA's estimation, "all but absolute power." Though the North Vietnamese did not retaliate against the air strikes, Khanh nevertheless imposed stricter censorship, severely curtailed civil liberties, and introduced a new constitution as a means of ousting Duong Van Minh from his largely ceremonial post as chief of state. These abrupt moves, about which Khanh first consulted with Maxwell Taylor, sparked an explosive reaction on the streets of Saigon. Buddhist militants and their student allies led massive demonstrations against Khanh, demanding that he establish a civilian government, ensure religious freedom, and schedule elections for the coming year. They were not satisfied when Khanh backed down a little and promised to revise the new constitution and relax censorship and other government controls.

By the last week of August, urban South Vietnam was in a state of acute crisis. On 25 August, after promising further liberalizing measures, Khanh suddenly resigned. Two days later, after no one had stepped forward to fill the vacuum, a triumvirate composed of Khanh, Minh, and Tran Thien Khiem assumed power and withdrew the controversial constitution. Two days after that, Khanh apparently suffered a mental and physical "breakdown" and abruptly left Saigon, whereupon Nguyen Xuen Oanh, a

Harvard-educated economist, was named acting premier to lead a caretaker government for the next two months. Five days, three government shake-ups: the worst turmoil in the era of Ngo Dinh Diem paled in comparison. And while the politicians jockeyed for power, the violence in the streets continued, not only in Saigon but in several other cities. Long-simmering hatreds and suspicions among the militants in the country's two main religious groups—the Buddhists and the Roman Catholics—flared into street fighting with sticks, stones, knives, rifles, and grenades. Students took to the streets in ever greater numbers, throwing rocks and shouting "Down with Nguyen Khanh." The NLF, not surprisingly, worked to foment the uprising. Its clandestine radio station urged the people of Saigon to take to the streets and continue to struggle against the "confused puppet government." Its leaders called again for a coalition government representing all segments of society.

Military matters were scarcely more encouraging for American leaders. On 21 August, an ARVN force was ambushed in Kien Hoa province with more than 150 casualties, including 80 dead. Four U.S. advisers were killed. General William Westmoreland, commander of U.S. operations in Vietnam, was deeply upset by the incident and by the fact that the Vietcong force that staged the ambush was able to move into position and remain concealed for more than twenty-four hours without a single member of the local population reporting the fact. Nor was that all, Westmoreland complained to an official at the British embassy in Saigon: in Phu Yen province, a detachment of ARVN armored vehicles was stopped and immobilized by a crowd of women and children with a Buddhist flag.[52]

For American officials, the nightmare scenario was coming true: South Vietnam was falling apart. In the midst of the crisis, Ambassador Taylor warned Washington that "the absence of effective governmental authority has led, in Saigon, to an advanced state of demoralization of [the] populace." Many government ministries were "grinding to a halt, dealing with only the most routine business," and the ministers themselves were "freely expressing to embassy officers their extreme pessimism regarding the future." And if the situation in Saigon was bad, it was even worse in the cities in central Vietnam. "In these cities," the ambassador noted, "it is actually difficult to tell where authority lies."[53] Taylor did not mention that he and the rest of U.S. officialdom shared responsibility for the disaster because they had endorsed Khanh's initial assumption of greater power in the apparent belief that a centralization of power could yield a more effective prosecution of the war. It is a measure of these officials' poor understanding of South Vietnamese political realities that they were taken aback by what resulted. Americans made the basic error, as Peter Grose put it at the time, "of assuming that the primary interest of the Vietnamese people was the same as the primary interest of the American mission in Vietnam: defeat of the Vietcong insurgency." The August crisis demonstrated again that Buddhist and Catholic leaders, for example, tended to see each other as a more immediate threat than the Vietcong and that students were more interested in fighting for political gains in the cities than in signing up to fight on behalf of a discredited regime in the rice paddies of the Mekong Delta. Army officers, it appeared, were more concerned about their personal positions than about waging a war. And among the general population, too many either sympathized with the NLF or were disillusioned with both sides; few were committed supporters of Nguyen Khanh.

Indeed, by late August, Khanh had only one real source of support left: the U.S. government. The Johnson administration, though deeply troubled by Khanh's bizarre antics during the previous week, and though aware that the mounting anger in South Vietnam against Khanh might turn into increased anti-U.S. sentiment, saw no alternative but to stick with him. Khanh may have lost all credibility in the eyes of his own people, but Americans saw no one else around whom to construct an effective war effort. National Security Adviser McGeorge Bundy advised Johnson on 31 August that every top adviser agreed that the United States should continue to provide Khanh with firm support, "so that if he falls it will in no sense be our doing." The same day, Taylor and U.S. Deputy Ambassador U. Alexis Johnson chased Khanh down in the town of Dalat and pressured him to return to Saigon to resume control of the government. "We assured him that further inactivity would be fatal, that his actions were being closely watched in Vietnam, in Washington, and other capitals abroad to see whether he could really govern this country," Taylor reported. "If he can give such evidence, the U.S. is still behind him. If we ever become convinced that he cannot lead his country to victory, he can no longer count upon us."[54]

The threat worked. Khanh, though initially noncommittal, returned to Saigon on 3 September, resumed his position as premier, dissolved the triumvirate, and reappointed Minh as chief of state. American officials had what they wanted, but they saw little reason to cheer. They were smart enough to know that the general had returned a drastically weakened man, whose reputation had been done perhaps irreparable harm by the events of August, and who no longer inspired respect. They themselves no longer respected him. They worried that he might stumble again, that he might move to openly embrace the Buddhists, and that a coalition government might emerge that would seek neutralist goals. "War weariness and a desire for a quick solution to the long struggle against the Vietcong may be an important factor underlying the current agitation," the CIA warned.

"The confused situation is extremely vulnerable to exploitation by the Communists and by the proponents of a negotiated settlement."[55] In the past, this kind of crisis situation would have resulted in Robert McNamara leading a fact-finding mission to Saigon. Now, because such whirlwind, high-publicity visits had been deemed counterproductive, it resulted instead in the return of Maxwell Taylor for high-level meetings in Washington. Could the situation be held together until "D day," on 1 January, or even until the November election, now mere weeks away? That, officials knew, would be the question at the center of these meetings.

8 Standing Logic on Its Head

On the evening of 13 August 1964, Sir Robert Thompson, head of the British Advisory Mission to South Vietnam (BRIAM), sat down at the mission's headquarters in Saigon to write a memorandum to his superiors in London. For more than two years, Thompson had been a close adviser on Vietnam to the Kennedy and Johnson administrations. He was that rare outsider to whom top U.S. officials actually listened and whose advice they genuinely sought. Throughout that time, Thompson had been a strong supporter of the American advisory effort, a believer in the notion that victory would ultimately come and that South Vietnam would survive as an independent, noncommunist entity. No longer. Thompson had changed his mind. He had come to the conclusion that the situation in South Vietnam was all but hopeless and that it was foolish to pretend otherwise. For the better part of a year, since the overthrow of Ngo Dinh Diem some ten months earlier, Thompson had feared the arrival of this day. Now that it was here, he wasted no time informing the Foreign Office of the fact. This transformation of Robert Thompson was yet one more sign of the growing isolation of the Johnson administration: though Washington emerged from the August crisis with its opposition to negotiations fully intact, increasing numbers of outside observers saw the chaotic situation that enveloped South Vietnam as demonstrating the need for precisely such a solution.

"I am now convinced that we are passing the point of no return," Thompson wrote. "Defeat by the Viet Cong, through subversion and increased guerrilla activity, is inevitable, and this prospect will become gradually more apparent over the next few months." Whether this defeat would remain "sufficiently obscure" until after the American election Thompson could not say, "but it will be plain for all to see early in 1965." Only a miracle such as the collapse of the Hanoi regime could alter this scenario, he suggested, though there existed a "faint ray of hope" that the defeat could perhaps be delayed if a group of officers under Duong Van Minh took control, ceded effective control to the Americans, and allowed the introduction of U.S. combat forces. But Thompson emphasized that this "ray" was too faint to put any faith in and that Americans should therefore seek negotiations right away, however "bleak and unpalatable" the prospect might be. If they refused, Thompson concluded, they "could be forced to insert combat troops in some strength not to retrieve the position but merely to extricate themselves."[1]

Both the nature of the message and the identity of the messenger guaranteed that the memorandum would receive widespread attention upon its arrival in London. Interestingly, however, its grim conclusions raised little ruckus at the Foreign Office. Thompson, it turned out, was preaching to the choir. The top figures in London had undergone much the same transformation as he had, over approximately the same period. They, too, believed that the situation was dire and the prognosis grim, and they were inclined to agree that Washington should seek negotiations while it still could—in other words, while a measure of control remained in South Vietnam. Indeed, by the late summer of 1964, a consensus had developed among British officials in London and Saigon with respect to the war, around several key points: that expanding the war to the North would be a mistake because it would not significantly affect the insurgency in the South but merely increase the risk of a large-scale war; that, *pace* the Americans, the Khanh coup in January had been a disaster for the war effort; that Minh, who had been overthrown in that coup and who did not want an expanded war, was the only viable leader in South Vietnam; that Americans had a poor understanding of the political and cultural realities in the country; and that Washington would suffer much less from a judicious withdrawal from the conflict than from fighting an inevitably long and costly war. Given that Beijing and Hanoi hoped to prevent an Americanized war and that neither had ruled out attending a reconvened Geneva conference, a face-saving agreement for the United States ought to be possible to arrange.

The Thompson report thus served primarily to reinforce attitudes already held in London. In this respect, the extraordinary thing about the document was that it was not extraordinary, its authorship aside. Neither in tone nor content did his missive differ much from the dispatches coming from the British embassy in Saigon—though no staffers there were quite prepared to follow Thompson's lead and declare defeat "inevitable." London officials received similar reports from Commonwealth members, most notably the Australians, reports detailing the low morale afflicting the general public and members of ARVN and the near-total absence of popular support for Khanh. Even American and South Vietnamese sources served to confirm British suspicions of impending doom. Her Majesty's officers in both Saigon and Washington found widespread defeatism among junior and middle-ranking State Department officials on the subject of Vietnam. Australians in South Vietnam reported the same pessimism among low- and midlevel Americans they encountered there. Bui Diem, later South Vietnam's ambassador to Washington, told a senior British official in August that the Vietcong would continue the struggle even if supplies from the North were cut off and that the United States had wrongly neglected the political aspects of the conflict.[2]

From a variety of sources, British policymakers heard the same grim message. The question was what to do next. Thompson seemed to be suggesting an immediate British approach to Washington to convince the administration that the game was up and some form of negotiated withdrawal the only viable option. Most, however, including Foreign Secretary R. A. B. Butler, said that it would be better not to say anything at all until the American elections were over. "With the electoral campaign as well as American prestige at stake, the U.S. government would not welcome advice from us and it might only result in our being made the scapegoat for their own failures," James E. Cable, the head of the Foreign Office's Southeast Asia Department, wrote in an internal memorandum. This argument won the day, as the formal instructions to the Saigon embassy made clear in late August: "Our present intention . . . is to lie low and say nothing. We do not intend to reveal to anyone else even that we have been making a fresh assessment of the outlook for Viet-Nam, much less that our prognosis is pessimistic." The instructions emphasized the need to be "extremely careful not to let the Americans have any inkling of the way our ideas are moving. Until their elections are over this is bound to be too sensitive a subject for frank discussion."[3]

Once again, the British were saying what they had said all year: that Johnson's election-year considerations had a huge influence on America's Vietnam policy and that domestic American political considerations mattered a great deal. (It is a central difference between the British and American documentary record for that year: what Americans almost never dared say—certainly not on paper—British officials articulated constantly.) Until the election was over, talking to Washington was pointless; it would do nothing but irritate the Americans. Given that London still desired U.S. support for its position in Malaysia, and given that British voters, too, would be going to the polls in the fall, friction with Lyndon Johnson was best avoided. But only until the American election. After 3 November, the British had decided, it would be imperative to confront the Johnson administration, along the lines suggested by Robert Thompson. Implicit in this decision was the notion (explored in chapter 9) that, after his election, Johnson would have options on Vietnam. In the words of a senior staffer at the British embassy in Washington, after election day Johnson would be able to "take stock afresh" and exercise the choice between a stepped-up war involving perhaps North Vietnam and China and "what could be presented as a realistic, statesmanlike attempt to achieve a settlement by negotiation, and attempt it from a position of renewed authority."[4]

This British "lie low" strategy was on display when Henry Cabot Lodge stopped in London on 1 September during his tour of European capitals. Even though Foreign Secretary Butler had scribbled, "The whole visit is worthless," on a list of talking points for his meeting with the American, he and other officials were careful not to articulate the full extent of their pessimism about the war. They bit their tongue when Lodge asserted that Khanh was an "above average" leader. They gently pressed Lodge on the possibility of a Geneva conference on Vietnam but said little when he ruled out the idea. They probed him on the meaning of the growing war-weariness among the South Vietnamese population but did not challenge his claim that the problem was not as bad as it had been made to appear. When Lodge said that the American commitment to Saigon remained very limited and that the number of U.S. service personnel killed was nothing compared with those killed in traffic accidents in the United States, they chose not to ask whether this fact might not make an American disengagement easier. Though Butler did say that Washington should not expect a significant increase in Britain's assistance to the GVN ("We are overextended," he said), both he and Prime Minister Douglas-Home voiced rhetorical support for the American advisory effort.[5]

One issue, however, did threaten to disrupt this British desire to avoid antagonizing Washington. That issue was Laos and the tripartite talks on its future that began in Paris in late August. The Johnson administration, acutely concerned that Souvanna Phouma might abandon his preconditions for a Geneva conference as laid down the previous spring, urged London to help in stiffening the prince's spine and convincing him to stick to the preconditions, or, should he modify them, to insist that he make no real concessions in doing so. Senior British officials were skeptical. For one thing, they knew that Souvanna looked kindly on a return to Geneva. A long-time admirer of de Gaulle, Souvanna was inclined to agree with the French view that a great-power meeting, touching also on the Vietnam conflict, represented the best chance to bring peace to the region. Just prior to departing for Paris, he told the British ambassador in Vientiane that he was prepared to drop the key precondition to a conference, the return to the territorial positions held before the Pathet Lao's May 1964 offensive. His recent gains in the area between Vientiane and Luong Prabang made such a demand unnecessary and unwarranted, he said. Upon his arrival in France, Souvanna asked de Gaulle to help bring about a return to Geneva.[6]

Even apart from Souvanna's position, British policymakers were predisposed to support a Geneva meeting on Laos, for precisely the reason Washington did not: because it could lead to a conference on Vietnam. "There may soon be a real need for another Geneva Conference, less on account of Laos than of Viet-Nam," James Cable wrote in a secret internal memorandum endorsed by several senior colleagues. "If Mr. Thompson is right and an early collapse of South Viet-Namese resistance is possible, it might be of great value to have an international Conference in progress on Laos." Its corridors would afford opportunities for informal exchanges on the Vietnam situation, and once the U.S. election was over, it could provide a precedent for a conference on Vietnam itself. "Because negotiations on Viet-Nam are unmentionable, but may nevertheless be urgently needed, I think it would be wrong for us to assist in creating fresh obstacles to a Conference on Laos."[7]

Once the Paris talks actually got under way, however, London chose to put its relationship with Washington before its desire for a conference. It adopted a hands-off stance that neither put "fresh obstacles" in the way of a Laos conference nor helped facilitate one. This policy of noninvolvement was potentially decisive, because the talks quickly became dominated by a behind-the-scenes struggle between Washington and Paris for the ear of Souvanna Phouma. The French worked hard to convince the prince to abandon the preconditions and agree to a fourteen-power conference, while the Johnson administration labored just as mightily to get him to maintain the preconditions. For a time, the French appeared to make headway, to the point that by 15 September Souvanna seemed on the verge of agreeing to the conference. At the last minute, however, Washington's twin threats— that the United States would not attend such a conference, and that Souvanna would likely be overthrown in a coup d'état if he agreed to a conference—had the desired effect: no Pathet Lao concessions, no conference, Souvanna declared. He had clearly been torn about what to do, and it is conceivable that a push from 1962 cochair Britain would have led him to agree to the French plan. But London stayed aloof, and the tripartite talks broke up without an agreement in late September. American officials breathed a sigh of relief.[8]

But the important fact remained: on Vietnam, the United States could not count on the active support of its closest and most important ally, at least not past the November election. The situation was scarcely better with other allies. In early September, Lodge returned from his European tour and proclaimed that only France among the countries he had visited opposed American involvement in the region. "Broadly speaking," Lodge said, "the governments which I visited expressed appreciation for the United States efforts in Vietnam, hoped for the success of these efforts, and gave assurances of help."[9] This statement was no doubt essentially true, but Lodge's cryptic phraseology meant that it was also essentially meaningless. Lodge actually found little encouragement on the trip. Some governments—notably those in Belgium and Denmark—openly expressed their opposition to the direction of American policy and their fear of a larger war. Others were perfectly prepared, à la London, to express vague appreciation for the U.S. effort—as long as it remained limited and defensive in nature—and to *hope* for its success. At the same time, however, they were more pessimistic than ever that it *would* succeed and more doubtful than ever that it was necessary to try.

In Rome, officials did not reveal to Lodge their deep doubts on the war (stemming, in part, from a stream of pessimistic telegrams from the Italian ambassador in Saigon) but urged that every avenue for a political solution be explored. In Bonn, Chancellor Erhard voiced strong support for American policy. According to the U.S. embassy, however, the Germans, "left to their own devices . . . would probably have chosen a course closer to that favored by the French." The reason: Bonn did not consider Vietnam a vital concern to the West.[10] And although many European leaders were happy to give Lodge "assurances of help," all continued to resist making meaningful contributions to the war effort. It was another sign of the failure of the administration's "more flags" campaign. Several weeks earlier, thirty-four countries, including some in Latin America and Africa, had been approached and asked to provide aid. Virtually nothing materialized. "Most countries have been reluctant to provide military assistance," a State Department report on the effort noted, "and where it has been given it has been of a largely token character."[11]

A common concern among all the Western European democracies was how the conflict played with their own populations. Gauging public opinion on the war in these countries in this period is difficult, but it is clear that major elements of the continent's press were alarmed and puzzled at the seemingly unshakable determination of the Johnson administration to continue to prop up what was widely seen as an incompetent, repressive, minority anticommunist Saigon government. The London *Times* spoke of "more cracks in the already disintegrating society of South Vietnam" and wondered, "On what sure ground can the U.S. build now?" *The Economist* of London, in general sympathetic to the American effort, called U.S. policy bankrupt and said that Lyndon Johnson faced a stark choice: to begin negotiations, "which would essentially be a disengagement operation," or to massively escalate the American commitment "to a miserably bad military situation." In Germany, the *Rheinische Post* of Düsseldorf said that a political settlement seemed America's only way out. And in France, Gaullist *La Nation* said that neutralization "would leave unaffected the American prestige and supremacy in the Pacific," while *Le Monde* wondered how long American policy could continue as it had. "Militarily, the situation gets worse. Politically, it is catastrophic. The U.S. will indeed have to negotiate, but Mr. Johnson seems in no hurry to admit this." If Johnson won the upcoming election, the paper predicted, he would be forced to agree to a new Geneva conference, "but we wonder if the evolution of the political and military situation will allow him to wait for the elections to be over."[12]

Pessimism was the word at the center of these foreign analyses, pessimism that the war could be won, pessimism that Washington could find South Vietnamese leaders who could bring unity and purpose to a crumbling society, and pessimism that Lyndon Johnson and his compatriots understood the magnitude of the obstacles they faced. Unfortunately for the White House, in late August, domestic speculation occurred along these same lines, in part because of the mounting chaos in Saigon and in part because of the simultaneous release of CIA analyst Willard Matthias's gloomy 8 June memorandum. The memo, it will be recalled, urged that consideration be given to a negotiated settlement for Vietnam, based on neutralization. Matthias had expressed "serious doubt that victory can be won" and suggested that at best a "prolonged stalemate" might be achieved. Other members of the CIA's Board of National Estimates had read the memo and approved it in general terms.[13]

On 21 August, the *Chicago Tribune* received a copy of the memo from an undisclosed source and indicated to government officials that it intended to publish excerpts. The administration immediately released the memo on its own, hoping thereby to suggest both that it was not a secret and that it was discursive in nature. Nevertheless, the story received wide newspaper coverage across the nation. Several papers, including the *New York Times*, editorially supported Matthias's analysis. Republican presidential nominee Barry Goldwater suggested that the memo indicated a secret administration plan to enter into negotiations, and *New York Times* reporter Jack Raymond said that it reflected views "widely held in the Government and the subject of recurrent discussion."[14] Goldwater and Raymond were wrong, or at least misleading. Senior officials were running as fast as they could away from negotiations, not to them. Matthias's pessimistic diagnosis might have been "widely held" among them, but his prescription was not. His analysis might have been "the subject of recurrent discussion," but only in terms of how to best thwart the kind of solution he advocated.

The administration's line of thinking was articulated by, ironically enough, Undersecretary of State George Ball, the one high-level official to have expressed precisely the misgivings articulated by Willard Matthias and by the London and Paris governments. On the morning of 29 August, as news of Khanh's supposed mental and physical breakdown arrived, Ball received a call from *New York Times* columnist James Reston. Ball confirmed that the situation in Saigon was very serious. What about finding a way to get out of Vietnam? Reston asked. "There is no talk of that kind," Ball replied. Nobody was thinking seriously about pulling out or initiating negotiations. What about a wider, Geneva-type conference taking in much of Southeast Asia? Reston continued. Unworkable, Ball answered. Such a solution presupposed that the Chinese wanted above all stability in Southeast Asia. De Gaulle thought they did; the United States thought they did not. In the administration's view, Beijing was in an aggressive, expansionist mood. Ball conceded that the dilemma for American policy was very real, especially because of the lack of support from other western powers, but he quickly added that "we really don't see how one checks Communist extension by negotiation at this point. . . . Therefore, one continues to support resistance as long as the resistance has a hope of success." De Gaulle's position contained an element of defeatism, Ball went on, based as it was on the assumption that Southeast Asia was a Chinese sphere of influence and would remain so, and that a conference would be a less painful way to accept the inevitable: a communist victory in Indochina. This was the wrong analysis, Ball maintained, particularly because it blithely assumed that communist expansion could stop with the Southeast Asian peninsula.[15]

It was an illuminating conversation, both for what it contained and for what it omitted. Ball and Reston were neighbors and close friends. They held similar reservations about the entire Vietnam enterprise and presumably knew that they did. But Ball gave no hint of his reservations in this conversation. He gave every indication that the key figures in the administration were unanimous in ruling out negotiations (for fear of an aggressive China and falling dominoes) and were committed to the war for the long haul. In including himself in this group, Ball contradicted what he had argued to Rusk, with considerable passion, the previous spring. Was Ball's unswerving loyalty to his president again coming to the fore? Perhaps. Or perhaps he feared that if he expressed his true feelings, Reston would write a column suggesting high-level sympathy for diplomacy, whereupon Johnson, always sensitive to leaks and knowing of Ball's friendship with the columnist, would suspect him of being the source for the story.[16] Perhaps he said what he did because he knew that the call was being taped. Perhaps all these considerations influenced him. Whatever the case, he adopted a determined tone.

What is striking, however, is that he did so even as he gave an utterly gloomy picture of the current situation. Ball correctly saw an element of defeatism in de Gaulle's position on the war, but his own analysis was hardly more optimistic. The difference, as always, was that whereas de Gaulle said, in effect, "cut your losses," the administration said it had to go on as long as there remained "a hope of success." Even if that hope, stated in percentage terms, descended to 20 percent? 10 percent? 5 percent? Presumably yes.

Reston did not address these questions in his column the next day. Instead, he focused on another issue that had become increasingly evident during the August chaos and that was implicit in Ball's comments: the limits of American power. In South Vietnam, Reston told his readers, the Johnson administration faced the problem of being very powerful but not quite powerful enough, with the result that it confronted problems beyond its control. The only way to increase that power—and thus increase U.S. control—was to have Americans take over the fighting. It was the logical next step, but Reston warned that anyone contemplating this move had to consider three key questions: first, did the American people really want to wage a large-scale war "in the jungles and rice paddies of Vietnam, 7,000 miles from home"? Second, would Asians really like to see Americans fighting on behalf of the South Vietnamese? And third, would an American war have the effect of healing the Sino-Soviet split? "No one knows the answer to these questions, but the Johnson administration has to face them," Reston wrote. He suggested that the current judgment in official quarters was that it was better to "take it easy" and stay the current course and perhaps "put up with the frustrations of a compromise" than to unleash the marines and the air force.[17]

On this point, the venerable columnist allowed wishful thinking to overtake reasoned, skeptical judgment, as he himself perhaps realized. For as America's top civilian and military officials prepared to convene in Washington in early September for the high-level meetings with Maxwell Taylor, they were in no mood to compromise. Almost to a man, they viewed as the central question not whether to escalate, but how far and fast to proceed.[18] Even before the meetings began, McGeorge Bundy urged the president to proceed with contingency planning to expand the American involvement by way of naval harassments along the coast of North Vietnam, air strikes over the panhandle in Laos, and a dispatch of the U.S. Navy into the Tonkin Gulf. Such actions were not needed for military reasons so much as to "heighten morale" and show America's "strength of purpose." Bundy suggested that Johnson even consider sending American troops to fight the Vietcong: "I myself believe that before we let this country go we should have a hard look at this grim alternative. It seems to me at least possible that a couple of brigade-size units put in to do specific jobs about six weeks from now might be good medicine everywhere."[19]

An important moment had arrived. A key member of Lyndon Johnson's inner circle had suggested sending Americans to fight in Vietnam. Johnson no doubt objected to the plan as stated—Bundy's six-week timetable would have put the U.S. troops on the ground in mid October, scarcely more than two weeks before the presidential election, an impossibility in the president's political judgment. But there is little reason to doubt that Johnson shared Bundy's fundamental conviction: eventual Americanization was preferable to letting South Vietnam go. The timing of the plan, not its substance, was the problem.

Others in Washington had independently come to the same conclusion as Bundy. John McNaughton, McNamara's top Vietnam deputy at the Defense Department and an important figure in the policy discussions in the succeeding months, produced a memorandum titled "Plan of Action for Vietnam" that presaged to a stunning degree the decisions the administration would make in 1965. The war was being lost, McNaughton wrote. The Vietcong were stronger than ever, whereas the ARVN and the Saigon government were weaker. War-weariness had increased. Khanh's prestige had been irreparably damaged. "The odds have therefore become very great," McNaughton cautioned, "that if we do not inject some major new elements—and perhaps even if we do—the situation will continue to deteriorate; there is a substantial chance that the situation will come completely apart, with dramatic VC military victories putting intolerable pressures on a weakened Saigon government. The result could be a succession of governmental changes ending in a demand for a negotiated settlement." To counteract this possibility, McNaughton recommended that active consideration be given to a significant U.S. troop presence in the South, and he outlined a specific series of provocative actions the United States might simultaneously take against the North, culminating in a sustained air war.[20]

But not everyone among Johnson's close aides was prepared to move this fast, this soon. Robert McNamara remained opposed to the dispatch of any American troops. Dean Rusk, too, believed such action to be prematuce. Equally important, Maxwell Taylor, the administration's man on the spot, differed with Bundy and McNaughton as to the timing of a dramatically escalated American military involvement in the war. Taylor, who had been forced to delay his return to Washington by a week because of the turmoil in Saigon, spent the final days before his departure frantically working to secure Khanh's place in power and assessing what the United States ought to do next. His faith in Khanh, never very high, had plummeted as a result of the recent events. He now doubted that the South Vietnamese leader could do the job and speculated that a neutralist coup could occur at any time. Khanh might even opt for a political accommodation with the NLF, which of course meant an end to the war.[21] Just hours before his departure for Washington, Taylor sent Rusk another mission report, which he hoped would be a "basic document in our coming discussions." The cable, labeled top secret, is surely one of the most remarkable ever written by an American envoy in Vietnam:

> We must accept the fact that an effective government, much beyond the capacity of that which has existed over the past several months, is unlikely to survive. We now have a better feel for the quality of our ally and for what we can expect from him in terms of ability to govern. Only the emergence of an exceptional leader could improve the situation and no George Washington is in sight.
>
> Consequently we can and must anticipate for the future an instrument of government which will have definite limits of performance. At the very worst, it will continue to seek a broadened consensus involving and attempting to encompass all or most of the minority elements with political aspirations until it approaches a sort of popular front. This amalgam, if it takes form, may be expected in due course to become susceptible to an accommodation with the Liberation Front. At best, the emerging governmental structure might be capable of maintaining a holding operation against the Viet Cong. This level of effort could, with good luck and strenuous American efforts, be expanded to produce certain limited pacification successes. . . . But the willingness and ability of such a government to exert itself or to attempt to execute an all-out National Pacification Plan would be marginal. . . .
>
> We may, therefore, expect to find ourselves faced with a choice of (a) passively watching the development of a popular front, knowing that this may in due course require the U.S. to leave Vietnam in failure; or (b) actively assuming increased responsibility for the outcome following a time-schedule consistent with our estimate of the limited viability of any South Vietnamese government.
>
> An examination of our total world responsibilities and the significance of Vietnam in relationship to them clearly rules out the option

of accepting course (a). If we leave Vietnam with our tail between our legs, the consequences of this defeat in the rest of Asia, Africa, and Latin America would be disastrous. We therefore would seem to have little choice left except to accept course (b).

A gloomier assessment can scarcely be imagined. The situation was desperate, Taylor was saying, and defeat might be inevitable. And yet, the United States had no choice but to persevere. It was precisely this kind of logic that raised eyebrows among critics in the United States and around the world: Was a "broadened consensus" leading to a deal with the NLF and a departure of the United States really the *worst* outcome from Washington's perspective? Would an American departure from Vietnam really be more "disastrous" than fighting a long, bloody, and likely futile war, on behalf of the South Vietnamese people, too many of whom lacked motivation for the struggle?

Ironically, the very fragility of the South Vietnamese political structure led Taylor to oppose the kind of immediate steep increase in American involvement suggested by McGeorge Bundy and John McNaughton. The structure might collapse altogether. The key word here is *immediate*, for Taylor agreed that a massively expanded U.S. presence might be needed soon. But first it would be necessary to try yet again to bring strength and effectiveness to the Saigon regime. Specifically, "we need two to three months to get any sort of government going which has any chance of being able to maintain order in the cities and to continue the pacification effort of past levels." An important consideration in Taylor's thinking may have been that Khanh and his associates, exhausted and frustrated by the recent events, had undergone a crucial change: they no longer wanted to "march north." (Did the desire for peace extend now even to Khanh himself? Later in the fall Taylor would suggest that it did.) The ambassador also knew that Johnson wanted no drastic measures before the November vote. In recommending against a rapid escalation, however, Taylor ran smack into the "too much versus too little" dilemma that had bedeviled him and other Americans for months. If too much activity could bring a collapse, so could too little. He concluded that, to build South Vietnamese morale, the administration should press ahead vigorously with the limited pressures outlined by William Bundy on 13 August, while preparing to move, sometime after 1 December, to heavier pressures.[22]

The Taylor suggestions won the day. When senior officials met in Washington without the president on 7 September, General Earle Wheeler, Taylor's successor as chairman of the Joint Chiefs of Staff, presented a JCS proposal for a series of "deliberately provocative actions" against North

Vietnam, followed by a systematic American bombing campaign of increasing severity to crush the will and capability of Hanoi to support the insurgencies in Laos and South Vietnam. Taylor immediately opposed the idea, for the reason outlined in his cable: the Khanh government was too weak for the United States to risk a dramatic escalation. The others in attendance agreed. Systematic bombing might be needed in the future, "depending on GVN progress and Communist reaction in the meantime," but it was not needed yet. Never stated but surely on these men's minds was a second reason to delay: Johnson's aversion to wider action before the election. Thus for now, it would be recommended to Johnson that he approve a series of limited actions designed to strengthen South Vietnamese morale and "show the Communists we mean business." These actions included the resumption of American naval patrols in the Tonkin Gulf as well as Oplan 34-A operations, consultations with Souvanna Phouma to allow limited South Vietnamese operation in Laos, and preparations "to respond on a tit-for-tat basis" to any provocative action against the United States by the Vietcong or North Vietnam.[23]

Johnson received these recommendations and met with top aides on 9 September. McNamara opened by saying that, with the exception of two members of the Joint Chiefs, who wanted to move immediately to sustained action against the North, all agreed that this was the way to go. Johnson was confused. If the situation in South Vietnam was as dire as everyone agreed it was, why the modest scale of the recommendations? Taylor responded that both he and General Westmoreland were in agreement on the question of timing. Johnson asked the others in the room to state their views. All voiced their support for the recommended action, on the grounds that the Saigon government was too fragile to support heavier measures. Dean Rusk assured the president that a major decision to go north could be taken at any time—"at 5-minutes notice"—but that now was not the time. CIA director John McCone, no doubt chastened by a pessimistic Special National Intelligence Estimate (SNIE) produced by his agency the day before, made no effort to hide his concerns.[24] While South Vietnam disintegrated, McCone told Johnson, Hanoi and Beijing were in a buoyant mood, confident that their policy would succeed. He added that the CIA was disturbed that the internal movement toward negotiations might be growing and that anti-American sentiment appeared likewise to be on the increase. It could be, McCone said, that the aims originally set forth by Dwight Eisenhower in 1954 were no longer supported by the South Vietnamese.

The president asked Taylor if the situation was better or worse than when he had assumed his position in Saigon. Taylor conceded that it was worse and that sooner or later the United States would have to "move forcefully" against the North. Now was simply not the right time. The rest of the group agreed. When Johnson asked if anyone doubted that Vietnam was worth all this effort, all emphatically said that it was. The war, they agreed, must be vigorously prosecuted. The reason for waiting, Johnson concluded, was that "with a weak and wobbly situation it would be unwise to attack until we could stabilize our base." He told the group that he did not want to enter the patient in a ten-round bout when he was in no shape to last even one round. "We should get him ready to face 3 or 4 rounds at least." NSAM 314, signed by the president the following day, authorized Taylor's recommended actions.[25]

The September 1964 policy discussions loom large in the history of American decision making on Vietnam. This is not because of the specific decisions that resulted—existing policy would be essentially maintained until the South Vietnamese political picture improved—but because the most important figures in that decision making had reached a general consensus that a dramatically increased American involvement would at some point be necessary. Reporter Peter Grose's contemporaneous assertion, that the Vietnam War as it had been waged for the previous three years was drawing to a close and that a turning point had come, has a large measure of truth to it. Foreign observers certainly thought so. And U.S. officials did as well; they had chosen the road they would follow, when the time was right. In the meantime, they would continue to rule out any diplomatic overture to North Vietnam. (It was in this period, it will be recalled, that the administration showed a total lack of interest in Canada's offer in September to send J. Blair Seaborn back to Hanoi to convey an American message and rebuffed U Thant's efforts to get bilateral U.S.–North Vietnamese talks going.) In South Vietnam, they would "play for the breaks," as Rusk put it, and work energetically to strengthen the Khanh regime.

If success or failure seemed to hinge largely on the political situation in Saigon, the administration also knew that it could not neglect its ongoing effort to win support for its policy from important audiences outside South Vietnam. In this context, it was no accident that Assistant Secretary of State for Public Affairs Robert J. Manning was one of only three assistant secretaries included in the top-level meeting on 9 September (McNaughton and William Bundy were the others). As the head of the administration's ongoing public information campaign on Vietnam, Manning had a crucial task: to put the best spin on the Saigon crisis and on Taylor's Washington visit to the press and to Congress. Accordingly, the administration came out of the September meetings actually professing cautious optimism about the state of the war. Taylor told a news conference on 9 September that the military outlook looked good, that the economic situation had been "relatively favorable" all along and, amazingly, that Nguyen Khanh faced tough challenges ahead but was doing an excellent job (Taylor also explicitly denied that the administration was considering air strikes over the Laotian panhandle). That night, Johnson told reporters that Taylor had described "continued progress" in the war effort, and a spokesperson from Manning's office suggested that the war had become so expensive to the Vietcong and Hanoi that they might give it up in the end rather than risk suffering further losses.[26]

Lest anyone believe that this supposed progress could result in negotiations or a reduced American commitment to Saigon, the administration at the same time stressed the unlimited nature of U.S. support and the vital importance of the region to American security. The U.S. commitment to South Vietnam "is flat and very firm," Dean Rusk told a news conference on 10 September. "I don't know of any negotiations now going on anywhere, overt or covert, about a settlement in Vietnam." (He had evidently forgotten about U Thant's efforts in that direction.) The White House also took the unusual step of releasing to the press a one-page summary of testimony by Taylor to the House Subcommittee on the Far East. In the excerpt, the ambassador said that an American withdrawal from Vietnam would be "a major disaster." Saigon would swiftly fall, and the remainder of Southeast Asia would soon go neutralist and perhaps communist. "Burma would be affected, India also. Indonesia would soon line up with the Communists. We could be pushed out of the Western Pacific, back to Honolulu. That would be the short-term effect over the next few years."[27]

This was the line the administration followed in its public utterances in the six weeks leading up to the November election: cautiously optimistic evaluations of the state of the war combined with energetic affirmations of the American stake in, and commitment to, the preservation of a noncommunist South Vietnam.[28] It was a strategy perfectly suited to the Johnson team's two long-standing and potentially contradictory aims vis-à-vis the public and the war. On the one hand, the notion of "steady progress" gave a sense of continuity to developments and kept Vietnam from becoming a compelling issue to the electorate. This was never more important than in these final weeks—"Let's keep the public debate on Vietnam to as low a level as possible," White House aide Bill Moyers told Johnson in advising against another McNamara trip to Vietnam. On the other hand, that same electorate had to be persuaded of the conflict's ultimate importance to American interests. Manning's information campaign had been launched back in June (in NSAM 308) because of concerns about the level of public commitment to the struggle; almost half a year later, those concerns remained. In late September the administration, at Johnson's request, had Henry Cabot Lodge, leading Republican and former Saigon ambassador, travel around the country to speak to groups about the stakes in Vietnam.[29]

There was danger in the strategy, for while administration spokesmen fanned out to convince audiences near and far of America's determination to prevail in the war and to oppose what Dean Rusk in Detroit called "a bogus neutralization," Johnson struck a decidedly peaceful tone in his campaign appearances, which began in earnest in mid September. It was not long before the discrepancies were noted. "There are those who say you ought to go North and drop bombs to try to wipe out the supply lines," Johnson said at Eufala, Oklahoma, on 25 September. "We don't want our American boys to do the fighting for Asian boys. . . . To get involved with 700 million people and get tied down in a land war in Asia." Four days later, in a speech in Tokyo, William Bundy left a different impression: "Expansion of the war outside South Vietnam, while not a course we want or seek, could be forced on us by the pressures of the Communists." Columnist Arthur Krock in the *New York Times* commented: "Political considerations do not justify the conflict between [Johnson's] implication of a settled policy against 'escalating' the Vietnam War and Assistant Secretary of State Bundy's implication to the contrary two [sic] days thereafter." Krock also noted another feature of administration policy: the effort to demonize Barry Goldwater as "trigger-happy" and a "war-monger" merely for pointing out, without endorsement, that the White House was considering a major expansion of the war.[30]

William's brother McGeorge Bundy worried about Krock's column. The following day, 1 October, he advised Johnson to "give a hint of firmness" on Vietnam. "It is a better than even chance that we will be undertaking some air and land action in the Laotian corridor and even in North Vietnam within the next two months, and we do not want the record to suggest even remotely that we campaigned on peace in order to start a war in November," Bundy told the president. Two days after that, he urged Johnson to have a TV conversation on foreign policy with Walter Lippmann. True, Bundy conceded, some regarded Lippmann as a "soft-liner," but "to most people he is simply the wisest publicist in the country. You could easily set yourself off a little bit from him on Vietnam or on national defense, and anyway the risk of contamination is low."

Johnson did not take up the suggestions. No doubt he felt he could handle a few Arthur Krocks, as long as the poll numbers looked favorable and as long as people like Dean Rusk and Henry Cabot Lodge were out there talking tough on the war. And besides, he could have told Bundy, most of his campaign speeches *were* leaving the door open for an expanded American involvement in Vietnam. Many were in fact models of ambiguity, seemingly foreclosing no option. In Manchester, New Hampshire, for example, he told the audience that *"just for the moment* I have not thought we were ready for American boys to do the fighting for Asian boys," and that "we are not going north and drop bombs *at this stage of the game.*"[31]

And indeed, Krock's criticism was echoed by few in the press in the final weeks of the campaign. Editors and columnists focused the bulk of their attention on the electioneering at home. When they did examine the war, many spoke of the looming (that is, postelection) choice between disengagement and escalation and said Barry Goldwater favored the latter. The *New York Times*, still giving the White House grief with its support for neutralization, told its readers that of the two major presidential candidates only the Republican sought a larger war. "In effect, Mr. Goldwater wants to convert an Asian war into an American war," the paper charged in early October. "The Republican candidate considers Vietnam as part of a worldwide Communist military threat which the United States must defeat." The editorial chided Goldwater for seeing no significance in the Sino-Soviet split and for failing to understand that the chief problems in Vietnam were in the South, not in the North. Though it also faulted Kennedy and Johnson for drifting "far from the original concept of advice and material aid, and toward Americanization of the war and of the governmental policies of South Vietnam," the overall message of the piece was clear: vote for Johnson if you want to avoid an American war in Vietnam.[32]

This was music to the ears of White House campaign strategists, but it only underlined Bundy's concern about what might happen after 3 November. The *Times* and other prominent voices might be falling all over themselves to secure a Johnson victory, but what about later, what about November and December? The *Times* editorial closed by declaring that the only viable solution in Vietnam was "a negotiated settlement based on neutralization of all four Indochinese states under suitable guarantees." Bundy understood that the real task was to change this sentiment or at least contain it, to keep it from spreading, and to anticipate the kinds of large questions that were certain to be asked once the election was over. Hence the importance that Bundy and other officials attached to the administration's information campaign on Vietnam.

It is difficult not to feel sympathy for Robert Manning and the other officials who toiled in the administration's information campaign. With every passing day, their chief task—to sell Congress, the press, and friends abroad on the essential wisdom of U.S. policy—became more difficult. Scarcely had the Taylor meetings concluded in Washington (with the administration preaching optimism) than a group led by a disgruntled South Vietnamese army officer, Lam Van Phat, launched a coup attempt against Khanh, ostensibly to prevent a takeover by pro-Vietcong neutralists. The coup failed, largely because of disorganization and poor execution, but it demonstrated for the world how Khanh was opposed by the military from which he came. Only the staunch support of the U.S. embassy kept him in power. By late September, morale among embassy staffers had sunk to a new low ("Let's get a government," had become the slogan of choice). Taylor now found that the situation was even worse than he had anticipated, and it was going steadily downhill. The Saigon government was a "lame duck," he reported, and Khanh lacked even basic leadership skills. Many government ministries were "rapidly grinding to a halt dealing with only the most routine business." Did this mean that Washington should cast about for another leader? No, Taylor advised. No one else had appeared who could do the job. In a series of cables, the ambassador hammered home his recommendations: the United States should hang on and hope for the best, should continue to plan for a "D day" on 1 January, and should be prepared to "drop Khanh" if necessary.[33]

The last line was telling. Though outside observers in Saigon, in particular the British, shook their heads at the staunch American backing of Khanh, U.S. officials had begun to entertain the idea that he might have to go. The cause of this shift in American thinking was Khanh's accommodationist policies toward the Buddhists, policies that grew stronger as September progressed. The Buddhists had emerged out of the August crisis as the most powerful political force in South Vietnam, and Khanh, mindful of his own political isolation and aware that he had become too dependent on American support, saw closer ties with them as a key to his political survival. Americans in Saigon and Washington were acutely concerned. The thing they had always found most attractive in Khanh—his willingness to follow American strictures—now appeared not merely threatened but destined to be replaced by a similar attachment to the Buddhist leadership.

What did the Buddhists want? This was the critical question for American intelligence officers in the autumn of 1964, as it had been a year earlier. The answer proved more elusive than ever, perhaps in part because Buddhists themselves were uncertain. Buddhist leaders liked to say that their goal was to "protect Buddhism," but neither the meaning of this phrase nor the means to realize it were made clear to nonbelievers. Bonzes tended to couch their declarations in religious terms—that is, they evaded difficult political questions by insisting that they were solely men of religion not competent to speak on matters of politics. Disingenuous though such statements may have been—the bonzes were deeply involved in bringing down the Diem regime and in forcing the removal of Khanh's draconian constitution in August—they made Buddhist attitudes with respect to the conflict against the Vietcong all the more difficult to ascertain.

Nevertheless, there were several signs of an accelerating Buddhist movement aimed at ending the war. On 2 September, Buddhist representatives demanded the release of all prisoners taken by the government during the disturbances in August. The timid Khanh government agreed, even though at least eleven of those released had been antiwar agitators with ties to the NLF. A few days later, an editorial in the important Buddhist weekly *Hai trieu am* (Voice of the Ocean Tide), blamed the August crisis in large part on American influences, accused the United States of fomenting troubles between the Catholics and Buddhists, and insisted that the pursuit of the war was the result of American intervention. Even as they made these charges, Buddhist leaders were anxious to avoid too close an identification with the Vietcong. Several times in early September, influential bonzes declared that they were anticommunist and denied that the Vietcong were using them to their own ends. Still, the desire to end the war appeared to outweigh the fear of communism in the minds of most Buddhist leaders. Another *Hai trieu am* editorial began by disavowing communism and neutralism but then called on the Vietnamese army and "our brothers" in the NLF to cut down their war efforts and agree to a cease-fire.[34]

The key figure in the Buddhist agitation was Thich Tri Quang, mastermind of the revolt against Ngo Dinh Diem in mid 1963 and widely described as the single most influential individual in South Vietnam. Preaching a kind of "national Buddhism" from his headquarters in Hué, Quang maintained that Buddhism, which expressed "so perfectly" the soul and aspiration of the Vietnamese people, should be recognized as the national religion, as it had been "in the most glorious epochs of Vietnamese history." In order to bring that about, Quang argued, it would be necessary to eliminate the foreign influences that perverted the body and soul of the nation. Principal among these was Catholicism, and the struggle against it took priority. But Quang and other Buddhist militants also opposed the steady increase of American influence in South Vietnam, and they became steadily more outspoken against it in the last half of 1964. They seemed unconcerned that their anti-American pronouncements played into the hands of the NLF, which had its own foreign influence, Marxism. The NLF, Quang believed, was merely the expression of the Vietnamese people's revolt against foreigners. As such, the NLF could be a short-term ally in the struggle for "national Buddhism," because it could help end the American influence in Vietnam and the materialism that went with it. To be sure, severe obstacles would remain after the Americans were gone, chief among them Marxism, but militant bonzes believed they could brave the storm. Peace was the first priority. So strong was the national hunger for peace, Quang believed, that the people would follow whoever brought an end to the fighting.[35]

Not all Buddhist leaders accepted this line of analysis. Those who were refugees from the North, such as Thich Tam Chau, powerful chairman of the Buddhist Secular Institute, were more wary of entering the messy world of politics and more inclined to espouse strong anticommunist views. The U.S. presence in the country might be unfortunate, Tam Chau asserted, but it was also necessary for the foreseeable future. But this was the weaker strain in the Buddhist movement in the early fall of 1964, as American and other foreign observers knew—the name that cropped up repeatedly in their analyses was not Tam Chau but Quang. In a series of reports in late August and September, the CIA maintained that Quang wanted the United States out of Vietnam and therefore liked neutralism. Ambassador Taylor agreed, as did Reggie Burrows, the British chargé d'affaires in Saigon. "Thich Tri Quang's influence should certainly not be underestimated, and I maintain the view that the Buddhists will ultimately move towards neutralism," Burrows told officials in London. Did this mean that Khanh, the Buddhists' newfound ally, might also move in that direction? The idea seemed less and less inconceivable. According to both the CIA and the U.S. embassy in Saigon, the increasingly anti-American Khanh could decide to turn his back on the war effort and pursue the Buddhist alliance even to the point of seeking a truce with the Vietcong.[36]

The parallel between this situation and the situation a year earlier could hardly be more striking. As then, the Buddhists were important players in the drama, with unpredictable implications. As then, severe friction had developed between Washington and its client government in Saigon, to the point where the GVN leadership was seeking alternative sources of support and Washington was contemplating the need for a new Saigon regime. And as then, Americans feared that the South Vietnamese government might opt for an accommodation with the enemy rather than a continuation of the war. Where there were differences between the two periods, they all pointed in the same negative direction from the U.S. perspective: Nguyen Khanh possessed even less popular support than Ngo Dinh Diem had possessed; the military outlook was even more grim than it had been a year earlier; anti-Americanism in South Vietnam was much more widespread; and Washington's international isolation with respect to the war had deepened appreciably.

Which brings us to the most important parallel between the autumn of 1964 and the same period in 1963. Despite the deterioration in the political and military situation, as measured from every conceivable angle, leading American officials were no less committed to the war in 1964 than they had been a year earlier. "What helps to win the war, we support; what interferes with the war effort, we oppose," John Kennedy had said. Lyndon Johnson felt no different now. The unchecked decline in the war effort in the weeks since the reprisal strikes, as reported in a series of breathtakingly gloomy assessments by the CIA and the Saigon embassy in late September, had not caused U.S. policymakers to change their minds. Nor had the dismal results of another JCS war game caused a reconsideration. Like its forerunner in the spring, Sigma II, which ran 8–17 September, found that major bombing of North Vietnam would actually stiffen Hanoi's determination and would not significantly harm the Vietcong effort in the South. The South Vietnamese ally would remain undependable, American ground troops would have to be dispatched in large numbers, and public support at home would erode. One team concluded that the American people would rather pull out of Vietnam than commit to a protracted war. The game's impact on administration planning, William Bundy would later say, "was not great."[37]

In speaking of the Johnson administration's isolation on Vietnam in the autumn of 1964, one must be careful to define terms. On one level, the administration was not "isolated" at all. A solid plurality of American voters supported the effort to contain communism in Indochina, as did most—though by no means all—of these voters' representatives in Congress. Most newspaper editors felt the same. As the administration had hoped, the Gulf of Tonkin episode had caused most Americans to rally around the flag and the president, at the perfect point in the campaign. But it is also true that the vast majority of these individuals knew neither the full extent of the problems in the war effort nor the secret plans that the White House was laying to rectify them. In supporting U.S. policy, most voters envisioned an American commitment that stayed roughly at its current level, which was one reason many rushed to the seemingly moderate Johnson and away from strident challenger Barry Goldwater—they did not know that privately the two men were nearly identical in their opinions on the war, that the president and his men were gearing up to do more or less what Goldwater suggested, namely, escalate the conflict. Support for the war effort was thus based in significant part on administration deception—deception about the current state of affairs, about the prospects, and about policy planning. In his column on 30 August, James Reston understood the shallow nature of the national consensus on Vietnam when he asked, with obvious skepticism, whether Americans would really back a full-scale war on behalf of a shaky regime seven thousand miles from the California coast.[38]

The better measure of administration isolation on the conflict is thus one that focuses on groups and individuals who were well informed about the actual situation on the ground in Vietnam. Viewed from this perspective, the picture is considerably murkier. Friendly governments around the world, with a few exceptions, saw the conflict as more or less a lost cause and were fearful of escalation, even though they sympathized with Washington's plight. American reporters in Saigon, again with some exceptions, were increasingly pessimistic about developments and increasingly doubtful that *any* political stabilization would be forthcoming in South Vietnam (though most were at the same time unprepared to counsel disengagement). The CIA, never optimistic about American prospects in the conflict, was more downbeat than ever—"It is still possible that the complex situation can improve, though the chances of such improvement are clearly very slim," a typical CIA report noted at the end of September. Even some State Department and NSC officials, as we have noted, were beginning to confess to British and other foreign observers that they saw no hope for the U.S.–South Vietnamese effort.[39]

The most important such official was Undersecretary of State George Ball. As the second-ranking official at the State Department, Ball operated just outside the inner circle of power, as close as one could get without being inside it. Like other advocates of a negotiated U.S. withdrawal, he watched the recent developments with growing dismay, certain that the United States was drifting toward a larger, bloodier version of France's *guerre sale* (dirty war). Ball was certain, he later wrote, that as matters then stood with regard to negotiations, "the administration really didn't have anything to say to the Vietnamese communists except for the modalities of their capitulation." As for the standard administration line that negotiations could not be undertaken because they would so shake the Saigon government that it might collapse, Ball thought that merely proved that the regime had not lived up to Eisenhower's 1954 aid stipulations and was not worth propping up.[40]

Ball detailed his concerns and recommendations in a memorandum dated 5 October.[41] Written over a succession of long nights and numbering sixty-seven pages, it closely paralleled the themes that Ball had articulated previously and also those put forth by other critics such as Lippmann, Mansfield, and, especially, de Gaulle. To the usual list of options presented to the president (continuation of current policy; air war against North Vietnam; and introduction of U.S. ground forces in the South), Ball added another: a course of action that would "permit a political settlement without direct U.S. military involvement." To continue to pursue a military solution carried unacceptable risks: "It is in the nature of escalation that each move passes the option to the other side, while at the same time the party which seems to be losing will be tempted to keep raising the ante," Ball wrote. "To the extent that the response to a move can be controlled, that move is probably ineffective. If the move is effective, it may not be possible to control—or accurately anticipate—the response. Once on the tiger's back we cannot be sure of picking the place to dismount."

Ball knew that the key members of the Johnson team were opposed to a political solution for one primary reason: it would require a withdrawal of the American military presence, which, they argued, would humiliate America and cripple its credibility among friends around the world. Ball took the opposite line. Far from damaging the country's credibility, a political settlement would actually enhance it, because the allies, most of whom questioned Vietnam's importance, would "applaud a move on our part to cut our losses." Ball noted that even Asian allies situated close to the war, such as Japan, Thailand, and the Philippines, were, at best, ambivalent. Neutrals, he insisted, would welcome a political solution. As for U.S. credibility vis-à-vis the communist powers, a settlement would be much less damaging over the long term than getting drawn into a bottomless quagmire.

There were several frameworks for achieving a political solution, Ball continued, all beginning with a cease-fire. Negotiations would follow in a number of possible contexts, from a localized settlement between the Saigon regime and the NLF to the kind of large-scale international conference proposed by de Gaulle. The former scenario, the undersecretary acknowledged, "might well be an uneasy coalition in which the communists would presumably be the most aggressive and dominant component. But the full effect of a Communist takeover would be diffused and postponed for a substantial period of time." (Recall that Ball explicitly rejected this argument in his talk with Reston a few weeks before.) Nor, Ball hastened to add, was a communist takeover necessarily inevitable. A government including elements of the NLF that operated free of external military intervention could very well win much support in the international community. U.S. allies uninterested in a war might welcome the chance to back a genuinely neutral government in Saigon, one that would join the ranks of the nonaligned nations. The result would be not a defeat for, but a fulfillment of, American objectives.

The necessary first step, Ball suggested, was for the United States to make abundantly clear to the South Vietnamese and to foreign governments (and presumably to the American public) that it would remain in South Vietnam only as long as the people there desired its help. At the same time, Washington should serve notice to the Saigon regime's leaders that "we are determined to continue the struggle . . . only if they achieve a unity of purpose in Saigon, clearly express that unity, and create a government free from factionalism and capable of carrying on the affairs of the country." In Saigon this would probably be seen as "a warning of ultimate United States disengagement," and this would hasten the formation of a neutralist government by accelerating "existing covert probing of the possibilities of a deal with the Viet Cong elements."

Ball conceded that he was offering only a "sketchy outline of the possibilities," but then there had been virtually no thought given to the option of a political solution and the ways to achieve it: "We have spent months of concentrated effort trying to devise ways and means to advance the present policy of winning the war in the South," he pointed out. "We have spent weeks trying to devise an effective strategy for applying increasing military pressure against the North. But we have given almost no attention to the possible political means of finding a way out without further enlargement of the war."

Here was a tightly argued plan for a negotiated American withdrawal from Vietnam, put forth by the number-two man at the State Department. It summarized all the arguments in favor of a political solution that Ball and others had articulated over the previous months. The fundamental objective, Ball later wrote, had been to show that his colleagues were "standing logic on its head."

> What we had charitably referred to as the government in Saigon was falling apart, yet we had to bomb the North as a form of political therapy. That was as absurd as Candide's account of hanging admirals *pour encourager les autres* [to encourage the others]. Such a tortuous argument was the product of despair—the last resort of those who believed we could not withdraw from Vietnam without humiliation. They still tenaciously believed that we did not dare negotiate until we had so battered the North that any settlement talks would concern only the terms of Hanoi's capitulation—which was out of the question.[42]

Ball's memorandum warrants extended discussion because of its extraordinarily prescient argumentation, because that argumentation so closely mirrored what many independent observers were saying, and because of the timing of the memo's appearance: early October 1964, with U.S.-GVN fortunes at a new low and with the American election only four weeks away. Had leading American policymakers given Ball's effort a full and careful hearing, it could have been used as a blueprint for a fundamental reevaluation of U.S. Vietnam policy once the election was over. But the memorandum did not figure prominently in top-level thinking on the war in the fall of 1964. Lyndon Johnson did not even see the memo until February 1965, by which time the broad policy review that he asked to be undertaken after election day had long since been completed. Ball's paper does not appear to have been seriously discussed at any of the high-level meetings in October, or even to have been read by anyone other than the hawkish group of McNamara, Rusk, and the Bundy brothers, along with a few second-tier State Department officials such as Benjamin Read and Thomas Hughes. In that respect, the memorandum was much less important in the policy process than Ball, and many other observers, later claimed.

This is not to suggest that the senior presidential advisers failed to take Ball's effort seriously. They worried about it a great deal. Intelligent men all, they could see the power of his analysis, could see the damage the report could cause if it began to gain adherents in the bureaucracies of the State and Defense departments or in the NSC. Had the memorandum been less cogent, less incisive, these men probably would have been much more willing to pass it on to Johnson. (Indeed, one can imagine them taking delight in showing the president a shoddy proposal for a political solution. "This," they then could have told him, "is the best that the skeptics can do.") As it was, neither McNamara, nor Rusk, nor either of the Bundys arranged for Johnson to see the Ball report. William Bundy drafted a response memorandum that, though it did not "attempt to meet all of Ball's arguments," addressed several of his points and all the other "apparent heresies" Bundy could think of. Bundy's effort is a fascinating historical artifact in its own right, and not only because it represented the only in-depth examination in this period of the stakes and options in Vietnam by a staunch proponent of standing firm in Vietnam. Equally fascinating is that Bundy endorsed many of Ball's assertions, implicitly if not explicitly. He agreed that all of America's options in the war were unpalatable and that the situation on the ground in South Vietnam was worse than ever. Allied nations in Europe did not think a major defense of South Vietnam was worth the trouble, Bundy conceded, believing as they did that the Soviet threat was reduced and that Indochina was not an area of vital concern to western security.

Even on the implications of a defeat in the war the two men were not far apart. Throughout the fall administration spokesmen, including Bundy (and Ball in his talk with Reston), had consistently warned of falling dominoes should South Vietnam be lost, but here Bundy said otherwise:

Other potentially beleaguered countries may not think we played our
cards too well in South Vietnam, but *in a general sense* none are likely
to feel that [a failure there] really proves that we cannot be counted on
in their individually different situations, or that they themselves cannot handle these situations with our help as needed. Their faith might
be somewhat shaken . . . but a strong case can be made that even the
loss of South Vietnam and Laos to Communist control would not shake
significant non-Communist nations in other areas, or encourage the
Communist side to think it had really found the answer to continuing
the cold war by neat little subversive operations to which we would
have no counter.

The basic point, of course, is that we have never thought we could
defend a government or a people that had ceased to care strongly about
defending themselves, or that were unable to maintain the fundamen-
tals of government. And the overwhelming world impression is that
these are the lacking elements in South Vietnam, and that its loss will
be due, if it comes, to their lack. . . . Let us accept that the domino theory is much too pat.

If South Vietnam were lost or given up, Bundy continued, it would be essential to hold Thailand and South Korea, and to have the British reinforce
the defense of Malaysia against Sukarno. Even here, however, he was sanguine, suggesting that much could be done to accomplish this aim.

As for the choices available to the United States, all were in the "Hobson
class," Bundy wrote. He ultimately gave a slight preference to the option of
"trying to get a negotiating balance by military action" against North Vietnam, but did so only after first casting strong doubts that a systematic air
campaign against the DRV would yield results (for the same reasons argued
by the Sigma II participants). Bundy tried to square this circle by stating
that the bombing would stop once negotiations got under way—the attacks
thus did not need to induce a capitulation by Hanoi. So why not just enter
negotiations immediately? Because Hanoi and its Chinese allies would have
no incentive to compromise, since the DRV would not be hurting in any
way. Early talks would thus be "a straight negotiation from weakness."

Most intriguing was Bundy's description of the status quo option, of
"carrying on unchanged." This would lead in short order to a neutralist outcome in South Vietnam, he declared, perhaps within only a couple
of months. Influential elements in Saigon would make contact with the
NLF, a deal would be struck, and a coalition government in Saigon would
take power. In a certain period of time—anywhere from a few months to
"just possibly" a year or two—the communists would become dominant
and Vietnam would be reunified under communist control. At some point

fairly early in the process the United States would be asked to withdraw. "These enormous disadvantages would appear to negate this course of action at the outset," Bundy wrote. He quickly acknowledged, however, that it also had two legitimate compensating advantages. First, it would be an all-Vietnamese solution, reached not at a great-power conference where the Chinese would be present but in Vietnam itself. Beijing would not have re-entered Southeast Asia in any significant sense, and a communist Vietnam might limit its own ambitions to Laos and act as a buffer against China. Sufficient time might be bought to allow Thailand's defenses to be bolstered. Second, under this solution the United States would not be directly associated with the negotiations—it could observe developments from a distance and not stake its prestige on the outcome of the talks.[43]

Ball and Bundy were thus not nearly as far apart in their analyses as one would have expected. Had Bundy in his memo withheld an explicit preference for any one option, a reader could indeed be forgiven for thinking he too backed an early American extrication from the conflict. But though he shared many of Ball's doubts about any program of expanded military action, he still thought it preferable to the alternatives. Ball did not.

Given the prophetic nature of the undersecretary's warnings in his memorandum, and in others he produced the following winter and spring, it was inevitable that he would in later years be regarded as a lonely, courageous dove in an administration full of hawks, as the one senior official who kept his senses, who understood the situation, and who could see beyond the immediate to the long term. Ball himself worked hard in his retirement years to cultivate this image of himself as a lone fighter who battled valiantly but in vain to prevent an American war in the jungles of Southeast Asia.

It is an attractive picture but a flawed one. That Ball genuinely believed what he argued is not in question—one glance at any of his missives in 1964 and 1965 removes all doubt as to the depth of his convictions, as do the later recollections of his colleagues.[44] Nor is there any dispute that he represented a minority of one in the upper reaches of policy making. The trouble pertains to how he saw his own role within that policy making, and how others saw his role, which in turn leads to questions of how hard he worked (or did not work) to build support for his views. Ball later strenuously denied that he had been assigned his role, that he had been appointed a "house dove," a resident devil's advocate, but it now appears certain that this is precisely what he was, and with his own full knowledge. The 5 October memorandum had been requested by Johnson at an NSC meeting some two weeks earlier and had been seen from the outset as a devil's advocate exercise. Johnson, wanting future historians to believe he had fully staffed out all the options, instructed the undersecretary to shoot holes in the contingency plans for stepped-up action then being laid down by McNamara, the JCS, and others. In telephone conversations in the days after he completed the memo, Ball and other officials expressed concern that James Reston had gotten wind of a "devil's advocate paper" and might say so in print. Tellingly, they did not dispute the columnist's characterization of the report.[45]

Ball's actions throughout 1964 and 1965 support this picture of him as a devil's advocate who could be safely counted on to remain on the team, come what may. Johnson, skilled judge of human (at least American) motivation that he was, had long since identified that key part of the George Ball persona: his unswerving loyalty. The president knew that, whatever Ball might feel inside, outwardly he would faithfully present the administration's position. And indeed, as we have seen, whenever he represented the administration—whether as undersecretary or, during Rusk's frequent absences, as acting secretary—Ball always talked tough on the war, tougher than almost anyone else. One wonders why Ball never made any attempt to get his October memorandum to the president, especially given that it had been written at Johnson's behest. Ball's own explanation, that he felt he owed it to his fellow senior advisers to let them see it first, does not satisfy—even if these men had to have first crack at it, and even if Johnson was too busy campaigning in October to pay attention to a sixty-seven-page report by a mere undersecretary of state, why did Ball make no effort to get it into Johnson's hands during the critical policy discussions in November?[46] Or in December? Nor did Ball make any attempt to build support for his position within the foreign-policy establishment, the way Clark Clifford would later do as secretary of defense. Whereas Ball remained content to make his pitch to the small coterie of senior policymakers, Clifford enlisted junior officials, former officials, reporters, and lawmakers in his cause to bring about a negotiated disengagement from the war. By all accounts, George Ball treasured his position in the administration and sought to do nothing that might jeopardize it. It was well known among administration insiders that he hoped one day to be Johnson's secretary of state.

It would be a mistake to take this argument too far. Loyalty to one's superiors is not a character flaw. Neither is ambition. Ball should not be faulted for wanting what almost any undersecretary would want, to be promoted to the top job. Nor should the difficulty of dissenting against the policies of a figure such as Lyndon Johnson be underestimated. McGeorge Bundy would emphasize this point in dismissing the idea that Ball could have tried harder. "Why do people hassle around with [Ball's] motives?" Bundy wondered in an interview. "I think George should be taken on the merits and also on who he was dealing with. You can't organize against Lyndon Johnson without getting bombed before breakfast, because in his view that's the final and ultimate conspiracy." Clifford operated as a cabinet member and at a time when the bulk of the eastern establishment had broken with the White House over the war, when antiwar demonstrations were commonplace across the country.[47]

Nevertheless, the fact remains that Ball accepted his devil's advocate role, which meant that his fulminations carried little weight—after all, he was merely fulfilling his assigned role, merely performing as the good lawyer that he was. He may even have reveled in his role, because it allowed him to stay true to his genuine convictions and at the same time remain on the team. Ball's own postwar assertion—that if he had resigned in a huff and publicly blasted the war from the outside, he would have lost all capacity to influence policy—does not get at the fundamental question of how hard he really tried to influence that policy from the inside. Ultimately, it seems, Ball's was a misplaced loyalty, one that put loyalty to boss before loyalty to nation. It put the short-term interests of the group and of self before the long-term interests of the country.

That Lyndon Johnson failed to see the 5 October memorandum until well into the new year tells us much about how the president viewed Ball's effort. If Ball failed to get the document to the president in the critical weeks after the election, Johnson also made no effort to get his hands on it, even though he was the one who requested that it be written. Johnson evidently thought it important that a dissenting analysis be written but less important that it be read. Already more or less committed to the plans he had instructed the undersecretary to critically analyze, Johnson primarily wanted the assurance that all sides of the Vietnam issue had been considered. It thus seems unlikely that it would have made much difference if the president had seen the memorandum in early October. In the final weeks of the presidential campaign, he continued to hope for signs of improvement in the war effort and to search for indications that present U.S. policy could be made to work. His watchword was *caution*. In campaign speeches, he stressed his desire to "stay out of a shooting war" and his intention to work for a peaceful solution to the conflict. He turned down Pentagon requests to increase American military and economic assistance to South Vietnam. And despite the urgings of advisers, he refused to retaliate when Vietcong guerrillas shelled the U.S. airbase at Bienhoa on 1 November.

The election was a landslide. Lyndon Johnson won forty-four states and 61 percent of the vote, and his plurality was the largest in history. The Democratic Party added two seats in the Senate, for a total of sixty-eight (against thirty-two for the Republicans) and thirty-seven in the House of

Representatives, giving it 297 (against the GOP's 140). It was an astonishing victory, more sweeping than all but the most optimistic administration insiders had anticipated, a glorious culmination of the campaign that Johnson had been waging since his arrival in the White House a year earlier. The president and his aides had succeeded in their election-year strategy of keeping the Vietnam problem at arm's length. Now, as the end of 1964 drew near, they readied themselves to face the road ahead. The fact that a general consensus existed among them, to the effect that expanding the war was preferable to disengagement, should not obscure the reality that genuine options existed. Various paths were open to them.

On 3 November, election day, an interdepartmental working group chaired by William Bundy convened for the first of several meetings to consider the next stage of the war and how to approach it. It would be the last, best chance to ask the really fundamental questions about the war, to deeply probe the policy alternatives available to the United States, to closely examine the implications of making Vietnam an American war.

9 The Freedom to Change

The most remarkable thing about the American presidential election of 1964 and the war in Vietnam is not that Lyndon Johnson and his foreign-policy advisers saw the two as closely connected; it is that practically everyone else did as well. All year long, outside observers of American policy had seen the election as certain to mark a key transition in the war. In London and Paris, Ottawa and Canberra, officials had operated on the assumption that Lyndon Johnson would try hard to avoid major new policy initiatives on Southeast Asia before November. In the United States, editorial writers and columnists had likewise suggested, albeit more circumspectly, that crucial decisions would have to await the outcome of the vote, and senior Democratic senators had tempered their concerns about American policy for fear of doing anything that might aid the Republican cause. Even the North Vietnamese, who paid close attention to American political developments, thought election considerations helped shape American policy. In August Premier Pham Van Dong assured Canadian diplomat J. Blair Seaborn that the U.S. air strikes in the wake of the Gulf of Tonkin incidents that month resulted partly from Johnson's need to "outbid" his election rival, Barry Goldwater. In September and October Hanoi officials concurred with western observers that Johnson would seek to avoid major policy departures through the end of the campaign.[1]

A difficult choice would confront American decision makers after the election, the vast majority of these outside observers agreed. Particularly as the war effort in South Vietnam deteriorated in the summer and early fall of 1964, and the political in-fighting in Saigon and general war-weariness among southerners increased, analysts both inside and outside the United States saw a fundamental choice facing whoever might be the victorious candidate: whether to dramatically expand the American involvement in the conflict or seek some kind of face-saving exit from South Vietnam. Judgments about the moral or geostrategic correctness of U.S. policy mattered little here: supporters as well as critics of America's commitment to the Saigon government agreed these were the likely alternatives.

Which way would the president go? To the international diplomatic community and to many close observers in the United States who did not know the details of the administration's secret planning, it was an open question. An expanded war was in no way preordained. Escalation versus disengagement constituted an odious choice but also a legitimate one, which meant that policymakers had considerable freedom of maneuver about which way to go. Had these analysts been able to predict the size of Johnson's victory they would no doubt have been further convinced of this fundamental maneuverability. On 3 November the voters placed a giant stamp of approval on the incumbent's performance, and the administration appeared to have a rock-solid mandate to continue its policies, both at home and abroad.

For Vietnam, the question was what that mandate constituted. There can be no doubt that millions who cast their ballots for Johnson did so precisely because he was not Barry Goldwater. The Republican candidate scared them with his ideologically tinged speeches and his seeming proclivity for a direct confrontation with communist forces in Vietnam. In contrast, Johnson ran as the candidate of peace, as the man who would continue to support South Vietnam but also keep the United States out of a major war in Southeast Asia. Notwithstanding the attempt by White House speechwriters to leave slightly ajar the door to a larger American involvement in the conflict, the dominant impression left by LBJ in the final weeks of the campaign was that of a president telling voters that if they wanted to avoid a larger war in Vietnam, he was their man. "If any American president had ever promised anything to the American people," Thomas Powers has written, "then Lyndon Johnson had promised to keep the United States out of the war in Vietnam."[2] Most voters thought not in terms of a large expansion of the American presence in the war, culminating perhaps in the dispatch of major U.S. fighting forces, but in terms of maintaining the status quo, of continuing the policy of providing aid and advisers to the Saigon government. The journalist James Reston, who followed Johnson all over the country during the campaign, observed that LBJ "was loudly cheered when he said over and over again that he wasn't going to 'send American boys to fight a war Asian boys should fight for themselves.'" As both the Reston and Powers assertions suggest, if Johnson's mandate provided for any kind of dramatic policy change on Vietnam it was in the opposite direction of escalation, toward disengagement.[3]

And disengagement was a policy option that won many new adherents in the United States in the wake of the election, less because of American than because of South Vietnamese political developments. November and December 1964 witnessed the almost total unraveling of the South Vietnamese socio-political fabric. Internal factional struggles among Saigon officials reached new levels of intensity, and intelligence agencies reported widespread support for some form of neutralist settlement leading to a coalition government. War-weariness became still more pervasive among the peasantry and many urban dwellers, and there occurred a pronounced increase in anti-American rhetoric, some of it uttered by top GVN officials. To longtime proponents of early negotiations these developments only confirmed what they had always said: that any American attempt to secure a GVN military victory over the Vietcong would inevitably fail, and that it was foolish to pretend otherwise.

Significantly, these critics now found vastly increased support for their views. In December 1964, dozens of newspapers across the United States, some of which had hitherto been unquestioning supporters of the American commitment (and would be again after the Americanization of the war in 1965), began to express deep doubts about the enterprise. Many of them endorsed a negotiated disengagement from the war. Others would not go that far but still explicitly ruled out any deeper American involvement. A troubling question began to echo in editorials across the land: Just what was America doing supporting a government and a people so demonstrably unwilling to contribute to their own defense? On Capitol Hill, meanwhile, support increased for a full-fledged reexamination of the country's commitment to South Vietnam.

Which suggests an additional reason why the last weeks of 1964 and the first of 1965 rank as crucial in the making of major war in Vietnam. If opponents of an expanded war thought Lyndon Johnson had increased freedom of maneuver in this period, they also now possessed greater freedom to challenge U.S. policy. Senate Democratic skeptics, for example, could not rationalize their self-muzzling quite so easily now that the Goldwater forces had been decimated. Before the election, prominent Georgia senator and Johnson mentor Richard Russell had revived the withdrawal plan he first articulated to LBJ the previous winter. Russell told Marine Corps commandant Wallace Greene in late October that the administration should move after the election to bring a man to the top of the South Vietnamese government "who would demand that the U.S. withdraw its forces from that country." Such a development, Russell said, would allow the United States to "save face" while disengaging from an untenable position.[4]

Would Russell and his large number of fellow Democratic skeptics press harder for a policy change along such lines now that the election was over? In the same way, would London officials, who time and again in previous months had said to one another that any challenge to the American position would have to await the November election, now force a showdown? Said one British official in mid November: "Although the problem is primarily an American one, we are clearly in a position to influence American thinking."[5] Would he and his colleagues now move to do so? Would the new Labour government under Harold Wilson make a major effort to head off an expansion of the war to North Vietnam? Would it work hard to convince Washington that early negotiations, even from a position of weakness, were preferable to escalation?

These questions take on additional historical significance when one considers that senior American policymakers shared many of the same judgments about the state of the war, and the prospects for a turnaround, as the British and other opponents of escalation. To say that Lyndon Johnson possessed freedom of action in the wake of his election would not mean all that much if he and his top aides were ignorant about the problems they faced in Vietnam, or at least were confident the measures they planned to adopt would have the desired effect. They were neither. American decision makers in 1964–1965 did not walk blindly into the Vietnam quagmire, as is sometimes claimed—their eyes were wide open. They were under no illusions about the chronic weakness of the GVN, about the absence of popular support for the government, about the growing strength of the Vietcong. They knew, most of them, that expanding the war on such a flimsy political foundation was fraught with peril. From their own intelligence and that of allies, they knew that Hanoi had not lessened in its determination to persevere in the conflict. And they were aware, finally, that the United States was increasingly isolated on the war among its allies. If they escalated the conflict, they understood, little international backing would be forthcoming.

On some level, Lyndon Johnson understood that he had options regarding Vietnam and that the immediate postelection period would present an opportunity to examine those options closely. The day before the election, he ordered the creation of an NSC "Working Group" to study "immediately and intensively" the American alternatives in Southeast Asia. The group, to be chaired by Assistant Secretary of State William P. Bundy, would be composed of eight middle-level officials from the State Department, the Pentagon, and the CIA—in addition to Bundy, they were Marshall Green, Robert H. Johnson, and Michael Forrestal, all from the State Department, John McNaughton and Vice Admiral Lloyd Mustin from the Pentagon, and Harold Ford and George Carver from the CIA. These men would report their conclusions to a group of NSC "principals" (Secretary of Defense Robert McNamara, Secretary of State Dean Rusk, National Security Adviser McGeorge Bundy, CIA Director John McCone, Undersecretary of State George Ball, and Joint Chiefs of Staff Chairman General Earle Wheeler), who would in turn make recommendations to the president. It resembled a bureaucratic layer cake, which suited the president fine—it allowed him to create something close to unanimity among his advisers.

Herein lay the crux of the matter. Lyndon Johnson not only wanted consensus on which way to proceed in Vietnam; he also wanted victory in the war, or at least something other than defeat. In the wake of his campaign triumph, he was no less adamant than before that he would not be the president who lost Vietnam. As William Bundy put it in a memorandum on 5 November, LBJ emerged from the election "clearly thinking in terms of maximum use of a Gulf of Tonkin rationale" to show American determination.[6] Presidential advisers, whether in the top or middle level, understood this Johnsonian idée fixe perfectly well, and it must have hung like a heavy blanket over the planning that November. In addition, almost all of these advisers had developed a deep stake in the success of the war effort. For several years in many cases, they had trumpeted the need to stand firm and proclaimed the certainty of ultimate victory; to suggest a new course now would mean going against all their previous recommendations and analyses. Vested interest, in other words, produced bias.

These pressures explain what in hindsight is the most defining characteristic of the postelection deliberations: their highly circumscribed nature. Whatever freedom of action other observers may have thought Johnson possessed after the crushing victory over Goldwater, it quickly became clear that there remained little latitude for reopening the basic questions about American involvement in Vietnam—about whether the struggle needed to be won or whether it could be won. NSAM 288, issued in March 1964, which committed the United States to defending and preserving an independent, noncommunist South Vietnam, remained the bedrock upon which all proposals were to be built. Thus, although the discussions in the Working Group and among the principals in November were indeed "immediate and intensive," the range of options under consideration was narrow: all of them presupposed the need to stand firm. Proposals of the type suggested by Richard Russell, in which the United States would seek an avenue out of the war, were no more palatable than they had ever been.

Even as they continued to embrace old assumptions about Vietnam's importance and the need to persevere, however, senior American officials also understood that the war had entered a new stage and required new measures. In fact, it was precisely the growing possibility that a Russell-type scenario could develop *without* American urging that gave special urgency to the Working Group's deliberations. So grave had the political situation in South Vietnam become that U.S. officials now thought it possible that the Saigon government might decide on its own to end the war through a deal with the Vietcong or Hanoi. Alternatively, the regime could be overthrown and replaced by a neutralist regime committed to the same result. (Note that Americans continued to be much more fearful of a political collapse in South Vietnam than of a military defeat.) Stepped-up American action to prevent such an outcome was plainly required. In the last weeks of 1964, Lyndon Johnson and his top aides made the final plans to go to war in Vietnam. It was a momentous decision, the most important of the entire mid-1963 to mid-1965 period, indeed of the entire war, but in their eyes it was also a logical one—for much of the year, they had anticipated that this day would come and had planned accordingly. Even the timing conformed to the prior planning. Since about the middle of the year, it will be recalled, officials had referred to 1 January 1965 as the likely "D day," or the day for initiating wider action against North Vietnam.

Before the NSC Working Group held its first meeting, in fact even before the election, this future direction of American policy could be seen. On 1 November, a State Department cable approved by Secretary of Defense Robert McNamara and by the White House asked Ambassador Maxwell Taylor in Saigon to recommend actions that would give the "right signal level to the North and keep up morale in the South." The cable requested Taylor's opinion about the use of air strikes against Vietcong units in South Vietnam and about the deployment of American ground forces, suggesting that such forces could give "the desirable appearance of securing decks for action." The following day, on the eve of the election, a second cable, authored by the Working Group's chairman, William Bundy, and approved by the White House, informed Taylor that the administration intended to seek the "earliest possible preparation for a later decision" to begin expanded action, and to authorize "interim actions" that would demonstrate America's unbending determination in the war. The cable added that the administration would try to have the various alternatives for wider action ready as soon as possible.[7]

Taylor welcomed the news. Earlier in the day he had written to McNamara that early military action against North Vietnam was essential, lest the war effort in the South collapse completely. Neither Taylor nor his colleagues in Washington were interested in waiting to see how the U.S. election turned out before making these plans for an expanded war. At 9:30 A.M. on election day, while millions of Americans were casting ballots against Goldwater—a good many of them because of his public stridency on the war—the Working Group convened for the first time to discuss how best to implement the expansion of the war that Goldwater advocated. Goldwater's general Vietnam policy before election day would become Johnson's Vietnam policy thereafter. A Herblock cartoon some months later got it right—it showed LBJ looking into a mirror and seeing Goldwater's face staring back at him.[8]

The Working Group thus began its work with the general assessment that an increased American participation in the war would be useful and necessary. The three basic options were outlined immediately and, with some modifications, were the ones presented to the principals in the final week of November. Option A would be to continue present policies, including, in John McNaughton's words, "maximum assistance within South Vietnam and limited external actions in Laos and by the GVN covertly against North Vietnam." Any American reprisal actions would be for the purpose of punishing large Vietcong actions in the South enough to deter future activity but not so much as to bring about strong international negotiating pressures. Basic to this option would the "continued rejection of negotiating in the hope the situation will improve." Option B would be early, heavy military pressure against the North, called "fast/full squeeze" by McNaughton. The actions would continue at a rapid pace and without interruption until the United States achieved its present objectives (that is, an end to the insurgency). At some point, Option B activity would be meshed with negotiation, Bundy and McNaughton wrote, "but we would approach any discussions or negotiations with absolutely inflexible insistence on our present objectives."[9]

Option C took the middle road between A and B. It called for a continuation of existing policies but with added military pressure. There would be communication with Hanoi, Beijing, or both, and graduated military moves against infiltration routes in Laos and North Vietnam and then against additional targets in the North. "The scenario should give the impression of a steady deliberate approach," McNaughton suggested. "It would be designed to give the U.S. the option at any point to proceed or not, to escalate or not, and to quicken the pace or not." Under Option C, the question of negotiations would be "played by ear," though the administration should probably indicate a willingness to talk under the right conditions. McNaughton and Bundy, the two dominant members of the Working Group, both preferred this option. Smart bureaucrats that they were, they plainly sought to control the outcome of the deliberations by utilizing what has been called the "Goldilocks principle," in which one choice is portrayed as too soft, one too hard, and one just right. The two men could reasonably expect the principals to join them in favoring the "just right" choice, Option C.[10]

Though these three options framed the debate throughout the Working Group's deliberations, there are intriguing hints that early in the process at least fleeting consideration was given to a "fall-back" position, to what we might call an "Option D," under which the United States would seek to disengage from the war. The unspoken rationale behind this line of thinking was that defeat in Vietnam was certain, or almost certain, regardless of what the administration did. An early position paper, drafted by William Bundy and borrowing heavily from portions of his "Heresies" memo of mid October, acknowledged that most of the world had written off South Vietnam and Laos in 1954; that South Vietnam was uniquely poor ground on which to make a stand, for reasons of geography, demography, and history; and that the present situation looked dismal. American policy had always been based on the notion that the South Vietnamese would care about defending themselves, the paper said, yet in the view of much of the world this will was precisely the lacking element in South Vietnam.[11]

Within this hypothetical "fall-back" position, two alternatives seemed most plausible, Bundy continued. The first would be to maintain support for the South Vietnamese but put a strict limit on the number of U.S. personnel in the country and take vigorous steps to build a stronger base in a more promising place, such as Thailand. The second would involve undertaking a highly visible supporting action (probably a limited-duration bombing campaign against the North) as a last effort to save the South, while simultaneously launching a propaganda campaign that proclaimed the unwinnability of the war given the Saigon government's apathy and ineptness. Once the bombing campaign failed, efforts would also be made to enter into negotiations for a face-saving neutralization agreement.[12]

It is not clear if any members of the Working Group actually thought this fall-back position merited serious consideration, but the group's intelligence panel held views that, if nothing else, seemed to confirm its pessimistic conclusions. The panel members noted that "the basic elements of Communist strength in South Vietnam remain indigenous" and that "even if severely damaged," North Vietnam could continue to support the insurgency at a reduced level. Equally important, Hanoi would endure great pain in any "test of wills with the United States over the course of events in South Vietnam." The North's leaders believed that Washington would encounter strong international pressure if it deliberately expanded the war, and both they and their Chinese allies felt that they could expect success in the South without initiating actions that might expose them to "the great weight of superior U.S. weaponry." Hanoi officials appeared to believe that America's will to stand firm in South Vietnam could in time be eroded and that Johnson's recent landslide victory would provide the administration with "greater policy flexibility" than it previously thought it had. As for the situation prevailing in the South, the intelligence panel members took a gloomy view. They described a Saigon regime "plagued by confusion, apathy, and poor morale," one that had a "better than even" chance of surviving in the short term but perhaps not much longer. In the countryside, the Vietcong continued to conquer government-held territory.[13]

The prescience of this assessment is starkly clear in hindsight, and its articulation early in the Working Group's discussions shows that the administration had access to remarkably accurate intelligence information about the current situation on the ground in Vietnam and about the probable impact of a major war on both North and South. Still more remarkable, most of the Working Group members appear to have agreed with the intelligence panel's grim diagnosis, even as they advocated a stepped-up American effort. William Bundy's early drafts, for example, incorporated many of the panel's assertions about the determination in the North and the dire situation in the South. And John McNaughton, in a 7 November memo in which he counseled wider American action, also made the following astonishing observation: "Progress inside South Vietnam is important, but it is unlikely despite our best ideas and efforts."[14]

Nevertheless, Bundy and McNaughton remained committed to pressing ahead, regardless of the odds. In this conviction they were joined by the Joint Chiefs of Staff's representative to the group, Vice Admiral Lloyd Mustin, who called for an end to the "dallying and delaying" in favor of expanded military action. Mustin's forceful advocacy no doubt helped remove any chance that serious consideration be given the "fall-back" position,[15] but it meant less to the deliberations than the position articulated in the cables of his former boss, Saigon ambassador Maxwell Taylor. Still a voice of major influence in American policy making on Vietnam, Taylor by the last two months of 1964 had become fully convinced that an air campaign against the North represented the magical missing ingredient in the war effort, and he followed his 1 November cable to McNamara with several that advocated sustained bombing action. On 9 November, for example, the ambassador called such action the only way to revive a "despondent country grown tired of the strains of the counterinsurgency struggle." He theorized that bombing could inflict significant damage on "the sources of VC strength" in North Vietnam and along the infiltration routes in Laos and that this damage would boost southern morale. Some American participation in the raids would be needed, Taylor emphasized, in order to "impart a sense of U.S. willingness in the future to share in the necessary action to stop DRV support and direction of VC."[16]

As these comments suggest, Taylor was in the process of undergoing a critical shift on the central dilemma with which he had grappled throughout the fall: how to escalate the war in the absence of any real governmental stability in Saigon. Wider military action, needed to bolster the South Vietnamese government, might prove too much for that government to bear. Having come no closer to resolving this Catch-22, Taylor opted, in effect, to bypass it. On 9 November, he acknowledged the danger of escalation at a time when the Saigon regime "is inadequate to provide leadership to the country" and to respond effectively to the likely Vietcong–North Vietnamese reaction to wider action. The next day, however, the ambassador asked Washington officials to contemplate the obvious question: what if a "minimum government"—which he defined as one keeping law and order in the cities, securing vital military bases from Vietcong attack, and cooperating with the United States—never materialized? "My own answer," Taylor said, "would be that it is highly desirable to have this kind of minimum government before accepting the risks inherent in any escalation program. However, if the government falters and gives good reason to believe that it will never attain the desired level of performance, I would favor going against the North anyway."[17]

It was an extraordinary assertion, and it must have had a powerful impact on planners back in Washington. Only a week had passed since the removal of one brake on escalated American involvement in Vietnam— namely, Johnson's election campaign. Now here was Taylor, the senior American official in Vietnam, a man whose opinion mattered more than perhaps any other presidential adviser's, suggesting that a second brake on such action—the requirement of a stable Saigon government—also be removed. Several top officials in Washington already adhered to this argument, but Taylor's blunt articulation of it surely had a powerful reinforcing effect. Even those inclined to question the message wanted to trust the messenger, who, after all, was in Vietnam and could see things from a perspective they could not.

Had Taylor been so inclined, he, more than any other presidential adviser, could have made a compelling argument in favor of pursuing a "fallback" strategy leading not to escalation but to disengagement. This had been true at the time of his appointment back in July—his impeccable military credentials gave him unique power to suggest bold alternatives—but it was even more true now in November, because he was the man on the scene. Unlike his senior colleagues in Washington, Taylor could see firsthand the war-weariness enveloping all levels of South Vietnamese society in November and could see that large numbers of southerners, spurred on by Buddhist (and, no doubt, NLF) agitation, plainly wanted an end to the war, if necessary through a compromise with the communists. More than his U.S.-based associates, he could see that this desire for peace appeared to reach right to the top of the regime. At the end of October, the High National Council had appointed a new government, headed by Phan Khac Suu as chief of state and Tran Van Huong as premier. Almost immediately, Suu began hinting that he was sympathetic to negotiations, telling the London *Observer* correspondent Denis Bloodworth that "the question of ending hostilities will be taken up by the future National Assembly and the elected Chief of State." Likewise, Ho Van That, a finalist for the premiership, let it be known that if he formed a government, his first task would be to see how an armistice could be arranged. Though Premier Huong appears to have rejected this line of thinking, he told American embassy officials that Buddhist pressures for a neutralist peace were a major source of concern to the government. The Huong regime also did something the previous government would never have done: it allowed an article advocating a "Vietnamese solution for the Vietnamese" to appear in a leading Saigon newspaper.[18]

For Gordon Etherington-Smith, the British ambassador in Saigon, the implications were clear. "In my view," he cabled London on 4 November, the day after the U.S. election, "the most significant aspect of what has happened [within South Vietnam] is the fact that for the first time the possibility of a negotiated settlement has emerged as a central factor (though not as yet openly acknowledged) in the political debate." Etherington-Smith noted the strong pressure being placed on members of the High National Council by Buddhist agitators allied with Thich Tri Quang, and he speculated that Huong "is being criticized in some quarters for being too far to the right (i.e. because he favors continuing the war)." In the ambassador's view, the new developments—including the fact that Suu and Huong had been appointed without American consultation—showed how little control Americans had over the political developments in Saigon and how little they were likely to have in the future. "In these circumstances," he concluded, "the possibility that the Americans may suddenly find themselves confronted with a Vietnamese Government determined to end the war by negotiation appears considerably greater than it has hitherto seemed."[19]

No less worrisome to British and other foreign observers in Saigon, this impotence of American power extended to the military sphere as well, where the ARVN continued to be plagued by low morale and apathy. On 6 November, ARVN officers resisted strong American pressure and refused to send their forces along a canal they considered militarily insecure, thereby delaying a major operation planned to break the Vietcong's hold on the Mekong Delta town of Nam Can. American officers expressed open disgust with this lack of aggression, but they were powerless to do anything about it, much as they had been powerless throughout 1964 to stem the general deterioration in the war effort.[20]

Indeed, the military picture in late 1964 looked worse than ever. The Vietcong attack on the Bienhoa airfield on 1 November showed the extent of enemy penetration even in areas close to the capital. Many important roads in the Mekong Delta, some only a few miles from Saigon (such as Route 13, which ran north through Ben Cat and Loc Ninh to Ban Me Thuot) were now more or less permanently cut off by Vietcong roadblocks or trenches dug across the right of way. The provincial capital of An Loc, center of a rubber growing area, received its food supplies over a circuitous detour of several hundred miles because the main road to Saigon had been cut. Long An province, directly south of Saigon, which had received the highest priority for American assistance of any province in South Vietnam during 1964, was now much less secure than it had been at the time of Diem's overthrow a year earlier. Inevitably, these problems around Saigon had a ripple effect. In October, the ARVN Twenty-Fifth Division was moved from Quang Ngai province, which was in the Second Corps area, to support forces defending the area around Saigon. As part of the redeployment, Quang Ngai was included in the area of responsibility of the First Corps. That command therefore now found itself having to face a greatly increased Vietcong threat in a larger area with no increase in its own forces.[21]

Remarkably, this poor military situation existed despite a relative lull in heavy Vietcong activity both before and after the Bienhoa attack. The NLF's strategy remained what it had been throughout the year, to maintain military pressure without seeking a military victory and to erode government authority to the point where the regime—or a successor regime—would opt for an end to the war through negotiations with the NLF. Continuing the policy they had followed throughout the summer and fall, NLF operatives worked to exacerbate the political instability in the cities and to encourage talk of a neutralist solution. As British officials understood, the absence of heavy military pressure against the government could thus represent a negative rather than a positive development: "It does seem as if a major reason for the absence of intensified Viet-Cong activity, of increased demoralisation in the South Viet-Namese army and of continued active opposition to the new Government, may be precisely the knowledge that the new Government, unlike their predecessors, have not closed their minds to the possibility of a negotiated solution."[22]

Taylor, however, remained adamantly opposed to the possibility, and he continued to frame the conflict in military terms. In mid November, he told Brigadier Robert G. K. Thompson of the British Advisory Mission that Washington was concerned about the Huong government and its prospects and about the government's stated promise to hold elections for a National Assembly. Neutralist and other left-wing elements opposed to a continuation of the war might win a majority of the seats in such an assembly, and thus it was vital to delay any elections for at least several months, so that the ARVN could first strengthen its position on the battlefield. In the meantime, Taylor suggested, a U.S.-directed bombing campaign should be launched against North Vietnam to slow down infiltration and boost morale in the South. Thompson disagreed. He said that even apart from the possible adverse reactions from Moscow and Beijing, a bombing campaign against the North would do little to stem the tide in South Vietnam. If anything, such action could hasten a government collapse in Saigon, because the government would quite likely be unable to handle the intensified war that would probably result. Moreover, the North Vietnamese leadership and populace were prepared for such attacks, and any damage to the North would be temporary. Hanoi would also be able to derive tremendous propaganda advantage from it, while America's international image would suffer. But Taylor was adamant. He told Thompson that the point could come when the Americans had to show that "crime does not pay." Even if South Vietnam went down to defeat, it would be better to have the North in "smoldering ruins" than in an easy position to take over the South.

Taylor had no patience with Thompson's suggestion that early negotiations were a viable option for ending the war. (Back in August, Thompson had privately called such a course Washington's only realistic choice.) The Gulf of Tonkin air strikes had shown the immensity of America's power, Thompson told him, and even though the actual use of such air power again in a sustained way would likely be counterproductive, the threat of employing it could facilitate a negotiated withdrawal for the United States. Thompson speculated that South Vietnam could in fact be quite difficult for Hanoi to digest, given the Cochin Chinese dislike of the North Vietnamese, but he conceded that the end result of any negotiations would likely be a single Vietnam under communist rule. Even so, such a Vietnam might prove, vis-à-vis China, to be a Yugoslavia rather than an East Germany, a Vietnam with which the West could live. Taylor retorted, "And still require one million dollars a day—not of my money!"[23]

Notwithstanding his dislike for any solution that would compromise Washington's fundamental objective—preserving an independent, noncommunist South Vietnam—Taylor professed to agree with Thompson that the pursuit of early negotiations was one of the three basic options open to the United States, the other two being staying the present course and attacking North Vietnam. Note that these were different from the three alternatives being considered at precisely this time some ten thousand miles away, in the Working Group's deliberations in Washington. In the group's formulation, the three options all involved doing the same or doing more; negotiations were to be expressly avoided in the near future and should only follow increased military action. Indeed, as the Working Group's discussions moved into their second and third weeks, a subtle but clear hardening occurred with respect to the negotiations issue, with all three options converging around the minimum demands that Hanoi cease its infiltration into the South, bring about an end to the Vietcong insurgency, and agree to the establishment of a secure noncommunist state. Though the United States would likely have to declare its willingness to negotiate, under all three options meaningful talks with Hanoi were to be avoided until wider military action had put the United States in a position to realize these core demands.

Secretary of State Dean Rusk thus misspoke at a White House meeting with the president on 19 November when he said that the Working Group had focused on exactly the three broad alternatives outlined by Thompson: first, a negotiated settlement on any basis obtainable (not, in fact, under consideration); second, a sharp increase in military pressure on the North (Option B); and third, an "in-between" alternative of increased pressure on the DRV coupled with simultaneous efforts to keep open the channels of communication in case Hanoi was interested in a settlement (a reasonable approximation of Option C, though Rusk failed to note that any settlement would have to be on America's terms). Why Rusk should claim early negotiations as one of the options is a mystery, but it proved a moot point because Working Group chairman William Bundy quickly articulated the actual three options under consideration. McGeorge Bundy noted the growing consensus around Option C and told Johnson that unless he said otherwise, the current thrust around that option would likely continue. Johnson did not respond. He appears to have made no effort in this meeting to broaden his options, to inquire about the differences between the Rusk and William Bundy articulations of Option A, or to probe his top advisers about implications of the expanded measures they were getting ready to recommend. According to the meeting notes, Johnson said nothing when McGeorge Bundy noted that work had not progressed on George Ball's "devil's advocate" exercise (which had begun with his 5 October memorandum, and which involved the preparation of a persuasive case for negotiation and withdrawal under the present circumstances), though that may have been because Rusk assured him that his advisers would not allow unstoppable momentum to develop in favor of any one option to the exclusion of the others.[24]

Once again, Rusk had misspoken. In reality, unstoppable momentum had developed in favor of bombing the North, and early negotiations leading to withdrawal had been ruled out. The fact that senior officials continued to refer to Ball's activity as a "devil's advocate" exercise suggests how little intellectual weight they attached to it. On 7 November, Ball had discussed the October memo with McNamara, Rusk, and McGeorge Bundy but had failed to move them. Likewise, Ball's mid-November suggestion that the administration develop a diplomatic strategy in the event of an imminent collapse by the Saigon regime got nowhere—the centerpiece of this strategy, an early great-power conference on the war convened by the British, at which the United States would play the best it could with lousy cards, was anathema to officials who still refused to contemplate seriously a retreat from core aims laid down in NSAM 288.[25]

Nor was Ball alone in hoping to restrain the move to a larger war. Several midlevel officials shared his basic position, among them James C. Thomson Jr. of the NSC; Thomas L. Hughes, who headed the Bureau of Intelligence and Research at the State Department; Allen Whiting, deputy director of the East Asian desk at the State Department; Carl Salans of the Legal Adviser's Office at the State Department; and the Working Group's Robert Johnson. No less than Ball, these men were distressed by the continuing administration pursuit of a military solution and by the complete unwillingness to negotiate on any terms except those that amounted to Hanoi's unconditional surrender. The United States was in no position to bargain from strength, they believed, and yet the administration had adopted a totally unyielding position on the question of negotiations. More important, the GVN's chronic and continuing weakness, and the growing war-weariness among the South Vietnamese people, suggested that no improvement in that bargaining position could be expected any time soon, especially given the doubts expressed by the U.S. intelligence community as to the benefits that could be expected from bombing the North.

Paul Kattenburg, whose suggestion of withdrawal back in the late summer of 1963 had been so swiftly quashed, later outlined the numerous disadvantages that such individuals worked from in terms of what he called the "bureaucratic-political warfare within the U.S. government." To begin with, Kattenburg argued, with the exception of Ball they were all middle-

or lower-ranking officials, which meant that they lacked pulling power against the president's senior advisers. (Even Ball, Kattenburg might have noted, stood outside the inner circle occupied by only Rusk, McNamara, McGeorge Bundy, and perhaps Taylor.) In addition, these men did not make up a coherent group within the bureaucracy but rather worked individually and apart, and they did not actively try to alter this situation by seeking allies in other agencies like the Defense Department or the CIA. Finally, in Kattenburg's view, they were all "just sufficiently career oriented not to dare pit their personal futures" on the single aim of stopping the momentum toward bombing.[26]

Kattenburg suggested that George Ball was the only one of the group not constrained by career considerations, but in fact the undersecretary was as anxious as anyone to preserve his position in the administration. Maintaining the posture to which he had adhered all year, Ball in November and December always took care not to rock the boat too much and to voice his strongest doubts outside Johnson's presence. This may explain why Ball, who attended the 19 November meeting at the White House, said nothing when McGeorge Bundy spoke of the growing consensus around Option C, and why he raised no objection to Bundy's use of the phrase "devil's advocate exercise" to describe what he was doing. Nor did Ball challenge Bundy's assertion that little progress had been made on the exercise, even though he had completed a sixty-seven-page report on the subject six weeks earlier, and even though he had produced another memo in November making the case for British-sponsored negotiations. Neither Ball nor anyone else at the meeting saw fit to mention to LBJ the existence of his October report. (Johnson, who had requested it be written in the first place, would not actually read it until late in February 1965.)[27]

Ball's special assistant on Vietnam, Thomas Ehrlich, would have been dismayed had he known of his boss's silence at the meeting. A day earlier, Ehrlich had bemoaned the "significant gaps in reasoning" and many unanswered questions in the Working Group's drafts. "Nowhere in these papers is there a consideration of your proposal for negotiations within the near future and without increased military action (although with the threat of such action)," he told Ball after reading what proved to be essentially the group's final recommendations. "As we have discussed, the third option [Option C, or graduated escalation] is full of dangers—I do not believe that they have received sufficient consideration in these papers. Most serious, however, is the lack of any real analysis of a negotiating track. In my judgment, at the very least a paper on this track should be prepared as a fourth option." Perhaps sensing that the point of no return was about to

be passed, Ehrlich worried that policy proposals of the type proposed by
the group tended to develop swiftly a strong bureaucratic momentum unless immediately challenged.[28]

Ehrlich's sense of foreboding was amply justified. By Thanksgiving, when
Ambassador Taylor returned to Washington to take part in the shaping of
the final report to be presented to Johnson on 1 December, a solid consensus had developed among the principals in favor of expanded action and
against early negotiations. One issue divided them, however: whether to
commit U.S. ground forces to Vietnam as part of the escalation. McGeorge
Bundy, Rusk, and McCone were sympathetic to the idea, whereas McNamara saw no military need for ground troops and stated his strong preference for bombing alone. Ball also argued against sending troops, pointing
to the French experience in the Indochina war. It is a measure of Taylor's
influence on the thinking in Washington that the principals looked to him
to help resolve this issue and to give his input on the final recommendations to the president. The ambassador's visit was thus extraordinarily important, more important even than his previous one in September—he
more than anyone could have challenged the consensus for escalation. He
did not. He was, to be sure, a troubled man as he boarded the plane for
Washington, and he carried with him a gloomy report he had written detailing the desperate military situation, the weakness of the GVN ("It is
impossible to foresee a stable and effective government under any name in
anything like the near future"), and the pronounced and mounting war-
weariness and hopelessness that pervaded South Vietnam. At the same
time, the report maintained that the United States should persist in its efforts in Vietnam and indeed should expand them, by working to "establish" a stronger Saigon government and by bombing the North. "Whatever the course of events," Taylor concluded, "we should adhere to three
principles":

   a. Do not enter into negotiations until the DRV is hurting.
   b. Never let the DRV gain a victory in South Viet-Nam without having
       paid a disproportionate price.
   c. Keep the GVN in the forefront of the combat and the negotiations.[29]

   It was essentially the message that Taylor had conveyed to Robert
Thompson a week earlier: North Vietnam, though it might win, should be
left in "smouldering ruins," negotiations should be avoided, and the main
combat forces should be South Vietnamese, not American. These were
principles that would drive Taylor's advocacy on the war in the months to
come. They also appear to have been ranked in order of importance, judg-

ing by the emphasis Taylor placed on them in his meetings with the principals in late November. The ambassador dominated these sessions, and at each of them he hammered away at the need to avoid a premature political solution and to take stronger action against Hanoi. When someone at the first meeting asked, with no evident sense of irony, whether the United States could carry on unilateral military action in the event that the GVN collapsed or told the United States to get out, Taylor, with equal seriousness, answered, "Probably not." He expressed relief that the proposed National Assembly in South Vietnam was at least some months away, but he warned his colleagues that such a body, once in place, could be expected to contain strong anti-American elements. Finally, he emphasized that the American message to the Saigon government must not be too forceful (in the manner of "Shape up or we get out"), because the regime might just call the Americans' bluff and demand withdrawal. The principals needed little convincing, and the Working Group's final policy recommendations put the matter plainly: "The U.S. would seek to control any negotiations," the report read, "and would oppose any independent South Vietnamese efforts to negotiate."[30]

There was less agreement on the question of whether to commit U.S. ground troops to the struggle, and the matter was left open in advance of the meeting with the president. The other remaining uncertainty had to do with the minimum government needed in Saigon to initiate the wider military action. Johnson's top advisers were in agreement that, if necessary, the new measures should be undertaken regardless of the strength of the regime, but they conceded that a more viable political foundation in South Vietnam had to be in place before too long. They accordingly recommended a two-phase policy, consistent with the general approach outlined in Option C. The first phase involved "armed reconnaissance strikes" against infiltration routes in Laos as well as retaliatory strikes against the North in the event of a Vietcong "spectacular" such as the one at Bienhoa, and the second phase would see "graduated military pressure" against North Vietnam. Phase one would begin as soon as possible. Phase two would come later, after thirty days, provided the Saigon government had bettered its effectiveness "to an acceptable degree." However, unwilling to contemplate the implications if the regime should fail to meet this standard, the advisory team then proceeded to waive this requirement: "If the GVN can only be kept going by stronger action," the final recommendations read, then "the U.S. is prepared . . . to enter into a second phase program." Escalation, in other words, should be undertaken regardless of the political picture in Saigon, either to reward the GVN or to keep it from disintegrating.[31]

Enter Lyndon Johnson. On 19 November, the president had indicated his

general agreement with the Working Group's early thinking; now, almost
two weeks later, he had the final recommendations in front of him. His
decision was never in serious doubt, though he plainly did not relish making it. At a long White House meeting on 1 December, he worried about
the absence of governmental stability in Saigon ("Basic to anything is stability," he said) and complained that he did not want to send "Johnson
City boys" out to die for a bunch of politicians who could not get their act
together. "Why not say, 'This is it?'" and withdraw, he wondered aloud.
These comments could be taken as proof that LBJ in this period remained
deeply uncertain about which way to proceed in the war, but his subsequent comments in the same meeting suggest that he still shared the same
mixture of gloom and determination that he and his top aides had possessed throughout 1964. It would be "easy to get in or out," he lectured
the men in the room, "but hard to be patient." The United States had to
stick it out. "The plans you've got now," he said, referring to the Working
Group's recommendations, "[are] all right." Johnson insisted that Taylor
"do [his] damnedest in South Vietnam" before the administration moved
into the second phase, but he signaled his intention to go ahead regardless. If the Saigon situation failed to improve, he declared, looking at JCS
chairman Wheeler, "then I'll be talking to you, General." Johnson further
noted that American dependents should be removed from Saigon; though
the meeting notes do not clearly indicate why, the context suggests that
it was because he feared for their safety in a wider war. And in ordering
Rusk to get military support from allies for the wider action, he tellingly
said, "If [the government?] fails, we want them in with us," and not merely
with a "chaplain and nurse."[32]

It would be hard to overestimate the importance of this presidential
decision. Johnson opted to fundamentally alter the American involvement
in Vietnam. Like his ambassador in Saigon, he was unhappy about the
prospect of moving against the North without a stronger South Vietnamese
government, but like him, he was prepared to do so if necessary. The decision contained deep contradictions. Washington policymakers had for a
long time conceded among themselves that the keys to victory in the war
lay in the South, but now they were seeking a solution through striking
the North, despite general skepticism in the intelligence community that
such a policy would yield results. They had consistently preached the need
for stable, effective government in Saigon prior to any action north of the
seventeenth parallel, but now they were opting to try to bring about that
stability by bombing the North. They had always declared that Americans should not be sent to fight in the war, and yet such a deployment
looked more and more likely—the position paper that emerged out of the

1 December meeting included the cryptic but suggestive line that the escalatory program would include "appropriate U.S. deployments to handle any contingency."[33]

And as always, there was the stark contradiction between the administration's publicly stated willingness to pursue a peaceful solution to the war and its profound private fear of such an outcome. American officials had always proclaimed their commitment to the notion of South Vietnamese self-determination, but the deliberations in November revealed just how empty that claim had become—"The U.S. would oppose any independent South Vietnamese moves to negotiate," said the report that Johnson approved. The establishment of a National Assembly in South Vietnam should be delayed as long as possible, because it might be dominated by pro-peace elements. It is clear that neither LBJ nor his top aides were prepared to accept the idea that to win the people, you had to let them express themselves, which meant risking a government that might negotiate an end to the war. Plainly put, the self-determination Washington claimed to be defending was what it feared most.

The most striking thing about the Johnson administration's decision to move to an escalated war was not that it contained contradictions, however, but that it came despite deep pessimism among many senior officials that the new measures would succeed in turning the war around. They were certainly hopeful that pressure on North Vietnam could improve morale in the South and perhaps cause Hanoi to end its support of the insurgency, but the internal record leaves little sense that they actually believed that these things would happen. Subsequent testimonials reinforce this picture. Michael Forrestal, Rusk's special assistant on Vietnam, recalled how John McNaughton would come see him almost nightly that November to stew over America's slide into a war that it would likely lose. In the same way, William Bundy subsequently acknowledged that Option C's chances of success were never deemed to be great.[34]

Why, then, did they proceed? Most officials coalesced around Option C because they liked its flexibility, liked the fact that one could—theoretically, at least—stop it at any time. McNaughton noted on 7 November that Option C would allow "maximum control at all stages" and permit interruptions if Hanoi showed a willingness to back down, "while seeking to maintain throughout a credible threat of further military pressures should such be required." But that still does not fully answer the question. The discarded Option A, which advocated no new action, could also be termed flexible, precisely because it committed the administration to no specific measures.

Critical to understanding the advocacy of a wider war in the face of general pessimism is the growing attachment among key officials to the theory of the "good doctor," first articulated by John McNaughton in a memo back in September in connection with the need to put the best possible face on what might be an unavoidable defeat. In this scenario, the United States should strive to project the image of a patient (South Vietnam) who died despite the heroic efforts of the good doctor (the United States). Even if bombing North Vietnam were expected to fail, it could serve an important purpose, which McNaughton phrased as follows in one of the early Working Group memoranda: "Even if Option C failed, it would, by demonstrating U.S. willingness to go to the mat, tend to bolster allied confidence in the U.S. as an ally." The next day, he added, "If Option C is tried and fails, we are in no worse position than we would be under Option A; but whatever form a failure took, Option C would leave behind a better odor than Option A: It would demonstrate that the U.S. was a 'good doctor' willing to keep promises, be tough, take risks, get bloodied, and hurt the enemy badly."[35]

Just how many senior American officials adhered to the "good doctor" metaphor as described by McNaughton is not clear. There is little doubt that William Bundy embraced it, as did Maxwell Taylor in Saigon—it probably lay at the root of his leave-the-North-in-smoldering-ruins comment to Thompson. Robert McNamara, McGeorge Bundy, and the JCS's General Wheeler appear likewise to have been sympathetic, judging by a discussion among the principals on 24 November. However, George Ball at the same meeting objected to the notion that the United States would receive international credit merely for trying to do something. Ever mindful of Charles de Gaulle's thinking on the war, Ball warned that the French president would portray the United States as foolish for adopting military measures with little or no hope of success. In Ball's view, American prestige would suffer if the administration tried either Option B ("fast/full squeeze") or C (graduated escalation) and failed. Dean Rusk echoed this sentiment, insisting that the harder America tried and failed, the worse the situation would be. The secretary of state was more optimistic than his colleagues that expanded military action could yield results, and therefore, he endorsed the two-phase escalation. Ball, sharing the others' pessimism but not their interpretation of the stakes, withheld support but raised no forceful objections.[36]

Lyndon Johnson was less inclined than his foreign-policy aides to see the war in terms of its international implications, and thus he likely did not frame the issue in the manner that McNaughton had. But Johnson, too, considered American prestige—and his own prestige—to be at stake in Vietnam, and he thought it vital for the administration to be perceived as doing all it could for the ailing patient in South Vietnam. There were important domestic audiences, after all, whose perceptions mattered a great deal, who could be counted on to launch a malpractice suit against LBJ and the Democrats if things went awry in Vietnam. It was partly with these audiences in mind, and partly because of the short period of time that had elapsed since his peace-oriented election campaign, that Johnson opted to conceal the new policy decision from the public, the Congress, and much of the foreign-policy bureaucracy. In a memo to Rusk, McNamara, and McCone, LBJ declared that he considered it "a matter of the highest importance that the substance of the decision should not become public except as I specifically direct." He ordered the three men to "take personal responsibility . . . for insuring that knowledge of all parts of it"—the immediate actions under phase one and the possible later actions against North Vietnam—be confined "as narrowly as possible to those who have an immediate working need to know."[37]

Among those midlevel government officials who learned of the decision, or at least had a general sense of the direction of policy, several voiced reservations. The State Department's William Jorden, whose current task involved assessing the extent of North Vietnamese infiltration into the South, expressed his preference for Option A and questioned the realism of the proposition, contained in the Working Group's final report, that North Vietnam could be induced to yield to America's terms in any negotiations. Hanoi's leaders would never agree to "turn off the faucet" and end infiltration into the South, Jorden told veteran diplomat W. Averell Harriman (who also preferred Option A), at least not for the foreseeable future, and it was foolish to pretend otherwise. Even if infiltration did cease, the war in the South would go on for a long time. Michael Forrestal professed general agreement with the thrust of the president's decision but lamented its military emphasis. "I should imagine that even among our friends in the area we are thought of more as harbingers of war rather than a force for social and economic development," Forrestal told Rusk. The same concern animated the NSC's James Thomson. Thomson felt certain that Asian governments were skeptical of U.S. intentions and, with some exceptions, opposed to a wider war, and he was convinced that historical Sino-Vietnamese friction precluded the possibility that a reunified, communist Vietnam would willingly come under Beijing's control. A Titoist Vietnam could in fact be an asset to American interests in the area, Thomson believed.[38]

A few days after the president's decision, McGeorge Bundy called Thomson into his office. "Sit down and read this report," Bundy instructed him. "This is the bombing plan, Option C, the preferred option." Thomson read it. "Well, what do you think?" Bundy asked. "I don't know anything about weapons," Thomson replied, "but I do know something about people, and about the Vietnamese. If we go down this road we will not bring them to their knees, or to the negotiating table. We could bomb them back to the stone age. They will disappear into jungle and they will wait us out. Because they know something we know deep down, and they know that we know, which is that some day we're going to go home." Bundy thought for a moment and responded, "Thomson, you may be right."[39]

What Forrestal and Thomson suspected about the attitude in Asia was true not only there but also in other parts of the world: few governments in late 1964 supported the military approach that Washington took to the Vietnam problem. Some continued to be sympathetic to the administration's broad objective in the struggle but did not think it could be achieved—at least at a reasonable price—given the weakness of the GVN, and others considered Vietnam an unimportant theater in the Cold War. Most rejected the notion that the "loss" of Vietnam would start a chain reaction in the rest of Southeast Asia—revolution, they insisted, was a homegrown product—and many feared that a larger war could lead to the intervention of China, the Soviet Union, or both. And there was something else: all friendly governments, even those most supportive of the U.S. intervention, tended to see Vietnam as fundamentally an American problem. It had been such for ten years, since 1954, and few allied leaders thought there was any reason to see the matter differently now.

This explained the embarrassingly meager results of the State Department's "more flags" initiative since its inception the previous spring, and it explained the shudder with which Johnson's aides must have now greeted his demand that the adoption of the two-phase escalation be accompanied by greater allied contributions to the war effort. These advisers knew that significant help would in all likelihood not be forthcoming. Johnson perhaps knew it as well, but he deemed it essential to spare no effort to get America's friends on board. He understood that it would be much more difficult to sustain public support for a unilateral American war in the jungles of Southeast Asia than for a multilateral one. And so, in early December, a new call went out for more third-country contributions. But this call contained two important differences than previous ones. First, it emphasized the need for *military* contributions to the war effort. Second, it targeted only those nations that might possibly oblige. The administration had plainly given up hope of getting tangible support from African, Arab, and Latin American nations. It likewise expected nothing meaningful from continental Europe, including the Germans. Canada, unsupportive of a larger war and in any event precluded from contributing because it was a mem-

ber of the ICC, was a lost cause. Many Asian nations, including Japan, had
ruled out sending troops. Even Taiwan's Chiang Kai-Shek, counted on to
be a staunch ally in the region, was reluctant to commit personnel.[40]

The list of possible contributors was thus a tiny one indeed: Thailand, the
Philippines, Australia, New Zealand, South Korea, and the United Kingdom.
Significantly, only the Australians and the New Zealanders among these
were to be told the full details of both phase one and phase two of the new
policy; the rest would be told only of Washington's "grave concern" or,
in the case of the British, of the first phase and the "possibility" that the
United States might at the end of it opt for additional measures. American
officials felt that only Australia and New Zealand were wholly dependable
allies on the war; only they were likely to be unstinting in their support
for the new actions. On 3 and 4 December, William Bundy met with John K.
Waller and George R. Laking, Canberra's and Wellington's respective ambassadors to Washington. He outlined phase one and told them that the
administration had decided, in principle, to move to phase two after thirty
days or more. What would this second phase entail? the ambassadors asked.
Primarily air attacks of mounting severity between the seventeenth and
nineteenth parallels in Vietnam, Bundy replied, though he noted that it
could also lead to the stationing of one division or two battalions of U.S.
ground forces in the northern part of South Vietnam, to be based in and
supplied from Danang.

With respect to negotiations, the administration would not actively pursue them, Bundy continued, but it would gladly take part in "satisfactory"
talks—that is, negotiations that would result in a noncommunist, independent South Vietnam left in peace by its neighbors. He then cut to the chase:
given the western world's stake in the struggle in Vietnam, and the burden
borne by the United States, it was imperative that other nations step up
their military contributions to a considerable degree. Could Lyndon Johnson count on increased participation by Australia and New Zealand? The
ambassadors were noncommittal but pledged to pass on the request to their
governments. Both hinted, however, that no substantial rise in contributions should be expected, given their countries' commitments in support of
the British in Malaysia. Laking added that in the New Zealand government's view, the North Vietnamese were unlikely to back down regardless
of the pressure put on them.[41]

That the administration should elect not to tell London about the full
range of its planning suggests that it worried about the Wilson government's level of support for escalation. It also had to be concerned that the
British, as cochair of the 1954 Geneva Conference, would feel compelled,
regardless of their own views, to issue a call for a return to Geneva should

the fighting escalate. The administration was nevertheless desperate for British support for its policy in Vietnam, more for psychological and diplomatic than for military reasons. As America's leading ally in international affairs, and as a major world power in its own right, Britain's position mattered to Washington in a way that no other government's stance mattered. Even Tokyo's importance paled in comparison. A British government publicly opposed to American policy could spell major trouble, U.S. decision makers knew, and they consequently attached tremendous importance to Harold Wilson's visit to Washington on 7–8 December, his first since becoming prime minister in October.

The British understood that the visit was occurring at a critical time of decision on Vietnam both for themselves and for the Americans. They also knew what the Americans knew: that their attitude with respect to the Johnson administration's policy in the coming weeks could have a highly important impact on the direction of that policy. Was this the time to put British cards squarely on the table? That was the question before London officials in the days prior to Wilson's departure.

Certainly British official thinking about the war had not grown more hopeful. If anything, Her Majesty's representatives in both Saigon and London were by early December even more pessimistic than before. Both Etherington-Smith of the British embassy and Robert Thompson of BRIAM sent home report after report detailing the floundering military effort and the spiraling political chaos and war-weariness in the South, and staffers at the British consulate-general in Hanoi reported the firm determination and sturdy morale evident among the North Vietnamese. Etherington-Smith professed to see a faint glimmer of light at the end of the tunnel, provided the GVN could get its act together, but his descriptions of the goings-on in the South seemed to argue against that possibility. For his part, Thompson saw only greater darkness the further he peered into the tunnel. He had been disturbed by Taylor's comments to him during their 17 November meeting, and the following week he penned a long cable to London, detailing his frustrations.

The cable began where Thompson's discussion with Taylor had left off: "We are clearly faced with three basic options"—to continue the present course, to attack the North in order to compel Hanoi to call off the war in the South, or to negotiate immediately on the best terms possible. The first option was theoretically possible but objectively impossible. "Both the Americans and Vietnamese failed in 1962 and 1963 in much better going and there is no sign that they can succeed in the vastly more difficult circumstances which now prevail," Thompson wrote. "It is a moot point also whether any form of 'winning' would now establish a politically viable

South Vietnam, capable of withstanding continuing communist subversion." The second option was no better, Thompson continued; indeed, it was worse. Plenty of excuses could be found for bombing the North, he conceded, all under "the law of brute force," but would it work? No. Thompson downplayed the risk of a direct confrontation with China or the Soviet Union under this option, but he insisted that its adoption would not improve the situation in the South. The ARVN would become increasingly likely to "down tools" and leave the work to the Americans. Xenophobic reactions would quite possibly occur in the South ("The Vietnamese may be callous about killing each other but there is no evidence that they like others doing it for them"). Vietcong activity would be stepped up. Infiltration from the North—which "no air action is going to prevent"—would increase. Worst of all, he noted, an intensified war could not be handled by the current government.

Nor did Thompson believe that the bombing would achieve its objective with respect to the North. Even if left in "smoldering ruins," the physical damage would be temporary, and besides, the North Vietnamese people were willing to accept this as the price of ultimate victory. They would also receive increased aid from the Soviets and Chinese. Under these circumstances, Thompson saw no possibility that Hanoi would feel compelled to negotiate on America's terms. "Why should they? The communists will have achieved a situation where America loses in South Vietnam and leaves Asia looking like a mad dog in the eyes of the world," he declared. "This will inevitably lead to a 'fortress America' policy, not because this would be a positive isolationist American reaction, but because she would herself be isolated by world opinion. Brute force is not effective force and I would sum up this option by calling it the bad-loser option." (John McNaughton's "good doctor" had become Robert Thompson's "bad loser.")

That left only the third alternative, early negotiations from an inferior position. Thompson did not doubt that the end result would be a unified, communist Vietnam, or that such a development would be a significant blow to the West's interests in Southeast Asia and in thwarting Maoist revolutions generally. "But if you are defeated," he wrote, "you have to accept some of the disastrous consequences and attempt to reduce them rather than increase them as in Option B." Now was the time, while there was still a government in Saigon, to use the *threat* of bombing the North but to move toward negotiations. Thompson speculated that the NLF would be ready to negotiate "solely on the basis of an American withdrawal with Hanoi concurring. It is to their advantage to achieve a respectable takeover and to keep the damage to a minimum, rather than to have a prolonged struggle." Nor would the communists blindly follow the Beijing line once the takeover was complete. Best of all, Thompson concluded, the negotiations option would actually give the West more time than the escalation option to strengthen other areas of Southeast Asia and give "America a better chance in other areas of the world where similar problems will have to be faced." Early negotiations might be a bitter pill to swallow, but because there was no viable alternative, it was the "good-loser option."[42]

London officials wholeheartedly agreed, as they had agreed with Thompson's similar message in August. A new party and a new prime minister had taken power in the interval, but the British outlook on the war was substantially the same. In late November, in preparation for Wilson's trip to Washington, the Foreign Office conducted its own analysis of the negotiations issue and concluded that sooner was better than later. The study deemed it "quite probable" that the current Saigon regime, or a successor one, would opt for negotiations rather than to continue "what now seems to [the South Vietnamese] a hopeless and interminable struggle." Because action against North Vietnam would not remedy the situation, the United States and the West should lay the groundwork now for a diplomatic solution, ideally through a reconvened Geneva conference that could simultaneously address the situations in neighboring Laos and Cambodia. The main American objection to a great-power conference—that it would harm South Vietnamese morale—would be moot, both because that morale was decimated already and because the Saigon government itself would quite likely want negotiations. As for the reaction in the rest of Southeast Asia, the report was sanguine: because many governments in the region were pessimistic and "had discounted the outcome in advance," they would not necessarily "regard as disastrous an American withdrawal from South Vietnam," especially if it took place at the wish of the Saigon government and not as a result of military defeat.[43]

All this seemed clear enough to most British officials, but the question remained how to broach the issue with Washington. Harold Wilson had come into office highly dubious about America's Vietnam enterprise but also determined to maintain good relations with the United States.[44] He had inherited a balance of payments crisis and an unstable currency, and as a trained economist he understood well Britain's dependence on U.S. support for the pound. In addition, both Wilson and the Foreign Office were loath to do anything that might threaten U.S. support for Britain's own involvement in Malaysia or complicate the various other issues facing Anglo-American relations in late 1964. Notable among these issues was the American-proposed Multilateral Force (MLF)—a mixed-European naval force carrying nuclear weapons, first introduced under John F. Kennedy—

which the British opposed and which appeared to be a key item for discussion at the Washington talks.[45]

From the start, then, the British game plan regarding the talks was to move gingerly on Vietnam, to express sympathy and general support for the U.S. position and yet at the same time provide an assessment "sufficiently slanted to lead, we hope, the Americans to what we think to be the inevitable conclusion"—that is, early negotiations. As the date of the talks grew nearer, however, London's trepidation about a confrontation increased and the "slant" began to disappear, particularly after Lord Harlech, the ambassador to Washington, reported home on 3 December that the Johnson administration had emerged from the November deliberations more determined than ever to stand firm in the war. (Australia and New Zealand the following day confirmed this point: good Commonwealth members that they were, they had reported to London the details of phase two, involving sustained attacks against the DRV, which U.S. officials had hoped they would keep to themselves.)[46]

By the time Harold Wilson's plane touched down in Washington on the evening of 6 December, the chances for an Anglo-American confrontation over Vietnam had disappeared. In advance of the trip the Foreign Office had produced two papers arguing "in detail the case for attempting a negotiated solution" and intended "as a basis for the Washington talks." Neither made it into the attaché cases of the British delegation, for the reason that senior London officials decided, shortly before the trip, that "it would be unwise to put these ideas to the U.S. Government."[47] The passing of the American election had not mattered much after all: British officials were no more willing afterward to stir up trouble than they had been before. In the talks Wilson pledged continued support for the administration's policy.

Nevertheless, the two countries' differing views on the Vietnam problem emerged clearly in the discussions. Johnson hit Wilson hard on the need for even a token contingent of British soldiers in South Vietnam, saying that they would have a tremendous psychological and political impact. The prime minister refused. He invoked the now-standard, two-part rationale: British forces were already heavily tied down in Malaysia, which left none available for Vietnam, and Britain's role as cochair of the Geneva Conference made it difficult to justify any kind of troop commitment. Wilson would go no further than to say that he might be able to arrange a modest increase in the existing British presence in South Vietnam (principally by adding individuals to Thompson's BRIAM), and he warned Johnson that a dramatically expanded war could compel Britain to activate its cochair role and to call for negotiations.[48]

If the British lack of enthusiasm for a full-fledged western commitment to South Vietnam was a letdown to Johnson and his Vietnam advisers (to him more than them; most aides had anticipated Wilson's reaction), they felt no such disappointment with respect to Charles de Gaulle's France. The Johnson administration had long since given up on getting support from the Paris government. Administration representatives continued to meet with French officials in the final months of 1964, but with the full realization that no movement on the fundamental issues could be expected. When Dean Rusk called on de Gaulle in Paris in mid December, the two men rehearsed their familiar arguments, with Rusk insisting that communists could not be trusted and could never be neutral, and with de Gaulle replying that neutralization was working, albeit imperfectly, in Cambodia and Laos, and that no one could be sure it would not work in Vietnam. The American countered that a loss in South Vietnam would hurt the West's position throughout Asia and beyond, to which the general responded that America could not win militarily in the region and that the United States should learn from the French experience in Indochina and Algeria and "eliminate this area from the Cold War."[49]

Walter Lippmann also met with de Gaulle in Paris in mid December. As always, he came away convinced of the Frenchman's essential wisdom on the war. The columnist had not altered his own belief that Vietnam was a looming disaster for the United States, but he had been less outspoken about the conflict in recent months, in large measure because of the presidential campaign and his determination to do his part to help defeat that "radical reactionary," Barry Goldwater. With Johnson safely returned to the White House, Lippmann refocused his attention on Vietnam. The war began to dominate his columns like never before. He still clung to the belief that Johnson was more dovish than his advisers, but he sensed that these men were pushing the president into a larger war. For their part, administration officials continued to woo the veteran journalist at every opportunity, to make him feel that they truly valued his input and that they were deeply desirous of finding a diplomatic solution to the war. Upon his return from Paris, they summoned him to the Oval Office, where Johnson grilled him on de Gaulle's neutralization plan and asked if it could prevent a communist takeover of the entire country. Lippmann responded that there was no other choice. He repeated what de Gaulle had said to him: that it would take a million Americans to pacify the country, and that a lasting military victory could never be achieved. The columnist made clear his support for this view, but Johnson remained doubtful. "This is a commitment I inherited," he complained. "I don't like it, but how can I pull out?"[50]

That question succinctly summarized Lyndon Johnson's predicament at the end of 1964. He was no more desirous of an American war in Southeast Asia than he had been when he assumed office a year earlier—had he been able to, he would have liked to flick a switch and make the whole mess in Vietnam go away. It may be that he already suspected that the war would ultimately be his undoing and would ruin his chances of leaving a legislative record greater than anyone's ever, greater even than his idol Franklin Roosevelt's. And yet he saw no alternative but to press ahead. The stakes were too high—both domestically and internationally—to consider withdrawal.

This brings us back to the issue with which this chapter began: Lyndon Johnson's freedom to maneuver on Vietnam in the wake of his election victory. Were the options as nonexistent as Johnson claimed to Lippmann? Many later students of the war have said yes—that when viewed in the international and domestic political context of the time, Johnson's course was the only viable one open to him.[51] In fact, however, a close examination of that context suggests that the president was far less constrained than he, and these later individuals, asserted.

Consider, first, the situation that Johnson faced at home as the year drew to a close. As journalists of the time remarked, he was in a dominant position politically, having decimated his Republican opponent and possessing huge majorities in both houses of Congress. His approval ratings were in the stratosphere. Polls in late 1964 and early 1965 revealed widespread popular support for his leadership. *Time* magazine exemplified this mood by naming LBJ its "Man of the Year" for 1964. The magazine praised the president and his leadership skills and, along with its cover story, printed a cartoon that showed Johnson standing by a White House window early in the morning, declaring: "I am the world—ready or not!"[52]

More important, the same public that gave the president high marks for his job performance expressed little inclination for a larger war in Vietnam. There is a prevailing argument in the literature on the war, an argument so dominant that it is frequently taken as a given, that says that there existed in the United States of 1964–1965 a near-unanimous consensus that the defense of South Vietnam was a vital national interest and thus worthy of a full military commitment. As proof, proponents point to poll numbers showing that, until well into 1966 and 1967, Americans supported the war and the use of U.S. ground forces, the implication being that they must have been similarly supportive at all points earlier on.

This is a faulty deduction, partly for reasons related to the inexactitudes of polling in general. It is difficult to gauge public attitudes toward a war, especially a limited one of the kind the United States waged in Vietnam.

Polls are not good at measuring intensity of feeling, at showing just how big a price people are willing to pay for victory. Also, respondents usually feel that they ought to be or at least appear to be patriotic—there is a war on, the flag is involved, and compatriots are out there being shot at. This last point is critical to the issue before us. The polling data cited in the literature is for the period after spring 1965—that, is *after* American ground forces had been committed.[53] As always happens in such instances, a rally-around-the-flag phenomenon resulted. Before the troop commitment, however, such a phenomenon was much less pronounced. At the end of 1964, a large percentage of Americans were apathetic about Vietnam, thanks at least in part to Johnson's peaceful assurances in the campaign; of those who were engaged, only a small minority favored the dispatch of American troops if a Saigon collapse seemed imminent. A Council of Foreign Relations (CFR) poll released in mid December showed that 25 percent of respondents did not know there was fighting in Vietnam. (A slightly larger number did not know China was communist. Of those who did, 71 percent favored talks with Beijing to improve relations.) Of the informed, close to half favored withdrawal, and only 24 percent were "definitely in favor" of using U.S. ground forces to avoid a communist victory.[54]

A University of Michigan study of public attitudes released in mid December showed similar results. Asked if the United States should get out of Vietnam immediately, 37 percent of those polled "strongly opposed" withdrawal, and 18 percent were "definitely" in favor of it. But when asked if American forces should be used in the struggle, 32 percent were opposed, and only 24 percent (the same figure as in the CFR study) were supportive. With respect to negotiations, 28 percent favored pursuing a settlement that might lead to a unified, neutral Vietnam, and only 23 percent rejected the idea. Likewise, a Louis Harris poll released the same week found that 18 percent favored bombing North Vietnam and that 20 percent backed withdrawal, perhaps via negotiations. Another Harris poll a few weeks later showed that a quarter of the respondents wanted to "negotiate and get out" and that another 45 percent were willing to do no more than "hold the line." Finally, an early January 1965 Gallup poll found that 81 percent answered yes to the question of whether Johnson should "arrange a conference with the leaders of Southeast Asia and China to see if a peace arrangement can be worked out?"[55]

More particular representations of public opinion also rose up against an expanded war. In late December, 105 religious leaders from various parts of the country joined forces to urge Johnson to avoid a war and seek instead a negotiated peace in Southeast Asia. Just before Christmas, a large advertisement in the *Boston Globe* asked the president to "call for a cease-fire agreement in Vietnam." Listed among the sponsors of the ad were such notable Brahmin names as Cabot, Forbes, Bainbridge, Amory, and Coolidge. In the academic community, likewise, significant rumblings could be heard. In December, a letter appealing for a neutralized Vietnam and an American withdrawal was signed by more than five thousand university faculty members from across the country. The letter, which was delivered to the White House, read, in part: "We . . . appeal to you, Mr. President, not to enlarge the scope of the war, but instead to work for a neutralized North and South Vietnam, as separate, federated, or reunified states, protected by international guarantees and peacekeeping forces against all outside interference." The same month, a rally against the war on the campus of the University of California at Berkeley drew a crowd of eight hundred people, and one in New York City attracted more than a thousand.[56]

The nation's newspapers also expressed concern about the direction of the war and U.S. policy. The elite *New York Times* in November and December sounded a drumbeat of gloom. Peter Grose, a *Times* correspondent in Saigon, wrote a series of pessimistic dispatches about the prospects in the war, noting in early November that the picture had become much bleaker in the one year since Diem's overthrow, and warning at the end of the month that "even a minimum of political stability [in Saigon] is absent." An editorial on 13 December accurately noted that Johnson had begun the shift to a wider war; another editorial, appearing a week later, spoke to the pervasive South Vietnamese war-weariness and apathy: "If the South Vietnamese themselves are not sufficiently aroused by the Vietcong threat to put aside their internal differences, the question must arise of why and how long American blood and treasure should be expended in the struggle."[57]

Of course, this line of argument was to be expected from the *Times*, which had been opposed to a larger war for the better part of a year. In late 1964, however, the opposition became a choir, a swelling chorus of criticism in the editorial columns of newspapers all across the nation, ranging from the liberal to the archconservative. By the start of the new year, the papers calling on the administration to rule out escalation and seek a negotiated exit from the war included, in addition to the *Times*, the *St. Louis Post-Dispatch*, the *Milwaukee Journal*, the *Miami Herald*, the *Salt Lake City Tribune*, the *Providence Journal*, the *Minneapolis Star*, the *Des Moines Register*, the *New York Post*, the *Indianapolis Times*, the *San Francisco Examiner*, the *Chicago Daily News*, and the *Hartford Courant*. Even the generally hawkish *Chicago Tribune* warned that the United States might be pushed out of Vietnam if it did not withdraw: "The irony of this impertinence," snorted the paper, "has rarely been exceeded in the checkered history of American global meddling and foreign aid doles."[58]

Consider also the *Washington Post*. In the past, the paper had always been a strong supporter of the American commitment to South Vietnam, and it would be again in the future—after the dispatch of U.S. ground troops, in a textbook example of the rally-around-the-flag effect, it would adopt a rigidly hawkish editorial position on the war. In this period, however, in November and December 1964 and January 1965, the *Post* warned against escalation and posed searching questions about the viability of any U.S. involvement in the conflict. An editorial in mid November said escalation would solve nothing and instead would invite "a host of extremely undesirable side effects," and it called on the administration to open informal talks with Hanoi to explore the terms of a political settlement. A month later the paper declared: "It is becoming increasingly clear that, without an effective government, backed by a loyal military and some kind of national consensus in support of independence, we cannot do anything for South Vietnam. . . . The economic and military power of the United States . . . must not be wasted in a futile attempt to save those who do not wish to be saved."[59]

The administration did not fail to perceive this trend in press thinking. James L. Greenfield of the Public Affairs desk at the State Department cautioned Rusk and McGeorge Bundy late in the year that a growing number of editors across the country, "hitherto staunch supporters of the U.S. commitment," were now convinced that "U.S. policy has become untenable" and that the administration should therefore seek to "make the best deal we can and get out." Greenfield noted that many papers, including those in the Hearst and Scripps-Howard chains, were urging Washington to "seek another 'friendly, politically stable base' elsewhere in Southeast Asia" and that other papers were arguing that the United States could withdraw from Vietnam with honor because "the Vietnamese refused to keep the terms of the agreement under which we went there."[60]

Given this rising dissatisfaction in American press opinion about the state and prospects of the war, it should come as no surprise that concerns grew also on Capitol Hill, especially within the president's own party. For at least the past six months, some two dozen Senate Democrats had felt deep concerns about the direction of American policy and a strong desire to contain and ideally reduce the nation's presence in the war. With two exceptions (Wayne Morse and Ernest Gruening), all of them nevertheless felt compelled to vote for the Gulf of Tonkin Resolution, and that show of support for administration policy, combined with the demands of the election campaign that followed, kept most of them quiet during the autumn. Now, however, with the election over and an expanded war in Vietnam increasingly likely, many understood that they would have to press harder.

They did not relish the task. Majority leader Mike Mansfield and Armed Services Committee chairman and Johnson mentor Richard Russell, for example, were reluctant to challenge Johnson publicly—their respect for presidential prerogative in foreign affairs, their loyalty to him personally, and their knowledge that he frowned on public dissent led them to keep their advocacy private if at all possible. Several times in November and December, both in Washington and at the LBJ Ranch in Austin, Russell told Johnson of his unhappiness with the war and his belief that every avenue for disengagement should be sought. Mansfield, alarmed by the determined posture he sensed emerging out of the November policy review, penned another one of his periodic pronegotiation memos to Johnson in early December. The United States was on a course in Vietnam "which takes us further and further out on a sagging limb," Mansfield wrote. The political foundations of South Vietnam were crumbling, and these could not be repaired by attacking the North. To redress America's "over-commitment" to the war, to avoid repeating the errors of the French, the president should initiate a process of reversal by way of a settlement. Otherwise, Mansfield warned, the administration could expect "years and years of involvement and a vast increase in the commitment."[61]

If the majority leader and the Armed Services chairman both opposed an expanded war, so did the chairman of the Senate Foreign Relations Committee. J. William Fulbright must have been discomfited as the year drew to a close. Just three months earlier, he had shepherded the Gulf of Tonkin Resolution through Congress, assuring skeptical colleagues that the measure would serve to prevent a larger war. Now talk of escalation was in the air. Aware of the general thrust of the Working Group's recommendations, and of Johnson's support for them, but in the dark about the specifics, Fulbright made clear his concerns when Ambassador Taylor testified before a closed session of the Foreign Relations Committee on 3 December, shortly before his return to Saigon. When Taylor noted a strong administration consensus that action against North Vietnam would at some point be necessary, Fulbright said that he would not support such action on behalf of a tottering regime in the South. Without a real government there, "What are you fighting for?" he asked Taylor. "If you want to go to war, I don't approve of it. I don't give a damn what the provocation is. I am not going to vote to send a hundred thousand men—or it would probably be 300,000 or 400,000. The French had 500,000." Taylor responded that the United States could attack by air, punish the North Vietnamese, "and let it go at that." Fulbright was dubious. What if that did not succeed? he asked. "America never fails—once it engages in [bombing] they will just go all out."[62]

Fulbright received confirmation of his fears ten days later, from the State

Department's David G. Nes, who had been Henry Cabot Lodge's chief deputy at the embassy in Saigon for the first half of 1964 and who even then
had expressed deep doubts that the U.S. effort could succeed. His skepticism
was even stronger now. After the two men shared their mutual concerns
during a round of golf, Nes wrote Fulbright a memorandum advocating an
American withdrawal from Vietnam by way of a diplomatic settlement. "I
am afraid," Nes wrote, "that too many of the top people responsible for the
extent and nature of current U.S. involvement in Vietnam are emotionally
reluctant to face the fact that we are striving for the impossible—on a bat-
tleground and with weapons chosen by the Communists." In selecting Vietnam as the place to show U.S. capability to challenge wars of liberation, the
administration could "not have chosen more disastrously." Geography, history, nationalism—all these worked against U.S. policy, Nes maintained,
in a way they did not in Greece or the Philippines, or in Malaya for the
British. The U.S. Air Force could level every square inch of territory in the
North, but that would not prevent the communization of the South. Hence
Charles de Gaulle's sound argument "for a 'political' rather than a 'military' solution." Fulbright received a similar message from the FRC's chief
of staff, Carl Marcy. A "planned, phased contraction of United States military assistance" ending with "neutralization and ultimate withdrawal" was
the only legitimate option for the United States, Marcy told him, given the
certain failure of any bombing campaign, the absence of political legitimacy
in Saigon, and the limited patience of the American people. Moreover, time
was short, for once Americans became directly involved in combat, disengagement would be impossible.[63]

Fulbright probably agreed with this, but he remained largely unwilling
to go public with his views. Largely, but not entirely—on 9 December, the
same day that Mansfield wrote the president, Fulbright told an audience at
Southern Methodist University in Dallas that expanding the war in Vietnam would be a "senseless effort" and that America should never have gotten involved there in the first place. In the main, however, he still shared
Mansfield's and Russell's extreme reluctance to challenge Johnson, a fellow
Democrat and close associate. LBJ understood this reticence, and he worked
hard to keep the trio quiet—in the days after his 1 December decision, he
instructed Rusk and McNamara to meet with them and other key lawmakers in small groups (so as not to generate publicity) to keep them on
board or at least keep them from dissenting openly. To a large extent the
effort succeeded, with the result that by Christmas 1964 the administration had managed to avoid a split with either of the two entities that had
the most power to thwart any move to escalate the war. Just as the British

government had chosen during the Wilson visit to avoid openly challenging the direction of American policy, so the Democratic leadership in the Senate opted to maintain a low profile.

Still, there was enough grumbling among lawmakers that the press by late December could report growing congressional unhappiness with the war, especially among Democrats. Some dissented openly. Frank Church of Idaho, in an interview with *Ramparts* magazine that had actually been done some weeks before but that now received front-page coverage in the *New York Times*, said that Washington should pursue a neutralization of Vietnam and perhaps all of Southeast Asia. Church avoided direct criticism of Johnson, but said that it would be an act of "folly" to escalate the war, especially given that the political crisis in Saigon gave "many signs of being beyond repair." Repeating themes he had enunciated in June, Church noted that "Vietnam is not our country and never has been" and that resentment among Asians would grow in direct proportion to the growth in the American presence. If the United States took over the war, he warned, it would be fighting "the tides of history" and ignoring the limits of its power. Church received praise for the interview from none other than Vice President–elect Hubert Humphrey, who was not prepared to speak out publicly but who shared many of Church's concerns. "You have performed a great service for American foreign policy," Humphrey wrote him after reading the interview. Other Democratic senators who went on record in November and December as opposing a wider war included Gaylord Nelson and Albert Gore, and they were joined by Republican John Sherman Cooper. And, of course, there was Oregon maverick Wayne Morse, who in characteristic fashion held nothing back. In late November, commenting on Maxwell Taylor's arrival in Washington, Morse called the ambassador a "warmonger" and said that the American role in Vietnam constituted "a bloody and shameful page in United States history."[64]

The point here is not to suggest that Lyndon Johnson faced a tidal wave of anti-escalation, pronegotiation sentiment on his home front in late 1964. He did not. Indeed, it is important to reiterate that roughly a quarter of the electorate indicated support for a wider military action, including the use of ground troops, to prevent a GVN collapse. Some Republican spokespeople, among them Strom Thurmond and Richard Nixon, advocated stepping up the military pressure and hinted darkly that Johnson would pay politically if he did not persevere in Vietnam. Moreover, if there were large and small newspapers recommending against escalation, there were also those that voiced support for a steadfast commitment to the cause. These included the

Los Angeles Times, the *Boston Globe*, the *Seattle Times*, the *Dallas Morning News*, the *Kansas City Star*, and the *St. Louis Globe-Democrat*.[65] Although the *New York Times* editorialized in favor of early negotiations, two of its star reporters, David Halberstam and Neil Sheehan, in this period resolutely opposed such a move. And at the same time that one leading columnist, Walter Lippmann, was urging Johnson to find a way out of the war, another one, Joseph Alsop, was questioning the president's manhood and warning readers of the disastrous consequences of "appeasement" in Vietnam. On 30 November, Alsop wrote that defeat in South Vietnam would cause the end of all U.S. influence anywhere in the Pacific, meaning the loss of "all that we fought for in the Second World War and in the Korean War."[66]

What the preceding analysis suggests is something more modest but hardly less important: that in terms of his domestic flank, Johnson had considerable freedom of action on Vietnam after the election. The political context he faced with respect to the war was a much more fluid one than is often suggested, with little or no national "consensus" about which way to proceed. The pressure for escalation was minimal. The fact that Nixon and Thurmond preached the need for victory is much less significant than that hardly anyone else in the GOP joined them. The same is true of the press, where the few newspapers advocating a stepped-up American involvement were vastly outnumbered by those that explicitly ruled out such a course. The latter group included not only those papers already referred to that urged a negotiated settlement but others that said that all options were equally bad—this group included the *Christian Science Monitor*, the *Baltimore Sun*, the *Philadelphia Inquirer*, the *San Francisco Chronicle*, the *Wall Street Journal*, and the Portland *Oregonian*.[67] In Middle America, ignorance and disengagement were the rule—it is doubtful that more than 20 percent of Americans could have placed Vietnam on a map, or provided concrete details about the ally on whose behalf the United States had intervened. Of those who paid attention, most were confused, not wanting to see a humiliating defeat for their country but seeing little sense in a land war on behalf of a weak government in a small country in a remote corner of the globe. In such instances, the natural inclination for people is to trust government to make the decision.

All of which suggests that William Bundy, one of the architects of the escalation, was correct when he later conceded that LBJ could have carried American public opinion with him "on whatever course he chose."[68] No doubt the president would have taken political heat had he opted for withdrawal, with Goldwater Republicans accusing him of "losing" Vietnam like Truman had "lost" China, but it would not have been debilitating heat.

Vietnam was not a deeply partisan issue at the end of 1964, and the Gold-water faction was but one wing of a Republican Party that lacked a singular vision of what should happen in Southeast Asia. His Democratic Party might have suffered in the 1966 midterm elections (though quite possibly not), but the in-party almost always loses seats in any nonpresidential election, especially following a landslide such as occurred in 1964.

For Bundy and most other Vietnam advisers, the domestic context mattered much less than the international one, and the next question to be considered is whether global considerations compelled Johnson to stay the course in Vietnam. Here again, the evidence suggests not. Among its friends in the world, America in late 1964 was largely isolated on Vietnam. Johnson's early-December demand that allied nations step up their assistance had by the end of the month yielded virtually nothing, despite the fact that special letters over Johnson's signature went out to targeted governments and despite the fact that the NSC joined what had up to this point been purely a State Department effort. The NSC's James Thomson and Chester Cooper succinctly summarized the situation at year's end: despite a "whirlwind of activity and a mass of cable traffic" on "third country assistance," they informed McGeorge Bundy on New Year's Eve, "very little has yet come out of the funnel."[69]

In later years, after America's isolation on the war had become plainly evident, Dean Rusk liked to argue that, even though friendly governments might be unwilling to contribute materially to the war effort, they nevertheless desperately wanted Washington to persevere in the fight. A decision to withdraw prematurely (in other words, before an independent, noncommunist South Vietnam had been ensured) would be taken by these countries as a sign that the United States could not be trusted to live up to its commitments. Even France? Especially France. "If we were to get out, de Gaulle would be the first to say, 'See, I told you one cannot depend on the United States under a security treaty,'" Rusk declared time and again during the height of the war.[70]

It was a tortuous line of reasoning. George Ball, Rusk's top deputy, was surely on the mark in making exactly the opposite argument in his October memo: American credibility vis-à-vis its allies, he declared, did not depend on adhering to prior commitments regardless of the odds but on showing intelligence and good judgment. Far from harming U.S. credibility, an early political settlement would actually enhance it, because the majority of allies would "applaud a move on our part to cut our losses." The New York Times, in an end-of-the-year assessment, accurately summarized European allied thinking on Vietnam as a mixture of "sympathy and bafflement": sympathy toward Washington's predicament, bafflement at its

dogged perseverance against long odds in a place of little import. Asian allies were perhaps less perplexed, given their proximity to the fighting, and
some of them hoped that the United States would stick it out. But few if
any viewed the outcome in Vietnam as vital to their own security, and there
is little evidence that they would have questioned an American decision to
withdraw support from what all saw as a hopeless Saigon government. Even
a "good doctor" cannot forever help a patient who has given up fighting for
life. As for de Gaulle, did Rusk really believe that the French leader would
invite certain ridicule by suddenly condemning the Americans for taking
the very action he had publicly advocated for so long?[71]

The more difficult aspect of the international context of Johnson's dilemma pertains to the views and intentions of the Soviet Union and, especially, China. In October, Nikita Khrushchev had been ousted as the USSR's
leader in a Kremlin power struggle. The new leadership under Leonid Brezhnev and Alexei Kosygin continued the basic two-part policy on Southeast
Asia followed by Khrushchev in his final months. On the one hand, they
sought to increase Soviet influence in the region, partly to counter growing Chinese influence and partly because they smelled a communist victory in Vietnam and wanted to claim part of the credit. On the other hand,
they feared a larger war that might force them to become more directly involved, or might bring the Chinese into the DRV in large numbers, and so
they hoped to restrain both Washington and Hanoi from initiating a major escalation. Moreover, there is little reason to believe that Soviet leaders
thought that American credibility was on the line in Vietnam or that they
would have viewed a negotiated American withdrawal as a sign of Washington's impotence and proof that the United States would no longer challenge communist expansion elsewhere. On 9 December, Foreign Minister
Andrei Gromyko, sounding much like de Gaulle, told Rusk that America
had no important stake in the Vietnam conflict and that none of the U.S.-
sponsored governments in Saigon had been worthy of the name. He told
Rusk that all outstanding questions on the war could be solved at a great-
power conference. (Rusk's response: If Hanoi and Beijing would "leave
their neighbors alone," peace would come.)[72]

Senior American officials were well aware of the depth of the Sino-
Soviet split and of Moscow's desire to discourage an expansion of the war
in Vietnam. In the November-December policy deliberations both the split
and the Soviet opposition to a wider war were taken as givens by most analysts. At the beginning of January 1965, William Bundy told Australian
officials that in the American estimation the increased Russian interest in
the war stemmed largely from the desire on the part of Kremlin leaders to

redress the Sino-Soviet balance in Hanoi. Brezhnev and Kosygin wanted to keep the Chinese from expanding their influence in North Vietnam, Bundy said, and were sympathetic to any course—including negotiations—that would accomplish this aim.[73]

As for China, there can be no doubt that its outlook and ambitions weighed on the minds of a majority of American officials. But not as much as one might think—in the many hundreds of pages of memoranda produced in the Working Group policy discussions, it is startling how seldom analyses of China's posture and aims appear. This relative lacuna is graphic proof of how fundamentally uninterested leading U.S. officials were in reopening basic questions about America's involvement in the war; their overriding concern was what to do next. On the rare occasion when Beijing's intentions did come up for discussion, little consensus emerged. Michael Forrestal of the Far East desk at the State Department, remarking on the lack of attention in the early Working Group papers to China's role, stated one view: "If China did not exist, the effect of our withdrawal from a situation in which the people we were trying to help seemed unable to help themselves might not be politically so pervasive in Asia." Much like the USSR after World War II, China possessed an "internal political necessity for ideological expansion," and a communist victory in Vietnam would encourage Beijing to pursue further successes. The U.S. aim, Forrestal argued, should therefore be to "contain" China for as long as possible, and the place to start was in Vietnam. James Thomson, the NSC's China expert, rejected this view of a Chinese expansionist imperative driven by internal need and countered the claim that containing the Chinese required the United States to remain in Vietnam. George Ball, though no China specialist, made the same argument as Thomson. With respect to both Moscow and Beijing, Ball maintained, U.S. credibility would in the long run suffer much less from a settlement than from getting drawn into a deep, perhaps bottomless, morass.[74]

More important, the two leading members of the Working Group appear to have possessed strong doubts about Forrestal's formulation. Near the end of the deliberations, John McNaughton and William Bundy, while arguing against the do-nothing Option A, conceded that its adoption might not bring disastrous results, especially given the deep Sino-Soviet split. Should the administration opt for Option A and against the new military measures, the two men wrote, "the most likely result would be a Vietnamese-negotiated deal, under which an eventually unified Communist Vietnam would reassert its traditional hostility to Communist China and limit its own ambitions to Laos and Cambodia." A prescient remark if ever there was one, this assertion suggests that senior American officials could see the logic of what critics were saying, that containing China did not necessarily depend on standing firm in South Vietnam.[75]

For each of the important audiences, both foreign and domestic, identified in the foregoing discussion, the actual situation on the ground in South Vietnam was of critical importance in their judgment of the American stake in the struggle. This brings us to the biggest reason why Lyndon Johnson had considerable freedom to maneuver in the months following his election: the continuing inability or unwillingness of the South Vietnamese leaders to live up to their end of the bargain. Since Dwight Eisenhower had first laid down aid stipulations a decade earlier, American officials had consistently maintained that continued U.S. support depended on the Saigon government performing effectively and doing its part in the struggle against the Vietcong. In December 1964, it was clearer than ever that it was doing neither. The situation that Taylor encountered upon his return from Washington was utterly dismal. He carried with him instructions to demand greater governmental stability and political cohesion from the South Vietnamese leaders, in return for which the United States would assume a major role in the war and pay for the increase of Saigon's armed forces by one hundred thousand men, bringing their total strength to 660,000.[76]

The effort failed, and South Vietnam in the final weeks of 1964 descended deeper into chaos. While Taylor was absent, Buddhist leaders initiated a campaign of nonviolent noncooperation with the Huong government, on the grounds that it was just another American creation that was pro-Catholic and anti-Buddhist. After his return, they stepped up their agitation, demanding that the United States withdraw its support from the regime and blaming Washington for selling out Vietnam to the anticommunist right wing. Taylor was at a loss about how to proceed. He assured LBJ on 16 December that "the Mission is giving this entire matter of the Buddhist opposition its priority attention," but in a follow-up cable the same day, he conceded that the monks "will not be greatly swayed by efforts at direct persuasion by us." Nor did the ambassador have much influence over the faction-ridden South Vietnamese military. He briefed Khanh and the other senior officers on Washington's new inducements for political unity and improved military performance, but the internecine warfare among the officer corps continued to rage.[77]

On 20 December, in a bid to enhance their own power, Khanh and a group of younger officers known as the "Young Turks" staged a bloodless coup d'état by arresting some three dozen high officers and civilian officials. In addition, they abolished the largely powerless civilian legislative body, the High National Council, and created an "Armed Forces Council" (AFC) to "oversee" (in other words, control) the actions of the Huong government. The AFC, the group declared, would act as a "mediator to achieve national unity." It was a transparent power grab, but the Huong regime, crippled by Buddhist opposition, was too weak to resist.[78]

Taylor was outraged. He cabled Washington that Khanh and his friends had "felt no reluctance in acting without consulting with U.S. representatives and in disregarding our advice on important matters. . . . Perhaps most serious of all is the deliberate disregard of the message which I brought from Washington and personally transmitted to most of these generals that continued and increased U.S. aid for S.V.N. depended upon governmental stability and evidence of national unity." That, of course, was untrue, and the generals knew it. They felt certain that continued and increased aid did *not* depend on their meeting this demand, that the Johnson administration felt too deeply committed to withdraw its support. When Taylor hauled four of them into the embassy and began making threats ("Now you have made a real mess," he barked. "We cannot carry you forever if you do things like this"), they were not unduly worried. Taylor's lecturing as if they were schoolboys offended them, however, and they responded by closing ranks behind Khanh, who in turn seized on the latent anti-Americanism that the episode brought to the surface to bolster his own position. Khanh accused Taylor of interfering in South Vietnam's internal affairs and publicly vowed independence from "foreign manipulation." American aid was no longer needed, he proclaimed, especially given that the United States had imposed a new colonialism on South Vietnam.[79]

It was an altogether bizarre state of affairs, with the de facto leader of South Vietnam, a man who early in the year Washington had hailed as a savior of his country, trading insults with Taylor and calling for anti-American demonstrations in Saigon. The Buddhists, meanwhile, continued their agitation against the rickety Huong government and its "American masters." Neutralist rumors were rampant, as were reports that former government leader Duong Van Minh might be orchestrating a coup to oust Khanh and place himself in power. ARVN operations in the field virtually ceased. So chaotic was the situation that when the Vietcong attacked the Brinks U.S. officers' billet in Saigon on Christmas Eve, killing two and injuring fifty, it took several days for the embassy to verify that the attack had been Vietcong-orchestrated and not the result of the intramural squabbling among South Vietnamese officials. That delay, coupled with Johnson's desire not to disrupt Americans' Christmas celebrations, led the White House to reject Taylor's recommendation for a reprisal strike against the North. "Under present conditions the American public might even doubt VC responsibility," Washington officials told Taylor in explaining the president's decision.[80]

Prominent outside observers saw the new developments as ample justification for an American extrication from the war. The *New York Times* put the matter bluntly: "The necessary, inevitable, inescapable consequence of not being wanted would be withdrawal." The *Washington Post* spoke in similar tones, as did a broad range of West European newspapers, among them pro–Social Democratic *Neue Rhein-Ruhr Zeitung* of Essen, centrist *Messaggero* of Rome, moderate-left *Frankfurter Rundschau* of Frankfurt, and conservative *Het Laatste Nieuws* of Brussels and *Muenchner Merkur* of Munich. Of special interest to officials at the United States Information Agency, who monitored press trends closely, the leading press organs in France and Britain now forcefully urged an American withdrawal. Said the Manchester *Guardian*, "Perhaps the least damaging decision for America and for those nations which now look to her primarily for their protection would be a withdrawal based on a clear and detailed statement explaining the impossibility of assisting a sovereign country to defend itself when it refuses to concentrate its own efforts for its own defense, or to abandon its internal factional struggles." *Le Monde* and the London *Times* made the same point and speculated that Washington was now actively considering extrication. The latter noted that the Buddhists in South Vietnam, who were an "approximation of public opinion," wanted an end to the war, and it further claimed that U.S. officials in Washington and Saigon were privately admitting defeat. The only question, the paper said, was whether a withdrawal would be possible in American domestic political terms. Leading American columnist James Reston said it would be. He noted that Johnson had most often explained American Vietnam policy in terms of the United States intervening to help a legal government defend its freedom. In view of the current in-fighting among South Vietnamese officials, and the rising anti-Americanism, such a defense was neither necessary nor warranted, Reston argued, and thus the president could justifiably withdraw.[81]

Reston was correct. A large window of opportunity on Vietnam existed for Lyndon Johnson in the wake of his 1964 election triumph. It is undeniable that he wanted to avoid a major American war in the jungles of Southeast Asia; it should be equally clear that he could have avoided one, and that a broad range of important observers saw this at the time. In due course, I examine precisely how disengagement might have been arranged; here it suffices to say that neither the domestic nor the international political context demanded a steadfast American commitment in Vietnam, es-

pecially given the almost surreal quality of the South Vietnamese political context in the final weeks of the year. No less a figure than General
William Westmoreland, commander of the Military Assistance Command,
Vietnam (MACV), later put it this way: "So obvious was the bickering,
the machination, the inefficiency, the divisiveness among the Vietnamese
that I suspect few in the world would have faulted us at that point had we
thrown up our hands in despair [and withdrawn]."[82]

That was Westmoreland several years later. In late 1964, however, neither
he nor any of his fellow senior American officials would consider withdrawal. It is this fact, this unwillingness to even explore in a meaningful
way the disengagement option, that would have puzzled so many outside
observers had they known about it. Almost everyone outside the administration could agree that escalation was legitimately one of the options before Lyndon Johnson; they would have been flabbergasted, however, had
they known that it was the only one under serious consideration. A theme
in this book is that American policymakers from mid 1963 onward were
not merely skeptical of the possibility of finding an early political solution
to the war but acutely fearful of such a prospect and strongly determined
to prevent one. Both the fear and the determination had increased by the
close of 1964. Nothing—not pessimistic intelligence reporting, not allied opposition, and not pervasive South Vietnamese war-weariness and burgeoning anti-Americanism—could dissuade these men from continuing their
pursuit of a military solution. Talk of a "fall-back" option had faded early in
the November deliberations, never to be resurrected. Option A, which contained no military escalation (but which also, significantly, ruled out early
negotiations), likewise found little support. A negotiations option never
emerged, even after important elements within South Vietnam expressed
support for it. On New Year's Eve, Maxwell Taylor suggested that the administration could consider withdrawing the bulk of American personnel
from Vietnam and focusing exclusively on air and maritime defense of the
South, thereby forcing the GVN "to walk on its own legs and be responsible for its own stumbles." The idea received no consideration, because of
what Taylor himself saw as a likely—and wholly unacceptable—result of
such a move: Saigon leaders "compet[ing] with each other in making a deal
with the National Liberation Front."

As for the option of pursuing bilateral talks with Hanoi, which now enjoyed sizable support on the nation's editorial pages, it was no more palatable to policymakers than it had ever been. In September UN Secretary General U Thant had won assurance from the DRV that it would enter talks but
had been rebuffed by the United States. In November, with Johnson safely
reelected, Thant tried again, telling the American ambassador to the UN,

Adlai Stevenson, that the Burmese government of Ne Win had agreed to serve as host for the talks. Stevenson was sympathetic and passed on the information to Dean Rusk. Now was not the time for talks with Hanoi, Rusk told him, and therefore the secretary general should be told to put the idea on the shelf. Thant had been rejected again.[83]

Also in late November, Canadian officials asked Washington for a substantive message that J. Blair Seaborn could deliver to North Vietnamese officials during his upcoming visit to Hanoi. Much to their dismay, the administration showed scant interest in the issue and gave Seaborn no real message to convey, beyond one affirming America's continued commitment to the GVN. The Johnson administration, Ottawa officials concluded among themselves, no longer had much use for the diplomatic track, preferring instead to pursue a military solution.[84]

Were the North Vietnamese sincere in professing a desire for talks aimed at finding a political solution to the war? There can be little doubt that they were. In the final weeks of 1964 they continued confident in their ability to prevail in South Vietnam. They were not keen on compromising their fundamental objectives in the struggle and saw little reason to do so, given the growing chaos in the South. At the same time, Hanoi's leaders still sought to avert an Americanization of the conflict and likely were prepared to compromise on nonfundamentals to achieve that objective—on the speed of the American withdrawal, for example, or the timing of reunification of the country. In October, the prospect of Americanization was a subject of discussion when Pham Van Dong met Mao Zedong in Beijing. The two leaders agreed that Washington did not want to fight a major war. "The United States is facing many difficulties, and it is not easy for it to expand the war," Pham Van Dong said, no doubt referring both to the weak GVN base upon which such an escalation would be launched and the lack of enthusiasm for such a move among many in the United States and in western capitals. "We must adopt a very skillful strategy, and should not provoke [the United States]," he said. This meant keeping the level of fighting at about its current level. "If the United States dares to start a [larger] war, we will fight it," Pham Van Dong assured Mao, "and we will win it." But it would be better if it did not come to that.[85]

Accordingly, in the aftermath of the American election Hanoi also sent subtle signals that it was open to peace talks. William Bundy acknowledged as much when he told Canadian officials in Washington on 3 December that Hanoi had been putting out hints in many quarters in November that it was interested in pursuing a settlement to the war, though only on its previously stated terms. What did Bundy think those terms to be? The record does not indicate.[86] Likely he believed them to involve (1) a coalition government in Saigon, with prominent NLF representation; (2) American withdrawal; and (3) eventual reunification of the country under Hanoi's control. But within these terms there were gray areas that could be the subject of discussion during bilateral talks or at a Geneva-type conference. For the past six months, since Pham Van Dong had met Blair Seaborn in June, Hanoi officials had emphasized that they were flexible on the question of diplomacy.[87] There was but one way to probe them on this. That was to meet with them.

A year later, in the late fall of 1965, U Thant's efforts in 1964 became public knowledge. When the story broke, senior officials in the Johnson administration instantly knew they faced a sticky problem. The disclosures, they realized, made them appear to have been not merely skeptical of a diplomatic settlement in Vietnam in late 1964, but actively opposed to such a solution. Critics were bound to pose one question above all, they knew, a question for which they had no ready answer. People were certain to ask, George Ball said to a colleague, "Why didn't you find out [what Hanoi had in mind]?" A satisfactory reply had to be found. Ball could not think of one.[88]

Looming over the policy process, as always, was Lyndon Johnson. He complained to Lippmann and others in late 1964 that he was trapped in a commitment he had inherited, a commitment he did not like but could not abandon. The question Lippmann might have asked him was why he made no attempt to break out of the trap. If Johnson felt that he had no options on Vietnam, why did he not deliberately externalize the conflict rather than internalize it? Why did he not encourage a national debate on the war, right now, when his political power was at its zenith and the Saigon political situation was at its nadir? If, as is likely, the American people wanted it both ways, wanted to win in Vietnam but did not want to fight for it, why did Johnson not put the burden on them to decide, after laying out the likely costs? Which did they want more?[89]

Johnson could have encouraged a congressional debate between hawks and doves, a debate wrangling over the pros and cons of maintaining the U.S. commitment. Given his mastery of the workings of Capitol Hill, he could have orchestrated such a debate to provide himself both with cover and with alternatives not to be found within his small and cloistered team of policy advisers. The three most influential Democratic foreign-policy thinkers on Capitol Hill—Mike Mansfield, Richard Russell, and William Fulbright—would have relished taking part in that debate, provided Johnson wanted it. Lippmann and Alsop, whose respective syndicated columns appeared in some two hundred American newspapers, could have duked it out before the public. At the very least, a debate would have made Vietnam a shared responsibility, not "Johnson's War." If things went badly, as he feared they would, the entire country would have to accept blame. But Johnson rejected a debate; indeed, he worked hard to avoid one. Why he did so is one of the great mysteries of the war.

Or maybe not. Maybe it is no mystery at all. Maybe Johnson failed to externalize the Vietnam problem because he was incapable of such a thing. "The role of public debate in securing popular assent to policies and, ultimately, national unity, was a concept he could not grasp," his former aide George Reedy has written. Talk, to Johnson, had true meaning "only when it was directed at getting something done." Other Johnson observers have argued likewise. But there was also something else, something deeper. Johnson's profound personal insecurity and his egomania led him not only to personalize the goals he aspired to but also to personalize all forms of dissent. Hence his vow not to be the president who lost Vietnam; hence his conviction that critics of the war were critics of him personally. In late 1964, Johnson's dislike of conflict, his need to create consensus and to avoid confrontation, remained unshaken, as did his insistence that Americans must support a president in foreign policy and unite behind a policy of anticommunism.[90] To reverse course in Vietnam would be to admit defeat, and that was something Johnson was loath to contemplate. Robert Thompson was more accurate than he ever could have realized when he referred to escalation in Vietnam as the "bad-loser" option.

At the end of December, while the turmoil in Saigon raged, Johnson held a meeting at the LBJ Ranch in Austin with McGeorge Bundy and Dean Rusk. Prior to its start, the president had told Bundy that the war in Vietnam was a civil war, that it had to be won in the South, and that the United States had to persevere. Now the three men discussed the next step. They probably discussed Taylor's growing estrangement from the South Vietnamese leadership and the need to get him to alter his approach. They almost certainly reached agreement that bombing the North would be insufficient to turn things around and that dispatching American ground forces would likely be necessary, though only after dependents had been removed. (It is surely significant that Robert McNamara, the fourth member of the "Awesome Foursome" and the only one strongly opposed to using U.S. ground troops, was not in attendance.) A postmeeting presidential memo to Taylor, drafted in Austin and dated 30 December, revealed a president determined in the new year to press on to victory in Vietnam, through escalation if necessary. In the memo, Johnson criticized Taylor for his handling of the Saigon political crisis and declared his belief that dependents should be removed in anticipation of expanded military action. "We are facing war in South Vietnam," Johnson wrote. "I have never felt that this war will be won from the air, and it seems to me that what is much more needed and would be much more effective is a larger and stronger use of Rangers and Special Forces and Marines, or other appropriate military strength on the ground and on the scene." Such a deployment would involve the acceptance of larger American sacrifice, the president acknowledged, but it was worth it. He vowed, "I myself am ready to substantially increase the number of Americans fighting in Vietnam."[91]

Nineteen-sixty-four, so often depicted as an "off year" in Vietnam but in reality the most crucial year of all, still had a few hours left in it. Already, it was becoming an American war.

10   "Stable Government or No Stable Government"

It was a day rich in symbolism. In Washington, Secretary of State Dean Rusk and National Security Adviser McGeorge Bundy were back at their desks after returning from meeting with the president in Texas. In that morning's *New York Times,* the two men could read that Senate heavyweight Richard Russell had come out publicly against any expansion of the war and in favor of a full-fledged reevaluation of the American commitment to South Vietnam. Later in the day, Rusk received aide James Greenfield's report that hitherto staunch supporters of American policy in the press were now advocating disengagement from the war, while at the White House Bundy learned from Chester Cooper and James C. Thomson Jr. that the push for third-country assistance had yielded virtually nothing. Bundy received more bad news in a prelunch meeting with British ambassador Lord Harlech. When Bundy complained of the British government's small commitment to the war, Harlech told him not to expect an increase. Disappointed, Bundy said that the administration would continue to seek allied assistance but that, regardless, Lyndon Johnson remained committed to making a major effort to turn the tide of battle. Afterward, Harlech returned to the embassy and cabled London that Bundy's description of the Texas meeting suggested "no disposition of any kind [among senior U.S. officials] to pull out and cut their losses" and no willingness to go to a conference, because any settlement resulting from such a meeting would eventually lead to the communist domination of South Vietnam. "My judgment is that the Americans are prepared to continue for a very long time their participation in the Vietnamese struggle," Harlech wrote. It was New Year's Eve, 1964.[1]

In New York City on this day, at the Manhattan offices of the *New York Times,* employees were busy at work putting together the next day's issue. Among the articles they were setting was one from the paper's London bureau, in which bureau chief Sydney Gruson reported that a survey by the *Times*'s European correspondents found no support for a wider war among America's leading allies. "The allies in Western Europe are convinced that no military solution favoring the United States is possible in Vietnam," Gruson wrote. Though few of them advocated immediate withdrawal, many endorsed the French view that neither neutralization nor a communist victory need have the long-feared "falling-domino" effect on the rest of Southeast Asia. Especially in view of the unchecked deterioration in South Vietnam, a negotiated settlement seemed more imperative than ever to European diplomats, Gruson noted. "These officials no longer see much point in the argument that the United States would be negotiating from weakness: in their opinion, the weakness only increases with time."[2]

In comparison to the beehive of activity at the New York Times Building, the LBJ Ranch in Austin was a quiet place on the final day of the year. But not all that quiet. Lyndon Johnson and the aides who remained behind when Bundy and Rusk left had much to think about, much to plan: the plethora of bills that would be introduced early in the next session of Congress; the State of the Union speech, to be delivered on 5 January; and the inauguration that would follow two weeks after that. And there was Vietnam. The war there had to be won, Johnson believed, or at least had to be kept from being lost. The South Vietnamese had to stop their bickering and unite behind the war effort. On the previous New Year's Eve, little more than a month after he assumed the Oval Office, he had sent a greeting to Saigon's then-leader, Duong Van Minh, vowing American opposition to neutralism and determination to defeat the Vietcong. This time he sent a letter of encouragement to the beleaguered prime minister, Tran Van Huong, and another one to Ambassador Maxwell Taylor. The one to Taylor was short and to the point: "I have thought all through the Christmas Season of you and of our effort there. As I said in our December meetings and in my cable yesterday, what I want is simply that we should use every resource that we have with our Allies and with our friends in Vietnam to get a government that is stable and to get on with the job of beating the Viet Cong."[3]

The time difference between Austin and Saigon meant that the embassy did not receive the message until after midnight, when 1964 had become 1965. But in South Vietnam, too, the final day of the year had seen developments that revealed much about where things had been and where they were going. When Taylor arrived for work that morning he found waiting for him the president's longer 30 December cable (it had arrived shortly before 2:00 A.M.), in which Johnson chided him for his handling of the Saigon political crisis and for his faith that bombing alone would do the job, and then declared both that American dependents should be removed from Vietnam in advance of wider action and that he was sympathetic to the use of U.S. ground forces in the conflict. For Taylor it was a double blow—not only had Johnson plainly faulted his performance, but he had indicated his willingness to do what Taylor strenuously wished to avoid: send Americans to fight in the war. Taylor also opposed the early removal of dependents, on the grounds that it would cause the GVN to think the Americans were getting ready to withdraw. This last point was clearly critical to Taylor as the year drew to a close—if Saigon leaders came to believe the United States was getting out, or even just reducing its assistance, he warned Washington later in the day, they might opt for a quick settlement with the NLF.[4]

The ambassador did not have much time to think about these matters, however, because of a more pressing matter that day. Binh Gia, a village of six thousand people, mostly Roman Catholics, about forty miles southeast of Saigon in coastal Phuoc Tuy province, was under attack by the Vietcong. Enemy attacks were routine events throughout South Vietnam in late 1964, but this one was different. Never before in the war had the Vietcong been deployed in such numbers. Two guerrilla regiments, comprising more than a thousand men, had set out weeks earlier from Tay Ninh province, northwest of Saigon, and slowly made their way into Phuoc Tuy. (To avoid detection, they had traveled in small groups.) At dawn on 28 December they struck, inflicting heavy casualties on government forces in the area, and then proceeded to occupy Binh Gia for eight hours before fading back into the jungle to avoid pursuit. The next day U.S. officials responded with a huge airlift of ARVN reinforcements and a swarm of U.S.-piloted helicopters. Smaller attacks and counterattacks followed. Three of the helicopters were shot down on the twenty-ninth and another one on the thirtieth, and ARVN forces suffered heavy losses, but by the evening of the thirtieth government forces seemed to be in control.[5]

The Vietcong, however, were far from finished. Early the next morning, 31 December, they hit hard, decimating an elite Saigon marine battalion of 326 officers and men in an ambush. Two hundred of the marines were killed, wounded, or captured. Twenty-nine of the battalion's thirty-five officers died. Another ARVN battalion operating in the vicinity, this one also an elite unit and one accompanied by tanks, suffered an even worse fate in another ambush later in the day, with nearly 400 men and officers injured. It was the heaviest day of fighting since the war had begun, and the government's forces had been trounced. Altogether, since the fighting had started on the twenty-eighth, seven battalions of Saigon's best troops had been thrown into the engagement; nearly two hundred were killed, along with five American advisers. In Saigon, American military officials were awed and perplexed. Said one: "The Vietcong fought magnificently, as well as any infantry anywhere. But the big question for me is how its troops, a thousand or more of them, could wander around the countryside so close to Saigon without being discovered. That tells something about this war." Taylor agreed, but he tried to put the best possible spin on the disaster. In reporting the results to Washington, he lamented the lackluster performance of the better-equipped Saigon forces and the political preoccupations of the senior ARVN generals, but he insisted that "we have not suffered a Dien Bien Phu as some describe it." The denial only served to underline the seriousness of the defeat—that someone, anyone, would compare the results to the great French debacle of 1954 suggested just how badly things had gone.[6]

Together these snapshots of a single day, coincidentally the very day of the year when it is customary in the West to reflect on the developments of the past year and look ahead to the new one, show in stark relief the determination of the Johnson administration to persist in Vietnam as 1965 began, and the formidable obstacles in its way. The growing uneasiness in the United States and among allies abroad about the developments in the war and the corresponding interest in negotiations; the deplorable performance of the Saigon regime and its military; the continuing administration fear of a negotiated deal between the GVN and the enemy; the strength and confidence of the Vietcong, as it tightened the noose around Saigon; the dogged perseverance of Lyndon Johnson—all these realities were in evidence on this day. The snapshots also demonstrate again the importance of viewing the war in its international context. (This applies even to those studies, like this one, that focus primarily on the development of American policy.) To fully understand the choices that Washington officials had, and the decisions they made, it is necessary to see how the war played elsewhere in the world—including, of course, in Vietnam itself—and how the views of outside observers affected (or did not affect) American decision making. As we shall see, the international isolation of the Johnson administration with respect to Vietnam would only increase in the key early months of 1965, as the South Vietnamese politico-military crisis deepened, as American opposition to an early negotiated settlement became steadily more apparent, and as Johnson's window of opportunity on Vietnam began to close.

No less important than the international picture was the domestic American context. Indeed, the one important theme not in evidence in these New Year's Eve developments, but which would become increasingly pronounced in the weeks and months thereafter, as the war escalated and the domestic and international pressure for negotiations grew, was Lyndon Johnson's demand for unity on the war, both among his advisers and in the country as a whole. Never one to look kindly on dissension, by nature impatient with intellectual give-and-take, and determined as always to emphasize the "continuity" of his Vietnam policy, Johnson in the first half of 1965 escalated the Vietnam War by stealth. More than that, he set out to quash debate on the war, to manufacture consensus. To a considerable degree he succeeded, so much so that students of the conflict have generally underplayed this critical dimension of the escalation, have exaggerated the consensus in the nation with respect to Vietnam in early 1965. Johnson's success in preventing a national debate owed much to his own unmatched skill at using flattery, needling, and threats to bend others to his will, and to the willingness of his three principal foreign-policy lieutenants, Bundy, Rusk, and Secretary of Defense Robert McNamara, who themselves possessed formidable talents for persuasion, to meet with critics and skeptics and warn them of the danger of disunity. But the effort also required a permissive context. That is, it required that the targets of the campaign *allow* themselves to be stifled, *allow* the debate to be effectively ended before it started.[7]

To be sure, some critics refused to be muzzled, and most others found ways to make their dissent known, albeit in muted tones. In this respect the permissive context that allowed Johnson to avoid a national debate on the war went beyond elite voices in American society to the public at large. The public could have forced a debate; it had enough information. Certainly any diligent reader of one of the nation's major newspapers could see the disconnect between the optimistic prognostications of senior American officials—on 1 January Maxwell Taylor told newsmen that the Saigon political crisis would soon end—and the actual situation on the ground in Vietnam. They could see that many Senate Democrats were nervous about the direction of the war and opposed to escalation. And they could see that America's allies failed to attach the same importance to Vietnam that the administration did. Even those who did not have access to an elite newspaper could in all likelihood read Walter Lippmann, whose syndicated column appeared in newspapers all over the country and who in early 1965 blasted the notion of an American war to save South Vietnam. That they could then read Joseph Alsop arguing the opposite, that it would be a crime to let South Vietnam be lost, should have only reinforced their desire for a true hashing out of the issues at stake. Of course, the public tends not to think in such terms. Murky public policy issues, especially those in the international realm, tend to keep the apathetic apathetic, and to make many others trust the "experts in government" to make the decision. Even after the nation's college campuses began to agitate against the war in March, few in middle America chose to join in.

That said, it warrants emphasizing that any such public-generated national debate would have occurred *in spite of* Johnson's efforts, not because of them. He and his aides worked hard in the first half of 1965 to keep the American people in the dark about Vietnam, to foster apathy, to conceal for as long as possible the Americanization of the war. Barely had Johnson returned to Washington in early January than he began leaning on Senate skeptics to get on the team or at least keep their reservations quiet. It proved a crucial effort, for in late December and early January numerous lawmakers, including some who fully backed the administration's policy, called for a full Senate debate on the war once the new session of Congress began. Said Republican leader Everett M. Dirksen, in suggesting a debate: "We are faced with a sharp reality: do we forsake what we have done? Do we go further and venture north and invite possible complications with Red China? Or do we just play along? These are not easily answered until there is a better evaluation of all the factors." Democrat Mike Monroney of Oklahoma, like Dirksen inclined to stand firm in the war and just returned from a visit to South Vietnam, likewise declared that he "would like to see a full-fledged Senate debate on it." Democrats Albert Gore, Stephen M. Young, Gaylord Nelson, Wayne Morse, and Ernest Gruening, all of them advocates of a U.S. disengagement from the conflict, also called for Congress to consider the issue in depth.[8]

What really gave sustenance to the notion of a Senate debate, however, was the public encouragement voiced by Armed Services Committee chairman Russell and Majority Leader Mike Mansfield. Perhaps spurred on by Frank Church's much-publicized *Ramparts* interview, though still unwilling to go as far as he did in articulating pessimism about the war and opposition to escalation, both men took small but significant steps as the year turned to openly distance themselves from the direction of U.S. policy. Russell followed up his call for a fundamental reevaluation of policy by telling reporters that his committee and the full Senate should take part in this exercise. He also told *Time* that he hoped a way could be found for the United States to cut its commitment to South Vietnam. Mansfield, appearing on NBC's *Meet the Press* on 3 January, said that neutralization for Southeast Asia by way of a great-power agreement might be the best solution and predicted there would be a "full-scale debate" on the war in the Senate. Three days later, Mansfield cautioned that "escalation will not solve the problem. It is more likely to enlarge it."[9]

That the upper chamber would have benefited from a genuine debate on the war cannot be doubted. An Associated Press poll of eighty-three Senators released on 6 January found no consensus whatsoever on what the Vietnam problem was or what the United States ought to do about it. Three of the respondents fully supported expansion of the war into North Vietnam, while five suggested American troops could be sent to the South at some future date if the situation warranted it. Ten advocated an immediate move to negotiations. Three wanted a unilateral American withdrawal. One of these three was no doubt Allen J. Ellender, Democrat of Louisiana, who told a reporter after the polling that it was time for the United States to get out of Vietnam "without any ifs and buts." Eight senators, possessing none of Ellender's certainty, said they simply did not know what to do. Others refused to comment for the present, many on the grounds that they wanted to wait for the results of inquiries by the Senate. The British embassy in Washington, commenting on the poll and on other congressional pronouncements, told London that more and more lawmakers hoped for a negotiated settlement to the war.[10]

What happened to the majority leader's call for a full-scale Senate debate? The timing for one was certainly right, given the calamitous state of the war effort and given the passing of the American election campaign. In addition, powerful lawmakers had gone on record in support, which led several leading publications, including *Time, Newsweek*, and, repeatedly, the *New York Times*, to predict that a debate would occur in January. Yet it failed to take place, in large measure because Lyndon Johnson and his senior aides worked hard to thwart it. The president, having emerged out of the November–December policy deliberations with a strong—and still largely secret—administration consensus in favor of pursuing the war, knew that a full Senate debate would greatly complicate matters by revealing a wide difference of opinion about what the American posture should be. He further knew that the anti-escalation side in the debate, with its formidable lineup of heavy hitters, could well draw a large proportion of the confused and the undecided to its side. Deep divisions would certainly emerge, and that could in turn threaten the swift passage of major pieces of his domestic legislation package. Johnson also had a deeper, philosophical aversion to open discussions of foreign policy, especially when they had to do with questions of war and peace. He remained unshaken in his belief in presidential supremacy in foreign affairs, and in the rule that politics should stop at the water's edge. Determined to persevere in the war, he thought a full airing of views among legislators would accomplish little except to embolden the communists in Hanoi.

Accordingly, Johnson instructed aides in early January to seek out Senate skeptics and persuade them not to press for a debate. On 5 January, he complained to his ambassador to the United Nations, Adlai E. Stevenson, that Mike Mansfield and Wayne Morse were causing him trouble over the war. A Senate debate would be a bad thing, Johnson said, and he asked Stevenson to talk to Morse, who was the leading exponent of taking the Vietnam matter to the UN (and who had been trying, along with Gruening, to get a debate started for the better part of a year). LBJ told Stevenson to remind Morse that it had been he, Johnson, who had given him a seat on the Foreign Relations Committee on the day Morse switched to the Democratic Party.

It was the chairman of that committee, however, J. William Fulbright, who mattered most to the president and his senior advisers. On 6 January, at the year's first top-level White House meeting on Vietnam, they determined that Dean Rusk should talk to the veteran Arkansas senator. Fulbright had performed brilliantly in acting as the administration's point man during the congressional resolution discussions the previous August, and LBJ appears to have determined that he should undertake a similar function now, this time to slow the momentum for a debate. Johnson knew of Fulbright's weakness for flattery and of his desire to remain on good terms with the administration, and he knew that Fulbright possessed his own doubts about public divisions over sensitive foreign-policy issues.[11]

The tactic worked. Rusk met with Fulbright on several occasions in January and got him to agree that now was not the time for the Senate to hold public hearings and engage in full discussion. For the second time in six months, Fulbright had done the administration's bidding on Vietnam, despite his deep doubts about the American involvement. It could be argued that this second Fulbright intervention (or, perhaps better, nonintervention) was every bit as important as the one during the Gulf of Tonkin affair, perhaps more important. Never again would there exist such a broad range of opinion on the war among senators as the AP poll revealed, for the simple reason that Lyndon Johnson had not yet taken a firm public position on the question of escalation. Once he did, many legislators would fall into line behind him. Until then, however, senators could agree on nothing but that the problems of Vietnam were intractable.[12] Also, the Democrats and the president who led them would never again possess the kind of freedom of maneuver on Vietnam and what to do there that they possessed in the first weeks of 1965. It was a prime time to have the kind of wide-ranging conversation on Vietnam that many in both parties had made clear they felt was needed.

The staff at the editorial desk of the *New York Times,* under editor John B. Oakes, quickly pounced on what they saw as an administration-Fulbright agreement to "stave off a public airing of the issue." In an editorial titled "Silence on Vietnam," the paper criticized Johnson for largely glossing over Vietnam in his State of the Union message. "Never in the decade of direct American involvement have the prospects of that unfortunate country looked less promising," the editorial read. "Nor has the internal political maneuvering within that fragmented society ever been more confused. Yet it is precisely for these reasons that American policies of the past decade need thorough reappraisal, rather than the vague reconfirmation that the President gave them." The paper noted that "the growing pressure in the United States Senate for a full-scale debate reflects a growing uneasiness in the country," and it faulted Fulbright for evidently agreeing with the White House view that a debate ought not to be held. "A 'great debate' undoubtedly would prove unsettling for Vietnam's factions and for American administrators in Saigon," the editorial conceded, but that did not negate the necessity of holding one.[13]

Whatever his public position, Fulbright showed little reticence in challenging the administration privately. On 7 January, the very day the *New York Times* editorial appeared, he and some other members of the Foreign Relations Committee heard secret testimony from General Edward Lansdale, Rufus Phillips, and two officials from the U.S. foreign aid mission in Vietnam, all of whom agreed that it was important to remain in Vietnam but that the keys to victory were political, not military. More men and material were not the answer. The following day, when Rusk and William Bundy appeared before the full committee in an executive session, Fulbright expressed his concerns. The reason he and others had contemplated the need for negotiations, he told the two men, was that the war effort looked hopeless. "It isn't because we want to [negotiate]," he said, but "we are faced with the fact that it just isn't working." Without mentioning the meeting with the Lansdale group the previous day, Fulbright wondered if perhaps the administration had "thought of this entirely as a military operation or practically so, and that we have not been . . . willing and able . . . to help them generate a stable political organization which could then be the basis with which we work." Others on the committee, including Gore, Morse, and Gruening, voiced their own opposition to wider military action, while some Republicans said no measures should be excluded from consideration. According to the Associated Press, the meeting left committee members "as divided as ever" regarding the best course to pursue in the crisis.[14]

The absence of a full Senate debate did not stop numerous lawmakers from publicly speaking out during January. As had been the case in December, what is especially striking about these pronouncements is that those advocating escalation were far less clamorous than those who opposed such a course. (On 26 January, once and future GOP presidential candidate Richard Nixon called for taking the war to North Vietnam and dismissed neutralization as "surrender on the installment plan.") Richard Russell, in remarks that made the front page of several leading newspapers, said on 11 January that without a stable GVN there could never be victory in Vietnam. Decrying the "changing chair" governments in Saigon, Russell foresaw nothing but an endless stalemate flowing from current American policy, and he repeated his call for a fundamental reevaluation of that policy. Kentucky Republican John Sherman Cooper, seen by some in the administration as a bellwether, agreed. "If these people in Vietnam will not fight and cannot stabilize their government," he declared, "I don't see how we can stay there." Gore, from neighboring Tennessee, told journalists in midmonth that "we should never have been there in the first place, but that is water over the dam. The search must be not for scapegoats but for a face-saving disentanglement." And Democrat George McGovern, in a Senate speech on 15 January, said that America was not winning in Vietnam, could not win a military victory, and therefore should seek to negotiate its way out. Responding to rumors of a planned expansion of the war to the North, McGovern said, "Attacks on North Vietnam will not seriously weaken guerrilla fighters 1,000 miles away, fighters who depend for 80 per cent of their weapons on captured United States equipment and for food on sympathetic peasants." In the absence of stability in Saigon, with stability looking more and more unlikely, expanding the American involvement would be "an act of folly designed in the end to create a larger, more inglorious debacle," McGovern declared.[15]

Newsweek magazine, surveying the opinions on Capitol Hill, saw something new in the growing expressions of dissent. "Thoughtful and responsible men who have long accepted the global responsibilities of the United States are now openly talking of a negotiated settlement, and some of them are at pains to make it clear that they are talking only of Vietnam," the magazine observed. No longer did such views come only from "predictable" groups such as liberal clergymen and students. What this meant, the magazine noted with remarkable prescience, was that "stirrings of doubt" were coming from those who "lead and shape public opinion. If past experience is any guide, those doubts will in time transmit themselves in magnified form to the public at large. . . . Historically, Americans have shown scant patience with wars that do not offer the clear possibility of unequivocal military victory." The noted Vietnam expert Bernard Fall also detected the change in Congressional thinking. "For the first time," he observed, "a broad spectrum of middle-of-the-roaders in the Senate and House want negotiated withdrawal."[16]

Among those skeptics who felt compelled to remain publicly silent, none occupied a more delicate position than Vice President–elect Hubert H. Humphrey. Opposed to an immediate American withdrawal from Vietnam but also to an escalated war, Humphrey in January kept his cards close to the vest. He was among those who attended the meeting with the Lansdale group, and he came away convinced of the futility of pursuing a military solution. How much Humphrey knew of the plans for escalation in this period is not clear, but he appears to have believed that a decision for war would in the end not have to be made. At a dinner two days before the 20 January inauguration that would make him the nation's second-highest-ranking official, Humphrey talked with James Thomson of the NSC staff about the war. Thomson was concerned. "I am very fearful," he told Humphrey, "that plans are going ahead to expand the war to bring Hanoi to its knees." The upper levels of the administration seemed united on the need for sustained bombing of the North. Humphrey nodded knowingly. "I know exactly what you're talking about," he replied, "but it'll never happen. Before it does, a neutralist government will come to power and ask us to leave. Don't worry, Jim."[17]

It was a provocative prediction, and a perfectly reasonable one. The neutralist possibility was stronger than ever in South Vietnam at the beginning of 1965. Pervasive war-weariness, growing anti-Americanism, expanding Vietcong strength—each of these fueled speculation by both Vietnamese and outside observers (American, British, and French) that there could emerge a government committed to ending the war immediately. "We are faced," Taylor told the president in a typical cable early in January, "with a seriously deteriorating situation characterized by continued political turmoil, irresponsibility and division within the armed forces, lethargy in the pacification program, some anti-U.S. feeling which could grow, signs of mounting terrorism by VC directly against U.S. personnel, and deepening discouragement and loss of morale throughout South Vietnam." The ambassador warned that unless these conditions were somehow changed and the trends reversed, the United States was "likely soon to face a number of unpleasant developments." These ranged from anti-American demonstrations, more civil disorders, and political assassinations, "to the ultimate installation of a hostile government which will ask us to leave while it seeks accommodation with the NLF and Hanoi."[18]

Officials in Washington needed little convincing. A State Department cable, cleared by Rusk, McNamara, and both Bundy brothers, instructed the embassy to do all it could to boost the civilian Huong-Suu government, since its demise could lead to a military (i.e., Khanh) government, which could have an "anti-U.S. bias," and which could, "by its victory, lend encouragement to the anti-American manifestations already evident in Buddhist and certain student groups." William Bundy, in a preparatory memo for Rusk in advance of the 6 January White House meeting, echoed Taylor in warning that "the most likely form of coming apart would be a government of key groups starting to negotiate covertly with the National Liberation Front or Hanoi," while the Pentagon's John McNaughton asserted that Vietnam was being "lost" and that, with time, a government "not unfriendly to the DRV will probably emerge."[19]

Nor was there much that embassy officials could do to remedy the situation. The events of December had made starkly clear their limited influence over the Saigon political scene. Even if Taylor and his cohorts had held greater sway over developments, however, it is unclear just what they could have accomplished. Everywhere they looked, things looked grim. The Huong government was nominally pro-American, but it insisted on maintaining a measure of independence from Washington, if only as a means of preserving some popular legitimacy. Accordingly, Huong and Suu continued in January to lay plans for a National Assembly, even though Taylor urged a delay—as before, he feared it could be dominated by elements favoring peace. For that matter, the Huong government possessed insufficient strength to withstand any kind of effort by the military to overthrow it. Nguyen Khanh was the commander in chief of South Vietnam, in every sense of the word, and American observers fully expected him to move to oust Huong before long. Senior U.S. officials in both Washington and Saigon had long since lost all respect for Khanh, and they knew he possessed little public support. So desperate were they for a marginally stable GVN, however, that they resigned themselves to backing him, should that become necessary. As Rusk wrote to Taylor on 11 January, the "eclipse of any form of meaningful civilian government in Saigon will create awkward and even serious problems for the Embassy." Even so, should a Khanh government get on with the war and agree "to work genuinely with the U.S. . . . we might well have to swallow our pride and work with it. Hence our only short-term guidance would be to avoid to the extent possible action that commits us one way or the other [in the leadership struggle]."[20]

The question was, which way would a Khanh government go? Khanh's rapprochement with the Buddhists, which had intensified in December in direct proportion to his loss of American support, continued to build in the first part of January, with the result that rumors flew that he planned to follow the bonzes' lead and seek a neutralist solution. American officials took these rumors very seriously, not because they believed Khanh had developed any kind of sudden intellectual affinity for neutralism, but because they thought he saw the Buddhist alliance as the key to preserving his power. This made it more imperative than ever to ascertain just what the Buddhist leaders wanted. McGeorge Bundy told Johnson in a handwritten note in midmonth that the Buddhists constituted "the central problem," and he pledged to press for a "new and more imaginative combined effort" in dealing with them. To that end, Bundy aide Chester Cooper looked for insights by consulting with psychiatrists who had "studied Buddhist psychology," while the embassy in Saigon sought increased contact with the bonzes. Given previous American failures to understand the monks' philosophy and objectives, it should come as no real surprise that the effort floundered.[21]

Still, the main outlines of the Buddhist campaign were clear enough. Most of its leaders remained opposed to the growing American presence in Vietnam, favored the overthrow of Huong (largely on the grounds that he was American-sponsored), and sought an early end to the war. Taylor's deputy, U. Alexis Johnson, conceded to British officials in Saigon that many Buddhist leaders wanted an end to the war by negotiation, and he agreed that a situation might arise in which the GVN would announce that an armistice had been reached and that the Americans were to leave. On 20 January one Buddhist leader, Thien Minh, told Taylor that Buddhists wanted peace, since a continuation of the war only brought useless suffering to the people if the regime for which they were fighting continued to oppress them. He added that the high members of the current regime were using American aid only for their own purposes and would be the first to negotiate surrender to the Vietcong. Taylor cabled Rusk that this "admission that the subject [of peace] is being actively discussed by the [Buddhist] hierarchy is disquieting." Even worse, Minh "seemed to be implying negotiation with Vietcong even by a strong GVN."[22]

Here the ambassador was putting his finger on one of the enduring truths of the war, a truth that neither he nor his senior colleagues in Washington ever fully understood, or, if they did, allowed themselves openly to acknowledge: namely, that a "strong" Saigon government meant a government with broad-based support, which meant a government neither created by nor sustained by the United States, which meant a government committed to ending twenty years of warfare. The more closely a government became tied to, and dependent on, the United States, the more it lost legitimacy. Taylor, more than many in Washington, grasped at least part of this reality—he objected to the possible introduction of U.S. ground forces partly because he felt certain the such an action would alienate many southerners. However, Taylor no less than his U.S.-based colleagues sought closer Washington-GVN collaboration, sought to prevent an early negotiated settlement, sought to delay democratic reforms by the Huong regime. Above all, Taylor and the top policymakers in Washington were in sync on the most fundamental point: that although a stable government should be sought prior to expanding the war, it should not be a prerequisite for such action. What the final recommendations of the Working Group had said in late November remained true in January: "If the GVN can only be kept going by stronger action, the U.S. is prepared . . . to enter into a second phase program [of sustained air strikes against North Vietnam]."[23]

Differences did exist among the top officials over when the phase two actions should be initiated, over how soon American dependents should be removed, and over whether U.S. ground forces should be deployed in the South in conjunction with the initiation of air strikes. But the important point here is that, as in previous months, no one among them viewed the disintegration in South Vietnam as a reason to *de*-escalate, to find some means to withdraw from the war. As before, no one among them even gave that option sustained appraisal. For these men, the discussion and debate in January concerned the best way to "clear the decks" (a phrase used frequently in the correspondence) for the expanded military action that all deemed necessary. In this context the dependents issue achieved special importance, especially for Johnson. He talked constantly about the need to get "the women and children" out, to get loved ones out of harm's way. In almost every meeting on the war in January, in virtually every cable that went out over his signature, he hammered away with the same message: get dependents out right away, before any reprisal strikes. It has been suggested that Johnson viewed the dependents issue as a stalling device, as a way to delay having to make a decision on escalation (i.e., no wider action without removal), but the better argument is that he had made up his mind and was merely laying the groundwork for the new military moves. He certainly was not viewing evacuation as the first stage of a general withdrawal—one White House–approved cable instructed Taylor to assure Huong that the removal would not mean a lessened U.S. commitment, while another noted that any evacuation "should give [the] correct impression of clearing the decks rather than withdrawal."[24]

The documentary record leaves no doubt as to Johnson's determination. His seeming insistence on securing a stable Saigon government before proceeding to escalation pales in importance next to his insistence on preventing defeat. Already in late December he had indicated his willingness to send American ground troops to Vietnam, if necessary. In January, when Fulbright and Humphrey met with him to convey the Lansdale team's concerns about the military emphasis of American policy, he showed no interest. When George Ball at a White House meeting said that the Vietnamese people were tired of war and that the GVN had "the smell of death," Johnson indicated firmness and told those in the room, "I hope you realize this may cost you your vacations." He may have glossed over Vietnam in his State of the Union message, as journalists complained, but what little he did say about it suggested no slackening in the commitment: "[Peace for Vietnam] shall come when the aggressors leave their neighbors in peace." When White House aide Douglass Cater—after hearing the *New York Times*'s Saigon correspondent Peter Grose tell him that the situation was hopeless and that the administration should explore every opportunity for a face-saving withdrawal—recommended to LBJ late in the month that he send a private emissary to Saigon "to give you a fresh assessment," Johnson agreed. But rather than sending someone who could reasonably be expected to provide such an assessment, he opted to follow Max Taylor's suggestion and send McGeorge Bundy, a fervent hawk and a man with a deep stake in seeing the American enterprise succeed.[25]

All the while, Johnson took care to hide from Congress and the nation the nature of the administration's thinking and planning. On 21 January, the day after his inauguration, he invited lawmakers to the White House to discuss foreign policy. They had barely sat down when Johnson asked for bipartisan support on the war ("There are no Democrats or Republicans on Vietnam") and darkly warned that public disclosures of the nature of the discussion would do grave damage to the national interest. Vietnam was the nation's most difficult foreign-policy problem, he said, one he wrestled with day and night, and one that would greatly benefit from the input of Congress. Never in recent history, he ringingly proclaimed, had there been an administration more willing to consider foreign and defense policy in terms of the national interest rather than party politics.

It was an extraordinary statement coming from someone whose every Vietnam decision in 1964 had been carefully considered in light of its potential impact on the election, and who now obsessed about erecting a Great Society, and it set the tone for the rest of the meeting. Dean Rusk misrepresented the administration's position on negotiations, telling the legislators that the State Department was keenly looking for any sign that the communists would agree to a new Geneva-type agreement (he failed to note that the administration opposed a return to Geneva) and wrongly stating that the United States welcomed a fourteen-power conference on Laos. Robert McNamara followed, exaggerating the success of recent covert operations against North Vietnam under Oplan 34-A and the Barrel Roll operations over Laos—neither had, in fact, yielded appreciable results, as McNamara knew. McNamara further suggested, contrary to reality, that ARVN's effectiveness had increased during 1964 and implied that it could be expected to continue to do so. Continuing in this reassuring tone, Johnson closed the meeting by stressing that the "war must be fought by the South Vietnamese. We cannot control everything that they do and we have to count on their fighting their war."[26]

The talent for duplicity exhibited by the president and his two most prominent cabinet members was not the only remarkable thing about this meeting; equally noteworthy was the list of who had not been invited, and who had. Though foreign-policy and defense issues were the sole subject matter, neither Armed Services Committee chairman Russell nor Foreign Relations Committee chair Fulbright were invited. Johnson explained the omission by telling the others that he wanted to limit the conference to a small number. This must have struck some in the room as odd, given that more than twenty people were in attendance, including thirteen lawmakers. Only one of the Democratic critics, Majority Leader Mike Mansfield, was there, while Russell, Fulbright, Church, Gore, Nelson, McGovern, and, of course, mavericks Morse and Gruening were nowhere to be found. The hawks, on the other hand, were well represented—Dirksen was in attendance, as were Senators Russell Long (D-LA) and George Smathers (D-FL), and House members Gerald Ford (R-MI), Melvin Laird (R-WI), and Speaker John McCormack (D-MA). Little wonder that Johnson received his treasured show of unity from those assembled (Mansfield remained silent, perhaps because of McNamara's and Johnson's comforting tone). Only a few hours had elapsed since the start of what Johnson had coveted for so long, his own four-year administration, and already the campaign of deception on Vietnam was in full swing.

To suggest that Lyndon Johnson in early 1965 was preparing to escalate the Vietnam War is not to suggest that he relished the idea, least of all at the start of his administration. He desperately hoped that the Saigon political situation could be held together for at least a few weeks, so that he could delay having to implement the escalatory measures under phase two and instead focus his energies on moving forward with his domestic legislative agenda.

It was not to be. Even while his meeting with the congressmen was going on, the turmoil in South Vietnam increased, as a ten-day-old, Taylor-brokered compromise agreement between Khanh and the Huong government began to break down, mainly owing to Buddhist opposition. Unalterably opposed to Huong's staying in power and thus unhappy with Taylor's action and Khanh's acquiescence, Buddhist leaders on 23 January called for a campaign to protest American support for Huong. Almost immediately, anti-U.S. protests erupted in the urban centers of South Vietnam. In Hué on that day, where leading bonze Quang was particularly influential, a mob of 5,000 attacked the U.S. Information Service (USIS) Library and destroyed some 8,000 books.[27]

Ambassador Taylor, anxious to show American determination, responded by convening a meeting with Huong and Khanh on the twenty-fifth to discuss reprisal plans for the next large-scale Vietcong attack. In Washington the next day, McGeorge Bundy suggested one last way to try to deal with the Buddhists: send Henry Cabot Lodge to reason with them. (Just what he thought Lodge could accomplish is not clear, but it proved a moot point—though LBJ agreed to the suggestion, Taylor later succeeded in killing it by arguing that it would be useless.) Bundy also noted the need for an immediate meeting among the top four—LBJ, Rusk, McNamara, and himself—and he gave Johnson a report from Chester Cooper suggesting that Khanh could be angling to make himself a neutralist "Sihanouk of South Vietnam" through a deal with the enemy. In a follow-up memo that afternoon, after LBJ had agreed to meet the next day, Bundy informed the president of intelligence reports predicting that Khanh, as part of a deal with the Buddhist leadership, would launch a coup within a matter of hours.[28]

Sure enough, in the early morning hours of 27 January, Saigon time, Khanh and the Armed Forces Council overthrew Tran Van Huong's government in a bloodless coup. Taylor immediately cabled Washington (where it was still the evening of the twenty-sixth) that an alliance between Khanh and the Quang–led Buddhist Institute had caused the coup, and that most senior generals had supported the action. He noted that the institute's leadership now appeared to be "in a position of dominant power and influence in the country," and speculated that, although Khanh hoped to use the alliance with the bonzes to his advantage, it looked much more likely that it would be the Buddhists who would use him. The result could be disastrous: "The most sinister aspect of this affair is the obvious danger that the Buddhist victory may be an important step toward the formation of a government which will eventually lead the country into negotiations with Hanoi and the National Liberation Front," Taylor wrote. The "Khanh-

Institute combination" thus represented a union of "two elements adverse to U.S. interests." The ambassador, up to this point opposed to the evacuation of American dependents, now supported such a move. Tellingly, he justified the removal not as part of an effort to "clear the decks" for military escalation but because he feared the dependents were in danger, less from the Vietcong than from the protesting mobs! The recent events in Hué, he noted, were "a reminder of the ease with which anti-American emotions can be whipped up."[29]

The Saigon crisis and the Taylor cable caused a frenzy of activity in Washington. At 7:45 A.M. on 27 January Robert McNamara and his chief Vietnam deputy, John McNaughton, discussed the situation. McNaughton, long pessimistic on prospects in the war, said Khanh's maneuverings gave the United States justification to "dump" Vietnam. But what about the effect on other countries? he wondered. Yes, McNamara replied, an American withdrawal would only shift the struggle to Malaysia and Thailand, both of which could be expected to "go fast." With withdrawal ruled out, McNaughton saw three choices: air strikes on North Vietnam, negotiations, and "plugging away along present lines." He preferred the last one, suggesting bombing would not work and negotiations promised little. McNamara disagreed. He said air strikes against the North could help bolster the situation in the South. As for negotiations, the defense secretary said that option would be better than the current "drifting," which characterized the "keep plugging" option.[30]

Later in the morning McNamara met with McGeorge Bundy, probably to plot strategy for the meeting with the president and Rusk scheduled for 11:30 A.M. The two must have conversed at some length prior to this, however, because Bundy had with him a memo that purported to represent both his and McNamara's point of view, which would be the subject of the discussion with Johnson. It was, McNamara later said, an "explosive memorandum," one that laid out in forceful prose what its author saw as the stark choice facing the United States: escalation or negotiation. "What we want to say to you," Bundy began, "is that both of us are now pretty well convinced that our current policy can lead only to disastrous defeat." Waiting for a stable Saigon regime before going further seemed fruitless, because "no one has much hope that there is going to be a stable government while we sit still." Echoing McNamara's complaint to McNaughton against continuing a policy of drift, Bundy said the worst course of action would be to continue in a passive role; such an approach could "only lead to eventual defeat and an invitation to get out in humiliating circumstances." This left two choices, to use military power to force a change in communist policy, or to "deploy all our resources along a track of negotiation, aimed at salvaging what little can be preserved with no major addition to our present military risks." Bundy said he and McNamara favored the first option, but he acknowledged that Rusk disagreed. The secretary of state, Bundy said, did not doubt that "things are going very badly [or] that the situation is unraveling" but felt "the consequences of both escalation and withdrawal are so bad that we must simply find a way of making our present policy work." (Rusk, in other words, shared McNaughton's preference for "plugging away.") "This would be good if it were possible," Bundy said. "Bob and I do not think it is."[31]

Neither, it quickly became clear, did Johnson. He read the memorandum prior to the meeting and when the three men joined him in the Oval Office he agreed to begin preparation for action. "Stable government or no stable government," he declared, "we'll do what we have to do. I'm prepared to do that. *We will move strongly*. Khanh is our boy" (emphasis in original). Rusk did not object, perhaps because he sensed the president's determination, perhaps because his own mind had been changed by the events of the previous hours—prior to the meeting he had received a State Department intelligence report that warned of a "rising crescendo of anti-American feelings" in South Vietnam and seconded Taylor's view that there was a serious risk that Khanh would opt for a neutralist solution. Such an outcome was for Dean Rusk no more palatable than it had ever been. That evening, he signed off on a presidential cable to Taylor in which Johnson pronounced himself "delighted" that the embassy now agreed on the need for the removal of dependents and vowed determination "to make it clear to all the world that the U.S. will spare no effort and no sacrifice in doing its full part to turn back the Communists in Vietnam."[32]

A key moment had arrived, the meaning of which must be clearly understood. The White House meeting's importance lay not in any assumptions articulated during it—the Bundy memorandum's claim that current policy could lead only to defeat had been suspected among senior officials for many months and had been fully anticipated in the president's 30 December cable to Taylor. Already at that time he and his chief advisers had concluded they would seek Saigon stability *through* escalation if they could not get it *before* escalation. Likewise, the assertion that expanding the fighting was preferable to negotiating from weakness had been the Johnson team's position from the start. Rather, the 27 January meeting mattered greatly because Johnson now moved to implement the policy he had agreed to in principle back in December. "We will move strongly," he had now decided, "stable government or no stable government." (Given the chaos in Saigon, this phrase really meant "government or no government.") And he did not stop there. Understanding that the administration needed a pretext to "move strongly," Johnson on this day also authorized the resumption of destroyer patrols in the Gulf of Tonkin, the first since September 1964, in the hope of provoking a North Vietnamese attack.[33]

Even before McGeorge Bundy and his team departed for Saigon at the beginning of February, therefore, the threshold had been crossed. Bundy informed Taylor that the team would seek the U.S. Mission's views on what military actions should be taken (note: not *if* they should be taken), on whether American fighting troops should be deployed, and on what should be done in the event of a total collapse and GVN-Hanoi deal. Disengagement from the war was clearly not an option—when Taylor sent a cable proposing that the possibility of reducing the U.S. role to mere policy guidance also be put on the agenda, Bundy wrote a question mark in the margin and later asked the ambassador "whether it is necessary to discuss this as a separate item." Taylor had sought to delay the visit for at least a week or two, on the grounds that there existed as yet no government to speak of in Saigon, but Bundy said that very fact necessitated an early visit. He hid from the ambassador the full conclusions of the 27 January meeting, stating merely that, on the need for a stable regime prior to escalation, "we [in Washington] now wonder whether this requirement is either realistic or necessary." (The meeting had decided it was neither.) The deception also continued at home. When the National Security Council convened on 1 February, neither Johnson nor Bundy made any mention of the policy change, and Bundy assured the group that his trip would be as low-key as possible. "No great new decisions are expected to result," he said, which was literally true—the decision had been made already.[34]

Recalled Bundy aide Chester Cooper, who accompanied the national security adviser on the trip: "The problem was that Johnson had already made up his mind. For all practical purposes he had dismissed the option of de-escalating and getting out, but he didn't want to say that he had, so the rationale for this trip was this was going to be decisive." But "he damn well had decided already what he was going to do."[35]

Even if we were to draw back from this conclusion that a firm decision had in fact been made, that is, even if we were to chalk up the strong statements of the 27 January meeting to characteristic Johnsonian bluster that he could retract if he saw fit, the impact of his words must still have been immense. That the president had chosen Bundy—in early 1965 probably the most hawkish among his senior advisers—to make the trip in the first place spoke volumes; that he now voiced firm and total support for the "explosive" recommendations in the Bundy memorandum said even more.

The man who boarded the airplane in Washington in the early evening of 2 February thus had every reason to believe that he and his president were in complete accord on what needed to be done in Vietnam. Why does this matter? It matters because Bundy knew, even before he arrived in Saigon, what essential message he would bring back to Washington—a rough draft of the trip report, bearing close approximation to the final version, was drafted early in his four-day stay.[36] It matters because, had Bundy traveled with a somewhat open mind, had he been instructed to provide Johnson with a truly fresh assessment of the war and its prospects, he might have been more affected by what he encountered.

What he encountered was a South Vietnam teetering on the brink of social and political disintegration. The ouster of Huong, it was already clear, had done nothing but plunge South Vietnam into further turmoil. In the coup's wake nobody knew which half of the Khanh-Buddhist alliance was really in charge; nobody knew whether the Americans would be asked to leave; nobody knew if a deal with the NLF was imminent. Rumors flew in all directions. But deeper changes also appeared under way. "South Vietnam is in the midst of a social and political revolution," a U.S. intelligence report noted on 4 February, with power passing to a much more "Vietnamese" element, "a militantly nationalistic and potentially xenophobic group" led by political-minded bonzes and students. It was a revolution exploited by, but also quite distinct from, the Vietcong-directed insurgency, the report continued, and it contained a strong element of anti-Americanism. Soon after arriving in Saigon, on the morning of 4 February, Bundy learned from Taylor and his deputy, U. Alexis Johnson, that mob action and anti-American demonstrations had become more menacing, so much so that U.S. citizens could be in physical danger.[37]

Nothing better indicated the bizarre state of American relations with its supposed ally than the snubbing Bundy received from Khanh after his arrival. Twice on 4 February the South Vietnamese leader turned down invitations to meet with Bundy and other American officials at a reception scheduled for the following day. He had clearly calculated that preserving good relations with Buddhist leaders mattered more than courting the Americans, but the action lent credence to Taylor's charge that Khanh likely intended to adopt a neutralist line and make himself the Sihanouk of South Vietnam. (Khanh eventually did agree to meet with Bundy.) When news of the snubbing reached Washington, Lyndon Johnson exploded with rage; barely a week earlier he had called Khanh "our boy," but now he said the administration should look to replace him, and he ordered aides to come up with a list of replacements. The State Department had by that point already reached the same conclusion. Incredibly, mere days after one coup

Washington officials were contemplating the need for another. But there were few capable replacements on the horizon, they knew. Also, what if Khanh got wind of a U.S.-sponsored effort to oust him? Might that not hasten his move toward neutralism? And even if the administration succeeded in removing him, there were the Buddhists to worry about, as a dejected Bundy reported home his first evening in Vietnam: "A day of inquiry reveals no present prospect of a government acceptable to us which would also be acceptable to the leaders of the Buddhist Institute. The current situation among non-Communist forces gives all the appearances of a civil war within a civil war."[38]

These various hostile actions directed against the United States—the mass urban protests, the sacking of the USIS Library, the snubbing of Bundy—should not give the impression that all South Vietnamese in early 1965 wanted the Americans out. As the notion of a civil war within a civil war suggests, opinions varied sharply. Clearly, there were sizable numbers who welcomed the U.S. presence, either because of genuine anticommunist conviction and fear of what a Vietcong takeover would bring, or because they had established careers for themselves serving the already-large American establishments that had sprung up in various parts of the South. For some, these twin considerations no doubt ran together. Others thought the American intervention unfortunate but necessary for the short term, until South Vietnam could withstand the communist threat on its own. (Among these were many who did not want the U.S. presence to become any larger than it was.) That said, there can be no doubt that active supporters of the U.S. intervention were a small minority in South Vietnam at the start of 1965, smaller than at any time previously, and that anti-American sentiments ran deeper and wider than ever before—U.S. intelligence agencies and embassy officials said so, foreign diplomatic observers said so, Saigon-based journalists said so. Add to that the more general war-weariness and apathy in both urban and rural areas and it becomes clear just how grim was the picture confronting the Bundy team. As Peter Grose aptly put it: "The oft-repeated American assumption that 'the South Vietnamese want to win this war as much as we do' becomes more and more hollow."[39]

With friends like these, Bundy might well have muttered, who needed enemies? As he well knew, however, the enemy lurked close by, more menacing than ever. In meetings with American military officials on 4 and 5 February, Bundy heard again what intelligence reports had already told him before he arrived: that the Vietcong were stronger than ever before; that they now controlled more than 50 percent of the territory in South Vietnam during the day, and perhaps 75 percent at night; that they had tightened their stranglehold on Saigon; that they were winning, if only by default, the battle for control of the population. Moreover, the Vietcong had achieved all this without significant material support from the North. To a large degree, the insurgency was self-sustaining. Whatever differences existed between the NLF/Vietcong and their allies in Hanoi, they agreed on the immediate goal: to defeat the GVN with as little bloodshed as possible and without causing a large-scale American intervention. In early February 1965, the objective appeared to be within reach, leaders believed. Not only had the GVN moved to the brink of collapse, but the clamor for peace among southerners—which the NLF had done its best to foment—had grown louder. Anti-Americanism had likewise mushroomed. In the United States, meanwhile, opposition to a larger war had grown more intense, suggesting that perhaps Lyndon Johnson would refrain from undertaking a major escalation. (As Pham Van Dong had made clear to Canadian diplomat J. Blair Seaborn the previous summer, Hanoi officials paid close attention to the mood in the United States and attached great weight to elite voices such as Walter Lippmann.) It is not surprising that DRV directives, which from the start of the insurgency in the late 1950s had stressed that the struggle in the South would be a long one, now cautiously suggested that victory could come soon.[40]

Ho Chi Minh and his colleagues were further encouraged by the knowledge that, in the event that Johnson did escalate the war, they could count on strong support from both China and the Soviet Union. On this front, too, early 1965 brought a positive development from the DRV's perspective, in the form of a deepening Sino-Soviet competition for influence in Southeast Asia that allowed Hanoi to play one off against the other. At precisely the same time that McGeorge Bundy visited Saigon, Soviet premier Alexei N. Kosygin traveled to Hanoi. The visit followed the signing of a Soviet–North Vietnamese trade agreement in January, and it sought to strengthen Moscow's claim that it was committed to helping North Vietnam. To that end, Kosygin pledged increased military and economic assistance to the Hanoi government, including surface-to-air missiles and other air defense equipment superior in quality to what Beijing could offer. In a joint appearance with the Hanoi leadership Kosygin condemned America's "aggression" against the Vietnamese people and vowed Soviet support for the Vietnamese "national liberation" movement and others like it around the world.[41]

But affirming Soviet support for the North Vietnamese cause did not constitute the sole objective of Kosygin's visit. He also sought to caution Hanoi officials against escalating the war and to inquire about their terms for a negotiated settlement, which suggests that he and co-leader Leonid

Brezhnev were no closer to resolving the vexing Vietnam dilemma that
they and Nikita Khrushchev before them had long confronted. As before,
the Soviets were not unhappy that things were going poorly for the United
States in Vietnam, that Asians and Africans resented the American intervention, that huge American sums were being spent there that otherwise
could be spent competing with the USSR elsewhere in the world. At the
same time, Moscow did not want the United States to get involved in another Korea-type war in Vietnam, a war in which the Kremlin would be
asked to honor its commitment to the DRV and that, from the Soviet viewpoint, would be the wrong war in the wrong place at the wrong time. Furthermore, what if the Chinese were drawn into such a war? Would that
compel Moscow to abide by the 1950 Sino-Soviet treaty and come in also?
Even if not, would Chinese intervention result in de facto Beijing control
of Indochina? The possibilities made Kosygin and his colleagues shudder
and exposed their problem: in order to deter a world conflagration they
had to constrain the North Vietnamese, but their need to compete with Beijing for the affection of Asian nationalists compelled them nevertheless to
pledge assistance to Hanoi.[42]

These conflicting Soviet goals brought up a third issue: how to approach the issue of negotiations. It seems likely, as the CIA reported in
early February, that the ideal solution for Moscow would be a Vietcong
victory without an American escalation, which explained Kosygin's urging Hanoi leaders to wait for political disintegration in the South to develop, and to do nothing that could provoke Washington. Though they were
not prepared to work to get one, Kremlin leaders saw real advantages in a
great-power conference, one that allowed for a face-saving American disengagement and put Hanoi in a strong position to win eventual control
of a reunified Vietnam. Almost certainly the Soviet Union would have welcomed for Vietnam in early 1965 the same kind of neutralization agreement it had helped arrange for Laos more than three years earlier, an agreement that, if nothing else, had ended the threat of Laos causing a major
Asian war.[43]

The historical implications are important. At the very moment when
American prospects in Vietnam looked their most dismal, when more and
more outside observers saw no light at the end of the tunnel but the Johnson administration nevertheless moved to escalate the war, Washington's
superpower rival, the rival Americans deemed responsible for starting and
perpetuating the Cold War, sought to restrain America's enemy in Vietnam and to provide a face-saving means for a U.S. withdrawal.

Had American policymakers paused as they reached the fork in the road, had they even slowed down slightly, they might have been more cognizant of the sizable group of individuals standing next to the sign marked "Withdrawal" and shouting, "Come this way." They might have seen that the group included prominent figures well schooled in international affairs— world leaders such as Charles de Gaulle, Harold Wilson, and U Thant; distinguished Americans such as Hans Morgenthau, Walter Lippmann, and Mike Mansfield. They might have actually contemplated the argument that the road to Withdrawal was the only one ultimately passable, and that it led to the destination the administration professed to want to go: to a land where Chinese ambitions in Asia were checked. But the Johnson administration did not pause or slow down. Instead, it turned swiftly onto the road to Escalation, a road all senior officials knew to be very treacherous indeed. Dean Rusk before the 27 January meeting had believed that the road was too treacherous to travel and had advocated staying on the current path. Once he learned his geography, however, learned that the current path ended right here and that a choice had to be made, he too saw only one way to go. That so few friends were willing to travel the road with them disappointed and angered the secretary and his colleagues, but they were not interested in really listening to the reasons why, not willing to hear the warnings of impending doom.

Shortly after turning onto the road (the crucial point is that it was after), the administration did pause, however, to wait for the provocation it felt was needed before going further. With almost miraculously good timing, the Vietcong obliged. At two o'clock in the morning on 7 February, mere hours before the Bundy party was scheduled to return to the United States and shortly after the end of a cease-fire to mark the Tet holiday, a company of Vietcong guerrillas launched an attack on a loosely guarded U.S. helicopter base and barracks near Pleiku in the Central Highlands. Eight Americans were killed, 126 were wounded, and ten U.S. aircraft were destroyed. It was one of about a dozen attacks on targets throughout South Vietnam launched by the Vietcong on this day, and it produced the highest number of American casualties of any incident in the conflict thus far. In Saigon, after conferring with Maxwell Taylor and William Westmoreland, Bundy called the White House on a secure telephone line and recommended the prompt initiation of air raids against the North.[44]

The pretext for action had arrived. Many American officials were not surprised by the attack, as Bundy himself implied in stating, a few weeks later, that "Pleikus are streetcars"—that is, you can count on one coming soon and are ready to board when it does. Not only had officials emerged out of the 27 January meeting looking to provoke an attack, but they also knew that it was customary for the Vietcong to launch major attacks on the heels of Tet cease-fires. In addition, American intelligence reports had indicated the very real possibility of an attack against a U.S. installation during Bundy's visit.[45]

Anticipated or not, the motives behind the attack were not easy to decipher, then or later. If, as Washington officials insisted, the raid had been initiated directly by Hanoi, the best explanation might be that DRV officials saw the assault as a way to involve Moscow more deeply in the war. Attacking an American base while Kosygin was in town might bring an American retaliation, which would more or less force the Soviet premier to pledge additional military assistance. This interpretation is complicated, however, by the fact that Kosygin had already pledged this increased support prior to the attack. Given the complexity of the Hanoi-Vietcong relationship, it is conceivable that the operation was solely the work of the southern insurgents. They may have feared that Hanoi, at Kosygin's urging, would negotiate a settlement with the United States at their expense and believed they could prevent such a settlement by attacking an American base and provoking a U.S. retaliation against the North. Charles Mohr, responding to administration claims that the attack differed from other Vietcong operations in size and intensity (and hence must have been the work of Hanoi), pointed out that a single Vietcong company of perhaps two to three hundred men had been involved, and that the principal weapon used had been the American-made eighty-one-millimeter mortars typically favored by the Vietcong.[46]

The relatively small size of the attacking force suggests another, simpler possibility: that the planners, whether in Hanoi or in the Vietcong command, viewed the Pleiku attack as merely another of the dozen raids that day, all designed to further destabilize the Saigon government and its army without provoking an American retaliation. After all, these officials could quite reasonably think, the Vietcong had staged assaults on American targets in recent months—Bienhoa in November and the Brinks billet on Christmas Eve—which had not prompted U.S. reprisals. Since then, antiwar sentiment in America had risen and Washington's international isolation grown. Hanoi and Vietcong leaders may well have surmised that the Pleiku offered another chance to strike without the risk of retaliation.[47]

If so, they miscalculated. On the evening of 6 February, Washington time, mere hours after news of the incident arrived, Johnson convened the NSC and secured near-unanimous assent for attacks on four preselected targets in southern North Vietnam (including Dong Hoi Barracks, where, JCS chairman Wheeler reported, some 3,600 casualties could be expected to result). George Ball, for months opposed to an expanded war but well aware of Johnson's desire for action, voiced strong support for the raids. He even said a new congressional resolution supporting wider action would be useful, though he also noted the need to consider the implications of Kosygin's presence in Hanoi and the problem of explaining to the public why the North was being bombed when Pleiku was in the South and its attackers were southern-based Vietcong.

Only one man in the room rose up in opposition: majority leader Mike Mansfield. The Pleiku attack had opened many eyes, he said, and the United States should be careful, especially as there existed no real government in Saigon. "We are not now in a penny-ante game. It appears that the local populace in South Vietnam is not behind us, [or] else the Viet Cong could not have carried out the surprise attack." Escalation might also bring in the Chinese, Mansfield added, and would put great pressure on the Soviets. As a result, the United States should think twice before acting. Johnson would have none of it. He probably welcomed Mansfield's dissent, however, because it permitted him, in David Halberstam's words, to "do his performance," which he promptly did: "We have kept our gun over the mantel and our shells in the cupboard for a long time now," he proclaimed. "And what was the result? They are killing our men while they sleep in the night. I can't ask our American soldiers out there to continue to fight with one hand tied behind their back." William Bundy, who was among those present, later called Johnson's response to the majority leader a deeply emotional "gut reaction" and said Mansfield never again took such a blunt position in an open meeting. Halberstam's conclusion rings true: "It was all flag, and as [Johnson] spoke the others nodded, and Mansfield nodded, as if he too knew, involuntarily or not, that he had somehow just played the role Johnson had prescribed for him, and that in a sense a curtain was coming down. The decisions had been made, all the questions had been asked, and now the answers were given."[48]

At the conclusion of the meeting, Johnson ordered the launching of retaliatory raids on the four targets (Operation Flaming Dart), to be carried out by 132 U.S. and 22 South Vietnamese planes. The South Vietnamese government was not consulted about the decision. Johnson asked those in attendance to return to the White House at 8:00 the next morning. The intensity of his feelings can be seen in his actions in the intervening hours. He retired to bed at midnight but awoke to talk on the phone with the Defense Department's Cyrus Vance, presumably about the results of the air strikes, at 3:40, 4:10, 4:55, and 5:10 in the morning, finally rising at 6:45.[49]

When the NSC reconvened a little more than an hour later, Mansfield made one last attempt to change the direction of policy, suggesting that the planned press release of the air strikes emphasize America's willingness to bring the matter to the United Nations or to a reconvened Geneva conference. Johnson said no. "This cannot be done," he declared in reference to the Geneva option; later a conference might be possible, but not now. As for the UN, he continued, going there would yield nothing. George Ball, again assuming the role of presidential mouthpiece, chimed in that the UN would indeed be hopeless and that any Geneva conference should be delayed until the United States could enter it from a stronger position than it possessed now. A lonely figure as he had been the night before, Mansfield was hopelessly overmatched by the Johnson-Ball one-two punch. At the conclusion of the nearly two-hour meeting, which contained no further substantive discussion of the U.S. commitment to the war and which produced agreement to immediately evacuate all 1,819 American dependents, the senator pledged his support. He wished to assure his president, he said, that he had spoken frankly but that he would work to support him, now that the decision had been made.[50]

Mansfield should not have been so lonely, of course. Ball privately shared all of his misgivings and all of his desire to get the United States out of the war and would have been a highly important ally, especially in his role as acting secretary of state. (Rusk was in Florida recovering from influenza.) But Ball gave no indication of support. On the contrary, he attacked Mansfield's position and portrayed himself—in both meetings—as not merely supportive of retaliation but as positively enthusiastic. Later, in his memoirs, Ball wrongly claimed the others in the room were "unanimous" in favoring reprisal and said he went along with the group in order not to destroy his effectiveness: "The demand for prompt retaliation was overwhelming and I realized that further frontal opposition would be not only futile but tactically unwise. I could gain nothing by antagonizing my colleagues. . . . [T]he President could no longer be deterred." Perhaps, but a skeptic could certainly be forgiven for thinking otherwise. No doubt Ball occupied a difficult position, sitting in the place of the hawkish Rusk, whose views he probably felt compelled to express. But was it really true that he could "gain nothing" by "antagonizing" his colleagues? Even if it were, was it necessary to cheer them on? Perhaps "full frontal opposition" was impossible, but what about voicing a mere modicum of concern?[51]

In several phone conversations that day, Ball revealed his talent for smoothly tailoring his remarks to suit the occasion. At 10:00 A.M., right after the meeting concluded, he called Rusk in Florida to report the results of the air strikes and to pass on the good news that a consensus had been reached. "Even Mike [Mansfield] having made his views felt says he will give all the support he can," he told Rusk. At 3:15 P.M. Ball listened sympathetically as William Fulbright expressed concerned over the unfolding events and said that perhaps the time had come for a Geneva conference.

Had there been any improvement in the Saigon political climate? Fulbright asked. "There will never be a stable government there," Ball replied. At 5:20 P.M., Ball told *New York Times* reporter Tom Wicker that LBJ needed Wicker to be helpful on Vietnam and wrongly said the NSC meetings had found unanimous support for the reprisal attacks.[52]

To the key players in the administration, reprisal bombing was not enough. That evening, McGeorge Bundy returned from South Vietnam. He went immediately to the White House, where he met with the president shortly before 11:00 P.M. and handed him the mission report. In it the national security adviser argued that the United States should move immediately to phase two, to a program of "sustained reprisal" bombing. The key paragraph revealed both Bundy's sense of urgency and his continuing fear of negotiations. "The situation in Vietnam is deteriorating, and without new action defeat appears inevitable," he wrote, echoing the central assertion in his 27 January memo. "There is still time to turn it around, but not much. The stakes in Vietnam are extremely high. The American investment is very large, and American responsibility is a fact of life which is palpable in the atmosphere of Asia, and even elsewhere. The international prestige of the United States, and a substantial part of our influence, are directly at risk in Vietnam." Bundy saw no way of "unloading the burden on the Vietnamese themselves," and no way of negotiating a U.S. withdrawal that offered any real promise at present. "It is possible that at some future time a neutral non-Communist force may emerge, perhaps under Buddhist leadership, but no such force currently exists, and any negotiated U.S. withdrawal today would mean surrender on the installment plan."[53]

This assessment of the indigenous possibilities for a negotiated settlement was, to say the least, disingenuous: a "neutral, non-Communist force" under "Buddhist leadership" had emerged, and that was the problem. Reaffirming the administration's negative stand on an early diplomatic settlement, Bundy stressed that "we should *not* now accept the idea of negotiations of any sort except on the basis of a stand-down of Viet Cong violence." Negotiations were to be avoided until the enemy surrendered, in other words, which would mean there would be nothing to negotiate.

The report was schizophrenic on the current situation in the war and the future prospects. The military effort had been deteriorating for the previous year, Bundy wrote, and anti-Americanism had increased. There existed a "worrisome lassitude among the Vietnamese generally," a "distressing absence of positive commitment to any serious social and political purpose. Outside observers are ready to write the patient off," he noted, while "to be an American in Saigon today is to have a gnawing feeling that time is against us." Then, as if trying to convince himself that all was not lost, Bundy professed to see some reasons for hope. Without offering a shred of evidence (because none existed), he declared that ARVN effectiveness in open combat "continues to grow," and that the South Vietnamese "readiness to quit" was not nearly as high as many thought. A policy of sustained reprisal, moreover, would address the "one grave weakness in our posture in Vietnam which is within our power to fix": the "widespread belief that we do not have the will and force and patience and determination to take the necessary action and stay the course." Once the policy was in place, U.S. influence on political and military developments in Vietnam would grow substantially.

Even Khanh received a boost in the report. Recognizing the need to have at least a minimal government in Saigon for the wider military action, and that Khanh would likely be heading that regime, Bundy mustered up words of support for the man whom he and other U.S. officials only hours earlier had discussed ousting: "We [in the Bundy team] believe that General Khanh, with all his faults, is by long odds the outstanding military man currently in sight—and the most impressive personality generally. We do not share the conclusion of Ambassador Taylor that he must somehow be removed from the military and political scene." True, Khanh was unscrupulous and power-hungry and lacking in support among both his colleagues and the public. True, he might opt for an "anti-American path" if U.S. support was withdrawn. But no adequate replacement existed.[54]

But what exactly would sustained reprisals accomplish? In an annex to the report prepared prior to the Pleiku attack, Bundy argued that bombing the North could be expected to improve the situation in the South. Initiation of the policy would bring a "sharp immediate increase in optimism in the South," he predicted, which would translate into increased American influence in pressing for a more effective Saigon government—at least in the short term. "The Vietnamese increase in hope could well increase the readiness of Vietnamese factions themselves to join together in forming a more effective government." Meanwhile, Bundy continued, Vietcong morale would go down, and Hanoi leaders might also be convinced to cease and desist. And what if none of these things happened and the policy failed? It would still be worth doing, Bundy the "good doctor" declared, because it would "damp down the charge that we did not do all that we could have done," an important consideration in many countries, including the United States. Beyond that, even a failed policy, by demonstrating U.S. steadfastness, would set a higher price for subsequent "adventures of guerrilla warfare" and perhaps increase America's ability to deter such adventures.[55]

It was an altogether rickety foundation upon which to build an expanded war. Each of the claims about the benefits of bombing North Vietnam went against the bulk of U.S. intelligence analysis dating back several months, as a clearly incredulous Thomas L. Hughes, of the State Department's Bureau of Intelligence and Research, reminded George Ball the next day after reading the report and the annex. (Ball's own memo the previous October had disputed virtually all the assertions now made by Bundy.) The DRV would fight on despite the bombing, Hughes predicted, and the Chinese would be obligated to offer support despite their aversion to a direct intervention. The Vietcong would remain as committed as ever. Moreover, Hughes added, Bundy had underestimated free-world opposition to an expansion of the war. He cited an intelligence report from November 1964 predicting that Washington would probably find itself "progressively isolated" in world opinion in the event the escalatory moves did not bring immediate results. James Thomson, no less perplexed than Hughes, likewise thought Bundy had underestimated the threat of Chinese intervention and also the domestic American implications. Were the American people really willing, Thomson asked, "to face a ground war in Vietnam—a conflict already fuzzed by national doubts far exceeding any that attached to the relatively clear-cut Korean conflict (invasion and 'UN' response)?" Also, Thomson wondered, "what has happened to the concept of 'negotiation' so earnestly pursued by our more thoughtful journalistic and Congressional critics, and previously pursued by many thoughtful people here and at State? Are we ruling it out, as the Annex suggests? If so, for how long?" To Thomson the situation was reminiscent of the Bay of Pigs debacle of 1961: the objective had not been worth the price then, and he seriously wondered if it was worth it now.[56]

Lyndon Johnson did not so wonder, or if he did, he did not show it. Whether he even read the Bundy report closely is open to question. When Bundy handed it to him he asked if the report contained anything new. "Well, we thought we made a sketch of a program that didn't exist," Bundy responded. Johnson disagreed. "No, that's where we are already," he said, accurately. "Let's not talk about it anymore." At a meeting of the NSC the next morning, the president declared his intention to endorse phase two. "It is our hope," he declared, "that current U.S. action may pull together the various forces in Saigon and thus make possible the establishment of a stable government." With Mike Mansfield looking on, Johnson vowed that he would not let the views of a few senators control his actions and said the legal power of the presidency, together with the Gulf of Tonkin Resolution, gave him the authority to act to deter aggression in Vietnam.

Mansfield said nothing. Instead he gave Johnson a memorandum after the meeting in which he again decried the absence of a functioning GVN and again advocated going to the UN or to Geneva, but in which he also repeated his pledge to support whatever policy Johnson adopted.[57]

Johnson later wrote that among those present there was unanimous support for the Bundy report's "principal recommendation: a program of sustained reprisal against the North." This was untrue: Mansfield certainly opposed it even if Johnson's treatment of him the day before had made him afraid to say so. In addition, Llewellyn Thompson, formerly ambassador to Moscow and now ambassador-at-large, voiced reservations about going to sustained actions before the Soviets had made their position clear (though he appears by the end of the meeting to have signed on). More important, the show of support was deceiving in that important critics who might have been expected to attend the session were not there. Hubert Humphrey, who as vice president held one of only four statutory seats on the NSC (the president and the secretaries of state and defense were the others) had been in Minnesota for several days and had not been asked to come back for the meeting. Nor were Fulbright or Russell asked to attend, despite their prominent foreign-policy positions in the Senate. The absence of Fulbright at all of the meetings on 6–8 February caused rumors on Capitol Hill—well-founded ones, it would seem—that Johnson was snubbing the Foreign Relations Committee chairman. Regardless, the views of the vice president, and of two leading legislators who were on record opposing an expanded war, were not heard at any time during the critical forty-eight-hour period following the Pleiku attack.[58]

On only one issue did Johnson differ with the Bundy mission report's recommendations. At the conclusion of it Bundy cautioned that "at the very best" the Vietnam struggle would be long, and that this fact should be made clear to the American people. Johnson refused. He wanted the new policy initiative to be kept as secret as possible, he told Bundy at their late-night White House meeting on 7 February, even within the administration. As Bundy got up to leave, Johnson asked, "How many copies are there?" When Bundy responded that several had been handed out, the president exploded, "Get them back!" The next day Bundy put the matter firmly to his brother William: "Look, get this straight, the President does not want this depicted as a change in policy." Johnson himself asked those at the NSC meeting that day to avoid mentioning that the administration had embarked on a new course. In brief public comments on the seventh and eighth he spoke in meaningless generalities, saying the United States sought no wider war, that it loved peace but also loved liberty. When White House aide Bill Moyers on the ninth suggested the need for a major presidential statement on Vietnam, Johnson said no.[59] America in early 1965 had entered a dangerous new stage in Vietnam, and Lyndon Johnson was determined to suggest otherwise.

11 Americanization

That anyone would have embarked on a major expansion of the war in Vietnam and tried to keep it a secret seems, at first glance, preposterous. All signs pointed to a protracted and costly struggle under the best of circumstances, on behalf of a people who, by and large, wanted nothing to do with such a war. It would be a war on behalf of a Saigon government that was unrepresentative and repressive, and whose leading figures were much more interested in political infighting than in battling the Vietcong. And it would be a war against an enemy of unshakable determination and proven ability, backed by the support of China and the Soviet Union. Of course, it was these very facts that caused Lyndon Johnson to opt for a strategy of stealth, to hide from the American people the new measures he had approved. And indeed, from a strictly short-term perspective, it made a strange kind of sense. For given Johnson's unshakable determination to avoid defeat in Vietnam, and given the general administration pessimism about the prospects in the war, it was natural that he would seek to damp down discussion of the policy as much as possible, at least until the new measures had had a chance to work. The growing divisions on Vietnam in the Congress and in the country as a whole only made him more anxious to avoid a debate— which he feared he might lose—and more anxious to pretend that no change in the American commitment had occurred.

Still, it was preposterous. It was preposterous because too many people could see through the deception, could see for themselves that the policy had changed and that the United States had plunged deeper into the Vietnamese morass. Immediately after the Pleiku reprisal strikes, the signs of such awareness were plentiful. Among the general public, while polls showed majority support for the air strikes, White House mail, heavy in volume, ran twelve to one in opposition. It had run two to one against the reprisal strikes during the Gulf of Tonkin crisis the previous August, which prompted McGeorge Bundy to tell Johnson that "the propensity of the American people to punch Communists in the nose over Vietnam is considerably less than six months ago" (when, he might have added, the propensity was not exactly high). Vietnam was too far away to matter to them, Bundy surmised, and thus "we have an education problem that bears close watching."[1]

In the press, too, many observers could see that the war had entered a new, more ominous, stage. In the days after the reprisal strikes, editorialists across the country said so, and although not all were displeased by the show of force, many noted that the choices between inaction and action were being whittled down. On 9 February, James Reston wrote that the United States had reduced its freedom of action by not only retaliating but proclaiming that future military action depended on the "action of the aggressors." Reston, echoing his colleague Charles Mohr, pointed to the presence of three aircraft carriers off the coast of Vietnam, rather than the usual one, as suggesting that the administration had been looking for provocation and had found it with Pleiku, and he informed his readers that Johnson had at last been able to accomplish what he had sought so long: to withdraw American dependents from Vietnam. "The president," he wrote, "seems prepared to escalate the war." Fellow columnist Arthur Krock said that a new war had begun and wondered how success could come when the South Vietnamese were so indifferent.[2]

But the most fervent alarms were raised in the international community by observers who saw the administration rejecting negotiations in favor of escalation. A late-1964 intelligence report had anticipated that Washington would become *progressively* isolated if the air strikes failed to show quick success, but the isolation was visible from the very start, as government after government expressed concern about the new developments. For many, Kosygin's presence in Hanoi had been a hopeful sign that perhaps a political settlement to the conflict could be worked out, but the Johnson administration had shown its complete noninterest in such a settlement by dispatching its bombers even before the premier left town. The danger level had been ratcheted up; the chances for peace had diminished.

Of course, decisions made can be unmade. To critics in the United States and elsewhere, it appeared that the Johnson administration had stepped over the threshold to an escalated American war, the president's claims to the contrary notwithstanding, but they hoped he might be induced to step back. In the weeks following the Pleiku incident, while the administration continued to try to manufacture consensus on the war, among audiences both at home and abroad, and continued to hide the direction of its policy, the advocates of diplomacy launched their most intensive effort to head off a full-scale war.

These weeks in the late winter of 1965 represent the climax to our story, for it was then that the Johnson administration moved to implement the policy decisions that had been taking shape since early 1964 but only now had been formally adopted; and it was then that the hopes for an early diplomatic solution all but ended. What more than a few observers perceived at the time and what is crystal clear today is that by the early spring of 1965 the last chance to prevent another full-scale war in Indochina had passed. By then the Americanization of the conflict had begun, and the negotiating positions of Hanoi and the National Liberation Front had hardened (exactly as U.S. intelligence analyses had anticipated). By then the Soviets had lost interest in promoting a settlement, and the Beijing government had become more intransigent. And by then even some longtime American proponents of a U.S. withdrawal, such as Senator Richard Russell, had conceded defeat in their efforts, had begun to say that although the original intervention had been a mistake and the future looked grim, there was now nothing to do but support the troops and hence the policy. Negotiating efforts did not cease with these developments—diplomatic activity would grow intense in the late spring and summer and would wax and wane for the next eight years—but thereafter these efforts would be about ending a major military conflict rather than preventing one. By the time a settlement was reached, at the beginning of 1973, under terms no better than Washington could have had in 1963 or 1964 or 1965, fifty-eight thousand Americans, and between 1.5 and three million Vietnamese, lay dead.

But it was not only the confluence of events—the initiation of sustained American bombing of North *and* South Vietnam, the dispatch of the first U.S. ground forces, the frenetic attempts to bring about negotiations—that make this four-week period following Pleiku so historically important in the three-decades-long struggle for control of Vietnam. There was also the towering presence throughout these weeks of Lyndon Baines Johnson. This may seem unexceptional, the idea that the president of the United States should be a decisive voice in matters relating to war and peace, and in a way it is: from the time he ascended to the presidency, as we have seen, Johnson's imprint guided and shaped American policy in the war. But his importance became even greater now, his imprint even deeper. Johnson, sometimes depicted in the literature as a restraining influence on U.S. decision making in this period, as a kind of lone dove in an inner circle of hawks, was in fact the biggest hawk of them all—not because he relished the idea of waging this war but because he, more than anyone, dreaded what would happen if he did not.[3] More than anyone in his administration, more even than Dean Rusk, it was Lyndon Johnson who opposed negotiations in February, March, April, who saw diplomacy as a sign of weakness and something to be avoided except on America's terms. When the bombing of North Vietnam failed to bring results and some of his top aides showed signs of doubt, Johnson plowed on. "Come hell or high water," he declared in early March, "we're gonna stay there." McGeorge Bundy would recall that the president "had decided to do whatever he had to do, but he had not decided how much he had to do."[4]

Johnson had help, of course. Whatever objections senior advisers had to his withholding the truth about the escalation, they quickly swallowed them and joined in the deception. Whatever doubts some of them developed about massive bombing, or about the dispatch of ground troops, or about committing those ground troops to combat, they pushed them aside and pledged enthusiastic support. External champions of escalation, individuals such as Joseph Alsop and Richard Nixon, also reinforced the president's determination. More important, LBJ had help from his opponents, from those who had always been against an Americanized war. The permissive context of earlier months was still there in the late winter and spring, and it mattered more now, because the real shooting was about to start. Some critics of escalation spoke out strongly against American policy, and the administration worried a great deal about how to respond to them, as we shall see. But the most important ones, the Senate Democratic leadership and the British government, time and again in these critical weeks showed themselves unwilling to state publicly what they believed privately, to challenge the administration's interpretation of the stakes, of the risks, of the costs. In that way, these dissenters, whose views of the conflict were to prove so prescient, helped carry out the deception, helped perpetuate the illusion of domestic American consensus and Anglo-American unity on the conflict, and thereby helped bring about the tragedy that was the Second Indochina War.

London's public support for American policy was all the more welcome in early 1965 since so many other important governments were openly distancing themselves from the U.S. position. Even before the Pleiku incident, the Japanese government, for example, had made clear its concerns about the direction of the fighting and the prospect of a larger American presence in South Vietnam. In advance of Prime Minister Eisaku Sato's mid-January visit to Washington, a National Security Council memo warned that even in conservative circles in Japan "there are serious misgivings about the prospects for success of U.S. Southeast Asia policies and the long-term risk to Japan in over-commitment to the U.S. position." During his talks with American officials Sato pledged support for current levels of U.S. assistance to South Vietnam but voiced strong opposition to American bombing attacks on the DRV, on the grounds that such attacks would fail to achieve their objectives and would send the wrong message to the peoples of Asia. After the meetings, Sato told a group of reporters that the solution for Vietnam must lie with Asians, not westerners. The "rational approach" of the western world would fail to resolve the issue, he said, which meant that the patience and forbearance of the Asian mind held the key.[5]

The Canadian government of Lester Pearson was inclined to agree. A few days after Sato returned to Tokyo, Prime Minister Pearson paid a visit to the LBJ Ranch in Austin, accompanied by his external affairs minister, Paul Martin. Pearson and Martin had been dubious of American aims in Vietnam since the previous spring, and they had been dismayed by the intransigent position Washington had adopted vis-à-vis the Seaborn missions to Hanoi. Even before they flew to Texas, the two men were apprehensive about what lay ahead, and the visit appears to have confirmed their fears. In the words of a Pearson biographer, "the discussions were a turning point in the Canadian perception of American involvement," as the president made clear his determination to continue the fight. The visit may also have been a turning point in Pearson's opinion of Johnson. The two had never been close, but Pearson was surprised and put off by his host's demeanor and actions, which included a wild automobile ride around the massive ranch and LBJ urging the prime minister to join him in "taking a leak" at the side of the car. (Pearson declined.) At dinner Johnson completely dominated the conversation and constantly interrupted anyone who tried to get a word in.[6]

Pearson's and Sato's fears of a larger war appeared confirmed with the Pleiku attack and American retaliation in early February. To them, and to numerous other world leaders, a dramatic increase in the fighting seemed imminent. They still hoped, however, that the incident would be a replay of the Gulf of Tonkin affair of the previous August, in which an apparent North Vietnamese attack on U.S. ships had led merely to a one-time American reprisal strike. Perhaps escalation could still be headed off. To that end, Indian prime minister Lal Bahadur Shastri on 7 February appealed to Johnson and Soviet premier Alexei Kosygin, then visiting Hanoi, to keep the peace in Vietnam. The following day, the Indian government issued a call for a cease-fire and the convening of a Geneva-type conference on the war. Pearson followed by pledging his government's support in arranging a conference and publicly distancing himself from U.S. policy. The Tokyo government urged the need for "restraint," and Pakistani leader Mohammad

Ayub Khan, long an opponent of America's growing involvement in the war, appealed for a diplomatic solution. In Paris, the de Gaulle government declared French support for Shastri's proposal and called for an end to foreign intervention in Vietnam. No amount of U.S. firepower would win the war, de Gaulle declared. Also in Paris, at a meeting of the North Atlantic Treaty Organization's Permanent Council, the European delegates, while generally supportive of U.S. aims in the conflict, left no doubt as to their anxiety in posing a series of searching questions to the American NATO ambassador, Thomas K. Finletter.[7]

Not all the foreign reactions to the reprisal strikes were hostile. Support came from expected quarters, from the Australians, the South Koreans, the Thais, the British. But in the British case, at least, it was the most grudging support imaginable. The Wilson government on 8 February issued a statement backing the air strikes, and new foreign secretary Michael Stewart did his best to defend the U.S. actions in spirited sparring with fellow Labourites in the House of Commons. Privately, however, British officials felt little different from their counterparts in France. Ever since his return from the Washington meetings of early December, Wilson had grown more concerned about the deepening politico-military deterioration in South Vietnam and the seeming proclivity of Lyndon Johnson to expand the fighting. At the end of December, he had sought the views of then–foreign secretary Patrick Gordon Walker on a possible British initiative aimed at allowing the United States to extricate itself from the mess in Vietnam. Walker was not enthusiastic, suggesting that any British move toward a conference should follow, not precede, the administration's acknowledgment that no other viable solution existed. "It would give great and probably lasting offence for us to suggest this idea to the United States at this stage," Walker had said. But Wilson continued to fret in January, continued to hear the drumbeat of pessimism from the Foreign Office and from many in the British press. Late in the month, he and other top British officials considered asking the Johnson administration if it thought the time opportune for a British diplomatic intervention aimed at getting a settlement.[8]

They were still discussing this option when the Pleiku attack occurred. For Wilson the audaciousness of this Vietcong attack on American forces spoke volumes about the dire state of the war, and he was acutely concerned by the U.S. decision to launch a retaliatory attack while Kosygin was still in Hanoi. The prime minister's apprehension increased on 10 February, when it became clear that the American reprisal would *not* be another isolated incident as in the Gulf of Tonkin. On this day, Lyndon Johnson ordered another major retaliatory strike, this time in response to a Vietcong attack on American barracks at Qui Nhon, seventy-five miles east of Pleiku on the central coast. (Guerrillas planted a hundred-pound bomb under a building, and the ensuing blast killed twenty-three American servicemen.) The expanded war anticipated in the Americans' November policy review appeared to have arrived, especially after McGeorge Bundy confirmed as much to Lord Harlech on the morning of the tenth. Wilson determined that he had to fly to Washington at once, to try to dissuade Johnson from going forward with escalation and, equally important, to show nervous Labour back-benchers and the British public that he was doing something to head off a major war.

At 1:00 A.M. London time on 11 February, Wilson called Lord Harlech in Washington, and the ambassador agreed to call the White House to request authorization for a Wilson visit. An hour later, Harlech called back. He had spoken to McGeorge Bundy, who told him the president was strongly against a visit on the grounds that it would smack too much of desperation. But Wilson would not be so easily deterred. He opted to call Johnson himself, right then, despite the lateness of the hour. Another call went into the White House. Could Wilson wait until morning to speak to the president? Bundy asked. No, Wilson replied, he needed to have something to bring to his cabinet at that time.[9]

At 3:15 A.M., London time, 10:15 P.M. in Washington, the call was finally put through on the "hot line." The conversation began poorly and got worse. A visit to Washington would be a serious mistake, Johnson said. There was nothing to get upset about, and nothing Britain could do to change the U.S. position. No gain could come from "jump[ing] around the Atlantic every time there is a critical situation." Wilson stood his ground. Britain had been a strong supporter of U.S. actions, he reminded Johnson, but now there was great concern in London about the recent developments and about the hazards of escalation, and great pressure on his government to do something. "We are under very strong pressure from both sides of Parliament about the long-term solution," he said. There had been heavy criticism "that we have not been taking the initiative in calling a conference. So far as any talks are concerned we do like to know what you think." Hence the need for a face-to-face meeting. Johnson was unmoved. "I won't tell you how to run Malaysia and you don't tell us how to run Vietnam," he snapped. Would Wilson like it if he, Johnson, told the American press tomorrow that he was going over to London to try to stop the British in Malaysia? What was the use of more talk? "If you want to help us some in Vietnam send us some men and send us some folks to deal with these guerrillas," the president declared. "And announce to the Press that you are going to help us. Now if you don't feel like doing that, go on with your Malaysian problem."

One can imagine the thoughts that ran through Wilson's mind as he took in these words. Here it was, the middle of the night, and he was getting a tongue-lashing from the president of the United States. Johnson was showing not the slightest sympathy for his predicament. He tried another tack, noting that there was concern also among friendly voices in the international community, but Johnson merely responded that none of these countries were great allies. ("France is a problem, and India has never taken up arms for us.") Sensing futility, Wilson said it was too bad he would have nothing to report to his cabinet except this phone call, and LBJ shot back that it was the prime minister and not he who had placed the call; all he had done was answer it.[10]

It was an altogether extraordinary conversation, whose perfunctory concluding pledges of mutual support could not hide the tension that had been present throughout. The call had laid bare the growing Anglo-American differences over the war. More than that, it had revealed something that would become increasingly pronounced in the coming months: Lyndon Johnson's impatience with critics of his Vietnam policy, especially foreign ones. Wilson had appealed to him as a close ally, as someone concerned about the rising tension who faced domestic pressure to be seen doing something, and Johnson had brusquely cut him off and told him to mind his own business. He rejected a Wilson visit because it would cause publicity and thus interfere with his plan to keep the escalation secret—as he said at one point during the call, a visit "would be very misunderstood here." (His real fear was that its meaning would be all too well understood.) But he also rejected it because he believed it would be pointless. No comment in the conversation spoke more loudly than his asking Wilson what use there could be in more talking about Vietnam. It suggested a man whose mind was made up. Moreover, it suggested a man tone-deaf to the subtleties of diplomacy. Close aides, even hawkish ones like McGeorge Bundy, would spend much time in the ensuing months urging Johnson to remember the importance of preserving outward British support for the war effort, and that Wilson therefore needed to be wooed just like any domestic critic. Bundy may even have made the plea this time, for the morning after the phone call Johnson sent Wilson a gracious note suggesting a visit a few weeks later (it would not occur for more than two months).[11]

Notwithstanding his ire with Harold Wilson, Johnson could be thankful the British leader continued to keep his advocacy private. Others were less reticent. When LBJ awoke the next morning, with Wilson's words perhaps still ringing in his ear, he got the same pro-diplomacy line from two voices he considered as important as the British leader: Walter Lippmann and the

New York Times. Lippmann had actually given tentative support for the
Pleiku reprisal raids three days earlier (on the grounds that they might
hasten a settlement), but he was fast losing faith in the one belief he had
clung to throughout 1964: that Lyndon Johnson, when push came to shove,
would rule out escalation, that the president was at heart more of a dove
than his advisers. Up to now, his tendency in columns on Vietnam had been
to condemn the proponents of a military solution while assuring readers
that Lyndon Johnson was not one of them. (His constant repetition of this
point in the period after the election suggests he was less confident than
he proclaimed.) As recently as the previous week, on 2 February, Lippmann
had lauded Johnson for grasping an essential truth, namely that the world
had entered a new era, marked by reduced Cold War tensions. The Soviet
threat was much diminished, which meant that American leaders, for the
first time in a quarter century, could shift their main attention from foreign
affairs to long-neglected domestic ills. Johnson, Lippmann had declared, was
a far-sighted leader whose focus was squarely on matters of the home front.[12]

On this day, however, Lippmann struck a different tone. The escalate-
or-withdraw decision, skillfully postponed by a president anxious to proceed by consensus, could be postponed no longer. "Desirable as the policy
of consensus is for dealing with the great domestic issues—such as civil
rights, labor and capital, the welfare state—for pressing problems in the
realm of great power politics there must be a decision and choice," the columnist maintained. "The choice which has to be decided is between full-
scale war and a negotiated truce. I say full-scale war because if the choice is
to seek a military solution the country must be prepared for the worst."
Returning to a point he had first made more than a year earlier, Lippmann
rejected as immaterial the administration's standard assertion that talk of
negotiations would only demoralize the South Vietnamese (why were they
so easily disheartened? he asked), and he called instead for a "diplomatic
offensive." Just what this phrase meant the columnist did not say, but he
insisted that the administration's practice of demanding what amounted to
North Vietnam's unconditional surrender was pointless.[13]

The *Times,* in a lead editorial entitled "Black Day in Vietnam," lamented
the "frightening 'normality' of the situation" in Vietnam, with events "occurring with the inexorability of a Greek tragedy." The paper lauded Charles
de Gaulle's claim the day before that the United States could never win
the war regardless of how much military power it committed, and it expressed grave doubts whether even the lesser objective of merely improving
America's negotiating position by hitting the DRV could ever be achieved.
"The greatest weakness of this reprisal policy against North Vietnam is

that while it [is] true the Vietcong gets [sic] orders, advice, some arms and some men from North Vietnam, the war is being fought in South Vietnam. . . . The Vietcong live and operate in South Vietnam, using American arms captured from the Vietnamese. The peasants either help them, or accept them, or are cowed into submission by them." Hence the soundness of the French president's assertion that a diplomatic solution had to be found: "There may still be a choice: talk or fight," the editorial concluded. "If everybody waits too long, the chance to talk will be gone."

A few blocks away from the New York Times Building, at the United Nations, a growing number of delegations concurred that de Gaulle's position on the war was correct and that the chance for diplomacy was fast disappearing. That morning, Secretary General U Thant conferred with several of the organization's top officials, including General Assembly president Alex Quaison-Sackey of Ghana and Security Council president Roger Seydoux of France. Both encouraged him to issue a public plea for UN-sponsored negotiations. The same day in Rome, Pope Paul VI called for a negotiated settlement to the war sponsored and guaranteed by the UN.[14]

Thant was ambivalent. On the one hand, he felt certain that a Security Council meeting on Vietnam would be a waste of time, because the North Vietnamese and the Chinese, neither of whom held membership in the UN, would deny the organization's competence, while Moscow, angered over the recent U.S. air strikes against the DRV, would say it was a war of liberation, an indigenous civil war against colonialist puppets in Saigon. The Soviets would veto any resolution calling for a cessation of infiltration and a cease-fire to be followed by negotiations, Thant believed. On the other hand, he had never been more convinced that America was fighting a losing battle in Vietnam, and he remained angry with Washington for repeatedly rejecting the bilateral talks he had tried to arrange with Hanoi. In early 1965 he was more convinced than ever that Ho Chi Minh could be weaned from Beijing and indeed become the Tito of Southeast Asia, and that an American escalation of the war would fail in its objectives and would drive the North Vietnamese into the arms of the Chinese.

In January, after having been ill for much of December, Thant had resumed pressing Stevenson for an indication that the administration would enter talks with Hanoi. Stevenson had replied that the United States was reluctant to enter into such a dialogue because of the embarrassment that would result if word of it leaked. Thant professed to see the cogency of this argument but said some risks had to be taken. Time was being wasted, and Hanoi might change its mind about negotiating at all. If bilateral talks were out of the question, he had asked Stevenson, what about a meeting of the five great powers (the United States, the Soviet Union, Britain, France, and

China) along with North and South Vietnam? Such a "five-plus-two" arrangement might be less cumbersome than a full-fledged Geneva-type conference. Stevenson was sympathetic, but as before, there was no response from Rusk or the White House.[15]

Thant decided the time had come to speak out publicly. He despaired at the rising tension in the conflict and welcomed the growing international clamor for negotiations. On 12 February, after conferring again with Seydoux and Quaison-Sackey and after reminding the deputy U.S. representative to the UN, Charles Yost, that he had still not heard back from Washington about talks with North Vietnam, even though Hanoi had responded positively, he held a televised press conference. "I am greatly disturbed by recent events in Southeast Asia, and particularly by the seriously deteriorating situation in Vietnam," Thant declared. "My fear, frankly, is in regard to the dangerous possibilities of escalation, because such a situation, if it should once get out of control, would obviously pose the gravest threat to the peace of the world." Informing his audience that he had publicly advocated a diplomatic solution for the past six months and more, Thant said recent developments had further convinced him that "means must be found, and found urgently, within or outside the United Nations, of shifting the quest for a solution away from the field of battle to the conference table."[16]

The administration had feared this development, in which leading international figures followed one another in clamoring for negotiations. How to respond to it became a central concern among senior officials in the days and weeks that followed. This was a significant change: although most officials were no more interested than before in actually pursuing an early political settlement of the war, they now strategized almost constantly about the negotiations issue and how to finesse it. Knowing that the diplomatic pressure would rise as the new military actions were implemented, U.S. officials sought, as a cable to the Saigon embassy put it, to lengthen the time before "negotiation pressure becomes extreme, or dangers of a sharp Communist response become substantial, or both, while at the same time maintaining the necessary pattern or response and pressure both to strengthen the South Vietnam situation and eventually to affect Hanoi attitudes." In order to keep down international "and even U.S." pressure for negotiations, another internal document stated, the bombing attacks on North Vietnam must not be too frequent or intense.[17]

On 11 February, the Joint Chiefs of Staff produced an eight-week plan for air strikes against North Vietnam, in conjunction with continued existing Oplan 34-A actions, resumption of Desoto patrols, and authorization of cross-border patrols. In keeping with instructions laid down by McNamara three days earlier, the air strike plan was much more limited than one the JCS had put forth in November. Whereas that one had urged the destruction of all ninety-four targets identified back in May 1964, this one called for U.S. and South Vietnamese aircraft to attack four fixed targets and to fly air interdiction missions over two road segments per week, almost all of them south of the nineteenth parallel. The Chiefs were far from confident that this program would work, stating merely that, although the plan "almost certainly would not lead Hanoi to restrain the Viet Cong . . . if the United States persevered in the face of threats and international pressures, and as the degree of damage inflicted on North Vietnam increased, the chances of a reduction in Viet Cong activity would rise." If the DRV did not cease supporting the insurgency, the air strikes would have to grow more frequent and move above the nineteenth parallel, the report said.[18]

The Chiefs' plan, code-named Rolling Thunder, won general favor from the president and his top aides, and at a meeting on 13 February Johnson formally approved the action that had been discussed for the past year and anticipated for almost as long: the sustained bombing of North Vietnam. Little discussion accompanied the decision, largely because the real choice had been made several weeks earlier but also because no one in a position to do so rose up to dissent. Undersecretary of State George Ball did produce a memo for the meeting, one he later said had been designed to "shake up" the president and "smoke out" the differences among the senior advisers, but which reads as if it was designed to do neither. That Ball felt deep pessimism about the prospects in the war cannot be doubted. Along with Vice President Hubert H. Humphrey he had tried in vain during the 10 February NSC meeting to delay the Qui Nhon reprisal strikes until Soviet premier Alexei Kosygin had departed North Vietnam. In a phone conversation the following day he and Humphrey determined that they had to try to take LBJ "down this road we are starting on and show him where it can lead," and to suggest the need for a genuine diplomatic track. To that end Ball, enlisting the help of fellow State Department skeptic Llewellyn Thompson, drafted a memo in time for the 13 February meeting.[19]

It was an odd piece of work. Short of a crushing military defeat, Ball and Thompson declared, Hanoi would "never abandon the aggressive course it has pursued at great cost for ten years and give up all the progress it has made in the Communization of South Vietnam." It was therefore wholly unrealistic to believe, as the "McNamara-Bundy position" posited, that North Vietnam could be coerced into calling off "the insurgency in the South and withdraw[ing] those elements infiltrated in the past." By insisting on such action the United States was demanding what amounted to "unconditional surrender." Moreover, Ball and Thompson said, escalation would not be supported by allied governments, and it would worsen the prospects for improved Soviet-American relations.

Even as they made these observations, however, the two men voiced support for the air strikes undertaken up until now and even for "a program of gradually increasing military pressure." Only by adopting such a program, they wrote, could the United States "achieve a bargaining position that can make possible an international arrangement that will avoid a humiliating defeat for the United States." With time, after the bombing had improved the bargaining position, a diplomatic settlement could be reached that would allow the United States to reduce its involvement in the war and also "stop the insurgency in South Vietnam and deliver the entire country south of the seventeenth parallel to the government in Saigon free and clear of insurgency." Just how much time? Months? Years? Ball and Thompson did not say.[20]

The Ball-Thompson memorandum thus did not raise too many hackles among senior officials; it seemed to allow for an indefinite delay in any move to negotiations. And delaying talks was exactly what Johnson and his closest advisers wished to do. They wanted, in essence, to fight first and talk later, to talk only once the military situation had been turned around. The question was whether it could be turned around. Lippmann and the *Times* suggested it could not, using arguments that would be made by countless critics in the months and years to come. Even now, several administration officials expressed doubts. Leonard Unger, William Bundy's top deputy at the Far East desk at the State Department, told a British embassy official that the United States was stepping up its efforts in the war but that he was pessimistic that there would ever be a politically stable South Vietnamese government. Robert H. Johnson of the Policy Planning Council agreed with the *New York Times*'s view that the time for diplomacy would soon pass—once escalation occurred, he told William Bundy, negotiation would be impossible. Hanoi would become intransigent, as would the Soviets and Chinese.[21]

James C. Thomson Jr., who was McGeorge Bundy's deputy at the NSC and who had long been convinced that South Vietnam was a lost cause, realized that time was running out on any alternative policy. To NSC colleague Chester Cooper he complained: "What has happened to the concept of 'negotiation' so earnestly pursued by our more thoughtful journalistic and Congressional critics, and previously pursued by many thoughtful people here and at State? Are we ruling it out? If so, for how long?" Those were not questions that Cooper could answer, so Thomson opted to write to

Bundy with his misgivings. Identifying his position as "one dove's lament," Thomson maintained that the administration was giving much too little attention to possible openings for negotiations—"the only rational alternative" to a major military commitment. The administration, he argued, had slipped into a gross overcommitment of national prestige and resources on political, military, and geographic terrain which should long ago have persuaded us to avoid such a commitment." What mattered most, therefore, was that the United States find itself a "face-saving avenue of retreat— that we marshal our imaginations and those of other powers to discover such an avenue." Thomson insisted that any policy of sustained bombing of the North entailed "greater risks than we have any right to take in terms of our world-wide interests."[22]

But the most significant effort aimed at stopping and reversing the move to war came from none other than Vice President Hubert Humphrey. On 11 February, the same day he and Ball had agreed to caution Johnson about the dangers ahead in the war, Humphrey told aide John Reilly that he intended soon to sit down with the president and his top aides "to discuss U.S. policy on Southeast Asia in all its implications." Humphrey must have known that time was short, but he misjudged just how short. On 13 February, while traveling in Georgia, he received a phone call from the State Department's Thomas Hughes, who headed the Bureau of Intelligence and Research and who knew that Humphrey shared his opposition to a larger war. The "die is cast," Hughes told him; any last attempt to head off major escalation must happen right away. The following day, Hughes joined Humphrey in Georgia and the two men spent the weekend looking at the latest cables and memos and deciding on a course of action. The only thing to do, they agreed, was for Humphrey to spell out his concerns in a memorandum to Johnson. With Hughes's help, Humphrey produced a document that detailed his fears of escalation and his reasons for believing that extrication was possible in domestic political terms.[23]

The result was a tour de force, a memorandum that must rank as one of the most incisive and prescient memos ever written on the prospect of an Americanized war in Vietnam. Less concerned than Ball and Thompson with the international implications of escalation, Humphrey emphasized the domestic political dilemmas that were sure to result. If the administration proved unable to limit the American military commitment, Humphrey warned, the nation would find itself "embroiled deeper in fighting in Vietnam over the next few months." Such an outcome could mean political trouble for the administration: "American wars have to be politically understandable by the American public. There has to be a cogent, convincing case if we are to enjoy sustained public support. In World Wars I and II we had this. In Korea we were moving under United Nations auspices to South Korea against dramatic, across-the-border, conventional aggression."

In Vietnam, Humphrey argued, the situation was different. Americans were confused by the perplexities of the conflict and by the administration's shifting rationale for U.S. involvement. The constant chaos in Saigon only increased this bewilderment, while undermining "political support for our policy." The public, Humphrey noted, "simply can't understand why we would run grave risks to support a country which is totally unable to put its house in order." The best solution, therefore, was for Johnson to reduce rather than increase an American commitment few Americans understood. Humphrey insisted that such a move would be politically possible. True, it was always hard to cut losses. "But the Johnson administration is in a stronger position to do so now than any administration in this century. Nineteen-sixty-five is the year of minimum political risk for the Johnson administration. Indeed, it is the first year when we can face the Vietnam problem without being preoccupied with the political repercussions from the Republican right." In the recent campaign, Humphrey reminded Johnson, "we stressed not enlarging the war"—and won by a landslide.[24]

The final draft of Humphrey's memo was submitted to the president on 17 February. It was a Wednesday, a day of feverish activity on Vietnam both inside and outside the American government. In London that morning, U.S. ambassador David Bruce called on Harold Wilson at 10 Downing Street. It was the second meeting in two days between them. The previous day Bruce had suggested that Washington would commence regular air action against the DRV but also would be open to "preliminary discussions" along the lines of the "five-plus-two" formula outlined by U Thant. The administration wanted to negotiate, Bruce had assured his host. This morning, however, the ambassador carried a different message. He told the prime minister that the State Department had recommended, and thought the president would concur in, continuing air and naval action against North Vietnam whenever and wherever necessary. American thinking had been and continued to be that any such action would be limited and fitting and adequate as a response to the continuous aggression in South Vietnam directed by Hanoi. Within twenty-four hours after the next military action the administration expected to make a statement, Bruce went on; very likely it would come from Dean Rusk rather than the president. The statement would make absolutely clear that the United States was committed to the South Vietnamese government, and it would call on Hanoi to leave its neighbors alone. A presentation would also be made to the UN Security Council detailing North Vietnam's aggression. The United States, Bruce said, did not plan to indicate a "readiness for talks or negotiations at this time."

Wilson listened with growing consternation. What had happened to the stated American willingness to negotiate? he asked when Bruce finished. The plan now appeared to be to step up military action without making any corresponding proposals for a political solution. This was "the pill without the jam." Britain and the whole outside world would have a hard time supporting the United States, he warned, if it could see no light at the end of the tunnel. Thus if Adlai Stevenson went before the Security Council and charged the DRV with aggression without also indicating any readiness to negotiate, he would be in for a very rough reception. Wilson said he was "deeply concerned" by this American rejection of early talks. Bruce expressed sympathy with the prime minister's comments and claimed he did not know the reasons for the administration's evident lack of interest in exploring a diplomatic solution. He pledged to report to Washington that in Britain's view American readiness to negotiate was a cardinal part of the equation.[25]

Later in the day, London got confirmation of the fundamental American intransigence on the question of diplomacy. In Washington, British ambassador Lord Harlech met with Dean Rusk and told him the Soviet government had expressed interest in a possible Soviet-British initiative to bring about a settlement in Vietnam. (Britain and the USSR, it will be recalled, were the cochairs of the 1954 Geneva Conference.) The British government thought this possibility should be explored, Harlech said, but also thought it would have little prospect of leading anywhere unless the United States spelled out more fully what its intentions were in Vietnam. Simply highlighting the iniquities of the other side would no longer suffice. Rusk was unmoved. He agreed that it might be useful for Britain to continue its cochair role with Moscow on Vietnam but said that the United States would not consider negotiations unless there was some possibility they would be successful—meaning, in Rusk's view, that South Vietnam would remain independent and secure from communist aggression. Moreover, to spell out publicly the conditions under which the United States would negotiate would be to lose flexibility and the possibility of probing the other side's attitude, he said. In the same way, if the administration proposed an agenda or conditions for a conference, these might be rejected out of hand by the communists, thereby closing off that possibility.[26]

Upon hearing of Rusk's comments British foreign secretary Michael

Stewart was bemused. What was needed from the secretary of state and the president, he wrote Harlech, "was some indication of American readiness to do something other than responsive military action. In brief, what were the circumstances in which they were ready to talk. . . . I cannot see that if the Americans were to spell this out in public they would lose flexibility and the possibility of probing the other side's attitude. It could and would be argued that exactly the opposite was the case, since it would then be for the other side to show where they stood."[27]

At the same time that Rusk and Harlech were meeting at Foggy Bottom, on Capitol Hill a "Vietnam debate" of sorts at last got under way in the Senate. Since the start of the year lawmakers and journalists had called for a debate, but it had taken until this day, 17 February, for it actually to begin. Up to now Johnson and his aides had successfully thwarted all moves to start the discussion, but during a dinner conversation at the home of Walter Lippmann a few days earlier several senators, including Frank Church and South Dakota Democrat George McGovern, decided they had to move. In the opening speech Church, adhering to his policy of not criticizing Johnson personally, faulted what he called America's "overinvolvement" in the excolonial regions of the world. The administration liked to claim that it had to prevent the fall of Southeast Asia, "but the hard fact of the matter is that there are limits to what we can do in helping any Government surmount a Communist uprising," he declared. "If the people themselves will not support the Government in power, we cannot save it. . . . The Saigon Government is losing its war, not for lack of equipment, but for lack of internal cohesion. The Viet Cong grow stronger, not because they are better supplied than Saigon, but because they are united in their will to fight. This spirit cannot be imported; it must come from within." The best solution from America's perspective, Church concluded, was a negotiated settlement leading to a neutral Indochina.[28]

Wisconsin Democrat Gaylord Nelson then took the floor to laud Church's speech, as did Democrats McGovern and Stephen Young of Ohio. McGovern said his mail was running fifteen to one in favor of a cease-fire and negotiations, and he noted: "It is not appeasement to recognize that the problem of Southeast Asia does not lend itself to a military solution. It is not appeasement for the mightiest military power in the world to recognize the limits of that power, and to commit itself reasonably and wisely. . . . We could pulverize the great cities of China and North Vietnam and still not end the guerrilla warfare." Missouri Democrat Stuart Symington did not mention negotiations in his speech but called for a "major reappraisal" of America's involvement in the war.[29]

There was also strong support offered for American policy that first day in the Senate chamber. It came from Wyoming Democrat Gale McGee, who had also attended the Lippmann dinner and who did not share his host's position on the war. "If Vietnam goes," McGee told his colleagues, "Cambodia goes, Thailand goes, Malaysia goes, Indonesia goes, the Philippines go. . . . We have risked too much to fritter it away with indecision at this moment; for fully as much rests on the right decision in Vietnam as rested on the right decision in Greece, Berlin, Germany, or Korea." McGee said he opposed negotiations over Vietnam at the current moment and lamented that the "resurgent isolationism of the 1960s jeopardizes the prospects of our ultimate triumph." He went on to advocate bombing of all military bases, air fields, and encampments in North Vietnam unless Vietcong infiltration into the South ceased. Should that not work, the United States ought to bomb bridges and supply lines, and if that too failed to do the job, industrial centers should be hit. Not long after he left the Senate floor, McGee received a telephone call from "a very high Administration official," thanking him for the speech.[30]

Even more welcome to the White House was the support that came on this day from Republicans. The joint Senate-House Republican leadership issued a statement that said "there can be no negotiations" in Vietnam as long as there was infiltration of South Vietnam from the North. "We urge the President to make this clear to the world," said the group, headed by the Senate minority leader, Everett M. Dirksen of Illinois, and the House minority leader, Gerald R. Ford of Michigan. Former president Dwight Eisenhower, meanwhile, in a morning meeting with Johnson in the White House Cabinet Room, voiced strong support for U.S. policy. Johnson read him the cable to Ambassador Bruce spelling out the immediate plans; Eisenhower, unlike Harold Wilson, found the wording appropriate. Do not negotiate from weakness, Eisenhower told LBJ. Wilson's attitude could be explained by the fact that the Briton did not have much experience with this kind of problem, whereas Americans had learned that Munichs won nothing. As a result, Eisenhower said, his answer to the British would be, "Not now, boys." What about the likelihood of Russian or Chinese intervention following U.S. escalation? Johnson asked. That was unlikely, Eisenhower responded, and regardless, it should not deter the administration from acting. He said he hoped the United States could avoid becoming overdeployed in Indochina but that ground troops should be sent if necessary, and he counseled Johnson to use any weapons available to turn the war effort around—even tactical nuclear weapons, he suggested, deserved serious consideration.[31]

Buoyed by Eisenhower's support, Johnson reaffirmed American determination near the end of a speech to the National Industrial Conference

Board early in the afternoon. "We seek no wider war," he declared, but "we will persist in the defense of freedom, and our continuing actions will be those which are justified and those that are made necessary by the continuing aggression of others. Those measures will be measured, fitting, and adequate. Our stamina and the stamina of the American people is equal to the task." Some aides had urged him to use the occasion to make a full presidential statement on the war, along the lines Britain had requested, but Johnson refused. (Thus the British reaction upon getting a transcript of the speech: Johnson's solemn assurances that he sought "no wider war" explained nothing, Michael Stewart complained to Harlech.)[32]

One other event of note took place on 17 February: a meeting in the afternoon between McGeorge Bundy and Walter Lippmann. The administration attached more importance than ever to courting the veteran journalist, to making him feel as if his counsel mattered, to keeping him from breaking fully with Johnson; more often than not, Bundy performed the duty. Lippmann, clearly sensing the direction of American policy, began the encounter by saying he would not be startled if air action across the seventeenth parallel continued even without Vietcong attacks in the South. Bundy skirted a direct answer. The administration, he assured Lippmann, was not planning any immediate all-out bombardment of Hanoi. When Lippmann said the situation in South Vietnam was hopeless, Bundy countered that it was difficult but in no sense hopeless. "Walter is not really happy about our present posture, but just the same he is doing his best to support it," Bundy informed the president that evening. "I gave him a lecture to the effect that calling a conference now was no way to get an honorable settlement, and he professed to see my point. He said that all he meant was that we must use the tools of diplomacy. I said I fully agreed, as long as it was understood that one of the major tools of diplomacy was the Seventh Fleet. He said he not only agreed but had repeatedly made this point." All in all, Bundy concluded, the meeting had gone well.[33]

Maybe so, but Lippmann's column, ready that evening for inclusion in the next morning's *Washington Post* and scores of other newspapers, minced no words. "The easy way to avoid the truth is to persuade ourselves that this is not really a civil war but is in fact essentially an invasion of South VietNam by North VietNam," the columnist wrote. "This has produced the argument that the way to stabilize South VietNam is [to] wage war against North VietNam." The strategy would never work. "Apart from the question of the morality and the gigantic risks of escalating the war, there is not sufficient reason to think that the Northern communists can be bombed into submission." Escalation was thus a disastrous prospect: "For this country to involve itself in such a war in Asia would be an act of supreme folly. While the warhawks would rejoice when it began, the people would weep before it ended." No viable option existed for the United States, Lippmann concluded, except a negotiated solution. The time had come when a settlement "should be the avowed objective, an objective pursued with all our many and very considerable diplomatic resources."[34]

At the *New York Times*, meanwhile, two stories on Vietnam were being prepared for the top of page one of the next morning's paper. Both concerned negotiations. In one, titled "Washington Still Rejects Any Vietnam Negotiations," reporter Max Frankel examined the growing pressure for a diplomatic solution and the continued White House intransigence on the issue. "In Congress, in the diplomatic corps, in the mail reaching Washington, there is more and more talk in favor of 'negotiations' over Vietnam," Frankel wrote. "But the Administration continued today to shun the word or any other suggestion that it might wish to bargain for peace." The second article, headlined "Johnson Asserts U.S. Will Persist in Vietnam Policy" and written by Charles Mohr, contrasted the president's reaffirmation of American policy before the National Industrial Conference Board with the Senate Democratic calls for a negotiated settlement. And on the editorial page, in what had become an almost-daily exhortation against escalation in Vietnam, the paper remarked that "the missing part of Johnson's policy is any hint of the circumstances under which a negotiated settlement, of the type proposed by Secretary General Thant of the United Nations, might be approached. Without such a move the potentiality of vastly expanded war increases each day."[35]

That was the way it would be in the two weeks that followed: continued pressure from important international and domestic voices for an American negotiating initiative to go along with any military action, coupled with administration resistance to any such move. On 18 February the administration did reach agreement with the British to have London propose to Moscow that the two cochairs ask the Geneva powers for their opinions on what ought to be done in Vietnam, but U.S. officials did not expect (or want) anything meaningful to result from the plan; they indeed saw it mostly as a means to delay any actual negotiations on the war, and as a way to placate the British and keep them on board in support of U.S. policy.[36]

Likewise, the administration continued to reject U Thant's offer to facilitate "five-plus-two" preliminary discussions on the war. Thant, feeling the heat from more and more UN delegations to do something to bring about a cease-fire, revealed his frustration during a press conference on 24 February. For several months he had acceded to American requests that he not publicize his efforts at starting talks; he could stay silent no longer.

He told the reporters that he had been conducting private discussions with various nations involved in the Vietnam conflict and had made "concrete ideas and proposals," the nature of which he could not publicly divulge. The chances for peace were becoming more remote, Thant warned, but time had not run out on gaining a diplomatic solution that would allow the United States to withdraw gracefully. "I am sure that the great American people, if only they know the true facts and the background to the developments in South Vietnam, will agree with me that further bloodshed is unnecessary."[37]

Johnson was livid when he heard of Thant's comments. He had White House press secretary George Reedy declare emphatically: "There are no authorized negotiations under way with Mr. Thant or any other government." In fact, said Reedy, the United States had yet to receive from any source any "meaningful" proposal for negotiations. At ten o'clock that evening, Dean Rusk called Thant and expressed the administration's dismay at his reference to truth being withheld from Americans. Compared to the other nations involved in the Vietnamese affair, Rusk said, Americans were certainly much more fully informed. Thant responded by asking if Rusk knew of his talks with Adlai Stevenson over the past eighteen months. Yes, Rusk replied, but the proposals were just procedural and did not give any indication that the talks would lead to an agreement. Thant said that whereas in September Hanoi had agreed to talks, the United States had avoided responding on the matter for six months now. Rusk replied that bilateral talks were out of the question, particularly since there were no signs they would be fruitful.[38]

The next afternoon, 25 February, Rusk held a press conference. He told a packed room of reporters that there could be no negotiations on the war until North Vietnam indicated it would halt its "aggression" against South Vietnam. "The key to peace in Southeast Asia," he said, "is the readiness of all those in that area to live at peace and to leave their neighbors alone. Now there is no mystery about that formulation. Those who are not leaving their neighbors alone know exactly what it means." America wanted peace, Rusk continued, but "what is still missing is any indication that Hanoi is prepared to stop doing what it is doing and what it knows it is doing against its neighbors." He concluded: "This question of calling a conference, under what circumstances—these are procedural matters. What we are interested in, what is needed to restore peace to Southeast Asia, is substance, content, an indication that peace is possible in terms of the appetites and attitudes of the other side."[39]

It would be the only major presentation of American policy surrounding the start of America's war against North Vietnam, and it summarized perfectly Washington's approach to diplomacy in Vietnam, not merely as it had been under Lyndon Johnson but under John F. Kennedy as well. Negotiations, Rusk was saying, could commence only when the enemy indicated he was prepared to give up the fight, to end the insurgency raging throughout the southern part of Vietnam. Talks, when they occurred, would be essentially about determining the terms of the communists' capitulation.

Not all high-level American analysts liked this inflexible posture. Indeed, in the days prior to Rusk's press conference there had occurred a debate of sorts within the administration, with some officials arguing that the United States had to couple its stepped-up military action with a more forthcoming position on negotiations.[40] On 17 February Rusk had received a memorandum from Assistant Secretary of State William Bundy on the pros and cons of an early U.S. "talking initiative." In it Bundy noted that Wilson was restive and that U Thant, as well as the Indian and Canadian governments, was agitating for negotiations. The Soviet Union, Bundy continued, likewise appeared to favor an immediate conference. The pressure was mounting on the administration to reciprocate in some way, and a U.S. initiative for talks might be necessary. Bundy reasoned that the talks would be preliminary and would last for a considerable period of time, during which military action would be continued to improve the U.S./GVN bargaining position. "On balance," he concluded, "I would strongly favor an early initiative."[41]

Adlai Stevenson favored one as well. Keenly aware that sentiment at the UN was running heavily against the American position, and himself sympathetic to U Thant's view of the war and frustrated by Rusk's uncompromising stance, Stevenson saw no option but to write to Johnson directly with his concerns. His letter seconded many of Bundy's points. "I do not believe that we should pursue a harder military line with all the risks it involves without at the same time making it emphatically clear that we prefer a peaceful solution and that we are ready to negotiate," Stevenson wrote. "Moreover, I believe that escalation of the war would diminish our maneuverability and that we should move quickly." Stevenson urged Johnson to accept Thant's proposed "five-plus-two" formula for talks while simultaneously affirming U.S. determination to support the GVN in its struggle. The North Vietnamese might reject the proposal, Stevenson conceded, but then the onus would be on them for the failure of diplomacy.[42]

Robert McNamara and George Ball appear to have thought along similar lines. On 18 February they discussed the British-Soviet cochairs' initiative on the phone and pronounced themselves pleased with it. The beauty of the plan, Ball said, was that it moved Vietnam onto a political track while avoiding a conference. The cochairs would merely ask the relevant parties for their views—no negotiations were involved. America's hands would not be tied. McNamara said that he liked the plan and that the United States had to move toward negotiations. Four days later, on 22 February, McNamara told Lord Harlech that he personally favored a policy of stepping up the military pressure while simultaneously seeking negotiations.[43]

Was McNamara looking for a way to gain the United States an early exit from Vietnam? Probably not, but he was more sympathetic to pursuing the diplomatic route than the other members of Johnson's inner circle—a few weeks hence, in a 5 March meeting with Rusk and McGeorge Bundy, McNamara would advocate seeking full-fledged negotiations in a great-power meeting. According to McGeorge Bundy, McNamara's idea was that "we will need a conference table if things get worse, as he expects."[44]

The other members of the "Awesome Foursome" showed no such inclination. McGeorge Bundy continued in the weeks after his Vietnam trip to advocate the same pro-escalation, antinegotiation posture he had adhered to before it. Do not appear eager for negotiations, he advised Johnson in mid February, as this would be interpreted as a sign of weakness. The sycophantic side of Bundy came to the fore in these weeks, as the national security adviser took every opportunity to praise Johnson for his handling of the war and to convey to the president his own toughness in dealing with administration critics.[45] After Pleiku Bundy had advised Johnson to spell out for the American public what would be required in Vietnam; when LBJ made clear he would do no such thing Bundy switched right around and called a stay-quiet policy the only sensible one. Dean Rusk, meanwhile, privately said pretty much the same thing he said publicly: that negotiations should be undertaken in Vietnam only when they were certain to yield an end to DRV aggression. "Negotiation as a cover for the abandonment of Southeast Asia to the Communist North cannot be accepted," he wrote on 23 February in a memo that advocated an expanded American involvement in the war effort, including if necessary the use of ground troops. At the meeting with Bundy and McNamara on 5 March, Rusk did advocate a somewhat more forthcoming American position on negotiations, but only in order to keep the British on the reservation.[46]

And then there was Lyndon Johnson, the fourth member of the group, the one who had been its dominant voice from the start, from the last week of November 1963. Johnson in February and March 1965 continued to fear the worst in Vietnam, continued to worry about the implications of an expanded U.S. role in the war. But he also continued to be committed to sticking it out. No diplomacy should be attempted, he told aides in the weeks after Pleiku, until the new military measures had been given a chance to work.[47]

Johnson would still on occasion tell the skeptics privately that he shared their sentiments and really wanted out of the war. He may have meant what he said. One reason for his insistence on keeping the escalation quiet was that he sought to preserve the option of pulling back at some point. And indeed, on 15 and 16 February he appears to have expressed some ambivalence about the air campaign and whether he ought to go through with it. As in previous months, however, he was not prepared to really consider the arguments of the skeptics, to explore the possibilities for disengagement from the conflict. Hubert Humphrey's memo of 17 February only infuriated LBJ and caused him to stop listening to the vice president's counsel on Vietnam. When Humphrey, not fully appreciating Johnson's ire, two weeks later gave him another cautionary memorandum, LBJ responded: "We don't need all these memos." From that point on, the vice president of the United States, the nation's second-ranking public official, was banished from all Vietnam policy discussions. He could not be barred from meetings of the National Security Council, of which the vice president is a member by law. But NSC meetings became rare after mid February and were mostly concerned with rubber-stamping decisions already made. Only after many months and after changing his tune and demonstrating utter devotion to the war effort was Humphrey allowed back into the picture.[48]

If Humphrey's banishment represented one sign of the president's inflexible position on the subject of diplomacy in Vietnam, there were many others. Johnson expressed anger at a Tad Szulc story in the *New York Times* on 15 February that suggested that the United States might be open to conference-table negotiations on the war; the administration should not appear eager to talk, he told George Ball, because that would convey weakness. The following day, Johnson summoned the Democratic House leadership—Speaker John McCormack of Massachusetts, Majority Leader Carl Albert of Oklahoma, and Majority Whip Hale Boggs of Louisiana—and gave them a special briefing on Vietnam. Talk of negotiations, he warned them, would only further weaken South Vietnamese morale, and besides, there was no indication that Hanoi or Beijing wanted negotiations anyway. When, the day after that, the proposal emerged for a British-Soviet cochairs' initiative, Johnson alone among the top American officials voiced serious reservations. He expressed the fear that supporting the initiative could somehow make Washington appear desperate for negotiations. And after another briefing for lawmakers on 18 February, Johnson cornered Frank Church and for an hour berated him for advocating a negotiated American withdrawal from Vietnam.[49]

In several meetings with allied government officials in February and March Johnson showed annoyance when asked about early negotiations, exhibiting the same impatience he had shown in his 11 February telephone encounter with Harold Wilson. On 19 February, for example, French foreign minister Maurice Couve de Murville told him in a White House meeting that North Vietnam was more willing than Beijing to enter negotiations on the war, but that the Chinese would likely agree as well. Johnson showed no interest in probing the point and responded that he would not run out on America's commitment to South Vietnam. "I'm not going to write the Vietcong a thank-you note for killing American boys at Pleiku," he declared. If the United States were to "abandon" South Vietnam, "we'd be forced to give up Laos, Thailand, Burma, and be back at Hawaii and San Francisco." Some weeks later Johnson took the same line in a meeting with British foreign secretary Stewart and told aides, after Stewart left, that he thought it insulting for foreign politicians to come "chasing over" to see him. And in a 6 March telephone conversation with George Ball, LBJ threatened to "get sick and leave town" rather than hear the peace proposals of U Thant and Harold Wilson. He told Ball that the negotiations proposals had him feeling as if he was getting "crowded into a corner," and that he expected Ball as his lawyer to diffuse pressure for negotiations until the North Vietnamese had been made to feel the effects of the bombing.[50]

Johnson's complete disavowal of negotiations distinguished him not only from some within his administration but also from a majority of those outside it. One survey of congressional attitudes in mid February revealed that the basics of the Church-McGovern position on the war were publicly shared by at least twenty Senate Democrats, and privately by as many as twenty-five more—a total, that is, of well over half of the party's senators.[51] According to *Newsweek*, there was among legislators in both houses "widespread evidence of a marked split between public support [for the war effort] and private disquiet." Thus although the administration can be said to have gotten the better of the Senate debate that began on 17 February and continued until early March—with impassioned speeches in support of the war by, in particular, McGee, Dirksen, and Connecticut Democrat Thomas Dodd—it was not a good measure of the state of thinking on Capitol Hill. The administration's all-out effort to win over lawmakers kept many senators at least nominally on board, and the floor debate may have ultimately benefited Johnson by forcing many who would rather have been silent to proclaim their support for the president and for expanded military action. Sympathetic senators were urged on by administration officials and were quietly told that the State Department was only too ready to crank out speeches for them to deliver. In the House of Representatives Johnson loyalists, acting with the White House's blessing (and perhaps prompting), used House rules and procedures to prevent potentially damaging hearings or votes from taking place. In mid February, for example, a request from twenty-five Democratic representatives for a hearing on the war, to be conducted by the Foreign Affairs Committee, was turned down.[52]

It amounted to a White House diplomatic offensive, waged not on the international stage in favor of negotiations but on Capitol Hill against them, and it was commanded by Lyndon Johnson himself. The centerpiece of the effort was the series of White House receptions for legislators and their spouses that were held on numerous evenings in the last half of February and early March. A standard script was followed: before a buffet supper, the spouses would go upstairs with Mrs. Johnson while the president assembled the legislators in the Blue Room for briefings with Dean Rusk and Robert McNamara. More often than not, LBJ proceeded to take charge of the discussion, using every ounce of his persuasive powers to make the points that withdrawal would be disastrous for American security, and negotiations were impossible until Hanoi ceased its aggression. Many came away awed. "For the first time in my experience," declared Senator Hugh Scott, Republican of Pennsylvania, "the present President of the United States not only gave us a briefing, but invited questions which he offered to answer himself. . . . [W]e received answers to which I found myself in agreement." Gushed Wisconsin Democratic senator William Proxmire: "There is simply no precedent for this kind of candid dialogue between congressmen and the President in the history of the Republic."[53]

The big success of the White House campaign was in keeping the key players in the Senate Democratic leadership, Mike Mansfield, William Fulbright, and Richard Russell—all of them opposed to a larger war—from voicing strong opposition in these crucial weeks. The three were seldom heard from in the Senate debate. Mansfield indeed publicly praised Johnson's handling of the war, even as he privately continued to urge the president to pursue a face-saving negotiated withdrawal.[54] Johnson, he told the press, should be commended for "trying to keep the lid on a dangerous volcano in Southeast Asia" and for "trying to prevent a great war in Asia." Mansfield also lauded the State Department's "White Paper," a sixty-four-page, ten-thousand-word report issued on 27 February, which explained American policy and said the choice of peace or war was up to Hanoi. The vast majority of observers, even those supportive of the U.S. commitment, called the White Paper an unpersuasive document that actually had the effect of making the administration's case appear flimsy. ("All the State Department's Himalayan labor has brought forth a mouse of an argument," the *New Republic* declared.) But on the same day that Oregon's Wayne Morse called the White Paper a rationalization best described as "a Swiss cheese," Mansfield endorsed it on the Senate floor, remarking that the paper helped to explain "why this nation has been compelled to take the steps it has in recent weeks." In mid March on NBC's *Meet the Press* William Fulbright defended the air strikes and said a public debate in Congress would be dangerous.[55]

For nervous Democrats, already feeling pressure to support the president in a time of crisis, and aware of the authorization they had granted him at the time of the Gulf of Tonkin affair the previous August, such words from their party's leaders in the Senate must have had a powerful impact and must have convinced many to simply go along. At least publicly; at one point a senator, identified by *Newsweek* as a "senior Democrat," declared on the floor of the chamber that the United States had rightly demonstrated its intention to stand firm in the war, for as long as necessary, and then abruptly changed his tone when he went off the record: "Oh, hell. I think the sooner we can get out the better."[56]

But not everyone allowed themselves to be taken in, or to swallow their misgivings. On 18 February, the day after Church's and McGovern's speeches, LBJ sent McGeorge Bundy to Capitol Hill to talk with the two of them and other skeptics (including Nelson, Young, and Minnesota Democrat Eugene McCarthy) and to try to limit the Senate debate. The president hoped to end the debate, Bundy told the group, in order that Hanoi not be misled by America's resolve. "Americans have to present a united front," Bundy said. The senators stood firm. A debate about war or peace in Asia, they insisted, would in the long run be in the president's best interests. Vice President Humphrey, who hosted the meeting and privately shared the senators' trepidation, welcomed their steadfastness. He exulted after Bundy left: " You boys don't scare easily, do you?" Indeed not, though most were careful in the days to follow to avoid criticizing Johnson directly or faulting his ordering reprisal strikes after Pleiku and Qui Nhon. By the time the Senate's debate ended in early March the number who publicly advocated early negotiations leading to withdrawal, though reduced, still numbered close to a dozen.[57]

Their opposition irked Johnson no end. "I'm getting kicked around by my own party in the Senate," he complained to Everett Dirksen on the phone in late February, "and getting my support from your side of the aisle." A week later, when another Republican remarked on the strong GOP support and asked him, "What about the people in your party—the cut-and-run boys?" Johnson grimly responded: "I'm going to talk to those boys personally—every one of them. The world shouldn't be misled by our differences of opinion. We are not going to negotiate at this time, and certainly not so long as the Communists continue to violate the Geneva accords." Already by the start of March, the press could report what would become very clear by the spring: that Lyndon Johnson's most solid support for his Vietnam policy came from what columnist William S. White called "The Loyal Opposition," the Republican Party. Even this was not quite accurate in that the GOP in this period was divided on Vietnam, with several moderates opposed to escalation. The "Loyal Opposition" referred primarily to the Goldwater wing of the party.[58]

If such was the state of opinion inside the Washington beltway, what about outside it? Here the picture was mixed. Johnson won generally high marks from Americans for his forceful response to the Pleiku and Qui Nhon attacks, but there was plainly great uneasiness in the land. On 16 February, a Gallup poll found that 67 percent of Americans supported the retaliatory air strikes, while White House mail was running fourteen to one against the actions. White House aide Gordon Chase, in reporting the figures to McGeorge Bundy, said he found the discrepancy startling. A few days later a Louis Harris survey reported that 83 percent of Americans supported the bombings but also that 75 percent favored asking for negotiations to end the war. The public, the pollsters noted, was deeply concerned that the conflict in Vietnam might escalate into a major war. A *San Francisco Chronicle* poll of Northern Californians in early March found overwhelming opposition to deeper American involvement: 80 percent of respondents opposed the introduction of ground troops and 82 percent favored following Charles de Gaulle's and U Thant's lead and arranging negotiations including the Soviet Union and China. Most notably, 76 percent said that they were not sympathetic to "the principles of the South Vietnamese government," while a mere 12 percent said that they were (the rest had "no opinion"). One finds the same phenomenon at work in many of the nation's newspapers: articles on the front pages detailing the strong support in national polls for the retaliatory air strikes and for negotiations and, on the back pages, thoughtful and knowledgeable letters to the editor (in both conservative and liberal papers) declaring that escalation would fail to yield the desired results in Vietnam and perhaps cause deep domestic frictions in the United States.[59]

Among that huge mass of people who never wrote letters to the editor, a high level of detachment was common, even now, after American soldiers had been attacked in their barracks and the president had ordered retaliation. When James Reston of the *New York Times* took a two-thousand-mile trip through some of the southern and middle Atlantic states at the beginning of March to survey Americans, he found a striking degree of nonengagement with the issues of the war, and willingness to leave the weighty decisions to the president. "President Johnson interprets this mood of acquiescence as approval of his policy, and he is probably right," Reston wrote after the trip. "But one has the impression that the mood would be about the same if he stepped up the bombing, or stopped it, or followed any other policy except ordering the American Army into battle on the ground."[60]

Reston was wrong or at least misleading on one point: outside the "larger cities," he wrote, even newspapers were giving scant attention to the war. In fact, press coverage and editorializing about Vietnam were abundant in February and early March, and not merely in major urban areas. Many papers lamented the continuing lack of popular agitation about the war, blamed this state of affairs partly on Lyndon Johnson's silence about the stakes involved, and urged readers to inform themselves about the key decisions that lay ahead. Most also staked out clear policy preferences in their editorials. As in previous months, one finds no consensus in these editorials on Vietnam and what should happen there, though there is evidence that some papers were rallying around the flag. Foremost among these was the *Washington Post*, which in February adopted an unflinchingly hawkish stance on the war. (It would seldom waver in the years that followed.) Others backing the administration's tough posture included the *Dallas Morning News*, the *Chicago Tribune*, the Portland *Oregonian*, the *Philadelphia Inquirer*, the *Omaha World-Herald*, the *Atlanta Journal*, the *Denver Post*, the *St. Louis Globe-Democrat*, the *Los Angeles Times*, and the *Houston Chronicle*. Even now, however, a large number of newspapers declared opposition to expanded military action and urged a vigorous American attempt at gaining a negotiated withdrawal from the war. These included the *New York Times*, the *Wall Street Journal*, the *Christian Science Monitor*, the *Louisville Courier-Journal*, the *Miami Herald*, the *Miami News*, the *Milwaukee Journal*, the *San Francisco Chronicle*, the *St. Louis Post-Dispatch*, the *Sacramento Bee*, the *Detroit Free Press*, the *Des Moines Register*, and the *Cleveland Plain Dealer*.

Nor was there anything approaching a consensus among the nation's columnists. Walter Lippmann and Joseph Alsop continued to present strikingly different visions of what should happen in the war. Whereas Lippmann said Americanization would fail and urged disengagement through negotiations, Alsop chafed with impatience for more and bigger U.S. attacks: "Where then is our common sense, that we shrink and fall back, shrink and fall back? We have waited overlong." Alsop added a warning: "Now what needs doing may perhaps be done at last. If not, we must expect dreadful trouble soon." William S. White, Marguerite Higgins, William F. Buckley Jr., and the team of Rowland Evans and Robert Novak were more muted than Alsop but echoed his call for a hard-line posture in the

war. Meanwhile, Lippmann's opposition to escalation and preference for disengagement were endorsed by Emmet John Hughes, Arthur Krock, Joseph
Kraft, and Drew Pearson. Pearson wrote in his column on the last day of
February: "The best long range hope for the United States in IndoChina is
Titoism. Ho Chi Minh could be another Tito if we don't drive him into the
hands of the Chinese, as we have been doing." Pearson labeled as "bunk"
the administration's suggestion that the United States was in South Vietnam at the request of the legitimate Saigon government—legitimacy was
precisely what the endless parade of regimes in Saigon lacked—and he said
there was no reason to believe bombing the North would appreciably help
matters in the South.[61]

On these two points Pearson was indisputably correct, judging by the situation on the ground at the end of February. Contrary to what McGeorge
Bundy and Maxwell Taylor had promised in recommending air strikes, the
bombings of North Vietnam were not inducing either greater stability in
the Saigon or greater dedication among southerners to prosecuting the war.
If anything, the bombings gave added impetus to the peace movement in
South Vietnam, as evidenced by an increase in February in both the number and the anti-American tone of peace demonstrations.[62] Nor did the new
U.S. action bring South Vietnamese leader Nguyen Khanh into line. Maxwell Taylor continued to fear that Khanh intended to negotiate a settlement with the NLF, and the ambassador began courting ambitious ARVN
officers in an attempt to promote a coup. Sensing danger, Khanh moved to
install a civilian ally, Phan Huy Quat, as prime minister. Though the effort
succeeded, Khanh himself was ousted a few days later by a group headed
by Air Vice Marshal Nguyen Cao Ky. Ky, who a few months later would
distinguish himself by expressing admiration for Adolf Hitler, would now
be the de facto major power in Saigon.

Ky's ascension to power coincided with the end of the crucial period of
American decision making in Vietnam. By the end of February 1965, the
most important U.S. policy initiatives were in place. On the thirteenth of
that month, the administration formally agreed to initiate regular, sustained
bombing of North Vietnam and enemy-held areas of South Vietnam. On
the nineteenth, U.S. planes attacked enemy-held areas in Bindinh province in the South, the first air attack on Vietcong forces in which no South
Vietnamese airmen were involved.[63] The assault, carried out by waves of
F-100s and B-57s, would last a week and would be expanded to targets
throughout the South. On the twenty-sixth, the White House, after minimal discussion and over Maxwell Taylor's strong objections, agreed to William Westmoreland's request for two battalions of marines to guard the

airbase at Danang, thus introducing the first U.S. ground troops to the war. Neither Congress nor the South Vietnamese government was consulted about the decision. On 2 March, six days before the marines would splash ashore, more than one hundred American planes hit targets inside North Vietnam. It was the first attack carried out not in retaliation, and it marked the start of Rolling Thunder.[64]

For those governments that had hoped to avert an American escalation of the war, the initiation of regular, sustained bombing of North Vietnam was a major blow. In late March the CIA cited reports that the permanent representatives to the UN were profoundly concerned about the rising tensions in Vietnam, with the image of the United States "at its lowest ebb today." In Japan, the Sato government objected strongly to the systematic bombing of the DRV and supported early negotiations; in the spring months U.S.-Japan relations would suffer markedly because of the war.[65] Britain and France, the leading Western nations in the group, were convinced that, with the tension ratcheted up, early negotiations would now be much more difficult to achieve. The stakes had increased, and each side would be more reluctant to compromise. Both London and Paris had representatives in Hanoi and Beijing and Moscow, and their discussions with officials in those capitals convinced them that the bombings would not compel the North Vietnamese to give in to American demands. Particularly given the chronic weakness of the South Vietnamese government and military, and the growing war-weariness in the South, British and French analysts doubted that the United States could improve its bargaining position with the new military moves.[66]

Charles de Gaulle was almost certain that major war was in the offing. On 18 March he told members of the French cabinet that the effort to prevent major fighting in Vietnam had failed. The war, the general declared, "will last a long, long, long time." The following month, he offered a more precise estimate: unless Washington stopped the war immediately, he told his ministers, the fighting would go on for ten years and would completely dishonor the United States. When U.S. ambassador Charles Bohlen called on de Gaulle in early May, he found the French leader in a philosophical mood, accepting the inevitable escalation of the war with "oriental fatalism."[67]

The Soviet Union, equally convinced that Vietnam was not worth a major war, all but abandoned hope for a political settlement in the weeks following the start of the air campaign in early March. Soviet officials were angry that the United States had bombed North Vietnam on 7 February while Alexei Kosygin was still in Hanoi, but their immediate reaction to the attack had nevertheless been relatively mild. In mid February Soviet officials let it be known that they supported U Thant's efforts to facilitate negotiations. They also gave hints to London of their interest in exploring some kind of cochairs' initiative, and London officials detected some Soviet disappointment that the British proposal of 20 February was not a call for substantive negotiations. In talks in Paris on 23–24 February, requested by Moscow, Soviet and French officials agreed on the nature of the struggle in South Vietnam (Charles de Gaulle and Soviet ambassador Sergei Vinogradov concurred that the American position was hopeless) and on the need for a conference to negotiate a settlement of the conflict.[68]

They did not agree on the question of preconditions for such a conference, however, and their differences on this score point to the difficult position in which Moscow found itself as the war escalated in the first half of 1965. Whereas the French thought it imperative that no preconditions be attached to the conference, the Soviets, committed to supporting the DRV, countered that American air attacks had to stop in advance of any meeting. No less desirous than the French of gaining a negotiated settlement to the war, Moscow knew it could not be seen to be abandoning an ally under attack—to do so would be to give Beijing a huge advantage in its bid to claim leadership of the world communist movement.[69]

In the weeks that followed the Paris talks, as sustained bombing of the North commenced and American marines arrived in the South, Moscow officials became increasingly frustrated. Like much of the rest of the world they had mistakenly assumed that Lyndon Johnson would never allow himself to be sucked into the Vietnamese morass, and it annoyed them that he would jeopardize continued improvement in Soviet-American relations for the sake of an incompetent and unrepresentative Saigon regime. Time and again in the late winter and spring months the Soviet ambassador to Washington, Anatoly Dobrynin, would ask American officials why the administration insisted on pursuing a futile mission in a place of marginal significance. The USSR had no option, he would say to them, but to support its ally in Hanoi. And so it would be. For almost a month, the Soviets delayed responding to the British cochair's proposal, most likely because they hoped that Johnson would stop the bombing and thereby allow Moscow to say yes. But the pace of the attacks only picked up, and on 16 March Foreign Minister Andrei Gromyko informed officials in London that the USSR would not agree to the proposal. Moscow would never abandon the North Vietnamese, Gromyko vowed, and no diplomacy on Vietnam was possible until Washington ceased its aggressive actions against the DRV. Gromyko's line would be repeated countless times by Soviet officials in the months to come.[70]

In Beijing, officials had never been as keen as their Soviet counterparts on gaining a political solution in Vietnam. China shared with the United States the distinction of being the most hostile to diplomacy on the conflict in early 1965, and its leaders much preferred to prolong an insurgency in which their allies were winning while Washington backed the loser. But if there was therefore a less marked change in the Chinese position after the onset of Rolling Thunder, a change there nevertheless was. Like the Soviets, leaders in Beijing had hoped to avoid a dramatic escalation of the war— acutely conscious of their own military weakness, they wanted to steer clear of a direct military confrontation with the mighty U.S. Seventh Fleet, and they did not relish the prospect of increased Soviet influence in Southeast Asia such as was certain to result in the event of large-scale war. Thus alongside their scathing denunciations of American policy in January and February were hints of moderation.

In a 9 January interview with the American journalist Edgar Snow, Mao Zedong sounded a flexible tone, welcoming the prospect of a conference on the war and even suggesting the possibility of American troops remaining around Saigon for its duration. He added that China would not "fight anyone" unless its own territory were attacked. On the same day, Foreign Minister Chen Yi told the French ambassador in Beijing, Lucien Paye, that a total U.S. withdrawal from Vietnam was not a precondition for a conference but might be a goal thereof. The French continued to meet with Chinese representatives in both Paris and Beijing later in January and in February and gained the firm impression that Beijing was not unalterably opposed to negotiations—hence Couve de Murville's comments to that effect in his talks in Washington.[71]

After the beginning of March such ambiguities in the Chinese position disappeared. Beijing continued studiously to avoid making direct pledges of support to the DRV and continued to pledge privately that it would not provoke the United States, but it also categorically ruled out a negotiated settlement. The Paris contacts that Beijing had seen as a useful way to probe the negotiations issue became much more infrequent, and Chinese leaders now demanded that the United States withdraw fully from both South Vietnam and Laos before any negotiations could occur. On 17 March Premier Zhou Enlai told Lucien Paye that the Americans were the personification of evil and that the United States had acted in bad faith on Indochina ever since 1954. Washington had now escalated the war, Zhou continued, but the worse the fighting got the better it would be for North Vietnam and China, which had right on their side. In Algiers on 30 March, Zhou rejected Algerian president Ben Bella's suggestion that U Thant visit Beijing with an eye toward facilitating negotiations. And three days later in

Karachi, Zhou told Pakistani leader Mohammad Ayub Khan that though China did not "fundamentally oppose holding negotiations," the current situation was not conducive to the convening of a conference. In phrasing the issue this way the premier no doubt wanted to keep open the possibility of talks in case the Vietcong position in South Vietnam suddenly deteriorated, but for the moment he and his colleagues would work to prevent a diplomatic solution and strengthen its ties to Hanoi.[72]

This brings us to the most important among those players hoping to avoid a major escalation of the war: North Vietnam. For its leadership, February 1965 was a watershed. Since the start of the insurgency in the South in the late 1950s, a chief objective of Ho Chi Minh and his colleagues had been to prevent an Americanization of the conflict. In late 1964 the North Vietnamese were confident that they were on the way to achieving this objective, and they continued in January and February to send out signals that they were willing to enter talks, the primary aim of which would be to gain an American withdrawal from the conflict. In December and again in January the North Vietnamese trade representative in Paris, Mai Van Bo, met with French officials and, according to the Quai d'Orsay, struck a conciliatory tone; Bo, the French reported, expressed his government's interest in negotiations aimed at creating an internationally guaranteed neutral South Vietnam. In February Pham Van Dong and Ho Chi Minh reportedly asked the French delegate general in Hanoi, Jacques de Buzon, to have Paris work for a Geneva-type conference; both were said to have told him that their government feared the increased Chinese influence in the DRV that likely would come with escalation. On 15 February, the government newspaper *Nhan Dan* approvingly reported the support for a Geneva conference expressed by the Canadians, the French, and the Indians.[73]

Whatever the exact nature of Hanoi's thinking with respect to negotiations in the first two months of the year, one thing is clear: its leaders became much less flexible after the systematic U.S. air strikes began. Having determined that Washington had now fully committed itself to a military solution, Hanoi vowed to give as good as it got. A State Department analyst would later describe what occurred in Hanoi in early March as a "sudden reversal from a more open-ended position on possible negotiations" to a hard position. On 3 March Hanoi closed off the French contacts and withdrew private overtures made to a western news correspondent in Phnom Penh. The next day Canadian diplomat J. Blair Seaborn, on one of his periodic visits to Hanoi as Ottawa's representative to the ICC, was denied permission to meet with Pham Van Dong; the midlevel official who spoke to him denounced U.S. actions in vituperative language. Seaborn told Ottawa he found a distinct stiffening in the government's position, and other foreign diplomats did the same as the month progressed. On 4 April Pham Van Dong told French diplomats in Hanoi that negotiations were impossible in the foreseeable future.[74]

For each of the communist powers, then, Johnson's February 1965 policy initiatives proved decisive. All three had been waiting to see which way Washington would go; by the start of March they had their answer. Late in the year a U.S. government report would highlight the shift in Moscow-Beijing-Hanoi thinking that occurred in February. The report, produced by an interagency planning group headed by Chester Cooper and Leonard Unger, read: "It can be seen in retrospect that Communist political moves and attitudes divide into two phases: the 'soft' period from early January to mid February 1965 (marked by reportedly positive attitudes privately expressed on possible negotiations), and the 'hard' period beginning in mid February and assuming greater severity with the 2 March initiation of air strikes against North Vietnam."[75]

Neither in North Vietnam nor in the South did the initiation of those air strikes bring the results that American officials had hoped to see. In the North, the main effect of the new show of American muscle was to strengthen the DRV's ties to Moscow and Beijing and to remove the constraints that had previously kept Hanoi from sending sizable numbers of its own combat units into the South. Though the Ho Chi Minh government had for some years infiltrated military and technical cadres into the South, only two regiments of combat troops had arrived in South Vietnam by the start of 1965. Now there seemed less reason to hold back. Over the next weeks and months, more North Vietnamese units began the trek to the South, though not yet in large numbers. (As late as July 1965 the Vietcong still made up approximately 97 percent of enemy combat forces.)[76]

In South Vietnam, the poor trends already evident in late February grew more pronounced in March and April. The rate of desertion from ARVN increased at an alarming rate in these months, approaching an all-time high of eleven thousand a month (at ARVN draft induction centers the rate was close to 50 percent). Behind the armed forces, the government continued to be weakened by corruption, assassination (carried out by the Vietcong), and constant political maneuvering. Neither the systematic bombing of the North nor the marines' arrival had any appreciable impact on these problems. In a draft memorandum written in the middle of March, McNamara's deputy John McNaughton noted that the Saigon government controlled only minimal parts of the northern part of South Vietnam and that U.S. officials on the scene saw a 50 percent chance of a coup within three weeks. The "prognosis," he warned, was for "a continued deterioration leading to more ARVN desertions and whole regions of South Vietnam being denied to the Saigon regime." Such setbacks would then lead regime officials to "adjust their behavior to an eventual VC takeover." Specifically, they would allow neutralist elements to enter the government, make concessions to the Vietcong, and invite the United States to leave.[77]

The boost in South Vietnamese morale that U.S. officials had hoped to see failed to materialize. Though some senior Saigon officials no doubt were heartened by the increased American commitment, the war-weariness of much of the population actually increased in the wake of the new military measures. Many Southerners worried that the bombs would drop on relatives in the North, while others feared what the influx of more Americans would do to Southern society and culture. "Yank, go fight your war somewhere else," became a slogan frequently heard in Saigon and elsewhere. A week before the marine landing at Danang, NSC staffer Chester Cooper informed Bundy that a Buddhist-sponsored "peace group" opposed to the bombing and pressing for negotiations was "causing troubles" in Saigon and in the northern provinces of South Vietnam. Cooper added that support for this group had grown in recent weeks and would likely continue to do so. Sure enough, on 11 March, three days after the landing, Ambassador Maxwell Taylor warned Rusk that there had been "a renewed flurry of 'peace' talk" in the preceding days. He would repeat the claim several times in the weeks to come.[78]

These results made the spring months a demoralizing time for several of the architects of the American escalation. Robert McNamara and John McNaughton, for example, grew steadily more gloomy in the period. In June McNamara told Britain's Patrick Gordon Walker that the key indicators were pointing in the wrong direction. In the short term the United States could hold on militarily, but over the long haul it was doubtful. "None of us at the centre of things [in U.S. policy making] talk about winning a victory," McNamara confessed to Walker, adding that it was not possible to tell the American people that the war was unwinnable. The only hope, McNamara suggested, was that Moscow would pressure Hanoi to soften its demands. "How can we get Russia to move?" he asked Walker several times in the conversation. Walker had no answer, and he asked McNamara if any consideration was being given to getting out of the war. None at all, the American replied.[79]

William Bundy detailed his disillusionment on several occasions in June. It is clear that the prospect of a deal behind America's back between the

Saigon government and the NLF was heavy on his mind. In a heartfelt letter to American envoys in East Asia dated 14 June, Bundy said that the war was going very badly; the prospects were poor, the options few. The dispatch of large numbers of American ground forces looked likely, but such a move might well cause the Vietnamese to slacken in their own effort. Even worse, Bundy wrote, Americanization might turn the population against the United States, as Americans appeared to the local population to be acting like the French had before them. "My own hunch," he continued, "is that the general weariness, combined with the high rate of activity and, to some extent, the exaggerated expectations originally held for the effective bombing of the North, have created a situation where morale is really much more brittle than at similar pressure periods in the past. We get reports that even the Catholics are thinking of ways to make a deal, in a few instances, and we have always supposed that such tendencies were present in the Buddhist groups." The most likely form of collapse would be a quiet deal with the NLF or Hanoi that would call for a coalition government and, "in fairly short order, a request for our withdrawal," Bundy noted, adding that such an outcome might be preferable to a U.S.-Hanoi deal or a conference that would end up "selling out South Viet-Nam." As did McNamara to Walker, Bundy made clear that no thought was being given in Washington to extrication from the war.[80]

And there was no such thought, not at the top level.[81] Beginning in March 1965 the escalation of the American commitment in Vietnam took on an inexorable quality. This should come as no surprise: for the past year observers both inside and outside the American government had said that once the war expanded and ground troops were sent, turning back would become infinitely harder. As Maxwell Taylor later put it with reference to the initial deployment of ground forces at Danang, they represented "the nose of the camel. You couldn't take that nose [out of the tent] once you landed those Marines at Danang."[82] Whereas civilian officials had been supreme in the months prior, now the military's needs drove U.S. decision making.

The choices had narrowed drastically. Already on 9 February James Reston had noted that American freedom of maneuver on Vietnam had been reduced by the military and diplomatic response to Pleiku; by a month later, the maneuverability had been reduced much more. It was not merely that the communist governments' political positions hardened after February, further raising the stakes; in addition, Johnson's domestic political constraints increased. The *Economist* of London, generally sympathetic to U.S. aims in the war, put it this way in its 3 April issue: "Short of sitting back and saying that everything since February 7th has been a mistake [Johnson] has no choice but [to] increase the pressure on North Vietnam."[83] American casualty figures started to increase rapidly in these months, further adding to the pressure on Johnson, and he now faced intensified partisan pressure, as the right wing became more voluble in demanding victory in the war.[84]

Did Johnson realize that his options on Vietnam had diminished? Probably. To Lady Bird and others he complained of feeling trapped, with nowhere to go. The lament had more legitimacy now than when he had uttered it in 1964. He was in any event more determined than ever in the weeks and months after the marine landing to prevail in the war. The war began to consume him. On 15 March, Johnson addressed a joint session of Congress to plead for passage of the Voting Rights Act. A member of the audience, enthralled by what he heard, later called it "Johnson's finest hour," a "great moral statement against discrimination." According to McGeorge Bundy and George Ball, however, that day LBJ's mind was elsewhere; Bundy and Ball conversed on the phone in the afternoon and concurred that the president was fixated on Vietnam. That same day, LBJ summoned the Joint Chiefs of Staff to the White House. His message to the military leaders was: "Kill more Vietcong." Johnson told the Chiefs that he wanted a weekly report totaling the Vietcong dead.[85]

The poor results of the air war in the spring months did not cause Johnson to change his mind, and neither did the continued deterioration in South Vietnam. The CIA reported again and again that these trends were likely to continue, but this mattered little as Johnson seldom read even the summaries of the agency's reports. (Director John McCone, frustrated by this presidential disregard for intelligence analysis, resigned in April.)[86] The lack of allied support did not deter Johnson, and neither did the first real stirrings of broad-based discontent within America's academic community—the first university teach-ins took place in March, and in April the escalation of the war was criticized by several prominent American thinkers, including Reinhold Niebuhr, George Kennan, Hans J. Morgenthau, and John Kenneth Galbraith.[87] Continued grumbling in Congress, among large numbers of Democrats and several moderate Republicans, only caused Johnson to redouble his efforts to convert them or at least keep them quiet. Major efforts were expended through the spring months in this direction, as George Ball and other administration officials met individually with scores of lawmakers to squelch planned antiwar speeches or, if the speech had already been given, to bring the critic around. (They did not bother with Oregon's Wayne Morse and Alaska's Ernest Gruening, judging them to be beyond persuasion.)[88]

Johnson grew especially resentful of foreign leaders' intrusions into Vietnam policy. After a meeting with Britain's Michael Stewart on 23 March he complained to aides that no foreigner had ever offered him practical or helpful advice. When Canadian prime minister Lester Pearson gingerly advocated a pause in the bombing and spoke to the desirability of negotiations in a speech at Temple University in Philadelphia on 2 April, Johnson exploded in anger. He berated Pearson in a meeting at Camp David the next day, at one point, according to an eye witness, even grabbing the prime minister by the lapels. "He strode the terrace, he sawed the air with his arms, with upraised fist he drove home the verbal hammer blows": that Pearson had joined with Morse, Lippmann, the *New York Times*, the ignorant liberals and "know nothing" do-gooders; that he had made the U.S. task more difficult; that he had dared give the speech without first checking with the White House. "You don't come here and piss on my rug," Johnson barked. Still angry two days later, Johnson ordered embarrassed aides to cancel the planned visits of India's Lal Bahadur Shastri and Pakistan's Mohammad Ayub Khan, whom Johnson knew also sought reduced tensions in Southeast Asia. Shastri and Ayub were outraged by the snub, and the United States squandered an opportunity to facilitate better relations between the two leaders, whose countries went to war later in 1965. On those occasions when LBJ did meet with foreign officials in these weeks, he adhered to his standard practice of defining the alternatives to current policy—either to "retreat to Hawaii" or "bomb the hell out of China"—in such a way as to not merely preclude their being adopted but also essentially end the discussion.[89]

Notwithstanding Johnson's hostile reaction to the Temple speech, Pearson's statement no doubt helped propel the one notable diplomacy-oriented move made by the United States in the spring of 1965. It was a move designed primarily to defuse the clamor from the international community and from domestic critics such as the *New York Times* and Walter Lippmann for some sign that the administration might be willing to enter negotiations. At Johns Hopkins University in Baltimore on 7 April, in a speech carefully prepared by White House wordsmiths over several days, Johnson declared that he remained ready for "unconditional discussions" and would propose to Congress a billion-dollar U.S. investment program for economic development in Southeast Asia. The speech won widespread praise from the American press and from many world leaders, including U Thant and Eisaku Sato. (On LBJ's orders, Thant's name was given favorable mention in the text.) White House mail went from five to one against U.S. policy to four to one in favor. More careful analysts saw that the president had in fact signaled no real change in administration policy, no slackening in the drive to defeat the Vietcong.[90] The day after the speech Johnson met with the JCS and again emphasized the need to kill more Vietcong. On 13 April, he startled a group of visiting diplomats with a long-winded and vociferous defense of the U.S. commitment to South Vietnam. He likened his challenge to the one the British and Winston Churchill had faced in 1939–1940 and said he would not give up the fight. The same day, Johnson overrode Taylor's objections and the reservations of several senior civilian aides and approved the dispatch of the 173d Airborne Brigade to the Bienhoa area for security and combat operations.[91]

The breathing room created by the Hopkins speech lasted barely a week. By the middle of the month the critics were back, louder than before. On 17 April, fifteen to twenty thousand protesters gathered in Washington for a march organized by the Students for a Democratic Society. Press criticism increased. Many observers were particularly put off by the revelation that Washington had failed to respond to a statement by North Vietnamese premier Pham Van Dong, outlining "Four Points" that would need to be recognized for a settlement to occur, and by the administration's staunch refusal to consider including the Vietcong in any talks.[92] On the twenty-first Chester Cooper, one of several midlevel officials who thought the Four Points could be a starting point for further exchanges, informed LBJ that the Hopkins honeymoon period was over.[93] The administration's propaganda position was being hurt, Cooper noted, by the harmful comments of Lippmann, Kennan, Galbraith, and Fulbright (the senator on 17 April had urged a bombing halt, even as he said he supported administration policy). Also unfortunate, Cooper continued, were the student demonstrations in the United States, the unhelpful comments by allies such as France and Canada, and the "worldwide fear of war," especially in key countries such as India and Japan.[94]

Cooper's memo came almost exactly a year after the launching of the American effort to get "more flags" involved in the defense of South Vietnam. His comments indicated once more how little had been accomplished. But Johnson refused to give up. As American fighting forces arrived in Vietnam in greater numbers, he knew it was more vital than ever to get increased third-country help, in order to show lawmakers and the American public that the defense of South Vietnam was indeed a Free World effort. In the spring of 1965, on LBJ's orders, the administration undertook a desperate effort to convince the few governments strongly supportive of the war effort to make significant manpower contributions. Little materialized, much as presidential advisers had expected.[95] By 15 June, Australia had committed one infantry battalion, a seventy-three-man air force unit, and one hundred combat advisers, and South Korea had agreed to send a twenty-two-hundred-man task force, which included one infantry battalion. New Zealand had committed an artillery battalion. All three told the administration to expect little more.[96]

These were not large contributions, but the White House could have been content with them had Great Britain come through with even a token troop commitment. Johnson was outraged by Wilson's steadfast refusal to bend on this issue, telling aides that he thought he had made it clear to the prime minister in their December 1964 meeting that the only effective contribution Britain could make to the war effort would be soldiers on the ground. Johnson said he wanted a few British soldiers to get killed in Vietnam alongside Americans so that their pictures could appear in the U.S. press to demonstrate to the public that America's principal ally was contributing to a joint effort. In June and July top American officials, including the big three of McNamara, Rusk, and McGeorge Bundy, leaned hard on the Wilson government to commit a brigade or at least a couple of battalions. Their hope was that London's dependence on American assistance in propping up the beleaguered pound would cause Wilson to yield on the issue. Dollars would be dangled. On the evening of 25 July, Bundy told Sir Patrick Dean, the new British ambassador in Washington, that what Johnson really wanted was a British military contribution in the form of ground troops. Such a contribution, he added, would be worth "several hundred million dollars." Dean said he would report the request to his government. McNamara, meanwhile, told colleagues he was prepared to give London a billion dollars in exchange for a brigade. Whether he actually made that offer to the British is not clear, but in any event Harold Wilson refused to go along. There would be no British fighting forces sent to Vietnam.[97]

On 9 June 1965, in the midst of the American buildup that by the end of the year would see 180,000 American ground troops in Vietnam, there appeared in the New York Times an editorial titled "Ground War in Asia." The editorial described how the Eisenhower and Kennedy policies of assisting the South Vietnamese to fight the Vietcong had been transformed into "an American war against Asians." Remarkably, however, there was "still no official explanation offered for a move that fundamentally alters the character of the American involvement in Vietnam." The president was silent, as crucial questions went unanswered. For example, the paper asked, what exactly were the new military measures intended to accomplish? The bombing had been started and the troop commitment made apparently because for the White House these represented the only way to shore up southern morale and halt the factional feuding in Saigon, "but is it not more likely that political irresponsibility will grow, rather than decline, as the main military responsibility for defending Vietnam is transferred increasingly to American hands?" Moreover, what was the emergency that ruled out a proper congressional debate on the war? There was none, the editorial declared. None of it was necessary, none of it inevitable: "It can all be made to sound like a gradual and inevitable outgrowth of earlier commitments. Yet the whole development occurred in a four-month span, just after the election in which the Administration campaigned on the issue of its responsibility and restraint in foreign military involvements."[98]

Exactly right. Lyndon Johnson, in the wake of his election victory, had taken the United States into a major war in Vietnam. He had inherited a difficult Vietnam problem but one that in no way compelled him to put the country on the course it was now following. Perhaps he understood that he could choose. Perhaps that is why he so feared a congressional debate, so feared telling the American people what they were being asked to do in a land 7,000 miles from the coast of California. Perhaps that is why he insisted on a policy designed to deceive the people who had given him his triumphant victory in November. The *Times*'s editorial writers understood what would only gradually become clear to a majority of their countrymen: that Americanization would not create a stable South Vietnamese government with popular legitimacy. And they understood that Americanization was nevertheless a reality. America was in a ground war in Southeast Asia. It would be seven long and bloody years before the bankruptcy and futility of the policy forced Johnson's successor to yield to reality and call a halt.

12 Choosing War

When the first contingent of American marines waded ashore near Danang in South Vietnam in the early part of March 1965, it signaled the end
of the most important period of policy deliberation in the history of American involvement in Vietnam. This period began some eighteen months
earlier, in the late summer of 1963, and it was characterized by a marked
deterioration in the politico-military position of the Saigon government
and a concomitant dilemma for Washington officials: whether to escalate
dramatically U.S. involvement in the war or get out of it altogether. The
landing of the marines and the initiation of regular, sustained bombing of
North Vietnam and Vietcong-controlled areas of South Vietnam were dramatic proof of which way they had gone.

That the significance of this development is clearer in hindsight than
it was at the time cannot be doubted. The question is how much clearer.
Neither senior officials nor anyone else could know in the late winter of
1965 how large the American commitment would eventually become, or
how long the war would go on, or how much blood would be shed before it was over. But all informed observers knew that a key moment had
come and a line had been crossed. Lyndon Johnson would publicly insist
otherwise and would instruct aides into the summer to say that the policy
had not changed, that the new measures were a substitute for escalation,
rather than escalation itself. But he really believed otherwise, as indicated
by his deepening hostility in these months to early negotiations and his
instructing top U.S. military officials in March to go out and "kill Vietcong." Few knowledgeable people, whether inside or outside the U.S. government, would have disagreed with Walter Lippmann's assertion early in
the spring: "It used to be a war of the South Vietnamese assisted by the
Americans. It is now becoming an American war very inefficiently assisted
by the South Vietnamese."[1]

THE CONTEXT

Nor is hindsight necessarily much of an advantage in understanding the nature of the escalate-or-withdraw choice that first John Kennedy and then Lyndon Johnson faced in Vietnam. Judging by the existing historical literature, indeed, contemporaneous observers generally had a surer sense of that choice than those who came later.[2] For Lippmann as for others writing at the time, whatever their position on the war, the outcome of the policy process in late 1964–early 1965 was in no way preordained. They were certain that Lyndon Johnson faced a genuine dilemma—that is, a choice between two or more unpalatable alternatives—and they devoted considerable attention in their analyses to each of the options before him. Historians, on the other hand, writing after the fact, have generally given short shrift to the dilemma if they have examined it at all. Some authors have identified the president's choice as a legitimate one and spoken vaguely of "missed opportunities" for withdrawal in the period, but they have asserted rather than demonstrated the viability of these opportunities. More commonly, students of the war have rejected the notion that there existed a viable choice for the administration—for them, Johnson's dilemma was not much of a dilemma at all. They have described an escalation process that was essentially an inevitable outcome of the domestic and international political climate of the time. More than that, most of these authors have implied that the president was justified in believing that each escalation might provide the critical increment—after all, practically everyone else thought so. Writes one distinguished historian: "What was most remarkable about the Vietnam War was that, with the exception of Charles de Gaulle, George Ball, and a handful of others, so few challenged the fundamental assumptions of the American vision."[3]

It would indeed be remarkable, if it were correct. Leaving aside for a moment the vexing issue of what exactly those "fundamental assumptions" were, in reality a veritable chorus of voices challenged the direction of American policy, albeit often in muted tones. In the executive branch of government, Ball's views were shared by a sizable number of midlevel bureaucrats in the State Department and the National Security Council, as well as by analysts in the CIA. In American elite opinion, views were divided on what to do in Vietnam should the Saigon regime move to the point of collapse, with powerful elements on record by February 1965 as opposing a major American escalation—the group included the bulk of the Senate Democratic leadership and many other lawmakers in the party; the vice president–elect; prominent commentators such as Lippmann, Drew Pearson, Arthur Krock, and Hans J. Morgenthau; and newspapers across the country, including the *New York Times*, the *Wall Street Journal*, and the *Washington Post*.

Some elites, of course, spoke out in *favor* of a stepped-up American military involvement, should that become necessary—notables included the columnist Joseph Alsop, who rivaled (but did not quite match) Lippmann in terms of national influence, and once-and-future GOP presidential candidate Richard Nixon. *Time* magazine generally struck a hawkish tone, as did the *Los Angeles Times* and several smaller regional papers. Famed Vietnam correspondents David Halberstam and Neil Sheehan, both of whom would later turn against the war, in late 1964 remained supportive of a strong U.S. commitment. In terms of staking out a firm position on what to do if a Saigon collapse threatened, however, the pro-escalation advocates were a small minority, especially on Capitol Hill—if there were "war hawks" in Congress at the end of 1964, they were a timid bunch indeed. For that matter, the existence of both points of view merely underscores a main theme in this book: the fluidity in establishment thinking about the war in the crucial months of decision.

Within the general public, too, it is very difficult to speak of any kind of meaningful "consensus" on the war in 1964; Americans, to the extent that they followed developments in Vietnam, tended to support the effort there, in large measure because they took candidate-for-president Johnson at his word when he said the nation's commitment would stay at about its current level and that South Vietnamese boys would have to fight their own war. When pressed on what should be done if defeat loomed, however, middle Americans were deeply ambivalent, with only a small minority favoring the use of U.S. ground troops. The common assertion, standard enough to be found in almost any textbook on recent U.S. history, that the war effort enjoyed broad popular support well into 1966 and 1967, is true enough but is fundamentally misleading: near-universal support for a full-scale military effort on behalf of the South Vietnamese was there *after* Americanization, courtesy of the rally-around-the-flag effect; it was not there before. As late as February 1965, polls of the public and Congress revealed widespread antipathy for the introduction of U.S. ground troops into the conflict, and broad support for some form of negotiations. More than that, surveys revealed a willingness on the part of lawmakers and their constituents to follow the administration's lead on the war, whichever way it chose to go.[4]

With respect to the international arena, the judgment quoted above would be more accurate if it were changed to read precisely the opposite: what is remarkable is how few *embraced* the "fundamental assumptions of the American vision." By the start of 1965, the United States was in large measure isolated on the Vietnam War. The key allied governments were sympathetic to Washington's dilemma and were prepared to offer tepid rhetorical support for American aims in the conflict (many because they thought it would smooth dealings with Washington on other issues). But they withstood strong and continuous U.S. pressure to make even a token manpower contribution to the conflict, in large measure because they were highly dubious about U.S. claims regarding Vietnam's importance to western security, and about whether any kind of meaningful "victory" there was possible in any event. Most thought absurd the standard American public claim that this was a case of external aggression against a freedom-loving, independent South Vietnam, considering it instead a civil war (whether between factions of southerners or between the North and South) in which the side with the least political legitimacy was the Saigon regime. Though few leaders in the West were prepared to follow de Gaulle's lead and openly challenge American policy, the majority of them saw things much the way he did—at the start of 1965 the Johnson administration could count on the firm backing of only Australia, Thailand, the Philippines, and South Korea. Of these only Australia could be considered unreservedly supportive. Out of 126 nations in the world in 1965, the United States had the unequivocal support for its Vietnam policy of exactly one.

Nothing speaks to this general American isolation on Vietnam more forcefully than this: even many Asian allies registered opposition to, or at least nonsupport for, a larger American effort in Vietnam. Early in 1966 the Central Intelligence Agency would report that the countries of the region were "permeated" with the views of American dissidents, and Lyndon Johnson would complain that "the countries [in Southeast Asia] don't want the war to go on." The situation was not markedly different a year earlier. When in December 1964 the administration launched an intensified campaign for increased third-country assistance, as a corollary to the planned American increase, it found almost no support, even among the governments in Asia. Only a handful of allies eventually contributed manpower to the war effort, and some demanded large payments for doing so, which is to say that they were not true allies.

The chief consideration for all of the skeptics of U.S. policy, whether domestic or foreign, whether in Asia or elsewhere, was the utterly dismal politico-military situation in South Vietnam. The essential prerequisite for any successful outcome to the struggle—a stable Saigon government enjoying reasonably broad-based popular support—was not merely absent but further away than ever from becoming reality. In such a situation, these critics believed, a stepped-up American military effort could probably help stabilize the situation on the battlefield but could not rectify the fundamental problem, the unwillingness of the mass of southerners to fight for the regime. If anything, a larger American presence in the South would exacerbate the problem by making the regime seem more like a puppet than ever before. Those resentful of the existing American involvement would become more resentful; those apathetic about the struggle would become more so, since they could now rely on Americans to do the job. Among Asians generally, sympathy for the Vietcong and its North Vietnamese allies would increase as they took on a very big, very white, western power, in the same way that the Vietminh before them had taken on the French.

Many allied governments might nevertheless have contributed to the war effort, and many domestic American critics supported the Johnson administration's escalation, had they not possessed deep doubts that the outcome in South Vietnam really mattered to western security. None questioned the need to contain possible Chinese communist expansion in Asia, only whether it was necessary or wise to fight in Vietnam to do it. For some, historic Chinese-Vietnamese friction precluded the possibility of Indochina falling under Beijing's actual or de facto control, a reality that suggested Washington should seek, if anything, to make common cause with North Vietnam rather than fighting it. Others were inclined to downplay the Chinese threat, arguing that Mao Zedong's main concern was internal development, not external expansion, and that Beijing's belligerent public rhetoric vis-à-vis the West did not signify any actual intention of moving southward. Still others thought the best way to control or modify China's behavior was to engage the Mao government, as de Gaulle had done in extending recognition in January 1964, not to isolate it as the United States insisted on doing. For some observers, all these considerations pertained. Most critics of American policy also rejected the standard administration assertion that the outcome in Vietnam would have a direct bearing on developments elsewhere in the region, that a Saigon defeat would start the dominoes falling. What mattered, they were convinced, was the constellation of forces within each individual country, not what occurred in a civil war in Vietnam. When Walter Lippmann wrote that "revolution is a home-grown product," whether in Algeria, Northern Ireland, or Vietnam, he expressed a view widely held outside American officialdom.[5]

The critics did not deny that the Johnson administration occupied a difficult situation in Vietnam at the start of 1965, the result of ten years of steadily increasing involvement in the affairs of the South and constant reaffirmations of America's determination to stand firm. The United States had staked a sizable chunk of its prestige on a successful outcome in the war, they agreed, and to abandon that goal would be a blow to American credibility on the world stage. But most of them did not think it would be a big blow, particularly if it happened before American troops were on the ground—once it became a full-fledged American war, all could see, withdrawal would be infinitely more difficult. Before then, the administration had a ready-made excuse for disengagement: the evident unwillingness of the South Vietnamese to live up to their end of the bargain. Who could blame the United States for pulling up stakes and getting out, given the chaos that prevailed in the South as the year turned? If a unilateral American withdrawal was too difficult for an American president to pursue, a fig-leaf extrication could in all likelihood be engineered, perhaps via a Geneva-type conference—so said not only de Gaulle's government in Paris, but Harold Wilson's in London, Lester Pearson's in Ottawa, and Eisaku Sato's in Tokyo; so said the UN's U Thant; so said leading lawmakers on Capitol Hill; so said numerous columnists and editorial writers in the United States. The fact that most of these voices failed to spell out in detail how this negotiated withdrawal would be secured (a subject we shall return to) should not obscure the fact that they believed that it could be. They believed North Vietnam, China, and, especially, the Soviet Union were anxious to avoid a dramatically escalated war, which boded well for the prospects of getting the United States some kind of face-saving agreement.

Thus the irony of America's credibility dilemma: far from it being enhanced or preserved by the decision to wage large-scale war in Vietnam, it suffered as a result, much as these outside observers predicted. The core component of the credibility imperative was an assumption that a failure to stand firm in the war would cause allies around the world to question, and perhaps lose faith in, America's commitment to their defense, and would embolden adversaries to act aggressively. It was a kind of "psychological domino theory," as Jonathan Schell has put it, and there was but one thing wrong with it: it did not reflect the realities of the international system of late 1964–early 1965.[6] Already then, in the months *before* the escalation, what allied and nonaligned governments questioned was not America's will but its judgment; already then, many wondered why, in the wake of Johnson's massive election victory over Barry Goldwater, he did not take the cover that this victory (and large Democratic majorities in Congress) provided him and opt for a de-escalation of American involvement. The attitudes of the USSR and China are harder to measure, but certainly the Soviets were no less desirous than the western allies of averting a major war. For that matter, it seems undeniable that George Ball and Mike Mansfield were correct in arguing in 1964 that U.S. credibility vis-à-vis these two powers would in the medium and long run suffer much less from a negotiated American withdrawal from South Vietnam, even if the deal led eventually to a reunified Vietnam under Hanoi's control, than from getting drawn into a deep and deadly morass.

American officials were well aware of these widespread and fundamental doubts about the direction of U.S. policy. Indeed, the best proof for the absence of support for a larger war is the phenomenal amount of energy American officials expended fretting about it. Beginning already in the early fall of 1963, they worried about the fluidity in domestic opinion generally, and about the growing antipathy among elite voices in the United States and among important actors abroad. Surveys showing broad support for the Vietnam commitment were scant comfort to them, because they knew the support was soft. This explains why, early in 1964, White House and State Department aides began speaking of the need for a "public information" campaign on the war (subsequently launched in late spring). And it explains why administration insiders paid so much attention to each new *New York Times* editorial advocating neutralization for Vietnam, each new Lippmann column calling the war unwinnable in any meaningful sense, each new pronouncement from de Gaulle or U Thant suggesting the need for a negotiated solution. The extensive efforts begun in mid 1963 and expanded in 1964 to pressure these critics to change their position or at least keep their objections silent is testimony to these official fears.

The pressure campaign produced mixed results. On the one hand, the administration succeeded in persuading many domestic dissidents to keep their objections quiet, partly by playing to their patriotism (true Americans do not challenge the commander in chief on global issues in a time of Cold War) and partly by seducing them into thinking their ideas were taken seriously. On the other hand, none of those targeted were converted to the administration's point of view, at least not fully—a few appear to have been half-converted, such as the *New York Times*'s James Reston, who would suggest in one column that wider U.S. military involvement would be folly and in the next that there might be no alternative. With the notable exception of Lyndon Johnson, who seems to have been genuinely mystified that domestic critics in particular would cling so stubbornly to their positions, senior officials were not really surprised at this lack of success. They faced a formidable group of dissidents, they knew, one that would not be easily swayed. Charles de Gaulle, U Thant, Hans Morgenthau, Walter Lippmann, Mike Mansfield, Frank Church, J. William Fulbright—no foreign-policy slouches these. In later years, supporters of the war would have considerable success dismissing leaders of the so-called antiwar movement as ignorant and naive, as innocent in the affairs of the world. They could not make that claim with these earlier critics, all of whom were acknowledged "realists" in world politics and almost all of whom fully embraced the need for a vigorous (if discriminating) western posture in the Cold War.[7]

But the key point here is not that policymakers shared, in many cases, the same backgrounds and foreign-policy experience as their detractors; the key point is that they also shared many of the same judgments about the state of the war in Vietnam and the prospects for a turnaround. Lyndon Johnson and his chief lieutenants fully agreed that the military picture was grim and getting grimmer, and though they liked to say (even privately among themselves) that bombing North Vietnam would make a major difference to the situation in the South, deep down they suspected otherwise. Most were not optimistic that Hanoi would succumb to this form of coercion and cease its support of the insurgency, and they knew that, regardless, the keys to victory lay below the seventeenth parallel. Even as they dispatched the first contingent of U.S. troops to the war, the president and his men understood that it would bring resentment from many southerners, including leaders in Saigon, and generate charges of "colonialism" from elsewhere in Asia and around the world. As for the quality of government in South Vietnam, U.S. leaders were no more sanguine than their critics: they knew it was less capable and less popular than ever, permeated with dissension, and—in some quarters at least—not altogether unsympathetic to an early end to the war through a deal with the NLF or Hanoi.

Even in their estimations of the regional and global implications of a defeat in Vietnam, many senior policymakers did not differ all that much from most of the dissenters—especially if the defeat occurred because of the perceived ineptitude or apathy of the South Vietnamese themselves. Hence the difficulty of speaking of "fundamental assumptions" in the American vision. Officials certainly worried about possible Chinese expansion in the wake of such an eventuality, but they too understood that historic Sino-Vietnamese friction and very current Sino-Soviet friction militated against that possibility. They were concerned about the possible increase in the appeal of Maoist revolutions in other newly emerging nations should Ho Chi Minh's be allowed to succeed, but they knew that the internal conditions that made Vietnam so ripe for a communist takeover did not exist in many other nations in the region. With regard to the likely Soviet reaction to a withdrawal without victory, it cannot be considered a major concern in the upper levels of the administration. Senior strategists believed that Moscow would want to continue steps toward improved bilateral relations with the United States regardless of the outcome in Vietnam, and they do not appear to have worried much about increased Soviet penetration in other Third World areas.

WHY AMERICANIZATION?

Seen in this light, the Americanization of the war becomes difficult to understand. The isolation of the United States on the war among its international allies at the end of 1964; the thin nature of domestic American popular support for the Vietnam commitment; the downright opposition to a larger war among many elite American voices; the spreading war-weariness and anti-Americanism in urban and rural areas of South Vietnam; and the political chaos in Saigon—add all these elements together, along with the fact that senior officials in Washington knew of them and worried about them, and you have a policy decision that is far less easily explained than many would suggest (and this author used to believe). This does not mean it is impossible to explain. If the war was not overdetermined, it was not "underdetermined" either. Major escalation was bound to be one of the options under consideration in the halls of power in Washington in the winter of 1964–1965. Ever since the initial decision to aid the French war effort some fifteen years earlier, U.S. policymakers had always, at points of decision, opted to expand the nation's involvement rather than decrease it, and it stands to reason that they would give serious thought to doing so again, even if this time the escalation would be of an entirely different magnitude. That Johnson and his aides operated without deep public support and isolated from most western governments is a significant consideration in our analysis, but it is not by itself decisive—they would hardly have been the first lonely warriors in history, or the first to press ahead despite long odds against success. They commanded the greatest military power in the history of the world, they knew, and it makes sense that they would be tempted therefore to forge ahead, despite their general lack of optimism about the prospects in the war.

The more discerning opponents of escalation understood this and were hardly surprised when they learned, at various points in 1964, that the administration had begun laying contingency plans for expanded military action against North Vietnam. Significantly, however, few of these critics appear to have believed that these contingency plans would actually be implemented in the end. Surely Lyndon Johnson would prevent such a thing from happening, most assumed, if not before the November election, then certainly after. He was too skillful a politician, and too committed to his ambitious domestic agenda, to allow himself to be thrust into a major war in a politico-military swamp like South Vietnam. Moreover, many of these critics took for granted that alongside the planning for wider military action there would be planning, of roughly equal scope and intensity, for disengagement from the war. In the crisis situation of late 1964, staffers at the British Foreign Office, for example, thought their counterparts in the State Department must be working day and night to come up with imaginative ways of getting the United States out of a disastrous situation with minimum loss to the nation's prestige. In reality, little such thinking was taking place. That part of Foggy Bottom dealing with diplomacy in Vietnam was a quiet place as the year drew to a close, whatever small staff might be on hand usually home in time for supper.

For by then, the issue had really been decided in the inner sanctum of power: the United States would pursue a military solution in Vietnam, through escalation if necessary. As early as the previous spring the top officials had reached that conclusion, and they had never deviated from it. The question is why. As should be obvious from the foregoing analysis, and from the narrative in the preceding chapters, I attach more explanatory power to the short-term and personal factors in that decision than to long-term and impersonal ones. To be sure, the longer history of American involvement in Indochina, dating back to at least 1945, laid the necessary foundation for the policies that came later. John F. Kennedy inherited a difficult situation in Vietnam in January 1961, and the one he handed to his successor was more difficult still. Americans had already begun to perish in the war, and that fact, along with constant public reaffirmations in the late 1950s and early 1960s of South Vietnam's importance to U.S. security, complicated the situation that Kennedy and, especially, Lyndon Johnson confronted.

In the same way it would be foolish to deny that the decision to go to war in Vietnam was partly the product of long-term, subterranean currents in American ideology and culture. Michael H. Hunt has described an American foreign-policy ideology that took shape at the nation's founding and from the start contained three principal components: a vision of national greatness; a belief in a racial hierarchy, in which Native Americans, blacks, and Asians ranked below whites; and fear of revolution.[8] That the men who took the nation to war adhered to this ideological triad, that it helped shape their approach to the Vietnam issue, cannot be doubted. They were also products of their past, a past that had witnessed a devastating world war, one seemingly the result of a failed appeasement of Hitler at Munich, and which had been followed by a postwar division of Europe, by a communist takeover in China, and by a major conflict against communist foes in Korea. Americans, never wholly comfortable in the murky world of European-style diplomacy, with its emphasis on pragmatic give and take leading to imperfect solutions, took these experiences in World War II and its aftermath as reasons to be doubly suspicious of compromising with adversaries.

Diplomacy indeed held almost no place in the containment policy that emerged after 1945. Since the Soviets were thought to be fanatics, foreign to western ideas and traditions, talking to them was essentially pointless. Since they also were bent on exporting their system and imposing it on unwilling peoples, the United States, as the leader of the free world, had a moral obligation to stop them. Perceptive observers like Walter Lippmann and George Kennan saw already in 1947, with the enunciation in that year of the Truman Doctrine, the possibility that there was but a short step between this containment policy and an indiscriminate globalism that could compel the United States to intervene militarily on behalf of weak puppet states in remote areas of the world—places, that is, like Vietnam. Both men understood that the mere possession of great national power, such as America enjoyed after 1945, would make it hard for leaders to resist projecting that power far and wide and intervening in the affairs of others.

It could be tempting, therefore, to draw a straight line between the Truman Doctrine and the landing of the marines at Danang. The temptation should be resisted. For one thing, containment did not turn out to be quite the undiscriminating policy that Lippmann and Kennan feared it would be, which was one reason both of them often ended up supporting it in practice (even as they continued to object to it in theory) in the two decades that followed. American policymakers, it turned out, did not challenge communist expansion at every point; when they did, they did not always use military means. Moreover, though the Cold War Consensus that emerged in the early postwar period had a powerful hold on American culture and society, it had begun to fracture by the early 1960s, in large measure because the Cold War itself had changed. By 1963, certainly, there was de facto recognition by both superpowers of the other's legitimacy and therefore reduced attachment to the notion of irreconcilable ideological differences. By then one could speak of mutually (if tacitly) agreed spheres of influence, and of a tacit agreement not to use nuclear weapons except as a last resort. This new atmosphere suggested an opportunity for at least a limited rapprochement, and Kennedy and Khrushchev initiated moves in that direction in the last year of JFK's life. In western capitals, including Washington, officials and informed outside observers by now understood that communism was not monolithic, that Moscow and Beijing often viewed each other with more suspicion than they viewed the United States. They understood, most of them, that in Vietnam Ho Chi Minh possessed nationalist credentials that his counterparts in Saigon lacked.

The problem with structural explanations for the American war in Vietnam is that they ultimately do not explain very much. The ideology that Hunt delineates must be taken into consideration, but it could be applied as easily to the opponents of large-scale war on behalf of South Vietnam as to those who supported it. The Western European leaders who advised against Americanization could be said to have operated within a roughly similar ideological triad. For virtually everyone in public life in the early 1960s the word *Munich* had bad connotations, but not everyone thought *appeasement* had applicability in Southeast Asia—hence the danger of speaking of a "Munich generation" that took the United States into Vietnam. The Korean War analogy meant different things to different people, even those at the highest levels of decision making. And although many Americans were inclined to doubt the relevance of the France-in-Indochina analogy, on the grounds that America's power was so much greater, its purposes so much more noble, a significant number thought it very important indeed.[9] Leaders in the later antiwar movement would say it was the "establishment," the "ruling elite," that got the United States into war, but this, too, explains little—the *New York Times* was a pillar of that establishment, as were Lippmann and Mansfield and others of like mind. Long before there were college sit-ins and draft-card burnings they were advising against a deeper involvement in Vietnam.

The same lack of explanatory power attends interpretations that emphasize the role played by American economic imperatives. The most sophisticated exponents of the neocolonialist model avoid crude economic determinism in their analysis. They acknowledge that Vietnam itself was not economically valuable to the United States and indeed make an argument that is essentially unassailable: that policymakers sought, as one author has put it, "to create an integrated, essentially capitalist world framework out of the chaos of World War Two and the remnants of the colonial systems."[10] Perfectly true, but not very helpful. Exactly how did this commitment to an integrated capitalist order require a military intervention in Vietnam? Presumably the same imperatives were there in 1973, when Richard Nixon *ended* U.S. military involvement; certainly they must have been there in the spring of 1961, when JFK chose to pursue neutralization in Laos (the Laos that Eisenhower had called "the cork in the bottle") rather than a military solution. In the high-level policy deliberations of 1964–1965 concerns for the fate of world capitalism appear to have been *entirely* absent, while the main worry about the American economy was that it would be harmed by a larger war. Corporate America appears to have felt likewise. On 11 February 1965 the U.S. stock market took its biggest plunge since the day of the Kennedy assassination. The reason: investor concerns, after the Pleiku attack and American retaliatory air strikes, that the United States was sliding into a major land war in Asia.

The best arguments for the primacy of long-term factors in the 1965 escalation are those that confine themselves to the conflict itself—that is, to the cumulative weight of fifteen-plus years of American involvement in Vietnamese affairs and the sheer momentum (or, some would say, inertia) this caused. This is the "phenomenon of escalation," in which an initial set of decisions starts a chain of processes, each more difficult to control than the predecessor, each widening the area of action. But the decisions and developments of these early years only serve to make the decision for war more likely; they by no means *ensure* it. This is true of the various steps the Eisenhower team took in 1954–1960; it is true of the Kennedy administration's implementation of NSAM 111 in November 1961; it is true of its support of the coup against Ngo Dinh Diem two years later. The latter decision is often called decisive, because it ostensibly made American officials feel "responsible" for making sure any and all subsequent governments succeeded.[11] This is going too far. The Diem coup's legacy was significant, no doubt, but claims about American responsibility for each regime that followed lose much of their luster when one considers the chronic apathy and lack of skill with which those regimes pursued the twin tasks of fighting the war and governing effectively. In the massive internal record of the policy deliberations of late 1964–early 1965, nary a mention is made of the coup and its legacy.

A quarter of a century ago, two students of the events described in this book rightly observed that it would be a mistake to look for a single cause of the Americanization of the Vietnam War.[12] But it will not do merely to list *x* number of causes. It is the task of the historian to reduce a given list of causes to order by establishing a causal hierarchy, and to relate the items in this hierarchy to one another. For the leading causes of the 1965 escalation we must look to the short term, and especially to the year 1964 and to the interaction in that period of Lyndon Baines Johnson and his most senior advisers, Robert McNamara, McGeorge Bundy, and Dean Rusk. They constituted the "Inner War Cabinet," to use Rusk's apt phrase; they were the "Awesome Foursome," as a newspaper scribe dubbed them. To a large extent these four men made the Vietnam policy, made it with input from various assistant secretaries, to be sure, and from the Joint Chiefs of Staff and the various members of the National Security Council, and, especially, from ambassador to Saigon General Maxwell Taylor, but with decisive power preserved for themselves.

Why did they choose war? Publicly they insisted they did it principally to defend a free people from external aggression, but this was false. Though policymakers constantly proclaimed that all they wanted for the South Vietnamese was the right of self-determination, they worked to thwart that right whenever it appeared that southern leaders might seek to broaden their base of support by shifting the emphasis of the struggle from the military to the political plane—hence the turning against the Ngo brothers in the late summer of 1963 and the Minh junta in early 1964, and the determination in late 1964 to prevent any Saigon move to end the war through a deal with the National Liberation Front. "We will oppose any independent South Vietnamese move to negotiate," said the interdepartmental Working Group's final report in late November 1964. By the start of 1964 certainly, and probably long before, the wishes of the very people the United States claimed to be defending in Vietnam had essentially ceased to matter to senior American officials. No doubt they believed that what they were doing served the Vietnamese people's ultimate interests, and that the inhabitants of the South would be grateful in the end. No doubt this assumption made them sleep better at night. But it had little to do with why they acted.

For the key consideration behind the decision for war we must look to the other rationale articulated by policymakers: *credibility* and the need to preserve it by avoiding defeat in Vietnam. This was the explanation typically advanced by officials when they addressed knowledgeable audiences in off-the-record meetings—one finds scant references to "moral obligations" or "defending world freedom" in the records of their interaction with congressional committees, with foreign government leaders, with journalists in private sessions. In these settings, the emphasis was almost always on abstract (and closely related) notions of prestige, reputation, and credibility and how these were on the line in Vietnam. Even here, however, the picture that emerges is incomplete, inasmuch as the "credibility" referred to was always a purely national concept, having to do with the position of the United States on the world stage. That is, it was *American* credibility that was at stake in Southeast Asia, *American* prestige that needed to be upheld there. Though it can be right and proper to define the credibility imperative in exclusively national terms, it will not suffice as an explanation for policy making in Vietnam. For Vietnam a broader definition is essential, one that also includes domestic political credibility and even personal credibility. For it was not merely the United States that had a stake in the outcome in Vietnam; so did the Democratic Party (or at least so Kennedy and Johnson believed), and so did the individuals who had helped shape the earlier commitment and who were now charged with deciding the next move.

We may go further and argue that, within this three-part conception of the credibility imperative, the national part was the least important. Geostrategic considerations were not the driving force in American Vietnam policy in The Long 1964, either before the election or after; partisan political considerations were; individual careerist considerations were. True, some officials did see Vietnam as a vital theater in the larger Cold War struggle against world communism, did see American credibility as very much on the line—Dean Rusk was one, Walt Rostow another. Most, however, were more dubious. William Bundy and John McNaughton, two of the key players in the policy deliberations in late 1964, not only shared much of George Ball's pessimism about the long-term prospects in the war but on several occasions endorsed his relatively benign view of the likely consequences of defeat in South Vietnam. (Ball's views were at once more widely shared in the government and less influential in decision making than is often assumed.) Robert McNamara and McGeorge Bundy worried about the implications for America's world position of a defeat in Vietnam and were highly effective exponents of a staunch U.S. commitment to the war—never more forthrightly than in their "Fork in the Y" memo of 27 January 1965. But they cannot be considered true believers on Vietnam, at least not after the latter part of 1964, in the sense of truly believing that the United States had a moral obligation to help the South Vietnamese or that American national interests were seriously threatened by events in Indochina. So why did they favor Americanization? Less out of concern for America's credibility, I believe, than out of fears for their own personal credibility. For more than three years, McNamara and Bundy had counseled the need to stand firm in the war (a relatively easy thing to do in, say, 1962, when the commitment was small and the Cold War situation considerably more tense), and to go against that now would be to expose themselves to potential humiliation and to threaten their careers. It is not difficult to imagine both men, and especially McNamara, arguing with equal effectiveness for the need to cut losses and get out of the conflict, had they served a president who sought such a result.

PRESIDENTIAL PRIMACY

Even if we draw back from this conclusion, even if we assume that all of the principal advisers meant it when they said that America's global credibility was on the line in Vietnam, it would still not necessarily mean that we had arrived at the main motivation behind the decision for war. For it would not tell us anything about the position and role of the central figure in the policy making, the president of the United States. And on this there can be no doubt: Kennedy and Johnson were the key players in this policy process, not merely in the obvious sense that they had to give final approval to any and all policy decisions but in the sense of actively shaping the outcome of the deliberations. Because Johnson was fated to be president when the critical choices came, it is his imprint on the policy that is our central concern in this book. It is commonplace to emphasize Johnson's dominance in the policy making in the later years of his tenure (1966–1968), when his obsession with the war became nearly total; the argument here is that his imprint was deeper than anyone else's in the early period as well. During the conflict itself and to some degree in the years after, much noise was made about Vietnam being "McNamara's War," but it was never the defense secretary's war. From 23 November 1963 it was "Lyndon Johnson's War."

This is not to deny that Johnson relied in important ways on the triumvirate of McNamara, Bundy, and Rusk. He obviously did, in all the ways outlined in previous chapters. Tom Wicker has captured it well: "He would look around him and see in Bob McNamara that it was technologically feasible, in McGeorge Bundy that it was intellectually respectable, and in Dean Rusk that it was historically necessary." Here, indeed, is another reason why the appellation "McNamara's War" is misleading: it exaggerates his importance in relation to the other two. Bundy, as both policy advocate *and* manager of the flow of foreign-policy information that reached the president, could and often did play a major role in determining what items would be up for discussion in policy deliberations—most notably, he eliminated the disengagement option from the agenda of topics for his meetings with Maxwell Taylor in Saigon in early February 1965.[13] Rusk, for his part, reinforced Johnson's conventional, inflexible approach to foreign-policy problems and shared his penchant for simplistic analogizing between Munich in 1938 and Saigon in 1965. As secretary of state, Rusk was the nation's chief diplomat, but he was as hostile as anyone in the administration to even exploring the possibilities for a diplomatic solution. Much of the responsibility for the rigidity of the American approach to negotiations throughout the period under study must be laid at his feet.

But Johnson was always first among equals, as the internal record makes clear. If his top Vietnam aides intimidated him with their accomplishments and academic pedigrees, he also intimidated them with his forceful presence and his frequent resort to bullying tactics, and he established firm control of his administration from the start. Furthermore, no president is a prisoner to his advisers—Eisenhower and Kennedy had rejected policy recommendations on Vietnam, and Johnson might have done the same had he so desired. (He showed a capacity to do so on non-Vietnam issues.) He did not. What, then, drove Johnson's approach to the Vietnam issue? Chiefly its potential to do harm to his domestic political objectives and to his personal historical reputation. Both concerns were there from the start—he determined already in late 1963 that Vietnam would be kept on the back burner in 1964, so as to avoid giving Republicans an issue with which to beat up on Democrats in an election year, and he vowed only hours after the Dallas assassination that he would not be the president who lost Vietnam.

Understanding this duality in Johnson's thinking about the war, in which partisan calculations competed for supremacy with concerns for his personal reputation, is essential to understanding the outcome of the policy process in Washington in the fifteen months that followed his taking office as president. The former explains his determination to keep Vietnam from being lost in an election year, a year in which he also sought to pass major pieces of the Democratic Party's legislative agenda. But it cannot by itself explain his willingness to proceed with a major military intervention—whose importance and viability he himself doubted—after the glorious election results, which brought not only a smashing victory over Barry Goldwater but also huge Democratic majorities in both houses of Congress. It cannot explain Johnson's refusal to even consider possible alternatives to a military solution, never more resolutely than in those important weeks after the election.

For this reason it would be wrong to overemphasize the importance of the Great Society in the decision to escalate the conflict—that is, to give too much weight to the idea that LBJ took the nation to war because of fears that if he did not, Republicans and conservative Democrats would oppose and possibly scuttle his beloved domestic agenda. Concerns along these lines certainly existed within Johnson, and they directly influenced the *way* in which he expanded the war—in particular, they dictated that the escalation be as quiet as possible so as to avoid the need for choosing between the war and the programs, between guns and butter. But strategizing of this sort cannot be considered the primary *cause* of the decision for escalation. McGeorge Bundy spoke well to this point years later: "I think if [Johnson] had decided that the right thing to do was to cut our losses, he was quite sufficiently inventive to do that in a way that would not have destroyed the Great Society. It's not a dependent variable. It's an independent variable." In Bundy's view, Johnson saw achieving victory in Vietnam as important for its own sake, not merely as something necessary to ensure the survival of some domestic agenda. LBJ had vowed steadfastness in Vietnam in his very first foreign-policy meeting in November 1963 and had adhered to that line at all points thereafter.[14]

A healthy dose of skepticism is always warranted when considering the recollections of former policymakers, especially when the subject is responsibility for policy mistakes. But here Bundy had it right. Lyndon Johnson was a hawk on Vietnam, and he was so for reasons that went beyond immediate domestic political or geostrategic advantage. For it was not merely his country's and his party's reputation that Johnson took to be on the line, but also his own. His tendency to personalize all issues relating to the war, so evident in the later years, in 1966 and 1967 and 1968, was there from the start, from the time he vowed to not be the first American president to lose a war. From the beginning, he viewed attacks on the policy as attacks on himself, saw American credibility and his own credibility as essentially synonymous. In so doing he diminished his capacity to render objective judgment, to retain the necessary level of detachment. He failed to see that the international and domestic political context gave him considerable freedom of maneuver, if not in the period before the November 1964 election then certainly in the weeks thereafter.

It would be difficult to exaggerate the importance of this conflation of the national interest and his own personal interest in Johnson's approach to Vietnam. Skeptical readers may nevertheless think I have done so, that I have overestimated LBJ's commitment to standing firm in Vietnam, especially in the early months of his presidency, and underestimated the influence of his top advisers on shaping that approach. It is true that Johnson did not come into office looking for a fight in Vietnam. He was no warmonger. There is no reason to doubt his frequent assertions that he hated the war, hated what it was doing to his country and his dreams for creating a Great Society that would eliminate poverty, illiteracy, and homelessness among his people (and they were always *his* people). It is also clear that he always possessed considerable skepticism about the prospects in Vietnam—not infrequently his doubts on that score surpassed those of his closest aides. But warriors need not be enthusiastic or optimistic to be committed. From the start of his tenure, perhaps even from the time he visited South Vietnam on Kennedy's behalf in mid 1961, Lyndon Johnson's position on the Vietnam issue did not deviate from the fundamental position that defeat there had to be avoided.

This included defeat disguised by some kind of negotiated settlement, one providing a "decent interval" before the reunification of the country under communist control. Had Johnson been concerned only with, or even primarily with, preserving *American* credibility and/or *Democratic* credibility, he surely would have ordered extensive contingency planning for some kind of fig leaf for withdrawal in the months leading up to escalation, when the outlook looked grimmer than ever. He would have actively sought, rather than actively avoided, the advice of allied leaders like Harold Wilson and Lester Pearson and given much deeper reflection to the urgings of anti-

Americanization voices on Capitol Hill and in the press community. His dislike of the war was hardly less intense than theirs, after all, his evaluation of the Saigon government's potential not significantly more rosy. But the end result of the scenario these critics espoused—American withdrawal without victory—was one Johnson could not contemplate, largely because of the damage such an outcome could do to his own personal reputation.

The concern here went deeper than merely saving his political skin. In private LBJ would sometimes say that he could not withdraw from Vietnam because it would lead to his impeachment, but he was too smart a politician to really believe such a thing. What he really feared was the personal humiliation that he believed would come with failure in Vietnam. He saw the war as a test of his own manliness. Many have commented on the powerful element of *machismo* in Johnson's world view, rooted in his upbringing and fueled by his haunting fear that he would be judged insufficiently manly for the job, that he would lack courage when the chips were down.[15] In his world there were weak and strong men; the weak men were the skeptics, who sat around contemplating, talking, criticizing; the strong men were the doers, the activists, the ones who were always tough and always refused to back down. Thus Mansfield could be dismissed as spineless, as "milquetoast"; thus Fulbright could be castigated as a "crybaby." Though Johnson on occasion showed himself quite capable of asking probing questions in policy meetings, he had little patience with those who tried to supply probing answers. His macho ethos extended to relations among states. "If you let a bully come into your front yard one day," he liked to say, in reference to the lesson of Munich, "the next day he will be up on your porch and the day after that he will rape your wife in your own bed." In such a situation, retreat was impossible, retreat was cowardly. Johnson's approach did not make him reckless on Vietnam—he was, in fact, exceedingly cautious—but it made him quite unable to contemplate extrication as anything but the equivalent of, as he might put it, "tucking tail and running."[16]

This personal insecurity in Johnson, so much a feature of the recollections of those who knew him and worked with him, might have been less important in Vietnam policy if not for the way it reinforced his equally well documented intolerance of dissent. Even in the early months of his presidency he was incredulous to learn that some Americans might be opposed to his policy of fully supporting South Vietnam; it was un-American, he believed, to make an issue during the Cold War of national security matters. Throughout his career Johnson had made his way in politics by intimidation, by dominating those around him, and he did not change this modus operandi once he got into the White House. "I'm the only president you have," he told those who opposed his policies. His demand for consensus and loyalty extended to his inner circle of advisers, a reality that, when combined with his powerful personality, must have had a chilling effect on anyone inclined to try to build support for a contrary view.[17] Recall the point made later by McGeorge Bundy, certainly no contrarian voice: "You can't organize against Lyndon Johnson without getting bombed before breakfast, because in his view that's the final and ultimate conspiracy."[18] When Vice President Hubert H. Humphrey (one of the "weak" men in Johnson's lexicon) in early 1965 gingerly began advocating a de-escalated American involvement and made the crucial mistake of voicing his concerns not merely in a private memo to LBJ but also in a meeting of the National Security Council, Johnson banned him from Vietnam policy discussions for a year. Canadian prime minister Lester Pearson suffered the same fate in April 1965 after suggesting a pause in the bombing of the DRV; for the remainder of the Johnson presidency, Canada would be in the dark about U.S. policy in the war.

Access thus did not equal influence. A large number of individuals had the former; only a few also had the latter. Johnson would hear the critics out—he frequently talked to them privately, often professed sympathy with their views, and accepted their private memos—but there is no evidence that he ever really considered their arguments. The implications for our analysis are enormous. Johnson's aversion to dissent and his obsessive fear of leaks created a cloistered decision-making system that effectively excluded contrarian voices from the deliberations and discouraged in-depth reexamination of the fundamental issues among those who remained. A conformist atmosphere reigned. (George Ball, the one high-level official to question the move to a larger war, was himself a conformist, willingly accepting the assignment of in-house "devil's advocate" and always making clear that he would remain the loyal insider regardless of what policy decision emerged.)

In this way, while responsibility for the outcome of the policy process rested with all of those who participated in it, it rested chiefly with the president. Johnson, no one else, ensured that the critical decisions on Vietnam were made by a small and insular group of individuals who by the latter part of 1964 had been involved in policy making for several years in most cases, who had overseen the steady expansion in the U.S. commitment to the war, and who had a large personal stake in seeing that commitment succeed. He more than anyone determined that there would be not a single NSC meeting from October 1964 to the eve of the Pleiku incident in February 1965, and that those that occurred after that date were mostly about rubber-stamping decisions already reached. (After February 16 there would be only four more until July.) Bundy and others may have encouraged him in this schedule, but it also corresponded with the way he liked to do business. Johnson was poorly served by his advisory system, but it was a system he in large measure created.

IF OSWALD HAD MISSED

One way to assess Johnson's importance in the decision for war, especially in a book that also examines the record of his predecessor, is to remove him from the equation, through consideration of what John F. Kennedy might have done in Vietnam had he returned from Texas alive. Counterfactual questions of this kind often make professional historians nervous, but they should not. Thinking about unrealized possibilities is an indispensable part of the historian's craft—we can judge the forces that prevailed only by comparing them with those that were defeated. All historians, whenever they make causal judgments, are engaging in speculation, are envisioning alternative developments, even when these alternatives are not stated explicitly. In this case, speculating about what Kennedy *might* have done in the conflict helps us better understand what his successor *did* do.

The Kennedy-in-Vietnam counterfactual is especially conducive to fruitful exploration because of the massive available documentary record for the period in question; because of the short period of time between the assassination and the moment of truth in the decision making; and because of the minimal number of likely changes in other key variables. The following base assumptions seem reasonable: that a surviving Kennedy would have kept his advisory team (which became Johnson's) more or less intact, at least through the 1964 election; that he likely would have faced Goldwater in that election, as Johnson did, and would have beaten him; that, like Johnson, he would have wanted to keep Vietnam on the back burner until voting day; that the situation in South Vietnam would have deteriorated at more or less the same rate as under his successor; and that, therefore, crunch time for him likely would have come at about the same time as for Johnson, as 1964 turned into 1965.

How would Kennedy have responded when the difficult choices came, when he could temporize no longer? A good argument can be made that he likely would have done more or less what Johnson did and Americanized the war, but a better one is that he probably would not have done so, that he would instead have chosen some form of disengagement.[19] None of the components that make up this argument hold persuasive power when standing alone; for full effect, they must be considered systematically and in terms of their *cumulative* impact.

Consider, first, one of the points articulated in chapter 1: that running through Kennedy's whole approach to the war was a fundamental ambivalence about the conflict and what to do in it. Chapter 2 suggested that JFK remained committed to the war effort at the time of his death, but this is not the contradiction it might appear to be. There are commitments and there are commitments. The Kennedy record reveals a man who sought victory in Vietnam from day one to the end, who opposed negotiations, and who helped overthrow Ngo Dinh Diem, but it also reveals a man who always had deep doubts about the enterprise and deep determination to keep it from becoming an American war. He may have significantly expanded the Eisenhower administration's assistance to the Saigon regime, but it still fit under the rubric of *assistance*; as such, it was a long way from the Johnson team's decision in 1964–1965 to Americanize the war, essentially to take over the fighting from the South Vietnamese. Johnson's doubts, though considerable, were less fundamental; they centered on whether the war effort would be successful rather than on whether it should be undertaken.

Kennedy's decision to pursue a negotiated settlement in Laos further demonstrated his disinclination to use American ground troops in Indochina. To be sure, Laos never mattered as much as Vietnam in American official and popular opinion, which made the decision to negotiate there comparatively easy. Likewise, it is possible, as some have argued, that the Laos decision only made Kennedy more determined to affirm U.S. support for South Vietnam—conciliation in one place necessitated standing firm somewhere else. Nevertheless, the Laos case is further evidence of JFK's opposition to large-scale interventions in that part of the world, even when senior associates called for them. Significant as well is that in opting against military intervention in Laos Kennedy relied heavily on the advice of America's leading allies. In particular, Britain's Harold Macmillan and France's Charles de Gaulle made a strong impression on him with their outright opposition to any kind of significant military action there, both in the spring of 1961 and at all points thereafter. For Kennedy this allied opposition was critical, because unilateral intervention by the United States would, he was convinced, bring sharp domestic criticism and widespread international condemnation. As a result, allied support became for JFK very much a prerequisite for large-scale military action in both Laos *and* Vietnam, without which he was deeply reluctant to proceed. Not so with his successor. As we have seen, the colossal failure of the "more flags" program did not deter

Johnson, and he exhibited a singular lack of interest in seeking allied advice on what to do in the war.

A post-Dallas Kennedy would have faced one significant disadvantage vis-à-vis Johnson, in terms of a greater stake in the war and a vested interest in seeing the administration's "flexible response" policy succeed. Overall, however, the greater disadvantages belonged to Johnson, and each of them served to reduce his freedom of action (real and imagined) on the war. First and most obvious, he was a new president in late November 1963, new and untested. Many in the foreign-policy establishment mistrusted him; many others questioned his qualifications. Just a few months hence Democrats would accept or reject him at the national convention, and not long after that the general public would pass their judgment on him. Johnson believed, no doubt accurately, that adversaries at home and abroad were watching him closely, watching his responses to problems and probing for signs of weakness. Little wonder that he perceived the need not only for "continuity" in his foreign policy but also for firmness.[20]

Kennedy, by contrast, could in no way be considered untried in the fall of 1963. He had faced an uncommon number of foreign policy crises in his tenure; to some of these he responded well, to others not, but all made him more battle-tested. A little over a year before his death, Kennedy had showed strength and gained prestige in forcing Khrushchev to withdraw Soviet missiles from Cuba; regardless of whether JFK's tough stance was wise or necessary, few could question his steadfastness after that point. Then in mid 1963 he signed the limited nuclear test ban treaty with Moscow, which he could cite as his commitment to peace. At the time of his death, therefore, he had a sizable fund of political credibility as a foreign-policy leader, something LBJ never possessed.

The timing of the assassination, occurring as it did only about a year before the 1964 election, also may have served to limit Johnson's perceived freedom of action. Whereas Kennedy would have faced the critical Vietnam decisions in his second (and final) term, when the domestic political implications of those decisions would be at least somewhat less pressing, Johnson faced them in what amounted to his first term—for him the eleven months between his taking office and the 1964 election were but a prelude, a kind of preliminary campaign for who would succeed the martyred leader. The relative freedom of maneuver that might have led a second-term Kennedy to reevaluate fundamentally Vietnam policy in, say, December 1964, thus did not exist to the same degree for LBJ, or at least so he believed. Nor was it merely electoral considerations that kept Johnson focused on the domestic political costs of his Vietnam decisions; there was also his ambitious legislative agenda.[21] The Great Society may not have been decisive in Johnson's strategizing on Vietnam, but it certainly mattered. It stands to reason that here, too, a post-Dallas Kennedy, possessing no real Great Society equivalent, would have been less constrained.

Kennedy was no expert on Southeast Asia, but he possessed a more sophisticated understanding of the dynamics of the region than his successor. As president he privately doubted the validity of a crude domino theory, whereby a defeat in Vietnam would lead to the loss of all Southeast Asia, and he perceived from early on that there were limits to what the United States could accomplish in that part of the world. He appears to have understood, well before many of his aides, the civil-war dimension of the Vietnam conflict and the problems this might cause for American intervention. Perhaps most important, Kennedy was more cognizant than Johnson of the need for genuine political reforms in South Vietnam if there were to be long-term success in the war effort. LBJ, in one of his first comments on Vietnam upon becoming president, said there had been too much emphasis on reforms and not enough on fighting the war; although he and his top advisers would spend much time in subsequent months fretting about the absence of governmental stability in Saigon, they did not let that dissuade them from Americanizing the war.

More elusive personality differences between the two men may also have made a difference when the difficult choices came. Kennedy did not share his successor's deep self-doubt in the role of commander in chief, or his general tendency toward self-pity. Moreover, Kennedy's world view contained a pronounced skepticism that the Texan's lacked—when Dean Rusk would speak apocalyptically of the need to save "Christian civilization" by persevering in Vietnam, his words resonated with Johnson in a way they would never have done with JFK. Both presidents were intelligent men, but Kennedy possessed the more flexible and reflective mind, at least with respect to foreign affairs. It is hard to imagine him exhibiting the pigheadedness and truculence with respect to Vietnam that Johnson so frequently showed in 1965 (and in the years that followed). It is hard to imagine him telling pro-negotiation British and French officials that the only alternatives to current policy were to "bomb the hell out of China" or to retreat to Hawaii and San Francisco, or telling aides it was insulting to have foreign politicians "chasing over" to see him, or reading to allied officials a letter from a supportive American soldier in Vietnam to his mom, all of which LBJ did. It is hard to imagine Kennedy doing what Johnson did and canceling imminent visits by important world leaders merely because they opposed the U.S. bombing of North Vietnam, or telling a top aide that he would rather "get sick and leave town" than hear the peace proposals of

United Nations Secretary General U Thant and British Prime Minister Harold Wilson.

What about those two facets of Johnson's approach to which we attached particular importance above, namely his tendency to personalize all facets of the Vietnam issue and his deep dislike of dissent? Here, too, a surviving Kennedy almost certainly would have been different. He would not have seen the war as a test of his manliness to the same degree as did Johnson, for though himself imbued with a good dose of *machismo*, he was less prone to extending it to the nation, to the complex world of foreign policy. Perhaps because he had proven himself in war—Johnson had not—he never viewed attacks on foreign policy as attacks on himself to the extent LBJ did. Though politicians as a rule are notoriously averse to abandoning failed policies and altering course, these Kennedy characteristics suggest he would have had an easier time doing so than Johnson. We can further assume that Kennedy's decision-making environment, comparatively open in the pre-Dallas period, would have kept that quality afterward as well, thus distinguishing it from Johnson's.[22] This is potentially critical, for the reason already suggested: a less constrained, more Kennedy-like environment would have made the Johnson team more inclined after November 1964 to ask the really fundamental questions about the war, to listen to—not just to hear—the many independent voices predicting giant, perhaps insurmountable, obstacles ahead, given the chronic weaknesses south of the seventeenth parallel.

In the end, it is this dismal South Vietnamese politico-military situation in late 1964–early 1965, more than any personal attributes of Kennedy, that stands as the single most important reason to suppose he would have opted against a large-scale American war in Vietnam. As noted in chapter 9, it is easy today to forget the despair that this situation generated in a broad cross-section of informed observers, both American and foreign, who saw first-hand the political infighting in Saigon and the pervasive war-weariness and burgeoning anti-Americanism throughout the South. Many who had always enthusiastically supported the U.S. commitment to South Vietnam, and who would do so again a few months later after the commitment of American troops, in these months freely stated that America had no obligation to persevere under such circumstances and that there might be no option but to withdraw. Recall the assertion in mid December 1964 by the *Washington Post*, later a staunchly hawkish voice on the war: "It is becoming increasingly clear that, without an effective government, backed by a loyal military and some kind of national consensus in support of independence, we cannot do anything for South Vietnam. The economic and military power of the United States . . . must not be wasted in a futile attempt to save those who do not wish to be saved."[23]

Wise words then as now, and ones that Kennedy, for all the reasons outlined above, would have been more likely than his successor to heed.

A PERMISSIVE CONTEXT

Johnson did not heed them, and that is what ultimately matters. At the top
of the causal hierarchy for the Americanization of the Vietnam War in
1964–1965 must go Lyndon Johnson's conception of the conflict and what
it meant for his domestic political and personal historical credibility, followed
by the workings of the advisory system, and, in particular, the centrality
within that system of Mssrs. McNamara, Bundy, and Rusk. The decision for
major escalation grew out of two decades of American involvement in Indochina, and two decades of containing global communism, and it emerged
out of still-older undercurrents in American culture and ideology, but it
was crucially dependent on the active intervention of this small group of men.
To a large extent they were responsible for the bloody war that followed.

But responsibility for war cannot be ascribed solely to the perceptions
and actions of senior American officials; it must also be given to the shortcomings of those who *opposed* Americanization. This group included the
leadership in Hanoi. Northern officials had always, since the days of the
Geneva Conference, sought to avert a large-scale American military intervention in Vietnam—this objective ranked second only to the overriding
quest for reunification of the country under their control. Right up to the
spring of 1965, they hoped to prevent such an eventuality, hoped that their
U.S. counterparts would conclude that the political and military mess in
the South made de-escalation the only option. They did not, however, do
much to push the Americans to this desired result. The preceding chapters have made much of the shortcomings of American diplomacy in Vietnam—where it existed at all it was unimaginative—but it is possible to
level the same charge against the government of Ho Chi Minh. In the re-
curring nightmare of Washington policymakers in 1964–1965, Hanoi would
launch a diplomatic offensive in which it grandly proclaimed its willingness to enter into "talks" on achieving an end to hostilities. Such a move
would cost Ho and his colleagues little, these strategists reasoned, since they
would enter any talks in a dominant position, and it assuredly would earn
them kudos on the international stage. Washington's hope of avoiding premature negotiations, at least until the American military had the chance to
show its capability, would be seriously threatened.[24] Luckily for the administration, nothing of the sort happened in the period up through March
1965, as the Hanoi government stayed largely silent on the issue of nego-

tiations. If the American government played a bad diplomatic hand poorly, the North's leaders played a good one no better. By April, with American intervention a reality and with the North Vietnamese determined not to appear rattled by it, the Ho government's belief in the possibility of early talks had faded.

Ironically, just as North Vietnamese abandoned the hope for an early diplomatic settlement, western critics of U.S. policy stepped up their efforts in that direction. The late spring and summer months of 1965 witnessed feverish attempts from several quarters to facilitate a political solution. But by then, it was really too late—no political settlement could be forthcoming, it is now clear, until the American military buildup had had a chance to show its effectiveness, which would take many months. After that, the inevitable rising body counts would likely incline both sides to dig in deeper rather than seek a way out. The stakes had increased dramatically. The key period for diplomacy is thus the period before the spring of 1965, and there can be no denying the failure in these months of western proponents of a political solution in Vietnam to challenge the administration in Washington directly with their views on the conflict and what should be done to settle it.

No doubt Lyndon Johnson's imprint mattered here: his craving for approbation coupled with his general aversion to unsolicited advice (attributes well known to important audiences both at home and abroad) must have caused many to stay silent and others to wait as long as possible to speak up and then to do so in the most circumspect manner possible. Also, the White House strategy of deception, ordered by LBJ and designed to make the critics believe that their ideas really were being taken seriously and that the administration really did want early negotiations and had no plans to expand the war, for a long time succeeded in inducing high-profile dissenters to keep their views quiet.

Nevertheless, the fact remains that many of those who foresaw a great calamity ahead should escalation occur failed to work hard to keep it from happening. Indeed, those domestic and foreign voices that would have had the greatest potential impact on top officials were precisely the ones that were most hesitant to speak out about forcing the administration to really confront the choice it was making. Particularly important in this regard was the British government, whose leaders shared the essentials of Charles de Gaulle's position on the war but not his willingness to speak out. The phrase "Now is not the best time for us to confront the Americans" became a kind of mantra among senior British officials in late 1964. Canadian decision makers, too, usually found reasons to avoid pressing their views on their U.S. counterparts, as did leaders in numerous other western capitals. UN Secretary General U Thant was convinced already in 1963 that no satisfactory military solution was possible for the United States and by the late summer of 1964 had assurances from Hanoi that it was willing to enter talks with Washington; nevertheless, into 1965 Thant agreed to American requests that he not push hard for negotiations.

In the United States Senate, many Democratic lawmakers—some two dozen, perhaps more—opposed Americanization and favored negotiations but too often were unwilling to say so. This congressional silence was critical in view of the essential role the legislative branch must play in the foreign-policy process, especially in those cases—like the Vietnam issue— where there is ample time for deliberation and consultation. As Paul Kattenburg has rightly noted, "if Congress does not fulfill the role of loyal opposition in foreign policy, that role does not seem to get fulfilled at all."[25] Majority Leader Mike Mansfield and Foreign Relations Committee chairman J. William Fulbright, for example, always took care to keep their concerns private and even to do the administration's bidding on occasion. Fulbright would later claim he had been deceived by the White House into believing there would be no wider war, which was true enough, but he also acted as he did because of his belief in executive branch supremacy in foreign affairs and his fear of incurring Johnson's wrath. Perhaps, too, his desire to be appointed secretary of state influenced his decision to lie low.

Outside Congress, as well, such thinking too often prevailed. Another aspirant for the top job at the State Department, Undersecretary George Ball, put loyalty to Johnson before principle; his hatred for the war was outweighed by his desire to stay on the team. Others in the government who shared Ball's views on the war, including midlevel officials in the State Department and NSC, usually chose to suffer in silence. Walter Lippmann, anxious to preserve his privileged White House access, for a long time allowed himself to be taken in by White House claims that it contemplated no major expansion of the war; as a result his columns often featured cogent and incisive assertions on the folly of escalation alongside assurances that Lyndon Johnson really sought a peaceful solution. Not until the spring of 1965, after the key decisions had been made, did Lippmann finally break fully with Johnson over the war (thereby forgoing any more White House dinner invitations).

The critics, especially those in the United States, can also be faulted for their general reluctance to spell out how a "political solution" would be reached, and with what terms. Articulate and forthright in explaining why a military solution could never succeed, many turned to mumbling when the subject of alternatives came up. Typically they offered "negotiations" leading to "neutralization" as the goal, but often with little explanation of what these words meant in the context of Vietnam. If a certain degree of fuzziness was to be expected on this score—Who could say what a final settlement would look like before negotiations had even commenced? Who knew in advance how long a coalition government in Saigon would survive before falling under Hanoi's control?—it remains true that too many opponents of Americanization failed to provide even a rudimentary roadmap for disengagement. Too many were reluctant to say what they privately believed: that the long-term result of American withdrawal (negotiated or otherwise) would likely be a reunified Vietnam under Hanoi rule; that reunification would take many months and perhaps years to occur, during which time the administration could work to shore up other parts of East Asia; and that it would be a Titoist Vietnam with which the United States could live.

All this suggests that the Americanization of the Vietnam War occurred in a permissive context. Influential observers, at home and abroad, could see the futility that lay ahead for any American military effort in South Vietnam but often were timid about saying so. Those who did speak up often gave few clues on how Washington could exit the morass. The posture of the British government and the Senate Democratic leadership, in particular, was crucial in allowing American policy to go forward, in allowing the Johnson administration to escalate by stealth. Harold Wilson and his colleagues in London were as anxious as the administration in Washington to avoid an Anglo-American rupture over Vietnam, and key Democrats shared LBJ's desire to avoid a full-fledged congressional debate on the conflict in the early weeks of 1965. If Lyndon Johnson faced a legitimate choice in the weeks after his 1964 election victory about which way to go on Vietnam, so did the London government and so did the leadership on Capitol Hill.

The permissive context extended to the general public as well, though here the problem was not timidity or vagueness but apathy. The vast majority of Americans during The Long 1964 knew little about Vietnam and cared less. The "public information campaign" launched by the administration in the late spring of 1964 to a large extent failed. Partly it failed because of the contradictions at the heart of the campaign itself—Johnson wanted to educate Americans about the importance of America's commitment to South Vietnam, but also to avoid giving them any sense that major war could be the result. (There were really two campaigns: a public information campaign and a public deception campaign.) But John Q. Citizen was also ignorant because he preferred it that way. Lyndon Johnson may have worked hard to avoid a national debate on the war in 1964–1965, but he had help from his constituents. The public, we observed in chapter 10, could have forced a debate had it wanted to; enough information existed. (The strikingly knowledgeable letters to the editor that appeared regularly in America's newspapers during the period are one proof of that.) The public did not want a debate and therefore must accept some responsibility for the debacle that followed.

There is of course one other dimension to this permissive context, and it pertains to the critics on Johnson's right, who argued strenuously that the war had to be pursued regardless of cost. In 1969 Richard Nixon and other Republicans would complain of inheriting a Vietnam mess not of their own making, of having to resolve somehow "The Democrats' War"; the assertion was specious, inasmuch as Johnson's strongest supporters in the escalation in 1965 were conservative Republicans.[26] The GOP right wing was a weaker entity in national politics in mid-decade than is often assumed, but its persistent push for a greater application of American military power in Vietnam nevertheless played a role in bringing about Americanization. The same goes for the senior leaders in the American military, who consistently chafed at restrictions on the use of military power and always warned of the disastrous consequences of allowing South Vietnam to fall. The exhortations of Nixon and Goldwater, of the Joint Chiefs of Staff, of Joseph Alsop, allowed LBJ in 1965 to claim that he was continuing to adhere to the middle road on Vietnam even as he dramatically expanded the war. It was a disinguous claim, to be sure—Johnson had always traveled much closer to the escalation side of the street than the withdrawal side—but for a time it worked.

THE UNREALIZED POSSIBILITIES

What, then, of the alternative to a major American military escalation in Vietnam in 1965? The historian who accepts that such an alternative existed is under no less of an obligation than contemporaneous critics to identify it and demonstrate its viability. That so few students of the war should have examined this question is testimony both to the widespread belief in inevitability (If it was bound to happen, why think about how it could have been avoided?) and the tendency among those who reject inevitability to stop their analysis prematurely. As historian John Prados has rightly noted, the question of how disengagement could have been arranged is not only underexamined in the literature; it is also exceedingly important, for historians as well as for the policymakers of tomorrow. "There is wisdom," Prados writes, "in knowing when to stop."

In the strategy of poker, the most skillful element lies in understanding when to hold your cards, when to bluff, when to fold your hand and walk away. American strategists have drawn about as much as possible from the illusion of victory in Vietnam, but there is vast unexplored territory in identifying points at which the U.S. might have stopped. It seems clear that in the post-cold war world, strategies for holding out amid uncertainty without damaging escalation; for defusing local crises by bluff and maneuver; for disengaging from crises by walking away— these are concepts that could be of enormous value in [America's] future.[27]

To pose disengagement as the lone option may seem unduly confining. But getting out really was the only alternative to the course the Johnson administration followed. Maintaining the status quo, in which the United States persisted in an advisory role, was no longer possible by the early weeks of 1965. U.S. officials knew that tinkering with the existing arrangements, perhaps through adding a few hundred additional American advisers, would not make an appreciable difference. What about a more rapid, more massive escalation? Could that have brought success? The Joint Chiefs then and some analysts after the war said yes, but it is hard to see this as a legitimate option in the political context of the time, given the then-reasonable official fears of the likely reaction of the Soviets and the Chinese and the larger international community (the State Department warned there would be worldwide condemnation if the United States went in with all guns blazing), and given senior policymakers' continuing doubts about the depth of the American public's support for the Vietnam commitment. Graduated pressure, for all its flaws, was the only possible escalatory strategy.[28] Nor would a hit-'em-early-and-hit-'em-hard approach have done anything to address the core problem in the war effort: the almost total absence of political legitimacy of the South Vietnamese government. Even the use of tactical nuclear weapons against the North would have made no appreciable difference in this regard.

If getting out was the only alternative to a larger war, the three months following the November 1964 election was the prime time to have opted for such a course. (Of the roughly one hundred such three-month periods in America's quarter-century involvement in Vietnam, it ranks supreme in importance.) Some fifteen months earlier, in the summer of 1963, John F. Kennedy had possessed an excellent opportunity for disengagement, given the Diem government's repression of the Buddhists and its blithe rejection of American advice, and given the constellation of forces in the international system. He chose not to take that opportunity, and it is difficult to imagine him or his successor doing anything drastic from then until after the

American election. Some authors have suggested that Johnson could have withdrawn immediately after his ascension to the White House in November 1963, but this seems unreasonable, and not only because of his (well-founded) instinct to seek continuity on all foreign-policy issues in those difficult weeks of transition. The American-sponsored coup against Diem had just occurred, and in the short term—that is, until the inertia and infighting that characterized the successor regimes became clear—this must have reinforced LBJ's inclination to stay the course. Most important, perhaps, like Kennedy, indeed like most politicians, Johnson sought to avoid making difficult policy decisions for as long as possible (prudence calls, in the bureaucratic phrase, for "keeping options open"); in late 1963, he could still stall. Not so a year later.

How might a withdrawal have been executed? The distinguished political scientist Hans Morgenthau outlined the possibilities in *Newsweek* in January 1965. (One can picture the magazine on a coffee table in the White House as officials sat nearby discussing how to expand the war.) The events of the previous months had confirmed for Morgenthau what he had begun saying early in 1964: that an American war in Vietnam was neither necessary nor winnable. "For a year," he told the magazine, "I have seen only one alternative: to get out without losing too much face. There are three possible ways this could happen. South Vietnam can tell us to get out—which is a distinct possibility. Secondly, you could have another Geneva conference which would neutralize all of Southeast Asia—which would really mean China would be recognized as the dominant power in Southeast Asia. Thirdly, you could make a bilateral deal with North Vietnam to establish a kind of coalition government, which would really be a Ho Chi Minh government with some trimmings. It would be Titoist—that is to say, Communist but not subservient to Peking or Moscow."[29]

To get out without losing too much face. That indeed was the alternative to expanding the war. Morgenthau's three suggested ways for achieving this result require closer examination. His first plan, the same one Richard Russell had suggested at various points since late 1963, may have been the best, if only because of its simplicity—it involved no intricate bilateral or multipower negotiations. It merely called for getting the current Saigon government—or, if necessary, a successor one—to ask the United States to leave. In view of the intense administration fear in late 1964–early 1965 that the United States could be asked to leave in spite of its best efforts to remain, and given the burgeoning anti-Americanism in South Vietnam, it seems entirely plausible that the Johnson administration could have secretly engineered this result if it had wanted to. It may not even have had to engineer it, given the downward trends in the South; merely doing nothing might have achieved this result. As the reliably conservative *U.S. News & World Report* put it, "if the U.S. is purposely looking for a way out of Vietnam, it can let the chaos continue to mount and then blame the failure on the South Vietnamese alone."[30]

A variant of this first plan, also involving no negotiations and potentially less embarrassing (in that it did not mean being asked by an ally to depart), would have had the administration declare on its own that it had regretfully determined that it could no longer help people who would not help themselves and therefore had no option but to withdraw. This had been the preferred option of more than a few editorial writers at the close of 1964, and many in Congress clearly viewed it sympathetically. The United States had already fulfilled any obligation it may have had to South Vietnam, the proponents of this view said, had already done more for a thoroughly uncooperative patient than any "good doctor" could be expected to do. Perhaps the best argument in favor of this plan's viability is that many South Vietnamese themselves appear to have endorsed it. As early as December 1964 Americans in Saigon were told by some in the GVN that they would not blame the administration if it decided to withdraw, and in the new year rumors were rampant in Saigon that the United States would soon disengage. The Pentagon's John McNaughton, who accompanied McGeorge Bundy to Vietnam, informed McNamara shortly before the end of the visit that the "belief is widespread among the South Vietnamese that the U.S. [is] on the verge of bugging out."[31]

Would Lyndon Johnson have had strong support among the majority Democrats on Capitol Hill if he had chosen this path? Without question. Could he have used his unsurpassed skills at persuasion to convince many skeptical Dixiecrats and moderate Republicans to go along, if necessary by showing them the stacks of intelligence analyses predicting that bombing the North would likely bring meager results and by assuring them that he was taking steps to strengthen the U.S. position in Thailand and elsewhere in Southeast Asia? Almost certainly. Could he have sold the general public on the plan, utilizing the help of respected figures such as Richard Russell, William Fulbright, Mike Mansfield, James Reston, Walter Lippmann, Drew Pearson, and Joseph Kraft? Undoubtedly. These lawmakers and journalists would have constituted an awesomely powerful voice in any national debate on the issue, and they would have won support in that debate from Morgenthau and other Realist heavyweights such as George Kennan and Reinhold Niebuhr, as well as from editorial writers at a large number of newspapers across the country.

The second possibility outlined by Morgenthau, a reconvened Geneva conference leading to an internationally guaranteed neutralization, had steadily gained adherents since French president Charles de Gaulle proposed it in 1963. Some proponents thought neutralization should be limited to South Vietnam, at least initially; others thought the conference should from the start consider neutralization for Indochina or even the whole of Southeast Asia. The Kennedy and Johnson administrations, as we have seen, opposed the idea from the start—indeed worked vigorously to thwart it—and it may be that the North Vietnamese leadership's desire to attend a multipower conference, never particularly high, had lessened by early 1965, given its growing confidence that it could achieve its objectives merely by staying put. As we observed in the previous chapter, however, Hanoi was more forthcoming on the issue than Washington, at least through the month of February, and it is hard to believe that it would have refused to attend a conference, despite its bad memories from the 1954 meeting.

The two major European powers at Geneva also supported reconvening the meeting, much to Washington's chagrin. In the view of both the French and the British, a great-power conference made sense for Washington if only because any agreement to come out of it would be preferable to whatever the U.S./GVN side could realistically achieve by military means. Paris and London officials believed, as did U Thant and others in the world community, that communist peace terms could be packaged at a conference in such a way as to allow the United States a reasonably graceful exit from South Vietnam. Veterans in many cases of the practice of complex international negotiations, these observers knew that the final shape of diplomatic agreements often do not reflect the overall politico-military balance on the ground. Many felt certain that although a coalition between enemies in a civil war seldom succeeds, it can work as a temporary settlement (especially in cases—such as the South Vietnam of 1965—in which both warweariness and a desire to be rid of foreigners are rampant at all levels of society). "No one can foretell the precise terms of an eventual settlement," Lyndon Johnson would declare much later, in March 1968, in calling for negotiations to end the conflict. A common-sensical line in 1968, it would have been no less so three years earlier.[32]

But the main reason the Geneva option held special appeal here, in the first two months of 1965, was the invigorated Soviet posture on the war, so vividly symbolized by the image of Alexei Kosygin traipsing around Hanoi in early February. The Soviet premier and his colleagues, for all their show of support of the DRV and their ritual denunciations of "imperialist aggression," supported a return to Geneva; more than that, they were now prepared, at least through the start of Rolling Thunder, to work to make it happen, in the same way that Khrushchev had done with respect to the Laos meeting. The Laos analogy is particularly pertinent in this time period, suggesting what might have been accomplished had Washington been seeking a way out of Vietnam. In 1961, Soviet and American officials had had parallel interests in a negotiated settlement in Laos in that both countries wanted to avert involvement that might lead to a major war in Asia. The Kennedy administration and its western allies accepted the 1962 accord despite reservations about its long-term viability because the civil war in Laos was being lost in any case and because Geneva gave the West time to shore up its defenses in the region. As several observers noted in early 1965, the current situation was analogous in important respects, not merely in terms of the military situation in Vietnam but in terms of the parallel interests once again held by the two superpowers.[33]

On a general level, both Washington and Moscow sought improved bilateral relations, sought to continue the steps toward détente begun under Kennedy and Khrushchev. In January there occurred much speculation in the world press that Johnson would visit the Soviet Union at some point in the year, and that Russian leaders would in turn come to the United States, and much talk about the possibility of progress on arms control, Berlin, and other issues. American officials were more hopeful than their Soviet counterparts that Vietnam could be kept separate from these efforts, but they too had to be concerned about what an escalated war would do to the prospects for improving Soviet-American relations. Most important, the two nations shared the same basic desire to check Chinese ambitions in Asia, and this, more than anything, could have allowed a subtle diplomacy of the kind practiced in the Laotian case. Said the *New York Times*, in seeing opportunities emerging out of Kosygin's mission: "A high American official was quoted the other day as saying that the ideal solution for Moscow would be 'to get the United States out of South Vietnam without letting the Chinese come in.' We think it would be ideal for the United States as well."[34]

How Beijing leaders would have reacted to a determined effort to reconvene the Geneva conference is difficult to say. Like their allies in Hanoi they appear to have become more opposed to a return to Geneva in the preceding months—they, too, smelled an American defeat and wanted to do nothing that might obfuscate things. It is doubtful, however, that they would have refused to go to a conference. (One reason the Johnson administration worked so hard to prevent a conference was that it suspected all others would say yes.) Early in 1965 the Chinese were careful to say merely that a great-power meeting on the war was unnecessary, not that they would never attend one. For that matter, the Chinese had reasons of their own to look with favor on a conference, if only as an alternative to major war. Notwithstanding their glee at Washington's troubles in Vietnam, and their scathing public denunciations of U.S. policy, they were not eager for a direct military confrontation with the United States. (Washington officials understood this as well as anyone; it is why they felt confident that Rolling Thunder would not bring a sharp Chinese response.) Nor was an increased American involvement the only thing that concerned the Beijing leadership; it also had to worry about the prospect of a revived Soviet influence on China's Southeast Asian border, influence certain only to increase in the event of a major war, since Moscow could offer the DRV much more in the way of economic and military assistance than China could.[35]

A decision to go to Geneva would have brought cries of "Appeasement!" from the Nixon-Alsop crowd at home, but it would have won powerful support as well. Senior American officials proclaimed constantly in early 1965 that they supported the principles of the 1954 Geneva accords and sought only to ensure that those principles were adhered to by all sides. Disingenuous though this claim was—the administration in fact sought to prevent the very reunification of Vietnam that was a centerpiece of the accords—it provided a useful means by which LBJ could have explained a decision to go to a conference. It is not hard to imagine Johnson giving a speech to the American people in which he reiterated this U.S. support for the Geneva principles and then said that the best way to ensure their implementation was through the convening of another multipower meeting. The speech would have been lauded by many opinion makers in the country, including the *St. Louis Post-Dispatch*. In early March, the paper declared that the Johnson administration kept contending that preserving the principles of Geneva was its only aim—"that the United States covets no territory, no military position, no bases, no political gains. The best, and the most honest way to realize such aspirations—if indeed we entertain them—is through an honorably negotiated peace settlement." At Geneva, "military neutralization of the whole of Indochina could be established, with more direct guarantees by all interested parties than in 1954. Under such terms American troops could be gradually withdrawn and the future of Viet Nam left to the decision of the Viet Namese people."[36]

Given the publicity attending any great-power conference, and the difficulties this inevitably posed for anyone in the sort of weak bargaining position occupied by the U.S./GVN side, the better negotiating avenue may have been the third plan suggested by Morgenthau, involving direct bilateral negotiations between Hanoi and Washington. This had long been the preferred form of negotiations of the North Vietnamese, who had readily agreed when U Thant late the previous summer had suggested direct talks with Washington. The Johnson administration, determined to delay negotiations until it could dictate the terms, had shown no interest, either then or after the November election, when Hanoi again expressed support.

Undoubtedly, the North Vietnamese would have taken a firm line in any bilateral talks and would have offered no major concessions. But the United States had at least some cards to play (though fewer in early 1965 than in 1964, when there had been at least the semblance of a government in Saigon), which could have allowed the "decent interval" needed to withdraw gracefully and to shore up other areas in the region. The big card was the Seventh Fleet. The retaliatory air strikes in the Gulf of Tonkin in August 1964 had shaken the Hanoi leadership, and they plainly did not relish the prospect of facing the full weight of American military power. Here the perspicacious Robert G. K. Thompson was undoubtedly correct in suggesting to Maxwell Taylor in December 1964 that the threat would be worse than the reality, that the time to try to bargain with the North was *before* you began bombing it. Respected Vietnam-watcher Bernard Fall argued likewise.[37] Given Hanoi leaders' repeated assurances to Canadian diplomat J. Blair Seaborn and others that they envisioned a coalition government in Saigon followed only gradually by reunification of the two zones, it seems likely that they would have agreed to such a deal in talks with the Americans—they could rightly expect communists to be very strong in any coalition. As the British and French governments and many second-tier U.S. officials stressed, and as several American journalists said in print, the reunified Vietnam would be a Titoist one, charting its own course and in no way a puppet of Beijing. It would thus actually be an asset in what these individuals took to be Washington's primary aim in Southeast Asia: containing China.

Morgenthau's argument, that any American war in Vietnam would be an unnecessary war, was a hopeful argument in the context of January 1965, before the carpet bombings had commenced, before U.S. fighting troops were on the scene, before the real bloodshed had started. But it is a profoundly troubling argument in hindsight (the comforting retrospective argument is the one that says it was all inevitable), less because the Johnson team failed to heed his advice than because they failed to even consider it. And there was every reason why they should have given it close consideration, given the realities of the situation in Vietnam and the realities of the domestic American and international political context. A move to extricate the United States from the war would have exacted a political price from Lyndon Johnson, but it would not have been an exorbitant price. ("Nineteen sixty-five is the year of minimum political risk for the Johnson administration," Hubert Humphrey had advised him.) It would have required moral courage, but no more of it than Americans should expect of their leaders. Moreover, the president and his team chose the war option not because

of any tangible foreign-policy concerns or moral attachment to the South
Vietnamese, but because of the threat of embarrassment—to the United
States and the Democratic Party and, most of all, to themselves personally.
They were willing to sacrifice virtually everything to avoid the stigma of
failure. If the morality of a policy is determined in large part by the com-
mensurateness of means to ends, that of the Johnson administration in Vietnam must be judged immoral.

The certainty that this was an unnecessary war, not merely in hindsight
but in the context of the time, also makes the astronomical costs that resulted from it during 1965–1973 that much more difficult to contemplate.
Foremost among these, of course, was the staggering number of deaths, especially among Vietnamese, and the utter destruction of much of the country
of Vietnam and large portions of Laos and Cambodia. The war also caused
deep social divisions within American society, fostered a destructive cynicism about government claims and actions that persists to this day, and
exacted staggering short- and long-term economic costs. (The diversion of
hundreds of billions of dollars to the war could have been used to fund, for
example, the total urban renewal of most large American cities.) Then there
were the diplomatic costs. The administration's obsession with Vietnam after early 1965 caused it to neglect other vital foreign-policy issues, including relations with Latin America, Europe, and the Middle East, as well as
the difficult frictions between rich and poor nations.[38] Most important, the
war was largely responsible for the lack of progress in East-West relations in
the Johnson years. It is entirely reasonable to suggest, as long-time Soviet
ambassador to Washington Anatoly Dobrynin has done, that had it not been
for the Vietnam War, détente between the superpowers might have come in
the mid 1960s, with potentially longer-lasting effects than the version that
came later.[39] The thawing in Moscow-Washington relations that occurred
in the year after the Cuban Missile Crisis might well have continued, leading,
if not to an outright end to the Soviet-American confrontation then at least
to something that could no longer be called a Cold War.

And there is this, finally, to say about America's avoidable debacle in
Vietnam: something very much like it could happen again. Not in the same
place, assuredly, and not in the same way, but potentially with equally destructive results. This is the central lesson of the war. The continued primacy of the executive branch in foreign affairs—and within that branch of
a few individuals, to the exclusion of the bureaucracy—together with the
eternal temptation of politicians to emphasize short-term personal advantage over long-term national interests, ensures that the potential will exist.
For it cannot be forgotten that, *given their priorities*, the decision by Lyndon
Johnson and his closest advisers for major war in Vietnam made a horrible

kind of sense. They were not evil individuals, but individuals who are not evil can enact policies that have evil consequences. A leader will assuredly come along who, like Johnson, will take the path of least immediate resistance and in the process produce disastrous policy—provided there is a permissive context that allows it. Lyndon Johnson's War was also America's War; the circle of responsibility was wide. If future Vietnams are to be prevented, the American people and their representatives in Congress will have to meet their responsibilities no less than those who make the ultimate decisions. Otherwise, American soldiers will again be asked to kill and be killed, and their compatriots will again determine, afterward, that there was no good reason why.

Abbreviations Used in the Notes

AFP	Agence France Presse
BRIAM	British Advisory Mission to South Vietnam
CF	Country File
CLV	Cambodge–Laos–Viêt-Nam
CR	*Congressional Record*
DoD	Department of Defense
EM	Entretiens et Messages
FO	Foreign Office
FRUS	*Foreign Relations of the United States*
HASC	House Armed Services Committee
HP	Handlingspapper
IMT	International Meeting and Travel File
INR	Bureau of Intelligence and Research, U.S. State Department
JFKL	John F. Kennedy Library, Boston, Massachusetts
JT	Johnson Tapes (of White House telephone conversations)
KT	Kennedy Tapes (of White House conversations)
LBJL	Lyndon Baines Johnson Library, Austin, Texas
MAE	Ministère des Affaires Etrangères
Memcon	Memorandum of conversation
MB	McGeorge Bundy
MPB	Memos to the President—McGeorge Bundy
NAC	National Archives of Canada
NF	Name File
NSAM	National Security Action Memorandum
NSF	National Security File
NYT	*New York Times*
OH	Oral History
POF	Presidential Office File

PP	*Pentagon Papers*
PPOP	*Papers of the President*
PREM	Prime Minister's Papers
PRO	Public Record Office
RSM	Robert S. McNamara
SEA	Southeast Asia
SG	Secrétariat général
SNIE	Special National Intelligence Estimate
Telcon	Telephone conversation
UD	Utrikesdepartementet
VN	Vietnam
WP	*Washington Post*
WPB	William P. Bundy

Notes

PREFACE

1. Robert S. McNamara, *In Retrospect: The Tragedy and Lessons of Vietnam* (New York: Times Books, 1995), xvi. For a rare opposing view, see Walt W. Rostow, "Vietnam and Asia," *Diplomatic History* 20, no. 3 (summer 1996): 467–471; Walt W. Rostow, *The United States and the Regional Organization of Asia and the Pacific* (Austin: University of Texas Press, 1986).

2. For the earlier period, see David L. Anderson, *Trapped by Success: The Eisenhower Administration and Vietnam, 1953–1961* (New York: Columbia University Press, 1991); Gary R. Hess, *The United States Emergence as a Southeast Asian Power, 1940–1950* (New York: Columbia University Press, 1987); Lloyd C. Gardner, *Approaching Vietnam: From World War II to Dienbienphu* (New York: Norton, 1988); Stein Tonnesson, *The Vietnamese Revolution of 1945: Roosevelt, Ho Chi Minh, and de Gaulle in a World at War* (Newbury Park, Calif.: Sage Publications, 1991); Andrew J. Rotter, *The Path to Vietnam: Origins of the American Commitment to Southeast Asia* (Ithaca, N.Y.: Cornell University Press, 1987); Ronald H. Spector, *Advice and Support: The Early Years, 1941–1960* (Washington, D.C.: Center for Military History, United States Army, 1983); Steven Hugh Lee, *Outposts of Empire: Korea, Vietnam, and the Origins of the Cold War in Asia* (Montreal: McGill-Queen's University Press, 1995); Robert D. Schulzinger, *A Time for War: The United States and Vietnam, 1941–1975* (New York: Oxford University Press, 1997); and Michael Schaller, "Securing the Great Crescent: Occupied Japan and the Origins of Containment in Southeast Asia," *Journal of American History* 69 (September 1982): 392–414. For the earliest U.S. involvement, pre–World War II, see Anne L. Foster, "Secret Police Cooperation and the Roots of Anti-Communism in Interwar Southeast Asia," *Journal of American–East Asian Relations* 4, no. 4 (winter 1995): 331–350.

3. It is curious that the developments in this year-and-a-half period have received comparatively little attention from students of the war. See Anne E. Blair, *Lodge in Vietnam: A Patriot Abroad* (New Haven, Conn.: Yale University

Press, 1995), x. A few recent scholars have begun to rectify this omission. See Blair, *Lodge in Vietnam*; Lloyd C. Gardner, *Pay Any Price: Lyndon Johnson and the Wars for Vietnam* (Chicago, Ill.: Ivan R. Dee, 1995); H. R. McMaster, *Dereliction of Duty: Lyndon Johnson, Robert McNamara, the Joint Chiefs of Staff, and the Lies That Led to Vietnam* (New York: HarperCollins, 1997); and Edwin E. Moïse, *Tonkin Gulf and the Escalation of the Vietnam War* (Chapel Hill, N.C.: University of North Carolina Press, 1996). Readers familiar with the literature on the war may be surprised that I give relatively little attention to the months of June and July 1965, which most authors have considered highly important in U.S. policy making. Well before June, I argue, the key decisions had been made; well before then, the United States had crossed the threshold from peace to war (see chapter 11).

4. According to George C. Herring, one of our foremost historiographers of the conflict, "The international aspects of the war have not been given the attention they deserve." George C. Herring, *America's Longest War: The United States and Vietnam, 1950–1975*, 3d ed. (New York: McGraw-Hill, 1996), 335. One who has studied this issue is Ralph B. Smith, *An International History of the Vietnam War*, 3 vols. (New York: St. Martin's Press, 1984–1990). Smith is persuasive in arguing for the importance of studying the war in its global context, and he makes good use of the documentation then available on North Vietnam and its allies. Unfortunately, he makes little use of the declassified American primary source material. Smith and I reach very different conclusions about the soundness of American policy. Older studies that also explore the international dimension include Janos Radvanyi, *Delusion and Reality: Gambits, Hoaxes, and Diplomatic One-Upmanship in Vietnam* (South Bend, Ind.: Gateway, 1978); and Gene T. Hsiao, ed., *The Role of the External Powers in the Indochina Crisis* (Edwardsville, Ill.: Southern Illinois University Press, 1973). Also useful is Joachim Arenth, *Johnson, Vietnam, und der Western: Transatlantische Belastungen, 1963–1969* (Munich: Olzog, 1994). Valuable studies of the Vietnam policies of individual countries are starting to appear. See, for example, Glen St. J. Barclay, *A Very Small Insurance Policy: The Politics of Australian Involvement in Vietnam, 1954–1967* (St. Lucia, Australia: University of Queensland Press, 1988); P. G. Edwards, *Crises and Commitments: The Politics and Diplomacy of Australia's Involvement in Southeast Asian Conflicts, 1948–1965* (North Sydney: Allen and Unwin in association with the Australian War Memorial, 1992); Ilya V. Gaiduk, *The Soviet Union and the Vietnam War* (Chicago, Ill.: Ivan R. Dee, 1996); Thomas R. Havens, *Fire across the Seas: The Vietnam War and Japan* (Princeton, N.J.: Princeton University Press, 1987); Douglas A. Ross, *In the Interests of Peace: Canada and Vietnam, 1954–1973* (Toronto: University of Toronto Press, 1984); Masaya Shiraishi, *Japanese Relations with Vietnam, 1951–1987* (Ithaca, N.Y.: Cornell University, Southeast Asia Program, 1990); Yngve Möller, *Sverige och Vietnamkriget: Ett unikt kapitel i svensk utrikespolitik* (Stockholm: Tidens Förlag, 1992); and Jian Chen, "China's Involvement in the Vietnam War, 1964–1969," *China Quarterly* 142 (June 1995): 356–389.

5. This point is effectively made in Michael H. Hunt, *Crises in U.S. Foreign*

Policy: An International History Reader (New Haven, Conn.: Yale University Press, 1996), 1–2, 7. Hunt notes elsewhere the critical importance of historians of U.S. foreign policy developing "the alternative, external perspective—whether domestic or international—critical to understanding the source of that policy and the consequences it unleashed." See Hunt, "Commentary: The Three Realms Revisited," in *America in the World: The Historiography of American Foreign Relations since 1941*, ed. Michael J. Hogan (New York: Cambridge University Press, 1995), 155.

6. For a perceptive examination of a rather slippery concept and its importance in post-1945 U.S. diplomacy, see Robert J. McMahon, "Credibility and World Power," *Diplomatic History* 15 (fall 1991): 455–471. Historians have been slower than political scientists in exploring the concept. Among the latter group, see, for example, Robert Jervis, *Perception and Misperception in International Politics* (Princeton, N.J.: Princeton University Press, 1976); Richard N. Lebow, *Between Peace and War: The Nature of International Crisis* (Baltimore, Md.: Johns Hopkins University Press, 1981); Michael Mandelbaum, *The Nuclear Revolution: International Politics before and after Hiroshima* (New York: Cambridge University Press, 1981); Lawrence Freedman, *The Evolution of Nuclear Strategy* (New York: St. Martin's Press, 1989); Robert Gilpin, *War and Change in International Politics* (Princeton, N.J.: Princeton University Press, 1981); William C. Wohlforth, *The Elusive Balance: Power and Perceptions during the Cold War* (Ithaca, N.Y.: Cornell University Press, 1993). See also Jonathan Schell, *The Time of Illusion* (New York: Knopf, 1976).

7. Hunt, *Crises*, 331. It is noteworthy that a June 1997 conference in Hanoi between Americans and Vietnamese (including former high-level officials) had as its main theme the issue of whether there were "missed opportunities" to end the conflict via a political solution at an earlier point. (The conferees reached no resolution on the matter.) See David K. Shipler, "Robert McNamara and the Ghosts of Vietnam," *New York Times Magazine*, 10 August 1997. A Cable News Network (CNN) television special, "The Vietnam War: Fighting Blind," which aired in December 1997, also posed as the central unanswered question whether major war might have been prevented.

8. Jeffrey Kimball, *To Reason Why: The Debate about Causes of the U.S. Involvement in the Vietnam War* (New York.: McGraw Hill, 1990), 1.

9. Jean Lacouture, *Vietnam: Between Two Truces* (New York: Random House, 1966), 224. The diplomacy of the war has received little scholarly attention. An important source, though not so much for the period under study here, is George C. Herring, ed., *The Secret Diplomacy of the Vietnam War: The Negotiating Volumes of the Pentagon Papers* (Austin, Tex.: University of Texas Press, 1983). The secondary sources, all of them at least two decades old and thus written without access to significant primary sources, include David Kraslow and Stuart H. Loory, *The Secret Search for Peace in Vietnam* (New York: Random House, 1968); Allan E. Goodman, *The Lost Peace: America's Search for a Negotiated Settlement of the Vietnam War*, Indochina Research Monograph Series no. 2 (Berkeley, Calif.: University of California, Institute of East Asian Studies, 1986); and Gareth Porter, *A Peace Denied: The United States, Vietnam,*

and the Paris Agreement (Bloomington, Ind.: Indiana University Press, 1975). All three are valuable works, but none gives much attention to the period under study. George Herring's fine essay, "Diplomacy," in Stanley I. Kutler, ed., *Encyclopedia of the Vietnam War* (New York: Scribners, 1996), 161–174, is notable for the fact that Herring begins the story in April 1965.

10. On congressional thinking in the period under study an essential source is William Conrad Gibbons, *The U.S. Government and the Vietnam War: Executive and Legislative Roles and Relationships,* 4 vols. (Princeton, N.J.: Princeton University Press, 1986–1995), vols. 2 and 3.

11. Leslie Gelb and Richard K. Betts, *The Irony of Vietnam: The System Worked* (Washington, D.C.: Brookings Institute, 1978), 244.

12. In addition to Gelb and Betts, *Irony of Vietnam,* see, for example, Robert Dallek, *Flawed Giant: Lyndon Johnson and His Times, 1961–1973* (New York: Oxford University Press, 1998); Robert Dallek, "Lyndon Johnson and Vietnam: The Making of a Tragedy," *Diplomatic History* 20, no. 2 (spring 1996): 147–162; Smith, *International History,* vols. 2 and 3; David M. Barrett, *Uncertain Warriors: Lyndon Johnson and His Vietnam Advisers* (Lawrence: University Press of Kansas, 1993); Gabriel Kolko, *Anatomy of a War: Vietnam, the United States, and the Modern Historical Experience* (New York: Pantheon, 1985); Noam Chomsky, *Rethinking Camelot: JFK, the Vietnam War, and U.S. Political Culture* (Boston: South End Press, 1993); Frank E. Vandiver, *Shadows of Vietnam: Lyndon Johnson's Wars* (College Station: Texas A&M Press, 1997); Gardner, *Pay Any Price.* See also Frank Ninkovich, *Modernity and Power: A History of the Domino Theory in the Twentieth Century* (Chicago: University of Chicago Press, 1994), 274–309; Michael S. Sherry, *In the Shadow of War: The United States since the 1930s* (New Haven, Conn.: Yale University Press, 1995), 241–250. For the argument that the Diem coup was crucial, see chapter 2, note 80.

13. The authors who have made this argument are too numerous to list. An important early version is Gelb and Betts, *Irony of Vietnam* (esp. pp. 213–214, 241–244, 353). Recent articulations include Robert Divine, "Vietnam: An Episode in the Cold War," in *Vietnam: The Early Years,* ed. Lloyd C. Gardner and Ted Gittinger (Austin: University of Texas Press, 1997), 11–22; Herring, *America's Longest War,* xi, 41–42; James T. Patterson, *Grand Expectations: The United States, 1945–1974* (New York: Oxford University Press, 1996), 604–610; Charles E. Neu, "Robert McNamara's Journey to Hanoi: Reflections on a Lost War," *Reviews in American History* 25 (1995): 729–730. The importance of the Cold War mindset in the escalation is also emphasized in Dallek, *Flawed Giant,* and Brian VanDeMark, *Into the Quagmire: Lyndon Johnson and the Escalation of the Vietnam War* (New York: Oxford University Press, 1990). See also the concluding chapter of the present volume.

14. Dallek, "Lyndon Johnson and Vietnam," 149.

15. The belief in inevitability may also have philosophical or methodological explanations, in addition to the empirical one described here. Some historians are inclined to see long-term causes as paramount in history, to see structures as more important than individuals. For these authors, powerful structural

forces pulled the United States into major war in Vietnam, forces largely immune to the whims of whoever might be occupying the Oval Office in 1963 or 1964 or 1965 (see chapter 12). The methodological explanation emerges out of the "vacuum" phenomenon referred to earlier, the overreliance by many researchers on official government documents—and then only American ones—in investigating the war and fashioning their arguments. Essential though these documents are, using them brings with it attendant risks. What one scholar has said about French diplomacy in an earlier period applies also to American diplomacy in Vietnam: "The abundant, well-arranged documentation validates the establishment's perception of its problems and policies. Thus the historian can [wrongly] conclude that ministers could have done only what they did." Anthony P. Adamthwaite, *Grandeur and Misery: France's Bid for Power in Europe, 1914–1940* (New York: St. Martin's Press, 1995), ix. Here is further proof of the essential importance of employing a wider lens: we need to examine the perceptions of ministers in other capitals and the perceptions of nonministers in the United States. That so many previous studies attach great importance to the U.S. documents pertaining to June and July 1965 may further explain the sense of inevitability in these works: by that point in time, major war does appear to have been virtually unavoidable.

16. The argument that Lyndon Johnson at the start of 1965 had considerable freedom of maneuver is made briefly in John P. Burke and Fred I. Greenstein, *How Presidents Test Reality: Decisions on Vietnam, 1954 and 1965* (New York: Russell Sage Foundation, 1989), 146–149.

17. Curiously, even veteran journalists of the Vietnam era perpetuate the image of a press that unquestioningly backed the expansion of the war. See David Halberstam, "Vietnam: Why We Missed the Story," *Washington Post National Weekly Edition*, 22–28 May 1995; Robert Scheer, "Democracy's Debt to Our Fringe Press," *Los Angeles Times*, 2 May 1995; Richard Harwood, "As Wrong as McNamara," *WP*, 19 April 1995.

18. The pessimism was first identified by authors writing in the wake of the leaking and subsequent publication of the so-called *Pentagon Papers*. See Daniel Ellsberg, *Papers on the War* (New York: Simon and Schuster, 1972); and Gelb and Betts, *Irony of Vietnam*. In my view, the huge mass of documentation that has been released since these authors wrote confirms and strengthens their argument.

19. INR (Hughes) to Rusk, 28 July 1965, box 31, NSF VN, LBJL. I thank Regina Greenwell for drawing this memorandum to my attention.

20. McNamara's role in the war is given close attention in Deborah Shapley, *Promise and Power: The Life and Times of Robert McNamara* (Boston: Little, Brown, 1993); McMaster, *Dereliction of Duty*; Paul Hendrickson, *The Living and the Dead: Robert McNamara and Five Lives of a Lost War* (New York: Knopf, 1996). On Bundy, see Kai Bird, *The Color of Truth: McGeorge and William Bundy, Brothers in Arms* (New York: Simon and Schuster, 1998), which appeared after the completion of the present volume.

21. Two useful biographies of Rusk are Warren I. Cohen, *Dean Rusk* (Totowa, N.J.: Cooper Square Publishers, 1980); and Thomas J. Schoenbaum,

Waging Peace and War: Dean Rusk in the Truman, Kennedy, and Johnson Years (New York: Simon and Schuster, 1988). A very sympathetic account is Francis L. Loewenheim, "Dean Rusk: Diplomacy and Principle," in *The Diplomats: 1939–1979,* ed. Gordon A. Craig and Francis L. Loewenheim (Princeton, N.J.: Princeton University Press, 1994), 499–537.

22. Examples include Dallek, *Flawed Giant;* Dallek, "Lyndon Johnson and Vietnam"; Gardner, *Pay Any Price;* Barrett, *Uncertain Warriors;* Vandiver, *Shadows of Vietnam;* George McT. Kahin, *Intervention: How America Became Involved in Vietnam* (New York: Knopf, 1986); Schulzinger, *A Time for War.* The existence of this trend is noted in David C. Hendrickson, "All the President's Acumen," *Foreign Affairs* 77 (May/June 1998): 112.

23. On Lippmann, see Ronald Steel, *Walter Lippmann and the American Century* (Boston: Little, Brown, 1980), 544–572; and Fredrik Logevall, "First among Critics: Walter Lippmann and the Vietnam War," *Journal of American–East Asian Relations* 4, no. 4 (winter 1995): 351–375. Lippmann's hesitation in opposing U.S. policy distinguished him from another early—and much less influential—journalist critic, I. F. Stone. See the remarkable collection of reports from 1963 to 1965 in *I. F. Stone's Newsletter,* many of which are reprinted in I. F. Stone, *In a Time of Torment* (New York: Random House, 1967).

24. McNamara, *In Retrospect.* The popular historian Barbara Tuchman, in her engaging study *The March of Folly: From Troy to Vietnam* (New York: Knopf, 1984), argues that the Vietnam escalation fits her criteria for folly (that the policy be widely seen as counterproductive in its own time; that viable alternatives be proposed at the time; and that the policy in question should be that of a group, not an individual ruler). She is right in this claim, but in the book she does little to back it up, with the result that many reviewers were unpersuaded. See, for example, John Mueller, "Vietnam Involvement Was a Failure, Not a Folly," *WSJ,* 10 April 1984.

25. I have argued elsewhere that careful counterfactual exploration is often essential to reaching the fullest historical understanding. Logevall, "Vietnam and the Question of What Might Have Been," in *Kennedy: Revisiting the New Frontier,* ed. Mark J. White (London: Macmillan, 1998).

CHAPTER 1

1. On the Franco-Vietminh war, see Jacques Dalloz, *The War in Indochina, 1945–1954* (Savage, Md.: Barnes & Noble Books, 1990); Alain Ruscio, *La guerre française d'Indochine: 1945–1954* (Brussels: Editions Complexes, 1992).

2. On the growth of American involvement in these years, see Kahin, *Intervention,* 3–121; William J. Duiker, *U.S. Containment Policy and the Conflict in Indochina* (Stanford, Calif.: Stanford University Press, 1994), 52–247; and Anderson, *Trapped by Success.* Less detailed but providing good overviews are Herring, *America's Longest War,* 3–79; and Gary R. Hess, *Vietnam and the United States: Origins and Legacy of War* (Boston, Mass.: G. K. Hale, 1990), 22–68. On the insurgency in South Vietnam, see Carlyle Thayer, *War*

by Other Means: National Liberation and Revolution in Vietnam, 1954–1960 (Winchester, Mass.: Unwin Hyman, 1989); William J. Duiker, *Sacred War: Nationalism and Revolution in a Divided Vietnam* (New York: McGraw-Hill, 1995), 95–137; Truong Nhu Tang, with David Chanoff and Doan Van Toai, *A Vietcong Memoir* (New York: Random House, 1985), 18–80.

3. *Le Monde,* 30 August 1963. Author's translation. See also *NYT,* 30 August 1963; Alain Peyrefitte, *C'était de Gaulle: La France reprend sa place dans le monde* (Paris: Fayard, 1997), 475–476; Saigon to Paris, 30 August 1963, CLV, sud-vietnam, #78, MAE. A slightly different translation of de Gaulle's pronouncement is in U.S. Department of State, *American Foreign Policy: Current Documents, 1963* (Washington, D.C.: GPO, 1967), 869.

4. Saigon to State, 29 August 1963, U.S. Department of State, *Foreign Relations of the United States 1961–1963—Vietnam* 4:20–22 (hereafter cited as *FRUS*); Memo of Telcon, JFK and Hilsman, 29 August 1963, *FRUS,* 1961–1963, 4:25–26; JFK to Lodge, 29 August 1963, *FRUS,* 1961–1963, 4:35–36. Earlier in the day, at noon, Kennedy met with his key aides to discuss Lodge's cable and how to proceed. Most in attendance favored a coup but also feared that it might fail. See Memcon, 29 August 1963, *FRUS,* 1961–1963, 4:26–31. *Washington Post* headlines cited in Richard Reeves, *President Kennedy: Profile of Power* (New York: Simon and Schuster, 1993), 574.

5. The conflict had entered that realm of urgency previously, notably in the spring of 1954 and the autumn of 1961, but only intermittently, and only briefly. Of mid 1963 William P. Bundy would write some years later: "Particularly after mid-August, the senior levels of the US Government from the President down were more preoccupied with Vietnam than at any previous time." Bundy MS, chapter 9, page 3. For another articulation of this point, see Forrestal OH, LBJL.

6. Jean Lacouture, *Vietnam,* 224.

7. The Franco-American conflict over Vietnam in the 1960s is also examined in Marianna P. Sullivan, *France's Vietnam Policy: A Study in French-American Relations* (Westport, Conn.: Greenwood, 1978); Fredrik Logevall, "De Gaulle, Neutralization, and American Involvement in Vietnam 1963–1964," *Pacific Historical Review* 41 (February 1992): 69–102; and Anne Sa'adah, "Idées Simples and Idées Fixes: De Gaulle, the United States, and Vietnam," in Robert O. Paxton and Nicholas Wahl, eds., *De Gaulle and the United States: A Centennial Reappraisal* (Providence, R.I.: Berg, 1994), 295–328, with comments by Pierre Mélandri, Jean-Marcel Jeanneney, Jean Lacouture, and Bernard Tricot.

8. These were the five countries United Nations secretary general U Thant would cite at the start of 1965 in proposing "preliminary discussions" by "the five major Geneva powers" plus North and South Vietnam. See chapter 11.

9. Washington to FO, 6 April 1963, FO 371/170111, PRO. On Diem's shortcomings as a leader, see Neil L. Jamieson, *Understanding Vietnam* (Berkeley: University of California Press, 1993), 234–246. On the U.S. decision to nevertheless back him, see Anderson, *Trapped by Success,* 82–86.

10. Washington to Paris, 17 May 1963, Amerique Etats-Unis, 1952–63, #399,

MAE; Saigon to Canberra, 9 April 1963, FO 371/170090, PRO; Bangkok (Saigon) to Stockholm, 26 April 1963, HP1, #XV, UD. According to Harry Hohler of the British embassy in Saigon, "Nhu is passionately anxious to reduce the number of American advisers in the provinces and is pressing [U.S. ambassador Frederick] Nolting hard." Saigon embassy to FO, 25 April 1963, FO 371/170111, PRO. Nhu continued pressing in the summer. See Washington to FO, 18 July 1963, FO 371/170111, PRO; Saigon to FO, 14 August 1963, FO 371/170091, PRO; Washington to FO, 27 August 1963, FO 371/170092, PRO; Saigon to FO, 31 August 1963, FO 371/170092, PRO; Saigon to Paris, 30 August 1963, cabinet du ministre #206, MAE. See also Warren Unna's front-page article in the *WP*, 12 May 1963.

11. According to R. G. K. Thompson, in July several provincial government leaders were dismissed by the Ngos merely because they were too pro-American and were replaced by officials who were anti-American. BRIAM to London, 19 December 1963, FO 371/170096, PRO.

12. On the deliberations in Washington in this period and in the early days of Lodge's tenure, an excellent account is Blair, *Lodge in Vietnam*, 24–47. See also Reeves, *President Kennedy*, 556–577; White House conversation, 21 August 1963, KT. On the Buddhist crisis, see John Prados, *The Hidden History of the Vietnam War* (Chicago: Ivan R. Dee, 1995), 88–92.

13. Both the U.S. State Department and the CIA reported such meetings taking place. See, for example, Lodge to Rusk, cable, 31 August 1963, box 198, NSF CF, JFKL; Lodge to Rusk, 13 September 1963, box 199, NSF CF, JFKL; CIA Report, 17 September 1963, box 200, NSF CF, JFKL; Memo of Telcon, Harriman and McCone, 13 September 1963, *FRUS*, 1961–1963, 4:204; CIA Report, 19 September 1963, box 200, NSF CF, JFKL. Author Geoffrey Warner finds "little doubt that the RVN government was negotiating with the Communists." Geoffrey Warner, "The United States and the Fall of Diem, Part I: The Coup That Never Was," *Australian Outlook* 28 (December 1974): 248–249. See also Kahin, *Intervention*, 153–155; Tang, *Vietcong Memoir*, 51.

14. Saigon to FO, 18 September 1963, FO 371/170091, PRO. The Maneli cable is excerpted in Mieczyslaw Maneli, *War of the Vanquished* (New York: Harper and Row, 1971), 126–129.

15. This is also the view in Tang, *Vietcong Memoir*, 51.

16. Lodge to State, 12 September 1963, *FRUS*, 4:204. FO to Saigon, 12 September 1963, FO 371/170107, PRO. On Madame Nhu's claims, see the French weekly *Candide*, 13 February 1964. See also Bernard B. Fall, "Our Options in Vietnam," *The Reporter*, 12 March 1964; Stanley Karnow, "Lost Chance in Vietnam," *New Republic*, 2 February 1974.

17. French ambassador Laloulette was among those who believed the Ngos *could* survive a deal with Hanoi. "[Diem] would have had to change the system if he stayed on [after a deal], but he had the government and administration, and he had good men," Laloulette later told author Ellen Hammer. "All he had to do was move toward a political solution." Ellen J. Hammer, *A Death in November: America in Vietnam, 1963* (New York: Dutton, 1987), 223.

18. CIA Memorandum, 9 August 1962, box 195, NSF CF, JFKL; "Demands

for an International Conference on Vietnam, 1960–September 1963," FO (South-East Asia Department), 20 September 1963, FO 371/170153, PRO; INR Research Memorandum, 20 January 1964, box 1, NSF VN, LBJL; *Newsweek*, 10 December 1962. The NLF also professed support for negotiations several times in the first half of 1962. See Robert K. Brigham, "The NLF's Foreign Relations and the Vietnam War," paper delivered at the Society for Historians of American Foreign Relations annual meeting, Charlottesville, Va., June 1994.

19. Duiker, *U.S. Containment Policy*, 287; William J. Duiker, *The Communist Road to Power in Vietnam* (Boulder, Colo.: Westview Press, 1981), 205–206. In yet another volume, *Sacred War*, 155–156, the prolific Duiker quotes at length from this very interesting letter by Le Duan, which was dated July 1962 and addressed to Nguyen Van Linh, the leader of the insurgency in the South.

20. The Pham Van Dong conversation is reported in Saigon to FO, 27 March 1963, FO 371/170103, PRO; Hanoi to FO, 12 April 1963, FO 371/170098, PRO. See also Maneli, *War of the Vanquished*, 121–122, 127–129, 187–191, 198–208. In June Blackwell told a Swedish diplomat in Beijing that his contacts with Hanoi leaders had convinced him that they wanted desperately to gain a U.S. withdrawal and would agree to neutralization in order to get such a result. Beijing to Stockholm, HP1, #XV, UD.

21. Hanoi to FO, 8 April 1963, FO 371/170097, PRO; Saigon to FO, 17 April 1963, FO 371/170103, PRO; Hanoi to FO, 25 January 1964, FO 371/175480, PRO. According to Blackwell, Khiem made a special effort to take him aside at a reception on 4 April to say there ought to be a conference on Vietnam, similar to the one on Laos.

22. Hanoi to FO, 8 April 1963, FO 371/170097, PRO; Hanoi to FO, 14 January 1963, FO 371/170103, PRO; Hanoi to FO, 23 May 1963, FO 371/170090, PRO. Officials at the Foreign Office in London agreed with this view. Said one report in July 1962: "The North Vietnamese are clearly bothered by the 10,000 American troops in South Vietnam and are looking for the easiest way to get rid of them. They are therefore trying to build up international pressure on the Americans to withdraw. They have suggested to both Prince Souvanna Phouma and Prince Sihanouk that the matter should be discussed at Geneva upon the conclusion of the Laos Conference. They have tried to blackmail these two characters with the suggestion that the Laotian settlement will never work so long as there is still a dangerous situation in Vietnam. . . . The North Vietnamese doubtless calculate that the success of the Laos conference will lead many people to urge that a similar pacific technique should be adopted for settling the situation in Vietnam also." "Vietnam Confidential," Minutes of 5 July 1962, FO 371/166763, PRO.

23. In the course of its fence-walking between Moscow and Beijing, the DRV would fluctuate in the tenor of its pronouncements. Sometimes government spokesmen would echo Russian proclamations in favor of "peaceful coexistence" and "world peace," at the expense of national liberation movements, while at other times they would adopt the more belligerent rhetoric of the Chinese. As 1963 progressed, they moved closer to Beijing. In mid April, for example, Le

Duan gave what a foreign diplomat called a "very Chinese-sounding speech," one that gave no impression "that the North Vietnamese were moving in the direction of calling off the military campaign in South Vietnam as part of some peaceful settlement." The same month the pro-Soviet Khiem was replaced as foreign minister by the more pro-Chinese Xuan Thuy. Later in the summer, Hanoi joined Beijing in denouncing the Test Ban Treaty. Although it would be a mistake to read too much into these developments—if the DRV got off the fence occasionally on the side of the Chinese, it soon got back on again, as evidenced, for example, by the pro-Soviet speeches in Hanoi during the October Revolution celebrations in the fall—they do suggest that Hanoi was anxious to keep its diplomatic cards very close to the vest, for fear of alienating the great power situated across its northern frontier. For good analyses, see Saigon to FO, 25 April 1963, FO 371/170107, PRO; Hanoi to FO, 9 December 1963, FO 371/170099, PRO; CIA Office of Current Intelligence Memo, 8 November 1963, box 202, NSF CF, JFKL. Bernard Fall used a different metaphor than the "tightrope"; according to him, the DRV was like a man "walking a straight zigzag path through the woods." Quoted in Douglas Pike, *Viet Cong: The Organization and Techniques of the National Liberation Party of South Vietnam*, rev. ed. (Cambridge, Mass.: MIT Press, 1972), 55. See also Bui Tin, *Following Ho Chi Minh: The Memoirs of a North Vietnamese Colonel*, trans. Judy Stowe and Do Van (Honolulu: University of Hawaii Press, 1995), 43–46.

24. Vo Nhan Tri, *Croissance économique de la Republique Democratique du Vietnam, 1945–1965* (Hanoi: Editions en langues étrangères, 1967), 421–422; Hammer, *A Death in November*, 223–224; Hanoi to FO, 1 March 1963, FO 371/170097, PRO; Saigon to FO, 5 September 1963, FO 371/170107, PRO.

25. According to Donald Zagoria, in the middle of 1963 Hanoi still hoped for a Laos-type settlement, and it scaled down military operations in the South in order to try to get such a result. Donald S. Zagoria, *Vietnam Triangle: Moscow, Peking, Hanoi* (New York: Pegasus, 1967), 108.

26. INR (Hughes) to Rusk, 11 September 1963, box 199, NSF CF, JFKL; Lodge to State, 12 September 1963, *FRUS, 1961–1963*, 4:204; Hammer, *Death in November*, 221–223.

27. Franco-American friction over Indochina went back to the Franco-Vietminh War, when the two nations disagreed frequently over the best approach to the war. The squabbles continued during and after the Geneva Conference. See Kathryn Statler, "The Diem Experiment: The Franco-American Conflict over South Vietnam, 1954–1955," paper presented at the annual meeting of the Society for Historians of Foreign Relations, Washington, D.C., June 1998. For de Gaulle's early position on Indochina, see Alfred Georges, *Charles de Gaulle et la guerre d'Indochine* (Paris: Plon, 1974).

28. Philippe Devillers, "Le General de Gaulle et l'Asie," *De Gaulle et le tiers Monde*, Institute Charles de Gaulle (Paris: Pédone, 1984), 299–306.

29. INR (Hughes) to Rusk, 11 September 1963, box 199, NSF CF, JFKL; INR Research Memo, 20 April 1964, box 171, NSF CF, LBJL; Paris to FO, 27 March 1963, FO 371/170103, PRO; Paris to FO, 25 April 1963, FO 371/170107,

PRO; Philippe Devillers, "French Policy and the Second Indochina War," *The World Today* 23 (June 1967): 251–262.

30. Paris to FO, 12 September 1963, FO 371/170107, PRO.

31. Saigon to Paris, 30 August 1963, cabinet du ministre #206, MAE; Lodge to Rusk, 30 August 1963, box 198, NSF CF, JFKL; Saigon to FO, 30 August 1963, PREM 11/4759, PRO; Sullivan, *France's Vietnam Policy*, 67; Maneli, *War of the Vanquished*, 120–122, 140–142, 150–152.

32. Accounts of de Gaulle's foreign-policy objectives upon returning to power include Jean Lacouture, *De Gaulle: Le souverain, 1958–1969* (Paris: Seuil, 1986); Alfred Grosser, *Affaires éxterieures: La politique de la France, 1944–1989* (Paris: Flammarion, 1989); Maurice Vaïsse, *La grandeur: Politique étrangère du général de Gaulle, 1958–1969* (Paris: Fayard, 1998), 13–110; Michael M. Harrison, *The Reluctant Ally: France and Atlantic Security* (Baltimore, Md.: Johns Hopkins University Press, 1981), 49–114; Edward A. Kolodziej, *French International Policy under de Gaulle and Pompidou: The Politics of Grandeur* (Ithaca, N.Y.: Cornell University Press, 1974), 235–291; Stanley Hoffmann, *Decline or Renewal: France since the 1930s* (New York: Viking, 1974), 283–331; A. W. DePorte, *Europe between the Superpowers: The Enduring Balance* (New Haven, Conn.: Yale University Press, 1986), 229–242; and Andrew Shennan, *De Gaulle* (London: Longman, 1993), 74–140.

33. Ball to Johnson and Rusk, 6 June 1964, box 170, NSF CF, LBJL. This was characteristic of de Gaulle's foreign policy in general, as a Canadian assessment would note in late 1963: "[De Gaulle] sees policy in terms not so much of precise solutions as of vaguely defined destinations, with certain signposts marked on the way, but with the itinerary and the time-table open to the development of events." "Review of French Foreign Policy," 19 December 1963, MG 26-135, file 313 45/F815, NAC.

34. Hanoi to FO, 24 May 1963, FO 371/170103, PRO; Hanoi to FO, 14 January 1963, FO 371/170103, PRO; Maneli, *War of the Vanquished*, 202–203.

35. *Newsweek*, 16 September 1963; *NYT*, 12 November 1963; Jean Daniel, "De Gaulle's Vietnam," *New Republic*, 14 September 1963.

36. INR (Hughes) to Rusk, 11 September 1963, box 199, NSF CF, JFKL; SEAD Study, "Demands for an International Conference on Vietnam, 1960–September 1963," 20 September 1963, FO 371/170153, PRO; INR Research Memorandum, 20 January 1964, box 1, NSF VN, LBJL; Maneli, *War of the Vanquished*, 209–210.

37. This is a theme in Gaiduk, *Soviet Union*.

38. Vietnam Minutes (F. A. Warner), Secret, FO, 3 April 1963, FO 371/170110, PRO.

39. Whitehall memo, 10 September 1963, FO 371/170092, PRO. On the earlier period of Anglo-American disagreement in Indochina, see Arthur Combs, "The Path Not Taken," *Diplomatic History* 19 (winter 1995): 33–57. On Geneva, see James E. Cable, *The Geneva Conference of 1954 on Indochina* (New York: St. Martin's Press, 1986).

40. Minutes by A. J. Williams, 13 September 1963, FO 371/170107, PRO;

Minutes by T. J. Everard, 12 September 1963, FO 371/170107, PRO; Extract from Record of a Meeting, 2 May 1963, PREM 11/4186, PRO.

41. Minutes by F. A. Warner, 5 July 1962, FO 371/166763, PRO; Minutes by F. A. Warner, 3 April 1963, FO 371/170110, PRO; Minutes by E. H. Peck, 4 April 1963, FO 371/170110, PRO.

42. See David Dimbleby and David Reynolds, *An Ocean Apart: The Relationship between Britain and America in the Twentieth Century* (New York: Random House, 1988), 237–261, 270–271.

43. Hanoi to FO, 13 February 1963, FO 371/170097, PRO. Blackwell repeated the point several times in 1963 and, with an increasing sense of futility, in 1964. Even as they failed to follow his suggestion, Foreign Office colleagues held him in high regard. "Mr. Blackwell is first-class, if a trifle long-winded," one commented after reading one of his dispatches. "I wish we could get 'think piece' of this calibre out of Saigon." Minutes by A. J. Williams, 22 March 1963, FO 371/170097, PRO.

44. SEAD Study, "Demands for an International Conference on Vietnam, 1960–September 1963," 20 September 1963, FO 371/170153, PRO. See also Minutes by E. H. Peck, 4 April 1963, FO 371/170110, PRO.

45. SEAD Study, ibid.; Daniel S. Papp, *Vietnam: The View from Moscow, Peking, Washington* (Jefferson, N.C.: McFarland, 1987), 21.

46. Chen, "China's Involvement in the Vietnam War," 359–360; Smith, *International History*, 2:161. For the view that Beijing was anxious to get a negotiated settlement, even after 1963, see Eugene K. Lawson, *The Sino-Vietnamese Conflict* (New York: Praeger, 1984), 65–69.

47. See Richard J. Walton, *Cold War and Counter-Revolution: The Foreign Policy of John F. Kennedy* (Baltimore, Md.: Johns Hopkins University Press, 1972); Louise FitzSimons, *The Kennedy Doctrine* (New York: Random House, 1972); Thomas G. Paterson, ed., *Kennedy's Quest for Victory: American Foreign Policy, 1961–1963* (New York: Oxford University Press, 1989). For the view that Kennedy was positively eager to wage war in Vietnam, see Noam Chomsky's polemical essay, *Rethinking Camelot: JFK, the Vietnam War, and U.S. Political Culture* (Boston: South End Press, 1993). Also depicting Kennedy as an unreconstructed hawk on Vietnam are Robert Buzzanco, *Masters of War: Military Dissent and Politics in the Vietnam War* (New York: Cambridge University Press, 1996); Kahin, *Intervention*, 129ff.

48. See here the powerful account in Aleksandr Fursenko and Timothy Naftali, *"One Hell of a Gamble": Khrushchev, Castro, and Kennedy, 1958–1964* (New York: Norton, 1997), 77–131.

49. Precisely what Eisenhower advocated doing in Laos during this meeting remains unclear because of the discrepancies in various notetakers' accounts. See Fred I. Greenstein and Richard H. Immerman, "What Did Eisenhower Tell Kennedy about Indochina? The Politics of Misperception," *Journal of American History* 79 (September 1992): 568–587. See also Clark Clifford to Kennedy, memorandum, 24 January 1961, President's Office Files, JFKL; Thomas C. Reeves, *A Question of Character: John F. Kennedy in Image and*

Reality (New York: Free Press, 1990), 281; Clark Clifford, *Counsel to the President: A Memoir* (New York: Random House, 1991), 342–344.

50. According to Kennedy aide Michael Forrestal, JFK told him that U.S. interests in Laos were minimal. "We couldn't care less, actually," Forrestal quoted him as saying. Forrestal OH, JFKL. A good, succinct examination of the Laos deliberations in this period is Duiker, *U.S. Containment Policy*, 253–263.

51. Record of Conversation, 28 January 1961, PREM 11/3279, PRO; Washington to FO, 1 March 1961, PREM 11/3326, PRO; Record of Conversation, 28 March 1961, PREM 11/3280, PRO; Macmillan to de Gaulle, 14 April 1961, PREM 11/3326, PRO; Alistair Horne, *Harold MacMillan* (New York: Viking, 1989), 2:294.

52. Charles de Gaulle, *Memoirs of Hope: Renewal and Endeavor* (New York: Simon and Schuster, 1971), 256. See also Lacouture, *Souverain*, 360–361. The Kennedy quotation is in Lawrence J. Bassett and Stephen E. Pelz, "The Failed Search for Victory: Vietnam and the Politics of War," in *Kennedy's Quest for Victory: American Foreign Policy, 1961–1963*, ed. Thomas G. Paterson (New York: Oxford University Press, 1989), 229.

53. The 1960–1962 Laos crisis awaits serious scholarly research using the vast available documentary record. A very brief recent study is Timothy N. Castle, *At War in the Shadow of Vietnam: U.S. Military Aid to the Royal Lao Government, 1955–1975* (New York: Columbia University Press, 1993). See also Charles A. Stevenson, *The End of Nowhere: American Policy toward Laos since 1954* (Boston: Beacon Press, 1973); Bernard B. Fall, *Anatomy of a Crisis: The Laotian Crisis of 1960–1961* (Garden City, N.Y.: Doubleday, 1969); and Arthur J. Dommen, *Conflict in Laos: The Politics of Neutralization*, rev. ed. (New York: Praeger, 1971).

54. These proposals are summarized in David Kaiser, "Men and Policies: 1961–1969," in *The Diplomacy of the Crucial Decade: American Foreign Relations during the 1960s*, ed. Diane Kunz, 11–41 (New York: Columbia University Press, 1994), 16–17.

55. Gibbons, *U.S. Government*, 2:38; Theodore C. Sorensen, *Kennedy* (New York: Harper and Row, 1965), 562–563; John M. Newman, *JFK and Vietnam: Deception, Intrigue, and the Struggle for Power* (New York: Warner Books, 1992), 82. Sorensen and Schlesinger, in their early volumes—which are thus perhaps more trustworthy, in that they appeared before the war turned incontrovertibly sour for the United States—note Kennedy's particular opposition to ground troops. Sorensen, *Kennedy*, 652–655. Schlesinger wrote that JFK told him that once troops were introduced, it would be "like taking a drink. The effect wears off, and you have to take another." Arthur M. Schlesinger Jr., *A Thousand Days: John F. Kennedy in the White House* (Boston: Houghton Mifflin, 1965), 547. Robert Kennedy, in an interview in 1964, said his brother was convinced that committing ground forces would be disastrous. On JFK perceiving the relevance of the French analogy, see Ellsberg, *Papers*, 69. See also Arthur Krock's column in *NYT*, 12 October 1961.

56. *The Pentagon Papers: The Defense Department History of Decision-making on Vietnam*, the Senator Gravel edition, 5 vols. (Boston: Beacon, 1971–1972), 2:70–71, 2:85–91 (hereafter cited as *PP* (Gravel); Taylor report, 3 November 1961, box 301, NSF CF, JFKL. For Taylor's perspective on the mission, see Maxwell Taylor, *Swords and Plowshares* (New York: Norton, 1972), chapter 18.

57. Mansfield to JFK, 2 November 1961, in *FRUS, 1961–1963,* 1:467–470; *FRUS, 1961–1963,* 1:547–548; George W. Ball, *The Past Has Another Pattern: Memoirs* (New York: Norton, 1982), 410, 366; David DiLeo, *George Ball, Vietnam, and the Rethinking of Containment* (Chapel Hill, N.C.: University of North Carolina Press, 1991), 53–56. According to Ball, Kennedy, upon hearing Ball's prediction that Vietnam might one day demand three hundred thousand U.S. troops who might never return home, laughed and said, "Well, George, you're supposed to be one of the smartest guys in town, but you're crazier than hell. That will never happen." The meaning of this last sentence is not clear. Either JFK meant that these three hundred thousand American troops would not get swallowed up by the jungle, or he meant that they would never be committed in the first place.

58. Chief of Defence Staff to FO, 10 November 1961, FO 371/160129, PRO; Geneva to FO, 4 November 1961, PREM 11/3739, PRO; Duiker, *U.S. Containment Policy,* 273. Similarly, Abram Chayes, the department's legal adviser, attacked the Taylor report for focusing principally on "military and semimilitary means." Past experience, Chayes noted, had indicated the difficulties of a military-centered approach. "In assessing the prospects for this course the long history of attempts to prop up unpopular governments through the use of foreign military forces is powerfully discouraging," Chayes argued. "The French experience in this very area, as well as our own efforts since 1955, reveal the essential inadequacy of the sort of program now proposed. The drawbacks of such intervention in Viet-Nam would be compounded, not relieved, by the United States penetration and assumption of co-responsibility at all levels of the Vietnamese Government suggested in the Taylor Report." Marilyn B. Young, *The Vietnam Wars, 1945–1990* (New York: HarperCollins, 1991), 81.

59. Memcon, 15 November 1961, *FRUS, 1961–1963,* 1:254.

60. Geneva to FO, 4 November 1961, PREM 11/3739, PRO.

61. Harriman to Kennedy, 11 November 1961, box 195, NSF CF, JFKL; Geneva to FO, 20 November 1961, FO 371/160128, PRO.

62. Washington to FO, 13 November 1961, PREM 11/4166, PRO; Galbraith to Kennedy, n.d., Box 128, NSF CF, JFKL; Kahin, *Intervention,* 136–137; Bassett and Pelz, "Failed Search," 236–237.

63. Bowles would soon be demoted from undersecretary to Kennedy's "Special Representative and Adviser on African, Asian, and Latin American Affairs." The title sounded important, but it proved an essentially meaningless post. Some have seen this demotion as evidence of Kennedy's fundamental hawkishness on Vietnam—he effectively silenced one of the few men counseling a nonmilitary approach. This theory is undermined by the fact that the man chosen to replace Bowles, George Ball, held views not too different from

Bowles's, and by the simultaneous promotion of Averell Harriman to a higher post at the State Department. The principal reasons for Bowles's demotion lay elsewhere. For an excellent treatment of his difficult tenure in the administration, see Howard B. Schaffer, *Chester Bowles: New Dealer in the Cold War* (Cambridge, Mass.: Harvard University Press, 1993), 164–258.

64. Bowles to Kennedy, 30 November 1961, box 297, Papers of Chester Bowles, Yale University, New Haven, Connecticut (hereafter cited as Bowles Papers). *FRUS*, 1961–1963, 1:322–325; Chester Bowles, *Promises to Keep* (New York: Harper and Row, 1971), 407–409.

65. Dean Rusk, *As I Saw It* (New York: W. W. Norton, 1990), 432. In the apt wording of Abram Chayes, who himself advocated a diplomacy-centered approach to Vietnam, the advocates of negotiations represented "all the non-power in the [State] Department," with the result that "it just never flew." Chayes quoted in Young, *Vietnam Wars*, 81.

66. Kennedy to Rusk and McNamara, 14 November 1961, box 128, POF, JFKL; *PP* (Gravel), 2:111.

67. Schell, *Time of Illusion*, 9–10.

68. Michael R. Beschloss, *The Crisis Years: Kennedy and Khrushchev, 1960–1963* (New York: HarperCollins, 1991), 62–353. On the reluctance of Kennedy officials to see the reality of the Sino-Soviet split, see Nancy Bernkopf Tucker, "Threats, Opportunities, and Frustrations in East Asia," in Warren I. Cohen and Nancy Bernkopf Tucker, eds., *Lyndon Johnson Confronts the World: American Foreign Policy, 1963–1968* (New York: Cambridge University Press, 1994), 103.

69. Said Michael Forrestal later about Johnson's 1961 description of Diem: "It's understandable that he would have admired Diem, because even by 1961, Diem convinced [Roger] Hilsman and myself . . . that he was a pretty great fellow. Everybody thought he was pretty good." Forrestal OHC, LBJL.

70. See Noam Chomsky, *Year 501: The Conquest Continues* (Boston: South End Press, 1993); Diane B. Kunz, "Camelot Continued: What if JFK Had Lived?" in Niall Ferguson, ed., *Virtual History: Alternatives and Counterfactuals* (New York: Macmillan, 1997). Stopping somewhat short of this position is Michael Cannon, "Raising the Stakes: The Taylor-Rostow Mission," *Journal of Strategic Studies* 12 (June 1989): 155–158.

71. Robert F. Kennedy quoted in Stanley Karnow, *Vietnam: A History* (New York: Viking, 1991), 272; Record of Honolulu meeting, 23 July 1962, in *FRUS*, 1961–1963, 2:548.

72. *The Pentagon Papers. United States–Vietnam Relations, 1945–1967: Study Prepared by the Department of Defense*, 12 vols. (Washington, D.C.: GPO, 1971), book 3, part 4B, chapter 4, pages 1–4 (hereafter *PP* [DoD]); Gibbons, *U.S. Government*, 2:125.

73. Frances FitzGerald has perceptively written that in its very conception, the hamlets program was "a study in misplaced analogy." The Malayan insurgency had virtually nothing in common with the one in South Vietnam. Frances FitzGerald, *Fire in the Lake: The Vietnamese and the Americans in Vietnam* (Boston, Mass.: Little, Brown, 1972), 123. In fairness to Thompson,

who helped plan the successful Malayan operation, Diem and Nhu did not follow his suggestions on how the program should be implemented. The failures of the program are described in Douglas S. Blaufarb, *The Counterinsurgency Era: U.S. Doctrine and Performance, 1950 to the Present* (New York: Free Press, 1977), 89–127, and ably summarized in Richard A. Hunt, *Pacification: The American Struggle for Vietnam's Hearts and Minds* (Boulder, Colo.: Westview, 1995), 20–23. For the problems in the program in specific provinces, see Jeffrey Race, *War Comes to Long An: Revolutionary Conflict in a Vietnamese Province* (Berkeley and Los Angeles: University of California Press, 1972), 192–194; and Eric M. Bergerud, *The Dynamics of Defeat: The Vietnam War in Hau Nghia Province* (Boulder, Colo.: Westview Press, 1991), 33–38, 50–53.

74. Herring, *America's Longest War,* 100–105.

75. Saigon to FO, 1 March 1962, FO 371/166720, PRO; Minutes by J. I. McGhie, 5 March 1962, FO 371/166720, PRO.

76. Galbraith to Kennedy, 4 April 1962, box 196, NSF CF, JFKL; John K. Galbraith, *A Life in Our Times* (Boston: Houghton Mifflin, 1981), 476–477; Gibbons, *U.S. Government,* 2:119–120. Galbraith to Kennedy, n.d. (likely March 1962), NSF CF, JFKL; also reprinted in William J. Rust, *Kennedy in Vietnam* (New York: Scribner's, 1985), 70.

77. Memo of Conversation between JFK and Harriman, 6 April 1963, in *FRUS, 1961–1963,* 2:309; *PP,* 12:464–465. The meeting with British officials took place on 24 May. In talks the following day, a senior British official repeated the question, and Rusk repeated the answer. Memo of Conversation, 25 May 1962, PREM 11/4583, PRO.

78. Walter Lippmann, *The Cold War: A Study in U.S. Foreign Policy* (New York: Harper, 1947), 60.

79. On Rusk's deep skepticism that the Laos talks would amount to anything, see his comments to British officials on 25 May 1962, in PREM 11/4583, PRO.

80. Schoenbaum, *Waging Peace and War,* 395.

81. This comment has been seized upon by those who argue that Kennedy was intent on withdrawing from Vietnam. See, especially, Newman, *JFK and Vietnam,* 236–238. For the problems in this argument, see Logevall, "What Might Have Been."

82. Draft Memo of Conversation, 1 May 1962, in *FRUS, 1961–1963,* 2:367.

83. Memcon, Harriman and Khiem, 22 July 1962, *FRUS, 1961–1963,* II, 543–546; Rudy Abramson, *Spanning the Century: The Life of W. Averell Harriman, 1891–1986* (New York: Morrow, 1992), 605–606.

84. Kenneth P. O'Donnell and David F. Powers, *Johnny, We Hardly Knew Ye: Memories of John Fitzgerald Kennedy* (Boston: Little, Brown, 1972), 15.

85. Kennedy's press conference is in *PP* (Gravel), 2:824.

86. During the aforementioned White House meeting in early April with Thompson and other British officials, the discussion focused principally on the best means by which to defeat the Vietcong, which caused a British notetaker to remark, "I was led to conclude that there was no immediate prospect of the

U.S. Administration withdrawing its support from President Diem within the next year or so." Washington to FO, 6 April 1963, FO 371/170111, PRO.

87. Reeves, *President Kennedy*, 484; Charles Bartlett, OH, LBJL. Kennedy's pessimism regarding Vietnam may also have played a role in his sending Republican stalwart Henry Cabot Lodge to be ambassador to Saigon in August. According to aide Kenneth O'Donnell, "The President told us that when Rusk suggested sending Lodge to Saigon, he decided to approve the appointment because the idea of getting Lodge mixed up in such a hopeless mess as Vietnam was irresistible." O'Donnell and Powers, *Johnny*, 16.

88. Bernard B. Fall, *Viet-Nam Witness* (New York: Praeger, 1966), 199–200; Gelb and Betts, *Irony of Vietnam*, 93.

89. Wrote William P. Bundy a few years later: "The summer of 1963 was a time of great success for the foreign policy of the Kennedy administration. As the outcome of the Cuban missile crisis had appeared to indicate an end to major Soviet pressures, so the signing of the Test Ban Treaty in August of 1963 seemed to mark a high point in the possibilities of agreement, and possibly a turning point in the whole U.S./Soviet relationship. This certainly was the feeling at the time, not only in Washington but widely at home and abroad, and much credit for the changed atmosphere was properly given to President Kennedy himself." Bundy MS, chapter 9, page 1.

90. One British official, writing with these earlier Geneva meetings in mind, said, "I think it is a mistake to assume that [the West is] going to be worsted in any conference." Blackwell to FO, 23 May 1963, FO 371/170090, PRO. In his memoir of the period, Mieczyslaw Maneli has several interesting excerpts of conversations with DRV leaders in the spring of 1963 on the possibility of a Laos-type settlement in Vietnam that would allow the United States to save face. See Maneli, *War of the Vanquished*, 187–191, 198–208.

91. One of the few who doubted that the long-term result of a Vietnam settlement would be a reunified country under Hanoi's control was Britain's Kenneth Blackwell. He wrote London in May 1963: "Even if the North Vietnamese do believe that in the long run that they would be able to subvert the South they need not necessarily be right. For once we could perhaps take them at their word and set up a neutral, independent and democratic (in our sense of the word) state in South Vietnam. It would perhaps be less than either side originally hoped for but it might well be the best solution for the people of South Vietnam." Blackwell to FO, 23 May 1963, FO 371/170090, PRO.

92. On the reporters in Vietnam in 1963, see Neil Sheehan, *A Bright Shining Lie: John Paul Vann and America in Vietnam* (New York: Random House, 1988); and William Prochnau, *Once Upon a Distant War* (New York: Times Books, 1995).

CHAPTER 2

1. On 21 August, after another crackdown on Buddhists, the State Department issued a strong condemnation of the GVN's handling of the issue. Next came another State Department announcement, this time to the effect that

American aid policy to the GVN remained unchanged. On 26 and 27 August, the Voice of America (VOA) declared that the action against the Buddhists had been taken by special forces controlled by Nhu without the knowledge or approval of the South Vietnamese army. On 26 August, the VOA said that aid might be cut; the next day, it quoted a State Department official as saying no such decision had been made. This series of pronouncements, and the fact that Lodge took four full days to present his credentials to the GVN after his arrival on 22 August, left at least British diplomats in Saigon shaking their heads. See Saigon to FO, 31 August 1963, FO 371/170092, PRO.

2. Bundy MS, chapter 9, pages 2–3.

3. The fullest explication of this view is Newman, *JFK and Vietnam*. See also Peter D. Scott, *Deep Politics and the Death of JFK* (Berkeley and Los Angeles: University of California Press, 1993); O'Donnell and Powers, *Johnny*, 16–18; Arthur M. Schlesinger Jr., *Robert Kennedy and His Times* (Boston: Houghton Mifflin, 1978); Arthur M. Schlesinger Jr., "What Would He Have Done?" *NYT Book Review*, 29 March 1992, 3, 31. Declares Newman: "The facts are that President Kennedy was withdrawing from Vietnam at the time of his murder." Letter to the editor, *NYT*, 20 January 1992. See also Roger Hilsman's letter to the editor on the same day. The incipient-withdrawal thesis got a big boost with the appearance in 1991 of Oliver Stone's motion picture *JFK*. See also Stone, "Was Vietnam JFK's War?" *Newsweek*, 21 October 1996.

4. For a more detailed analysis of this argument, see Logevall, "What Might Have Been."

5. Former *New York Times* columnist Leslie Gelb, who as a Defense Department official in the 1960s played a key role in the Pentagon Papers project, has written: "The coup was fully supported, if not inspired, by the U.S. in good part because of the fear that Nhu was conspiring with North Vietnam to neutralize South Vietnam. In other words, the Kennedy team felt that Diem and Nhu might be selling out the Communists." Leslie H. Gelb, "Kennedy and Vietnam," *NYT*, 6 January 1992. See also Karnow, "Lost Chance." In the days after the coup, many in Saigon saw fear of a Nhu-NVN deal as motivating the United States. Lodge to State, 8 November 1963, *FRUS, 1961–1963*, 4:588.

6. Such unambiguous language suggests the utter implausibility, to put it charitably, of Hilsman's claim after the war that he would have welcomed a Hanoi-Saigon deal in the fall of 1963 as an excuse to get out of Vietnam. Karnow, "Lost Chance."

7. Hilsman to Rusk, 30 August 1963, box 198, NSF CF, JFKL. At a State Department meeting on the same day, de Gaulle's statement was discussed, and the CIA's William Colby said that it was possible that Nhu had been in contact with North Vietnam with French help. Memo of Conversation, 30 August 1963, Hilsman Papers, box 12, JFKL.

8. Lodge to Rusk, 30 August 1963, box 198, NSF CF, JFKL; Lodge to Rusk, cable, 31 August 1963, box 198, NSF CF, JFKL. For Lodge's concern about the overall developments in the South, see his comments to Roger Laloulette, as reported in Saigon to Paris, 4 September 1963, CLV, sud-vietnam #78, MAE.

9. Memcon, Rusk-Alphand, 30 August 1963, *FRUS, 1961–1963*, 4:59–60.

Hervé Alphand, *L'étonnement d'être: Journal, 1939–1973* (Paris: Fayard, 1977), 408. Alphand apparently never made the announcement.

10. FO (F. A. Warner) to Saigon, 12 September 1963, FO 371/170107, PRO; Washington to FO, 6 September 1963, FO 371/170092, PRO.

11. MB to JFK, 1 September 1963, box 199, NSF CF, JFKL.

12. The full text of the interview is in *FRUS*, 1961–1963, 4:93–95. See also Washington to FO, 6 September 1963, FO 371/170092.

13. An exasperated Kennedy official summarized American thinking when he complained in early 1963 that de Gaulle's bid for European leadership "cuts directly across U.S. interests all along the board." Quoted in Frank Costigliola, "The Pursuit of Atlantic Community: Nuclear Arms, Dollars, and Berlin," in *Kennedy's Quest for Victory: American Foreign Policy, 1961–1963*, ed. Thomas G. Paterson (New York: Oxford University Press, 1989), 33. A good treatment of Franco-American relations under Kennedy is Frank Costigliola, "The Failed Design: Kennedy, de Gaulle, and the Struggle for Europe," *Diplomatic History* 8, no. 3 (summer 1984): 227–251. See also Costigliola, *France and the United States: The Cold Alliance since World War II* (New York: Twayne, 1992), 118–159.

14. Responding to such speculation, one administration official who was convinced that de Gaulle had widespread support for his policy said: "[The] U.S. should not assume that everything which de Gaulle stands for is merely a product of his peculiar outlook and state of mind; that if it weren't for de Gaulle, France would be a docile and reasonable ally." William Tyler to MB, 3 March 1964, box 169, NSF CF, LBJL. Similarly, Marianna Sullivan has demonstrated that most political leaders and journalists in France agreed with de Gaulle's analysis of Vietnam and supported his policy. Sullivan, *France's Vietnam Policy*, 75–79.

15. See also Maneli, *War of the Vanquished*, 202; and Hughes to Rusk, 11 September 1963, box 199, NSF CF, JFKL. France maintained a *délégute-général* in Hanoi, which had no standing in international law but which performed diplomatic and consular functions.

16. INR (Hughes) to Rusk, 11 September 1963, box 199, NSF CF, JFKL.

17. CIA cable, 2 September 1963, *FRUS*, 1961–1963, 4:88–89; Saigon to FO, 19 September 1963, FO 371/170107, PRO. Fall quoted in the State Department's American Opinion Survey for the week of 2 October. In box 23, Thomson Papers, JFKL. In an article in *The New Republic* in 1979, journalist Stanley Karnow wrote that "sources familiar with the North Vietnamese" had recently told him of Hanoi's desire for negotiations in late 1963. Karnow, "Lost Chance." Geoffrey Warner finds "little doubt that the RVN government was negotiating with the Communists." Warner, "The Coup That Never Was," 248–249.

18. CIA cable, 2 September 1963, *FRUS*, 1961–1963, 4:88–89; Saigon to FO, 19 September 1963, FO 371/170107, PRO; Karnow, *Vietnam*, 307–308; Hammer, *A Death in November*, 227–229; Saigon to FO, 31 August 1963, FO 371/170092. See also Karnow, "Lost Chance." Alsop's column appeared in the *New York Herald Tribune* on 18 September 1963.

19. CIA cable, 2 September 1963, *FRUS, 1961–1963*, 4:88–89; CIA Memo, 19 September 1963, box 200, NSF CF, JFKL; CIA Report, 17 September 1963, box 200, NSF CF, JFKL.

20. Lodge to State, 13 September 1963, *FRUS, 1961–1963*, 4:203.

21. Hilsman to Rusk, 16 September 1963, box 199, NSF CF, JFKL; Hughes to Rusk, memorandum, 11 September 1963, box 199, NSF CF, JFKL.

22. *PP* (Gravel) 3:444.

23. Attorney General Robert Kennedy also may have floated the withdrawal idea at a top-level meeting in September. Some years later in an interview, Kattenburg recalled the 31 August meeting: "There was not a single person there that knew what he was talking about. They didn't know Vietnam. They didn't know the past. They had forgotten the history. They simply didn't understand the identification of nationalism and Communism, and the more the meeting went on the more I sat there and thought, 'God, we're walking into a major disaster.'" See his cryptic comments, as recorded in Memcon, 6 September 1963, *FRUS, 1961–1963*, 4:117–120.

24. Memcon, 31 August 1963, *FRUS, 1961–1963*, 4:69–74; *PP* (Gravel), 2:741–743; David Halberstam, *The Best and the Brightest* (New York: Random House, 1972), 266–267.

25. Congressional Research Service interview, cited in Gibbons, *U.S. Government*, 2:161. Kattenburg would later write an exceptionally useful and insightful book on the American intervention. See Paul Kattenburg, *The Vietnam Trauma in American Foreign Policy* (New Brunswick, N.J.: Transaction Books, 1980).

26. *Public Papers of the Presidents of the United States: John F. Kennedy, 1963* (Millwood, N.Y.: KTO Press, 1977), 652, 659, 676 (hereafter *PPOP-1963*).

27. Minutes, "President's Press Conference of 12/9," 17 September 1963, FO 371/170112.

28. Memo of Conference, 3 September 1963, box 199, NSF CF, JFKL; State to Lodge, 3 September 1963, *FRUS, 1961–1963*, 4:101, 104–106; Rusk to Lodge, 4 September 1963, box 199, NSF CF, JFKL; Harriman to Lodge, 14 September 1963, box 461, Harriman Papers, Library of Congress. JFK received praise for his interview also from Michael Forrestal, who said that JFK had proven with his words that "our determination to resist Communist incursion in SEA remains unchanged." Forrestal to Kennedy, 4 September 1963, box 199, NSF CF, JFKL.

29. Hilsman to Rusk and McNamara, 16 September 1963, box 317, NSF Meetings and Memoranda File, JFKL. In a memo to Rusk, INR director Thomas Hughes noted that an assessment by the State Department's Country Team had concluded that actual power was in the hands of Nhu. Hughes to Rusk, 15 September 1963, *FRUS, 1961–1963*, 4:213. Four days later, Hilsman wrote Rusk that there was an "overwhelming feeling among Vietnamese" that Nhu was "the real power" in the government. Hilsman to Rusk, 19 September 1963, box 202, NSF CF, JFKL. The divisions on the administration are described in Washington to FO, 12 September 1963, FO 371/170112.

30. Herring, *America's Longest War*, 100–102; McCone to Johnson, 26 Sep-

tember 1963, box 317, NSF Meetings and Memoranda File, JFKL. The depth of the split was dramatically demonstrated by the findings of an interdepartmental mission to Vietnam, which reported to Kennedy on 10 September. The Pentagon's General Victor Krulak minimized the possibilities of a coup and painted a rosy picture of the state of the war. Victory would be achieved, he insisted, if the United States fully backed Diem. The State Department's Joseph Mendenhall, in contrast, reported a "virtual breakdown of the civil government in Saigon" and warned of a possible religious civil war in the South or a "slow turning of the South Vietnamese people to the Viet Cong." Nhu had to go, Mendenhall insisted, if the war was to be won. Kennedy heard the two men out and then issued his famous remark: "Did you two gentlemen visit the same country?" Memcon, 10 September 1963, box 316, NSF CF, JFKL.

31. Reeves, *President Kennedy*, 602–603. In his instructions to McNamara prior to the trip, Kennedy again indicated his determination to defeat the Vietcong. Kennedy to McNamara, 21 September 1963, *FRUS*, 1961–1963, 4:278.

32. McNamara Notes of Conversation with "Professor Smith," 26 September 1963, *FRUS*, 1961–1963, 4:293–295; Lodge to SecState, 30 September 1963, box 316, NSF CF, JFKL; Henry C. Lodge, *The Storm Has Many Eyes* (New York: Norton, 1973), 207. For the problem of relying on easily manipulated statistical indices in determining progress and policy, see John Lewis Gaddis, *Strategies of Containment: A Critical Appraisal of Postwar American National Security Policy* (New York: Oxford University Press, 1982), 255–258.

33. McNamara-Taylor Report, 2 October 1963, *PP* (Gravel), 2:751–766.

34. Bundy MS, chapter 9.

35. Summary Record of NSC Meeting, 2 October 1963, box 314, NSF Meetings and Memoranda File, JFKL; White House conversations, 2 October 1963 (6:05 P.M.), KT.

36. Department of State, "American Opinion Survey," 18 September 1963, box 200, NSF CF, JFKL.

37. *WP*, 3 and 5 September 1963.

38. *New Republic*, 14 September 1963.

39. *U.S. News and World Report*, 9 September 1963.

40. *NYT*, 19 October 1963; State Department American Opinion Survey, 2 and 9 October 1963, box 23, Thomson Papers, JFKL. Kennedy, too, perceived the increasing pessimism among journalists, whether or not they were critics of the war. He told McNamara, "The only way to confound the press is to win the war." Memo for the Record, 23 September 1963, box 200, NSF CF, JFKL.

41. State to Saigon, 5 September 1963, *FRUS* 1961–1963, IV, 113. On 13 September, Hilsman told officials at the British embassy in Washington that he had had a rough passage at a hearing of the Senate Foreign Relations Committee the previous week. Washington to FO, 14 September 1963, FO 371/170112, PRO.

42. Robert David Johnson, "Ernest Gruening and the American Dissenting Tradition," unpublished manuscript, chapter 7. On the concerns about making a good case to Congress, see JFK cable to Saigon, 17 September 1963, *FRUS*, 1961–1963, 4:252–254. See also Reeves, *President Kennedy*, 613–614.

43. On Church's resolution, see LeRoy Ashby and Rod Gramer, *Fighting the Odds: The Life of Senator Frank Church* (Pullman, Wash.: Washington State University Press, 1994), 168–171; and Gibbons, *U.S. Government*, 2:166–169, 191–195.

44. *U.S. News and World Report*, 16 September 1963; Memorandum by Sullivan, 30 September 1963, *FRUS, 1961–1963*, 4:325–326; Hilsman to Ball (acting secretary of state), 1 October 1963, *FRUS, 1961–1963*, 4:331.

45. Saigon to FO, 19 September 1963, FO 371/170093, PRO.

46. Bohlen to State, 2 October 1963, box 202, NSF CF, JFKL; Bohlen to State, 16 September 1963, box 72, NSF CF, JFKL. Couve's comments are in *Le Monde*, 9 October 1963.

47. On the worldwide reaction, see Direction Asie-Océanie, "Réactions dans le monde à la déclaration du Général de Gaulle," 6 September 1963, CLV, sud-vietnam #91, MAE; Bangkok to Stockholm, 2 September 1963, HP1, #XV, UD.

48. Paris to State, 8 January 1964, box 169, NSF CF, JFKL; *Le Monde*, 19 September 1963. For a fascinating account of Laloulette's recall, see Saigon to FO, 25 September 1963, FO 371/170107, PRO.

49. An alarmist CIA memorandum accurately identified de Gaulle's two chief claims: that North Vietnam would never be militarily defeated, even with U.S. help, and that in the not-too-distant future North Vietnam would become the predominant power in Indochina. The agency said that Paris was actively working for a neutral solution and that this effort would likely "accelerate in the event that the U.S. outlook in South Vietnam should darken." CIA Memorandum, 23 October 1963, box 73, NSF CF, JFKL.

50. State to Bohlen, 25 September 1963, NSF CF, JFKL; Bohlen to State Department, 2 October 1963, NSF CF, JFKL.

51. Memorandum of Conversation, 7 October 1963, box 73, NSF CF, JFKL.

52. Report by the CIA Working Group, 30 September 1963. This report, declassified in 1993 and numbering thirty-one pages (some of which are still sanitized), can be examined at the JFKL. I am grateful to William Gibbons for providing me with a copy of it. A memo by State Intelligence and Research bureau dated 22 October 1963 spoke in similar terms. The memo says that each of the major indices of progress showed deterioration: Vietcong casualties, weapons losses, and defections had all moved downward, and the number of Vietcong attacks was up. In addition, sharp political deterioration had taken place. For a fascinating discussion of this memo and the Pentagon's response to it, see Thomas L. Hughes, "Experiencing McNamara," *Foreign Policy* 5 (1995): 160–163.

53. CIA to Lodge, 6 October 1963, *PP* (Gravel), 2:769; White House conversation, 8 October 1963, KT.

54. CIA Information Report, 14 October 1963, box 200, NSF CF, JFKL. A marginal note in McGeorge Bundy's handwriting shows that Kennedy read this report. In a *Times of Vietnam* interview on 17 October, Nhu declared that the South Vietnamese people "have lost confidence in the United States." Lodge to Rusk, 7 October 1963, box 204, NSF CF, JFKL.

55. Sullivan to Hilsman, 3 October 1963, box 519, Papers of W. A. Harri-

man, Library of Congress; Lodge to Rusk, 7 October 1963, box 204, NSF CF, JFKL; Saigon to FO, 28 October 1963, FO 371/170112, PRO. See also Washington to Paris, 6 November 1963, CLV, sud-vietnam #78, MAE.

56. This fear is amply demonstrated in section 3 of *FRUS, 1961–1963,* 4: 427–537. RFK quotation is from Memcon with President, 29 October 1963, *FRUS, 1961–1963,* 4:470. See also White House conversations, 8 and 25 October 1963, KT.

57. Spokesman Robert McCloskey read the line to the press on 22 October. U.S. Department of State, *American Foreign Policy: Current Documents, 1963* (Washington: GPO, 1964), 877. Four days earlier, Roger Hilsman had uttered a variant of it on NBC's *Today* show. "We're there to win a war," Hilsman said, "to help the Vietnamese fight the communist aggression," and it was within this context that the withdrawal plan had to be understood. The 1965 target date did not mean that the United States was pulling out, or that there would be no American aid past 1965, only that the Vietnamese could gradually take over the responsibilities currently held by Americans. NBC transcript, 18 October 1963, box 8, Thomson Papers, JFKL.

58. White House Discussion, 30 October 1963, KT. MB to Lodge, 30 October 1963, box 200, NSF CF, JFKL. A South Vietnamese diplomat, Tran Van Dinh, would later claim that Diem in his last days decided to try to make a deal with Hanoi. According to Dinh, Diem recalled him from his post at the Vietnamese embassy in Washington in late October and ordered him to proceed to New Delhi to meet with a North Vietnamese official on 15 November. The coup intervened and prevented the meeting. Karnow, "Lost Chance"; Hammer, *A Death in November,* 268–270; Seymour Hersh, *The Dark Side of Camelot* (Boston: Little, Brown, 1997), 433–434.

59. In the days after the coup, many in Saigon saw fear of a Nhu-DRV deal as motivating the United States. Lodge to State, 8 November 1963, *FRUS, 1961–1963,* 4:588; Bangkok to Stockholm, 7 February 1964, HP1, #XV, UD.

60. State to Paris, 4 November 1963, *FRUS, 1961–1963,* 4:565.

61. Kahin, *Intervention,* 183.

62. Ibid., 183–184; Young, *Vietnam Wars,* 106–107. According to Kahin, Minh insisted in an interview that he and his group were noncommunist rather than anticommunist and stressed, "You must understand the distinction, because it is an important one." Kahin, *Intervention,* 185. On Buddhist attraction to the NLF, see William J. Duiker, *Vietnam: Nation in Revolution* (Boulder, Colo.: Westview Press, 1983), 68–69, 369.

63. CIA Memorandum, 6 November 1963, box 202, NSF CF, JFKL.

64. CIA Report, 16 November 1963, box 202, NSF CF, JFKL; CIA Memorandum, 26 November 1963, box 202, NSF CF, JFKL.

65. State to Bohlen, 4 November 1963, box 204, NSF CF, JFKL; Bohlen to State, 5 November 1963, box 204, NSF CF, JFKL; State to Paris, 15 November 1963; *FRUS, 1961–1963,* 4:662; Entretien Couve-Moffat, 6 November 1963, CLV, sud-vietnam #78, MAE.

66. Peyrefitte, *C'était de Gaulle,* 480–481; Bohlen to State, 5 November 1963, *FRUS, 1961–1963,* IV, 568–569; Vaïsse, *La grandeur,* 526.

67. *NYT*, 3, 6, and 10 November 1963. For an interesting discussion among former officials meeting in Austin in 1991 that the Frankel piece might have been "planted" by the administration, see Ted Gittinger, ed., *The Johnson Years: A Vietnam Roundtable* (Austin, Tex.: Lyndon Baines Johnson Library, Lyndon B. Johnson School of Public Affairs, 1993), 8–9. It is also worth noting that the paper's famed correspondent in Vietnam, David Halberstam, although critical of U.S. strategy, was still hawkish in late 1963 and would remain so for many months. See Halberstam, *The Making of a Quagmire* (New York: Random House, 1990), 177; and the introduction to the 1991 edition of Halberstam, *Best and the Brightest.*

68. Harrison Salisbury, *Without Fear or Favor: The New York Times and Its Times* (New York: Times Books, 1980), 44–46; Daniel C. Hallin, *The "Uncensored War": The Media and Vietnam* (New York: Oxford University Press, 1986), 6.

69. Forrestal to MB, 7 November 1963, box 202, NSF CF, JFKL. In the margin, Bundy noted that he agreed with Forrestal's suggestion. So, apparently, did Kennedy; at a press conference on 14 November, he restated the U.S. goal of preserving an independent South Vietnam and blamed the conflict on an assault "manipulated from the North." *PPOF-1963*, 848–853; Mendenhall to Hilsman, 12 November 1963, box 202, NSF CF, JFKL.

70. Forrestal to MB, 7 November 1963, box 202, NSF CF, JFKL.

71. State to Lodge, 13 November 1963, box 202, NSF CF, JFKL. The cable was repeated to embassies in London, Paris, Bangkok, Ottawa, New Delhi, Vientiane, and Phnom Penh.

72. Dallas speech is in *Public Papers of the Presidents: Kennedy*, 890–894.

73. Thompson to FO, 13 September 1962, FO 371/166723, PRO. Emphasis added.

74. Newman, *JFK and Vietnam*, 456. Likewise, Peter Dale Scott maintains that "Johnson redirected U.S. Vietnam policy from this graduated disengagement (NSAM 263) to graduated escalation (NSAM 273)." Scott, *Deep Politics*, 24.

75. State to Saigon, 5 October 1963, Presidential Office File, box 128, JFKL (emphasis added), White House conversation, 2 November 1963, KT.

76. I have benefited here from the analysis in Larry Berman, "Counterfactual Historical Reasoning: NSAM 263 and NSAM 273," paper delivered at conference on "Vietnam: The Early Decisions, 1961–1964," LBJL, 15 October 1993. A recently declassified memorandum on the discussion at the Honolulu meeting shows no mention of a withdrawal; on the contrary, the conferees appear to presuppose a continued American advisory effort. Summary of Discussion, 20 November 1963, box 1, NSF, Vietnam, LBJL. I am grateful to William C. Gibbons for kindly providing me with a copy of this memo.

77. Rusk, *As I Saw It*, 441–442; Walt W. Rostow, letter to the editor, *NYT*, 15 February 1992; William P. Bundy, letter to the editor, *NYT*, 12 February 1992; Robert Kennedy OH, JFKL. LBJ aide George Reedy has also cast doubt on the withdrawal notion. "If JFK was preparing to pull out of Vietnam after the election, his top assistants in the White House failed to inform LBJ of that

fact. I sat in on many meetings where it was taken for granted that the war would be prosecuted." George E. Reedy, letter to the editor, *NYT*, 8 March 1992.

78. In an early message to Lodge after the coup, Kennedy said that the United States had a "responsibility" to make the new government succeed. JFK to Lodge, 6 November 1963, *FRUS, 1961–1963*, 4:579–580.

79. Report by the CIA Working Group, 30 September 1963.

80. The list includes journalists, scholars, and former officials. See Henry Kissinger, *Diplomacy* (New York: Simon and Schuster, 1994), 655–657; Richard Nixon, *No More Vietnams* (New York: Arbor House, 1985), 62–84; Frederick Nolting, *From Trust to Tragedy: The Political Memoir of Frederick Nolting, Kennedy's Ambassador to Diem's Vietnam* (New York: Praeger, 1988), 132–144; Robert H. Miller, "Vietnam: Folly, Quagmire, or Inevitability?" *Studies in Conflict and Terrorism* 15 (1992): 114; Stanley Karnow, "Commentary: The Two Vietnams," in *Vietnam as History: Ten Years after the Paris Peace Accords*, ed. Peter Braestrup (Washington, D.C.: University Press of America, 1984), 81–83; William C. Gibbons, "Lyndon Johnson and the Legacy of Vietnam," in *Vietnam: The Early Years*, ed. Lloyd C. Gardner and Ted Gittinger (Austin: University of Texas Press, 1997), 138–139; Col. William Wilson, "Perspectives," *Vietnam* 10 (April 1997): 56–60; William C. Westmoreland, "Vietnam in Perspective," *The Retired Officer* (October 1978): 21–24. Likewise, Lloyd Gardner writes that "American involvement in Vietnam was sealed by a decision in 1963 to intervene—against Ngo Dinh Diem, whose government had proved incapable of waging America's war in Vietnam." Gardner, *Pay Any Price*, 542. The most breathtakingly categorical argument along these lines is in Francis Winters's study of JFK and Vietnam in 1963. Referring to the certainty that U.S. complicity in the coup sealed the deal, the author states: "The banality of this lesson of Vietnam—its seemingly uncomplicated clarity—is now at last being registered by a surprising, and therefore persuasive, chorus of commentators." Francis X. Winters, *The Year of the Hare: America in Vietnam, January 25, 1963–February 15, 1964* (Athens: University of Georgia Press, 1997), 205. Others do not point to the coup specifically but make the same larger argument: that by the time of JFK's death, the Rubicon had been crossed. See here Dallek, "Lyndon Johnson and Vietnam"; Buzzanco, *Masters of War*; Chomsky, *Rethinking Camelot*.

81. According to figures compiled by the CIA, Vietcong attacks had increased from about 375 per week in September and October to more than 1,000 during the week from 6 to 13 November. Honolulu Briefing Book, November 1963, box 204, NSF CF, JFKL; Memorandum of Discussion, Honolulu, 20 November 1963, *FRUS, 1961–1963*, 4:608–624.

CHAPTER 3

1. In 1960, President Eisenhower told the *New York Times* that he could not understand how the Democrats could consider nominating an "inexperienced

boy" like Kennedy, "or for that matter [Stuart] Symington or [Adlai] Stevenson. Lyndon Johnson . . . would be the best Democrat of them all as president
from the viewpoint of responsible management of national affairs." Quoted in
Robert Dallek, "The President We Love to Blame," *Wilson Quarterly* (winter
1991): 106. See also George E. Reedy, *Lyndon B. Johnson: A Memoir* (New York:
Andrews and McMeel, 1982), 47; and Dean Rusk OH, LBJL, tape 1.

2. Karnow, *Vietnam*, 337.

3. LBJ to Taylor, 2 December 1963, *FRUS, 1961–1963*, 4:651. On another
occasion in the early days of his presidency, Johnson confessed to press secretary Bill Moyers that he had "the terrible feeling that something has grabbed
me around the ankles and won't let go." Quoted in Bill Moyers, "Flashbacks,"
Newsweek, 10 February 1975.

4. William H. Chafe, *The Unfinished Journey: America since World War
II*, 3d ed. (New York: Oxford University Press, 1991), 271; Ronnie Dugger,
The Politician: The Life and Times of Lyndon Johnson (New York: Norton,
1982).

5. Johnson's 1961 quote is in *PP* (Gravel), II, 57–58. Johnson is often cred-
ited with helping to prevent a U.S. intervention at the time of French defeat at
Dien Bien Phu in 1954, when he was minority leader in the Senate. He did
contribute to that decision, by posing some tough questions to the Eisenhower
administration regarding allied support for the endeavor, but he was not against
intervention per se. Moreover, he asserted that the fall of Indochina "would be
disastrous to all our plans in Southeast Asia." Prados, *Hidden History*, 13–17.

6. Chafe, *Unfinished Journey*, 274; Doris Kearns, *Lyndon Johnson and the
American Dream* (New York: Harper and Row, 1976), 252–253.

7. Memorandum for the Record, 24 November 1963, *FRUS, 1961–1963*, IV,
635–637; Lyndon B. Johnson, *The Vantage Point: Perspectives of the Presidency* (New York: Holt, Rinehart, and Winston, 1971), 43–44; National Security Action Memorandum No. 273, 26 November 1963, *FRUS, 1961–1963*, IV,
637–640.

8. McNamara, *In Retrospect*, 102; David Nes telephone interview with the
author, 20 February 1994; Blair, *Lodge in Vietnam*, 119. Johnson's determination is also evident in LBJ–Donald Cook telcon, 30 November 1963, in Michael
Beschloss, ed., *Taking Charge: The Johnson White House Tapes, 1963–1964*
(New York: Simon and Schuster, 1998), 73–74. And see Johnson's comments
at the State Department on 5 December, as recorded in *NYT*, 6 December 1963.

9. State to Lodge, 27 November 1963, *FRUS, 1961–1963*, IV, 640–642;
Lodge to State, 30 November 1963, box 1, NSF VN, LBJL; Rusk to Lodge, 6 December 1963, box 1, NSF VN, LBJL.

10. James Reston, *Deadline: A Memoir* (New York: Random House, 1991),
310–311; Reedy, *Lyndon B. Johnson*, 121; David Wise, *The Politics of Lying:
Government Deception, Secrecy, and Power* (New York: Random House, 1973),
296–297; Tom Wicker, *JFK and LBJ: The Influence of Personality upon Politics*
(New York: Morrow, 1968), 199.

11. Reedy, *Lyndon B. Johnson*, 25, 52; Reston, *Deadline*, 304; James Deakin,

"I've Got a Secret," *New Republic,* 30 January 1965; Philip Geyelin, *Lyndon B. Johnson and the World* (New York: Praeger, 1966), 15–17; Anatoly F. Dobrynin, *In Confidence: Moscow's Ambassador to America's Six Cold War Presidents, 1962–1986* (New York: Times Books, 1995), 120; Richard J. Barnet, *The Alliance: America, Europe, Japan: Makers of the Postwar World* (New York: Simon and Schuster, 1983), 236. A thoughtful and perceptive essay on Johnson's approach to world affairs, albeit one that underplays his aversion to dissent, is Waldo Heinrichs, "Lyndon Johnson: Change and Continuity," in *Lyndon Johnson Confronts the World: American Foreign Policy, 1963–1968,* ed. Warren I. Cohen and Nancy Bernkopf Tucker (New York: Cambridge University Press, 1994), 9–30.

12. MB to LBJ, 11 February 1964, box 1, NSF MPB, LBJL; MB to LBJ, 14 May 1964, NSF MPB, LBJL. On the roots of Johnson's insecurities, and the ways in which these fueled his urge to dominate those around him, see Robert A. Caro, *The Path to Power,* vol. 1 of *The Years of Lyndon Johnson* (New York: Knopf, 1982).

13. Reedy, *Lyndon B. Johnson,* 6. See here also, for example, Kearns, *Lyndon Johnson and the American Dream,* 315–318; James David Barber, *The Presidential Character: Predicting Performance in the White House,* 2d ed. (Englewood Cliffs, N.J.: Prentice-Hall, 1977), 30–42, 78–98, 129–140; George C. Herring, *LBJ and Vietnam: A Different Kind of War* (Austin: University of Texas Press, 1994), 48; Christopher M. Andrew, *For the President's Eyes Only: Secret Intelligence and the American Presidency from Washington to Bush* (New York: HarperCollins, 1995), 328; Henry F. Graff, *The Tuesday Cabinet: Deliberation and Decision on Peace and War under Lyndon B. Johnson* (Englewood Cliffs, N.J.: Prentice-Hall, 1970), 6; Irving L. Janis, *Victims of Groupthink: A Psychological Study of Foreign-Policy Decisions and Fiascoes* (Boston: Houghton Mifflin, 1972), 106; Schoenbaum, *Waging Peace and War,* 414; Hyman L. Muslin and Thomas H. Jobe, *Lyndon Johnson: The Tragic Self: A Psychohistorical Portrait* (New York: Plenum Press, 1991), 183–200; Burke and Greenstein, *How Presidents Test Reality,* 291.

14. Michael Forrestal OH, LBJL; McGeorge Bundy interview with the author, New York City, 15 March 1994; Chester L. Cooper, *The Lost Crusade: America in Vietnam* (New York: Dodd, Mead, 1970), 223.

15. CIA Information Report, 2 December 1963, box 1, NSF VN, LBJL; JCS to Felt, 2 December 1963, box 1, NSF VN, LBJL; Cooper to McCone, 6 December 1963, *FRUS, 1961–1963,* 4:680–684; State to Saigon, 6 December 1963, box 1, NSF VN, LBJL; Lodge to State, 7 December 1963, box 1, NSF VN, LBJL.

16. Maxwell Taylor, OH, LBJL; Bundy MS, chapter 10.

17. *PP* (Gravel), 3:498–499; Kahin, *Intervention,* 188. On Minh's dislike for the hamlets program, see also his comments to the British embassy on 3 December. Saigon to FO, 5 December 1963, FO 371/170095, PRO.

18. Saigon to FO, 5 December 1963, FO 371/170095, PRO; *NYT,* 10 December 1963; Saigon to Paris, 15 November 1963, CLV, sud-vietnam #91, MAE.

19. CIA Intelligence Memorandum, 26 November 1963, box 1, NSF VN,

LBJL. The NLF appeal is quoted in full in George McT. Kahin and John W. Lewis, *The United States in Vietnam* (New York: Dial Press, 1969), 473–476. See also Duiker, *Sacred War*, 161.

20. Russell quoted in Gibbons, *U.S. Government*, 2:215. See also LBJ-Russell telcon, 7 December 1963, JT; Blair, *Lodge in Vietnam*, 75.

21. Mansfield to LBJ, 7 December 1963, box 6, NSF NF, LBJL. Mansfield seems to have been unaware that senior military officials agreed that the war could not be won in the South alone. Unlike the senator, of course, many of them favored an extension of the war to the North.

22. Ibid. Emphasis in original. Mansfield's memo was a follow-up to a conversation the two men had held on the previous Thursday.

23. Johnson, *Vantage Point*, 212; Ball, *Past Has Another Pattern*, 336. For other references to the baseball analogy, see H. W. Brands Jr., "Johnson and de Gaulle: American Diplomacy *Sotto Voce*," *The Historian* 49 (1987): 482–485; and Charles Bohlen OH, LBJL. For the administration's handling of de Gaulle, see also H. W. Brands Jr., *The Wages of Globalism: Lyndon Johnson and the Limits of American Power* (New York: Oxford University Press, 1995), 85–121.

24. Bohlen to Rusk, 13 December 1963, box 169, NSF CF, LBJL; Charles E. Bohlen, *Witness to History, 1929–1969* (New York: Norton, 1973), 503. Bohlen often reiterated his belief that de Gaulle was all-powerful in French foreign policy, to the degree that even Foreign Minister Couve de Murville often had no input on policy decisions. See, for example, the cable cited previously; and Bohlen, *Witness to History*, 502.

25. Paris to State, 16 December 1963, box 169, NSF CF, LBJL; *WP*, 8 December 1963; *NYT*, 8 December 1963.

26. Sihanouk's break with the United States is ably covered in David P. Chandler, *The Tragedy of Cambodian History: Politics, War, and Revolution since 1945* (New Haven, Conn.: Yale University Press, 1991), 130–141. Older but still useful is Michael Leifer, *Cambodia: The Search for Security* (New York: Praeger, 1967). See also Couve, *Une politique étrangère*, 124.

27. Chandler, *Tragedy*, 132.

28. Lodge to Rusk, 3 December 1963, box 1, NSF VN, LBJL.

29. Lodge to Harriman, 4 December 1963, *FRUS*, 1961–1963, 4:661–662; Saigon to FO, 23 December 1963, FO 371/170079, PRO.

30. State to Lodge, 10 December 1963, box 1, NSF VN, LBJL. Lodge responded the following day, with reference to a pro-diplomacy editorial in the *Times* on 8 December: "I definitely believe U.S. should make a public statement, making it absolutely clear without mentioning the *New York Times'* name, that we do not agree with the thought in the editorial." Lodge to State, 11 December 1963, *FRUS*, 1961–1963, IV, 697.

31. Hughes to Rusk, 7 December 1963, box 236, NSF VN, LBJL; State to Kohler, 10 December 1963, box 236, NSF CF, LBJL; Memcon Zinchuk-Forrestal, 16 December 1963, box 461, Papers of W. A. Harriman, Library of Congress (hereafter Harriman Papers).

32. FO to Bangkok, 5 December 1963, FO 371/170077, PRO; FO to Bang-

kok, 20 December 1963, FO 371/170078, PRO; Minutes by J. E. Cable, 31 December 1963, FO 371/170096, PRO.

33. Lodge to State, 13 December 1963, box 1, NSF VN, LBJL; Lodge to State, 15 December 1963, box 1, NSF VN, LBJL; State to Lodge, 16 December 1963, *FRUS*, 1961–1963, 4:710.

34. McNamara, *In Retrospect*, 103; Forrestal to MB, 10 December 1963, box 1, NSF, Memos to the President—McGeorge Bundy, LBJL (hereafter cited as NSF MPB). In a cable to Lodge, McNamara said that he was coming to finalize plans designed to "make clear to the North Vietnamese that the U.S. will not accept a communist victory in South Vietnam and that we will escalate the conflict to whatever level is required to insure their defeat." RSM to Lodge, 12 December 1963, box 1, NSF VN, LBJL.

35. FO to Saigon, 11 December 1963, FO 371/170095, PRO. On French views, see the memo from the Australian embassy in Paris to Canberra, 20 December 1964, FO 371/170107, PRO.

36. Washington to FO, 27 December 1963, FO 371/170096; Saigon to State, 1 December 1963, box 1, NSF VN, LBJL. McCone's report is in *FRUS*, 1961–1963, IV, 736–738. See here also the very gloomy report of Britain's Robert Thompson, BRIAM to FO, 19 December 1963, FO 371/170107, PRO. Commented one Foreign Office member upon reading the report: "Mr. Thompson is now an on-balance pessimist regarding the future of Vietnam." T. J. Everard Minute, 23 December 1963, FO 371/170096, PRO.

37. RSM to LBJ, 21 December 1963, box 1, NSF VN, LBJL. A more optimistic public statement given by McNamara is printed in *American Foreign Policy*, 883–884.

38. Hanoi to FO, 27 November 1963, FO 371/170115, PRO; *Newsweek*, 2 December 1963.

39. RSM to LBJ, 21 December 1963, box 1, NSF VN, LBJL; McCone to LBJ, 23 December 1963, box 1, NSF VN, LBJL; Rusk to LBJ, 27 December 1963, *FRUS*, 1961–1963, 4:745.

40. LBJ to Duong Van Minh, 31 December 1963, box 12, NSF, Head of State Correspondence File, LBJL. Along with his New Year's greeting, Johnson had a confidential message for Minh. He instructed Lodge to tell Minh that "it is vitally important to act rapidly to reverse the trend of the war within the next 60–90 days." LBJ to Lodge, 26 December 1963, box 12, NSF, Head of State Correspondence, LBJL. The message was reported, in almost exactly the same language, in State to Lodge, 31 December 1963, *FRUS*, 1961–1963, 4:745–747.

41. Mansfield to LBJ, 6 January 1964, box 1, NSF VN, LBJL.

42. MB to LBJ, 6 January 1964, box 1, NSF MPB, LBJL; MB to LBJ, 9 January 1964, box 1, NSF VN, LBJL. Emphasis in original.

43. RSM to LBJ, 7 January 1964, box 1, NSF VN, LBJL; Rusk to LBJ, 8 January 1964, box 1, NSF VN, LBJL.

44. Rostow to Rusk, 10 January 1964, box 170, NSF VN, LBJL; Sorensen to LBJ, 14 January 1964, box 1, NSF VN, LBJL. Interestingly, Sorensen did agree

with Mansfield on one point: that the United States should do more to emphasize that South Vietnam had ultimate responsibility for victory in the war.
That way, "if during the next four months the new government fails to take
the necessary political, economic, social, and military actions, it will be their
choice and not our betrayal or weakness that loses the area."

45. McNamara, *In Retrospect*, 106–107.

46. On New Year's Eve, William Jorden reported that "talk of neutralism
has spread like wildfire through the Vietnamese community." He noted that
the actual amount of support for the concept could not be determined. A few
days later, McGeorge Bundy informed Johnson that "neutralist elements"
were gaining in strength in Saigon. Jorden to Rusk, 31 December 1963, *FRUS*,
1961–1963, 4:753; *PP* (Gravel), 3:37.

47. CIA Report, 8 January 1964, box 1, NSF VN, LBJL; Lodge to State, 10
January 1964, box 1, NSF VN, LBJL; Lodge to State, 14 January 1964, *FRUS*,
1964–1968, 1:24. In a 1989 interview with Australian scholar Anne Blair, Minister of Defense Tran Van Don said his main difference with General Harkins
had been over Harkins's efforts to push the MRC into a larger war. The MRC,
Don said, had welcomed U.S. material and technical advice but wanted no U.S.
troops and no escalation of the scale and nature of the war. Anne Blair, "No
Time to Stop: Henry Cabot Lodge in Vietnam," Ph.D. dissertation, Monash
University, Australia, 1992, page 220.

48. *PP* (Gravel), 3:150–153; Gibbons, *U.S. Government*, 2:213–214. An excellent summary of early covert operations and the formulation and implementation of OPLAN 34-A is Moïse, *Tonkin Gulf*, 2–19.

49. Hanoi to FO, 27 January 1964, FO 371/175480, PRO; Duiker, *Sacred
War*, 161–164.

50. INR (Hughes) to Rusk, 20 January 1964, box 1, NSF VN, LBJL. According to Duiker, in December 1963 Hanoi "began to send out peace feelers to
the [Minh] government." Duiker, *Communist Road*, 221.

51. Paris to FO, 8 January 1964, FO 371/175923, PRO; Peyrefitte, *C'était
de Gaulle*, 480–494; Vaïsse, *La grandeur*, 514–521. According to Philippe Devillers, de Gaulle's talks with Johnson and Rusk at the time of Kennedy's fu-
neral convinced him that U.S. Asian policy would henceforth be more unrealistic than ever and that France must resume contact with Beijing as soon
as possible. Philippe Devillers, "French Policy in the Second Vietnam War,"
The World Today 23 (June 1967): 249–263. For French recognition of China,
see also Lacouture, *Souverain*, 439–443; Edgar Faure, *Mémoires* (Paris: Plon,
1982), 2:673–674. According to Lacouture, de Gaulle had been influenced by a
book written by Faure many years earlier, titled *Le serpent et la tortue: Les
problèmes de la Chine populaire* (Paris: Julliard, 1957). In it, Faure advocated
the establishment of diplomatic relations between France and China. See also
de Gaulle's comments to Bohlen on 5 November 1965, in SG, EM, #19, MAE.

52. CIA Report, "France Reassessing Policy toward Communist China?"
6 September 1963, box 72, NSF CF, JFKL; Bohlen to State, 16 October 1963,
box 73, NSF CF, JFKL; CIA Memorandum for the Director, "Gaullist France and

Communist China," 23 October 1963, box 73, NSF CF, JFKL; State to Bohlen, 3 January 1964, box 461, Harriman Papers.

53. See "Talking Points for Douglas Home Visit," 4 February 1964, box 212, NSF CF, LBJL. In January 1964, the JCS warned that an American failure to stand up to China in Vietnam would damage American credibility throughout Asia and have "a corresponding unfavorable effect upon our image in Africa and Latin America." CIA Memorandum, January 1964, box 1, NSF VN, LBJL.

54. State to Bohlen, 3 January 1964, box 461, Harriman Papers; Bohlen to State, 8 January 1964, box 169, NSF CF, LBJL.

55. Harriman to Rusk, 8 January 1964, box 454, Harriman Papers; MB to LBJ, 8 January 1964, box 1, NSF MPB, LBJL; Memcon, Tyler and Bohlen, 7 January 1964, box 1, NSF VN, LBJL. Bohlen had initially favored intervention by LBJ. On 30 December 1963, he had even drafted a suggested letter from Johnson to de Gaulle. Bohlen to Harriman, 30 December 1963, box 454, Harriman Papers.

56. See LBJ-Russell telcon, 15 January 1964, JT. In mid January, Harriman spoke bluntly to Hervé Alphand, the French ambassador in Washington, about the connection made by Paris between recognition of China and a neutralist settlement in Indochina and the uneasiness this caused in Washington. *FRUS,* 1964–1968, 1:32. See also Alphand, *L'étonnement d'être,* 420–423.

57. Most of Martin's comments in the conversation remain sanitized, but Ball's phraseology indicates considerable Canadian skepticism about U.S. policy. Memcon, Ball and Martin et al., 22 January 1964, box 167, NSF CF, LBJL. A few days earlier in Paris, Canadian prime minister Lester Pearson had told de Gaulle that Ottawa had no objection to French recognition of China. Canada indeed hoped to take the same action itself before too long, Pearson said, and he assured de Gaulle that Ottawa would not take part in any U.S.-sponsored anti-French action. Paris to FO, 17 January 1964, FO 371/175923, PRO. See also Couve-Martin Meeting Notes, 15 January 1964, SG, EM, #20, MAE.

58. Rusk and McNamara statements are from "Chronology on Vietnam," November 1965, box 38, NSF NSC History, LBJL. On McNamara before the House Armed Services Committee, see also Shapley, *Promise and Power,* 295–296.

59. Lodge to State, 19 January 1964, box 1, NSF VN, LBJL; Lodge to State, 21 January 1964, box 1, NSF VN, LBJL. The State Department lauded Lodge for his comments. The United States, it said in a cable, was "180 degrees opposed" to the recommendations in the AFP article, believed the war could be won, and saw the "French approach as avenue of disaster which could lead to communist control of all Viet-Nam and Southeast Asia." State to Lodge, 21 January 1964, box 1, NSF VN, LBJL.

60. Lodge to State, 21 January 1964, box 1, NSF VN, LBJL; Lodge to State, 1 February 1964, box 1, NSF VN, LBJL; Lodge to State, 21 January 1964, box 236, NSF CF, LBJL; Lodge to State, 23 January 1964, box 236, NSF CF, LBJL.

61. *PP* (Gravel), 2:308–309, 3:37–38.

62. CIA Station in Saigon to Agency, 28 January 1964, *FRUS, 1964–1968,* 1:36–37. See also Saigon to Ottawa, 31 January 1964, FO 371/175468, PRO.

63. Lodge to State, 28 January 1964, box 1, NSF VN, LBJL.

64. State to Lodge, 28 January 1964, box 1, NSF VN, LBJL; Lodge to Rusk, 29 January 1964, box 1, NSF VN, LBJL.

65. *PP* (Gravel), 3:39. In his first press conference, Khanh justified his action on this ground, attacking those in the previous regime "who took a subservient attitude, paving the way for neutralization and thereby selling out the nation." *Le Monde,* 31 January 1964.

66. Ball-LBJ telcon, 29 January 1964, box 7, Ball Papers, LBJL; Ball-McNamara telcon, 29 January 1964, box 7, Ball Papers, LBJL; Ball-Clifton telcon, box 7, Ball Papers, LBJL; State to Lodge, 29 January 1964, *FRUS, 1964–1968,* 1:42. The State Department's Intelligence and Research desk also gave considerable weight to Khanh's neutralization fears, though it also listed personal ambition and concerns about the Minh regime's lackluster effort in the war as motivating him to act. See George C. Denney to Ball, 29 January 1964, *FRUS, 1964–1968,* 1:40–41.

67. Quai d'Orsay officials, when pressed on the issue, said that naturally they could not stop neutralist Vietnamese emigrés from telephoning them or writing letters to them or inviting them to lunch. They insisted, however, that they were scrupulous in never allowing emigrés to visit the Quai, and they scorned the notion of an incipient French-inspired plot that required Khanh to act. British officials in Saigon to FO, 5 February 1964, FO 371/175467, PRO; Paris to FO, 12 February 1964, FO 371/175488, PRO. Available French documentation also gives no indication of a concerted French effort, which of course does not preclude the possibility that Paris was trying to indirectly push developments in that direction.

68. Lodge to State, 30 January 1964, box 2, NSF VN, LBJL; *PP* (Gravel), 3: 37–39; Lodge to Rusk, 31 January 1964, box 169, NSF CF, LBJL; Lodge to State, 3 February 1964, box 169, NSF CF, LBJL.

69. *NYT,* 31 January 1964; Forrestal to LBJ, 31 January 1964, box 1, NSF CF, LBJL. Press speculation on the possibilities of a peaceful resolution to the conflict had picked up during the four days since Paris announced its recognition of China. Both the *NYT* and *Le Monde* reported that the neutralist movement in Vietnam experienced significant growth only after the French president's well-publicized August announcement (the *Times* went so far as to suggest that fear of a Gaullist neutralization lay behind the ouster of Diem in November), and they predicted a similar boost this time. *NYT,* 30 and 31 January 1964; *Le Monde,* 30 and 31 January 1964. On 2–3 February, *Le Monde* editorially supported de Gaulle's Vietnam policy, hailing his neutralization proposal. However, the paper doubted that France could by itself do much to bring about a settlement.

70. The de Gaulle quotation is in French Embassy, Press and Information Division, *Chronology of Charles de Gaulle's Press Conferences, 1958–1966* (New York: French Embassy, Press and Information Division, 1968), 89. A State Department statement issued the day of the announcement described the French

action as an "unfortunate step, particularly at a time when the Chinese communists are actively promoting aggression and subversion in Southeast Asia and elsewhere." *NYT,* 31 January 1964.

71. Peyrefitte, *C'était de Gaulle,* 494; CIA Report: Indications of French Policy, 5 February 1964, box 169, NSF CF, LBJL; Paris to FO, 12 February 1964, FO 371/175488, PRO; Paris to FO, 13 February 1964, FO 371/175488, PRO; Hanoi to FO, 13 November 1963, FO 371/170107, PRO.

72. Rusk-Manning telcon, 1 February 1964, *FRUS, 1964–1968,* 1:57–58; State to Saigon, 1 February 1964, box 2, NSF VN, LBJL; LBJ to Khanh, 2 February 1964, box 2, NSF VN, LBJL; Lodge to State, 31 January 1964, box 1, NSF VN, LBJL. The emphasis on continuity extended to the potentially prickly recognition issue. On 31 January, the administration announced that the United States was "continuing relations with the new leaders of the Government of the Republic of Vietnam" and that "accordingly no question of recognition" was involved.

73. Lacouture, *Vietnam,* 83, as cited in Franz Schurmann et al., *The Politics of Escalation in Vietnam* (Greenwich, Conn.: Fawcett Publications, 1966), 26.

74. *WP,* 4 February 1964. In his column the following week, Lippmann returned to the theme: "There are, I submit, compelling reasons why we must open our minds to the possibilities of a political solution in Southeast Asia. . . . The current policy of the United States—in which the alternatives are military victory or military defeat—is catastrophic. . . . The real problem is how to negotiate a political settlement before the situation deteriorates, as it is now deteriorating, into a military defeat." *WP,* 11 February 1964.

75. LBJ-Stone telcon, 31 January 1964, JT. Johnson used similar language in another telephone conversation the same day. See LBJ–Marshall McNeil telcon, 31 January 1964, JT.

CHAPTER 4

1. McGeorge Bundy interview with the author, 15 March 1994, New York City.

2. Michael Forrestal OH, LBJL; McGeorge Bundy interview with the author, 15 March 1994, New York City. British officials had few doubts on this score, judging by the casual way in which they would mention it in their internal memos. To cite but one example, in midspring Foreign Secretary R. A. B. Butler told Prime Minister Alec Douglas-Home of an "atmosphere in the White House dictated almost exclusively by considerations about the election next November." Butler to Prime Minister, Top Secret, 29 April 1964, PREM 11/4789, PRO.

3. *PP* (Gravel), 2:307–309; Lodge to State, 4 February 1964, box 2, NSF VN, LBJL. On 8 February, Khanh announced the formation of his government, with himself as premier and Minh as chief of state.

4. Saigon to FO, 6 February 1964, FO 371/175468, PRO; Saigon to FO, 16 March 1964, FO 371/175495, PRO; Saigon to FO, 8 April 1964, FO 371/

175495, PRO; Saigon to FO, 12 February 1964, FO 371/175493, PRO; Record of Meeting, Washington, 10 February 1964, FO 371/175090, PRO.

5. Forrestal to McNamara, 14 February 1964, box 2, NSF VN, LBJL; Defense Intelligence Agency Memorandum, 12 February 1964, *FRUS*, 1964–1968, 1:71–72; Helms to Rusk, 18 February 1964, box 2, NSF VN, LBJL.

6. CIA Saigon Station to McCone, 10 February 1964, box 2, NSF VN, LBJL; CIA Station (Kirkpatrick and de Silva) to McCone, 12 February 1964, as reported in *PP* (Gravel), 3:41–42; CIA Report, 20 February 1964, box 2, NSF VN, LBJL.

7. BRIAM to FO, 5 February 1964, FO 371/175493, PRO.

8. Nes to Lodge, 17 February 1964, box 1, Papers of David G. Nes, LBJL (hereafter cited as Nes Papers). Despite his pessimistic appraisal of the situation and his belief that de Gaulle might be right, Nes was not prepared to counsel an immediate American exit from Vietnam. Defeat was not absolutely certain, he suggested; if the Vietcong were deprived of all outside support, both material and psychological, and if the U.S. assured continued and massive support for "any and all anti-communist regimes" which might emerge in Saigon, "we might see the VC movement wither in 5–10 years." Neutralist sentiment might wither also, but only if the United States made clear a willingness to escalate toward a direct confrontation with Hanoi and Peking.

9. The Perruche meeting is reported in CIA Memorandum, 20 February 1964, box 2, NSF VN, LBJL. On the growing pessimism among Saigon-based U.S. officials, see Saigon to Stockholm, 5 March 1964, HP1, #XV, UD.

10. LBJ-Knight telcon, 3 February 1964, JT; LBJ-Ellender telcon, 16 February 1964, JT; LBJ-RSM telcon, 25 February 1964; LBJ-Fulbright telcon, 4 March 1964, JT. See also LBJ-MB telcon, 6 February 1964; MB to LBJ, 10 February 1964, box 1, NSF MPB, LBJL.

11. Washington to FO, 17 February 1964, FO 371/175493, PRO; Memo for the President, "Visit of Prime Minister," 7 February 1964, box 212, NSF CF, LBJL; "Talking Points Outline," February 1964, box 212, NSF CF, LBJL; LBJ to Lodge, 18 February 1964, box 3, NSF VN, LBJL; Memorandum of Record, 20 February 1964, box 2, NSF VN, LBJL; *Public Papers of the Presidents: Kennedy*, 304; Geyelin, *Lyndon B. Johnson and the World*, 187–188.

12. Lodge to LBJ, 19 February 1964, box 2, NSF VN, LBJL; Lodge to Rusk, 27 February 1964, box 2, NSF VN, LBJL. It should come as no surprise that relations between Lodge and Nes were strained. The ambassador had not liked the selection of Nes as his underling, and the tension manifested itself almost immediately after Nes arrived in December 1963. As 1964 progressed, the two men communicated less and less. Nes telephone interview with the author, 20 February 1994; Blair, *Lodge in Vietnam*, 120–121.

13. Lodge to LBJ, 10 February 1964, box 169, NSF CF, LBJL; Lodge to State, 14 February 1964, box 2, NSF VN, LBJL; Lodge to LBJ, 22 February 1994, box 1, NSF MPB, LBJL; Lodge to State, 24 February 1964, box 2, NSF VN, LBJL. In the 24 February cable, Lodge claimed with no apparent evidence that France was considering recognizing North Vietnam and that the Khanh government would certainly break relations with Paris if that occurred.

14. "French Proposals for Neutralization of South-East Asia: Departmental Analysis," Australian Department of External Affairs, 11 February 1964, FO 371/175091, PRO.

15. LBJ to Lodge, 22 February 1964, box 2, NSF VN, LBJL. The first draft of Johnson's telegram phrased the matter somewhat differently, but the gist was the same: "Let me say at once that [Rusk and I] agree entirely with the purpose of your recommendation and that the problem is simply to find the right ways and means of getting the French to understand the damage done by their current position. Ambassador Bohlen has tried repeatedly on this, but I agree with you that we must leave no stone unturned in this effort." Draft telegram, LBJ to Lodge, 22 February 1964, *FRUS, 1964–1968*, 1:104.

16. State Department Circular, 8 February 1964, box 236, NSF VN, LBJL.

17. Cohen, *Dean Rusk*, 246; Schoenbaum, *Waging Peace and War*, 358–359, 396. Schoenbaum claims that dealing with de Gaulle "brought out a closely guarded aspect of Rusk's personality: his anger." He quotes Rusk telling journalist C. L. Sulzberger after a NATO meeting: "You have found me in a bad mood. I'm so goddamned sore at de Gaulle." Schoenbaum, *Waging Peace and War*, 359.

18. David Nes, telephone interview, 20 February 1994. Rusk's views and disposition, and their impact on Vietnam policy, are explored in Halberstam, *Best and the Brightest*, 307–346.

19. LBJ to Bohlen, 25 February 1964, box 169, NSF CF, LBJL; Rusk to Bohlen, 25 February 1964, box 169, NSF CF, LBJL. In what was presumably a draft version, penned the preceding day and cleared by Rusk, Bohlen was told that the United States faced "increasingly critical decisions in Southeast Asia. The nature of our responses to communist provocations in that part of the world will have profound consequences everywhere." Should Vietnam fall, the cable noted, "the work of generations of Westerners and the immediate interests of our nations will suffer humiliating, and possibly irreversible, losses." LBJ to Bohlen, 24 February 1964, box 169, NSF CF, LBJL.

20. Bohlen to LBJ, 26 February 1964, box 169, NSF CF, LBJL; Rusk to Bohlen, 28 February 1964, box 169, NSF CF, LBJL; Bohlen to Rusk, 3 March 1964, box 2, NSF VN, LBJL; Bohlen to the White House, 4 March 1964, box 169, NSF CF, LBJL. A State Department summary of the meeting described Couve's reaction as "not very satisfactory." Michael Forrestal to MB, 9 March 1964, box 1, NSF MPB, LBJL.

21. CIA Report, 28 February 1964, box 2, NSF VN, LBJL; Saigon to State, 16 February 1964, box 2, NSF VN, LBJL; *NYT*, 5 and 8 March 1964.

22. Saigon to State, 16 February 1964, box 2, NSF VN, LBJL; *NYT*, 5 and 8 March 1964.

23. Hanoi to Paris, 11 February 1964, "Visite au president Ho Chi Minh et au premier Pham Van Dong," RDVN, #78, MAE. According to the CIA, a key French contact for the North Vietnamese was former minister of justice Edmond Michelet, a lifelong friend and associate of de Gaulle, who viewed the war very much the same as he did. Michelet, the CIA reported, "argues that any solution must involve a settlement in which the West comes to term with

the Viet Cong, and that by encouraging nationalist elements in the Viet Cong, it should be possible to preserve the formal independence of South Vietnam under a Viet Cong or coalition regime." The CIA noted that the Far East chief of the Quai d'Orsay felt the same: that "the only solution in South Vietnam is political—specifically, negotiation leading to neutrality." CIA Memorandum, 20 February 1964, box 2, NSF VN, LBJL.

24. Concern about adding fuel to Khanh's ire helps explain why Dean Rusk, at a news conference on March 6, refused to directly criticize the French government. Rusk said merely that constant talk of neutralization had the effect of undermining morale in South Vietnam. *NYT*, 7 March 1964.

25. *NYT*, 8 March 1964. "I do not think," Johnson told reporters on 29 February, "that the speculation that has been made that we should enter into a neutralization of that area, or that we are losing the fight in that area, or that things have gone to pot there, are at all justified. I think they do our cause a great disservice, but we are keeping in touch with it daily." Dean Rusk used similar language in press conferences on 27 February and 6 March. And in a letter to British foreign secretary Michael Stewart, Rusk called neutralization a "phony," vowed that U.S. support would not be withdrawn, and said that peace would come if North Vietnam would leave its neighbors alone. Transcript of Johnson Press Conference, 29 February 1964, box 9, NSF Intelligence File, LBJL; Chronology on Vietnam, November 1965, box 38, NSF NSC History, LBJL; Rusk to London embassy, 1 March 1964, *FRUS*, 1964–1968, 1:110.

26. Bundy MS, chapter 12; Halberstam, *Best and the Brightest*, 355–358; Gibbons, *US Government*, II, 6, 121; "SIGMA I-64 Final Report," box 30, NSF Agency File, LBJL.

27. Meeting Notes, 12 February 1964, PREM 11/4789, PRO.

28. The United States Government and South Viet-Nam," FO, 27 February 1964, FO 371/175495, PRO; Hanoi to FO, 29 February 1964, FO 371/175493, PRO. See also FO to Saigon, 10 March 1964, FO 371/175494, PRO.

29. "Our principal concern," the Foreign Office cabled the embassy in Saigon, "is that our support for U.S. policy in Viet-Nam is really understood by the U.S. Government to apply to the original defensive policy and not to constitute any implied commitment to support a new offensive strategy." FO to Saigon, 10 March 1964, FO 371/175494, PRO.

30. See Johnson's comments in LBJ-Ellender telcon, 16 February 1964, JT.

31. Hilsman to Rusk, 14 March 1964, box 3, NSF VN, LBJL. Some authors, including Hilsman himself, have claimed that he and Averell Harriman were effectively squeezed out of key administration posts in early 1964 because of their skeptical views on Vietnam and their questioning of whether the war effort ought to be pursued. See Roger Hilsman, *To Move a Nation: The Politics of Foreign Policy in the Administration of John F. Kennedy* (Garden City, N.Y.: Doubleday, 1967), 534–537; Halberstam, *Best and the Brightest*, 369–375. In fact, neither differed fundamentally with their colleagues on the need to pursue the war to a successful conclusion. A year later, Hilsman wrote a letter to the editor of the *New York Times* that declared Vietnam vital to American security and advocated the use of U.S. ground troops if necessary. *NYT*, 14 March 1965.

32. See here Johnson's comments to McNamara on 2 March. "Let's make a record on this thing, Bob," LBJ said. "I'd like to have a wire out there to him nearly every day or so on something. Either approving what Lodge is recommending, or either trying to boost them up to do a little extra." LBJ-RSM telcon, 2 March 1964, JT. See also MB to Rusk, 16 April 1964, box 9, NSF Intelligence File, LBJL.

33. Saigon to FO, 11 March 1964, FO 371/175495, PRO.

34. This includes the authors who have looked most closely at McNamara's role in the war. Paul Hendrickson, *The Living and the Dead: Robert McNamara and Five Lives of a Lost War* (New York: Knopf, 1996), 297–298. Deborah Shapley gives hints that McNamara's doubts came early in 1965; but she too gives prime emphasis to late 1965. Shapley, *Promise and Power*, 355–360.

35. LBJ-RSM telcon, 25 February and 2 March 1964, JT; Washington to FO, 6 March 1964, FO 371/175494, PRO. According to Henry Brandon, McNamara had been pessimistic about the prospects in Vietnam already in February, voicing deep doubts during a dinner party in Georgetown. Henry Brandon, *Special Relationships: A Foreign Correspondent's Memoirs from Roosevelt to Reagan* (New York: Atheneum, 1988), 227.

36. Bundy MS, chapter 12, 28; RSM to LBJ, 16 March 1964, box 3, NSF VN, LBJL. The first draft was completed on 1 March, with revised versions appearing on 4, 5, and 13 March. See *FRUS, 1964–1968*, I, 153–167.

37. NSC Meeting Notes, 17 March 1964, box 3, NSF VN, LBJL; Gibbons, *U.S. Government*, 2:238.

38. *PP* (Gravel), 3:50; *NYT*, 21 March 1964.

39. *PP* (Gravel), 2:312; CIA Profile of Khanh, 20 March 1964, box 3, NSF VN, LBJL. According to George Kahin, neutralist plots against Khanh were reported by U.S. intelligence as early as the first week in February and continued thereafter. Kahin, *Intervention*, 206.

40. LBJ to Lodge, 17 March 1964, box 3, NSF VN, LBJL; Lodge to LBJ, 19 March 1964, box 170, NSF CF, LBJL; LBJ to Lodge, 20 March 1964, box 3, NSF VN, LBJL; *The Pentagon Papers as Published by the New York Times*, ed. Neil Sheehan et al. (New York: Quadrangle Books, 1971), 285. Cited hereafter as *PP* (*NYT*).

41. Lodge to Rusk, 27 March 1964, box 169, NSF CF, LBJL; Lodge to Rusk, 8 April 1964, box 3, NSF VN, LBJL; Harriman to Rusk, 18 March 1964, box 169, NSF CF, LBJL. In another cable, Lodge hammered the point home again: "No amount of verbiage," he charged, "can alter the fact that de Gaulle is frankly opposing the vital interests of the U.S. as effectively as he can." Lodge to Rusk, 7 April 1964, box 3, NSF VN, LBJL. Later in April Lodge told Swedish diplomat Jean-Christophe Öberg that negotiations for an end to the conflict were out of the question. Saigon to Stockholm, 24 April 1964, HP1, #XV, UD.

42. LBJ to Bohlen, 24 March 1964, *FRUS, 1964–1968*, 1:191–193; State to Paris, 25 March 1964, box 3, NSF VN, LBJL. See also Rusk-WPB telcon, 25 March 1964, *FRUS, 1964–1968*, I, 195.

43. Bohlen to LBJ, 2 April 1964, box 169, NSF CF, LBJL. It is a measure of

the administration's concern over de Gaulle's potential influence in Vietnam—and over Khanh's susceptibility to neutralism—that it opted to tell the Saigon government as little as possible about Bohlen's lack of success. Lodge to Rusk, 7 April 1964, box 3, NSF VN, LBJL. Bohlen also told his British counterpart in Paris that it was most important that the poor outcome of his meeting with de Gaulle not become known. Paris to FO, 7 April 1964, FO 371/175488, PRO.

44. A few days prior to the SEATO meeting, French minister Georges Pompidou also promoted neutralization publicly. In a speech to the Tokyo Foreign Press Club on 9 April, he declared: "We think the countries of the former Indo-China are part of a vast group of countries which by [virtue of their] size, [and the] devastation they have undergone, need tranquility and can only find it in neutrality. . . . " Pompidou dismissed the notion that U.S. policy could work: "I don't want to seem to be a prophet of doom to our United States allies, but we have kept the memory of the bitter experiences in the Indochinese and Algerian wars. We are convinced that such a war, even if victorious, does not solve anything, and the solution can only be political." The text of Pompidou's speech is in *Le Figaro*, 10 April 1964. Bohlen to Rusk (in Manila), 10 April 1964, box 169, NSF CF, LBJL. See also *NYT*, 10 April 1964.

45. Manila to Paris, 15 April 1964, CLV, sud-vietnam, #71, MAE; Bundy MS, chapter 12; Memcon, 12 April 1964, box 169, NSF CF, LBJL. See also Peyrefitte, *C'était de Gaulle*, 496.

46. Despite this forthrightness, Rusk claimed to find a good deal of fuzziness in the French position. "We are still punching a feather bed in trying to find out what the French really have in mind about South Vietnam," he wrote the White House after the meeting. "[Couve] apparently believes, as we have known before, that present course in Vietnam cannot succeed and that real choice lies between larger war . . . or some sort of political solution." Rusk to LBJ and Ball, 14 April 1964, box 3, NSF VN, LBJL.

47. Pakistani officials in Beijing told British officials there that a U.S. decision to expand the war into North Vietnam would be a mistake, for it would give the Communists an immeasurable propaganda advantage. Beijing to FO, 8 April 1964, FO 371/175513, PRO.

48. Rusk to LBJ and Ball, 14 April 1964, box 3, NSF VN, LBJL; Manila to FO, 25 August 1965, FO 371/31744, PRO.

49. FO to Paris, 25 May 1964, FO 371/175091, PRO; Bonn to FO, 14 May 1964, FO 371/175496, PRO. For Canada's position, see chapter 6.

50. In response to Butler's letter of 29 February, Rusk had written: "Unfortunately, there is not the sense of solidarity in the free world which would give this [present] course the greatest chance of success." Rusk to Butler, 2 March 1964, FO 371/175494, PRO.

CHAPTER 5

1. *Christian Science Monitor*, 9 May 1964. See also the paper's editorial on 1 April 1964. *Los Angeles Times*, 23 April 1964; *Newsweek*, 6 April 1964. The *Washington Post* said on 20 May that "the country is not ready either to give

up the South Viet-Nam fight or to enlarge the war by offensive operation against North Viet-Nam." See also *WP*, 15 May 1964.

2. The evangelist Billy Graham, no expert on Vietnam but an authority figure for millions of Americans, declared that the time for decision was at hand: "It is my candid opinion that we ought to get in with all we've got, or get out," Graham said in a talk before the Southern Baptist Convention in late May. *U.S. News and World Report*, 1 June 1964.

3. On 1 April CBS aired a documentary entitled "Vietnam: The Deadly Decision," which framed the choice as one of finding an "honorable way out" or accepting the costs and staying the war for what could be a very long time. A perceptive analysis of the program is in Young, *Vietnam Wars*, 110–113.

4. *NYT* 3, 4, 6, and 10 April 1964; *U.S. News and World Report*, 1 June 1964. (Halberstam's article, "News Analysis: U.S. Policy in Vietnam," appeared on 6 March alongside one by military correspondent Hanson W. Baldwin. Baldwin, in later years a strong defender of U.S. intervention, wrote that "the commitment of United States ground forces to warfare on the Asian mainland is opposed by most military men.") Alsop was especially vociferous. At various times throughout the spring he criticized the administration for timidity on the Vietnam issue and called for a vigorous prosecution of the war. He labeled neutralization a sell-out and criticized de Gaulle for trying to expel U.S. power and influence from South Vietnam. Alsop said the United States had to achieve victory in Vietnam "despite de Gaulle." See, for example, *WP*, 6 May 1964. See also Robert W. Merry, *Taking on the World: Joseph and Stewart Alsop, Guardians of the American Century* (New York: Viking, 1996), 414–415. For his part, Sulzberger argued in early May that "a continued policy of neither war nor peace" would lead to the neutralization of Vietnam, which would be a "humiliating sham." He said, "The time for a showdown [with the North] has come." *NYT*, 9 May 1964.

5. *Los Angeles Times*, 21 April 1964; *Christian Science Monitor*, 1 April 1964.

6. *CR* 110, 4831–4835. Morse and Gruening had little respect for Khanh, describing him variously as a "little tinhorn tyrant," a "tyrannical military dictator," and a U.S. "puppet." Thomson to MB, 24 April 1964, box 24, Thomson Papers, JFKL. On May 13, Morse accused the administration of trying to "pick up the failure of Great Britain, France, the Dutch, and every other colonial power in Asia of the last 50 years, and we will end with the same failure. Asia will not be run by white men. . . . In trying to fight on ground and terms alien to the United States, we are needlessly killing Americans for an objective we eventually will have to abandon." *CR*, 110, 10826ff. On the positions of Gruening and other Democratic skeptics in this period, see also Johnson, "Ernest Gruening," chapter 7.

7. Morse's speeches, in particular, were a frequent topic of discussion among the president and top aides in the spring, as is clear from the tapes of White House telephone conversations. See, for example, LBJ-RSM telcon, 27 April 1964, JT.

8. Thomson to WPB, 24 April 1964, box 24, Thomson Papers, JFKL.

9. Johnson, "Ernest Gruening," chapter 7; *Newsweek*, 6 April 1964.

10. Thomson to WPB, 24 April 1964, box 24, Thomson Papers, JFKL. See also *U.S. News and World Report*, 18 May 1964; *NYT*, 21 March 1964. On a television program on 26 April, Church did register public opposition to an expansion of the war and said it would mean "a hopeless entanglement, the end of which is difficult to see." *NYT*, 27 April 1964.

11. LBJ-Russell telcon, 27 May 1964, JT.

12. In late May, as the fighting flared up in Laos, Mansfield did take to the Senate floor to urge that de Gaulle's diplomatic initiatives on Indochina not be lightly dismissed. These initiatives, Mansfield maintained, were "designed to preserve a measure of peace, stability, and national sovereignty in Southeast Asia, where all three are on the brink of collapse in the gathering chaos." The senator suggested that de Gaulle's plan was "consistent in every respect" with American interests in Asia, and he wondered why the administration seemed to fear a conference. "Are we afraid of words of criticism from China and the Vietnamese Communists at an international conference? That would hardly be a new experience. We have been raved and ranted at before and have always managed to survive." Mansfield concluded with a warning: negotiation, he said, may be "the last train out for peace in Southeast Asia." He urged Johnson to welcome a conference. *CR*, 110, 11552. See also *NYT*, 20 February 1964.

13. See LBJ-Fulbright telcon, 2 March 1964, JT; LBJ-RSM telcon, 21 March 1964, JT; Lee Riley Powell, *J. William Fulbright and His Time: A Political Biography* (Memphis, Tenn.: Guild Bindery Press, 1996), 215. "Spouting off" quote is in *NYT*, 21 March 1964. For a good examination of the Fulbright speech and the response to it, see Randall B. Woods, *Fulbright: A Biography* (New York: Cambridge University Press, 1996), 333–339. An interesting contemporaneous analysis of the speech is in *Newsweek*, 6 April 1964.

14. *WP*, 15 March 1964. Morgenthau criticized an article written by Columbia professor Zbigniew Brzezinski that appeared in the *Post* on March 1 in which he suggested the need for deeper U.S. involvement in the war. On Morgenthau, see also Greg Russell, *Hans J. Morgenthau and the Ethics of American Statecraft* (Baton Rouge: Louisiana State University Press, 1990), 199–205.

15. *The Reporter*, 16 March 1964. This period also witnessed the first stirrings of an antiwar movement among American college students. On 13 to 15 March 1964, participants in a student conference on socialism at Yale University formed an ad hoc May Second Committee to organize a demonstration against the war in New York City on 2 May. On 20 May, a group of students at the University of California at Berkeley sent a telegram to Senator Ernest Gruening asking for the withdrawal of U.S. military personnel from Vietnam.

16. *New Republic*, 7 and 28 March, 2 May 1964; *Newsweek*, 18 May 1964; *Harper's*, spring 1964. Some commentators not deemed particularly influential also attacked U.S. policy, none more so, or with more perspicacity, than I. F. Stone. On 16 March, for example, he wrote: "In the headlines which mould the public mind Rusk and McNamara continue to pour a picture of the conflict as an invasion from the North, supplied by arms from China. So long as they

fear to tell the truth about the war, they cannot free themselves from the undertow pulling them toward its suicidal extension." Stone, *In a Time of Torment*, 195.

17. "[T]he *Times* editorial page is a soft page, Mr. President," National Security Adviser McGeorge Bundy told Johnson in one phone conversation in early February. "It makes Walter Lippmann look like a warmonger. [The editors are] clever, but they don't have a whole lot of judgment. You've got to show them you're a man of peace without letting them call the tune, I think, and you're damned good at that." LBJ-MB telcon, 6 February 1964, JT.

18. Forrestal to MB, 20 April 1964, box 3, NSF VN, LBJL.

19. In April a veteran political analyst warned Johnson that the Washington press corps was like a "bunch of sheep" who always followed the "bellwether sheep." The analyst said, "The only two newspapermen practically all of them admire are Walter Lippmann and [James] Scotty Reston. As long as these two are for Lyndon Johnson he will, on the whole, get a good press from the rest of them. You certainly have Lippmann and Reston in your pocket now. I hope you do not lose them." Rowe to LBJ, 9 April 1964, White House Central File, Ex PR 18, box 356, LBJL. Joseph Alsop's biographer, Robert Merry, refers to Lippmann as *primus inter pares*. Merry, *Taking on the World*, 401. On LBJ's view of Lippmann's importance, see also Melvin Small, *Johnson, Nixon and the Doves* (New Brunswick, N.J.: Rutgers University Press, 1986), 40–41.

20. Logevall, "First among Critics"; Steel, *Walter Lippmann*, 557–584.

21. Logevall, "First among Critics"; Steel, *Lippmann*, 541–550. For Lippmann's critique of Nixon and other advocates of a larger war, see his column of 21 April. *WP*, 21 April 1964.

22. Steel, *Walter Lippmann*, 549–550; *WP*, 21 May 1964. The reaction to the 21 May column provides good evidence of the astonishing international reach of Lippmann's columns. When J. Blair Seaborn, Canada's representative to the ICC, visited Hanoi in June to confer with North Vietnamese officials (see chapter 6), North Vietnamese premier Pham Van Dong cited the column in arguing that the U.S.–South Vietnamese effort would never succeed. Wallace J. Thies, *When Governments Collide: Coercion and Diplomacy in the Vietnam Conflict* (Berkeley and Los Angeles: University of California Press, 1980), 37–38. Also in June, Thai foreign minister Thanat Khoman asked U.S. officials about the meaning of the 21 May column and its potential impact on American public opinion. Martin to Rusk, 8 June 1964, box 53, NSF VN, LBJL.

23. LBJ-MB telcon, 27 May 1964, JT.

24. These accounts of the 19 and 27 May meetings are taken from Steel, *Walter Lippmann*, 550.

25. *WP*, 28 May 1964.

26. On 30 May, McNamara told a sympathetic Robert Thompson of BRIAM that if no wider military action were taken the war effort would deteriorate quickly and the GVN would lose. McNamara agreed with Thompson's contention that the situation was grim and close to the point of no return, and he told the Briton that on each of his recent visits to South Vietnam the outlook had been worse than the time before. Washington to FO, 30 May 1964, PREM 11/4759, PRO.

27. According to McNamara, Khanh now controlled only eight (including two in Saigon) of the fourteen million people who inhabited South Vietnam. Significantly, he also conceded that 90–95 percent of the Vietcong forces were recruited in South Vietnam, with only cadres being sent from North Vietnam. NSC Meeting Summary, 15 May 1964, box 1, NSC Meetings File, LBJL.

28. NSC Meeting Summary, 15 May 1964, box 1, NSC Meetings File, LBJL; McNamara Notes for Report to President, 14 May 1964, box 4, NSF VN, LBJL. RSM-McCone-WPB to LBJ, draft memo, 18 May 1964, box 4, NSF VN, LBJL. For a devastating portrait of the politico-military situation from a British perspective, see Saigon to FO ("South Viet-Nam: Situation and Prospects"), 28 April 1964, FO 371/157469, PRO. For an even more downbeat one from a Swedish perspective, see Saigon to Stockholm, 5 May 1964, HP1, #XV, UD.

29. CIA Memorandum, 15 May 1964, *FRUS, 1964–1968*, 1:336; McCone-Rusk telcon, 16 May 1964, *FRUS, 1964–1968*, 1:336; CIA Situation Report, 18 May 1964, box 4, NSF VN, LBJL; State to Lodge, 21 May 1964, box 4, NSF VN, LBJL; Lodge to Rusk, 7 May 1964, box 4, NSF VN, LBJL; Lodge to Rusk, 14 May 1964, box 4, NSF VN, LBJL; Lodge to Rusk, 22 May 1964, box 4, NSF VN, LBJL.

30. LBJ-RSM telcon, 30 April 1964, JT; LBJ-MB telcon, 13 May 1964, JT; LBJ-MB telcon, 20 May 1964, JT.

31. LBJ-MB telcon, 27 May 1964, JT; LBJ-Russell telcon, 27 May 1964, JT.

32. White House special assistant Michael Forrestal recalled: "There was a bad thing in this period. The government was extremely scared of itself. There was tremendous nervousness that if you expressed an opinion it might somehow leak out . . . and the president would be furious and everyone's head would be cut off. ∴ . It inhibited an exchange of information and prevented the president from getting a lot of the facts that he should have had." Forrestal OH, LBJL. See here also McMaster, *Dereliction of Duty*, 88–89.

33. The four preconditions were: (1) a cease-fire; (2) a withdrawal of the Pathet Lao to the position it had held before its recent advances; (3) the affirmation of Souvanna Phouma's position and powers; and (4) "the effective functioning of the ICC." At a tense meeting with French ambassador Alphand on 22 May, Rusk denied that Washington was turning down the idea of a conference a priori but maintained that the four preconditions had to be met in advance. In reply, Alphand wondered if the four points should not be the first thing on the agenda *at* the conference. Memcon, 22 May 1964, box 266, NSF CF, LBJL.

34. State Circular cable, 25 May 1964, box 266, NSF CF, LBJL; State to Vientiane, 6 May 1964, box 266, NSF CF, LBJL; State Circular Cable, 28 May 1964, box 266, NSF CF, LBJL; Paris to State, 25 May 1964, box 172, NSF CF, LBJL; Marshall Green to MB, 29 May 1964, box 53, NSF VN, LBJL; Ball to Rusk, 29 May 1964, box 53, NSF VN, LBJL; State Dept. "Outline of Diplomatic Actions," 4 June 1964, box 7, Warnke Papers, LBJL. The United States did agree to a Polish proposal for more informal "consultations," strictly limited to Laos (see chapter 6).

35. Summary Record of NSC Meeting, 24 May 1964, box 38, NSF NSC

History, LBJL; MB to LBJ, 25 May 1964, box 1, Reference File, Vietnam, LBJL. Those present at the 25 May NSC meeting, during which the plans were discussed, were Rusk, McNamara, McGeorge and William Bundy, John McCone, General Maxwell Taylor, George Ball, AID administrator David Bell, Assistant Secretary of State Robert Manning, Assistant Secretary of Defense John McNaughton, General Andrew Goodpaster, William Sullivan, Chester Cooper, William Colby, Douglass Cater, and notetaker Bromley Smith.

36. *PP* (Gravel), 3:72–74; State to Lodge, 27 May 1964, box 53, NSF VN, LBJL.

37. The notion that legislative endorsement for wider American action would eventually be needed had begun several months before. (Perhaps as much as a year before. According to the State Department's William H. Sullivan, he and NSC staffer Michael Forrestal had produced a draft of a congressional resolution already back in the middle part of 1963. William H. Sullivan, *Obbligato, 1939–1979: Notes on a Foreign Service Career* [New York: Norton, 1984], 182.) Walt Rostow of the State Department's Policy Planning Staff called for a congressional resolution as early as 13 February. Rostow to Rusk, 13 February 1964, box 2, NSF VN, LBJL. In the weeks that followed, the idea gathered more adherents. In a 1 March memorandum to LBJ, for example, William Bundy outlined a comprehensive plan to punish North Vietnam into "stopping its assistance" to the Vietcong and thereby both demonstrate U.S. resolve and discourage moves toward neutralism in Saigon. Bundy stressed, however, that it would be "unsatisfactory" to proceed without a congressional resolution. WPB to LBJ, 1 March 1964, box 3, NSF CF, LBJL. For a perceptive examination of the background to the resolution idea, see Andrew L. Johns, "Opening Pandora's Box: The Genesis and Evolution of the 1964 Congressional Resolution on Vietnam," *Journal of American–East Asian Relations* (forthcoming).

38. MB to LBJ, draft memo, 25 May 1964, box 53, NSF VN, LBJL; Forrestal Memorandum on South Vietnam, 29 May 1964, box 5, NSF VN, LBJL; Defense Department Memorandum, likely 30 May 1964, box 53, NSF VN, LBJL.

39. "Discussions with Mr. Bundy," 28 May 1964, PREM 11/4761, PRO; "Record of Discussions with Mr. Bundy," 29 May 1964, PREM 11/4761, PRO; For Bundy's own perspective on the meetings, see Bundy MS, chapter 13.

40. According to the *Pentagon Papers*, "The [Honolulu] conference concluded that the crucial actions for the immediate future were (1) to prosecute an urgent information effort in the United States toward dispelling the basic doubts of the value of Southeast Asia which were besetting key members of Congress and the public in the budding 'great debate,' and (2) to start diplomatic efforts with the Thais, Australians, New Zealanders, Filipinos, and the French on matters within their cognizance which impinged on our effort in South Vietnam." *PP* (Gravel), 2:325. See also MB to LBJ, 3 June 1964, box 1, Reference File, Vietnam, LBJL.

41. WPB to Rusk, 3 June 1964, box 53, NSF VN, LBJL. A copy of this memo in the Johnson Papers contains the following marginal comment, penned by McGeorge Bundy: "Hitting the North is required."

42. Dutton to MB, 2 June 1964, box 6, NSF VN, LBJL.

43. *PP* (DoD), vol. 4, part B, chapter 4, page 2. The editors quote Dean Rusk as telling his fellow Honolulu conferees that public opinion on Vietnam was "badly divided in the United States at the moment." *PP* (Gravel), 3:174. On the Gallup poll, see *WP*, 27 May 1964.

44. Manning to LBJ, 15 June 1964, box 54, NSF VN, LBJL.

45. The domestic political implications of any policy departure at this time were succinctly articulated by former Secretary of State Dean Acheson, whose counsel Johnson valued greatly, during a conversation with White House aide Douglass Cater on 18 May. According to Cater, Acheson expressed great concern that the "situation in Viet Nam will soon enter [a] phase when new initiatives become impossible because of the convention and campaign period here at home. He urged that any assessment of stepping up involvement in Indo-China take into account that we must act quickly or be prepared to stall for awhile." Cater to LBJ, 19 May 1964, as cited in Gibbons, *U.S. Government*, 2:252.

46. Summary Record of NSC Meeting, 10 June 1964, box 5, NSF VN, LBJL; Draft Resolution (WPB), 11 June 1964, box 5, NSF VN, LBJL; Bundy MS, chapter 13, pp. 23ff.

47. *Newsweek*, 18 May 1964; Memorandum for the Record, 27 April 1964, box 3, NSF VN, LBJL; State to Bonn, 8 June 1964, box 5, NSF VN, LBJL.

48. Bonn to FO, 14 May 1964, FO 371/175496, PRO; Bonn to FO, 25 May 1964, FO 371/175091, PRO; State to Bonn, 8 June 1964, box 5, NSF VN, LBJL. *Die Welt* quote is from *Newsweek*, 25 May 1964. See also *NYT*, 27 May 1964.

49. J. E. Cable memo, 9 March 1964, FO 371/175494, PRO.

50. Minutes by E. H. Peck, 17 April 1964, FO 371/175506, PRO. James Cable had by May come to agree with the wisdom of a wait-and-see approach until November. "The possibility of negotiations on Viet-Nam is not a subject that we can broach with the Americans at present, with their entire effort devoted to the survival of South Viet-Nam," he acknowledged in a memo to Gordon Etherington-Smith in Saigon. "However, when the presidential elections are over the next administration (assuming it is a Democratic one) will no doubt consider very carefully the long term implications of continuing the military struggle and may give some thought to the possibilities of a diplomatic solution as an alternative." Administration officials might not even then seek a face-saving exit, Cable conceded, "but they must be as conscious as we are of one uncomfortable possibility: that the growing war-weariness of the South Viet-Namese people will find expression in a third coup d'état and the emergence of a government in Saigon eager to attempt a negotiated solution. If this happened, the existence of the Geneva Agreement, and the basis for contact with the Russians it provides, might be very useful in enabling the West to salvage something—above all United States prestige—from the wreck." FO to Saigon, 1 May 1964, FO 371/175496, PRO.

51. On Australia's position in this period, see Edwards, *Crises and Commitments*, chapter 15.

52. RSM-McCone-WPB to LBJ, draft memo, 18 May 1964, box 4, NSF VN,

LBJL. Charles Bohlen had heard more of de Gaulle's "drumfire" earlier that month. In a meeting on 5 May, the French leader had told him that the United States was in the wrong war in the wrong way, and that a U.S. defeat was inevitable. David Klein to MB, 5 May 1964, box 171, NSF CF, LBJL.

53. Hilsman to Rusk, 14 March 1964, box 53, NSF VN, LBJL.

54. The policy planning staff's Walt Rostow, in addition to being among the first to urge the need for a congressional resolution, was ahead of his time here as well. He had suggested the need for a public information campaign back in April, and then again in early May. See Rostow to Rusk, 6 May 1964, box 24, Thomson Papers, JFKL.

CHAPTER 6

1. Manning to LBJ, 16 June 1964, box 54, NSF VN, LBJL.

2. Memcon, 19 April 1964, box 9, NSF VN, LBJL. Among those in attendance were Dean Rusk and his chief Vietnam deputy, William Bundy, who were visiting South Vietnam on their way back from the SEATO meeting in Manila. Bundy, describing the 19 April meeting, said that it had concluded that the emissary "should tell (not negotiate with) Hanoi" that, if necessary, the United States was prepared to escalate. WPB Memorandum for the Record, 27 April 1964, box 3, NSF VN, LBJL.

3. The scholarly literature on coercive diplomacy is large. Excellent introductions to the concept are Alexander L. George and William E. Simons, eds., *The Limits of Coercive Diplomacy* (Boulder, Colo.: Westview Press, 1994), which includes a chapter by William E. Simons on Vietnam; and Gordon A. Craig and Alexander L. George, *Force and Statecraft: Diplomatic Problems of Our Time* (New York: Oxford University Press, 1995), 197–211. See also Paul G. Lauren, "Ultimata and Coercive Diplomacy," *International Studies Quarterly* 16 (1972): 135–165; Paul G. Lauren, *Diplomacy: New Approaches in History, Theory, and Policy* (New York: Free Press, 1979); and Lebow, *Between Peace and War*, chapters 8–10. Thies, *When Governments Collide*, a study based largely on the *Pentagon Papers*, examines the strategy as employed by the United States in Vietnam.

4. Memcon, 19 April 1964, box 9, NSF VN, LBJL; WPB Memorandum for the Record, 27 April 1964, box 3, NSF VN, LBJL. Lodge implied, and others have suggested, that he and Seaborn knew each other from past diplomatic posts. According to Seaborn, however, they had never met. J. Blair Seaborn, interview with the author, Ottawa, Canada, 16 September 1995.

5. Memcon, Rusk and Pearson, 30 April 1964, 1980-81/22, box 50, 20-22-VIET S-2-1, Possibility of Terminating the War 1964, National Archives of Canada, Ottawa (hereafter 20-22-VIET S, NAC); "M.C." to Martin, 28 May 1964, 20-22-VIET S, NAC; Rusk to Lodge, cable, 1 May 1964, box 4, NSF VN. The Seaborn channel would be code-named BACON.

6. Emphasis added. Lodge to Rusk, 4 May 1964, box 4, NSF VN, LBJL; Lodge to LBJ, 15 May 1964, *FRUS*, 1964–1968, 1:333. Lodge described his idea for a preliminary bombing run in a conversation on 11 May in Saigon

with the State Department's William H. Sullivan. Memcon, 11 May 1964, *FRUS*, 1964–1968, 1:305.

7. Goldwater had suggested that "low yield atomic weapons" be used as defoliants along the South's borders and that the United States use conventional bombs to attack roads, bridges, and railroads in the North used to supply the insurgency in the South. See *NYT*, 25 May 1964.

8. Memcon, 28 May 1964, box 4, NSF CF, LBJL; Washington to Ottawa, 30 May 1964, 20-22-VIET S, NAC. After the meeting, McGeorge Bundy told a Canadian official that the main reason for scheduling the meeting was to underline the importance LBJ attached to having Seaborn go as soon as possible to Hanoi. Bundy also noted that Johnson was running for election as a man of peace and was not about to start a war and that the administration was "playing this day by day" and not about to engage in the kind of "five-act play" advocated by Walter Lippmann and Joseph Alsop. H. B. Robinson Memcon, 29 May 1964, 20-22-VIET S, NAC. See also John English, *The Wordly Years: The Life of Lester Pearson*, vol. 2, *1949–1972* (Toronto, Canada: Knopf, 1992), 358–359.

9. Rusk to Lodge, 22 May 1964, *FRUS*, 1964–1968, 1:348–349; Lodge to Rusk, 26 May 1964, *FRUS*, 1964–1968, 1:348–349. Pearson and Rusk were old acquaintances and fellow alumni of St. John's College, Oxford. According to Pearson's biographer, however, the Canadian was troubled by what he saw as Rusk's obsession with East Asia. English, *Worldly Years*, 358.

10. State Department, "Talking Paper for Canadians," 22 May 1964, 20-22-VIET S, NAC. Also printed in *FRUS*, 1964–1968, 1:352–355.

11. Summary Record of Conversation, Sullivan and Martin, 29 May 1964, Record Group 25, Volume 3092, #29-39-1-2-A, North Vietnam–USA Relations—Special Project (BACON), NAC (hereafter 29-39-BACON, NAC); State to Saigon, 30 May 1964, *FRUS*, 1964–1968, 1:395.

12. Seaborn interview with the author, Ottawa, Canada, 16 September 1995; Michael Maclear, *The Ten-Thousand-Day War: Vietnam, 1945–1975* (New York: St. Martin's Press, 1981), 102. In a letter dated 30 May, Pearson impressed on Seaborn the importance of the mission and emphasized that "nothing be overlooked which could prevent a serious confrontation." Pearson to Seaborn, 30 May 1964, 29-39-BACON, NAC.

13. Summary Record of State Department meeting, 30 May 1964, *FRUS*, 1964–1968, 1:399; Green to WPB, 30 May 1964, box 53, NSF VN, LBJL; Ball-Cleveland telcon, box 7, Ball Papers, LBJL.

14. Summary Record of Conversation, Sullivan and Martin, 29 May 1964, 29-39-BACON, NAC; Record of Conversation, Sullivan and Arnold Smith et al., 28 May 1964, 29-39-BACON, NAC.

15. On this point, see Craig and George, *Force and Statecraft*, 197–227. At least one American, Henry Cabot Lodge, perceived this problem. At the Honolulu meetings in early June, he told Sullivan that the Seaborn message would be effective only if it contained "explicit" information about American plans. See Washington to Ottawa, 5 June 1964, 29-39-BACON, NAC.

16. In making his remarks, Seaborn followed closely a thirteen-point "Outline of Subjects for Mr. Seaborn," submitted by Sullivan to the Canadian em-

bassy in Washington on 30 May. A copy is in 29-39-BACON, NAC. In an attempt to lend credibility to Seaborn's message, the administration released on that same day congressional testimony by William Bundy maintaining that Washington was committed to driving the communists out of the South, even if that involved military attacks on the North. Thies, *When Governments Collide*, 36–40.

17. Seaborn to Ottawa, 20 June 1964, 29-39-BACON, NAC.

18. Thies, *When Governments Collide*, 37–38; Seaborn to Ottawa, 20 June 1964, 29-39-BACON, NAC.

19. Seaborn to Ottawa, 22 June 1964, 20-22-VIET S, NAC; Seaborn interview with the author, Ottawa, Canada, 16 September 1995.

20. Washington to Ottawa, 24 June 1964, 20-22-VIET S, NAC.

21. Henry Cabot Lodge recommended demonstrating that steadfastness before Seaborn's return to Hanoi by giving the North Vietnamese "a very neat bloody nose by knocking out a machine tool factory or a bridge or something" in response to "some Viet Cong outrage here." Lodge to State, 24 June 1964, *FRUS*, 1964–1968, 1:526. On the administration's decision to delay a return visit by Seaborn, see Washington to Ottawa, 22 June 1964, 29-39-BACON, NAC.

22. Also on the list were Sargent Shriver, whom Johnson had already named to head the effort to eradicate poverty, and former Deputy Secretary of Defense Roswell Gilpatrick. Bundy did not exactly trumpet McNamara's candidacy. The defense secretary, he wrote, has "been trying to think of ways of dealing with the problem for so long that he has gone a little stale. . . . He has rather mechanized the problem so that he misses some of its real political flavor." Describing himself, Bundy pointed to his fluency in French, his understanding of the issues, and his "heavy dose of the ways of thinking of all branches of the U.S. team in South Vietnam." Bundy to LBJ, 6 June 1964, box 5, MPB, LBJL.

23. Halberstam, *Best and the Brightest*, 465; Sheehan, *Bright Shining Lie*, 379.

24. Before Taylor departed, Johnson emphasized that he wanted the "strongest possible effort to move ahead *within* South Vietnam. Large scale moves 'to the North' are not the present answer." LBJ to Taylor, 2 July 1964, *FRUS*, 1964–1968, 1:538.

25. The Matthias memo was leaked to the press later that summer (see chapter 7). See *NYT*, 23 August 1964; *Chicago Tribune*, 23 August 1964; *WP*, 24 August 1964.

26. Nes to Lodge, 21 May 1964, box 1, Nes Papers, LBJL (emphasis in original); Nes to U. A. Johnson, 26 June 1964, box 1, Nes Papers, LBJL. Of the Seaborn mission, Nes would later say: "We were talking to Hanoi through the Canadians at that time, but in a very desultory way, and I don't think we ever offered the Ho Chi Minh regime anything that was sufficiently attractive for them to forebear for awhile." Nes OH, LBJL.

27. *NYT*, 18 June 1964. Unlike Nes, the officer advocated a massive increase in the American presence in Vietnam. The key problem, he told the reporters, was getting the South Vietnamese government and armed forces to

take American advice. For the administration's alarmist response to the comments by the officer (later identified as Col. Wilbur Wilson, the U.S. army's senior adviser in the II and III corps tactical zones), see William M. Hammond, *Public Affairs: The Military and the Media, 1962–1968* (Washington, D.C.: Center for Military History, U.S. Army, 1988), 94–95.

28. *NYT,* 12 June 1964; Manning to Saigon, 12 June 1964, box 5, NSF VN, LBJL. To what extent the *Times*'s long-standing editorial opposition to an expanded war and support for neutralization affected the paper's readership is difficult to determine. Printed "letters to the editor" are probably not too helpful in this regard. But it is noteworthy that the vast majority of Vietnam-related letters in the first half of 1964 supported the paper's position. A common theme in these letters was that the conflict was a civil war, not a case of external aggression, and that the Saigon regime represented the less-popular side. Several spoke of Ho Chi Minh as an "Asian Tito," under the control of neither Moscow nor Beijing, and others asserted that the French experience taught that the United States could never win a lasting victory in Vietnam.

29. *NYT,* 11 July 1964. See also Hans J. Morgenthau, "The Realities of Containment," *The New Leader,* 8 June 1964. In the article Morgenthau wrote: "It is tiresome but necessary to say again what has been said so many times before: it is impossible to win the war in Vietnam without the political support of at least a very substantial segment of the population." The statesmen Richelieu and Bismarck would never have allowed themselves to get ensnared à la Johnson in a civil war that could not be won short of a political miracle, he declared, nor would they have followed Washington's foolish policy of opposing any and all communist governments for no other reason than that they were communist.

30. Manning to Saigon, 14 June 1964, box 5, NSF VN, LBJL; Woods, *Fulbright,* 347; *NYT,* 29 June 1964.

31. Gibbons, *U.S. Government,* 2:275–276.

32. *CR,* volume 110, pages 14790–14796. For Church's ambivalence on speaking out, see also the comments by his aide Bryce Nelson in Gibbons, *U.S. Government,* 2:277. See also Ashby and Gramer, *Fighting the Odds,* 181–183.

33. Hubert H. Humphrey, *The Education of a Public Man: My Life and Politics* (Garden City, N.Y.: Doubleday, 1976), 482–483. In a 1979 interview, Humphrey aide John Reilly said that he advised Humphrey to avoid discussing Vietnam with Johnson or becoming one of his spokesmen on the subject. Reilly said that he told Humphrey: "(1) Do not make any speech on the subject of Vietnam. (2) Do not present to the President any memoranda on Vietnam. (3) Do not permit yourself, if at all possible, to be maneuvered into a position by the president where you become the principal defender of the Administration's policy in the Senate against critics like Mansfield, Church, Morse, Gruening and others." Gibbons, *U.S. Government,* 2:278.

34. *NYT,* 30 June 1964; *CR,* volume 110, page 15666.

35. *PP* (Gravel), 3:291; *NYT,* 21 June 1964.

36. *PP* (Gravel), 3:291.

37. Saigon to FO, 25 June 1964, FO 371/175470, PRO.

38. Saigon to FO, 23 June 1964, PREM 11/4759, PRO. On Khanh's con-

tacts with the Vietcong in this period, see also State Department memo, "Summary of Positions on Negotiations, and Key Issues," 12 June 1967, box 94, NSF VN, LBJL; and J. E. Cable, Minutes, 5 February 1965, FO 371/180555, PRO.

39. On U.S. fears of a large-scale Geneva conference on Laos, see the comments by Deputy Assistant Secretary of State for Far Eastern Affairs Marshall Green to British Ambassador Lord Harlech, as reported in Washington to FO, 23 June 1964, PREM 11/4762, PRO.

40. Ambassador Charles Bohlen thought it was obvious how the general would react: with disdain. Since the disastrous Rusk-Alphand meeting in Manila in April, the French had continued to speak out against U.S. policy. On several occasions in April and May, Foreign Minister Maurice Couve de Murville and Minister of Information Alain Peyrefitte publicly called neutralization the only answer for the region. Both claimed to be speaking on behalf of de Gaulle. *Le Monde,* 21 May 1964; Bohlen to State, 21 May 1964, box 170, NSF CF, LBJL; Bohlen to State, 28 April 1964, box 169, NSF CF, LBJL.

41. LBJ-Bundy telcon, 1 June 1964, JT. Bundy also advised LBJ to invite French prime minister Pompidou for a visit to the United States, perhaps in August. Bohlen advised against it. MB to LBJ, 15 June 1964, box 2, NSF MPB, LBJL. The visit did not take place.

42. Ball to Rusk, 31 May 1964, *FRUS,* 1964–1968, 1:400–404.

43. Ball, *Past Has Another Pattern,* 377–378. See also Geyelin, *Lyndon B. Johnson and the World,* 210.

44. Johnson instructed Ball to "get across" four main points. First, he should make clear to de Gaulle that the United States was in Southeast Asia because it believed it essential to maintain peace in the region and preserve the independence of vital allies. Second, increasing threats from North Vietnam and Communist China, combined with doubts about "American strength and the strength of those who depend on us," could easily lead to a situation in which, "against all my desires and intent, the U.S. government would have to prove its determination by military action." Third, de Gaulle should realize the harmful effect of Franco-American division on this issue. Finally, should the United States find itself "forced to act in defense of peace and independence in Southeast Asia," Johnson wrote, "I am confident that I could place reliance upon the firmness of General de Gaulle as a friend and an ally, as America properly did in the Cuba crisis of '62, and if by chance I am wrong on this point, it is a matter of great importance that we should know it now." LBJ to Ball, 2 June 1964, box 170, NSF CF, LBJL.

45. Ball to LBJ and Rusk, 5 June 1964, box 170, NSF CF, LBJL; Ball, *Past Has Another Pattern,* 378. See also Peyrefitte, *C'était de Gaulle,* 497; and Couve-Ball Meeting Notes, 5 June 1964, SG, EM, #21, MAE.

46. Ball to LBJ and Rusk, 5 June 1964, box 170, NSF CF, LBJL. Some two weeks later, de Gaulle told British officials that he had told Ball that local inhabitants in South Vietnam would never be prepared to fight as long as it was an American-led war, that it was a mistake to think that white men could lead the Southeast Asians into battle. Even if the United States bombed Hanoi and Beijing, it would never achieve its objectives. Paris to FO, 17 June 1964, FO

371/175091, PRO. For another articulation of the same general point, see de Gaulle's comments to aides after a cabinet meeting on 10 June in Peyrefitte, *C'était de Gaulle*, 497. For the Americans in Vietnam, Peyrefitte quotes de Gaulle as saying, "It is not possible to win. It is only possible to lose."

47. Ball to LBJ and Rusk, 6 June 1964, box 170, NSF CF, LBJL; Ball, *Past Has Another Pattern*, 378. The Ball visit received significant coverage in *Le Monde* and the *New York Times*. Both papers predicted, erroneously, that the visit would serve to bring an improvement in Franco-American relations, to the point where a de Gaulle–LBJ meeting could be expected after the American election in November. For another record of the Ball–de Gaulle meeting, see Record of Conversation, Ball and R. A. Butler, London, 8 June 1964, PREM 11/4759, PRO.

48. Ball to LBJ and Rusk, 6 June 1964, box 170, NSF CF, LBJL; Ball, *Past Has Another Pattern*, 378.

49. Memcon, 1 July 1964, box 170, NSF CF, LBJL; Memcon, 20 July 1964, box 6, NSF VN, LBJL; Alphand, *L'étonnement d'être*, 431–434.

50. The eleven were Tokyo, Bonn, London, Rome, Brussels, Ottawa, Copenhagen, Bangkok, Taipei, Karachi, and Athens. For obvious reasons, Paris was not on the list, though the embassy did receive a copy of the cable.

51. LBJ circular cable, 2 July 1964, box 6, NSF VN, LBJL.

52. On 29 July, British prime minister Douglas-Home wrote Khanh with the following happy news: Britain would provide £6,000 for marine diesel engines. PREM 11/4760, PRO.

53. Wright to the Prime Minister, 18 June 1964, PREM 11/4759, PRO.

54. Hughes to Rusk, 25 July 1964, box 170, NSF CF, LBJL; *NYT*, 7 August 1964; Robert J. McMahon, "Toward Disillusionment and Disengagement in South Asia," in Cohen and Tucker, *Lyndon Johnson*, 138–139; Yaacov Vertzberger, *The Enduring Entente: Sino-Pakistani Relations, 1960–1980* (New York: Praeger, 1983), 7–14.

55. Thomas R. Havens, *Fire across the Sea: The Vietnam War and Japan, 1965–1975* (Princeton, N.J.: Princeton University Press, 1987), 19–22; Nancy Bernkopf Tucker, "Threats, Opportunities, and Frustrations in East Asia," in Cohen and Tucker, *Lyndon Johnson*, 116–119; Walter LaFeber, *The Clash: A History of U.S.-Japan Relations* (New York: Norton, 1997), 339–341.

56. Edwin O. Reischauer, *The Japanese* (Cambridge, Mass.: Belknap Press, 1977), 347; Edwin O. Reischauer, *My Life between Japan and America* (New York: Harper and Row, 1986), 257, as cited in Tucker, "Threats," 116.

57. On several occasions in June and July, Souvanna Phouma of Laos privately predicted defeat for the United States and endorsed a reconvened Geneva conference. For Sukarno's position, see H. W. Brands Jr., "The Limits of Manipulation: How the United States Didn't Topple Sukarno," *Journal of American History* (December 1989): 790–797. Burma's government of Ne Win declared its neutrality in the conflict and predicted defeat for any American attempt to secure a military victory for the GVN.

58. Kahin, *Intervention*, 333–334. On the phenomenally high price exacted

by Seoul, see Tucker, "Threats," 130–132. On Manila's demands, see Stanley Karnow, *In Our Image: America's Empire in the Philippines* (New York: Random House, 1989), 376–377.

59. Ball-MB telcon, 9 July 1964, box 1, Ball Papers, LBJL.

60. The discussion at a White House meeting on 10 June, a summary record of which is printed in *FRUS, 1964–1968*, 1:487–492, is very revealing in this context. See also Sullivan to Rusk, 16 June 1964, box 5, NSF VN, LBJL; Bundy to LBJ, 25 June 1964, box 5, NSF VN, LBJL; CIA Memo, 18 July 1964, box 6, NSF VN, LBJL; State to Taylor, 24 July 1964, box 6, NSF VN, LBJL. In early July, Dhong Van Minh told a Swedish diplomat that bombing the North would be foolish and catastrophic. Saigon to Stockholm, 9 July 1964, HP1, #XV, UD.

61. Taylor to State, 25 July 1964, box 6, NSF VN, LBJL.

62. Taylor to State, successive cables, 25 July 1964, box 6, NSF VN, LBJL; State to Taylor, 25 July 1964, box 6, NSF VN, LBJL; Taylor to State, 26 July 1964, box 6, NSF VN, LBJL.

63. Brian Urquhart, *A Life in Peace and War* (New York: Harper and Row, 1987), 189ff; Mario Rossi, "U Thant and Vietnam: The Untold Story," *New York Review of Books* (17 November 1966), 8–13. See also U Thant, *View from the UN* (Garden City, N.Y.: Doubleday, 1978), 57–65.

64. *NYT*, 9 July 1964; Rossi, "U Thant"; Thant, *View from the UN*, 57–65.

65. *NYT, Le Monde,* and London *Times,* 9 July 1964; *NYT,* 11 July 1964. The *New York Times* editorial took for granted that the upcoming U.S. election influenced administration thinking: "The United States Government certainly is unlikely to extend the scope of the conflict in this period just before a Presidential election unless it is faced with the most extreme provocation or necessity." The editorial concluded by warning that no military solution was likely to be found, now or later. William C. Berman, *J. William Fulbright and the Vietnam War: The Dissent of a Political Realist* (Kent, Ohio: Kent State University Press, 1988), 22.

66. See the LBJ-Stevenson telcon, 27 May 1964, JT; Rusk quotation is in Gardner, *Pay Any Price*, 146.

67. Stevenson to Rusk, 11 July 1964, box 6, NSF VN, LBJL. Thant may have been unaware that Seaborn was planning a second mission to Hanoi.

68. Paris to FO, 22 July 1964, FO 371/178227; *Le Monde,* 22 July 1964. On 23 July Thant met with Douglas-Home and expressed concerns that the United States might escalate the war. Meeting notes, 23 July 1964, FO 371/178227, PRO. Thant spoke out publicly again a few days after that, upon arriving in his native Rangoon to sound out Ne Win about finding a suitable channel to Hanoi. Force was not the answer in Southeast Asia, he said. A political solution had to be found. Thant also said that he expected France to play an increasingly active role in UN affairs. *NYT,* 26 July 1964.

69. Although de Gaulle addressed a broad range of issues, newspapers in Europe and the United States emphasized his comments on Southeast Asia in

their headlines and analysis. The press conference was the lead item in both *Le Monde* and the *New York Times* the following day. *NYT,* 24 July 1964; *Le Monde,* 24 July 1964; London *Times,* 24 July 1964; Marcus G. Raskin and Bernard Fall, eds., *The Vietnam Reader: Articles and Documents on American Foreign Policy and the Vietnam Crisis* (New York: Vintage, 1965), 270; Hughes to Rusk, memorandum, 25 July 1964, box 170, NSF CF, LBJL. See also Peyrefitte, *C'était de Gaulle,* 497–498.

70. For example, CIA director John McCone: De Gaulle's interpretation of events since 1954 was frequently "unjustified." The State Department's Thomas L. Hughes: De Gaulle may have chosen this time to move because of his growing fear that U.S. escalation was imminent. White House aide David Klein: "The president must make it clear that he does not share many of the General's views" and that on Southeast Asia "there is no common ground." McGeorge Bundy: Bohlen should revisit the Elysée Palace and say, "Here's our policy—we have wings of peace but also have the arm of firm military action." McCone to MB, 24 July 1964, box 170, NSF CF, LBJL; Hughes to Rusk, 25 July 1964, box 170, NSF CF, LBJL; Klein to MB, 23 July 1964, box 170, NSF CF, LBJL; MB-Ball telcon, 30 July 1964, box 3, Ball Papers, LBJL.

71. The Johnson quotation is in *NYT,* 25 July 1964; the Saigon government's quotation is in *Le Monde,* 26–27 July 1964.

72. INR (Hughes) to Rusk, 25 July 1964, box 170, NSF CF, LBJL.

73. Manac'h-Mai Van Bo Meeting Notes, 25 July 1964, SG, EM, #45, MAE; Hanoi to FO, 6 July 1964, FO 371/175480, PRO; *Le Monde,* 20, 26–27 July 1964. INR (Hughes) to Rusk, 25 July 1964, box 170, NSF CF, LBJL.

74. A transcript of the Zhou conversation, which occurred on 19 July, is contained in FO 371/180988. The Japanese delegation was led by Toshio Kuroda. On the Rangoon meeting, see Roberts (Hong Kong) to Ottawa, 17 July 1964, 20-22-VIET S, NAC. In November 1964, Hughes would tell Dean Rusk that Chen Yi had made a "private suggestion in July 1964" of interest in a negotiated settlement. Hughes to Rusk, 20 November 1964, box 8, book 4, Warnke Papers, LBJL. It is not clear what "private suggestion" Hughes was referring to. See also Couve-Huang Chen Meeting Notes, 21 July 1964, SG, EM, #22, MAE.

75. Warsaw to FO, 30 July 1964, FO 371/175926, PRO; D. K. Timms comments on Warsaw meeting, 13 August 1964, FO 371/175926, PRO; Qiang Zhai, "An Uneasy Relationship: China and the DRV during the Vietnam War," unpublished paper, 12–13; INR (Hughes) to Rusk, 25 July 1964, box 170, NSF CF, LBJL. The representatives in Warsaw were John Moors Cabot for the United States and Wang Kuo-Chuan for China. On Chinese statements not committing them to doing anything, see Roberts (Hong Kong) to Ottawa, 17 July 1964, 20–22-VIET S, NAC.

76. INR (Hughes) to Rusk, 25 July 1964, box 170, NSF CF, LBJL; *Le Monde,* 28 July 1964. See also Gaiduk, *Soviet Union,* 11–12.

77. INR (Hughes) to Rusk, 25 July 1964, NSF CF, LBJL; Taylor to State, 25 July 1964, NSF VN, LBJL.

78. Seaborn to Ottawa, 27 July 1964, 20-22-VIET S, NAC; Saigon to FO,

30 July 1964, FO 371/175499, PRO. See also Washington to FO, 24 July 1964, FO 371/175497, PRO. The *Saigon Daily News* extract is in FO 371/175499, PRO.

CHAPTER 7

1. *NYT*, 4 September 1964; Taylor to State, 18 August 1964, *FRUS, 1964–1968*, 1:689; *PP* (DoD), vol. 4, part C, chapter b, page ii.

2. Barry Goldwater, *The Conscience of a Conservative* (New York: Macfadden Books, 1964); *NYT*, 19 March 1964.

3. *NYT*, 17 July 1964; Thomas Powers, *The War at Home: Vietnam and the American People, 1964–1968* (New York: Grossman, 1973), 3–4. Powers's book remains one of the best on the domestic impact of the war.

4. Any inquiry into the Gulf of Tonkin affair should begin with Moïse, *Tonkin Gulf*. See also the accounts in Prados, *Hidden History*, 48–59, and Karnow, *Vietnam*, 372–392. Also useful is James Stockdale, *In Love and War* (New York: Harper and Row, 1984); Anthony Austin, *The President's War: The Story of the Tonkin Gulf Resolution and How the Nation Was Trapped in Vietnam* (New York: Lippincott, 1971); Joseph C. Goulden, *Truth Is the First Casualty: The Gulf of Tonkin Affair—Illusion and Reality* (Chicago: Rand-McNally, 1969); Gibbons, *U.S. Government*, volume 2, chapter 5; *PP* (Gravel), 5:320–341.

5. Karnow, *Vietnam*, 381; Prados, *Hidden History*, 49.

6. State to Saigon, 3 August 1964, *FRUS, 1964–1968*, 1:603. On the morning of 3 August, LBJ told former treasury secretary Robert Anderson: "There have been some covert operations in that area that we have been carrying on—blowing up some bridges and things of that kind, roads and so forth. So I imagine they wanted to put a stop to it." LBJ-Anderson telcon, 3 August 1964. A few minutes later, Johnson spoke to McNamara, who said: "There's no question [the Oplan 34-A covert operations] had a bearing on it." LBJ-McNamara telcon, 3 August 1964. When Hubert Humphrey, LBJ's likely choice for vice president, that morning suggested the same thing publicly, LBJ was livid. See LBJ-Rowe telcon, 4 August 1964.

7. Moïse, *Tonkin Gulf*, esp. 106–207. For a contrary view, see Edward J. Marolda and Oscar P. Fitzgerald, *The United States Navy and the Vietnam Conflict*, vol. 2, *From Military Assistance to Combat, 1959–1963* (Washington, D.C.: GPO, 1986), 393–462.

8. A few months later, Johnson would phrase it slightly differently: "For all I know, our Navy was shooting at whales out there." On the pilots' accounts, see also Stockdale, *In Love and War*, 20–23; and *U.S. News and World Report*, 23 July 1984.

9. Notes on Meeting with Congressional Leaders, 4 August 1964, NSF Meeting Notes File, box 5, LBJL; *NYT*, 5 August 1964; *Public Papers of the Presidents of the United States: Lyndon B. Johnson, 1963–1964* (Millwood, N.Y.: KTO Press, 1978), 927–928. On Mansfield's and Aiken's position in this meeting, see Mark Stoler, "Aiken, Mansfield, and the Tonkin Gulf Crisis: Notes from the Congressional Leadership Meeting at the White House, August 4, 1964," *Vermont History* 50, no. 2 (1982): 80–94.

10. Gittinger, ed., *Johnson Years*, 28; Moïse, *Tonkin Gulf*, 209–221. Johnson termed the reprisal attacks "limited and fitting." It can reasonably be asked, however, whether the punishment fit the crime, whether the U.S. response adhered to the doctrine of proportionality. Though the total U.S. damage suffered in the gulf was one inconsequential bullet to the *Maddox* on 2 August and no casualties, the administration unleashed fifty-nine planes from two carriers. Four North Vietnamese patrol boat bases were hit and about twenty-five vessels were damaged or destroyed, which amounted to about 50 percent of the North's high-speed patrol boats. In addition, an oil depot containing 10 percent of North Vietnam's oil capacity was judged to be 90 percent destroyed. Two American planes were shot down. One pilot died and the other was taken prisoner. See William F. Levantrosser, "Tonkin Gulf Revisited," in *Lyndon Johnson and the Use of Power*, ed. Bernard J. Firestone and Robert C. Vogt (Westport, Conn.: Greenwood Press, 1988), 303.

11. Historian Lloyd Gardner has argued that the administration also saw in the crisis an opportunity to quiet de Gaulle. Gardner, *Pay Any Price*, 135, 145. Maybe, but it seems doubtful that many U.S. officials really believed the French leader would alter his posture in response to a military skirmish in the Gulf of Tonkin.

12. Bundy comments were made on PBS's *McNeil-Lehrer Newshour*, 17 April 1995. In November 1995, McNamara said that had he been certain that no attack occurred on 4 August, "we would not have carried out that military attack." *WP*, 11 November 1995.

13. Prados, *Hidden History*, 51.

14. Moïse, *Tonkin Gulf*, 211; Gibbons, *U.S. Government*, 2:288.

15. W. Berman, *Fulbright*, 22; Woods, *Fulbright*, 348. U. A. Johnson's comment is in Washington to FO, 24 July 1964, FO 371/175497, PRO. Saigon to State, 27 July 1964, box 6, NSF VN, LBJL.

16. Summary Notes of NSC Meeting, 4 August 1964, box 8, NSF VN, LBJL. Another potential piece of evidence for "conspiracy fans" has been brought forth by historian John Prados. This is a secondhand report involving a purported cable on 31 July from Admiral David L. McDonald, chief of naval operations, direct to Herrick, ordering him to *make sure* he got in harm's way by going in prepared to support the Oplan 34-A raids. At the same time, parallel orders through special channels informed the Oplan 34-A crafts that they could count on support from the two destroyers. The source for the story reportedly heard that the order came from the White House—Admiral McDonald supposedly visited the White House late one night in July, where Johnson virtually ordered him to send the *Maddox* into action. Prados notes that expert sources give the report little credence and doubt that McDonald would have held a personal meeting with the president; tantalizingly, however, Prados found that Johnson's diary notes indicate a meeting with Admiral McDonald on 31 July 1964, though it was in the daytime and with the other members of the JCS present. Prados concludes: "The session with the Joint Chiefs may have been innocuous, and this story apocryphal, but it remains true that more than one former communications operator recalls strange traffic during those days up to and through the Tonkin Gulf incident." Prados, *Hidden History*, 58.

17. Saigon to London, 6 August 1964, FO 371, 175498, PRO; Hanoi to London, 11 August 1964, FO 371, 175499, PRO; Paris to London, 6 August 1964, FO 371, 175498, PRO; Canberra to London, 10 August 1964, FO 371, 175499, PRO.

18. Haig's comments were made on a CNN television special, *Vietnam: Twenty Years Later*, May 1995.

19. For McNamara's later explanation of these comments, see McNamara, *In Retrospect*, 137–138.

20. Fulbright quoted in Karnow, *Vietnam*, 392.

21. The crucial passages of the resolution read: "Congress approves and supports the determination of the President, as Commander in Chief, to take all necessary measures to repel any armed attack against the forces of the United States and to prevent further aggression. . . . The United States is . . . prepared, as the President determines, to take all necessary steps, including the use of armed force, to assist any member or protocol state of the Southeast Asia Collective Defense Treaty requiring assistance in defense of its freedom." It should be noted that the House vote was unanimous only because two Congressmen, Democrat Adam Clayton Powell of New York and Republican Eugene Siler of Kentucky, chose not to cast votes.

22. For the debate in the Senate, see *CR*, volume 110, 18399–18471.

23. Powers, *War at Home*, 13; Goulden, *Truth Is the First Casualty*, 49. Wrote James Reston a couple of days later: "The Congress was free in theory only." *NYT*, 9 August 1964.

24. Nicholas deB. Katzenbach, then the deputy attorney general and subsequently the undersecretary of state, later said that the 1964 election was key: "There is no question in my mind that that is what motivated Bill Fulbright and other good Democrats to go along with it and to vote for it." The same resolution, Katzenbach suggested, would not have passed any time thereafter. See Gibbons, *U.S. Government*, 2:308.

25. John M. Blum, *Years of Discord: American Politics and Society, 1961–1974* (New York: W. W. Norton, 1991), 232. For an excellent discussion of press coverage of the affair, see Moïse, *Tonkin Gulf*, 229–236. For an argument that Congress had not really been misled, see Gardner, *Pay Any Price*, 138.

26. Halberstam, *Best and the Brightest*, 414.

27. *NYT*, 6 August 1964. See also Herring, *America's Longest War*, 123.

28. Canberra to London, 10 August 1964, FO 371/175499, FO; *PP* (*NYT*), 270. Influential *New York Times* columnist James Reston spoke directly to this point later in the year: "President Johnson is in a particularly difficult position now because he has given two quite different reasons for his policy in Vietnam. On the one hand, he has said that the U.S. [is] there to help [the South Vietnamese] win the war, not to replace them or win it for them. . . . On the other hand, at the president's request, the Senate and House of Representatives passed a Joint Resolution which defined U.S. aims in Vietnam in much different terms. . . . If he follows the lines of the Congressional Resolution, he is bound to regard Vietnam as vital to America's national interest and to world peace." *NYT*, 23 December 1964.

29. "If United States action is criticized in the [Security] Council," the Foreign Office cabled its UN mission in New York, "you should certainly support the United States position. Quite apart from other considerations, we may one day need their support for similar action in the event of intensified Indonesian aggression against Malaysia." London to UN Mission, 5 August 1964, FO 371/175498, PRO.

30. *NYT*, 6, 7 August 1964; Tokyo to London, 6 August 1964, FO 371/175498, PRO. In several countries, newspapers voiced criticism of the reprisal strikes. Major Japanese papers expressed anxiety about the actions, as did leading papers in Belgium, Switzerland, Sweden, and Denmark. In Brussels, the British embassy observed that "the press reaction here to the U.S. reprisals has been strong [in other words, negative] enough to call for comment." Brussels to London, 7 August 1964, FO 371/175499, PRO. The Vatican's official newspaper, *L'Osservatore romano*, labeled the reports from Vietnam "disquieting not only for the future of Southeast Asia but for the peace of the world." It called on world leaders to preserve the peace.

31. MB to LBJ, 7 August 1964, box 8, NSF VN, LBJL; *NYT*, 6 August 1964; *FRUS*, 1964–1968, 1:647.

32. Duiker, *U.S. Containment Policy*, 323–324; Duiker, *Sacred War*, 166–169; William Turley, *The Second Indochina War: A Short Political and Military History, 1954–1975* (Boulder, Colo.: Westview Press and New American Library, 1986), 61.

33. Moïse, *Tonkin Gulf*, 236–237; *NYT*, 7 August 1964. The day before this statement, on the morning of 5 August, McNamara told LBJ that the Chinese reaction had been less than he had anticipated. LBJ-McNamara telcon, 5 August 1964.

34. Mao Zedong and Le Duan, 13 August 1964, in Odd Arne Westad, et al., "77 Conversations between Chinese and Foreign Leaders on the Wars in Indochina," working pa-per, Cold War International History Project, Washington, D.C., 1998, 84. I am grateful to Chen Jian for providing me with an early copy of this fascinating collection of documents.

35. Seaborn interview with the author, Ottawa, 16 September 1995; Seaborn to Ottawa, 15 August 1964, 20-22-VIET S, NAC; Seaborn to Ottawa, 13 August 1964, 29-39-BACON, NAC; Seaborn to Ottawa, 17 August 1964, 29-39-BACON, NAC; Seaborn to R. Louis Rogers, 31 August 1964, 20-22-VIET S, NAC; State to Ottawa, 8 August 1964, box 7, McNaughton file, Warnke Papers, LBJL. See also Maclear, *Ten-Thousand-Day War*, 118–119.

36. Memo for the Minister, 12 August 1964, 20-22-VIET S, NAC; Washington to Ottawa, 8 August 1964, 20-22-VIET S, NAC; Ottawa to Seaborn, 8 August 1964, 20-22-VIET S, NAC; Ottawa to Saigon, 12 August 1964, 20-22-VIET S, NAC; Seaborn to R. Louis Rogers, 31 August 1964, 20-22-VIET S, NAC.

37. INR Research Memorandum, "North Vietnam and Negotiations," 28 July 1965, box 31, NSF VN, LBJL; Kraslow and Loory, *Secret Search*, 97–99; Herring, *LBJ and Vietnam*, 91–92; *NYT*, 7 August 1964.

38. BKS(?) to MB, 10 July 1965, box 71, NSF Agency File, LBJL; Memo of

Conversation, Stevenson and Thant, 16 February 1965, box 71, Agency File, LBJL; State Circular Telegram, 13 August 1964, box 294, NSF UN, LBJL; CIA Report, "U Thant: An Assessment," 25 September 1964, box 287, NSF UN, LBJL; Kraslow and Loory, *Secret Search*, 98.

39. Ball-Yost telcon, 17 November 1965, box 7, Ball Papers, LBJL; Thant, *View from the UN*, 63–64. See also Walter Johnson, "The U Thant–Stevenson Peace Initiatives on Vietnam," *Diplomatic History* 1 (Fall 1977), 286.

40. State Department Memorandum, n.d., box 8, NSF VN, LBJL; State Department Circular re Thant visit, 13 August 1964, box 294, NSF CF UN, LBJL; Ilya Gaiduk, "Turnabout: The Soviet Policy Dilemma in the Vietnam Conflict," in *Vietnam*, ed. Gardner and Gittinger, 207–219.

41. Ball-Yost telcon, 17 November 1965, box 7, Ball Papers, LBJL; Ball-MB telcon, 17 November 1965, box 7, Ball Papers, LBJL; Ottawa to Washington, 23 September 1964, 20-22-VIET S, NAC; Ottawa to Saigon, 30 September 1964, 20-22-VIET S, NAC; Washington to Ottawa, 2 October 1964, 20-22-VIET S, NAC; "Memo for the Minister," 6 October 1964, 20-22-VIET S, NAC.

42. On CIA figures, see Ball to Rusk, McNamara, and Bundy, 5 October 1964, box 9, NSF VN, LBJL.

43. Taylor to State, 10 August 1964, box 8, NSF VN, LBJL; WPB memorandum, "Next Courses of Action in Southeast Asia," 13 August 1964, *FRUS*, 1964–1968, 1:673–679. On 11 August, Marshall Green of the State Department expressed great pessimism about the war and the prospects in a conversation with Australian officials. FO to Washington, 12 August 1964, FO 371/175499, PRO.

44. See the narrative in *PP* (DoD), vol. 4, part C, chapter b, pages 16–18; WPB memorandum, "Next Courses of Action in Southeast Asia," 13 August 1964, *FRUS*, 1964–1968, 1:673–679.

45. Washington to London, 12 August 1964, FO 371/175499, PRO; Taylor to State, 9 August 1964, box 8, NSF VN, LBJL.

46. WPB memorandum, "Next Courses of Action in Southeast Asia," 13 August 1964, *FRUS*, 1964–1968, 1:673–679.

47. Representative of the *NYT* reporting is the following account, in a Peter Grose article on 30 August: "The head of an American agency in Vietnam told a small group shortly after his arrival, 'Our underlying assumption is that the Vietnamese people are as eager to win this war as the United States is.' As he said it, he faltered, for he knew as well as those listening to him how feebly grounded was this assumption." The same day, Tad Szulc wrote: "The awesome, and perhaps insoluble, problem of inspiring a disintegrating society to pursue with determination a patriotic defensive war is facing the United States in Vietnam." *NYT*, 30 August 1964.

48. McNamara, *In Retrospect*.

49. Gittinger, ed., *Johnson Years*, 24–25.

50. WPB memorandum, "Next Courses of Action in Southeast Asia," 13 August 1964, *FRUS*, 1964–1968, 1:673–679.

51. JCS to McNamara, 14 August 1964, *FRUS*, 1964–1968, 1:681–682; Taylor to State, 18 August 1964, *FRUS*, 1964–1968, 1:689–693; McNamara, *In Retrospect*, 151.

52. Saigon to London, 24 August 1964, FO 371/175472, PRO.

53. Taylor to Rusk, 28 August 1964, box 8, NSF VN, LBJL.

54. MB to LBJ, 31 August 1964, box 8, NSF VN, LBJL; Taylor to State, 31 August 1964, *FRUS*, 1964–1968, 1:719–721.

55. CIA memorandum, 27 August 1964, as cited in Kahin, *Intervention*, 228; Thomson to MB, 29 August 1964, Thomson Papers, JFKL.

CHAPTER 8

1. BRIAM to FO, 13 August 1964, FO 371/175501, PRO. Thompson was not the most consistent commentator on Vietnam. He would have occasional periods of hopefulness about the war in the years to come, and he was still around in 1969 preaching the virtues of Vietnamization to Richard Nixon. But there is no reason to doubt that his pessimism in late 1964 and early 1965 was genuine and deeply felt. Already in late December 1963, it will be recalled, a colleague had called him "an on-balance pessimist regarding the future of Vietnam." See chapter 3, note 36.

2. Saigon to FO, 31 August 1964, FO 371/175472, PRO; Saigon to FO, 2 September 1964, FO 371/175474, PRO; Saigon to FO, 14 August 1964, FO 371/175500, PRO; FO to Saigon, 12 August 1964, FO 371/175471, PRO.

3. J. E. Cable memorandum, 17 August 1964, FO 371/175501, PRO; London to Saigon, 21 August 1964, FO 371/175501, PRO.

4. Washington to FO, 1 September 1964, FO 371/175502, PRO.

5. Peck to Butler, 28 August 1964, FO 371/175501, PRO; Meeting Notes, Visit of Mr. Lodge, 1 September 1964, FO 371/175501, PRO.

6. Vientiane to State, 30 August 1964, box 268, NSF CF, LBJL; State Circular, 17 August 1964, box 268, NSF CF, LBJL; State Circular, 12 August 1964, box 268, NSF CF, LBJL; Vientiane to State, 6 August 1964, box 268, NSF CF, LBJL; Vientiane to FO, 17 August 1964, FO 371/175172, PRO; Vientiane to FO, 24 August 1964, FO 371/175173, PRO; Paris to FO, 21 August 1964, FO 371/175173, PRO; Paris to FO, 24 August 1964, FO 371/175173, PRO; *NYT*, 4 September 1964.

7. J. E. Cable memorandum, 19 August 1964, FO 371/175182, PRO.

8. For various appraisals of the course of the Laos talks see FO 371/175500–175502. See also Benjamin Read to WPB, 18 September 1964, box 268, NSF CF, LBJL; Vientiane to State, 16 September 1964, box 268, NSF CF, LBJL.

9. *NYT*, 11 September 1964. On Lodge's encounter with the French, see Joxe-Lodge Meeting Notes, 17 August 1964, SG, EM, #22, MAE.

10. Bonn to FO, 27 August 1964, FO 371/175501, PRO; Hughes to Rusk, 28 August 1964, box 7, NSF VN, LBJL; Rome to London, 10 September 1964, FO 371/175502, PRO; Bonn to State, 20 August 1964, box 7, NSF VN, LBJL; Bonn to FO, 3 September 1964, FO 371/175501, PRO. Shortly before Lodge's arrival in Rome, the Vatican issued an appeal from Pope Paul IV for peace through diplomacy in Vietnam and in the other contemporaneous hot spots, Cyprus and the Congo.

11. Hughes to Rusk, 28 August 1964, box 7, NSF VN, LBJL; Bonn to FO, 27 August 1964, FO 371/175501, PRO; Rusk to LBJ, 14 August 1964, box 7, NSF VN, LBJL. On 10 October, a conference of nonaligned nations meeting in Cairo urged a reconvened Geneva conference to negotiate an end to the war.

12. *WP,* 12 September 1964; *NYT,* 6 September 1964; *Le Monde,* 25 August 1964; the quotations from the London *Times* and the *Economist* are in Rowan to Johnson, USIA Daily Summary Report, 4 and 14 September 1964, box 73, NSF Agency File, LBJL.

13. See chapter 6.

14. *NYT,* 23 and 24 August 1964; *Chicago Tribune,* 23 August 1964. The *San Francisco Chronicle* gave the story a huge headline on the front page of its 23 August edition. See also *Christian Science Monitor,* 25 August 1964.

15. Ball-Reston telcon, 29 August 1964, box 7, Ball Papers, LBJL.

16. Reston himself knew well of Johnson's anger at leaks. See Reston, *Deadline,* 305.

17. *NYT,* 30 August 1964.

18. As a chronicler of the *Pentagon Papers* put it, by early September "a general consensus had developed among high-level Administration officials that some form of additional and continuous pressure should be exerted against North Vietnam." *PP* (Gravel), 3:192.

19. MB to LBJ, 31 August 1964, box 5, NSF MPB, LBJL.

20. McNaughton to RSM, 3 September 1964, box 8, NSF VN, LBJL. The memo was apparently drafted by Daniel Ellsberg, a McNaughton aide who later leaked the *Pentagon Papers* to the press and became an active member of the antiwar movement.

21. In this context Taylor encountered the "powerlessness of power" that Reston had identified. When the ambassador complained to Khanh that an all-civilian government—such as the Buddhists demanded and Khanh in principle agreed to work toward—would be weak and prone to neutralism, Khanh responded that he simply had to have Buddhist support. Hence, it would be necessary to work to meet their demands. Taylor to State, 4 September 1964, box 8, NSF VN, LBJL.

22. Taylor to Rusk, 6 September 1964, box 8, NSF VN, LBJL.

23. William Bundy summarized the results of the meeting in an attachment to a memo by his brother. In the memo, McGeorge Bundy advised Johnson that top aides had reached a consensus around the suggested actions. "Our consensus," he wrote, "now runs against any plan to force substantial escalation before October, at the earliest. My own guess is that unless there is a very marked change in Saigon, we will still be cautious a month from now, although Bob McNamara is a little more aggressive than the rest of us." MB to LBJ, 8 September 1964, *FRUS,* 1964–1968, 1:746–749. For more on the meeting, see Taylor, *Swords and Plowshares,* 320–321.

24. The SNIE, titled "Chances for a Stable Government in South Vietnam," called the current situation "far more serious than that of November 1963, for the Viet Cong are now stronger, and in 1963 popular enthusiasm over Diem's ouster gave his immediate successors a degree of general support and period

of grace the present shaky government does not have. . . . Beyond the immediate crisis over governmental arrangements, however, there is the question of whether any stable regime can emerge, capable of effectively prosecuting the war. On present evidence, chances of this outcome must be rated as less than even." Given the current political climate, the report said, neutralist sentiment could be expected to increase, and there was a danger that "a loosely organized coalition would emerge which could take advantage of frustration and war weariness to seek a neutralist solution." The report noted that "some of the recent agitation against Khanh's government had anti-American undertones," and it speculated that French agents had encouraged these sentiments. The one bright spot in the SNIE was that the situation in rural areas looked relatively good, though this too would change if the discord in the cities continued. SNIE 53-64, 8 September 1964, *FRUS*, 1964–1968, 1:742–746.

25. CIA Cable from Saigon, 25 August 1964, box 8, NSF VN, LBJL; Memorandum for the Record, 9 September 1964, box 1, Meeting Notes File, LBJL. See also LBJ-McNamara telcon, 8 September 1964, JT.

26. Memorandum for the Record, 9 September 1964, box 1, Meeting Notes File, LBJL; *NYT*, 10 and 11 September 1964.

27. *NYT*, 12 September 1964.

28. See Dean Rusk's comments to the Commonwealth Club in San Francisco on 22 September, as reported in *NYT*, 23 September 1964.

29. Moyers to LBJ, 3 October 1964, box 8, Reference File, LBJL. MB to LBJ, 1 October 1964, box 2, NSF MPB, LBJL; MB to LBJ, 23 October 1964, box 2, NSF MPB, LBJL.

30. *NYT*, 30 September 1964. For Bundy's recollection of the Japan speech, se Bundy OH, LBJL. Bundy rightly notes in the oral history that he said nothing in Tokyo that was not administration policy. See also Kraslow and Loory, *Secret Search*, 93–94.

31. Emphasis added. On this point, see Eric F. Goldman, *The Tragedy of Lyndon Johnson* (New York: Knopf, 1969), 233–237. MB to LBJ, 3 October 1964, box 2, NSF MPB, LBJL.

32. *NYT*, 8 October 1964.

33. Taylor to State, 24 September 1964, box 9, NSF VN, LBJL; Taylor to State, 28 September 1964, box 9, NSF VN, LBJL.

34. *NYT*, 3 September 1964; Lacouture, *Vietnam*, 194–195.

35. An insightful discussion is in Lacouture, *Vietnam*, 207–223.

36. CIA Report, 25 August 1964, as cited in Kahin, *Intervention*, 233; CIA Weekly Report, 18 September 1964, box 9, NSF VN, LBJL; CIA Report, 28 September 1964, box 9, NSF VN, LBJL; Taylor to State, 24 September 1964, box 9, NSF VN, LBJL; Saigon to FO, 28 August 1964, FO 371/175472, PRO. See also *NYT*, 28 September 1964. On 1 October McGeorge Bundy wrote to LBJ about "a particularly serious point": the "increasing signs that the Vietnamese are blaming us for their troubles." MB to LBJ, 1 October 1964, box 2, NSF MPB, LBJL.

37. McMaster, *Dereliction of Duty*, 156–158; Bundy MS, chapter 15, appendix, pp. 2–3. LBJ's determination, even in the face of unrelievedly gloomy

reports from Saigon, is clear in his recorded telephone conversations with top advisers in late September.

38. In early October Reston was still skeptical. "Is it really true," he asked then, "that the situation would be made better by putting American forces into the battle and expanding the war to North Vietnam?" *NYT*, 4 October 1964.

39. CIA Memorandum, 28 September 1964, box 9, NSF VN, LBJL. For the pessimism pervading the international community in Saigon, see Saigon to Stockholm, 24 September 1964, NP1, #XV, UD.

40. George Ball, "A Light That Failed," *Atlantic*, July 1972, 33–49; Kahin, *Intervention*, 242. See also DiLeo, *George Ball*, 66–77.

41. Ball to McNamara, Rusk, and Bundy, 5 October 1964, box 9, NSF VN, LBJL. A part of the memorandum is also reprinted in Ball, "A Light That Failed," 36–49. Subsequent quotations are from this memorandum.

42. Ball, *Past Has Another Pattern*, 383.

43. Large portions of the memo are excerpted in Bundy MS, chapter 17, pp. 9–26.

44. McGeorge Bundy, interview with author, 15 March 1994, New York City; McNamara, *In Retrospect*, 156–158.

45. MB Meeting Notes, 20 September 1964, box 8, NSF VN, LBJL; Ball-MB telcon, 8 October 1964, box 7, Ball Papers, LBJL; Ball-Forrestal, 8 October 1964, box 7, Ball Papers, LBJL. Dean Rusk OH (vol. 2), LBJL. Michael Forrestal, in his oral history for the LBJL, alluded to the devil's advocate role and said, "You could never tell about George." Forrestal OH, LBJL. See also James C. Thomson Jr., "How Could Vietnam Happen? An Autopsy," *Atlantic*, April 1968, 49. For a more sympathetic treatment of Ball's posture, see James A. Bill, *George Ball: Behind the Scenes in U.S. Foreign Policy* (New Haven, Conn.: Yale University Press, 1997), 163–175.

46. Ball, *Past Has Another Pattern*, 383.

47. McGeorge Bundy, interview with author, 15 March 1994, New York City.

CHAPTER 9

1. On North Vietnamese thinking in the period, see, for example, Saigon (Seaborn) to Ottawa, 1 October 1964, 20-22-VIET S, NAC.

2. Powers, *War at Home*, 17. See also Kattenburg, *Vietnam Trauma*, 129, 212; Reston, *Deadline*, 301; and Michael Barone, *Our Country: The Shaping of America from Roosevelt to Reagan* (New York: Free Press, 1990), 405. Ronald Steel wrote two years later that, in the campaign, Johnson "was the voice of compassion and restraint, was blasting the folly of a presidential candidate who sought to win the war in Vietnam by bombing the North and napalming the South. What provocation, what madness, what futility. One could hardly take the Goldwater proposals seriously—until they were adopted a few months after the election by the president himself." Steel, "A Visit to Washington," *New York Review of Books*, 6 October 1966.

3. Reston, *Deadline*, 301. See also Wicker, *JFK and LBJ*, 216–217.

4. On Russell's position, see Wallace Greene, Memorandum for the Record, Resumé of Conversation between Commandant of the Marine Corps and Senator Russell, 26 October 1964, page 114; papers of Wallace Green, as cited in McMaster, *Dereliction of Duty*, 165.

5. Lord Walston confidential memo, 17 November 1964, FO 371/180557, PRO.

6. Summary Memo, William Bundy, 5 November 1964, box 11, NSF VN, LBJL. On LBJ's determination, see also U. A. Johnson, *The Right Hand of Power* (Englewood Cliffs, N.J.: Prentice-Hall, 1984), 415. According to journalist Chalmers Roberts, LBJ told him already in October that he had decided to expand the war by initiating regular bombing of the North. See Geyelin, *Lyndon B. Johnson and the World*, 214.

7. State to Taylor, 1 November 1964, box 11, NSF VN, LBJL; State to Taylor, 2 November 1964, box 11, NSF VN, LBJL.

8. Taylor to Defense, 2 December 1964, *FRUS*, 1964–1968, 1:882.

9. McNaughton memo, 7 November 1964, box 54, NSF VN, LBJL; Bundy/McNaughton memo, 14 November 1964, box 54, NSF VN, LBJL.

10. McNaughton memo, 7 November 1964, box 54, NSF VN, LBJL; Bundy/McNaughton memo, 14 November 1964, box 54, NSF VN, LBJL.

11. *PP* (DoD), vol. 4, part C, chapter 3, pages 14–29.

12. Ibid.

13. Ibid., pp. 35–36.

14. McNaughton memo, 7 November 1964, box 7, McNaughton Papers, Warnke Papers, LBJL.

15. This is asserted in *PP* (DoD), vol. 4, part C, chapter 3, page 38.

16. Taylor to State, 9 November 1964, box 11, NSF VN, LBJL.

17. Taylor to State, 9 and 10 November 1964, box 11, NSF VN, LBJL.

18. Saigon to FO, 11 November 1964, FO 371/175503, PRO; Lacouture, *Vietnam*, 76. Said the British embassy in Saigon in mid November: "As we know, peace talk is already current in Government circles. . . . [W]e may well find ourselves with a Government which considers that it has a mandate to negotiate with the Communists and decides to exercise it." Saigon to FO, 12 November 1964, FO 371/175502, PRO.

19. Saigon to FO, 4 November 1964, FO 371/175477, PRO. In his lengthy summary of developments for the whole of 1964, Etherington-Smith wrote as follows of the final weeks of the year: "For the first time . . . the possibility of ending the war by negotiation became a subject of open discussion and was even hinted at by the new Chief of State. Pressure increased for an early convening of a national congress, at least partially elected, which could decide the issues of war and peace. All political groups, as well as the armed forces, officially support the convocation of such an assembly." Saigon to FO, 1 January 1965, FO 371/180511, PRO.

20. *NYT*, 7 November 1964. On the low morale of the ARVN in this period, see also Robert Shaplen, *The Road from War: Vietnam, 1965–1971* (New York: Harper and Row, 1970), 14.

21. See the reporting from the British embassy in Saigon in early Novem-

ber, as contained in FO 371/175503, PRO. The French perspective is in Perruche to Couve, 30 November 1964, CLV, sud-vietnam, #150, MAE.

22. London to Saigon, 12 November 1964, FO 371/175503, PRO. See also Tang, *Vietcong Memoir*, 94–96.

23. BRIAM to FO, 18 November 1964, FO 371/175503, PRO.

24. Meeting Notes, 19 November 1964, *FRUS*, 1964–1968, 1:914.

25. *PP* (DoD), vol. 4, part C, chapter 3, page 44; Shapley, *Promise and Power*, 313–314.

26. Kattenburg, *Vietnam Trauma*, 129–130.

27. Ibid.; Meeting Notes, 19 November 1964, box 12, NSF VN, LBJL.

28. Ehrlich to Ball, 18 November 1964, box 42, NSF VN, LBJL.

29. Paper prepared by Taylor, November 1964, *FRUS*, 1964–1968, 1: 948–955.

30. Meeting Notes, James C. Thomson Jr., 27 November 1964, box 12, Thomson Papers, JFKL. Thomson later said "the whole neutralism thing" was "hovering" during Taylor's visit, with some fearful of the prospect, and some hopeful. All agreed, Thomson said, that a solution might come without the United States. Thomson, interview with author, 18 October 1993, Cambridge, Mass. For a different set of notes of the 27 November 1964 meeting, taken by William Bundy, see *FRUS*, 1964–1968, 1:958–960.

31. Working Group, "Draft Position Paper on Southeast Asia," 29 November 1964, in *PP* (Gravel), 3:678–679.

32. See the handwritten notes of these meeting by McGeorge Bundy, in box 1, Bundy Papers, LBJL. See also the notes by John McNaughton in box 1, Meeting Notes File, LBJL.

33. Executive Committee Position Paper, 2 December 1964, *FRUS*, 1964–1968, I: 970. The paper, approved by LBJ on 3 December, began by declaring that U.S. goals in Vietnam remained unchanged and was unambiguous on the subject of diplomacy: "Concurrently [with the wider military action] the US would be alert to any sign of yielding by Hanoi, and would be prepared to explore negotiated solutions that attain US objectives in an acceptable manner."

34. See Forrestal OH, LBJL; Bundy MS, chapter 20. In addition, the British embassy in Saigon reported in late November that their counterparts at the American embassy were pessimistic about the prospects.

35. Daniel Ellsberg, at the time McNaughton's deputy and later an outspoken opponent of the war, commented in 1970: "Read today—six million tons of bombs later—these judgments seem astounding, to use as neutral a word as possible. It is evident . . . that the sort of reputation to be guarded by such means is not that of a 'doctor' but of a Mafia chieftain." Ellsberg, *Papers*, 86.

36. Meeting Notes, 24 November 1964, *PP* (Gravel), 3:237–239.

37. LBJ to Rusk, RSM, McCone, 7 December 1964, *FRUS*, 1964–1968, 1:984.

38. Jorden to Harriman, box 595, Harriman Papers, Library of Congress; Forrestal to Rusk, 4 December 1964, box 12, NSF VN, LBJL; Thomson to MB, 28 November 1964, box 12, Thomson Papers, JFKL.

39. Thomson, interview with author, 18 October 1993, Cambridge, Mass. See also Thomson OH, LBJL.

40. Robert M. Blackburn, *Mercenaries and Lyndon Johnson's "More Flags": The Hiring of Korean, Filipino, and Thai Soldiers in the Vietnam War* (Jefferson, N.C.: McFarland, 1994); McNaughton notes of 1 December 1964 White House meeting, in box 1, Meeting Notes File, LBJL.

41. ExCom Position Paper on SEA, 2 December 1964, box 12, NSF VN, LBJL; Washington to FO, 4 December 1964, FO 371/ 175503, PRO; Canberra to FO, 4 December 1964, FO 371/175503, PRO.

42. BRIAM to FO, 25 November 1964, FO 371/175503, PRO.

43. "Prospects for a Settlement to the Vietnam Conflict," Foreign Office, FO 371/175503, PRO.

44. As a Labour member of parliament in May 1954, Wilson had declared that Vietnam was undergoing a revolution and that Britain should "march on the side of the peoples in that revolution and not on the side of the aggressors." Wilson added that "not a man, not a gun, must be sent from this country," and that Britain "must not join or in any way encourage an anti-Communist crusade in Asia under the leadership of the Americans or anyone else." Quoted in Ken Coates, *The Crisis of British Socialism* (Nottingham: Partisan Press, 1971), 123. I am grateful to Sandra Sharman for drawing this Wilson speech to my attention.

45. Ben Pimlott, *Harold Wilson* (London: HarperCollins, 1992), 382–385. On Britain's economic dependence on the United States, see Diane B. Kunz, "Lyndon Johnson's Economic Diplomacy," *History Today* 42 (April 1992): 45–51.

46. FO to Saigon, 24 November 1964, FO 371/175503, PRO; Washington to FO, 3 December 1964, FO 371/175503, PRO; Washington to FO, 4 December 1964, FO 371/175503, PRO.

47. J. E. Cable memo, 1 January 1965, FO 371/180539, PRO.

48. Record of Conversation, Washington, 7 December 1964, FO 371/175503, PRO; *FRUS*, 1964–1968, 1:492. See also Wilson's recollections in Harold Wilson, *The Labour Government, 1964–1970: A Personal Record* (London: Weidenfeld and Nicolson, 1971), 46–51.

49. Rusk to LBJ, 16 December 1964, box 170, NSF CF, LBJL; Couve-Rusk Meeting Notes, 17 December 1964, SG, EM, #23, MAE. Bernard Ledwidge, *De Gaulle et les Américains: Conversations avec Dulles, Eisenhower, Kennedy, Rusk, 1958–1964* (Paris: Flammarion, 1984), 146–151.

50. Steel, *Walter Lippmann*, 555–556; Logevall, "First among Critics," 365–367. See also Lippmann's column in *WP*, 22 December 1964. For other Johnson expressions of feeling trapped, see Reedy, *Lyndon B. Johnson*, 149; Goldman, *Tragedy*, 491; and Richard N. Goodwin, *Remembering America: A Voice from the Sixties* (Boston, Mass.: Little, Brown, 1988), 403–404.

51. For the argument that escalation was an all-but-inevitable outcome of the political climate of the time, see the works cited in Preface, note 12.

52. *Time*, 1 January 1965, as cited in Burke and Greenstein, *How Presidents Test Reality*, 115.

53. Many scholars have noted the methodological difficulties in analyzing American public opinion on the war, especially in this early period. See John E.

Mueller, *War, Presidents, and Public Opinion* (New York: Wiley, 1973); William L. Lunch and Peter W. Sperlich, "American Public Opinion and the War in Vietnam," *Western Political Quarterly* 32 (March 1979): 21–44; and John M. Benson, "The Polls: U.S. Military Intervention," *Public Opinion Quarterly* 49 (winter 1982): 592–598. Mueller suggests that the beginning of the Vietnam War, for the purpose of public opinion analysis, is mid 1965. Philip E. Converse and Howard Schuman have argued in favor of what might be called a "rally-around-the-president" phenomenon; the public, they convincingly argue, tend to support the president when he takes a strong initiative, "whether it is in the direction of escalation or a reduction of the commitment." Howard Schuman and Philip E. Converse, "Silent Majority and the Vietnam War," *Scientific American* 22 (June 1970): 21.

54. *NYT*, 15 December 1964. On the "striking" ignorance of Americans regarding Vietnam through 1964, see also Mueller, *War*, 35.

55. *WP*, 21 December 1964; *Newsweek*, 8 January 1965; *NYT*, 5 January 1965.

56. *Newsweek*, 8 January 1965. The academics' letter and list of signatures is contained in box 24, Thomson Papers, JFKL.

57. *NYT*, 30 November 1964, 13 and 21 December 1964.

58. See, for example, the *St. Louis Post-Dispatch*, 5 and 11 January 1965; *Minneapolis Star*, 24 December 1964; *Detroit News*, 23 December 1964; *Salt Lake City Tribune*, 31 December 1964; *Des Moines Register*, 22 December 1964; *Hartford Courant*, 22 and 24 December 1964. See also *Newsweek*, 8 January 1964; and Greenfield to Rusk, 31 December 1964, box 12, NSF VN, LBJL.

59. *WP*, 15 November and 22 December 1964. Histories of the *Post* have mistakenly said that the paper was always hawkish on Vietnam in the early years of the war. See Chalmers Roberts, *The Washington Post: The First 100 Years* (Boston: Houghton Mifflin, 1977), 373–374; Tom Kelly, *The Imperial Post: The Meyers, the Grahams, and the Paper That Rules Washington* (New York: Morrow, 1973), 141.

60. Greenfield to Rusk and MB, 31 December 1964, box 42, NSF VN, LBJL.

61. Mansfield to LBJ, 9 December 1964, box 6, NSF Name File, LBJL. Upon reading the Mansfield memorandum, McGeorge Bundy advised Johnson to reject its premises and stay the course, though he conceded that success might be some years away. MB to LBJ, 16 December 1964, box 2, NSF MPB, LBJL.

62. Gibbons, *U.S. Government*, 2:377. It should be noted that France in fact never had five hundred thousand troops in Vietnam. Counting only French nationals, the number never exceeded one hundred thousand; including also non-French troops, the figure rises closer to the half million mark.

63. Nes to Fulbright, 16 December 1964, box 1, Nes Papers, LBJL; Marcy to Fulbright, 22 December 1964, as cited in Woods, *Fulbright*, 361.

64. *NYT*, 27 December 1964; Ashby and Gramer, *Fighting the Odds*, 191. Morse quoted in *NYT*, 27 November 1964.

65. See, for example, *Los Angeles Times*, 31 December 1964; *Boston Globe*, 23 November 1964; *Seattle Times*, 23 December 1964. And see American Opinion Survey, 25 November 1964, box 11, NSF VN, LBJL.

66. *WP*, 30 November 1964. See also, notably, the Alsop columns on 13 and 23 November, and 14 and 18 December, all in *WP*.

67. For example,*Christian Science Monitor*, 6 January 1965; *Baltimore Sun*, 31 December 1964; *Philadelphia Inquirer*, 12 and 22 December 1964; *San Francisco Chronicle*, 24 December 1964; *Wall Street Journal*, 30 December 1964; *Oregonian*, 8 January 1965.

68. Bundy MS, chapter 18, page 20. See here also Barone, *Our Country*, 399; Thomson Jr., "How Could Vietnam Happen?" 52.

69. Thomson/Cooper to MB, 31 December 1964, box 13, Thomson Papers, JFKL.

70. For one version of Rusk's comment on de Gaulle, see Geyelin, *Lyndon B. Johnson and the World*, 122. For the view that Rusk was correct in this assertion, see Ninkovich, *Modernity and Power*, 296.

71. Ball memo, 5 October 1964; *NYT*, 1 January 1965. See also Marquis Childs, "Scant Sympathy for U.S. in Asia," *WP*, 9 December 1964.

72. Memcon, 9 December 1964, *FRUS*, 1964–1968, 1:502. On Soviet policy in the period, see Gaiduk, *Soviet Union*, 86–88.

73. Washington to FO, 8 January 1965, FO 371/180539, PRO.

74. Forrestal to WPB, 4 November 1964, box 10, NSF VN, LBJL; Thomson to MB, 30 October 1964, box 13, Thomson Papers, JFKL. For Ball's position, see his 5 October 1964 memo, as discussed in chapter 8.

75. Summary of Working Group Report, 21 November 1964, box 11, NSF VN, LBJL.

76. LBJ to Taylor, 3 December 1964, box 12, NSF VN, LBJL.

77. Taylor to State, 9, 11, and 16 December 1964; Taylor to LBJ, 16 December 1964, all in box 12, NSF VN, LBJL.

78. *Le Monde*, 21 December 1964; *NYT*, 21 and 22 December 1964; *PP* (DoD), vol. 4, part C, chapter 3, page 70.

79. Taylor to State, 20, 21, 22, and 23 December 1964, box 12, NSF VN, LBJL. For the Taylor-Khanh crisis, see also the reporting in *NYT*, 20–27 December 1964; and Lacouture, *Vietnam*, 146, 163–164.

80. State to Saigon, 25 and 26 December 1964, box 12, NSF VN, LBJL. For a different interpretation of Johnson's decision, see Gardner, *Pay Any Price*, 161. On the circumstances of the Brinks bombing, see Karnow, *Vietnam*, 423–425.

81. *NYT*, 24 December 1964; *WP*, 22 December 1964; USIA Daily Reaction Report, 24 December 1964, box 73, NSF Agency File, LBJL; *Le Monde*, 23 December 1964; London *Times*, 23 December 1964; *Manchester Guardian*, 29 December 1964.

82. William C. Westmoreland, *A Soldier Reports* (New York: Dell, 1980), 225. See also U. A. Johnson, *Right Hand of Power*, 415. The argument that Johnson had freedom to maneuver is made briefly but well in Burke and Greenstein, *How Presidents Test Reality*, 148.

83. Ball-LBJ telcon, 16 November 1965, box 7, Ball Papers, LBJL; Ball-Yost telcon, 17 November 1965, box 7, NSF VN, LBJL; Editorial Note, *FRUS*, 1964–1968, I: 957–958. Walter Johnson, ed., *The Papers of Adlai Stevenson*, 8 vols.

(Boston: Little, Brown, 1972–1979), 8:661–666; Yost (UN) to State, 25 February 1965, box 1, Gibbons Papers, LBJL.

84. Saigon (Seaborn) to Ottawa, 19 November 1964, 29-39-1-2-A, NAC; Washington to Ottawa, 3 December 1964, 20-22-VIETS-2-1, NAC; Ottawa to Seaborn, 4 December 1964, 20-22-VIETS-2-1, NAC. This 4 December cable read, in part, "[W]e are concerned about lack of substance in position you are being asked to adopt in forthcoming visit to Hanoi." On 23 December, the Canadian embassy in Washington reported to Ottawa that the State Department's Michael Forrestal doubted that the United States would have anything to communicate to the DRV in the near future. Washington to Ottawa, 23 December 1964, 20-22-VIETS-2-1, NAC. For the curious argument that Johnson in this period made "continuing efforts to negotiate a settlement," see Dallek, *Flawed Giant*, 226.

85. Memcon, Mao Zedong and Pham Van Dong, Beijing, 5 October 1964, Westad et al., "77 Conversations," 83–84.

86. Washington to Ottawa, 3 December 1964, 20-22-VIETS-2-1, NAC; Saigon to FO, 28 December 1964, FO 371/180555, PRO. See also Bundy's comments to Australian official Alan Renouf in January 1965, as recorded in Washington to FO, 8 January 1965, FO 371/180539, PRO.

87. See Hanoi to FO, 13 February 1965, FO 371/180511, PRO; Bettelheim–Pham Van Dong Meeting Notes, 10 November 1964, SG, EM, #47, MAE.

88. Ball-Goldberg telcon, 17 November 1965, box 7, Ball Papers, LBJL; Ball-Rusk telcon, 17 November 1965, box 7, Ball Papers, LBJL.

89. On forcing the people to decide, see Powers, *War at Home*, 9. See also the perceptive analysis in Ronald A. Heifetz, *Leadership without Easy Answers* (Cambridge, Mass.: Harvard University Press, 1994).

90. Reedy, *Lyndon B. Johnson*, 5–7, 42, 156. See also Reston, *Deadline*, 310–311; Chafe, *Unfinished Journey*, 223–226, 244.

91. LBJ to Bundy, 29 December 1964, box 12, NSF VN, LBJL; LBJ to Taylor, 30 December 1964, *FRUS*, 1964–1968, I: 1057. This cable was likely drafted by Bundy. For more on the Austin meeting, see Washington to FO, 31 December 1964, FO 371/175503, PRO.

CHAPTER 10

1. *NYT*, 31 December 1964; Greenfield to Rusk, 31 December 1964, box 42, NSF VN, LBJL; Thomson and Cooper to Bundy, 31 December 1964, box 13, Thomson Papers, JFKL; Harlech to FO, 31 December 1964, FO 371, 175503.

2. *NYT*, 1 January 1965.

3. LBJ to Taylor, 31 December 1964, box 12, NSF VN, LBJL.

4. Taylor to State, 31 December 1964, *FRUS*, 1964–1968, 1:1060–1063. The cable was repeated to the CIA for John McCone, to the Department of Defense for Robert McNamara, and to the White House for Bundy.

5. Sheehan, *Bright Shining Lie*, 382; Karnow, *Vietnam*, 422–423; *NYT*, 3 January 1965.

6. Karnow, *Vietnam*, 423; Taylor to State, 6 January 1965, box 13, NSF VN, LBJL. The battle finally ended on 2 January, when the Vietcong, having accomplished their aim of showing their increased strength and delivering a hard blow to government forces, melted back into the jungle.

7. For a good study of this phenomenon, see Valdimer O. Key, *Public Opinion and American Democracy* (New York: Knopf, 1961). Key, whose book appeared in 1957, well before the Vietnam War, labeled this willingness to allow debate to be stifled "the permissive consensus." See also Mueller, *War*.

8. Dirksen and Monroney quoted in *Newsweek*, 18 January 1965. See also *NYT*, 6 and 8 January 1965.

9. *NYT*, 1, 4, and 7 January 1965; *Time*, 8 January 1965; Manchester *Guardian*, 31 January 1964.

10. *NYT*, 7 January 1965; Gibbons, *U.S. Government*, 2:399; Washington to FO, 8 January 1965, FO 371/180539, PRO.

11. LBJ-Stevenson conversation is in John B. Martin, *Adlai Stevenson and the World: The Life of Adlai E. Stevenson* (Garden City, N.Y.: Doubleday, 1977), 812; *FRUS, 1964–1968*, 2:37–38; Gibbons, *U.S. Government*, 3:33.

12. On this point, see Powers, *War at Home*, 41.

13. *NYT*, 7 January 1965.

14. Gibbons, *U.S. Government*, 2:398–399; *NYT*, 9 January 1965.

15. Nixon in *WP*, 27 January 1965; Russell in *WP* and *NYT*, 12 January 1965; Cooper in *NYT*, 7 January 1965; Gore in *Newsweek*, 18 January 1965, page 28; McGovern in *NYT*, 16 January 1965. For Cooper as bellwether, see Jonathan Moore to WPB, January 1965, box 3, Thomson Papers, JFKL.

16. *Newsweek*, 18 January 1965, 33; Bernard Fall in *The New Republic*, 16 January 1965.

17. Thomson interview with the author, 18 October 1993, Cambridge, Mass. See also Thomson's article, "How Could Vietnam Happen?" 51, where he attributes the remark to "one of the very highest figures in the administration."

18. Taylor to Johnson, 6 January 1965, box 45, NSF VN, LBJL. In another top-secret cable, Taylor stated that a top South Vietnamese official (the name remains sanitized) told him that Khanh, together with the Buddhists, intended to lead the country to a neutralist solution. Taylor to Rusk, 2 January 1965, box 11, NSF VN, LBJL.

19. WPB to Rusk, 6 January 1965, box 1, Gibbons Papers, LBJL; McNaughton Observations on Vietnam, 4 January 1965, box 1, Warnke Papers—McNaughton File, LBJL; see also Robert Shaplen, "Plotting to Neutralize Vietnam," *New York Herald Tribune*, 20 December 1964.

20. State to Saigon, 11 January 1965, box 12, NSF VN, LBJL.

21. MB to LBJ, 15 January 1965, box 2, NSF MPB, LBJL; Cooper and Thomson to MB, 15 January 1965, box 45, NSF VN, LBJL.

22. Saigon to FO, 31 January 1965, FO 371/180539, PRO; Taylor to Rusk, 20 January 1965, box 12, NSF VN, LBJL.

23. Summary report, 29 November 1964, box 11, NSF VN, LBJL. Taylor's deputy, U. Alexis Johnson, told British officials in Saigon in mid January that

the situation was desperate and that, in his view, bombing of the DRV should be undertaken. Saigon to FO, 16 January 1964, FO 371/180558, PRO.

24. MB meeting notes, 6 January 1965, NSF MPB, box 1, LBJL; State to Saigon, 14 and 25 January 1965, box 12, NSF VN, LBJL. On the dependents issue, see also Bundy MS, chapter 20.

25. Memcon, 6 January 1965, in *FRUS, 1964–1968,* 2:37; *NYT,* 7 January 1964; Cater to LBJ, 26 January 1965, box 13, NSF VN, LBJL.

26. Memcon, 21 January 1965, box 13, NSF VN, LBJL.

27. *Le Monde,* 24 January 1965; *NYT,* 24 January 1965.

28. Saigon to State, 25 January 1965, box 13, NSF VN, LBJL; MB to LBJ, 26 January 1965, box 2 NSF MPB, LBJL; MB to LBJ, 26 January 1965, box 2, NSF MPB, LBJL; Cooper to MB, 26 January 1965, box 13, NSF VN, LBJL.

29. Taylor to Rusk, 27 January 1965, box 45, NSF VN, LBJL.

30. *PP* (Gravel), 3:667–668.

31. McNamara, *In Retrospect,* 166; MB to LBJ, 27 January 1965, box 2, NSF MPB, LBJL. On Rusk's view, see also Rusk, *As I Saw It,* 447.

32. MB meeting notes, 27 January 1965, box 2, NSF MPB, LBJL; LBJ to Taylor, cable, 27 January 1965, box 45, NSF VN, LBJL.

33. MB meeting notes, 27 January 1965, box 2, NSF MPB, LBJL.

34. MB to Saigon, 30 January and 1 February 1965, box 45, NSF VN, LBJL; Taylor to MB, 30 January 1965, box 13, NSF VN, LBJL; Summary Notes of NSC Meeting, 1 February 1965, box 1, NSC Meetings File, LBJL. William Bundy would later make the claim that when his brother departed for Vietnam, "every possible ball was in play." Bundy MS, chapter 21.

35. Gibbons, *U.S. Government,* 3:51.

36. Cooper, *Lost Crusade,* 314. British officials in Saigon remarked that from the start Bundy made clear that the United States remained fully committed to victory against the Vietcong. Saigon to FO, 10 February 1965, FO 371/180539, PRO.

37. SNIE 53-65, 4 February 1964, *FRUS, 1964–1968,* 2:143–148; Memcon Saigon, 4 February 1965, box 13, NSF VN, LBJL.

38. Smith to MB, 4 February 65, box 10, NSF IMT, LBJL; *WP,* 5 February 1965; Saigon to State, 4 February 1965, box 13, NSF VN, LBJL; MB to McCone, 4 February 1965, box 10, NSF IMT, LBJL.

39. *NYT,* 10 January 1965.

40. Memcon Saigon, 4 February 1965, *FRUS, 1964–1968,* 2:133; Editorial Note, *FRUS, 1964–1968,* 2:139; Maxwell Taylor to State, 4 February 1965, box 13, NSF VN, LBJL; Duiker, *Sacred War,* 170–173.

41. SNIE 53-10, "Kosygin's Visit to DRV"; *Le Monde,* 4 February 1965; FO to Washington, 4 February 1965, FO 371/182757, PRO; Moscow to FO, 12 February 1965, FO 371/180539, PRO; Bundy MS, chapter 21, page 7.

42. Intelligence Memo, "The Kosygin Delegation to North Vietnam," 1 February 1965, box 10, NSF IMT, LBJL; Denney to Rusk, 1 February 1965, box 10, NSF IMT, LBJL; CIA Memo 7-65, 5 February 1965, box 13, NSF VN, LBJL; SNIE 10-65, 3 February 1965, box 10, NSF IMT, LBJL; *The Economist,* 13 February 1965. See also Moscow to FO ("Mr. Kosygin's Visits to Peking, Hanoi, and

Pyongyang: An Assessment of Aims and Achievements"), 22 February 1965, FO 371/182757, PRO.

43. CIA Memo 7-65, 5 February 1965, box 13, NSF VN, LBJL; Moscow to FO, 22 February 1965, FO 371/182757, PRO.

44. Cyrus Vance, Memo for the Record, 7 February 1965, *FRUS, 1964–1968*, 2:160–164; Kahin, *Intervention*, 276.

45. Townsend Hoopes, *The Limits of Intervention: An Inside Account of How the Johnson Policy of Escalation in Vietnam Was Reversed* (New York: Norton, 1987), 30; Kahin, *Intervention*, 277. Veteran Vietnam correspondent Charles Mohr, formerly of *Time* magazine and now with the *New York Times*, suggested strongly that the administration was looking for action when he pointed out, a couple of days later, that at the time of the Pleiku attack the three aircraft carriers of the Seventh Fleet were conveniently located off the Vietnamese coast in the South China Sea, not widely dispersed as they usually were. *NYT*, 8 February 1965. In fact, the carriers were conveniently gathered there to be in a position to retaliate should the DRV attack the destroyer patrols in the Tonkin Gulf authorized by Johnson in January. See Moïse, *Tonkin Gulf*, 253.

46. *NYT*, 8 February 1965. In 1997, Hanoi officials would endorse the theory that it was a "spontaneous attack by a local commander." See Shipler, "McNamara."

47. SNIE 10-65, 3 February 1965, box 10, NSF IMT, LBJL; Duiker, *Sacred War*, 172.

48. Summary notes of NSC Meeting, 6 February 1965, box 1, NSC Meetings File, LBJL; Memo for Record, 6 February 1965, box 3, McCone Memos of Meetings, LBJL; Bundy MS, chapter 22B, page 6; Halberstam, *Best and the Brightest*, 522, as cited in Gibbons, *U.S. Government*, 2:63.

49. Burke and Greenstein, *How Presidents Test Reality*, 133; Bui Diem and David Charnoff, *In the Jaws of History* (New York: Houghton Mifflin, 1987), 130–132. Because of bad weather, only forty-nine of the U.S. planes were able to deliver their bombs and rockets. The twenty-two South Vietnamese aircraft also failed to get off the ground because of the weather, but they made their attack the following day. See *PP* (Gravel), 3:286.

50. Summary Notes of NSC meeting, 7 February 1965, box 1, NSC Meetings File, LBJL; Memo for Record, 7 February 1965, box 3, McCone Memos of Meetings, LBJL.

51. Ball, *Past Has Another Pattern*, 389–390.

52. Ball-Rusk telcon, Ball-Fulbright telcon, Ball-Wicker telcon, all 7 February 1965, all in box 7, Ball Papers, LBJL.

53. MB to LBJ, 7 February 1965, box 13, NSF VN, LBJL. Note that the "surrender on the installment plan" phrase had been used ten days earlier by Bundy's fellow Republican, Richard Nixon.

54. Ibid.

55. Annex to MB Memo ("A Policy of Sustained Appraisal"), 7 February 1965, box 13, NSF VN, LBJL.

56. Hughes to Ball, 8 February 1965, *FRUS, 1964–1968*, 2:199–201; Thomson to Cooper, 10 February 1965, box 13, Thomson Papers, JFKL.

57. Gittinger, ed., *Johnson Years*, 60; Summary Notes of NSC meeting, 8 February 1965, box 1, NSC Meetings File, LBJL; Memo for Record, 8 February 1965, box 3, McCone Memos of Meetings, LBJL.

58. Johnson, *Vantage Point*, 126; Summary Notes of NSC Meeting, 8 February 1965, box 1, NSC Meetings File, LBJL; *NYT*, 9 February 1965.

59. Gittinger, ed., *Johnson Years*, 59–60; VanDeMark, *Into the Quagmire*, 71; *NYT*, 8 and 9 February 1965; Moyers to LBJ, 9 February 1965, box 13, NSF VN, LBJL.

CHAPTER 11

1. MB to LBJ, 9 February 1965, box 22, NSF NSC History File—Deployment of Forces, LBJL.

2. Reston and Kraft columns are in *NYT*, 9 February 1965.

3. For Johnson as dove see, notably, Kahin, *Intervention*, 260–305.

4. MB Meeting Notes, 10 March 1965, box 2, NSF MPB, LBJL; Gittinger, ed., *Johnson Years*, 53.

5. Thomson to MB, 11 January 1965, box 12, Thomson Papers, JFKL; "Background Paper, Sato Visit," 7 January 1965, box 253, NSF CF, LBJL; *WP*, 13 January 1965.

6. English, *Worldly Years*, 232–233.

7. *NYT*, 10 and 11 January 1965; Manning to Rusk, 14 January 1965, box 202, NSF VN, LBJL; Record of Conversation, George Thomson and Kewal Singh, 10 February 1965, FO 371/180594, PRO.

8. J. E. Cable, Minutes, 1 February 1965, FO 371/180539, PRO. Gordon Etherington-Smith, the ambassador in Saigon, was a rare exception among British officials in believing that the domino theory was valid, that a GVN victory in the war was still possible, and that the Americans should be encouraged to stand firm. See his cable, Saigon to FO, 14 January 1965, FO 371/180558, PRO. On Australia's position, see Edwards, *Crises and Commitments*, 346.

9. Washington to FO, 10 February 1965, FO 371/180594, PRO; Note for the Record, 11 February 1965, PREM 11/692, PRO; Memo of LBJ-Wilson telcon, 10 February 1965, *FRUS*, 1964–1968, 2:229–232.

10. Record of Telephone Conversation, 11 February 1965, PREM 11/692, PRO.

11. LBJ to Wilson, 11 February 1965, box 3, NSF MPB, LBJL. Other officials shared McGeorge Bundy's desire to keep the British on board. On 11 February, mere hours after the Johnson-Wilson telephone encounter, William Bundy told Australian and New Zealand officials that British opinion was crucial. If the British government stood firm in public in support of American action, the pressure for early talks would be measurably lessened, Bundy said. Washington to Office of the High Commissioner for Australia, London, 11 February 1965, FO 371/180594, PRO.

12. *WP*, 9 and 2 February 1965.

13. *WP*, 11 February 1965.

14. USUN to State, 12 February 1965, box 71, NSF Agency File, LBJL; *NYT*, 11 February 1965.

15. USUN to State, 25 February 1965, box 1, Gibbons Papers, LBJL; Record of Conversation, Thant-Stewart, 23 March 1965, PREM 11/693, PRO; Memcon, Thant-Stevenson, 16 February 1965, box 71, NSF Agency File, LBJL; Ball-Yost telcon, 17 November 1965, box 7, Ball Papers, LBJL; Ball-MB telcon, 17 November 1965, box 7, Ball Papers, LBJL; Thant, *View from the UN*, 65–66.

16. *NYT*, 13 February 1965; Memcon, Thant-Stevenson, 16 February 1965, box 71, NSF Agency File, LBJL.

17. State to Saigon, 11 February 1965, box 1, Gibbons Papers, LBJL.

18. The plan is in *PP* (Gravel), 3:318–320.

19. Record of NSC Meeting, 10 February 1965, *FRUS*, 1964–1968, 2:216–220; Ball-Humphrey telcon, 11 February 1965, box 6, Ball Papers, LBJL.

20. Ball-Thompson Memorandum, 13 February 1965, box 40, NSF NSC History, LBJL.

21. Washington to FO, 12 February 1965, FO 371/180539, PRO; Robert Johnson to WPB, 11 February 1965, box 202, NSF VN, LBJL. See also Johnson to WPB, 31 March 1965, box 25, Thomson Papers, JFKL. Johnson would later say that all he sought in early 1965 was a "decent interval" between a U.S. withdrawal and a Hanoi takeover. See Gibbons, *U.S. Government*, 3:120.

22. Thomson to Cooper, 10 February 1965, *FRUS*, 1964–1968, 2:228–229; Thomson to MB, 19 February 1965, box 13, Thomson Papers, JFKL; Thomson interview with the author. See also Larry Berman, *Planning a Tragedy: The Americanization of the War in Vietnam* (New York: Norton, 1982), 44–45.

23. Carl Solberg, *Hubert Humphrey: A Biography* (New York: Norton, 1984), 271–272; Gibbons, *U.S. Government*, 3:92–95.

24. The memorandum is reprinted in full in Humphrey, *Education of a Public Man*, 320–324.

25. Record of Conversation, Bruce and Wilson, 16 February 1965, PREM 13/692, PRO; Record of Conversation, Bruce and Wilson, 17 February 1965, PREM 13/692, PRO; State to London, 16 February 1965, box 45, NSF VN, LBJL; London to State, 17 February 1965, box 13, NSF VN, LBJL; Bundy to LBJ, 17 February 1965, box 13, NSF VN, LBJL.

26. Washington to FO, 17 February 1965, FO 371/180580, PRO; Moscow to FO, 16 February 1965, FO 371/180580, PRO; Memo of Conversation, Rusk and Harlech, 17 February 1965, *FRUS*, 1964–1968, 2:313–315.

27. FO to Washington, 18 February 1965, FO 371/180580, PRO.

28. *CR*, 111:2869ff; *Newsweek*, 1 March 1965. See also Church's article, "We Are in Too Deep in Africa and Asia," *New York Times Magazine*, 14 February 1965.

29. *WP*, 18 February 1965; *Time*, 26 February 1965.

30. *CR*, 111:2884ff; *Newsweek*, 1 March 1965.

31. Memo of a Meeting, 17 February 1965, *FRUS*, 1964–1968, 2:298–308; *WP*, 18 February 1965; Gibbons, *U.S. Government*, 3:130n.

32. *NYT*, 18 February 1965; FO to Washington, 18 February 1965, FO 371/180580, PRO.

33. MB to LBJ, 17 February 1965, box 2, NSF MPB, LBJL.

34. *WP*, 18 February 1965.

35. *NYT*, 18 February 1965.

36. In a cable to Saigon the State Department said the initiative would allow the United States "to make clear how stiff our views are. We of course have no thought holding back on basic program." State to Saigon, 20 February 1965, box 45, NSF VN, LBJL. See also *PP* (Gravel), 3:329; and MB to LBJ, 14 March 1965, box 3, NSF MPB, LBJL.

37. *NYT*, 25 February 1965.

38. Memo of Conversation, Rusk and Thant, 24 February 1965, box 71, NSF Agency File, LBJL.

39. *Time*, 5 March 1965; *WP*, 26 February 1965; Gibbons, *U.S. Government*, 3:113. See also USUN to State, 27 February 1965, box 1, Gibbons Papers, LBJL; Bundy MS, chapter 22B, page 32.

40. Johnson alluded to this schism in his talk with Eisenhower on 17 February.

41. Bundy to Rusk, 17 February 1965, *FRUS*, 1964–1968, 2:295–297. In an uncompleted memo written the next day, 18 February, Bundy made clear that any American initiative would be intended less to reach an early settlement than to postpone one. See *PP* (Gravel), 3:692–693. On 15 February, he wrote that there was "great merit in the idea that getting into 'preliminary discussions' on a seven-power basis would give us a strong lightning rod against pressures for an immediate conference and would permit us to continue our actions during the prolonged period that such preliminary discussions would take." WPB to Rusk, 15 February 1965, box 1, Gibbons Papers, LBJL.

42. USUN to State, 13 February 1965, box 89, NSF Agency File, LBJL; Stevenson to LBJ, 17 February 1965, box 71, NSF Agency File, LBJL. See also Stevenson's memo dated 1 March 1965, "Negotiations on Vietnam," box 71, NSF Agency File, LBJL. In it Stevenson wrote: "The essential point, as history shows, is that negotiations, after the agony of getting them under way is over, are themselves *a stabilizing factor* in the overall politico-military picture, even if they drag on for many months . . . without a satisfactory conclusion." See also Martin, *Adlai Stevenson and the World*, 826–836, and Henry Brandon, *Anatomy of Error: The Inside Story of the Asian War on the Potomac* (Boston: Gambit, 1969).

43. Ball-McNamara telcon, 18 February 1965, box 6, Ball Papers, LBJL; Washington to FO, 24 February 1965, FO 371/180581.

44. MB to LBJ, 6 March 1965, *FRUS*, 1964–1968, 2:402–405; Shapley, *Promise and Power*, 332–333.

45. MB to LBJ, 13 February 1965, box 1, NSF MPB, LBJL; MB to LBJ, 17 February 1965, box 2, NSF MPB, LBJL; MB to LBJ, 19 February 1965, box 2, NSF MPB, LBJL; MB to LBJ, 19 February 1965, box 2, NSF MPB, LBJL.

46. MB to LBJ, 19 February 1965, box 2, NSF MPB, LBJL; Rusk memorandum, 23 February 1965, *FRUS*, 1964–1968, 2:355–359. MB to LBJ, 6 March 1965, *FRUS*, 1964–1968, 2:402–405. In late March Rusk once again ruled out negotiations in a meeting with Britain's Stewart. Stewart asked: Why not indicate support for a conference, since if Hanoi said no, Washington would score

points in world opinion by appearing more forthcoming? Rusk answered: Because the United States did not want a conference that would be fruitless. Record of Conversation, Rusk and Stewart, 23 March 1965, FO 371/180540, PRO. See also Schoenbaum, *Waging Peace and War*, 452.

47. On 10 March, for example, LBJ ruled out negotiations on the grounds that "we haven't done anything [militarily] yet." MB Meeting Notes, 10 March 1965, box 1 NSF MPB, LBJL.

48. MB to LBJ, 16 February 1965, box 40, NSF NSC Histories—Deployment of Major Forces, LBJL; Solberg, *Hubert Humphrey*, 273–274; Humphrey, *Education of Public Man*, 327.

49. LBJ-Ball telcon, 15 February 1965, box 6, NSF VN, LBJL; RSM-Ball telcon, 18 February 1965, box 7, NSF VN, LBJL; Frank Church OH, LBJL; *Time*, 12 March 1965; Ashby and Gramer, *Fighting the Odds*, 194–196.

50. Memcon, 19 February 1965, box 15, NSF VN, LBJL; Memcon, 23 March 1965, box 207, NSF CF, LBJL; LBJ-Ball telcon, 6 March 1965, box 6, Ball Papers, LBJL.

51. *Newsweek*, 1 March 1965. On 24 February, Carl Rowan of the U.S. Information Agency informed LBJ that there was a "widespread notion, voiced even by U.S. congressmen, that we are waging a futile effort in Vietnam." Rowan to LBJ, 24 February 1965, box 71, NSF Agency File, LBJL.

52. *Time*, 12 March 1965; *Newsweek*, 22 February 1965. On 1 March, Louisiana Democrat Russell Long asked George Ball for information with which to rebut Wayne Morse's charges. Ball pledged to do it right away. Ball-Long telcon, 1 March 1965, box 6, Ball Papers, LBJL.

53. *Newsweek*, 15 March 1965; *Time*, 5 March 1965; Frank Church OH, LBJL.

54. On 10 February, Mansfield warned Johnson in a letter that the South Vietnamese would become less helpful as American involvement grew and that, therefore, a cease-fire followed by negotiations was the only viable solution. Mansfield to LBJ, 10 February 1965, box 2, NSF MPB, LBJL. See also Mansfield to LBJ, 8 February 1965, box 2, NSF MPB, LBJL.

55. *Newsweek*, 15 March 1965; *New Republic*, 13 March 1965; *CR*, 111: 3685; Woods, *Fulbright*, 366. According to Tristram Coffin, Fulbright tried in late March to get Russell's help in pressing Johnson to negotiate, but Russell refused. Tristram Coffin, *Senator Fulbright: Portrait of a Public Philosopher* (New York: Dutton, 1966), 241–242. For a piercing contemporaneous critique of the White Paper, see I. F. Stone, "A Reply to the White Paper," *I. F. Stone's Weekly*, 8 March 1965, reprinted in Stone, *In a Time of Torment*, 212–218.

56. *Newsweek*, 1 March 1965.

57. George McGovern, *Grassroots: The Autobiography of George McGovern* (New York: Random House, 1977), 106; Ashby and Gramer, *Fighting the Odds*, 193–194.

58. *Newsweek*, 1 and 15 March 1965; *Time*, 5 March 1965. William S. White's column is in *WP*, 22 February 1965. See also the article by James Reston in *NYT*, 27 February 1965.

59. Chase to MB, 16 February 1965, box 13, NSF VN, LBJL; *Newsweek*, 1 March 1965; *San Francisco Chronicle*, 9 March 1965.

60. *NYT*, 7 March 1965. See also Marquis Childs, "A Vietnam Poll in a Supermarket," *WP*, 19 March 1965.

61. Alsop quotation is from his column in *WP*, 8 February 1965. Pearson's column appeared in *WP* and numerous other papers on 28 February and under varying titles. On Titoism as the best solution, see also "TRB" in *New Republic*, 27 February 1965. For Krock's position, see *NYT*, 14 February 1965. A common concern among the skeptics was that the administration had no real rationale for the new policy. Hughes wrote in *Newsweek*: "The essential riddle, of course, remains: what are [the] air strikes supposed to *say* to the Communist foe? Call off the war he is winning? Promise never to attack by surprise? Kill slightly fewer Americans? The answer eludes." *Newsweek*, 22 February 1965.

62. See *Le Monde*, 26 February 1965.

63. Some six months later, *New York Times* reporter Jack Langguth would call 19 February the turning point in the war for this reason—it marked the first American air attacks on *South* Vietnam, attacks that would continue virtually uninterrupted in the months that followed. See his article in the *New York Times Magazine*, 19 September 1965.

64. On the South Vietnamese not being consulted, see Bui Diem and Charnoff, *In the Jaws of History*, 127, 131–133.

65. CIA Intelligence Information Cable, 30 March 1965, box 294, NSF United Nations File, LBJL; Thomson to MB, 29 March 1965, box 11, Thomson Papers, JFKL; Thomson to MB, 11 June 1965, box 13, Thomson Papers, JFKL; Barnet, *Alliance*, 267. On 6 April, Shunichi Matsumoto, formerly Japan's ambassador to Britain, issued a report strongly critical of American policy and assumptions. Many thought the report represented the government's position on the war. A description of the report is in *New Republic*, 1 May 1965.

66. CIA Cable, 26 August 1965, box 171, NSF CF, LBJL; E. H. Peck, Minutes, 3 June 1965, FO 371/180528, PRO; Paris to FO, 25 March 1965, FO 371/180584, PRO; Paris to State, 24 April 1965, box 171, NSF CF, LBJL. On Britain believing that time for early negotiations had passed, see London to Ottawa, 22 March 1965, 845/I41V666, NAC; and J. E. Cable, Minutes, 1 June 1965, FO 371/180586, PRO. See also the "Notes from Abroad" section in *NYT*, 27 June 1965.

67. Peyrefitte, *C'était de Gaulle*, 501; Paris to State, 5 May 1965, box 171, NSF CF, LBJL.

68. E. H. Peck, Minutes, 18 February 1965, FO 371/180556, PRO; Record of Conversation, Thant and Wilson, 9 July 1965, PREM 13/696, PRO; Paris to FO, 25 February 1965, FO 371/180581, PRO; Paris to FO, 26 February 1965, FO 371/180582, PRO; De Gaulle-Vinegradov Meeting Notes, 23 February 1965, SG, EM, #24, MAE. Vaïsse, *La grandeur*, 529.

69. Memo of Conversation, Alphand and Thompson, 2 March 1965, box 171, NSF CF, LBJL; Paris to FO, 8 March 1965, FO 371/180581, PRO; Paris to State, 11 March 1965, box 171, NSF CF, LBJL; Peyrefitte, *C'était de Gaulle*, 500. On the Soviet dilemma, see also Moscow to Stockholm, 6 April 1965, HP1, #XV, UD.

70. Ball-Fulbright telcon, 10 March 1965, box 6, Ball Papers, LBJL; Ball–Chalmers Roberts telcon, 9 April 1965, box 6, Ball Papers, LBJL; Washington

to FO, 30 March 1965, FO 371/180583, PRO; Record of Conversation, Gromyko and Stewart, Vienna, 15 May 1965, PREM 13/695, PRO; FO to Washington, 26 June 1965, FO 371/180535, PRO; Moscow to FO, 30 June 1965, PREM 13/695, PRO; CIA Memorandum, 19 July 1965, box 20, NSF VN, LBJL; Dobrynin, *In Confidence*, 138–145; Gaiduk, *Soviet Union*, 40–41. On the Soviets wanting negotiations but being unwilling to work for them, see also SNIE 10-5-65, "Communist Reactions to Certain U.S. Actions," 6 April 1965, box 1, NSF SNIE, LBJL. And see Couve-Gromyko Meeting Notes, 26 April 1965, SG, EM, #24, MAE.

71. WPB Draft Paper, 23 February 1965, box 13, NSF VN, LBJL; INR (Hughes) to Rusk, 26 February 1965, box 171, NSF CF, LBJL; Washington to FO, 26 February 1965, FO 371/180581, PRO; Paris to Canberra, 16 January 1965, FO 371/180530, PRO; Paris to London, 20 February 1965, FO 371/180581. The Snow interview is in *The New Republic*, 27 February 1965. It appeared earlier, on 14 February, in the London *Times*.

72. Beijing to FO, 9 March 1965, FO 371/180988, PRO; Beijing to FO, 1 May 1965, FO 371/180527, PRO; Beijing to FO, 20 March 1965, FO 371/180989, PRO; Zhou Enlai–Ben Bella transcript, 30 March 1965, in Westad et al., "77 Conversations," 86; Zhou Enlai–Ayub Khan transcript, 2 April 1965, in Westad et al., "77 Conversations," 86–92. See also the *Economist*, 6 March 1965; and Qiang Zhai, "Beijing and the Vietnam Peace Talks, 1965–1968: New Evidence from Chinese Sources," Cold War International History Project Working Paper, June 1997.

73. CIA Intelligence Memorandum, 23 February 1965, box 14, NSF VN, LBJL; Moscow to FO, 7 April 1965, FO 371/180524, PRO; Paris to Canberra, 16 January 1965, FO 371/180530, PRO; Hanoi to FO, 16 February 1965, FO 371/180524, PRO; INR (Hughes) to Rusk, 26 February 1965, box 171, NSF CF, LBJL. See also Drew Middleton article in *NYT*, 23 February 1965. The British ambassador to the UN, Lord Caradon, reported that his contacts at the UN said that the DRV appeared to be willing to negotiate. See Record of Conversation, Wilson and Bruce, 16 February 1965, PREM 13/692, PRO. See also Bundy MS, chapter 23, page 37.

74. INR (Hughes) to Rusk, 28 July 1965, box 31, NSF VN, LBJL; Saigon to Ottawa, 5 March 1965, 29-39-1-2-A, NAC; Hanoi to FO, 8 March 1965, FO 371/180584, PRO; Hanoi to FO, 18 March 1965, FO 371/180584, PRO; Hanoi to FO, 29 March 1965, FO 371/180595, PRO; Hanoi to FO, 23 April 1965, FO 371/180519, PRO; Hanoi to FO, 9 June 1965, FO 371/180519, PRO; Moscow to FO, 7 April 1965, FO 371/180524, PRO. See also Duiker, *Sacred War*, 173–175.

75. Planning Group Report, "A Settlement in Vietnam," 3 November 1965, box 24, NSF VN, LBJL.

76. For a number of years South Vietnamese governments had insistently reported People's Army of Vietnam (PAVN) units fighting in the South, but American intelligence had regularly discounted these claims, describing them as a ploy to win greater U.S. support. In fact, it was not until 21 April 1965 that U.S. intelligence confirmed that a single North Vietnamese combat unit—a bat-

talion—was operating in the South. *PP* (Gravel), 3:392, 498. See also Kahin, *Intervention*, 308.

77. McNaughton draft memorandum, 10 March 1965, box 14, NSF VN, LBJL; McNaughton memo, 24 March 1965, box 14, NSF VN, LBJL.

78. Cooper to MB, 1 March 1965, box 14, NSF VN, LBJL; Taylor to Rusk, 11 March 1965, box 46, NSF VN, LBJL. "Yank" quotation is in the *Economist*, 17 April 1965. See also Beverly Deepe's article in *New York Herald Tribune*, 25 April 1965; and Peer De Silva, *sub rosa: The CIA and the Uses of Intelligence* (New York: New York Times Book Co., 1978), 275.

79. Walker summary of talks in Washington, 30 June 1965, FO 371/180542, PRO. See also MB handwritten meeting notes, 8 June 1965, box 1, Bundy Papers, LBJL; MB-Ball telcon, 31 May 1965, box 7, Ball Papers, LBJL. On McNaughton, see Gibbons, *U.S. Government*, 3:155. U.S. diplomats based in Southeast Asia, meeting in the Philippines in March, were all but unanimous in the belief that the outlook was exceedingly grim, that South Vietnam was essentially a nonstate, and that the Vietcong and Hanoi were extremely confident. See the meeting notes by James Thomson, box 25, Thomson Papers, JFKL. For a different account, see Bundy MS, chapter 23, page 13.

80. WPB to Reischauer et al., 14 June 1965, box 1, Gibbons Papers, LBJL. See also WPB to Ball, 21 June 1965, box 20, NSF VN, LBJL. It is noteworthy that Bundy contributed material to what was by far the strongest of the many "devil's advocate" memoranda George Ball wrote in the spring and summer of 1965. Titled "Cutting Our Losses in Vietnam" and dated 29 June 1965, the memo can be found in NSF NSC Histories—Deployment of Forces, LBJL. For Bundy's view of the 1964–1965 period from the perspectives of three decades later, see William Bundy, *A Tangled Web: The Making of Foreign Policy in the Nixon Presidency* (New York: Hill and Wang, 1998), 499–500.

81. Below the top level, sizable numbers advocated a serious effort at gaining a negotiated withdrawal in the spring of 1965. They included James Thomson and Chester Cooper at the NSC, Thomas Hughes, Allen Whiting, Carl Salans, Robert Johnson, Abram Chayes, and Edward Rice at State, and White House aides Richard Goodwin and Bill Moyers. Prominent Democrat and future defense secretary Clark Clifford twice counseled LBJ to think twice about escalating the war. See Clifford to LBJ, 17 May 1965, *FRUS*, 1964–1968, 2:672; Ball-Clifford telcon, 23 July 1965, box 7, Ball Papers, LBJL.

82. Gibbons, *U.S. Government*, 3:125. On 22 February 1965, upon learning of Westmoreland's request for troops, Taylor cabled the JCS: "Such action would be a step in reversing the long-standing policy of avoiding the commitment of ground combat forces in South. Once this policy is breached, it will be very difficult to hold the line." Taylor to JCS, 22 February 1965, *FRUS*, 1964–1968, 2:347.

83. *Economist*, 3 April 1965. See also the magazine's 24 April issue.

84. On rising casualty figures influencing Johnson, see Reedy, *Lyndon B. Johnson*, 147; and Taylor Branch, *Pillar of Fire: America in the King Years 1963–1965* (New York: Simon and Schuster, 1998), 594–595.

85. Lady Bird Johnson, *A White House Diary* (New York: Holt, Rinehart,

and Winston, 1970), 247–248; Thomas P. O'Neill Jr., *Man of the House: The Life and Political Memoirs of Speaker Tip O'Neill* (New York: Random House, 1987), 185; Ball-MB telcon, 15 March 1965, box 6, Ball Papers, LBJL; McMaster, *Dereliction of Duty*, 248–250.

86. Andrew, *For the President's Eyes Only*, 321–324. According to Andrew, Johnson's choice of William F. "Red" Raborn to succeed McCone "reflected his growing impatience with the discordant notes struck by the CIA's Vietnam estimates." Raborn, he writes, "knew little about, and had little interest in, foreign affairs" and was widely perceived to be unqualified for the post (pp. 323–324). On the CIA's basic skepticism about the prospects, and its lack of influence on decision making, see also Evan Thomas, *The Very Best Men: Four Who Dared: The Early Years of the CIA* (New York: Simon and Schuster, 1995), 326–327.

87. Johnson, *White House Diary*, 247–248; Cooper to LBJ, 21 April 1965, box 16, NSF VN, LBJL; Hans J. Morgenthau, "We Are Deluding Ourselves in Vietnam," *New York Times Magazine*, 18 April 1965. In late April Kennan gave a lecture in England in which he said that Soviet-American relations were being harmed by U.S. escalation in Vietnam, that Vietnam was a poor place to make a stand, and that the United States was wrong to refuse negotiations. See J. A. L. Morgan, Minutes, 29 April 1965, FO 371/180541, PRO. On 23 April Dean Rusk, perhaps referring to Morgenthau's article, publicly scolded academic critics for spreading "nonsense" about the war. He spoke of "the gullibility of educated men and the stubborn disregard for plain facts by men who are supposed to be helping our young to learn." *NYT*, 24 April 1965. Countered I. F. Stone: "Never have plainer facts been more stubbornly disregarded than by Rusk, McNamara, and Johnson since Johnson called Diem the 'Churchill of Asia.'" Stone, "The Secretary of State and the Academic Community," *I. F. Stone's Weekly*, 3 May 1965, reprinted in Stone, *In a Time of Torment*, 227–231.

88. See the article by Tom Wicker in *NYT*, 27 April 1965. The congressional thinking in the spring months is well handled in Gibbons, *U.S. Government*, 3:205–216, 237–252, 300–308. On 30 May Carl Marcy, chief of staff of the Senate Foreign Relations Committee, informed Fulbright that at least nine of the FRC members agreed with Walter Lippmann's article that morning. In it Lippmann said that it would be a mistake for the United States to get further involved in the war. The bombing was not working, he wrote, and major ground forces would not get the job done either. "If we had an army of 350,000 men in South Vietnam, and extended the war in the air, we would have on our hands an interminable war without the prospect of a solution. To talk of freedom and national independence amidst such violence and chaos would be to talk nonsense." *WP*, 30 March 1965. At least four other members of the FRC probably agreed, Marcy continued. "Yet everyone is silent." Gibbons, *U.S. Government*, 3:210–211.

89. English, *Worldly Years*, 362–369; Washington to FO, 23 March 1965, FO 371/180594, PRO; Bundy MS, chapter 23, page 32; Lester B. Pearson, *Mike: The Memoirs of the Right Honourable Lester B. Pearson* (Toronto: University of Toronto Press), 3:138–141.

90. Logevall, "First among Critics," 367–370; Sato to LBJ, 10 April 1965, box 250, NSF CF, LBJL; MB to LBJ, 13 April 1965, box 3, NSF MPB, LBJL; Ball-LBJ telcon, 6 April 1965, box 7, Ball Papers, LBJL; Ball-MB telcon, 6 April 1965, box 7, Ball Papers, LBJL; Ball-MB telcon, 7 April 1965, box 7, Ball Papers, LBJL. See also the interesting account of George Reedy's meeting with the press a few hours before the speech, in "TRB" in *The New Republic*, 17 April 1965.

91. Britain's Sir Patrick Dean, one of the diplomats, reported to London: "There is no doubt at all that the President is very heavily preoccupied with Viet-Nam and has the strongest personal feelings about it." Johnson, Dean added, was "extremely sensitive to any form of criticism." Washington to FO, 13 April 1965, FO 371/180541, PRO. On the decision for additional troops, see the succession of documents in *FRUS*, 1964–1968, 2:553–571. On 17 April Johnson agreed, after further urgings from Taylor, to suspend the action until after McNamara met with Westmoreland in Hawaii on 20 April. At that meeting the troop increase plan approved on 13 April was affirmed.

92. For the text of the Four Points, see Kahin, *Intervention*, 326. See also Kattenburg, *Vietnam Trauma*, 131–133.

93. For the suggestion that the United States ought to probe the meaning of the Four Points, see, for example, Cooper/Thomson to MB, 24 April 1965, box 11, Thomson Papers, JFKL; Cooper/Thomson to MB, 29 June 1965, box 19, NSF VN, LBJL; Cooper to LBJ, 25 May 1965, box 41, NSF NSC Histories—Deployment of Forces, LBJL; Thomson to MB, 24 July 1965, box 20, NSF VN, LBJL; Goodwin to LBJ, 27 April 1965, box 2, NSF MPB, LBJL. Even McGeorge Bundy, after describing North Vietnam's response as "quite unacceptable to us," acknowledged that the Hanoi message had referred to the four points as "a basis for discussions" and that he, Ray Cline (acting CIA director), and Llewellyn Thompson all agreed that there existed "at least a hint of real interest from Hanoi in eventual discussions." Bundy to LBJ, 20 April 1965, box 16, NSF VN, LBJL. See also Cooper, *Lost Crusade*, 274–275; Herring, ed., *Secret Diplomacy*, 46.

94. Cooper to LBJ, 21 April 1965, box 16, NSF VN, LBJL. To defuse the renewed criticism and to set the stage for further escalation, the administration would in mid May make another "peaceful" gesture, this time not a presidential speech but a brief bombing pause, code-named Operation Mayflower. See Fredrik Logevall, "Fear to Negotiate: Lyndon Johnson and the Escalation of the Vietnam War, 1963–1965" (Ph.D. diss., Yale University, 1993), pp. 251–252.

95. LBJ letter to Holyoke, 8 April 1965, box 12, Thomson Papers, JFKL; Taylor (Washington) to Saigon, 30 March 1965, box 45, NSF VN, LBJL; Ball-MB telcon, 6 April 1965, box 7, Ball Papers, LBJL; Bundy MS, chapter 23, page 21, and chapter 24, page 16; MB to LBJ, 1 April 1965, *FRUS*, 1964–1968, 2:506–510. In the memo Bundy noted that help was likely to come only from Australia, New Zealand, and South Korea, and that the Canberra and Wellington commitments would be small. Even the Korean situation, he said, was "touchy." See also White House Meeting Notes, 21 July 1965, *FRUS*, 1964–1968, 3:189–197.

96. "Free World Assistance to Vietnam," 15 June 1965, FO 371/180578,

PRO; Wellington to Commonwealth Relations Office, 6 August 1965, PREM 13/697, PRO; Canberra to Commonwealth Relations Office, 2 July 1965, PREM 13/696, PRO.

97. Canberra to Commonwealth Relations Office, 2 July 1965, PREM 13/696, PRO; Washington to FO, 26 July 1965, FO 371/180542, PRO; Washington to FO, 29 July 1965, FO 371/180543, PRO; A. M. Palliser, Minutes, 28 July 1965, FO 371/180543, PRO; Ball-Fowler telcon, 29 July 1965, box 7, Ball Papers, LBJL; Ball-MB telcon, 29 July 1965, box 7, Ball Papers, LBJL.

98. *NYT*, 9 June 1965.

CHAPTER 12

1. *Newsweek*, 12 April 1965.

2. For this reason some of the earliest literature on the war is also some of the most instructive. See, for example, Hans J. Morgenthau, *Vietnam and the United States* (Washington: Public Affairs Press, 1965); Stone, *In a Time of Torment*; Howard Zinn, *Vietnam: The Logic of Withdrawal* (Boston: Beacon Press, 1967); Hoopes, *Limits of Intervention*; Wicker, *JFK and LBJ*; Kahin and Lewis, *The United States in Vietnam*; Ronald Steel, *Pax Americana* (New York: Norton, 1967).

3. Gardner, *Pay Any Price*, 158.

4. On Capitol Hill, especially, there was a growing sense that the situation in South Vietnam had reached a crisis point, which required some kind of bold action, in one direction or another. "In the crisis atmosphere" of late 1964–early 1965, former assistant secretary of state Roger Hilsman has argued, "Mr. Johnson could have gone to Geneva as easily as he escalated the war." Hilsman OH, LBJL.

5. *WP*, 18 March 1965.

6. Schell, *Time of Illusion*, 9–10.

7. It is remarkable that those early critics have received virtually no attention in the large literature of antiwar agitation. Students of the movement against the war have tended to focus on just that, the so-called Movement, which came into full flower only after the winter of 1965—too late, that is, to have an impact on the key decisions for Americanization. See Logevall, "First among Critics," 354–355.

8. Michael H. Hunt, *Ideology and U.S. Foreign Policy* (New Haven, Conn.: Yale University Press, 1987).

9. For an interpretation that stresses the vital importance of analogies— especially the Korean War one—in the making of the Americanization decisions, see Yuen Foong Khong, *Analogies at War: Korea, Munich, Dien Bien Phu, and the Vietnam Decisions of 1965* (Princeton, N.J.: Princeton University Press, 1992).

10. Kolko, *Anatomy of a War*, 72.

11. See chapter 2.

12. Gelb and Betts, *Irony of Vietnam*.

13. This point is well made in Burke and Greenstein, *How Presidents Test Reality*, 136–137.

14. McGeorge Bundy interview with the author, New York City, 15 March 1994.

15. Kearns, *Lyndon Johnson and the American Dream*; Reedy, *Lyndon B. Johnson*, esp. 31–38; Goldman, *Tragedy*; Chafe, *Unfinished Journey*, 273–276; Halberstam, *Best and the Brightest*, esp. 528–533.

16. Halberstam, *Best and the Brightest*, 531–532. See also Blema S. Steinberg, *Shame and Humiliation: Presidential Decision Making on Vietnam* (Pittsburgh: University of Pittsburgh Press, 1996), 78–79. The "crybaby" reference is in Dallek, *Flawed Giant*, 289.

17. An attempt at refuting this view of a closed presidency in which debate was not tolerated is Barrett, *Uncertain Warriors*. See also Heinrichs, "Lyndon Johnson," 24. But see also Chafe, *Unfinished Journey*, 276, 284–285; and Karnow, *Vietnam*, 414.

18. McGeorge Bundy interview with the author, New York City, 15 March 1994; Gibbons, *U.S. Government*, 3:95; Humphrey, *Education of a Public Man*, 320–327.

19. I have examined both possibilities in more detail elsewhere. Logevall, "What Might Have Been."

20. Wicker, *JFK and LBJ*, 206–207.

21. Larry Berman, *Planning a Tragedy*, esp. 145–153.

22. On this point, see Robert L. Gallucci, *Neither Peace nor Honor: The Politics of American Military Policy in Vietnam* (Baltimore, Md.: Johns Hopkins University Press, 1975), 131.

23. *WP*, 22 December 1964.

24. See here Leonard Unger's cover note on a seventy-seven-page Planning Group paper, "A Settlement in Vietnam," 3 November 1965, box 24, NSF VN, LBJL.

25. Kattenburg, *Vietnam Trauma*, 234.

26. See here Stephen Ambrose, *Nixon: The Triumph of a Politician* (New York: Simon and Schuster, 1989), 61. Nixon's national security adviser, equally inclined to grumble in 1969 about the hand he had been dealt, also backed the escalation in 1965. See Walter Isaacson, *Kissinger: A Biography* (New York: Simon and Schuster, 1992), 117–118.

27. Prados, *Hidden History*, 297.

28. For a different view, see Harry G. Summers, *On Strategy: A Critical Analysis of the Vietnam War* (Novato, Calif.: Presidio Press, 1982).

29. *Newsweek*, 18 January 1965.

30. *U.S. News & World Report*, 4 January 1965.

31. McNaughton to RSM, 7 February 1965, *FRUS*, 1964–1968, 1:166. Officials in the British Foreign Office also speculated in early 1965 that Washington was considering this option, and wondered if it might include a provision offering resettlement outside Vietnam to those Saigon officials who had been committed to the war effort and did not wish to remain in the country following a U.S. withdrawal.

32. Johnson's speech is in *WP,* 1 April 1968. Officials in the South-East Asia Department of the British Foreign Office even thought it possible that the western powers could get a quid pro quo from Hanoi: a U.S. withdrawal from South Vietnam in exchange for a North Vietnamese withdrawal from Laos (on the theory that Hanoi would have less need for a presence in Laos with the Americans out of South Vietnam) and the admission of Souvanna Phouma's officials and soldiers to all parts of Laos. SEAD Paper, "Seeking a Solution in Viet-Nam," 15 February 1965, FO 371/180580, PRO. See also WPB Draft Paper, 23 February 1965, box 13, NSF VN, LBJL; Bundy MS, chapter 21.

33. See Seymour Topping's article in *NYT,* 5 February 1965; C. L. Sulzberger's column in *NYT,* 3 February 1965; *Le Monde,* 5 February 1965; *The Economist,* 13 February 1965.

34. *NYT,* 7 February 1965.

35. As a British diplomat in Beijing put it in early March, surely the Chinese knew "that further escalation of Viet Nam hostilities will lead to an increased Soviet stake in Viet Nam's defence and thereby to an increased Soviet voice in the conduct of the war and the discussion of peace." Beijing to FO, 9 March 1965, FO 371/180988, PRO.

36. *St. Louis Post-Dispatch,* 9 March 1965. For a different view of the viability of this kind of presidential speech in the context of 1965, see Richard E. Neustadt and Ernest R. May, *Thinking in Time: The Uses of History for Decision-Makers* (New York: The Free Press, 1986), 88–89.

37. Bernard Fall in *The New Republic,* 16 January 1965. Roger Hilsman spoke well (if disingenuously, given his own position in 1965) to this point a few years later, at the time of the 1968 negotiations in Paris: "My feeling was that [Johnson's failure to negotiate] was his great mistake, because I think, quite frankly, that we'd have gotten more out of those negotiations of 1965 than we'll get out of these. And the reason is because the North Vietnamese had never experienced the bombing, never experienced five hundred thousand Americans, and they could have been fearful of it. They would have been under the threat. The threat is always worse than the reality." Hilsman OH, LBJL. See also Goodwin, *Remembering America,* 379.

38. The heavy toll of the war on all other foreign-policy issues is a theme that runs through the essays in Cohen and Tucker, eds., *Lyndon Johnson.* See also Gaddis, *Strategies of Containment,* 269.

39. Dobrynin, *In Confidence,* 181. See also Adam Yarmolinsky, "Cold War Stories," *Foreign Policy* 97 (winter 1994–1995): 162.

Bibliography

PRIMARY SOURCES

Archival, Manuscript, and Oral History Sources

Alsop, Joseph W., and Stewart Alsop. Papers. Library of Congress, Washington, D.C.

Ball, George W. Papers. Lyndon Baines Johnson Library, Austin, Tex.

Bowles, Chester. Papers. Yale University Library, New Haven, Conn.

Bundy, McGeorge. Author's Interview, New York, N.Y., 15 March 1994.

Bundy, William P. Papers. Lyndon Baines Johnson Library, Austin, Tex.

Gibbons, William C. Papers. Lyndon Baines Johnson Library, Austin, Tex.

Harriman, W. Averell. Papers. Library of Congress, Washington, D.C.

Hilsman, Roger. Author's Interview, Old Lyme, Conn., 18 February 1994.

———. Papers. John Fitzgerald Kennedy Library, Boston, Mass.

Johnson, Lyndon Baines. Papers. Lyndon Baines Johnson Library, Austin, Tex.

Kennedy, John Fitzgerald. Papers. John Fitzgerald Kennedy Library, Boston, Mass.

Lippmann, Walter. Papers. Yale University Library, New Haven, Conn.

McNaughton, John. Papers. Lyndon Baines Johnson Library, Austin, Tex.

Ministère des Affaires Etrangères, Paris, France.

National Archives of Canada, Ottawa.

National Security Council. Meetings Files. Lyndon Baines Johnson Library, Austin, Tex.

National Security Files. Lyndon Baines Johnson Library, Austin, Tex.

Nes, David G. Author's Phone Interview, 20 February 1994.

———. Papers. Lyndon Baines Johnson Library, Austin, Tex.

Oral History Collection. John Fitzgerald Kennedy Library, Boston, Mass.

Oral History Collection. Lyndon Baines Johnson Library, Austin, Tex.

President's Office Files. John Fitzgerald Kennedy Library, Boston, Mass.

Public Record Office, Kew, England.

Seaborn, Blair J. Author's Interview, Ottawa, Canada, 16 September 1995.

Thomson, James C. Jr. Author's Interview, Boston Mass., 17 October 1993.
———. Papers. John Fitzgerald Kennedy Library, Boston, Mass.
Utrikesdepartementet, Stockholm, Sweden.
Warnke, Paul C. Papers. Lyndon Baines Johnson Library, Austin, Tex.

Government Publications

Congressional Record. Washington, D.C.: GPO.
The Pentagon Papers. United States–Vietnam Relations, 1945–1967: Study Prepared by the Department of Defense. 12 vols. Washington, D.C.: GPO, 1971. Cited as PP (DoD).
The Pentagon Papers as Published by the New York Times. Ed. Neil Sheehan et. al. New York: Quadrangle Books, 1971. Cited as PP (NYT).
The Pentagon Papers: The Defense Department History of Decisionmaking on Vietnam. The Senator Gravel edition. 5 vols. Boston: Beacon, 1971–1972. Cited as PP (Gravel).
U.S. Department of State, American Foreign Policy: Current Documents, 1963. Washington, D.C.: GPO, 1964.
U.S. Department of State. Foreign Relations of the United States, 1961–1963— Vietnam. 4 vols. Washington, D.C.: GPO, 1988–1991.
U.S. Department of State. Foreign Relations of the United States, 1964–1968— Vietnam. 4 vols. Washington, D.C.: GPO, 1993–1995.

Newspapers

Baltimore Sun
Boston Globe
Candide
Chicago Tribune
Christian Science Monitor
Dallas Morning News
Des Moines Register
Detroit News
Espresso
Le Figaro
Hartford Courant
Los Angeles Times
Manchester Guardian
Miami Herald
Minneapolis Star
Le Monde
New York Daily News
New York Herald Tribune
New York Times
L'Osservatore romano
The Oregonian
Philadelphia Inquirer

The Reporter
Salt Lake City Tribune
San Francisco Chronicle
Seattle Times
St. Louis Post-Dispatch
The Times (London)
Times of Vietnam
Wall Street Journal
Washington Post

Periodicals

Atlantic Monthly
The Economist
The New Republic
Newsweek
New York Times Magazine
Time
U.S. News and World Report
World Today

SECONDARY SOURCES AND PUBLISHED MEMOIRS

Abramson, Rudy. *Spanning the Century: The Life of W. Averell Harriman, 1891 1986.* New York: Morrow, 1992.

Adamthwaite, Anthony P. *Grandeur and Misery: France's Bid for Power in Europe, 1914–1940.* New York: St. Martin's Press, 1995.

Alphand, Hervé. *L'étonnement d'être: Journal, 1939–1973.* Paris: Fayard, 1977.

Ambrose, Stephen. *Nixon: The Triumph of a Politician.* New York: Simon and Schuster, 1989.

Anderson, David L. *Trapped by Success: The Eisenhower Administration and Vietnam, 1953–1961.* New York: Columbia University Press, 1991.

Andrew, Christopher M. *For the President's Eyes Only: Secret Intelligence and the American Presidency from Washington to Bush.* New York: HarperCollins, 1995.

Arenth, Joachim. *Johnson, Vietnam, und der Western: Transatlantische Belastungen, 1963–1969.* Munich: Olzog, 1994.

Ashby, LeRoy, and Rod Gramer. *Fighting the Odds: The Life of Senator Frank Church.* Pullman: Washington State University Press, 1994.

Austin, Anthony. *The President's War: The Story of the Tonkin Gulf Resolution and How the Nation Was Trapped in Vietnam.* New York: Lippincott, 1971.

Ball, George. "A Light That Failed." *Atlantic* (July 1972): 33–49.

———. *The Past Has Another Pattern: Memoirs.* New York: Norton, 1982.

Barclay, Glen St. J. *A Very Small Insurance Policy: The Politics of Australian Involvement in Vietnam, 1954–1967.* St. Lucia, Australia: University of Queensland Press, 1988.

Barber, James David. *The Presidential Character: Predicting Performance in the White House*, 2d ed. Englewood Cliffs, N.J.: Prentice-Hall, 1977.

Barnet, Richard J. *The Alliance: America, Europe, Japan: Makers of the Postwar World*. New York: Simon and Schuster, 1983.

Barone, Michael. *Our Country: The Shaping of America from Roosevelt to Reagan*. New York: Free Press, 1990.

Barrett, David M. *Uncertain Warriors: Lyndon Johnson and His Vietnam Advisers*. Lawrence: University Press of Kansas, 1993.

Bassett, Lawrence J., and Stephen E. Pelz. "The Failed Search for Victory: Vietnam and the Politics of War." In *Kennedy's Quest for Victory: American Foreign Policy, 1961–1963*, ed. Thomas G. Paterson. New York: Oxford University Press, 1989.

Benson, John M. "The Polls: U.S. Military Intervention." *Public Opinion Quarterly* 49 (winter 1982): 592–598.

Bergerud, Eric M. *The Dynamics of Defeat: The Vietnam War in Hau Nghia Province*. Boulder, Colo.: Westview Press, 1991.

Berman, Larry. "Counterfactual Historical Reasoning: NSAM 263 and NSAM 273." Unpublished paper delivered at conference on "Vietnam: The Early Decisions, 1961–1964," LBJL, 15 October 1993.

———. "NSAM 263 and NSAM 273: Manipulating History." In *Vietnam: The Early Years*, ed. Lloyd C. Gardner and Ted Gittinger. Austin: University of Texas Press, 1997.

———. *Planning a Tragedy: The Americanization of the War in Vietnam*. New York: Norton, 1982.

Berman, William C. *J. William Fulbright and the Vietnam War: The Dissent of a Political Realist*. Kent, Ohio: Kent State University Press, 1988.

Beschloss, Michael R. *The Crisis Years: Kennedy and Khrushchev, 1960–1963*. New York: HarperCollins, 1991.

———, ed. *Taking Charge: The Johnson White House Tapes, 1963–1964*. New York: Simon and Schuster, 1998.

Bill, James A. *George Ball: Behind the Scenes in Foreign Policy* (New Haven, Conn.: Yale University Press, 1997).

Blackburn, Robert M. *Mercenaries and Lyndon Johnson's "More Flags": The Hiring of Korean, Filipino, and Thai Soldiers in the Vietnam War*. Jefferson, N.C.: McFarland, 1994.

Blair, Anne E. *Lodge in Vietnam: A Patriot Abroad*. New Haven, Conn.: Yale University Press, 1995.

———. "No Time to Stop: Henry Cabot Lodge in Vietnam." Ph.D. diss., Monash University, Australia, 1992.

Blaufarb, Douglas S. *The Counterinsurgency Era: U.S. Doctrine and Performance, 1950 to the Present*. New York: Free Press, 1977.

Blum, John M. *Years of Discord: American Politics and Society, 1961–1974*. New York: Norton, 1991.

Bohlen, Charles E. *Witness to History, 1929–1969*. New York: Norton, 1973.

Bowles, Chester. *Promises to Keep*. New York: Harper and Row, 1971.

Braestrup, Peter, ed. *Vietnam as History: Ten Years after the Paris Peace Accords.* Washington, D.C.: University Press of America, 1984.

Branch, Taylor. *Pillar of Fire: America in the King Years, 1963–1965.* New York: Simon and Schuster, 1998.

Brandon, Henry. *Anatomy of Error: The Inside Story of the Asian War on the Potomac.* Boston: Gambit, 1969.

———. *Special Relationships: A Foreign Correspondent's Memoirs from Roosevelt to Reagan.* New York: Atheneum, 1988.

Brands, H. W. Jr. "Johnson and de Gaulle: American Diplomacy *Sotto Voce.*" *The Historian* 49 (1987): 482–485.

———. "The Limits of Manipulation: How the United States Didn't Topple Sukarno." *Journal of American History* (December 1989): 790–797.

Brigham, Robert K. "The NLF's Foreign Relations and the Vietnam War." Unpublished paper delivered at the Society for Historians of American Foreign Relations annual meeting, Charlottesville, Va., June 1994.

———. *The Wages of Globalism: Lyndon Johnson and the Limits of American Power.* New York: Oxford University Press, 1995.

Bui Tin. *Following Ho Chi Minh: The Memoirs of a North Vietnamese Colonel.* Trans. Judy Stowe and Do Van. Honolulu: University of Hawaii Press, 1995.

Bundy, William. *A Tangled Web: The Making of Foreign Policy in the Nixon Presidency.* New York: Hill and Wang, 1998.

Burke, John P., and Fred I. Greenstein. *How Presidents Test Reality: Decisions on Vietnam, 1954 and 1965.* New York: Russell Sage Foundation, 1989.

Buzzanco, Robert. *Masters of War: Military Dissent and Politics in the Vietnam War.* New York: Cambridge University Press, 1996.

Cable, James E. *The Geneva Conference of 1954 on Indochina.* New York: St. Martin's Press, 1986.

Cannon, Michael. "Raising the Stakes: The Taylor-Rostow Mission." *Journal of Strategic Studies* 12 (June 1989): 153–158.

Caro, Robert A. *The Years of Lyndon Johnson: The Path to Power.* Vol. 1, New York: Knopf, 1982.

Castle, Timothy N. *At War in the Shadow of Vietnam: U.S. Military Aid to the Royal Lao Government, 1955–1975.* New York: Columbia University Press, 1993.

Chafe, William H. *The Unfinished Journey: America since World War II,* 3d ed. New York: Oxford University Press, 1991.

Chandler, David P. *The Tragedy of Cambodian History: Politics, War, and Revolution since 1945.* New Haven, Conn.: Yale University Press, 1991.

Chen, Jian. "China's Involvement in the Vietnam War, 1964–1969." *China Quarterly* 142 (June 1995): 356–387.

Chomsky, Noam. *Rethinking Camelot: JFK, the Vietnam War, and U.S. Political Culture.* Boston: South End Press, 1993.

———. *Year 501: The Conquest Continues.* Boston: South End Press, 1993.

Clifford, Clark. *Counsel to the President: A Memoir.* New York: Random House, 1991.

Coates, Ken. *The Crisis of British Socialism.* Nottingham: Partisan Press, 1971.

Coffin, Tristram. *Senator Fulbright: Portrait of a Public Philosopher.* New York: Dutton, 1966.

Cohen, Warren I. *Dean Rusk.* Totowa, N.J.: Cooper Square Publishers, 1980.

Cohen, Warren I., and Nancy Bernkopf Tucker, eds. *Lyndon Johnson Confronts the World: American Foreign Policy, 1963–1968.* New York: Cambridge University Press, 1994.

Combs, Arthur. "The Path Not Taken: The British Alternative to U.S. Policy in Vietnam, 1954–1956." *Diplomatic History* 19, no. 1 (winter 1995): 33–57.

Cooper, Chester L. *The Lost Crusade: America in Vietnam.* New York: Dodd, Mead, 1970.

Costigliola, Frank. "The Failed Design: Kennedy, de Gaulle, and the Struggle for Europe." *Diplomatic History* 8 (summer 1984): 227–251.

———. *France and the United States: The Cold Alliance Since World War II.* New York: Twayne, 1992.

———. "The Pursuit of Atlantic Community: Nuclear Arms, Dollars, and Berlin." In *Kennedy's Quest for Victory: American Foreign Policy, 1961–1963,* ed. Thomas G. Paterson. New York: Oxford University Press, 1989.

Couve de Murville, Maurice. *Une politique étrangère, 1958–1969.* Paris: Plon, 1971.

Craig, Gordon A., and Alexander L. George. *Force and Statecraft: Diplomatic Problems of Our Time.* New York: Oxford University Press, 1995.

Dallek, Robert. *Flawed Giant: Lyndon Johnson and His Times, 1961–1973.* New York: Oxford University Press, 1998.

———. "Lyndon Johnson and Vietnam: The Making of a Tragedy." *Diplomatic History* 20, no. 2 (spring 1996): 147–162.

———. "The President We Love to Blame." *Wilson Quarterly* 15 (winter 1991): 100–108.

Dalloz, Jacques. *The War in Indochina, 1945–1954.* Savage, Md.: Barnes & Noble, 1990.

De Gaulle, Charles. *Memoirs of Hope: Renewal and Endeavor.* New York: Simon and Schuster, 1971.

DePorte, A. W. *Europe between the Superpowers: The Enduring Balance.* New Haven, Conn.: Yale University Press, 1986.

De Silva, Peer. *Sub rosa: The CIA and the Uses of Intelligence.* New York: New York Times Book Co., 1978.

Devillers, Philippe. "French Policy and the Second Vietnam War." *World Today* (London) 23 (June 1967): 249–262.

———. "La General de Gaulle et l'Asie." In *De Gaulle et le tiers monde.* Institute Charles de Gaulle. Paris: Pédone, 1984.

Diem, Bui, and David Charnoff. *In the Jaws of History.* New York: Houghton Mifflin, 1987.

DiLeo, David. *George Ball, Vietnam, and the Rethinking of Containment.* Chapel Hill: University of North Carolina Press, 1991.

Dimbleby, David, and David Reynolds. *An Ocean Apart: The Relationship*

Between Britain and America in the Twentieth Century. New York: Random House, 1988.

Divine, Robert. "Vietnam: An Episode in the Cold War." In *Vietnam: The Early Years*, ed. Lloyd C. Gardner and Ted Gittinger. Austin: University of Texas Press, 1997.

Dobrynin, Anatoly F. *In Confidence: Moscow's Ambassador to America's Six Cold War Presidents, 1962–1986*. New York: Times Books, 1995.

Dommen, Arthur J. *Conflict in Laos: The Politics of Neutralization*. Rev. ed. New York: Praeger, 1971.

Dugger, Ronnie. *The Politician: The Life and Times of Lyndon Johnson*. New York: Norton, 1982.

Duiker, William J. *The Communist Road to Power in Vietnam*. Boulder, Colo.: Westview Press, 1981.

———. *Sacred War: Nationalism and Revolution in a Divided Vietnam*. New York: McGraw-Hill, 1995.

———. *U.S. Containment Policy and the Conflict in Indochina*. Stanford, Calif.: Stanford University Press, 1994.

———. *Vietnam: Nation in Revolution*. Boulder, Colo.: Westview Press, 1983.

Edwards, P. G. *Crises and Commitments: The Politics and Diplomacy of Australia's Involvement in Southeast Asian Conflicts, 1948–1965*. North Sydney: Allen and Unwin in association with the Australian War Memorial, 1992.

Ellsberg, Daniel. *Papers on the War*. New York: Simon and Schuster, 1972.

English, John. *The Worldly Years. The Life of Lester Pearson*. Vol. 2, *1949 1972*. Toronto, Canada: Knopf, 1992.

Fall, Bernard B. *Anatomy of a Crisis: The Laotian Crisis of 1960–1961*. Garden City, N.Y.: Doubleday, 1969.

———. "Our Options in Vietnam." *The Reporter*, 12 March 1964.

———. *Viet-Nam Witness*. New York: Praeger, 1966.

Faure, Edgar. *Mémoires*. Paris: Plon, 1982.

———. *Le serpent et la tortue: Les problèmes de la Chine populaire*. Paris: Julliard, 1957.

Firestone, Bernard J., and Robert C. Vogt, eds. *Lyndon Johnson and the Use of Power*. Westport, Conn.: Greenwood Press, 1988.

FitzGerald, Frances. *Fire in the Lake: The Vietnamese and the Americans in Vietnam*. Boston: Little, Brown, 1972.

FitzSimons, Louise. *The Kennedy Doctrine*. New York: Random House, 1972.

Foster, Anne L. "Secret Police Cooperation and the Roots of Anti-Communism in Interwar Southeast Asia." *Journal of American–East Asian Relations 4*, no. 4 (winter 1995): 331–350.

Freedman, Lawrence. *The Evolution of Nuclear Strategy*. New York: St. Martin's Press, 1989.

French Embassy, Press and Information Division. *Chronology of Charles de Gaulle's Press Conferences, 1958–1966*. New York: French Embassy, Press and Information Division, 1966.

Fursenko, Aleksandr, and Timothy Naftali. *"One Hell of a Gamble": Khrushchev, Castro, and Kennedy, 1958–1964*. New York: Norton, 1997.

Gaddis, John Lewis. *Strategies of Containment: A Critical Appraisal of Postwar American National Security Policy*. New York: Oxford University Press, 1982.

Gaiduk, Ilya V. *The Soviet Union and the Vietnam War*. Chicago: Ivan R. Dee, 1996.

———. "Turnabout: The Soviet Policy Dilemma in the Vietnam Conflict." In *Vietnam: The Early Years*, ed. Lloyd C. Gardner and Ted Gittinger. Austin: University of Texas Press, 1997.

Galbraith, John K. *A Life in Our Times*. Boston: Houghton Mifflin, 1981.

Gallucci, Robert L. *Neither Peace nor Honor: The Politics of American Military Policy in Vietnam*. Baltimore, Md.: Johns Hopkins University Press, 1975.

Gardner, Lloyd C. *Approaching Vietnam: From World War II to Dienbienphu*. New York: Norton, 1988.

———. *Pay Any Price: Lyndon Johnson and the Wars for Vietnam*. Chicago: Ivan R. Dee, 1995.

Gelb, Leslie, and Richard K. Betts. *The Irony of Vietnam: The System Worked*. Washington, D.C.: Brookings Institute, 1978.

George, Alexander L., and William E. Simons, eds. *The Limits of Coercive Diplomacy*. Boulder, Colo.: Westview Press, 1994.

Georges, Alfred. *Charles de Gaulle et la guerre d'Indochine*. Paris: Nouvelles éditions latines, 1974.

Geyelin, Philip. *Lyndon B. Johnson and the World*. New York: Praeger, 1966.

Gibbons, William Conrad. "Lyndon Johnson and the Legacy of Vietnam." In *Vietnam: The Early Years*, ed. Lloyd C. Gardner and Ted Gittinger. Austin: University of Texas Press, 1997.

———. *The U.S. Government and the Vietnam War: Executive and Legislative Roles and Relationships*. 4 vols. Princeton, N.J.: Princeton University Press, 1986–1995.

Gilpin, Robert. *War and Change in International Politics*. Princeton, NJ: Princeton University Press, 1981.

Gittinger, Ted, ed. *The Johnson Years: A Vietnam Roundtable*. Austin, Tex.: Lyndon Baines Johnson Library, Lyndon B. Johnson School of Public Affairs, 1993.

Goldman, Eric F. *The Tragedy of Lyndon Johnson*. New York: Knopf, 1969.

Goldwater, Barry M. *The Conscience of a Conservative*. New York: Macfadden Books, 1964.

Goodman, Allan E. *The Lost Peace: America's Search for a Negotiated Settlement of the Vietnam War*. Indochina Research Monograph Series, no. 2. Berkeley, Calif.: University of California, Institute of East Asian Studies, 1986.

Goodwin, Richard N. *Remembering America: A Voice from the Sixties*. Boston: Little, Brown, 1988.

Goulden, Joseph C. *Truth Is the First Casualty: The Gulf of Tonkin Affair—Illusion and Reality*. Chicago: Rand-McNally, 1969.

Graff, Henry F. *The Tuesday Cabinet: Deliberation and Decision on Peace and War under Lyndon B. Johnson.* Englewood Cliffs, N.J.: Prentice-Hall, 1970.

Greenstein, Fred I., and Richard H. Immerman. "What Did Eisenhower Tell Kennedy about Indochina? The Politics of Misperception." *Journal of American History* 79 (September 1992): 568–588.

Grosser, Alfred. *Affaires éxterieures: La politique de la France, 1944–1989.* Paris: Flammarion, 1989.

Halberstam, David. *The Best and the Brightest.* New York: Random House, 1972.

———. *The Making of a Quagmire.* New York: Random House, 1990.

———. "Vietnam: Why We Missed the Story." *Washington Post National Weekly Edition,* 22–28 May 1995.

Hallin, Daniel C. *The "Uncensored War": The Media and Vietnam.* New York: Oxford University Press, 1986.

Hammer, Ellen J. *A Death in November: America in Vietnam, 1963.* New York: Dutton, 1987.

Hammond, William M. *Public Affairs: The Military and the Media, 1962–1968.* Washington, D.C.: Center for Military History, United States Army, 1988.

Harrison, Michael M. *The Reluctant Ally: France and Atlantic Security.* Baltimore, Md.: Johns Hopkins University Press, 1981.

Havens, Thomas R. *Fire across the Sea: The Vietnam War and Japan, 1965–1975.* Princeton, N.J.: Princeton University Press, 1987.

Heifetz, Ronald A. *Leadership without Easy Answers.* Cambridge, Mass.: Harvard University Press, 1994.

Heinrichs, Waldo. "Lyndon Johnson: Change and Continuity." In *Lyndon Johnson Confronts the World: American Foreign Policy, 1963–1968,* ed. Warren I. Cohen and Nancy Bernkopf Tucker. New York: Cambridge University Press, 1994.

Hendrickson, David C. "All the President's Acumen." *Foreign Affairs* 77 (May/June 1998).

Hendrickson, Paul. *The Living and the Dead: Robert McNamara and Five Lives of a Lost War.* New York: Knopf, 1996.

Herring, George C. *America's Longest War: The United States and Vietnam, 1950–1975.* 3d ed. New York: McGraw-Hill, 1996.

———. "Diplomacy." In *Encyclopedia of the Vietnam War,* ed. Stanley I. Kutler. New York: Scribners, 1996, 161–174.

———. *LBJ and Vietnam: A Different Kind of War.* Austin: University of Texas Press, 1994.

———, ed. *The Secret Diplomacy of the Vietnam War: The Negotiating Volumes of the Pentagon Papers.* Austin: University of Texas Press, 1983.

Hersh, Seymour. *The Dark Side of Camelot.* Boston: Little, Brown, 1997.

Hess, Gary R. *The United States Emergence as a Southeast Asian Power, 1940–1950.* New York: Columbia University Press, 1987.

———. *Vietnam and the United States: Origins and Legacy of War.* Boston: G. K. Hale, 1990.

Hilsman, Roger. *To Move a Nation: The Politics of Foreign Policy in the Administration of John F. Kennedy.* Garden City, N.Y.: Doubleday, 1967.

Hoffmann, Stanley. *Decline or Renewal: France since the 1930s.* New York: Viking, 1974.

Hoopes, Townsend. *The Limits of Intervention: An Inside Account of How the Johnson Policy of Escalation in Vietnam Was Reversed.* New York: Norton, 1987.

Horne, Alistair. *Harold MacMillan.* Vol. 2, *1957–1986.* New York: Viking, 1989.

———. *A Savage War of Peace: Algeria, 1954–1962.* London: Macmillan, 1977.

Hsiao, Gene T., ed. *The Role of the External Powers in the Indochina Crisis.* Edwardsville: Southern Illinois University, 1973.

Hughes, Thomas L. "Experiencing McNamara." *Foreign Policy* 5 (1995).

Humphrey, Hubert H. *The Education of a Public Man: My Life and Politics.* Garden City, N.Y.: Doubleday, 1976.

Hunt, Michael H. "Commentary: The Three Realms Revisited." In *America in the World: The Historiography of American Foreign Relations since 1941,* ed. Michael J. Hogan. New York: Cambridge University Press, 1995.

———. *Crises in U.S. Foreign Policy: An International History Reader.* New Haven, Conn.: Yale University Press, 1996.

———. *Ideology and U.S. Foreign Policy.* New Haven, Conn.: Yale University Press, 1987.

Hunt, Richard A. *Pacification: The American Struggle for Vietnam's Hearts and Minds.* Boulder, Colo.: Westview, 1995.

Isaacson, Walter. *Kissinger: A Biography.* New York: Simon and Schuster, 1992.

Jamieson, Neil L. *Understanding Vietnam.* Berkeley and Los Angeles: University of California Press, 1993.

Janis, Irving L. *Victims of Groupthink: A Psychological Study of Foreign-Policy Decisions and Fiascoes.* Boston: Houghton Mifflin, 1972.

Jervis, Robert. *Perception and Misperception in International Politics.* Princeton, N.J.: Princeton University Press, 1976.

Johns, Andrew L. "Opening Pandora's Box: The Genesis and Evolution of the 1964 Congressional Resolution on Vietnam." *Journal of American–East Asian Relations* (forthcoming).

Johnson, Lady Bird. *A White House Diary.* New York: Holt, Rinehart, and Winston, 1970.

Johnson, Lyndon B. *The Vantage Point: Perspectives of the Presidency, 1963–1968.* New York: Holt, Rinehart, and Winston, 1971.

Johnson, Robert David. "Ernest Gruening and the American Dissenting Tradition." Unpublished manuscript.

Johnson, U. A. *The Right Hand of Power.* Englewood Cliffs, N.J.: Prentice-Hall, 1984.

Johnson, Walter, ed. *The Papers of Adlai Stevenson.* 8 vols. Boston: Little, Brown, 1972–1979.

———. "The U Thant–Stevenson Peace Initiatives on Vietnam." *Diplomatic History* 1 (fall 1977).

Kahin, George McT. *Intervention: How America Became Involved in Vietnam.* New York: Knopf, 1987.

Kahin, George McT., and John W. Lewis. *The United States in Vietnam.* New York: Dial Press, 1969.

Kaiser, David. "Men and Policies: 1961–1969." In *The Diplomacy of the Crucial Decade: American Foreign Relations during the 1960s,* ed. Diane Kunz, 11–41. New York: Columbia University Press, 1994.

Karnow, Stanley. "Commentary: The Two Vietnams." In *Vietnam as History: Ten Years after the Paris Peace Accords,* ed. Peter Braestrup. Washington, D.C.: University Press of America, 1984.

———. *In Our Image: America's Empire in the Philippines.* New York: Random House, 1989.

———. "Lost Chance in Vietnam." *The New Republic,* 2 February 1974, 19–22.

———. *Vietnam: A History.* New York: Viking, 1991.

Kattenburg, Paul. *The Vietnam Trauma in American Foreign Policy.* New Brunswick, N.J.: Transaction Books, 1980.

Kearns, Doris. *Lyndon Johnson and the American Dream.* New York: Harper and Row, 1976.

Kelly, Tom. *The Imperial Post: The Meyers, the Grahams, and the Paper That Rules Washington.* New York: Morrow, 1983.

Key, Valdimer O. *Public Opinion and American Democracy.* New York: Knopf, 1961.

Khong, Yuen Foong. *Analogies at War: Korea, Munich, Dien Bien Phu, and the Vietnam Decisions of 1965.* Princeton, N.J.: Princeton University Press, 1992.

Kimball, Jeffrey. *To Reason Why: The Debate about Causes of the U.S. Involvement in the Vietnam War.* New York: McGraw Hill, 1990.

Kissinger, Henry. *Diplomacy.* New York: Simon and Schuster, 1994.

Kolko, Gabriel. *Anatomy of a War: Vietnam, the United States, and the Modern Historical Experience.* New York: Pantheon, 1985.

Kolodziej, Edward A. *French International Policy under de Gaulle and Pompidou: The Politics of Grandeur.* Ithaca, N.Y.: Cornell University Press, 1974.

Kraslow, David, and Stuart H. Loory. *The Secret Search for Peace in Vietnam.* New York: Random House, 1968.

Kunz, Diane B. "Camelot Continued: What if JFK Had Lived?" In *Virtual History: Alternatives and Counterfactuals,* ed. Niall Ferguson. New York: Macmillan, 1997.

———. "Lyndon Johnson's Economic Diplomacy." *History Today* 42 (April 1992): 45–51.

Lacouture, Jean. *De Gaulle: Le souverain, 1958–1969.* Paris: Seuil, 1986.

———. *Vietnam: Between Two Truces.* New York: Random House, 1966.

LaFeber, Walter. *The Clash: A History of U.S.-Japan Relations.* New York: Norton, 1997.

Lauren, Paul G. *Diplomacy: New Approaches in History, Theory, and Policy.* New York: Free Press, 1979.

———. "Ultimata and Coercive Diplomacy." *International Studies Quarterly* 16 (1972): 135–165.

Lawson, Eugene K. *The Sino-Vietnamese Conflict*. New York: Praeger, 1984.

Lebow, Richard N. *Between Peace and War: The Nature of International Crisis*. Baltimore, Md.: Johns Hopkins University Press, 1981.

Ledwidge, Bernard. *De Gaulle et les américains: Conversations avec Dulles, Eisenhower, Kennedy, Rusk, 1958–1964*. Paris: Flammarion, 1984.

Lee, Steven Hugh. *Outposts of Empire: Korea, Vietnam, and the Origins of the Cold War in Asia*. Montreal: McGill-Queen's University Press, 1995.

Leifer, Michael. *Cambodia: The Search for Security*. New York: Praeger, 1967.

Levantrosser, William F. "Tonkin Gulf Revisited." In *Lyndon Johnson and the Use of Power*, ed. Bernard J. Firestone and Robert C. Vogt. Westport, Conn.: Greenwood Press, 1988.

Lippmann, Walter. *The Cold War: A Study in U.S. Foreign Policy*. New York: Harper, 1947.

Lodge, Henry C. *The Storm Has Many Eyes*. New York: Norton, 1973.

Loewenheim, Francis L. "Dean Rusk: Diplomacy and Principle." In *The Diplomats: 1939–1979*, ed. Gordon A. Craig and Francis L. Loewenheim. Princeton: Princeton University Press, 1994.

Logevall, Fredrik. "De Gaulle, Neutralization, and American Involvement in Vietnam, 1963–1964." *Pacific Historical Review* 41 (February 1992): 69–102.

———. "Fear to Negotiate: Lyndon Johnson and the Escalation of the Vietnam War, 1963–1965." Ph.D. diss., Yale University, 1993.

———. "First among Critics: Walter Lippmann and the Vietnam War." *Journal of American–East Asian Relations* 4, no. 4 (winter 1995): 351–375.

———. "Vietnam and the Question of What Might Have Been." In *Kennedy: The New Frontier Revisited*, ed. Mark J. White. London: Macmillan, 1998.

Lunch, William L., and Peter W. Sperlich. "American Public Opinion and the War in Vietnam." *Western Political Quarterly* 32 (March 1979): 21–44.

Maclear, Michael. *The Ten-Thousand-Day War: Vietnam, 1945–1975*. New York: St. Martin's Press, 1981.

Mandelbaum, Michael. *The Nuclear Revolution: International Politics before and after Hiroshima*. New York: Cambridge University Press, 1981.

Maneli, Mieczyslaw. *War of the Vanquished*. New York: Harper and Row, 1971.

Marolda, Edward J., and Oscar P. Fitzgerald. *The United States Navy and the Vietnam Conflict*. Vol. 2, *From Military Assistance to Combat, 1959–1963*. Washington, D.C.: GPO, 1986.

Martin, John B. *Adlai Stevenson and the World: The Life of Adlai E. Stevenson*. Garden City, N.Y.: Doubleday, 1977.

McGovern, George. *Grassroots: The Autobiography of George McGovern*. New York: Random House, 1977.

McMahon, Robert J. "Credibility and World Power." *Diplomatic History* 15 (fall 1991): 455–471.

———. "Toward Disillusionment and Disengagement in South Asia." In *Lyndon Johnson Confronts the World: American Foreign Policy, 1963-1968*, ed. Warren I. Cohen and Nancy Bernkopf Tucker. New York: Cambridge University Press, 1994.

McMaster, H. R. *Dereliction of Duty: Lyndon Johnson, Robert McNamara, the Joint Chiefs of Staff, and the Lies That Led to Vietnam.* New York: HarperCollins, 1997.

McNamara, Robert S. *In Retrospect: The Tragedy and Lessons of Vietnam.* New York: Times Books, 1995.

Merry, Robert W. *Taking on the World: Joseph and Stewart Alsop, Guardians of the American Century.* New York: Viking, 1996.

Miller, Robert H. "Vietnam: Folly, Quagmire, or Inevitability?" *Studies in Conflict and Terrorism* 15 (1992).

Moïse, Edwin E. *Tonkin Gulf and the Escalation of the Vietnam War.* Chapel Hill: University of North Carolina Press, 1996.

Möller, Yngve. *Sverige och Vietnamkriget: Ett unikt kapitel i svensk utrikespolitik.* Stockholm: Tidens Förlag, 1992.

Morgenthau, Hans J. *Vietnam and the United States.* Washington, D.C.: Public Affairs Press, 1965.

Mueller, John E. *War, Presidents, and Public Opinion.* New York: Wiley, 1973.

Muslin, Hyman L., and Thomas H. Jobe, *Lyndon Johnson: The Tragic Self: A Psychohistorical Portrait.* New York: Plenum Press, 1991.

Neu, Charles E. "Robert McNamara's Journey to Hanoi: Reflections on a Lost War." *Reviews in American History* 25 (1995).

Neustadt, Richard, and Ernest R. May. *Thinking in Time: The Uses of History for Decision-Makers.* New York: Free Press, 1986.

Newman, John M. *JFK and Vietnam: Deception, Intrigue, and the Struggle for Power.* New York: Warner Books, 1992.

Ninkovich, Frank. *Modernity and Power: A History of the Domino Theory in the Twentieth Century.* Chicago: University of Chicago Press, 1994.

Nixon, Richard. *No More Vietnams.* New York: Arbor House, 1985.

Nolting, Frederick. *From Trust to Tragedy: The Political Memoir of Frederick Nolting, Kennedy's Ambassador to Diem's Vietnam.* New York: Praeger, 1988.

O'Donnell, Kenneth P., and David F. Powers. *Johnny, We Hardly Knew Ye: Memories of John Fitzgerald Kennedy.* Boston: Little, Brown, 1972.

O'Neill, Thomas P., Jr. *Man of the House: The Life and Political Memoirs of Speaker Tip O'Neill.* New York: Random House, 1987.

Papp, Daniel S. *Vietnam: The View from Moscow, Peking, Washington.* Jefferson, N.C.: McFarland, 1987.

Paterson, Thomas G., ed. *Kennedy's Quest for Victory: American Foreign Policy, 1961–1963.* New York: Oxford University Press, 1989.

Patterson, James T. *Grand Expectations: The United States, 1945–1974.* New York: Oxford University Press, 1996.

Paxton, Robert O., and Nicholas Wahl, eds. *De Gaulle and the United States: A Centennial Reappraisal.* Providence, R.I.: Berg, 1994.

Pearson, Lester B. *Mike: The Memoirs of the Right Honourable Lester B. Pearson. Volume III: 1957–1968.* Toronto: University of Toronto Press, 1975.

Peyrefitte, Alain. *C'était de Gaulle: La France reprend sa place dans le monde.* Paris: Fayard, 1997.

Pike, Douglas. *Viet Cong: The Organization and Techniques of the National Liberation Party of South Vietnam.* Rev. ed. Cambridge, Mass.: MIT Press, 1972.

—————. *Vietnam and the Soviet Union.* Boulder, Colo.: Westview Press, 1987.

Pimlott, Ben. *Harold Wilson.* London: HarperCollins, 1992.

Porter, Gareth. *A Peace Denied: The United States, Vietnam, and the Paris Agreement.* Bloomington: Indiana University Press, 1975.

Powell, Lee Riley. *J. William Fulbright and His Time: A Political Biography.* Memphis, Tenn.: Guild Bindery Press, 1996.

Powers, Thomas. *The War at Home: Vietnam and the American People, 1964–1968.* New York: Grossman, 1973.

Prados, John. *The Hidden History of the Vietnam War.* Chicago: Ivan R. Dee, 1995.

Prochnau, William. *Once upon a Distant War.* New York: Times Books, 1995.

Public Papers of the Presidents of the United States: John F. Kennedy, 1963. Millwood, N.Y.: KTO Press, 1977.

Public Papers of the Presidents of the United States: Lyndon B. Johnson, 1963–1964. Millwood, N.Y.: KTO Press, 1978.

Race, Jeffrey. *War Comes to Long An: Revolutionary Conflict in a Vietnamese Province.* Berkeley and Los Angeles: University of California Press, 1972.

Radvanyi, Janos. *Delusion and Reality: Gambits, Hoaxes, and Diplomatic One-Upmanship in Vietnam.* South Bend, Ind.: Gateway, 1978.

Raskin, Marcus G., and Bernard Fall, eds. *The Vietnam Reader: Articles and Documents on American Foreign Policy and the Vietnam Crisis.* New York: Vintage, 1965.

Reedy, George E. *Lyndon B. Johnson: A Memoir.* New York: Andrews and McMeel, 1982.

Reeves, Richard. *President Kennedy: Profile of Power.* New York: Simon and Schuster, 1993.

Reeves, Thomas C. *A Question of Character: John F. Kennedy in Image and Reality.* New York: Free Press, 1990.

Reischauer, Edwin O. *The Japanese.* Cambridge, Mass.: Belknap Press, 1977.

—————. *My Life between Japan and America.* New York: Harper and Row, 1986.

Reston, James. *Deadline: A Memoir.* New York: Random House, 1991.

Roberts, Chalmers. *The Washington Post: The First 100 Years.* Boston: Houghton Mifflin, 1977.

Ross, Douglas A. *In the Interests of Peace: Canada and Vietnam, 1954–1973.* Toronto: University of Toronto Press, 1984.

Rossi, Mario. "U Thant and Vietnam: The Untold Story." *New York Review of Books* 17 (November 1966): 8–13.

Rostow, Walt W. *The United States and the Regional Organization of Asia and the Pacific, 1965–1985.* Austin: University of Texas Press, 1986.

—————. "Vietnam and Asia." *Diplomatic History* 20, no. 3 (summer 1996): 467–471.

Rotter, Andrew J. *The Path to Vietnam: Origins of the American Commitment to Southeast Asia*. Ithaca, N.Y.: Cornell University Press, 1987.

Ruscio, Alain. *La guerre française d'Indochine: 1945–1954*. Brussels: Editions Complexes, 1992.

Rusk, Dean. *As I Saw It*. New York: Norton, 1990.

Russell, Greg. *Hans J. Morgenthau and the Ethics of American Statecraft*. Baton Rouge: Louisiana State University Press, 1990.

Rust, William J. *Kennedy in Vietnam*. New York: Scribner's, 1985.

Sa'adah, Anne. "Idées Simples and Idées Fixes: De Gaulle, the United States, and Vietnam." In *De Gaulle and the United States: A Centennial Reappraisal*, ed. Robert O. Paxton and Nicholas Wahl. Oxford, Eng.: Berg, 1994.

Salisbury, Harrison. *Without Fear or Favor: The New York Times and Its Times*. New York: Times Books, 1980.

Schaffer, Howard B. *Chester Bowles: New Dealer in the Cold War*. Cambridge, Mass.: Harvard University Press, 1993.

Schaller, Michael. "Securing the Great Crescent: Occupied Japan and the Origins of Containment in Southeast Asia." *Journal of American History* 69 (September 1982): 392–414.

Schell, Jonathan. *The Time of Illusion*. New York: Knopf, 1976.

Schlesinger, Arthur M. Jr. *Robert Kennedy and His Times*. Boston: Houghton Mifflin, 1978.

———. *A Thousand Days: John F. Kennedy in the White House*. Boston: Houghton Mifflin, 1965.

Schoenbaum, Thomas J. *Waging Peace and War: Dean Rusk in the Truman, Kennedy, and Johnson Years*. New York: Simon and Schuster, 1988.

Schulzinger, Robert D. *A Time for War: The United States and Vietnam, 1941–1975*. New York: Oxford University Press, 1997.

Schuman, Howard, and Philip E. Converse. "Silent Majority and the Vietnam War." *Scientific American* 22 (June 1970): 17–25.

Schurmann, Franz, et al. *The Politics of Escalation in Vietnam*. Greenwich, Conn.: Fawcett Publications, 1966.

Scott, Peter D. *Deep Politics and the Death of JFK*. Berkeley and Los Angeles: University of California Press, 1993.

Shaplen, Robert. *Lost Revolution: The U.S. in Vietnam, 1946–1966*. New York: Harper and Row, 1966.

———. *The Road from War: Vietnam, 1965–1971*. New York: Harper and Row, 1970.

Shapley, Deborah. *Promise and Power: The Life and Times of Robert McNamara*. Boston: Little, Brown, 1993.

Sheehan, Neil. *A Bright Shining Lie: John Paul Vann and America in Vietnam*. New York: Random House, 1988.

Shennan, Andrew. *De Gaulle*. London: Longman, 1993.

Sherry, Michael S. *In the Shadow of War: The United States since the 1930s*. New Haven, Conn.: Yale University Press, 1995.

Shipler, David K. "Robert McNamara and the Ghosts of Vietnam." *New York Times Magazine,* 10 August 1997.

Shiraishi, Masaya. *Japanese Relations with Vietnam, 1951–1987.* Ithaca, N.Y.: Cornell University, Southeast Asia Program, 1990.

Small, Melvin. *Johnson, Nixon, and the Doves.* New Brunswick, N.J.: Rutgers University Press, 1986.

Smith, Ralph B. *An International History of the Vietnam War.* 3 vols. New York: St. Martin's Press, 1984–1990.

Solberg, Carl. *Hubert Humphrey: A Biography.* New York: Norton, 1984.

Sorensen, Theodore C. *Kennedy.* New York: Harper and Row, 1965.

Spector, Ronald H. *Advice and Support: The Early Years, 1941–1960.* Washington, D.C.: Center for Military History, United States Army, 1983.

Statler, Kathryn. "The Diem Experiment: The Franco-American Conflict over South Vietnam, 1954–1955." Unpublished paper delivered at the Society for Historians of American Foreign Relations annual meeting, Washington, D.C., June 1998.

———. *Walter Lippmann and the American Century.* Boston: Little, Brown, 1980.

Steel, Ronald. *Pax Americana.* New York: Norton, 1967.

———. *Walter Lippmann and the American Century.* Boston: Little, Brown, 1980.

Steinberg, Blema S. *Shame and Humiliation: Presidential Decision Making on Vietnam.* Pittsburgh: University of Pittsburgh Press, 1996.

Stevenson, Charles A. *The End of Nowhere: American Policy toward Laos since 1954.* Boston: Beacon Press, 1973.

Stockdale, James. *In Love and War.* New York: Harper and Row, 1984.

Stoler, Mark. "Aiken, Mansfield, and the Tonkin Gulf Crisis: Notes from the Congressional Leadership Meeting at the White House, August 4, 1964." *Vermont History* 50, no. 2 (1982): 80–94.

Stone, I. F. *In a Time of Torment.* New York: Random House, 1967.

Sullivan, Marianna P. *France's Vietnam Policy: A Study in French-American Relations.* Westport, Conn.: Greenwood, 1978.

Sullivan, William H. *Obbligato, 1939–1979: Notes on a Foreign Service Career.* New York: Norton, 1984.

Summers, Harry G. *On Strategy: A Critical Analysis of the Vietnam War.* Novato, Calif.: Presidio Press, 1982.

Tang, Truong Nhu, with David Chanoff and Doan Van Toai. *A Vietcong Memoir.* New York: Random House, 1985.

Taylor, Maxwell. *Swords and Plowshares.* New York: Norton, 1972.

Thant, U. *View from the UN.* Garden City, N.Y.: Doubleday, 1978.

Thayer, Carlyle. *War by Other Means: National Liberation and Revolution in Vietnam, 1954–1960.* Winchester, Mass.: Unwin Hyman, 1989.

Thies, Wallace J. *When Governments Collide: Coercion and Diplomacy in the Vietnam Conflict, 1964–1968.* Berkeley and Los Angeles: University of California Press, 1980.

Thomas, Evan. *The Very Best Men: Four Who Dared: The Early Years of the CIA*. New York: Simon and Schuster, 1995.

Thomson, James C. Jr. "How Could Vietnam Happen? An Autopsy" *Atlantic* (April 1968): 47–53.

Tonnesson, Stein. *The Vietnamese Revolution of 1945: Roosevelt, Ho Chi Minh, and De Gaulle in a World at War*. Newbury Park, Calif.: Sage Publications, 1991.

Tri, Vo Nhan. *Croissance économique de la République Democratique du Vietnam, 1945–1965*. Hanoi: Editions en langues étrangères, 1967.

Tuchman, Barbara W. *The March of Folly: From Troy to Vietnam*. New York: Knopf, 1984.

Tucker, Nancy Bernkopf. "Threats, Opportunities, and Frustrations in East Asia." In *Lyndon Johnson Confronts the World: American Foreign Policy, 1963–1968*, ed. Warren I. Cohen and Nancy Bernkopf Tucker. New York: Cambridge University Press, 1994.

Turley, William. *The Second Indochina War: A Short Political and Military History, 1954–1975*. Boulder, Colo.: Westview Press and New American Library, 1986.

Urquhart, Brian. *A Life in Peace and War*. New York: Harper and Row, 1987.

Vaïsse, Maurice. *La grandeur: Politique étrangère du général de Gaulle, 1958–1969*. Paris: Fayard, 1998.

VanDeMark, Brian. *Into the Quagmire: Lyndon Johnson and the Escalation of the Vietnam War*. New York: Oxford University Press, 1990.

Vandiver, Frank E. *Shadows of Vietnam: Lyndon Johnson's Wars*. College Station: Texas A&M Press, 1997.

Vertzberger, Yaacov. *The Enduring Entente: Sino-Pakistani Relations, 1960–1980*. New York: Praeger, 1983.

Walton, Richard J. *Cold War and Counter-Revolution: The Foreign Policy of John F. Kennedy*. Baltimore, Md.: Johns Hopkins University Press, 1972.

Warner, Geoffrey. "The United States and the Fall of Diem, Part I: The Coup That Never Was." *Australian Outlook* 28 (December 1974): 245–258.

Westad, Odd Arne, Chen Jian, Stein Tønnesson, Nguyen Vu Tung, and James G. Hershberg, eds. "77 Conversations between Chinese and Foreign Leaders on the Wars in Vietnam." Cold War International History Project working paper, 1998.

Westmoreland, William C. *A Soldier Reports*. New York: Dell, 1980.

———. "Vietnam in Perspective." *The Retired Officer* (October 1978): 21–24.

Wicker, Tom. *JFK and LBJ: The Influence of Personality upon Politics*. New York: Morrow, 1968.

Wilson, Harold. *The Labour Government, 1964–1970: A Personal Record*. London: Weidenfeld and Nicolson, 1971.

Wilson, William. "Perspectives." *Vietnam* 10 (April 1997): 56–60.

Winters, Francis X. *The Year of the Hare: America in Vietnam, January 25, 1963–February 15, 1964*. Athens: University of Georgia Press, 1997.

Wise, David. *The Politics of Lying: Government Deception, Secrecy, and Power*. New York: Random House, 1973.

Wohlforth, William C. *The Elusive Balance: Power and Perceptions during the Cold War.* Ithaca, N.Y.: Cornell University Press, 1993.

Woods, Randall B. *Fulbright: A Biography.* New York: Cambridge University Press, 1995.

Yarmolinski, Adam. "Cold War Stories." *Foreign Policy* 97 (winter 1994–95).

Young, Marilyn B. *The Vietnam Wars, 1945–1990.* New York: HarperCollins, 1991.

Zagoria, Donald S. *Vietnam Triangle: Moscow, Peking, Hanoi.* New York: Pegasus, 1967.

Zhai, Qiang. "Beijing and the Vietnam Peace Talks, 1965–1968: New Evidence from Chinese Sources." Cold War International History Project working paper, June 1997.

———. "An Uneasy Relationship: China and the DRV during the Vietnam War." Unpublished paper.

Zinn, Howard. *Vietnam: The Logic of Withdrawal.* Boston: Beacon Press, 1967.

Index

Acheson, Dean, 460n45
Aiken, George, 137, 199
Albert, Carl, 356
Algeria, 131–32, 280
Alphand, Hervé, 45, 52, 177, 458n33
Alsop, Joseph, 48, 135, 136, 288,
  297–98, 304, 336, 361, 377, 455n4
Armed Forces Council, 293, 316
Army of the Republic of Vietnam
  (ARVN), xviii, 2, 14, 34, 109, 262,
  263, 302, 367
Australia, 110, 111, 117, 151, 179,
  182, 206, 275, 279, 338, 372–73,
  378
Ayub Khan, Mohammad, 180, 338,
  366, 371

Ball, George, 6, 30, 68, 98, 160, 168,
  201, 256, 297, 314, 330, 370, 376,
  380; on American credibility, 289,
  291; anxious to preserve position
  in administration, xxiii, 267, 402;
  argues against escalation, 344–45;
  criticism of "good doctor" theory,
  272; interview with Reston, 229–
  30; on Johnson and de Gaulle, 84;
  on Khanh coup, 101–2; as loyal in-
  house "dove," xxiii, 394; meets with
  de Gaulle, 175–76; meets with Fulbright, 327–28; meets with prominent legislators, 168; misgivings
  about war, 173–75, 176; October

1964 report recommending political
  solution, 243–46, 248–50, 265–66,
  267; on French recognition of
  China, 98; pessimism about war
  widely shared, 389; pleased with
  British-Soviet cochairs' initiative,
  354; supports raids on North, 325–
  26, 327; warning to Kennedy about
  committing too deeply to Vietnam,
  27
Bartlett, Charles, 38
Bay of Pigs, 31
Bella, Ben, 365
Betts, Richard K., xvi–xvii
Bienhoa, 250, 263, 325
Binh Gia, 302–3
Blackwell, J. Kenneth, 16, 17–18, 20,
  156, 428n43; bombing of North
  would have no effect, 124; on North
  Vietnamese interest in negotiation,
  9–10, 20, 425n20; on possibility of
  neutral South Vietnam, 433n91; on
  U.S. provocation of North Vietnam,
  202
Bloodworth, Denis, 262
Boggs, Hale, 356
Bohlen, Charles E., 61, 66, 84, 97, 117,
  119–20, 129, 130–31, 363
Bombing of North Vietnam: delay
  in implementing, 152; increasing
  attraction of, 122–23; initial recommendations and list of targets

Compositor: Prestige Typography
Text and display: Aldus
Display: Franklin
Printer and binder: Haddon Craftsmen